The
Rhododendron
Handbook
1998

Rhododendron Species in Cultivation

The Royal Horticultural Society

Published in 1997 by The Royal Horticultural Society, 80 Vincent Square,
London SW1P 2PE

ISBN 1-874431-63-9

Authors:
Dr George Argent
Mr John Bond
Dr David Chamberlain
Mr Peter Cox
Mr Alan Hardy

RHS Editor: Karen Wilson

Bibliographical note
The present handbook is the successor to the Year Books of the
Rhododendron Association, which were published annually from 1929 to
1939 and available to members of the Association. This Association became
the Rhododendron Group of the Royal Horticultural Society, and since 1947
the Society has undertaken publication of the Handbook. There were
revised editions published in 1947, 1952, 1956, 1967, 1980 and now 1997.

Designed by Grahame Dudley Associates, Middlesex

Printed in Great Britain by BAS Printers, Hampshire

Contents

Foreword

Since the publication of the last *Rhododendron Handbook* in 1980 there has been a period of considerable activity in the study of the genus. As China opened its boundaries, it again became possible for Western scientists to study rhododendrons in the field. Exchange agreements have facilitated collaboration with Chinese scientists and this has led to significant advances in the study of the genus. Moreover, research methods have been refined and developed, especially DNA analysis and the application of molecular and information technology to studies of classification and evolutionary biology.

A further factor has been a renaissance, since 1980, of interest in the cultivation of the tropical rhododendrons of Sect. Vireya. This, in turn, has coincided with a period of active field studies in South East Asia, leading to significant new information about the biology and classification of the group.

For all of these reasons, the Royal Horticultural Society considered that it was time to update the 1980 edition of the Handbook. The Society, through Alan Hardy and John Bond, commissioned the production of the present edition to build on the expertise of the Royal Botanic Garden Edinburgh in studies of *Rhododendron* in the field and in the laboratory, embracing both the temperate and tropical members of the genus. While the major authors, Dr David Chamberlain, and Dr George Argent, both of the Royal Botanic Garden Edinburgh, have prepared the text, advice on the species in cultivation has been sought from the Royal Horticultural Society itself, and from Mr Peter Cox of Glendoick, Perthshire.

Indeed, the Handbook would not have been possible without active collaboration between scientists with a technical knowledge of classification and horticulturists with an in-depth knowledge of the species in cultivation.

The 1980 edition of the Handbook marked the transition from the old Series Classification to one with Subsections, Sections and Subgenera. The latter is based on the classification proposed by Sleumer in 1949 and revised in a series of monographic treatments of *Rhododendron* written at the Royal Botanic Garden Edinburgh. The present handbook is now firmly anchored onto this 'Edinburgh' system of classification. A comprehensive list of accepted species, subspecies, and varieties is published up to the end of 1996. The classification used incorporates the findings of much recent experimental research, not only in Edinburgh but elsewhere in the world.

The Handbook also attempts to include all the species of *Rhododendron* in general cultivation in Europe and America and, for the first time, includes a significant proportion of the tropical species. The accounts have been redrafted and up-to-date distributions are included. This information is supplemented with a comprehensive list of synonyms published up to the end of 1996. The lists of collectors' numbers cover the many expeditions to India and China that have taken place since 1980.

The new Handbook therefore represents a major contribution to the literature dealing with the genus *Rhododendron*, not only summarising the scientific advances in *Rhododendron* taxonomy, but marrying this to clear practical information that will be of great value to *Rhododendron* cultivators around the world. It is thus a milestone publication, drawing together the threads of 100 years of *Rhododendron* research at the Royal Botanic Garden Edinburgh, the Royal Horticultural Society, and elsewhere. It paves the way for significant future publications on *Rhododendron* taxonomy, including the in-depth monographic treatments of both temperate and tropical rhododendrons that will be produced from Edinburgh in subsequent years.

I wish to thank Alan Hardy for all his hard and patient work as project co-ordinator and editor, David Chamberlain and George Argent who have borne the huge job of compiling and writing all the entries, and John Bond and Peter Cox who have worked closely with David Chamberlain and George Argent in compiling the descriptions and nomenclature. Finally, we are all grateful to the Iris Darnton Foundation for the donation which has contributed to the cost of the colour illustrations.

DAVID S INGRAM
REGIUS KEEPER OF THE
ROYAL BOTANIC GARDEN EDINBURGH,
PROFESSOR OF HORTICULTURE OF THE
ROYAL HORTICULTURAL SOCIETY

Introduction

The last edition of the *Rhododendron Handbook*, published in 1980 marked the transition from the essentially artificial Balfourian Series to a classification substituting Subgenera, Sections and Subsections, based on a system proposed by Sleumer in 1949. Since 1980 the deliberations of four international conferences on rhododendrons have been published, alongside a considerable amount of scientific research using experimental techniques, from analysis of chemical constituents and DNA sequencing to anatomical, electron microscopic and embryological studies.

These studies have led to the refined Sleumer classification proposed here. However, it should be realised that the integration of future research will undoubtedly lead to a continuing stream of modifications. Furthermore, there are recent classifications that to some extent conflict with that used here, notably those proposed by Spethmann (1987) and by the Chinese Authors of the *Rhododendron* accounts in the *Flora of China* (Hu & Fang, 1994).

There has been a burgeoning of interest in Vireya rhododendrons in cultivation, particularly in the USA, Australia and New Zealand. Many new hybrids have appeared very recently as a result of the large number of species that have been brought into cultivation in the last 30 years. This increasing interest is reflected in the larger entry of Vireya species.

Over the past 17 years travel within China has become possible, resulting in a number of international expeditions. This has allowed *Rhododendron* populations to be studied in the wild. From these studies it has become clear that some taxa traditionally recognized as species represent selections from hybrid swarms. A number of recent expeditions to SE Asia, including the Philippines, Borneo and Indonesia have also added much to our knowledge of *Rhododendron* Sect. Vireya in the field.

This classification has gained acceptance in the horticultural world and has been used in some of the more popular recently published accounts of the genus, for example the well illustrated publication by Cox, P.A. & Cox, K.N.E. (1997 - see Selected Bibliography, p. 351).

Thus the classification and species accounts presented here incorporate some of the knowledge gained over the past 17 years, justifying the final break with the Series and Subseries of the Balfourian System.

The Classification of Rhododendron

C= in cultivation

Subgenus Azaleastrum *Planch.*

Shrubs, to 8m, indumentum, when present, composed of simple or glandular hairs. Scales absent. Leaves evergreen. Inflorescence lateral below terminal or subterminal vegetative buds. Calyx obsolete or large. Corolla 5-lobed, rotate to tubular-campanulate. Stamens 5 or 10. Seeds with or without appendages.

Section Azaleastrum *(Planch.) Maxim.*

Flowers solitary. Calyx lobes large, fringed with stalked glands and/or hairs, or glabrous. Corolla broadly funnel-shaped to rotate, rarely narrowly tubular-campanulate. Stamens 5. Ovary with style base impressed. Capsule equalling the persistent calyx. Seeds without appendages.

    R. hangzhouense *W.P.Fang & M.Y.He*
C R. hongkongense *Hutch.*
C R. leptothrium *Balf.f. & Forrest*
    R. medoense *W.P.Fang & M.Y.He*
    R. ngawchangense *M.N.Philipson & Philipson*
C R. ovatum *(Lindl.) Maxim.*
C   var. ovatum
      var. setuliferum *M.Y.He*
    R. sanidodeum *P.C.Tam*
    R. tianlinense *P.C.Tam*
    R. uwaense *H.Hara & T.Yamanaka*
C R. vialii *Delavay & Franch.*
    R. xinganense *G.Z.Li*

Section Choniastrum *Franch.*

Inflorescence 1-several-flowered. Calyx minute to well-developed, ciliate or glabrous. Corolla narrowly funnel-shaped. Stamens 10. Ovary not impressed below style. Capsule elongate. Seeds with appendages at both ends.

    R. cavaleriei *H.Lév.*
C R. championiae *Hook.f.*
C   var. championiae
      var. ovalifolium *P.C.Tam*
    R. detampullum *Chun ex P.C.Tam*
    R. esquirolii *H.Lév.*
    R. feddei *H.Lév.*
    R. hancockii *Hemsl.*
    R. henryi *Hance*
      var. dunnii (E.H.Wilson) *M.Y.He*
      var. henryi
      var. pubescens *K.M.Feng & A.L.Chang*
    R. huguangense *P.C.Tam*
    R. kaliense *W.P.Fang & M.Y.He*
C R. latoucheae *Franch.*
      var. latoucheae
      var. ionanthum *(W.P.Feng) G.Z.Li*
    R. linearicupulare *P.C.Tam*
    R. mitriforme *P.C.Tam*
      var. mitriforme
      var. setaceum *P.C.Tam*
C R. moulmainense *Hook.f.*
    R. shiwandashanense *P.C.Tam*
C R. stamineum *Franch.*
      var. lasiocarpum *R.C.Fang & C.H.Yang*
C   var. stamineum
    R. subestipitatum *Chun & P.C.Tam*
    R. taiense *Hutch.*
    R. taishunense *B.Y.Ding & Y.Y.Fang*
    R. tutcherae *Hemsl. & E.H.Wilson*
      var. gymnocarpum *A.L.Chang*
      var. tutcherae

Subgenus Candidastrum (*Sleumer*) *N.M. Philipson & Philipson*

Deciduous shrub. Scales absent. Inflorescences lateral below vegetative buds, 1-2-flowered. Calyx with 5 large leaf-like gland-fringed lobes. Corolla rotate-campanulate more or less regular. Stamens 10, equal. Ovary globose, impressed below the style. Capsule globose. Seed with appendages at both ends.

C   R. albiflorum *Hook.*

Subgen. Hymenanthes (*Blume*) *K.Koch*

Dwarf shrubs to large trees, glabrous or with an indumentum composed, at least partly, of compound hairs. Scales absent. Leaves generally evergreen, rarely deciduous. Flowers in a terminal inflorescence; rhachis present or absent. Calyx obsolete or well-developed. Corolla 5-10-lobed, open- to tubular-campanulate, sometimes ventricose, with or without nectar pouches. Stamens 10-20, declinate. Ovary 5-20-locular. Capsule with hard woody valves. Seeds winged or unwinged.

Unplaced Names of Uncertain Affinity

   R. blumei *Nutt.*
C   R. chlorops *Cowan*
   R. chrysolepis *Hutch.*
   R. dimidiatum *Balf.f.*
C   R. dimitrium *Balf.f. & Forrest*
C   R. inopinum *Balf.f.*
   R. kansuense *Millais*
   R. magorianum *Balf.f.*
   R. maximowiczianum *H.Lév.*
C   R. paradoxum *Balf.f.*
C   R. peregrinum *Tagg*
C   R. planetum *Balf.f.*
   R. potaninii *Batalin*
C   R. purdomii *Rehder & E.H.Wilson*
   R. pyrrhoanthum *Balf.f.*
C   R. serotinum *Hutch.*
   R. venosum *Nutt.*

R. wallaceanum *Millais*

Sect. Ponticum *G.Don*

The only section in subgenus Hymenanthes; description as for subgenus.

Subsect. Arborea *Sleumer*

Trees, to 30m. Lower surface of leaves covered with a dense, generally white to fawn, spongy to compacted, one- to two-layered indumentum composed of dendroid hairs (rarely with upper layer rufous and floccose). Inflorescence dense, 10-25-flowerd. Calyx minute. Corolla 5-lobed, campanulate to tubular-campanulate, with nectar pouches. Stamens 10. Ovary densely tomentose, occasionally also glandular; style glabrous.

C   R. × agastum *Balf.f. & W.W.Sm.*
C   R. arboreum *Sm.*
C   subsp. albomentosum *(Davidian) D.F.Chamb.*
C   subsp. arboreum
    subsp. cinnamomeum *(Lindl.) Tagg*
C   var. cinnamomeum *(Wall. ex G.Don) Lindl.*
C   var. roseum *Lindl.*
C   forma album *Wall.*
    subsp. delavayi *(Franch.) D.F.Chamb.*
C   var. delavayi
C   var. peramoenum *(Balf.f. & Forrest) D.F.Chamb.*
    var. pilostylum *K.M.Feng*
C   subsp. nilagiricum *(Zenker) Tagg*
C   subsp. zeylanicum *(Booth) Tagg*
C   R. lanigerum *Tagg*
C   R. niveum *Hook.f.*

Subsect. Argyrophylla *Sleumer*

Shrubs or small trees, to 11m. Lower surface of leaves covered with a thin one-layered indumentum composed of rosulate hairs, or with a two-layered indumentum, the upper layer of ramiform hairs. Inflorescence lax or dense, 4-30-flowered;

rhachis 3-40mm. Calyx usually minute, rarely to 15mm. Corolla 5-lobed, open- to funnel-campanulate, nectar pouches usually absent (present in *R. ririei*). Stamens usually 10(-20). Ovary glabrous or with a thin white to dense rufous indumentum; style glabrous or glandular to tip.

C R. adenopodum *Franch.*
C R. argyrophyllum *Franch.*
C   subsp. argyrophyllum
C   subsp. hypoglaucum *(Hemsl.)* *D.F.Chamb.*
C   subsp. nankingense *(Cowan)* *D.F.Chamb.*
C   subsp. omeiense *(Rehder & E.H.Wilson) D.F.Chamb.*
    R. brevipetiolatum *M.Y.Fang*
C R. coryanum *Tagg & Forrest*
C R. denudatum *H.Lév.*
    R. ebianense *M.Y.Fang*
    R. fangchengense *P.C.Tam*
    R. farinosum *H.Lév.*
C R. floribundum *Franch.*
C R. formosanum *Hemsl.*
C R. haofui *Chun & W.P.Fang*
C R. hunnewellianum *Rehder & E.H.Wilson*
C   subsp. hunnewellianum
    subsp. rockii *(E.H.Wilson)* *D.F.Chamb.*
C R. insigne *Hemsl. & E.H.Wilson*
    var. hejiangense *(W.P.Fang)* *M.Y.Fang*
    var. insigne
C R. longipes *Rehder & E.H.Wilson*
    var. chienianum *(W.P.Fang)* *D.F.Chamb.*
C   var. longipes
    R. oblancifolium *M.Y.Fang*
C R. pingianum *W.P.Fang*
C R. ririei *Hemsl. & E.H.Wilson*
    R. shimenense *Q.X.Liu & C.M.Zhang*
C R. simiarum *Hance*
    var. deltoideum *P.C.Tam*
C   var. simiarum
    var. versicolor *(Chun & W.P.Fang)* *M.Y.Fang*
C R. thayerianum *Rehder & E.H.Wilson*

Subsect. Auriculata *Sleumer*

Small tree, to 6m; young shoots densely glandular-setulose. Leaves with rounded to cordate base, lower surface with scattered hairs or a pubescence that does not persist. Inflorescence dense, 6-15-flowered. Calyx minute. Corolla 7-lobed, funnel-shaped or infundibular-campanulate. Stamens 14-15. Ovary densely stalked-glandular; style glandular to tip.

C R. auriculatum *Hemsl.*
    R. chihsinianum *Chun & W.P.Fang*

Subsect. Barbata *Sleumer*

Shrubs or small trees; young shoots setose or glabrous. Leaves elliptic to broadly obovate, lower surface glabrous or with coarse bristles or stalked glands, sometimes also with a thin continuous dendroid indumentum. Inflorescence dense, 10-20-flowered. Calyx minute to large and cupular. Corolla 5-lobed, red, fleshy, tubular-campanulate, with nectar pouches. Stamens 10. Ovary glabrous to densely stalked-glandular, with or without a rufous dendroid indumentum.

C R. argipeplum *Balf.f. & R.E.Cooper*
C R. barbatum *Wall. ex G.Don*
C R. erosum *Cowan*
C R. exasperatum *Tagg*
C R. succothii *Davidian*

Subsect. Campanulata *Sleumer*

Shrubs or small trees. Leaves ovate to broadly elliptic, lower surface covered with a dendroid indumentum, to (rarely) more or less glabrous. Inflorescence lax or dense, 5-15-flowered. Calyx small. Corolla 5-lobed, whitish to pale mauve, open- to funnel-campanulate, nectar pouches absent. Stamens 10. Ovary and style glabrous.

C R. campanulatum *D.Don*
C   subsp. aeruginosum *(Hook.f.)*

D.F.Chamb.
C   subsp. campanulatum
      R. gannanense *Z.C.Feng & X.G.Sun*
C R. wallichii *Hook.f.*

Subsect. Campylocarpa *Sleumer*

Shrubs or small trees, 0.6-6.5m; young shoots shortly stalked-glandular or glabrous. Leaves narrowly obovate to orbicular, both surfaces glabrous when mature. Inflorescence loose or dense, 4-15-flowered. Calyx minute to well-developed and cupular. Corolla 5-lobed, yellow or pink to white, campanulate to saucer-shaped, nectar pouches absent. Stamens 10. Ovary stalked-glandular; style glabrous or glandular to tip.

C R. callimorphum *Balf.f. & W.W.Sm.*
C   var. callimorphum
C   var. myiagrum *(Balf.f. & Forrest)*
      D.F.Chamb.
C R. campylocarpum *Hook.f.*
C   subsp. caloxanthum *(Balf.f. & Farrer) D.F.Chamb.*
    subsp. campylocarpum
      R. henanense *W.P.Fang*
      subsp. henanense
      subsp. lingbaoense *W.P.Fang*
      R. longicalyx *M.Y.Fang*
C R. souliei *Franch.*
C R. wardii *W.W.Sm.*
C   var. puralbum *(Balf.f. & W.W.Sm.) D.F.Chamb.*
C   var. wardii

Subsect. Falconera *Sleumer*

Large shrubs or trees, 2.5-12m. Leaves large, oblanceolate to broadly obovate, lower surface covered with a white to rufous indumentum composed of cup-shaped hairs, sometimes also with a compacted lower layer. Inflorescence dense, 10-25-flowered. Calyx minute. Corolla (5-)7-10-lobed, yellow or white to pink, funnel- to oblique- or ventricose-campanulate, nectar pouches lacking. Stamens (10-)14-18. Ovary tomentose, glandular or

glabrous; style glabrous.

C R. arizelum *Balf.f. & Forrest*
C R. basilicum *Balf.f. & W.W.Sm.*
C R. coriaceum *Franch.*
C R. falconeri *Hook.f.*
C   subsp. eximium *(Nutt.) D.F.Chamb.*
C   subsp. falconeri
C (R. fictolacteum *Balf.f.*
C   var. miniforme *Davidian)*
C R. galactinum *Balf.f. ex Tagg*
C R. Hodconeri Group
C R. hodgsonii *Hook.f.*
C R. preptum *Balf.f. & Forrest*
C R. rex *H.Lév.*
C   subsp. fictolacteum *(Balf.f.) D.F.Chamb.*
    subsp. gratum *(T.L.Ming) M.Y.Fang*
C   subsp. rex
C R. rothschildii *Davidian*
C R. semnoides *Tagg & Forrest*
C R. sinofalconeri *Balf.f.*

Subsect. Fortunea *Sleumer*

Shrubs or trees, to 18m. Leaves oblanceolate, to orbicular, lower surface usually glabrous when mature, though sometimes with a floccose indumentum on midrib, rarely with a thin covering of stellate hairs on lamina. Inflorescence lax or dense, 5-30-flowered, rhachis sometimes well-developed, to 70mm long. Calyx minute or well-developed. Corolla 5-7(-8)-lobed, white to pink, funnel- to open-campanulate, nectar pouches usually absent. Stamens 10-16. Ovary stalked-glandular or glabrous; style glabrous or glandular to tip.

    R. asterochnoum *Diels*
      var. asterochnoum
      var. brevipedicellatum *W.K.Hu*
C R. calophytum *Franch.*
C   var. calophytum
      var. jinfuense *M.Y.Fang*
C   var. openshawianum *(Rehder & E.H.Wilson) D.F.Chamb.*
C   var. pauciflorum *W.K.Hu*
    R. davidii *Franch.*
C R. decorum *Franch.*

C subsp. cordatum *W.K.Hu*
C subsp. decorum
C subsp. diaprepes *(Balf.f. & W.W.Sm.) T.L.Ming*
subsp. parvistigmatis *W.K.Hu*
R. faithae *Chun*
C R. fortunei *Lindl.*
C subsp. fortunei
C subsp. discolor *(Franch.) D.F.Chamb.*
C R. × geraldii *Ivens*
C R. glanduliferum *Franch.*
R. gonggashanense *W.K.Hu*
C R. griffithianum *Wight*
C R. hemsleyanum *E.H.Wilson*
var. chengianum *W.P.Fang ex Ching*
C var. hemsleyanum
C R. huianum *W.P.Fang*
R. jingangshanicum *P.C.Tam*
R. magniflorum *W.K.Hu*
R. maoerense *W.P.Fang & G.Z.Li*
R. miyiense *W.K.Hu*
R. nymphaeoides *W.K.Hu*
C R. orbiculare *Decne.*
subsp. cardiobasis *(Sleumer) D.F.Chamb.*
subsp. oblongum *W.K.Hu*
C subsp. orbiculare
C R. oreodoxa *Franch.*
var. adenostylosum *M.Y.Fang & H.K.Hu*
C var. fargesii *(Franch.) D.F.Chamb.*
C var. oreodoxa
C var. shensiense *D.F.Chamb.*
R. platypodum *Diels*
C R. praeteritum *Hutch.*
var. hirsutum *W.K.Hu*
C var. praeteritum
C R. praevernum *Hutch.*
C R. serotinum *Hutch.*
C R. sutchuenense *Franch.*
C R. vernicosum *Franch.*
R. verruciferum *W.K.Hu*
R. wolongense *W.K.Hu*
R. xiaoxidongense *W.K.Hu*

Subsect. Fulgensia *Sleumer*

Shrubs or small trees, 1.5-6m. Leaves elliptic to broadly obovate, lower surface covered with a dense reddish-brown indumentum composed of fasciculate hairs. Inflorescence lax or dense, 4-14-flowered. Calyx minute to well-developed. Corolla 5-lobed, crimson, fleshy, funnel- to tubular-campanulate, with nectar pouches. Stamens 10. Ovary and style glabrous.

C R. fulgens *Hook.f.*
R. miniatum *Cowan*

Subsect. Fulva *Sleumer*

Large shrubs or small trees, 2-10m. Leaves elliptic to oblong, lower surface covered with a dense one- to two-layered indumentum, the lower composed of dendroid hairs, the upper, when present, of capitellate hairs. Inflorescence dense, 6-30-flowered. Calyx minute. Corolla 5-lobed, white to pale pink, usually with a basal blotch, campanulate. Stamens 10. Ovary and style glabrous.

C R. fulvum *Balf.f. & W.W.Sm.*
C subsp. fulvoides *(Balf.f. & Forrest) D.F.Chamb.*
C subsp. fulvum
C R. uvariifolium *Diels*
C var. griseum *Cowan*
C var. uvariifolium

Subsect. Glischra *(Tagg)* D.F.Chamb.

Shrub or small tree, 2-6m; young shoots glandular-setose. Leaves ovate to oblanceolate, lower surface covered with stalked glands and bristles, or with a dense matted indumentum composed of ramiform hairs. Inflorescence lax, 6-14-flowered. Calyx well-developed, 5-15mm. Corolla 5-lobed, white, sometimes flushed pink, usually with a basal blotch, campanulate to funnel-campanulate, lacking nectar pouches. Stamens 10. Ovary densely stalked-glandular; style glabrous, glandular at base or setose-glandular

C R. adenosum *Davidian*

C R. crinigerum *Franch.*
C var. crinigerum
C var. euadenium *Tagg & Forrest*
C R. diphrocalyx *Balf.f.*
C R. glischroides *(Tagg & Forrest) D.F.Chamb.*
C R. glischrum *Balf.f. & W.W.Sm.*
C subsp. glischrum
C subsp. rude *(Tagg & Forrest) D.F.Chamb.*
C R. habrotrichum *Balf.f. & W.W.Sm .*
C R. recurvoides *Tagg & Kingdon-Ward*
C R. spilotum *Balf.f. & Farrer*
C R. vesiculiferum *Tagg*

Subsect. Grandia *Sleumer*
Large shrubs to large trees, to 30m. Leaves large, oblanceolate to broadly elliptic, lower surface covered with a one- to two-layered usually compacted indumentum, the upper layer, when present, composed of rosulate or dendroid hairs. Inflorescence dense, 12-30-flowered. Calyx minute. Corolla 6-10-lobed, white or yellow to rosy-purple, tubular- or funnel- to ventricose-campanulate, nectar pouches usually absent. Stamens 12-18. Ovary tomentose, glandular or glabrous; style glabrous.
C R. balangense *W.P.Fang*
C R. grande *Wight*
C R. kesangiae *D.G.Long & Rushforth*
C var. album *D.G.Long*
C var kesangiae
R. oreogonum *L.C.Hu*
C R. macabeanum *Watt ex Balf.f.*
C R. magnificum *Kingdon-Ward*
C R. montroseanum *Davidian*
C R. praestans *Balf.f. & W.W.Sm.*
C R. protistum *Balf.f. & Forrest*
C var. giganteum *(Forrest ex Tagg) D.F.Chamb.*
C var. protistum
C R. pudorosum *Cowan*
C R. sidereum *Balf.f.*
C R. sinogrande *Balf.f. & W.W.Sm.*
C R. watsonii *Hemsl. & E.H.Wilson*
R. wattii *Cowan*

Subsect. Griersoniana *Davidian ex D.F.Chamb.*

Shrub, 1.5-3m. Leaves herbaceous, elliptic, lower surface covered with a dense whitish to pale brown tomentum composed of dendroid hairs. Inflorescence lax, 5-12-flowered. Calyx minute. Corolla 5-lobed, deep rose to scarlet, tubular- to funnel-campanulate, nectar pouches absent, outer surface densely hairy. Stamens 10. Ovary with a dense dendroid indumentum intermixed with a few glands; style glabrous.

C R. griersonianum *Balf.f. & Forrest*

Subsect. Irrorata *Sleumer*
Shrubs or small trees. Leaves ovate to oblanceolate, elliptic or oblong, lower surface usually glabrous when mature though with persistent hair bases, occasionally with a thin veil of dendroid hairs. Inflorescence lax or dense, 4-20-flowered. Calyx minute or cupular. Corolla 5-7-lobed, white or (rarely) yellow to mauve or deep crimson, tubular- to open-campanulate, with or without nectar pouches. Stamens 10. Ovary glabrous to tomentose and/or stalked-glandular; style glandular to tip.

C R. aberconwayi *Cowan*
C R. annae *Franch.*
C R. anthosphaerum *Diels*
C R. araiophyllum *Balf.f. & W.W.Sm.*
C var. araiophyllum
var. lapidosum *(T.L.Ming) M.Y.Fang*
R. brevinerve *Chun & W.P.Fang*
R. excelsum *A.Chev.*
R. gongshanense *T.L.Ming*
R. guizhouense *M.Y.Fang*
C R. irroratum *Franch.*
C subsp. irroratum
subsp. kontumense *(Sleumer) D.F.Chamb.*
C subsp. pogonostylum *(Balf.f. & W.W.Sm.) D.F.Chamb.*
C R. kendrickii *Nutt.*

R. korthalsii *Miq.*
R. laojunense *T.L.Ming*
R. leptopeplum *Balf.f. & Forrest*
C   R. lukiangense *Franch.*
R. mengtszense *Balf.f. & W.W.Sm.*
C   R. papillatum *Balf.f. & Cooper*
R. pingbianense *M.Y.Fang*
C   R. ramsdenianum *Cowan*
R. spanotrichum *Balf.f. & W.W.Sm.*
C   R. tanastylum *Balf.f. & Kingdon-Ward*
var. lingzhiense *M.Y.Fang*
C   var. pennivenium *(Balf.f. & Forrest)*
D.F.Chamb.
C   var. tanastylum
R. wrayi *King & Gamble*

Subsect Lanata *D.F.Chamb.*

Shrubs or small trees, to 7.5m. Leaves obovate to elliptic, lower surface covered with a dense one-layered, light brown to rufous, lanate or crisped tomentum composed of dendroid hairs. Inflorescence lax or dense, 3-15-flowered. Calyx minute. Corolla 5-lobed, yellow or white to pink, campanulate to open-campanulate, lacking nectar pouches. Ovary densely tomentose or (rarely) predominantly glandular; style glabrous.

R. circinnatum*Cowan & Kingdon-Ward*
R. flinckii *Davidian*
C   R. lanatoides *D.F.Chamb.*
C   R. lanatum *Hook.f.*
C   R. luciferum *(Cowan) Cowan*
C   R. tsariense *Cowan*
C   var. trimoense *Davidian*
C   var. tsariense

Subsect. Maculifera *Sleumer*

Large shrubs or small trees; young shoots tomentose or glandular-setose. Leaves elliptic or oblong to obovate, lower surface with a more or less persistent to evanescent, tomentum composed of fla-gellate, folioliferous, long-rayed or stellate hairs. Inflorescence lax or dense, 5-20-flowered. Calyx usually minute, rarely to 10mm. Corolla 5-lobed, white to pink or deep red, with or without a basal blotch,

narrowly to widely campanulate, with nectar pouches. Stamens 10. Ovary tomentose to stalked-glandular; style glabrous or at least partly glandular.

C   R. anwheiense *E.H.Wilson*
C   R. longesquamatum *C.K.Schneid.*
C   R. maculiferum *Franch.*
C   R. morii *Hayata*
C   var. morii
var. taitunense *(T.Yamaz.)*
D.F.Chamb.
C   R. ochraceum *Rehder & E.H.Wilson*
var. brevicarpum *W.K.Hu*
C   var. ochraceum *Rehder &*
E.H.Wilson
R. oligocarpum *W.P.Fang & X.S.Zhang*
R. pachyphyllum *W.P.Fang*
C   R. pachysanthum *Hayata*
C   R. pachytrichum *Franch.*
C   var monosematum *(Hutch.)*
D.F.Chamb.
C   var. pachytrichum
var. tenuistylosum *W.K.Hu*
R. pilostylum *W.K.Hu*
R. polytrichum *W.P.Fang*
C   R. pseudochrysanthum *Hayata*
var. nankotaisanense *(Hayata)*
T.Yamaz.
forma rufovelutinum *T.Yamaz.*
C   var. pseudochrysanthum
C   R. sikangense *W.P.Fang*
C   var. exquisitum *(T.L.Ming)*
T.L.Ming
C   var. sikangense *W.P.Fang*
C   R. strigillosum *Franch.*
R. ziyuanense *P.C.Tam*

Subsect. Neriiflora *Sleumer*

Shrubs, sometimes dwarf and creeping, or small trees. Leaves narrowly elliptic to orbicular, lower surface glabrous to dense-ly covered with a whitish or buff to rufous indumentum that is either compacted or lanate, composed of rosulate, dendroid or ramiform hairs. Inflorescence lax or dense, 1-12(-20)-flowered. Calyx minute to well-developed and cupular, often coloured. Corolla 5-lobed, white or yel-low to pink or deep red, usually fleshy, tubular-campanulate to campanulate, with nectar pouches. Stamens 10. Ovary tomentose, with or without stalked glands, or glabrous; style glabrous.

C R. albertsenianum *Forrest*
C R. aperantum *Balf.f. & Kingdon-Ward*
C R. beanianum *Cowan*
   R. bijiangense *T.L.Ming*
C R. catacosmum *Balf.f. ex Tagg*
C R. chamaethomsonii *(Tagg & Forrest) Cowan & Davidian*
   var. chamaedoron *(Tagg & Forrest) D.F.Chamb.*
C   var. chamaethauma *(Tagg) Cowan & Davidian*
C   var. chamaethomsonii
C R. chionanthum *Tagg & Forrest*
C R. citriniflorum *Balf.f. & Forrest*
C   var. citriniflorum
C   var. horaeum *(Balf.f. & Forrest) D.F.Chamb.*
C R. coelicum *Balf.f. & Farrer*
C R. dichroanthum *Diels*
C   subsp. apodectum *(Balf.f. & W.W.Sm.) Cowan*
C   subsp. dichroanthum
C   subsp. scyphocalyx *(Balf.f. & Forrest) Cowan*
C   subsp. septentrionale *Cowan*
   R. erastum *Balf.f. & Forrest*
   R. euchroum *Balf.f. & Kingdon-Ward*
C R. eudoxum *Balf.f. & Forrest*
C   var. brunneifolium *(Balf.f. & Forrest) D.F.Chamb.*
C   var. eudoxum
C   var. mesopolium *(Balf.f. & Forrest) D.F.Chamb.*
C R. floccigerum *Franch.*
C R. forrestii *Balf.f. ex Diels*
C   subsp. forrestii
C   subsp. papillatum *D.F.Chamb.*
C R. haematodes *Franch.*
C   subsp. haematodes
C   subsp. chaetomallum *(Balf.f. & Forrest) D.F.Chamb.*
C R. × hillieri *Davidian*
C R. mallotum *Balf.f. & Kingdon-Ward*
C R. microgynum *Balf.f. & Forrest*
C R. neriiflorum *Franch.*

C   subsp. agetum *(Balf.f. & Forrest) Tagg*
C   subsp. neriiflorum
C   subsp. phaedropum *(Balf.f. & Farrer) Tagg*
C R. parmulatum *Cowan*
C R. piercei *Davidian*
C R. pocophorum *Balf.f. ex Tagg*
C   var. hemidartum *(Tagg) D.F.Chamb.*
C   var. pocophorum
C R. sanguineum *Franch.*
C   subsp. didymum *(Balf.f. & Forrest) Cowan*
   subsp. sanguineum
C   var. cloiophorum *(Balf.f. & Forrest) D.F.Chamb.*
C   var. didymoides *Tagg & Forrest*
C   var. haemaleum *(Balf.f. & Forrest) D.F.Chamb.*
C   var. himertum *(Balf.f. & Forrest) D.F.Chamb.*
C   var. sanguineum
C R. sperabile *Balf.f. & Farrer*
C   var. sperabile
C   var. weihsiense *Tagg & Forrest*
C R. sperabiloides *Tagg & Forrest*
C R. temenium *Balf.f. & Forrest*
C   var. dealbatum *(Cowan) D.F.Chamb.*
C   var. gilvum *(Cowan) D.F.Chamb.*
C   var. temenium
   R. trilectorum *Cowan*
   R. × xanthanthum *(Tagg & Forrest) D.F.Chamb.*

Subsect. Parishia *Sleumer*

Shrubs or small trees, 2-10m. Leaves elliptic to broadly obovate, lower surface glabrescent or with a thin tomentum composed of stellate hairs and sometimes also a few stalked glands, that persists, especially around the midrib. Inflorescence lax, 5-15-flowered. Calyx usually small (though to 17mm and cupular in *R. schistocalyx*). Corolla 5-lobed, fleshy, deep red, tubular- to funnel-campanulate, with nectar pouches. Stamens 10. Ovary densely tomentose, usually also with stalked glands; style glabrous.

C R. elliottii *Watt ex Brandis*

C   R. facetum *Balf.f. & Kingdon-Ward*
    R. flavoflorum *T.L.Ming*
    R. huidongense *T.L.Ming*
C   R. kyawii *Lace & W.W.Sm.*
    R. parishii *C.B.Clarke*
    R. schistocalyx *Balf.f. & Forrest*
    R. urophyllum *W.P.Fang*

Subsect. Pontica *Sleumer*

Shrubs or small trees. Leaves linear to broadly elliptic or obovate, lower surface glabrous or with a one-layered indumentum composed of dendroid hairs. Inflorescence lax or dense, 5-20-flowered. Calyx 1-9mm. Corolla usually 5-lobed (-7-lobed in R. degronianum), lobes divided to half the length of the corolla, yellow or white to pink or lilac-purple, campanulate to funnel-campanulate, nectar pouches lacking. Stamens 10. Ovary glabrous or glandular and/or tomentose; style glabrous.

C   R. aureum *Georgi*
C   var. aureum
C   var hypopytis *(Pojark.)*
            D.F.Chamb.
C   R. brachycarpum *D.Don ex G.Don*
C   subsp. brachycarpum
C   subsp. fauriei *(Franch.) D.F.Chamb.*
            forma nematoanum *(Makino)*
                Murata
C   R. catawbiense *Michx.*
C   R. caucasicum *Pall.*
    R. × charadzeae *A.P.Khokhr. &*
        Mazurenko
C   R. degronianum *Carrière*
C   subsp. degronianum
        subsp. heptamerum *(Maxim.)*
            H.Hara
C   var. heptamerum *(Maxim.) Sealy*
C   var. hondoense *(Nakai) H.Hara*
C   var. kyomaruense *(T.Yamaz.)*
            H.Hara
            forma amagianum *(T.Yamaz.)*
                H.Hara
        subsp.yakushimanum *(Nakai)*
            H.Hara
C   var. intermedium *(Sugim.)*
            H.Hara
C   var. yakushimanum

C   R. hyperythrum *Hayata*
    R. × kurokimense *Arakawa*
C   R. macrophyllum *D.Don ex G.Don*
C   R. makinoi *Tagg*
C   R. maximum *L.*
C   R. × nikomontanum *(Komatsu) Nakai*
C   R. ponticum *L.*
C   R. smirnowii *Trautv.*
C   R. × sochadzeae *Char & Davlianidze*
C   R. ungernii *Trautv.*

Subsect. Selensia *Sleumer*

Shrubs or small trees; young shoots stalked- to setulose-glandular. Leaves obovate to elliptic, lower surface glabrous or with a thin indumentum composed of dendroid hairs. Inflorescence lax, (1-)5-10-flowered. Calyx 1-10mm. Corolla 5-lobed, white or pale yellow to pink, not fleshy, funnel-campanulate to campanulate, nectar pouches lacking. Stamens 10. Ovary stalked-glandular, sometimes also with dendroid hairs; style glabrous.

C   R. bainbridgeanum *Tagg & Forrest*
C   R. calvescens *Balf.f. & Forrest*
C   var. calvescens
        var. duseimatum *(Balf.f. & Forrest)*
            D.F.Chamb.
    R. dascycladoides *Hand.-Mazz.*
C   R. × erythrocalyx *Balf.f. & Forrest*
C   R. esetulosum *Balf.f. & Forrest*
C   R. hirtipes *Tagg*
C   R. martinianum *Balf.f. &Forrest*
C   R. selense *Franch.*
C   subsp. dasycladum *(Balf.f. &*
            W.W.Sm.) D.F.Chamb.
C   subsp. jucundum *(Balf.f. &*
            W.W.Sm.) D.F.Chamb.
C   subsp. selense
        subsp. setiferum *(Balf.f. & Forrest)*
            D.F.Chamb.
    R. xizangense *(W.P.Fang & W.K.Hu)*
        Q.Z.Yu

Subsect. Taliensia *Sleumer*

Shrubs, sometimes dwarf, to small trees. Leaves linear to broadly elliptic, lower surface covered with a dense one- or two-layered, lanate, felted or compacted indumentum composed of radiate, ramiform or fasciculate hairs, or (more rarely) sparse or lacking. Inflorescence usually dense, 5-20-flowered. Calyx minute, to 12 mm. Corolla 5(-7)-lobed, white or yellow to pink or purplish, campanulate or funnel-campanulate, nectar pouches lacking. Stamens 10(-14). Ovary glabrous to densely tomentose, sometimes also glandular, style glabrous or glandular.

C R. adenogynum *Diels*
C R. aganniphum *Balf.f. & Kingdon-Ward*
C var. aganniphum
C var. flavorufum (*Balf.f. & Forrest*) *D.F.Chamb*
C R. alutaceum *Balf.f. & W.W.Sm.*
C var. alutaceum
C var. iodes (*Balf.f. & Forrest*) *D.F.Chamb.*
C var. russotinctum (*Balf.f. & Forrest*) *D.F.Chamb.*
C R. balfourianum *Diels*
   var. aganniphoides *Tagg & Forrest*
C var. balfourianum
   R. barkamense *D.F.Chamb.*
C R. × bathyphyllum *Balf.f. & Forrest*
C R. beesianum *Diels*
C R. bhutanense *D.G.Long & Bowes Lyon*
C R. bureavii *Franch.*
C R. bureavioides *Balf.f.*
C R. clementinae *Forrest*
   subsp. aureodorsale *W.P.Fang ex J.Q.Fu*
C subsp. clementinae
   R. codonanthum *Balf.f. & Forrest*
C R. coeloneuron *Diels*
   R. comisteum *Balf.f. & Forrest*
   R. danbaense *L.C.Hu*
   R. detersile *Franch.*
C R. dignabile *Cowan*
C R. × detonsum *Balf.f. & Forrest*
   R. dumicola *Tagg & Forrest*
C R. elegantulum *Tagg & Forrest*
C R. faberi *Hemsl.*
C R. lacteum *Franch.*
   R. lulangense *L.C.Hu & Y.Tateishi*

C R. mimetes *Tagg & Forrest*
C var. mimetes
C var. simulans *Tagg & Forrest*
   R. montiganum *T.L.Ming*
C R. nakotiltum *Balf.f. & Forrest*
   R. nhatrangense *Dop*
C R. nigroglandulosum *Nitz.*
C R. phaeochrysum *Balf.f. & W.W.Sm.*
C var. agglutinatum (*Balf.f. & Forrest*) *D.F.Chamb.*
C var. levistratum (*Balf.f. & Forrest*) *D.F.Chamb.*
C var. phaeochrysum
   R. pomense *Cowan & Davidian*
   R. potaninii *Batalin*
C R. prattii *Franch.*
C R. principis *Bureau & Franch.*
C R. pronum *Tagg & Forrest*
C R. proteoides *Balf.f. & W.W.Sm.*
C R. przewalskii *Maxim.*
   subsp. chrysophyllum *W.P. Fang & M.Y.He*
C subsp. dabanshanense (*W.P.Fang & Wang*) *W.P.Fang & Wang*
   subsp. huzhuense *W.P.Fang & S.X.Wang*
C subsp. przewalskii
   subsp. yushuense *W.P.Fang & S.X.Wang*
   R. pubicostatum *T.L.Ming*
   R. pugeense *L.C.Hu*
   R. punctifolium *L.C.Hu*
C R. roxieanum *Forrest*
C var. cucullatum (*Hand.-Mazz.*) *D.F.Chamb.*
C var. oreonastes (*Balf.f.*) *T.L.Ming*
C var. parvum *Davidian*
C var. roxieanum
   R. roxieoides *D.F.Chamb.*
C R. rufum *Batalin*
   R. shanii *W.P.Fang*
C R. sphaeroblastum *Balf.f. & Forrest*
C var. sphaeroblastum
C var. wumengense *K.M.Feng*
C R. taliense *Franch.*
   R. torquatum *L.C.Hu, nom. illegit.*
C R. traillianum *Forrest & W.W.Sm.*
C var. dictyotum (*Balf.f. ex Tagg*) *D.F.Chamb.*

C var. traillianum
  R. trichogynum *L.C.Hu*
C R. wasonii *Hemsl. & E.H.Wilson*
C var. wasonii
  var. wenchuanense *L.C.Hu*
C R. wightii *Hook.f.*
C R. wiltonii *Hemsl. & E.H.Wilson*
  R. zhongdianense *L.C.Hu*

Subsect Thomsonia *Sleumer*

Shrubs or small trees. Leaves orbicular to elliptic, lower surface glabrous at maturity, sometimes with fasciculate hairs overlying the veins, or covered with a thin dendroid indumentum. Inflorescence lax or dense, 1-15-flowerd. Calyx usually well-developed and cupular, to 15mm. Corolla 5-lobed, white or cream to deep blackish-crimson, funnel- to tubular-campanulate, with nectar pouches. Stamens 10. Ovary glabrous, tomentose and/or stalked-glandular, style glabrous or glandular to tip.

  R. bonvalotii *Bureau & Franch.*
C R. × candelabrum *Hook.f.*
C R. cerasinum *Tagg*
C R. cyanocarpum *(Franch.)*
  W.W.Sm.
C R. eclecteum *Balf.f. & Forrest*
C var. bellatulum *Balf.f. ex Tagg*
C var. eclecteum
C R. eurysiphon *Tagg & Forrest*
C R. faucium *D.F.Chamb.*
C R. hookeri *Nutt.*
C R. hylaeum *Balf.f. & Farrer*
C R. meddianum *Forrest*
C var. atrokermesinum *Tagg*
C var. meddianum
  R. megalanthum *M.Y.Fang*
  R. populare *Cowan*
  R. ramipilosum *T.L.Ming*
C R. sherriffii *Cowan*
C R. stewartianum *Diels*
C R. subansiriense *D.F.Chamb. &*
  P.A.Cox
C R. thomsonii *Hook.f.*
C subsp. lopsangianum *(Cowan)*
  D.F.Chamb.
C subsp. thomsonii
C R. viscidifolium *Davidian*

Subsect Venatora *D.F.Chamb.*

Straggling shrub, 2-3m. Leaves elliptic, glabrous except for a thin indumentum composed of folioliferous hairs overlying the lower surface of the midrib. Inflorescence 7-10-flowered. Calyx with broad lobes 3-5mm long. Corolla 5-lobed, fleshy, crimson, tubular-campanulate, with nectar pouches. Stamens 10. Ovary densely tomentose and stalked-glandular, style glabrous.

C R. venator *Tagg*

Subsect. Williamsiana *D.F.Chamb.*

Dwarf shrub; young shoots setose-glandular. Leaves ovate-orbicular to broadly oblong, lower surface with lamina glabrous though with some glands, midrib sometimes setulose. Inflorescence lax, 2-3(-5)-flowered. Calyx small. Corolla 5-lobed, pink to purple, campanulate, lacking nectar pouches. Stamens 10. Ovary stalked-glandular to setulose-tomentose, style glabrous or glandular to tip.

  R. leishanicum *W.P.Fang & X.S.Chang*
C R. williamsianum *Rehder &*
  E.H.Wilson

Subgen. Mumeazalea *(Sleumer)* M.N.Philipson & Philipson

Deciduous shrubs; scales lacking; indumentum of simple hairs. Inflorescence lateral, below vegetative buds, 1-flowered. Calyx with gland-fringed lobes. Corolla rotate. Stamens 5, strongly dimorphic, the three lower long, divergent, slightly pubescent below, and with large anthers, the upper two shorter, erect, densely pilose, and with small anthers. Ovary subglobose, impressed below the style. Capsule subglobose. Seeds without appendages.

C R. semibarbatum *Maxim.*

Subgen. Pentanthera *(G.Don)* Pojark.

Deciduous shrubs or small trees; scales lacking; indumentum, when present, of simple hairs. Inflorescence terminal, racemose, 1-15-flowered. Calyx minute to well-developed. Corolla tubular- or rotate-campanulate to broadly funnel-shaped, zygomorphic or actinomorphic. Stamens 5-10 usually declinate. Ovary with a variable amount of indumentum; style usually declinate. Capsule ovoid to cylindrical. Seeds with or without terminal appendages and/or fringes.

Sect. Pentanthera *G.Don*

Corolla zygomorphic, outer surface covered with multicellular and/or unicellular hairs. Stamens 5. Seeds lacking tails, the coat usually more or less loose.

Subsect. Pentanthera

Corolla narrowly funnel-shaped, outer surface with both unicellular and multicellular hairs, upper lobe sometimes with a blotch but lacking spots. Stamens strongly exserted.

C   R. alabamense *Rehder*
C   R. arborescens *(Pursh) Torr.*
C   R. atlanticum *(Ashe) Rehder*
C   R. austrinum *(Small) Rehder*
C   R. × bakeri *(Lemmon & McKay) Hume*
C   R. calendulaceum *(Michx.) Torr.*
C   R. canescens *(Michx.) Sweet*
C   R. cumberlandense *E.L.Braun*
C   R. flammeum *(Michx.) Sargent*
C   R. luteum *Sweet*
C   R. occidentale *(Torr. & A.Gray) A.Gray*
C   R. periclymenoides *(Michx.) Shinners*
C   R. prinophyllum *(Small) Millais*
C   R. prunifolium *(Small) Millais*
C   R. viscosum *(L.) Torr.*

Subsect. Sinensia *(Nakai)* K.Kron

Corolla broadly funnel-shaped, outer sur-face with unicellular hairs only, the upper corolla lobe spotted. Stamens not or only slightly exserted.

C   R. molle *(Blume) G.Don*
C   subsp. japonicum *(A.Gray) Kron*
C   subsp. molle

Sect. Rhodora *(L.) G.Don*

Corolla zygomorphic, two-lipped as a result of the fusion of the three upper lobes, the outer surface glabrous; Stamens (5-)7-10. Seeds with a tail at each end and a conspicuous wing-like fringe, the coat tightly appressed to the seed body.

C   R. canadense *(L.) Torr.*
C   R. vaseyi *A.Gray*

Sect. Sciadorhodion *Rehder & E.H.Wilson*

Corolla zygomorphic, not 2-lipped, the outer surface glabrous. Stamens 10. Seeds lacking tails and a wing-like fringe, the coat tightly appressed to seed body.

C   R. albrechtii *Maxim.*
C   R. pentaphyllum *Maxim.*
C   var. pentaphyllum
         var. shikokianum *T.Yamaz.*
C   R. quinquefolium *Bisset & S.Moore*
C   forma quinquefolium
         forma speciosum *N.Yonez.*
C   R. schlippenbachii *Maxim.*

Sect. Viscidula *Matsumi & Nakai*

Corolla regular, tubular-campanulate, the outer surface glabrous. Stamens 10, included. Seeds with tessellate tails at either end, the coat tightly appressed to the seed body.

C   R. nipponicum *Matsum.*

Subgen. Rhododendron

Shrubs, sometimes dwarf, to trees; leaves persistent or (occasionally) deciduous.

Indumentum, when present, of simple or dendroid hairs; scales always present. Inflorescence terminal, or if lateral then borne in the axils of the upper leaves. Calyx obsolete to well-developed. Corolla rotate to funnel-shaped, campanulate or tubular. Stamens 5-10. Ovary scaly, glabrous, hairy and/or glandular, tapering into the style or with style base impressed. Capsule soft or woody. Seeds with or without appendages.

Sect. Pogonanthum *G.Don*

Aromatic shrubs, generally dwarf. Scales with lacerate margins. Hairs fringing inflorescence bud scales dendroid. Corolla hypocrateriform. Capsule valves soft, usually twisted on dehiscence; seeds with long caudate appendages that are usually longer than the body of the seed.

C   R. anthopogon *D.Don*
     subsp. anthopogon
C   var. album *Davidian*
C   var. anthopogon
C   subsp. hypenanthum *(Balf.f.)*
       Cullen
C   R. anthopogonoides *Maxim.*
C   subsp. anthopogonoides
     subsp. hoi *(W.P.Fang) W.P.Fang &*
       Xiong
     R. atropunicum *H.P.Yang*
C   R. cephalanthum *Franch.*
C   subsp. cephalanthum
C   subsp. platyphyllum *(Franch. ex*
       Balf.f. & Kingdon-Ward) Cullen
C   R. collettianum *Aitch. & Hemsl.*
     R. fragrans *(Adams) Maxim.*
C   R. hedyosmum *Balf.f.*
     R. heteroclitum *H.P.Yang*
C   R. kongboense *Hutch.*
C   R. laudandum *Cowan*
C   var. laudandum
C   var. temoense *Kingdon-Ward ex*
       Cowan & Davidian
     R. luhuoense *H.P.Yang*
     R. mainlingense *S.H.Huang &*
       R.C.Fang
     R. nyingchiense *S.H.Huang &*
       R.C.Fang

     R. pogonophyllum *Cowan & Davidian*
     R. praeclarum *Balf.f. & Farrer*
C   R. primuliflorum *Bureau & Franch.*
     R. radendum *W.P.Fang*
     R. rufescens *Franch.*
C   R. sargentianum *Rehder & E.H.Wilson*
C   R. trichostomum *Franch.*
     R. tubulosum *Ching & W.Y.Wang*

Sect. Rhododendron

Shrubs or trees, only occasionally aromatic. Scales entire, crenulate or undulate. Corolla very rarely hypocrateriform. Hairs fringing inflorescence bud scales simple. Capsule valves hard and woody at dehiscence; seeds variously winged, rarely with caudate appendages that are shorter than the body of the seed.

Subsect. Afghanica *Cullen*

Low shrub. Leaves evergreen, scales on lower surface well-spaced. Inflorescence terminal, a distinct and elongate many-flowered raceme. Calyx conspicuously lobed. Corolla campanulate; stamens 10, regularly arranged; style impressed sharply deflexed. Seeds unwinged, obscurely finned.

C   R. afghanicum *Aitch. & Hemsl.*

Subsect. Baileya *Sleumer*

Small shrub. Leaves evergreen, scales on lower surface crenulate, overlapping and flaky. Inflorescence terminal, with an elongate rhachis. Calyx well-developed. Corolla campanulate; stamens 10, regularly arranged; ovary impressed below the sharply deflexed style. Seeds unwinged and obscurely finned.

C   R. baileyi *Balf.f.*

Subsect Boothia *Sleumer*

Free-growing or epiphytic shrubs; young growth setose. Leaves evergreen, lower surface whitish-papillose, scales rimmed or vesicular, deeply sunk in pits. Inflorescence terminal, 1-many-flowered.

Calyx well-developed. Corolla broadly campanulate; stamens 10, regularly arranged, not declinate; ovary tapering into the sharply deflexed style. Seeds prominently winged and finned.

C R. boothii *Nutt.*
C R. chrysodoron *Tagg ex Hutch.*
   R. dekatanum *Cowan*
C R. leptocarpum *Nutt.*
C R. leucaspis *Tagg*
C R. megeratum *Balf.f.*
   R. nanjianense *K.M.Feng & Z.H.Yang*
C R. sulfureum *Franch.*

Subsect. Camelliiflora *Sleumer*

Shrubs, often epiphytic. Leaves evergreen, scales on lower surface broad-rimmed, touching. Inflorescence terminal, 1-2-flowered. Calyx conspicuous. Corolla open-campanulate; stamens 11-16; regularly arranged; ovary tapering into the sharply deflexed style. Seeds conspicuously winged and finned.

C R. camelliiflorum *Hook.f.*

Subsect. Campylogyna *Sleumer*

Dwarf, usually prostrate shrubs; young growth scaly, glabrous or pubescent. Leaves evergreen, lower surface papillose, often whitsh, scales for the most part deciduous, distant, vesicular. Inflorescence terminal, 1-3-flowered. Corolla campanulate; stamens 10, regularly arranged; ovary impressed below the sharply deflexed style. Seeds lacking wings and only obsurely finned.

C R. campylogynum *Franch.*

Subsect. Caroliniana *Sleumer*

Shrubs, 2(-5)m; young growth scaly. Leaves evergreen, lower surface with dense small-rimmed scales. Inflorescence terminal, several-flowered. Calyx small.

Corolla narrowly to openly funnel-shaped. Stamens 10, declinate; ovary impressed below the declinate style. Seeds unwinged and very obscurely finned.

C R. minus *Michx.*
C   var. chapmanii *(A.Gray)*
         W.H.Duncan & Pullen
C   var. minus

Subsect. Cinnabarina *Sleumer*

Shrubs, to 7m; young shoots scaly. Leaves evergreen or partly deciduous, scales on lower surface dense but not touching, small, broadly or narrowly winged. Inflorescence terminal or axillary, 2-5-flowered. Calyx inconspicuous. Corolla fleshy, tubular to campanulate; stamens 10, declinate; ovary impressed below the declinate style. Seeds unwinged and obscurely finned.

C R. cinnabarinum *Hook.f.*
      subsp. cinnabarinum
C   var. cinnabarinum
C   var. breviforme *Davidian*
C   subsp. tamaense *(Davidian) Cullen*
C   subsp. xanthocodon *(Hutch.)*
         Cullen
C R. keysii *Nutt.*
   R. lateriflorum *R.C.Fang &*
      A.L.Zhang
   R. tenuifolium *R.C.Fang &*
      S.H.Huang

Subsect. Edgeworthia *Sleumer*

Shrubs, epiphytic or scrambling over rocks; young shoots hairy. Leaves evergreen, often bullate above, lower surface covered with a relatively thick indumentum, scales distant, small. Inflorescence terminal, 2-3-flowered. Calyx well-developed. Corolla funnel-campanulate or campanulate; stamens 10, regularly arranged or declinate; ovary densely tomentose, style declinate or sharply deflexed downwards. Seeds winged and finned.

C R. edgeworthii *Hook.f.*
C R. pendulum *Hook.f.*
C R. seinghkuense *Kingdon-Ward*

Subsect. Fragariiflora *Cullen*

Small shrubs. Leaves evergreen, minute, crenulate, lower surface with distant vesicular scales. Inflorescence terminal, 2-3-flowered. Calyx conspicuous. Corolla open-campanulate; stamens 10, declinate; ovary impressed below the declinate style. Seeds without wings or fins.

C R. fragariiflorum *Kingdon-Ward*

Subsect. Genestieriana Sleumer

Free-growing shrubs; young shoots scaly, glabrous. Leaves evergreen, lower surface white-papillose, scales distant, small. Inflorescence terminal, many-flowered, racemose. Calyx rim-like. Corolla campanulate; stamens (8-)10, regularly arranged; style impressed, sharply deflexed. Seeds unwinged and obscurely finned.

C R. genestierianum *Forrest*

Subsect. Glauca *Sleumer*

Shrubs, to 2m. Leaves evergreen, small, lower surface whitsh-papillose, with dimorphic scales, the smaller more numerous, the larger long-stalked. Inflorescence 3-10-flowered. Calyx well-developed. Corolla campanulate to tubular-campanulate; stamens 10; style impressed, sharply deflexed or (rarely) declinate. Seeds unwinged, with obscure appendages.

C R. brachyanthum *Franch.*
C   subsp. brachyanthum
C   subsp. hypolepidotum *(Franch.)* Cullen
C R. charitopes *Balf.f. & Farrer*
C   subsp. charitopes
C   subsp. tsangpoense *(Kingdon-Ward)* Cullen

C R. glaucophyllum *Rehder*
        subsp. glaucophyllum
C   var. album *Davidian*
C   var. glaucophyllum
C   subsp. tubiforme *(Cowan & Davidian)* D.G.Long
C R. luteiflorum *(Davidian)* Cullen
C R. pruniflorum *Hutch. & Kingdon-Ward*
C R. shweliense *Balf.f. & Forrest*

Subsect. Heliolepida *Sleumer*

Shrubs or small trees, 1-10m; young shoots scaly, glabrous. Leaves evergreen, often aromatic, scales on lower surface dense, large. Inflorescence terminal 4-10-flowered. Calyx usually disc-like. Corolla funnel-shaped, sometimes openly so; stamens 10, declinate; ovary impressed below the declinate or straight style.

C R. bracteatum *Rehder & E.H.Wilson*
C R. heliolepis *Franch.*
C   var. brevistylum *(Franch.) Cullen*
C   var. heliolepis
   R. hirsutipetiolatum *R.C.Fang & A.L.Zhang*
   R. invictum *Balf.f. & Farrer*
C R. rubiginosum *Franch.*
       var. ptilostylum *R.C.Fang*
C   var. rubiginosum *Franch.*

Subsect. Lapponica *Sleumer*

Small shrubs; young shoots scaly, glabrous or (in *R. setosum*) setose. Leaves evergreen, usually papillose beneath, scales on lower surface of one or two types, distant or dense, broadly rimmed. Inflorescence a terminal umbellate raceme, 1-several-flowered. Calyx minute to conspicuous. Corolla usually open-campanulate, rarely hypocrateriform. Stamens 5-10(-11), usually regularly arranged. Style impressed, straight or declinate. Seeds unwinged and obscurely finned.

   R. amundsenianum *Hand.-Mazz.*
C R. bulu *Hutch.*

23

R. burjaticum *Malyschev*
C R. capitatum *Maxim.*
C R. complexum *Balf.f. & W.W.Sm.*
C R. cuneatum *W.W.Sm.*
C R. dasypetalum *Balf.f. & Forrest*
R. dawuense *H.P.Yang*
R. declivatum *Ching & H.P.Yang*
C R. × edgarianum *Rehder & E.H.Wilson*
C R. fastigiatum *Franch.*
C R. flavidum *Franch.*
C var. flavidum
var. psilostylum *Rehder & E.H.Wilson*
C R. hippophaeoides *Balf.f. & W.W.Sm.*
C var. hippophaeoides
C var. occidentale *M.N.Philipson & Philipson*
C R. impeditum *Balf.f. & W.W.Sm.*
C R. intricatum *Franch.*
R. joniense *Ching & H.P.Yang*
R. labolengense *Ching & H.P.Yang*
C R. lapponicum *(L.) Wahlenb.*
R. lungchiense *W.P.Fang*
C R. × lysolepis *Hutch.*
R. maowenense *Ching & H.P.Yang*
R. minyaense *M.N.Philipson & Philipson*
C R. nitidulum *Rehder & E.H.Wilson*
C var. nitidulum
C var. omeiense *M.N.Philipson & Philipson*
C R. nivale *Hook.f.*
C subsp. australe *M.N.Philipson & Philipson*
C subsp. boreale *M.N.Philipson & Philipson*
C subsp. nivale
C R. orthocladum *Balf.f. & Forrest*
var. longistylum *M.N.Philipson & Philipson*
C var. microleucum *(Hutch.) M.N.Philipson & Philipson*
C var. orthocladum
C R. polycladum *Franch.*
R. qinghaiense *Ching & W.Y.Wang*
C R. rupicola *W.W.Sm.*
C var. chryseum *(Balf.f & Kingdon-Ward) M.N.Philipson & Philipson*
C var. muliense *(Balf.f. & Kingdon-Ward) M.N.Philipson &*

Philipson
C var. rupicola
C R. russatum *Balf.f. & Forrest*
C R. setosum *D.Don*
R. taibaiense *Ching & H.P.Yang*
C R. tapetiforme *Balf.f. & Kingdon-Ward*
C R. telmateium *Balf.f. & W.W.Sm.*
C R. thymifolium *Maxim.*
R. tsaii *W.P.Fang*
R. × verruculosum *Rehder & E.H.Wilson*
C R. websterianum *Rehder & E.H.Wilson*
C var. websterianum
var. yulongense *M.N.Philipson & Philipson*
R. xiguense *Ching & H.P.Yang*
R. yulingense *W.P.Fang*
C R. yungningense *Balf.f.*
R. zheguense *Ching & H.P.Yang*

Subsect. Ledum *Kron & Judd*

Small shrubs, to 2m; young shoots scaly, covered with a ferrugineous indumentum, or puberulous, sometimes also with glands. Leaves evergreen, usually strongly revolute, lower surface with epidermis white-papillate and often also with a white setulose indumentum, sometimes also with a varying amount of ferrugineous tomentum. Inflorescence a many-flowered terminal corymb. Calyx obsolete or small. Corolla rotate, 4-10mm; stamens 7-12, regularly arranged; style straight.

C R. groenlandicum *(Oeder) Kron & Judd*
C R. hypoleucum *(Kom.) Harmaja*
C R. neoglandulosum *Harmaja*
C R. tolmachevii *Harmaja*
C R. tomentosum *(Stokes) Harmaja*
C subsp. subarcticum *(Harmaja) G.Wallace*
C subsp. tomentosum

Subsect. Lepidota *Sleumer*

Small shrub, to 2m; young shoots scaly, setose and pubescent to glabrous. Leaves evergreen or deciduous, scales on lower surface distant or touching, with broad translucent rims. Inflorescence terminal, 1-5-flowered. Calyx well-developed. Corolla campanulate; stamens 10, regularly arranged; ovary impressed below the very short, sharply deflexed style. Seeds unwinged and obscurely finned.

C   R. cowanianum *Davidian*
    R. lepidotum *Wall. ex G.Don*
C   var. album *Davidian*
C   var. lepidotum
C   var. minutiforme *Davidian*
C   R. lowndesii *Davidian*

Subsect. Maddenia *Sleumer*

Shrubs, sometimes epiphytic, or small trees, to 12m; young shoots scaly, often also setose. Leaves evergreen, lower surface whitish- or greyish-papillose, scales distant or dense, sometimes with crenulate margins. Inflorescence 1-7-flowered. Calyx usually conspicuous. Corolla funnel-campanulate to campanulate; stamens 8-27 though usually c.10, declinate; ovary tapering into style or impressed below the declinate style. Seeds winged and finned.

    R. amandum *Cowan*
C   R. burmanicum *Hutch.*
C   R. carneum *Hutch.*
    R. changii *(W.P.Fang) W.P.Fang*
    R. chunienii *W.P.Fang*
C   R. ciliatum *Hook.f.*
C   R. ciliicalyx *Franch.*
    R. ciliipes *Hutch.*
C   R. coxianum *Davidian*
    R. crenulatum *Hutch. ex Sleumer*
C   R. cuffeanum *Hutch.*
C   R. dalhousiae *Hook.f.*
C   var. dalhousiae
C   var. rhabdotum *(Balf.f. & R.E.Cooper) Cullen*
C   R. dendricola *Hutch.*
C   R. excellens *Hemsl. & E.H.Wilson*
C   R. fletcherianum *Davidian*
    R. fleuryi *Dop*
C   R. formosum *Wall.*
C   var. formosum
C   var. inaequale *C.B.Clarke*
C   R. goreri *Davidian*
C   R. grothausii *Davidian*

C   R. horlickianum *Davidian*
C   R. johnstoneanum *G.Watt ex Hutch.*
    R. kiangsiense *W.P.Fang*
C   R. levinei *Merr.*
C   R. liliiflorum *H.Lév.*
C   R. lindleyi *T.Moore*
    R. linearilobum *R.C.Fang & A.L.Zhang*
C   R. ludwigianum *Hosseus*
C   R. lyi *H.Lév.*
C   R. maddenii *Hook.f.*
C   subsp. crassum *(Franch.) Cullen*
C   subsp. maddenii
C   R. megacalyx *Balf.f.*
    R. mianningense *Z.J.Zhao*
    R. nemorosum *R.C.Fang*
C   R. nuttallii *Booth*
C   R. pachypodum *Balf.f. & W.W.Sm.*
C   R. parryae *Hutch.*
    R. pseudociliipes *Cullen*
    R. rhombifolium *R.C.Fang*
C   R. roseatum *Hutch.*
    R. rufosquamosum *Hutch.*
C   R. scopulorum *Hutch.*
    R. surasianum *Balf.f. & Craib*
C   R. taggianum *Hutch.*
C   R. valentianinum *Forrest ex Hutch.*
C   var. oblongilobatum *R.C.Fang*
C   var. valentinianum
C   R. veitchianum *Hook.f.*
C   R. walongense *Kingdon-Ward*
    R. wumingense *W.P.Fang*
    R. yaogangxianense *Q.X.Liu*
    R. yizangense *Q.X.Liu*
    R. yungchangense *Cullen*

Subsect. Micrantha *Sleumer*

Shrubs, to 2m; young shoots scaly, puberulent. Leaves evergreen, scales on lower surface touching or overlapping, broad-rimmed. Inflorescence terminal, a many-flowered raceme. Calyx small. Corolla funnel-campanulate, 5-8mm; stamens 10, more or less straight; ovary impressed below the straight style. Seeds prominently winged and finned.

    R. brevicaudatum *R.C.Fang & S.S.Chang*
    R. liaoxigensis *S.L.Tung & Z.Lu*
C   R. micranthum *Turcz.*

Subsect. Monantha *Cullen*

Epiphytic or free-growing shrubs; young shoots scaly, otherwise glabrous. Leaves evergreen, scales on lower surface dense, broad-rimmed. Inflorescence terminal, 1-3-flowered. Calyx minute. Corolla tubular-funnel-shaped to tubular-campanulate, with scarcely spreading lobes; stamens 10; style impressed, straight. Seeds winged and finned.

> R. concinnoides *Hutch. & Kingdon-Ward*
> R. flavantherum *Hutch. & Kingdon-Ward*
> R. kasoense *Hutch. & Kingdon-Ward*
> R. monanthum *Balf.f. & W.W.Sm.*

Subsect. Moupinensia *Sleumer*

Epiphytic or free-growing shrubs, to 1m; young shoots scaly and setose. Leaves evergreen, scales on lower surface dense, medium-sized to small. Inflorescence terminal, 1-2-flowered. Calyx conspicuous. Corolla open-funnel-campanulate; stamens 10, declinate; ovary tapering into the declinate style. Seeds winged and finned.

C R. dendrocharis *Franch.*
C R. moupinense *Franch.*
   R. petrocharis *Diels*

Subsect. Rhododendron

Small shrubs, to 1.5m; young shoots densely scaly, sometimes also with a few hairs. Leaves evergreen, lower surface covered with large golden or reddish-brown scales. Inflorescence terminal, with a conspicuous rhachis. Calyx small but clearly lobed. Corolla tubular-campanulate; stamens 10, declinate; style straight or declinate. Seeds unwinged and obscurely finned.

C R. ferrugineum *L.*
C R. hirsutum *L.*
C R. myrtifolium *Schott & Kotschy*

Subsect. Rhodorastra *(Maxim.) Cullen*

Small to moderately sized shrubs, to 1.5m; young shoots scaly and puberulous; new vegetative growth from bud below those that produce the inflorescences. Leaves partially or entirely deciduous, rarely all evergreen, lower surface densely or laxly covered in medium-sized scales. Inflorescence axillary, at the end of the branches, 1-flowered. Calyx rim-like. Corolla open-funnel-shaped; stamens 10, declinate; ovary impressed below the declinate style. Seeds unwinged and obscurely finned.

C R. dauricum *L.*
C R. ledebourii *Pojark.*
C R. mucronulatum *Turcz.*
C   var. mucronulatum
      var. taquetii *(H.Lév.) Nakai*
   R. sichotense *Pojark.*

Subsect. Saluenensia *Sleumer*

Prostrate to erect shrubs, to 1.5m; young shoots densely scaly, glabrous, or if setose then the setae quickly deciduous. Leaves evergreen, scales on lower surface of leaves overlapping, arranged in several tiers, the upper tier sometimes with stalks. Inflorescence terminal, 1-3(-5)-flowered. Calyx deeply 5-lobed. Corolla open-funnel-campanulate; stamens 10, declinate; ovary impressed below the declinate style. Seeds unwinged and obscurely finned.

C R. calostrotum *Balf.f. & Kingdon-Ward*
C   subsp. calostrotum
C   subsp. keleticum *(Balf.f. & Forrest) Cullen*
C   subsp. riparioides *Cullen*
C   subsp. riparium *(Kingdon-Ward) Cullen*
C R. saluenense *Franch.*
C   subsp. chameunum *(Balf.f. & Forrest) Cullen*
C   subsp. saluenense

Subsect. Scabrifolia *Cullen*

Small shrubs, to 3m; young shoots scaly, pilose and/or setose. Leaves evergreen, usually with a persistent indumentum on the upper surface, lower surface sometimes white-papillose, covered with vesicular glands, sometimes also setose, at least on midrib. Inflorescence axillary, 2-3(-5)-flowered. Calyx rim-like or with lobes to 3mm. Corolla open- to funnel-campanulate, or tubular; stamens (8-)10, declinate; ovary impressed below the usually declinate style. Seeds unwinged, fins small and obscure.

C   R. hemitrichotum *Balf.f. & Forrest*
C   R. mollicomum *Balf.f. & W.W.Sm.*
C   R. pubescens *Balf.f. & Forrest*
C   R. racemosum *Franch.*
C   R. scabrifolium *Franch.*
C   var. pauciflorum *Franch.*
C   var. scabrifolium
C   var. spiciferum *(Franch.) Cullen*
C   R. spinuliferum *Franch.*
      var. glabrescens *K.M.Feng*
C   var. spinuliferum *Franch.*

Subsect. Tephropepla *Sleumer*

Small to moderately sized shrubs; young shoots scaly. Leaves evergreen, lower surface papillose, scales broad-rimmed, sometimes sunk in pits, uniform or of two kinds. Inflorescence usually terminal, occasionally axillary. Calyx conspicuous. Corolla campanulate or funnel-campanulate; stamens 10, declinate; ovary tapering into the declinate style or ovary impressed below the style. Seeds unwinged, with obscure fins.

C   R. auritum *Tagg*
C   R. hanceanum *Hemsl.*
C   R. longistylum *Rehder & E.H.Wilson*
      subsp. decumbens *R.C.Fang*
C   subsp. longistylum
C   R. tephropeplum *Balf.f.*
      R. tsinlingense *W.P.Fang & J.Q.Fu*
C   R. xanthostephanum *Merr.*

Subsect. Trichoclada *(Balf.f.)* *Cullen*

Small shrubs, to 2m; young shoots often setose. Leaves evergreen or deciduous, glabrous or pilose, scales on lower surface distant, vesicular, large. Inflorescence terminal, 2-5-flowered. Calyx rim-like to clearly lobed. Corolla funnel-campanulate; stamens 10, regularly arranged; ovary impressed below the sharply deflexed style. Seeds unwinged and obscurely finned.

C   R. caesium *Hutch.*
C   R. lepidostylum *Balf.f. & Forrest*
C   R. mekongense *Franch.*
C   var. mekongense
C   var. rubrolineatum *(Balf.f. & Forrest) Cullen*
C   R. trichocladum *Franch.*
C   var. longipilosum *Cowan*
C   var. trichocladum
C   R. viridescens *Hutch.*

Subsect. Triflora *Sleumer*

Shrubs, often large, to 10m; young shoots scaly, sometimes setose. Leaves usually evergreen, occasionally deciduous, sometimes pubescent, especially on midrib and veins, scales on lower surface lax or dense, rimmed or rimless, sometimes of two kinds. Inflorescence terminal and axillary, 1-3-flowered, occasionally with several inflorescences coalescing to form a compound inflorescence. Calyx usually minute. Corolla strongly zygomorphic, openly funnel-shaped; stamens 10, declinate; ovary impressed below the declinate style. Seeds unwinged and with very small obscure fins.

C   R. ambiguum *Hemsl.*
C   R. amesiae *Rehder & E.H.Wilson*
C   R. augustinii *Hemsl.*
C   subsp. augustinii
C   subsp. chasmanthum *(Diels) Cullen*
C   subsp. hardyi *(Davidian) Cullen*
C   subsp. rubrum *(Davidian) Cullen*

R. brachypodum *W.P.Fang & P.S.Liu*
C R. concinnum *Hemsl.*
C R. davidsonianum *Rehder &
   E.H.Wilson*
   R. gemmiferum *M.N.Philipson &
   Philipson*
   R. guangnanense *R.C.Fang*
   R. kangdingense *Z.J.Zhao*
C R. keiskei *Miq.*
   var. hypoglaucum *Suto & Suzuki*
C   var. keiskei
   var. ozawae *T. Yamaz*
C R. lutescens *Franch.*
C R. oreotrephes *W.W.Sm.*
C R. pleistanthum *Balf.f. ex Wilding*
C R. polylepis *Franch.*
C R. rigidum *Franch.*
C R. searsiae *Rehder & E.H.Wilson*
   R. seguinii *H.Lév.*
   R. shaanxiense *W.P.Fang & Z.J.Zhao*
   R. shimianense *W.P.Fang & P.S.Liu*
C R. siderophyllum *Franch.*
C R. tatsienense *Franch.*
   var. nudatum *R.C.Fang*
C   var. tatsienense
C R. trichanthum *Rehder*
C R. triflorum *Hook.f.*
   subsp. multiflorum *R.C.Fang*
   subsp. triflorum
C   var. bauhiniiflorum *(Watt ex
     Hutch.) Cullen*
C   var. triflorum
   R. wongii *Hemsl. & E.H.Wilson*
   R. xichangense *Z.J.Zhao*
C R. yunnanense *Franch.*
C R. zaleucum *Balf.f. & W.W.Sm.*
C   var. flaviflorum *Davidian*
   var. pubifolium *R.C.Fang*
C   var. zaleucum

Subsect. Uniflora *Sleumer*

Small shrubs, often prostrate; young shoots scaly, sometimes also pubescent. Leaves evergreen, revolute, margins sometimes crenulate, scales on lower surface dense, unequal or equal, rimless or with undulate rims. Inflorescence terminal, 1-3-flowered, leaves beneath inflorescence bract-like. Calyx with definite lobes. Corolla funnel-campanulate; stamens 10, declinate; style impressed, decli-

nate, or straight.

C R. ludlowii *Cowan*
C R. pemakoense *Kingdon-Ward*
C R. pumilum *Hook.f.*
C R. uniflorum *Kingdon-Ward*
C   var. imperator *(Kingdon-Ward)
     Cullen*
C   var. uniflorum

Subsect. Virgata *(Hutch.)* Cullen

Small shrubs; young shoots scaly, otherwise glabrous. Leaves evergreen, lower surface papillose, the dense scales unequal and flaky. Inflorescence borne in the axils of the upper leaves, the terminal bud vegetative, each 1(-2)-flowered. Calyx lobes 2-3mm. Corolla funnel-shaped; stamens 10, declinate; ovary impressed below the declinate style. Seeds unwinged but caudate-appendaged at both ends.

C R. virgatum *Hook.f.*
   subsp. oleifolium *(Franch.) Cullen*
   var. glabriflorum *K.M.Feng*
C   var. oleifolium
C   subsp. virgatum

Section Vireya *(Blume)* H.F.Copel.

Small creeping shrubs to trees to 10m. Flowers solitary to many together in an umbellate inflorescence which never has a rhachis. Corolla very variable but never with spots of colour (although they may be spotted with scales). Stamens 5 or 10-14. The ovary normally tapering gradually into the style. Seeds with a long tail at both ends.

Subsection Albovireya *Sleumer*

Scales very dense, large, not markedly different in size and without dark centres, touching or overlapping to form a continuous layer on the undersurface of at least submature leaves and usually fairly per-sistent. Corolla shape various but the lobes more than ¼ of the total length of the flower.

C R. aequabile *J.J.Sm.*
C R. album *Blume*
   R. arenicolum *Sleumer*
   R. cernuum *Sleumer*
   R. comptum *C.H. Wright*
      var. comptum
      var. trichodes *Sleumer*
   R. correoides *J.J.Sm.*
   R. giulianettii *Laut.*
   R. lagunculicarpum *J.J.Sm.*
   R. lampongum *Miq.*
   R. proliferum *Sleumer*
   R. pudorinum *Sleumer*
   R. versteegii *J.J.Sm.*
C R. yelliotii *Warb.*
   R. zollingeri *J.J.Sm.*

Subsection Malayovireya
Sleumer

Scales very dense, usually of two, or at least very different sizes, at least some touching and mostly overlapping to com-pletely cover the underside of submature leaves and usually very persistent there. Corolla shape various but the lobes more than ¼ of the total length of the flower.

C R. acuminatum *Hook.f.*
C R. apoanum *Stein*
C R. durionifolium *Becc.*
C R. fallacinum *Sleumer*
   R. fortunans *J.J.Sm.*
C R. himantodes *Sleumer*
C R lineare *Merr.*
C R. malayanum *Jack*
C   var. axillare *J.J.Sm.*
      var. infrapilosum *Sleumer*
      var. malayanum
C   var. pilosifilum *Sleumer*
      var. pubens *Sleumer*
C R. micromalayanum *Sleumer*
   R. nortoniae *Merr.*
   R. obscurum *Sleumer*
C R. variolosum *Becc.*
      var. andersonii *(Ridl.)Sleumer*

   var. variolosum
   R. vinicolor *Sleumer*
   R. wilhelminae *Hochr.*

Subsection Phaeovireya
Sleumer

Scales more or less dendroid, each on top of a distinct and persistent epidermal tubercle, the scales themselves often quickly falling off. Corolla shape various, but the lobes always more than ¼ of the total length of the flower.

   R. asperrimum *Sleumer*
   R. asperum *J.J.Sm.*
C R. beyerinckianum *Koord.*
C R. bryophilum *Sleumer*
   R. bullifolium *Sleumer*
C R. caliginis *Kores*
   R. delicatulum *Sleumer*
      var. lanceolatoides *Sleumer*
C R. dianthosmum *Sleumer*
C R. dielsianum *Schltr.*
C   var. dielsianum
      var. stylotrichum *Sleumer*
   R. extrorsum *J.J.Sm.*
   R. eymae *Sleumer*
C R. gardenia *Schltr*
   R. gillardii *Sleumer.*
   R. haematopthalmum *Sleumer*
C R. hellwigii *Warb.*
   R. hooglandii *Sleumer*
C R. hyacinthosmum *Sleumer*
C R. konori *Becc.*
C   var. konori
C   var. phaeopeplum *(Sleumer) Argent*
C R. leptanthum *F.Muell.*
C   var. leptanthum
C   var. warianum *(Schltr.)Argent*
   R. melantherum *Schltr.*
   R. neobritanicum *Sleumer*
   R. neriifolium *Schltr.*
   R. opulentum *Sleumer*
C R. phaeochitum *F. Muell.*
   R. phaeochristum *Sleumer*
   R. phaeops *Sleumer*
   R. prainianum *Koord.*
   R. psilanthum *Sleumer*
   R. rappardii *Sleumer*
C R. rarum *Schltr.*

R. revolutum *Sleumer*
R. rhodochroum *Sleumer*
R. rubellum *Sleumer*
C R. schoddei *Sleumer*
C R. solitarium *Sleumer*
R. spondylophyllum *F. Muell.*
R. stelligerum *Sleumer*
R. stolleanum *Schltr.*
C R. superbum *Sleumer*
R. thaumasianthum *Sleumer*
R. truncicolum *Sleumer*
R. tuberculiferum *J.J.Sm.*

Subsection Pseudovireya (Clarke) *Sleumer*

Scales disk-shaped with a relatively large swollen centre and narrow entire to slightly lobed margin or flange, sometimes on persistent stalks; dense to sparse on the undersides of the leaves but rarely touching and never overlapping in the submature state. Corolla shape various but never white and trumpet-shaped and the lobes generally more than ¼ of the total length of the flower.

R. adinophyllum *Merr.*
R. asperulum *Hutch.& Kingdon-Ward*
C R. borneense *(J.J.Sm.)Argent,*
    A.L.Lamb & Phillipps
C   subsp. angustissimum *(Sleumer)*
    Argent
C   subsp. borneense
C   subsp. villosum *(J.J.Sm.)Argent*
    A.L.Lamb & Phillipps
R. buxoides *Sleumer*
R. capellae *Kores*
R. ciliilobum *Sleumer*
C R. cuneifolium *Stapf*
R. cyrtophyllum *Wernh.*
R. datiandingense *Z.J.Feng*
R. densifolium *K.M.Feng*
R. detznerianum *Sleumer*
C R. emarginatum *Hemsl.& Wilson*
C R. ericoides *Low ex Hook.f.*
R. erosipetalum *J.J.Sm.*
C R. gaultheriifolium *J.J.Sm.*

var. expositum *Sleumer*
var. gaultherifolium
R. hameliiflorum *Wernh.*
R. insculptum *Hutch. &*
    Kingdon-Ward
C R. kawakamii *Hayata*
R. leiboense *Z.J.Zhao*
R. lindaueanum *Koord.*
var. bantaengense *J.J.Sm.*
var. lindaueanum
R. maguanense *K.M.Feng*
C R. meliphagidum *J.J.Sm.*
R. nanophyton *Sleumer*
var. nanophyton
var. petrophilum *Sleumer*
R. nummatum *J.J.Sm.*
R oreites *Sleumer*
var. chlorops *Sleumer*
var. oreites
C R. perakense *King & Gamble*
R. pulleanum *Koord.*
var. maiusculum *Sleumer*
var pulleanum
C R. quadrasianum *Vidal*
var. davaoense *(H.F.*
    Copel.)Sleumer
var. intermedium *Merr.*
C   var. malindangense *(Merr.)Sleumer*
C   var. marivelesense *(H.F.*
    Copel.)Sleumer
C   var. quadrasianum
C   var. rosmarinifolium
    (Vidal)H.F.Copel.
var. selibicum *J.J.Sm.*
C R. retusum *(Blume)Benn.*
var. epilosum *J.J.Sm.*
C   var. retusum
var. trichostylum *Sleumer*
R. rupivalleculatum *P.C.Tam*
C R. rushforthii *Argent &*
    D.F.Chamberlain
C R. santapaui *Sastry et al.*
R. saruwagedicum *Foerster*
R. schizostigma *Sleumer*
R. scortechinii *King & Gamble*
R. seimundii *J.J.Sm.*
R. sororium *Sleumer*
R. spathulatum *Ridl.*

R. taxoides *J.J.Sm.*
C   R. vaccinioides *Hook.f.*
R. vanderbiltianum *Merr.*
R. vinkii *Sleumer*

Subsection Siphonovireya

Sleumer

Scales disk-shaped with a relatively large swollen centre and narrow entire to slightly lobed margin or flange, dense to sparse on the undersides of the leaves but rarely touching and never overlapping in the mature state. Corolla trumpet-shaped, the tube narrow and elongate with the lobes less than ¼ of the total length of the flower, white or white flushed pink.

R. agathodaemonis *J.J.Sm.*
R. cinchoniflorum *Sleumer*
R. habbemae *Koord.*
C   R. herzogii *Warb.*
R. incommodum *Sleumer*
R. inundatum *Sleumer*
R. protandrum *Sleumer*

Subsection Solenovireya

H.F. Copel.

Scales deeply lobed, star-shaped or sub-dendroid, sometimes minute and then hardly lobed, rarely touching in the submature state. Corolla trumpet-shaped, the tube narrow and elongate with the lobes less than ¼ of the total length of the flower, white or pink.

C   R. alborugosum *Argent & J.Dransf.*
R. amabile *Sleumer*
R. archboldianum *Sleumer*
C   R. armitii *F.M.Bailey*
R. brachypodarium *Sleumer*
C   R. carrii *Sleumer*
C   R. carringtoniae *F. Muell.*
R. carstensense *Wernh.*
R. chamaepitys *Sleumer*
R. cinerascens *Sleumer*
C   R. cruttwellii *Sleumer*
R. edanoi *Merr.*
C   R. goodenoughii *Sleumer*
R. hartleyi *Sleumer*
C   R jasminiflorum *Hook.*

C   var. copelandii *(Merr.)Sleumer*
C   var. heusseri *(J.J.Sm.)Sleumer*
C   var. jasminiflorum
C   var. oblongifolium *Sleumer*
C   var. punctatum *Ridl.*
C   R. loranthiflorum *Sleumer*
R. macrosiphon *Sleumer*
C   R. maius *(J.J.Sm.)Sleumer*
C   R. multinervium *Sleumer*
R. natalicium *Sleumer*
C   R. orbiculatum *Ridl.*
R. oliganthum *Sleumer*
R. oreadum *Wernh.*
C   R. pleianthum *Sleumer*
C   R. pneumonanthum *Sleumer*
R. pseudotrichanthum *Sleumer*
R. pubitubum *Sleumer*
R. radians *J.J.Sm.*
var. minahasae *Sleumer*
var. radians
R. retrorsipilum *Sleumer*
R. rhodoleucum *Sleumer*
R. rhodosalpinx *Sleumer*
R. roseiflorum *P.F.Stevens*
C   R. ruttenii *J.J.Sm.*
C   R. searleanum *Sleumer*
C   R. stapfianum *Hemsl. ex Prain*
C   R. suaveolens *Sleumer*
C   forma roseum *Argent, A.L.Lamb & Phillipps*
C   forma suaveolens
R. syringoideum *Sleumer*
C   R. tuba *Sleumer*

Subsection Vireya *H.F. Copel.*

Scales irregularly lobed to star-shaped, mostly widely spaced in submature leaves and with small centres. Corolla various but the lobes more than ¼ of the total length of the flower.

C   R. abietifolium *Sleumer*
C   R. acrophilum *Merr. & Quisumb.*
R. alternans *Sleumer*
C   R. alticolum *Sleumer*
C   R. anagalliflorum *Wernh.*
R. angulatum *J.J.Sm.*
R. arfakianum *Becc.*
C? R. atropurpureum *Sleumer*
C   R. aurigeranum *Sleumer*
C   R. baconii *Argent, A.L.Lamb & Phillipps*

C R. baenitzianum *Laut.*
C R. bagobonum *H.F.Copel.*
R. banghamiorum *(J.J.Sm.)Sleumer*
R. beccarii *Sleumer*
C R. blackii *Sleumer*
R. bloembergenii *Sleumer*
R. brachygynum *H.F.Copel.*
C R. brassii *Sleumer*
R. brevipes *Sleumer*
C R. brookeanum *Low ex Lindl.*
C   subsp. brookeanum
    var. cladotrichum *Sleumer*
    var. extraneum *Sleumer*
C   var. kinabaluense *(Argent,*
    A.L.Lamb & Phillipps)Argent
C   var. moultonii *(Ridl.)Argent*
C   subsp. cockburnii *(Argent, A.L.*
    Lamb & Phillipps)Argent
C   subsp. gracile *(Lindl.)Argent*
C R. burttii *P.Woods*
R. buruense *J.J.Sm.*
C R. buxifolium *Low ex Hook.f.*
    var. buxifolium
    var. robustum
C R. caespitosum *Sleumer*
R. calosanthes *Sleumer*
R. celebicum *(Blume)DC.*
R. chevalieri *Dop*
C R. christi *Foerster*
C R. christianae *Sleumer*
C R. citrinum *(Hassk.)Hassk.*
C   var. citrinum
    var. discoloratum *Sleumer*
R. coelorum *Wernh.*
C R. commonae *Foerster*
R. comparabile *Sleumer*
R. cornu-bovis *Sleumer*
C R. crassifolium *Stapf*
C R. culminicolum *F. Muell.*
    var. angiense *(J.J.Sm.)Sleumer*
C   var. culminicolum
    var. nubicola *(Wernh.) Sleumer*
C R. curviflorum *J.J.Sm.*
R. cuspidellum *Sleumer*
R. disterigmoides *Sleumer*
R. englerianum *Koord.*
C R. exuberans *(Sleumer)Argent*
R. flavroviride *J.J.Sm.*
R. frey-wysslingii *J.J.Sm.*
R. glabriflorum *J.J.Sm.*
C R. gracilentum *F. Muell.*

R. hatamense *Becc.*
R. helodes *Sleumer*
R. hirtolepidotum *J.J.Sm.*
R. impositum *J.J.Sm.*
R. impressopunctatum *J.J.Sm.*
C R. inconspicuum *J.J.Sm.*
C R. intranervatum *Sleumer*
C R. javanicum *(Blume)Benn.*
C   subsp. javanicum
C   var. javanicum
    var. teysmannii *(Miq.)King &*
    Gamble
C   subsp. schadenbergii
    (Warb.)Argent
R. kemulense *J.J.Sm.*
C R. kochii *Stein*
C R. laetum *J.J.Sm.*
R. lamii *J.J.Sm.*
C R. lanceolatum *Ridl.*
R. leptobrachion *Sleumer*
R. leptomorphum *Sleumer*
C R. leucogigas *Sleumer*
R. leytense *Merr.*
    var. loheri *(H.F. Copel.)Sleumer*
    var. leytense
R. loboense *H.F.Copel.*
C R. lochiae *F.Muell.*
R. loerzingii *J.J.Sm.*
R. lompohense *J.J.Sm.*
C R. longiflorum *Lindl.*
    var. bancanum *Sleumer*
C   var. longiflorum
C   var. subcordatum *(Becc.)Argent*
C R. lowii *Hook. f.*
C R. luraluense *Sleumer*
R. luteosquamatum *Sleumer*
C R. macgregoriae *F. Muell.*
    var. glabrifilum *(J.J.Sm.)Sleumer*
    var. mayrii *(J.J.Sm.)Sleumer*
    var. macgregoriae
C R. maxwellii *Gibbs*
C R. meijeri *Argent, A.L.Lamb &*
    Phillipps
R. microphyllum *J.J.Sm.*
C R. mindanaense *Merr.*
R. mollianum *Koord.*
C R. multicolor *Miq.*
C R. muscicola *J.J.Sm.*
R. myrsinites *Sleumer*
C R. nervulosum *Sleumer*
C R. nieuwenhuisii *J.J.Sm.*

C R. notiale *Craven*
R. oxycoccoides *Sleumer*
R. pachycarpon *Sleumer*
R. pachystigma *Sleumer*
R. papuanum *Becc.*
R. parvulum *Sleumer*
C R. pauciflorum *King & Gamble*
    var. calocodon *(Ridl.)Sleumer*
C   var. pauciflorum
R. perplexum *Sleumer*
C R. polyanthemum *Sleumer*
R. poremense *J.J.Sm.*
R. porphyranthes *Sleumer*
C R. praetervisum *Sleumer*
R. psammogenes *Sleumer*
R. pseudobuxifolium *Sleumer*
R. pseudomurudense *Sleumer*
C R. pubigermen *J.J.Sm.*
R. purpureiflorum *J.J.Sm.*
R. pusillum *J.J.Sm.*
R. pyrrhophorum *Sleumer*
C R. rarilepidotum *J.J.Sm.*
    var. ootrichum *Sleumer*
C   var. rarilepidotum
C R. renschianum *Sleumer*
R. retivenium *Sleumer*
R. rhodopus *Sleumer*
R. rhodostomum *Sleumer*
R. ripleyi *Merr.*
    var. basitrichum *Sleumer*
    var. cryptogonium *Sleumer*
    var. ripleyi
C R. robinsonii *Ridl.*
R. rosendahlii *Sleumer*
C R. rubineiflorum *Craven*
R. rubrobracteatum *Sleumer*
C R. rugosum *Low ex Hook.f.*
C R. salicifolium *Becc.*
C R. sarcodes *Argent & Madulid*
C R. saxifragoides *J.J.Sm.*
R. sayeri *Sleumer*
C R. scabridibracteum *Sleumer*
R. scarlatinum *Sleumer*
R. schlecteri *Laut.*
R. seranicum *J.J.Sm.*
C R. sessilifolium *J.J.Sm.*
R. simulans *Sleumer*
C R. stenophyllum *Hook.f. ex Stapf*
C   subsp. angustifolium
      (J.J.Sm.)Argent, A.L.Lamb &
      Phillipps

C   subsp. stenophyllum
C R. stevensianum *Sleumer*
R. stresemannii *J.J.Sm.*
R. subcrenulatum *Sleumer*
R. subuliferum *Sleumer*
R. subulosum *Sleumer*
C R. sumatranum *Merr.*
C R. taxifolium *Merr.*
R. toxopei *J.J.Sm.*
R. triumphans *Yersin & Cheval.*
R. ultimum *Wernh.*
R. vanvuurenii *J.J.Sm.*
C R. verticillatum *Low ex Lindl.*
C   forma velutinum *(Becc.)*
      Sleumer
    forma verticillatum
C R. vidalii *Rolfe*
R. villosulum *J.J.Sm.*
C R vitis-idaea *Sleumer*
R. wentianum *Koord.*
R. whiteheadii *Rendle*
C R. williamsii *Merr. ex Copel.f.*
C R. womersleyi *Sleumer*
C R. wrightianum *Koord.*
C   var. cyclopense *J.J.Sm.*
    var. insulare *Sleumer*
C   var. wrightianum
R. xanthopetalum *Merr.*
C R. yongii *Argent*
C R. zoelleri *Warb.*

Subgen. Therorhodion *(Maxim.) Gray*

Dwarf, evergreen or deciduous shrubs; indumentum of simple, sometimes glandular, hairs, scales absent. Inflorescence buds terminal, opening to produce a 1-3-flowered raceme; peduncles bearing leaf-like bracts. Calyx lobes well-developed. Corolla 5-lobed, rotate, divided to base on the lower side. Stamens 10. Ovary pubescent; style base impressed. Capsule ovoid. Seeds without appendages.

C R. camtschaticum *Pall.*
C   subsp. camtschaticum
    subsp. glandulosum *(Small)*
      Hultén
R. redowskianum *Maxim.*

Subgen. Tsutsusi *(Sweet)*

Pojark.

Shrubs, sometimes dwarf; indumentum of simple hairs or bristles that are sometimes ribbon-like and flattened or of stiff glandular hairs. Leaves persistent and/or deciduous. Leaves and inflorescence arising from within the same bud scales; inflorescence terminal, 1-several-flowered. Calyx lobes minute to well-developed. Corolla rotate to tubular-campanulate. Stamens (4-)5-10(-12). Ovary strigose to glandular. Seeds unornamented, without appendages.

Sect. Brachycalyx *Sweet*

Leaves rhombic to rhombic-ovate, arranged in pseudowhorls of (2-)3 at the ends of the branches, of one kind, deciduous in winter; flowers appearing before or with the leaves, corolla funnel-shaped to funnel-campanulate.

C   R. amagianum *(Makino) Makino ex H.Hara*
    R. amakusaense *(Takada ex T.Yamaz.) T.Yamaz.*
    R. daiyunicum *P.C.Tam*
C   R. decandrum *(Makino) Makino*
C   R. dilatatum *Miq.*
C   forma dilatatum
      forma hypopilosum *Sa.Kurata*
C   R. farrerae *Tate*
C   R. hidakanum *H.Hara*
    R. huadingense *B.Y.Ding & Y.Y.Fang*
    R. hyugaense *(T.Yamaz.) T.Yamaz.*
C   R. kiyosumense *(Makino) Makino*
C   R. lagopus *Nakai*
C   var. lagopus
      var. niphophilum *(T.Yamaz.) T.Yamaz.*
C   R. mariesii *Hemsl. & E.H.Wilson*
C   R. mayebarae *Nakai & H.Hara*
C   R. nudipes *Nakai*
      var. kirishimense *T.Yamaz.*
      var. nagasakianum *(Nakai) T.Yamaz*
C   var. nudipes
    R. osuzuyamense *T.Yamaz.*.
C   R. reticulatum *D.Don*

      var. bifolium *T. Yamaz.*
C   var. reticulatum
C   R. sanctum *Nakai*
      var. lasiogynum *Nakai ex Sugim.*
C   var. sanctum
    R. tsurugisanense *(T.Yamaz.) T.Yamaz.*
      var. nudipetiolatum *T.Yamaz.*
      var. tsurugisanense
    R. viscistylum *Nakai*
C   R. wadanum *Makino*
C   R. weyrichii *Maxim.*
      var. psilostylum *Nakai*
C   var. weyrichii
    R. yakumontanum *(T.Yamaz.) T.Yamaz.*

Sect. Tsutsusi

Leaves linear to broadly ovate, scattered along the stems (pseudo-whorled in *R. tashiroi*), usually of two kinds, the spring leaves larger and deciduous, the summer leaves smaller and persistent through the winter, sometimes with all the leaves apparently uniform and persistent. Corolla rotate to tubular-campanulate.

    R. adenanthum *M.Y.He*
    R. apricum *P.C.Tam*
    R. arunachalense *D.F.Chamb. & S.J.Rae*
C   R. atrovirens *Franch.*
    R. bellum *W.P.Fang & G.Z.Li*
    R. bicorniculatum *P.C.Tam*
    R. boninense *Nakai*
    R. chaoanense *D.C.Wu & P.C.Tam*
    R. chrysocalyx *H.Lév. & Vaniot*
      var. chrysocalyx
      var. xiushanense *(W.P.Fang) M.Y.He*
    R. chunii *W.P.Fang*
    R. crassistylum *M.Y.He*
    R. cretaceum *P.C.Tam*
C   R. eriocarpum *(Hayata) Nakai*
    R. florulentum *P.C.Tam*
    R. flosculum *W.P.Fang & G.Z.Li*
C   R. flumineum *W.P.Fang & M.Y.He*
    R. fuchsiifolium *H.Lév.*
    R. fuscipilum *M.Y.He*
    R. gratiosum *P.C.Tam*
    R. hainanense *Merr.*
    R. hejiangense *M.Y.He*
    R. huiyangense *W.P.Fang & M.Y.He*
    R. hunanense *Chun ex P.C.Tam*

C R. indicum *(L.) Sweet.*
R. jasminoides *M.Y.He*
R. jinpingense *W.P.Fang & M.Y.He*
R. jinxiuense *W.P.Fang & M.Y.He*
C R. kaempferi *Planch..*
C var. kaempferi
C var. macrogemma *Nakai*
var. saikaiense *(T.Yamaz.) T.Yamaz.*
var. tubiflorum *Komatzu*
C R. kanehirae *E.H.Wilson*
C R. kiusianum *Makino*
C var. kiusianum
C var sataense *(Nakai) D.F.Chamb.*
& *S.J.Rae*
R. kwangtungense *Merr. & Chun*
R. lasiostylum *Hayata*
R. litchiifolium *T.C.Wu & P.C.Tam*
R. longifalcatum *P.C.Tam*
R. longiperulatum *Hayata*
R. loniceriflorum *P.C.Tam*
R. malipoense *M.Y.He*
R. mariae *Hance*
subsp. kwangsiense *(P.C.Tam)*
D.F.Chamb.
subsp. mariae
R. matsumurai *Komatsu*
R. meridionale *P.C.Tam*
var. meridionale
var. minor *P.C.Tam*
C R. microphyton *Franch.*
R. minutiflorum *Hu*
C R. mucronatum *(Blume) G.Don*
R. myrsinifolium *Ching ex W.P.Fang*
& *M.Y.He*
R. naamkwanense *Merr.*
var. cryptonerve *P.C.Tam*
var. naamkwanense
C R. nakaharae *Hayata*
R. nanpingense *P.C.Tam*
C R. noriakianum *Suzuki*
C R. obtusum *(Lindl.) Planch.*
R. octandrum *M.Y.He*
C R. oldhamii *Maxim.*
R. petilum *P.C.Tam*
R. pinetorum *P.C.Tam*
R. polyraphidoideum *P.C.Tam*
var. montanum *P.C.Tam*
var. polyraphidoideum
R. pulchroides *Chun & W.P.Fang*
R. qianyangense *M.Y.He*
R. rhodanthum *M.Y.He*

R. rhuyuenense *Chun*
C R. ripense *Makino*
R. rivulare *Hand.-Mazz.*
C R. rubropilosum *Hayata*
C var. breviperulatum *(Hayata)*
T.Yamaz.
var. grandiflorum *T. Yamaz.*
C var. rubropilosum
R. rufo-hirtum *Hand.-Mazz.*
R. rufulum *P.C.Tam*
C R. saisiuense *Nakai*
R. saxatile *B.Y.Ding & Y.Y.Fang*
C R. saxicolum *Sleumer*
C R. scabrum *G.Don*
C subsp. amanoi *(Ohwi) D.F.Chamb.*
& *S.J.Rae*
C subsp. scabrum
R. seniavinii *Maxim.*
C R. serpyllifolium *(A.Gray) Miq.*
R. sikayotaisanense *Masam.*
C R. simsii *Planch.*
var. mesembrinum *(Balf.f. &*
Forrest) Rehder
C var. simsii
R. sparsifolium *W.P.Fang*
R. subcerinum *P.C.Tam*
C R. stenopetalum *(Hogg) Mabb.*
R. subenerve *P.C.Tam*
R. subflumineum *P.C.Tam*
C R. subsessile *Rendle*
R. taipaoense *T.C.Wu & P.C.Tam*
R. taiwanalpinum *Ohwi*
C R. tashiroi *Maxim.*
var. lasiophyllum *Hatus. ex*
T.Yamaz.
C var. tashiroi
R. tenuilaminare *P.C.Tam*
C R. tosaense *Makino*
C R. tschonoskyi *Maxim.*
var. trinerve *(Franch.) Makino*
C var. tschonoskyi
R. tsoi *Merr.*
C R. tsusiophyllum *Sugim.*
R. unciferum *P.C.Tam*
R. viscidum *C.Z.Guo & Z.H.Liu*
R. viscigemmatum *P.C.Tam*
R. yangmingshanense *P.C.Tam*
R. yaoshanicum *W.P.Fang & M.Y.He*
C R. yedoense *Maxim.*
C var. poukhanense *(H.Lév.) Nakai*
C var. yedoense

List of Synonyms with the Corresponding Accepted Names

Synonyms, Invalid and Unpublished Names

The list contains all traced synonyms published up to the end of 1996, each with the corresponding accepted name following the = sign (excl. those found in the species descriptions (p.81). It also contains those names that are not validly published, usually as there is no accompanying description. Wherever possible the corresponding accepted names are also given.

Some names published in Latin and referring to garden hybrids, or only known in horticulture, are also included, with the corresponding cultivar names, so that as complete a list as possible is available.

For an explanation of the form of these names see Introduction to Temperate Rhododendrons (p.74).

Anthodendron
A. **ponticum** *(L.) Rchb.*=
  R. luteum *Sweet*

Azalea
A. **alabamense** *(Rehder) Small*=
  R. alabamense *Rehder*
A. **albrechtii** *(Maxim.) Kuntze*=
  R. albrechtii *Maxim.*
A. **amagiana** *Makino* =
  R. amagianum *(Makino) Makino ex H.Hara*
A. **amoena** *Lindl.*=
  R. kiusianum *Makino* 'Amoenum'
A. **arborescens** *Pursh*=
  R. arborescens *(Pursh) Torr.*
A. **arborescens** *Pursh* var. **richardsonii** *(Rehder) Ashe*=
  R. arborescens *(Pursh) Torr.*
A. **atlantica** *Ashe*=
  R. atlanticum *(Ashe) Rehder*
A. **atlantica** *Ashe* var. **luteo-alba** *Coker* =
  R. atlanticum *(Ashe) Rehder*

A. **aurantiaca** *F.Dietr.* =
  R. calendulaceum *(Michx.) Torr.*
A. **austrina** *Small* =
  R. austrinum *(Small) Rehder*
A. **bakeri** *Lemmon & McKay* =
  R. × bakeri *(Lemmon & McKay) Hume*
A. **bicolor** *(Aiton) Pursh* =
  R. canescens *(Michx.) Sweet*
A. **brookeana** *(Low ex Lindl.) Kuntze* =
  R. brookeanum *Low ex Lindl.* var. brookeanum
A. **calendulacea** *Michx.* =
  R. calendulaceum *(Michx.) Torr.*
A. **calendulacea** *Michx.* var. **crocea** *Michx.* =
  R. calendulaceum *(Michx.) Torr.*
A. **calendulacea** *Michx.* var. **flammea** *Michx.* =
  R. flammeum *(Michx.) Sargent*
A. **californica** *Torr. & A.Gray ex Durand* =
  R. occidentale *(Torr. & A.Gray) A.Gray*
A. **canadensis** *(L.) Kuntze* =
  R. canadense *(L.) Torr.*
A. **candida** *Small* =
  R. canescens *(Michx.) Sweet*
A. **canescens** *Michx.* =
  R. canescens *(Michx.) Sweet*
A. **canescens** *Michx.* var. **candida** *(Small) Ashe* =
  R. canescens *(Michx.) Sweet*
A. **citrina** *Hassk.* =
  R. citrinum *(Hassk.) Hassk.* var. citrinum
A. **coccinea** *Lodd.* =
  R. calendulaceum *(Michx.) Torr.*
A. **crispiflora** *Hook.f.* =
  R. 'Crispiflorum'
A. **crocea** *Hoffmanns.* =
  R. calendulaceum *(Michx.) Torr.*
A. **cumberlandensis** *(E.L.Braun) Copel.* =
  R. cumberlandense *E.L.Braun*

A. **danielsiana** *Paxton* =
R. 'Danielsianum'
A. **dianthiflora** *Carrière* =
R. 'Dianthiflorum'
A. **farrerae** *(Tate) K.Koch.* =
R. farrerae *Tate*
A. **fastigifolia** *Lemmon* =
R. × fastigifolium *(Lemmon) Hume*
A. **flava** *Hoffmanns.* =
R. luteum *Sweet*
A. **fragrans** *Adams* =
R. fragrans *(Adams) Maxim.*
A. **fragrans** *Raf.* =
R. arborescens *(Pursh) Torr.*
A. **furbishii** *Lemmon* =
R. × furbishii *(Lemmon) Leach*
A. **glauca** *Lam.* =
R. viscosum *(L.) Torr.*
A. **glauca** *Lam.* **var. hispida** *(Pursh)*
Heynh. =
R. viscosum *(L.) Torr.*
A. **hispida** *Pursh* =
R. viscosum *(L.) Torr.*
A. **indica** *L.* =
R. indicum *(L.) Sweet*
A. **indica** *L.* **var. calycina** *Lindl.* =
R. 'Omurasaki'
A. **indica** *L.* **var. lateritia** *Lindl.* =
R. 'Lateritium'
A. **japonica** *A.Gray* =
R. molle *(Blume) G.Don* subsp.
japonicum *(A.Gray) Kron*
A. **jasminiflora** *(Hook.) Kuntze* =
R. jasminiflorum *Hook.* var.
jasminiflorum
A. **javanica** *(Blume) Kuntze* =
R. javanicum *(Blume) Benn.* subsp.
javanicum var. javanicum
A. **kaempferi** *(Planch.) André* =
R. kaempferi *Planch.*
A. **kiyosumensis** *Makino* =
R. kiyosumense *(Makino) Makino*
A. **lamponga** *(Miq.) Kuntze* =
R. lampongum *Miq.*
A. **lapponica** *L.* =
R. lapponicum *(L.) Wahlenb.*
A. **ledifolia** *Hook.* =
R. ripense 'Mucronatum' *(Blume)*
G.Don var. mucronatum
A. **ledifolia** *Hook.* **var. phaenicea**
Hook. =
R. 'Phoeniceum'

A. **liliiflora** *Poit.* =
R. ripense 'Mucronatum' *(Blume)*
G.Don var. mucronatum
A. **lutea** *L.* =
R. periclymenoides
(Michx.) Shinners
A. **macrantha** *Bunge* =
R. 'Macranthum'
A. **makinoi** *(Tagg) Makino* =
R. makinoi *Tagg*
A. **makinoi** *(Tagg) Makino* var.
muranoana *Makino* =
R. makinoi *Tagg*
A. **malayana** *(Jack) Kuntze* =
R. malayanum *Jack*
var. malayanum
A. **mollis** *Blume* =
R. molle *(Blume) G.Don*
subsp. molle
A. **mollis** *Blume* **var. glabrior**
Miq. ex Regel =
R. molle *(Blume) G.Don*
subsp. japonicum *(A.Gray)*
Kron
A. **mucronata** *Blume* =
R. ripense 'Mucronatum' *(Blume)*
G.Don
A. **multicolor** *(Miq.) Kuntze* =
R. multicolor *Miq.*
A. **myrtifolia** *Champ.* =
R. hongkongense *Hutch.*
A. **neglecta** *Ashe* =
R. atlanticum *(Ashe) Rehder*
A. **nipponica** *(Matsum.) Copel.* =
R. nipponicum *Matsum.*
A. **nitida** *Pursh* =
R. viscosum *(L.) Torr.*
A. **nudiflora** *L.* **var. alba** *Aiton* =
R. periclymenoides *(Michx.)*
Shinners
A. **nudiflora** *L.* **var. bicolor** *Aiton* =
R. canescens *(Michx.) Sweet*
A. **nudiflora** *L.* **var. calycosa** *Wood* =
R. periclymenoides *(Michx.)*
Shinners
A. **nudiflora** *L.* **var. carnea** *Aiton* =
R. periclymenoides *(Michx.)*
Shinners
A. **nudiflora** *L.* **var. ciliata** *Kellogg* =
R. occidentale *(Torr. & A.Gray)*
A.Gray
A. **nudiflora** *L.* **var. coccinea** *Aiton* =

R. flammeum *(Michx.) Sargent*

A. nudiflora *L.* **var. glandulifera**
Porter =
R. periclymenoides *(Michx.)*
Shinners

A. nudiflora *L.* **var. papilionacea**
Aiton =
R. periclymenoides *(Michx.)*
Shinners

A. nudiflora *L.* **var. partita** *Aiton =*
R. periclymenoides *(Michx.)*
Shinners

A. nudiflora *L.* **var. periclymenoides**
(Michx.) Heynh. =
R. periclymenoides *(Michx.)*
Shinners

A. nudiflora *L.* **var. polyandra**
(Pursh) DC. =
R. periclymenoides *(Michx.)*
Shinners

A. nudiflora *L.* **var. rosea**
Hoffmanns. =
R. periclymenoides *(Michx.)*
Shinners

A. nudiflora *L.* **var. rutilans** *Aiton =*
R. periclymenoides *(Michx.)*
Shinners

A. oblongifolia *Small =*
R. viscosum *(L.) Torr.*

A. obtusa *Lindl. =*
R. Obtusum Group

A. occidentalis *Torr. & A.Gray =*
R. occidentale *(Torr. & A.Gray)*
A.Gray

A. ovata *Lindl. =*
R. ovatum *(Lindl.) Maxim.*

A. parvifolia *(Adams) Kuntze =*
R. lapponicum *(L.) Wahlenb.*

A. pennslyvanica *Gable =*
R. × pennsylvanicum *(Gable)*
Rehder

A. pentaphylla *(Maxim.) Copel. =*
R. pentaphyllum *Maxim.*

A. periclymena *Pers. =*
R. periclymenoides *(Michx.)*
Shinners

A. periclymenoides *Michx. =*
R. periclymenoides *(Michx.)*
Shinners

A. periclymenoides *Michx.* **var. alba**
Pursh =
R. periclymenoides *(Michx.)*

Shinners

A. periclymenoides *Michx.*
var. carnea *Pursh =*
R. periclymenoides *(Michx.)*
Shinners

A. periclymenoides *Michx.* **var.**
coccinea *(Aiton) Pursh =*
R. flammeum *(Michx.) Sargent*

A. periclymenoides *Michx.* **var.**
papilionacea *(Aiton) Pursh =*
R. periclymenoides *(Michx.)*
Shinners

A. periclymenoides *Michx.* **var.**
partita *(Aiton) Pursh =*
R. periclymenoides *(Michx.)*
Shinners

A. periclymenoides *Michx.* **var.**
polyandra *Pursh =*
R. periclymenoides *(Michx.)*
Shinners

A. periclymenoides *Michx.* **var.**
rutilans *(Aiton) Pursh =*
R. periclymenoides *(Michx.)*
Shinners

A. pontica *L. =*
R. luteum *Sweet*

A. pontica *L.* **var. autumnalis**
K.Koch =
R. luteum *Sweet*

A. pontica *L.* **var. sinensis** *(Lodd.)*
Lindl. =
R. molle *(Blume) G.Don* subsp.
japonicum *(A.Gray) Kron*

A. prinophylla *Small =*
R. prinophyllum *(Small) Millais*

A. prunifolia *Small =*
R. prunifolium *(Small) Millais*

A. punicea *Sweet =*
R. × puniceum *(Sweet) Planch.*

A. quinquefolia *(Bisset & S.Moore)*
Olmsted, Coville & H.P.Kelsey =
R. quinquefolium *Bisset & S.Moore*

A. ramentacea *Lindl. =*
R. 'Album'

A. retusa *(Blume) Kuntze =*
R. retusum *(Blume) Benn.* var.
retusum

A. rosmarinifolia *Burm. =*
R. mucronatum *(Blume) G.Don* var.
mucronatum

A. schlippenbachii *(Maxim.)*
Kuntze =

R. schlippenbachii *Maxim.*
A. semibarbata *(Maxim.) Kuntze* =
R. semibarbatum *Maxim.*
A. serpyllifolia *A.Gray* =
R. serpyllifolium *(A.Gray) Miq.*
A. serrulata *Small* =
R. viscosum *(L.) Torr.*
A. serrulata *Small* **var. georgiana**
(Rehder) Ashe =
R. viscosum *(L.) Torr.*
A. sinensis *Lodd.* =
R. molle *(Blume) G.Don* subsp.
japonicum *(A.Gray) Kron*
A. sinensis *Lodd.* **var. glabrior** *(Miq.)*
Maxim. =
R. molle *(Blume) G.Don* subsp.
japonicum *(A.Gray) Kron*
A. speciosa *Willd.* **var. aurantia**
Lodd. =
R. calendulaceum *(Michx.) Torr.*
A. squamata *Lindl.* =
R. farrerae *Tate*
A. stenopetala *Hogg* =
R. stenopetalum *(Hogg) Mabb.*
A. teysmannii *(Miq.) Kuntze* =
R. javanicum *(Blume) Benn.* var.
teysmannii *(Miq.) K. & G.*
A. tomentosa *Dum.Cours.* =
R. viscosum *(L.) Torr.*
A. tubiflora *Blume ex DC.* =
R. malayanum *Jack* var.
malayanum
A. vaseyi *(A.Gray) Rehder* =
R. vaseyi *A.Gray*
A viscosa *Marshall* =
R. arborescens *(Pursh) Torr.*
A. viscosa *L.* =
R. viscosum *(L.) Torr.*
A. viscosa *L.* **var. aemulans** *(Rehder)*
Ashe =
R. viscosum *(L.) Torr.*
A. viscosa *L.* **var. floribunda** *Aiton* =
R. viscosum *(L.) Torr.*
A. viscosa *L.* **var. glauca** *Aiton* =
R. viscosum *(L.) Torr.*
A. viscosa *L.* **var. hispida**
(Pursh) Hook. =
R. viscosum *(L.) Torr.*
A. viscosa *L.* **var. montana** *(Rehder)*
Ashe =
R. viscosum *(L.) Torr.*
A. viscosa *L.* **var. nitida** *(Pursh)*

Britton =
R. viscosum *(L.) Torr.*
A. viscosa *L.* **var. palustris** *Marshall* =
R. viscosum *(L.) Torr.*
A. viscosa *L.* **var. pubescens** *Lodd.* =
R. viscosum *(L.) Torr.*
A. viscosa *L.* **var. rubescens** *Lodd.* =
R. viscosum *(L.) Torr.*
A. viscosa *L.* **var. virens** *Michx.* =
R. viscosum *(L.) Torr.*

Azaleastrum
A. albiflorum *(Hook.) Rydberg* =
R. albiflorum *Hook.* var.
albiflorum
A. warrenii *A.Nelson* =
R. albiflorum *Hook.* var. warrenii
(A.Nelson) M.A.Lane

Biltia
B. vaseyi *(A.Gray) Small* =
R. vaseyi *A. Gray*

Cladothamnus
C. campanulatus *Greene* =
R. albiflorum *Hook.*

Hochenwartia
H. canadensis *(L.) Crantz* =
R. canadense *(L.) Torr.*

Hymenanthes
H. japonica *Blume* =
R. degronianum *Carrière* var.
heptamerum *(Maxim.) Sealy*

Ledum L.
= *R.* Subsection Ledum *(L.) Kron*
& Judd
L. californicum *Kellogg* =
R. tolmachevii *Harmaja*
L. columbianum *Piper* =
R. columbianum *(Piper) Harmaja*
L. glandulosum *Nutt.* =
R. neoglandulosum *Harmaja*
L. groenlandicum *Oeder* =
R. groenlandicum *(Oeder) Kron &*
Judd
L. hypoleucum *Kom.* =
R. hypoleucum *(Kom.) Harmaja*
L. macrophyllum *Tolm.* =
R. tolmachevii *Harmaja*

L. palustre *L.* **var. decumbens** *Aiton=*
R. tomentosum *(Stokes) Harmaja*
var. subarcticum *(Harmaja)*
G.Wallace

L. palustre *L.* **var. diversipilosum**
Nakai =
R. hypoleucum *(Kom.) Harmaja*

L. palustre *L.* **var. palustre** =
R. tomentosum *(Stokes) Harmaja*
var. tomentosum

Rhodazalea crouxii *Croux =*
R. × crouxii *(Croux) Rehder*

Rhododendron

R. aberrans *Tagg & Forrest =*
R. traillianum *Forrest & W.W.Sm.*
var. traillianum

R. achroanthum *Balf.f. & W.W.Sm.* =
R. rupicola *W.W.Sm.* var. rupicola

R. acraium *Balf.f. & W.W.Sm.* =
R. primuliflorum *Bureau & Franch.*

R. acrocline *Sleumer =*
R. culminicolum *F.Muell.* var.
nubicola *(Wernham) Sleumer*

R. adamsii *Rehder =*
R. fragrans *(Adams) Maxim.*

R. adansonii *Pépin =*
R. ponticum *L.*

R. adenostemonum *Balf.f. &*
W.W.Sm. =
R. irroratum *Franch.* subsp.
pogonostylum *(Balf.f. & W.W.Sm.)*
D.F.Chamb.

R. admirabile *Balf.f. & Forrest =*
R. lukiangense *Franch.*

R. adoxum *Balf.f. & Forrest =*
R. vernicosum *Franch.*

R. adroserum *Balf.f. & Forrest =*
R. lukiangense *Franch.*

R. aechmophyllum *Balf.f. & Forrest =*
R. yunnanense *Franch.*

R. aemulorum *Balf.f.* =
R. mallotum *Balf.f. &*
Kingdon-Ward

R. aeruginosum *Hook.f.* =
R. campanulatum *D.Don* subsp.
aeruginosum *(Hook.f.) D.F.Chamb.*

R. aganniphum *Balf.f. &*
Kingdon-Ward **var. glaucopeplum**
(Balf.f. & Forrest) T.L.Ming =
R. aganniphum *Balf.f. &*

Kingdon-Ward var. aganniphum

R. aganniphum *Balf.f. & Kingdon-*
Ward **var. schizopeplum** *(Balf.f.*
& Forrest) T.L.Ming =
R. aganniphum *Balf.f. & Kingdon-*
Ward var. aganniphum

R. agapetum *Balf.f. & Kingdon-Ward* =
R. kyawii *Lace & W.W Sm.*

R. × agastum *Balf.f. & W.W.Sm.*
var. pennivenium *(Balf.f. &*
Forrest) T.L.Ming =
R. tanastylum *Balf.f. & Kingdon-*
Ward var. pennivenium *(Balf.f. &*
Forrest) D.F.Chamb.

R. agathodaemonis *J.J.Sm., non J.J.Sm.*
1913 =
R. herzogii *Warb.*

R. agetum *Balf.f. & Forrest =*
R. neriiflorum *Franch.* subsp.
agetum *(Balf.f. & Forrest) Tagg*

R. aiolopeplum *Balf.f. & Forrest =*
R. phaeochrysum *Balf.f. &*
W.W.Sm. var. levistratum *(Balf.f. &*
Forrest) D.F.Chamb.

R. aiolosalpinx *Balf.f. & Farrer =*
R. stewartianum *Diels*

R. aischropeplum *Balf.f. & Forrest =*
R. roxieanum *Forrest* var.
roxieanum

R. × albicans *Waterer ex Zabel =*
R. Albicans *Group*

R. albicaule *H.Lév.* =
R. fortunei *Lindl.* subsp. fortunei

R. albrechtii *Maxim.* **forma canescens**
Sugim. =
R. albrechtii *Maxim.*

R. album *Buch.-Ham. ex D.Don =*
R. arboreum *Sm.* forma album
Wall.

R. album *Hoffmanns.* =
R. albiflorum *Hook.*

R. album *Ridl., non Blume =*
R. aequabile *J.J.Sm.*

R. album *Zoll., non Blume =*
R. zollingeri *J.J.Sm.*

R. algarvense *Page =*
R. ponticum *L.*

R. alpicola *Rehder & E.H.Wilson* **var.**
strictum *Rehder & E.H.Wilson* =
R. nivale *Hook.f.* subsp. boreale
M.N.Philipson & Philipson

R. × altaclarense *Lindl.* =

R. 'Altaclarense'

R. amamiense *Ohwi* =
R. latoucheae *Franch.* var.
latoucheae

R. amanoi *Ohwi* =
R. scabrum *G.Don* subsp. amanoi
(Ohwi) D.F.Chamb. & S.J.Rae

R. amaurophyllum *Balf.f. & Forrest* =
R. saluenense *Franch.* subsp.
saluenense

R. amoenum *(Lindl.) Planch.* =
R. kiusianum *Makino* 'Amoenum'

R. andersonii *Ridl.* =
R. variolosum *Becc.* var.
andersonii *(Ridl.) Sleumer*

R. angiense *J.J.Sm.* =
R. culminicolum *F.Muell.* var.
angiense *(J.J.Sm.) Sleumer*

R. angustiflorum *Hoppe* =
R. hirsutum *L.*

R. annae *Franch.* **subsp. laxiflorum**
(Balf.f. & Forrest) T.L.Ming =
R. annae *Franch.*

R. × anneliesii *Rehder* =
R. Anneliesi Group

R. anthopogon *D.Don* **var.**
haemonium *(Balf.f. & R.E.Cooper)*
Cowan & Davidian =
R. anthopogon *D.Don* subsp.
anthopogon

R. anthopogon *D.Don* **var.**
hypenanthum *(Balf.f.) H.Hara* =
R. anthopogon *D.Don* subsp.
hypenanthum *(Balf.f.) Cullen*

R. anthosphaerum *Diels* **var.**
eritimum *(Balf.f. & W.W.Sm.)*
Davidian =
R. anthosphaerum *Diels*

R. aperantum *Balf.f. & Kingdon-Ward*
var. subpilosum *Cowan* =
R. aperantum *Balf.f. & Kingdon-*
Ward

R. apiculatum *Rehder & E.H.Wilson* =
R. concinnum *Hemsl.*

R. apodectum *Balf.f. & W.W.Sm.* =
R. dichroanthum *Diels* subsp.
apodectum *(Balf.f. & W.W.Sm.)*
Cowan

R. apricum *P.C.Tam* **var. falcinellum**
P.C.Tam =
R. rufulum *P.C.Tam*

R. araliiforme *Balf.f. & Forrest* =

R. vernicosum *Franch.*

R. arborescens *(Pursh) Torr.* **var.**
richardsonii *Rehder* =
R. arborescens *(Pursh) Torr.*

R. arboreum *Sm.* **subsp. kingianum**
(Watt ex Hook.f.) Tagg =
R. arboreum *Sm.* subsp.
zeylanicum *(Booth) Tagg*

R. arboreum *Sm.* **subsp. windsori**
(Nutt.) Tagg =
R. arboreum *Sm.* subsp. arboreum

R. arboreum *Sm.* **var. kingianum**
Watt ex Hook.f. =
R. arboreum *Sm.* subsp.
zeylanicum *(Booth) Tagg*

R. × arbutifolium *Rehder* =
R. Arbutifolium Group

R. argenteum *Hook.f.* =
R. grande *Wight*

R. argyi *H.Lév.* =
ripense 'Mucronatum'*(Blume)*
G.Don

R. argyrophyllum *Franch.* **subsp.**
hejiangense *W.P.Fang* =
R. insigne *Hemsl. & E.H.Wilson*
var. hejiangense *(W.P.Fang)*
M.Y.Fang

R. argyrophyllum *Franch.* **var.**
cupulare *Rehder & E.H.Wilson* =
R. argyrophyllum *Franch.* subsp.
argyrophyllum

R. argyrophyllum *Franch.* **var.**
leiandrum *Hutch.* =
R. argyrophyllum *Franch.* subsp.
nankingense *(Cowan) D.F.Chamb.*

R. argyrophyllum *Franch.* **var.**
nankingense *Cowan* =
R. argyrophyllum *Franch.* subsp.
nankingense *(Cowan) D.F.Chamb.*

R. argyrophyllum *Franch.* **var.**
omeiense *Rehder & E.H.Wilson* =
R. argyrophyllum *Franch.* subsp.
omeiense *(Rehder & E.H.Wilson)*
D.F.Chamb.

R. arizelum *Balf.f & Forrest* **var.**
rubicosum *Cowan & Davidian* =
R. arizelum *Balf.f. & Forrest*

R. artosquameum *Balf.f. & Forrest* =
R. oreotrephes *W.W.Sm.*

R. ashleyii *Coker* =
R. maximum *L.*

R. asmenistum *Balf.f. & Forrest* =

R. sanguineum *Franch.* var.
cloiophorum *(Balf.f. & Forrest)*
D.F.Chamb.

R. asparagoides *Wernham* =
R. zoelleri *Warb.*

R. asteium *Balf.f. & Forrest* =
R. eudoxum *Balf.f. & Forrest* var.
mesopolium *(Balf.f. & Forrest)*
D.F.Chamb.

R. astrapiae *Foerster ex Schltr.* =
R. konori *Becc.* var. konori

R. atentsiense *Hand.-Mazz.* =
R. dendricola *Hutch.*

R. atjehense *Sleumer* =
R. irroratum *Franch.* subsp.
kontumense *(Sleumer) D.F.Chamb.*

R. atlanticum *(Ashe) Rehder*
forma confusum *Fernald* =
R. atlanticum *(Ashe) Rehder*

R. atlanticum *(Ashe) Rehder* **forma
luteo-album** *(Coker) Fernald* =
R. atlanticum *(Ashe) Rehder*

R. atlanticum *(Ashe) Rehder* **forma
neglectum** *(Ashe) Rehder* =
R. atlanticum *(Ashe) Rehder*

R. atlanticum *(Ashe) Rehder* **forma
tomolobum** *Fernald* =
R. atlanticum *(Ashe) Rehder*

R. atlanticum *(Ashe) Rehder* **var.
luteo-album** *(Coker) Rehder* =
R. atlanticum *(Ashe) Rehder*

R. aucklandii *Hook.f.* =
R. griffithianum *Wight*

R. aucubaefolium *Hemsl.* =
R. stamineum *Franch.* var.
stamineum

R. augustinii *Hemsl.* **forma
grandifolia** *Franch.* =
R. augustinii *Hemsl.* subsp.
chasmanthum *(Diels) Cullen*

R. augustinii *Hemsl.* **forma hardyi**
(Davidian) R.C.Fang =
R. augustinii *Hemsl.* subsp. hardyi
(Davidian) Cullen

R. augustinii *Hemsl.* **forma rubrum**
(Davidian) R.C.Fang =
R. augustinii *Hemsl.* subsp.
rubrum *(Davidian) Cullen*

R. augustinii *Hemsl.* **forma subglabra**
Franch. =
R. augustinii *Hemsl.* subsp.
chasmanthum *(Diels) Cullen*

R. augustinii *Hemsl.* **var.
chasmanthum** *(Diels) Davidian* =
R. augustinii *Hemsl.* subsp.
chasmanthum *(Diels) Cullen*

R. augustinii *Hemsl.* **var. rubrum**
Davidian =
R. augustinii *Hemsl.* subsp.
rubrum *(Davidian) Cullen*

R. augustinii *Hemsl.* **var. yui**
W.P.Fang =
R. augustinii *Hemsl.* subsp.
augustinii

R. aureum *Franch.* =
R. xanthostephanum *Merr.*

R. australe *Balf.f. & Forrest* =
R. leptothrium *Balf.f. & Forrest*

R. austrokiusianum *Hatus.* =
R. kiusianum *Makino* var. sataense
(Nakai) D.F.Chamb. & S.J.Rae

R. axium *Balf.f. & Forrest* =
R. selense *Franch.* subsp. selense

R. baeticum *Boiss. & Reut.* =
R. ponticum *L.*

R. balsaminaeflorum *T.Moore* =
R. 'Balsaminiflorum'

R. barbatum *Wall. ex G.Don* **forma
imberbe** *(Hutch.) H.Hara* =
R. × imberbe *Hutch.*

R. basirotundatum *J.J.Sm.* =
R. javanicum *(Blume) Benn.* subsp.
javanicum var. teysmannii
(Miq.) King & Gamble

R. batangense *Balf.f.* =
R. nivale *Hook.f.* subsp. boreale
M.N.Philipson & Philipson

R. bauhiniflorum *G.Watt ex Hutch.* =
R. triflorum *Hook.f.* var.
bauhiniiflorum *(G.Watt ex Hutch.)*
Cullen

R. beanianum *Cowan* **var. compactum**
Cowan =
R. piercei *Davidian*

R. beimaense *Balf.f. & Forrest* =
R. × erythrocalyx *Balf.f. & Forrest*

R. benthamianum *Hemsl.* =
R. concinnum *Hemsl.*

R. bergii *Davidian* =
R. augustinii *Hemsl.* subsp.
rubrum *(Davidian) Cullen*

R. beyerinckianum *Koord.* **var.
longipetiolatum** *J.J.Sm.* =
R. beyerinckianum *Koord.*

R. bhairopatium *Ham. ex Madden* =
R. lepidotum *Wall. ex G.Don*

R. bhotanicum *C.B.Clarke in Hook.f.* =
R. lindleyi *T.Moore*

R. bicolor *P.C.Tam* =
R. simsii *Planch.* var. simsii

R. bicolor *(Aiton) Sweet* =
R. canescens *(Michx.) Sweet*

R. bilsianum *hort. ex Lavallée* =
R. 'Bylsianum'

R. blandfordiiflorum *Hook.f.* =
R. cinnabarinum *Hook.f.* subsp.
cinnabarinum

R. blandulum *Balf.f. & W.W.Sm.* =
R. selense *Franch.* subsp.
jucundum *(Balf.f. & W.W.Sm.)*
D.F.Chamb.

R. blepharocalyx *Franch.* =
R. intricatum *Franch.*

R. blinii *H.Lév.* =
R. lutescens *Franch.*

R. bodenii *Wernham* =
R. habbemae *Koord.*

R. brachyandrum *Balf.f. & Forrest* =
R. eclecteum *Balf.f. & Forrest* var.
eclecteum

R. brachyanthum *Franch.* **var.**
hypolepidotum *Franch.* =
R. brachyanthum *Franch.* subsp.
hypolepidotum *(Franch.) Cullen*

R. brachycarpum *D.Don ex G.Don*
forma normale *Kitam.* =
R. brachycarpum *D.Don ex G.Don*
subsp. brachycarpum

R. brachycarpum *D.Don ex G.Don*
subsp. tigerstedtii *Nitz.* =
R. brachycarpum *D.Don ex G.Don*
subsp. brachycarpum

R. brachycarpum *D.Don ex G.Don* **var.**
lutescens *Koidz.* =
R. × nikomontanum *(Komatsu)*
Nakai

R. brachycarpum *D.Don ex G.Don* **var.**
nematoanum *Makino* =
R. brachycarpum *D.Don ex G.Don*
subsp. fauriei *(Franch.) D.F.Chamb.*
forma nematoanum *(Makino)*
Murata

R. brachycarpum *D.Don ex G.Don* **var.**
nematoanum *Makino* **forma**
fauriei *(Franch.) Murata* =
R. brachycarpum *D.Don ex G.Don*

subsp. fauriei *(Franch.) D.F.Chamb.*
forma nematoanum *(Makino)*
Murata

R. brachycarpum *D.Don ex G.Don* **var.**
nematoanum *Makino* **forma**
nematoanum =
R. brachycarpum *D.Don ex G.Don*
subsp. fauriei *(Franch.) D.F.Chamb.*
forma nematoanum *(Makino)*
Murata

R. brachycarpum *D.Don ex G.Don* **var.**
roseiflorum *Miyoshi* =
R. brachycarpum *D.Don ex G.Don*
subsp. fauriei *(Franch.) D.F.Chamb.*

R. brachycarpum *D.Don ex G.Don* **var.**
roseum *Koidz.* =
R. brachycarpum *D.Don ex G.Don*
subsp. brachycarpum

R. brachystylum *Balf.f. & Kingdon-*
Ward =
R. trichocladum *Franch.* var.
trichocladum

R. brettii *Hemsl. & E.H.Wilson* =
R. longesquamatum *C.K.Schneid.*

R. brevistylum *Franch.* =
R. heliolepis *Franch.* var.
brevistylum *(Franch.) Cullen*

R. brevitubum *Balf.f. & Cooper* =
R. maddenii *Hook.f.* subsp.
maddenii

R. brevitubum *J.J.Sm.* =
R. crassifolium *Stapf*

R. brookeanum *Low ex Lindl.* **var.**
gracile *(Low ex Lindl.) G.Henslow* =
R. brookeanum *Low ex Lindl.*
subsp. gracile *(Lindl.) Argent,*
A.L.Lamb & Philpps

R. brookeanum *Stapf., non Low ex*
Lindl. =
R. retivenium *Sleumer*

R. bullatum *Franch.* =
R. edgeworthii *Hook.f.*

R. burmannii *G.Don* =
ripense 'Mucronatum'*(Blume)*
G.Don

R. burriflorum *Balf.f. & Forrest* =
R. diphrocalyx *Balf.f.*

R. buxifolium *Low ex Hook.f.*
var. robustum *Sleumer* =
R. buxifolium *Low ex Hook.f., non*
Low ex Lindl.

R. caeruleo-glaucum *Balf.f. &*

Forrest =
R. campylogynum Franch.

R. caespitulum *P.C.Tam* =
R. myrsinifolium *Ching ex W.P.Fang & M.Y.He*

R. calceolariodes *Wernham* =
R. macgregoriae *F.Muell.* var. macgregoriae

R. calendulaceum *(Michx.) Torr.* **forma aurantiacum** *(Dietr.) Rehder* =
R. calendulaceum *(Michx.) Torr.*

R. calendulaceum *(Michx.) Torr.* **forma croceum** *(Michx.) Rehder* =
R. calendulaceum *(Michx.) Torr.*

R. calendulaceum *(Michx.) Torr.* **var. aurantiacum** *(Dietr.) Zabel* =
R. calendulaceum *(Michx.) Torr.*

R. californicum *Hook.f.* =
R. macrophyllum *D.Don ex G.Don*

R. calleryi *Planch.* =
R. simsii *Planch.* var. simsii

R. callichilioides *Wernham* =
R. wentianum *Koord.*

R. callichilioides *Wernham* **var. minor** *Wernham* =
R. wentianum *Koord.*

R. calocodon *Ridl.* =
R. pauciflorum *King & Gamble* var. calocodon *(Ridl.) Sleumer*

R. calophytum *Franch.* **subsp. jinfuense** *M.Y.Fang* =
R. calophytum *Franch.* var. jinfuense *M.Y.Fang & W.K.Hu*

R. calostrotum *Balf.f. & Kingdon-Ward* **var. calciphilum** *(Hutch. & Kingdon-Ward) Davidian* =
R. calostrotum *Balf.f. & Kingdon-Ward* subsp. riparium *(Kingdon-Ward) Cullen*

R. calostrotum *R.C.Fang* **var. riparioides** *(Cullen) R.C.Fang* =
R. calostrotum *Balf.f. & Kingdon-Ward* subsp. riparioides *Cullen*

R. calycinum *(Lindl.) Planch.* =
R. 'Omurasaki'

R. campanulatum *D.Don* **var. aeruginosum** *(Hook.f.) Cowan & Davidian* =
R. campanulatum *D.Don* subsp. aeruginosum *(Hook.f.) D.F.Chamb.*

R. campanulatum *D.Don* **var.**

campbellii *Millais* =
R. arboreum *Sm.* × R. wallichii *Hook.f.*

R. campbelliae *Hook.f.* =
R. arboreum *Sm.* var. cinnamomeum *(Wall. ex G.Don) Lindl.*

R. campylocarpum *Hook.f.* **subsp. telopeum** *(Balf.f. & Forrest) D.F.Chamb.* =
R. campylocarpum *Hook.f.* subsp. caloxanthum *(Balf.f. & Farrer) D.F.Chamb.*

R. campylogynum *Franch.* **var. celsum** *Davidian* =
R. campylogynum *Franch.*

R. campylogynum *Franch.* **var. charopoeum** *(Balf.f. & Forrest) Davidian* =
R. campylogynum *Franch.*

R. campylogynum *Franch.* **var. cremastum** *(Balf.f. & Forrest) Davidian* =
R. campylogynum *Franch.*

R. campylogynum *Franch.* **var. eupodum** *Ingram* =
R. campylogynum *Franch.*

R. campylogynum *Franch.* **var. leucanthum** *Ingram* =
R. campylogynum *Franch.*

R. campylogynum *Franch.* **var. myrtilloides** *(Balf.f. & Kingdon-Ward) Davidian* =
R. campylogynum *Franch.*

R. canadense *(L.) Torr.* **forma albiflorum** *(E.L.Rand & Redf.) Rehder* =
R. canadense *(L.) Torr.*

R. canadense *(L.) Torr.* **forma album** *Voss* =
R. canadense *(L.) Torr.*

R. canadense *(L.) Torr.* **forma viridifolium** *Fernald* =
R. canadense *(L.) Torr.*

R. candidapiculatum *Wernham* =
R. pusillum *J.J. Sm.*

R. candidum *Rehder* =
R. canescens *(Michx.) Sweet*

R. canescens *Porter* =
R. prinophyllum *(Small) Millais*

R. canescens *(Michx.) Sweet* **forma subglabrum** *Rehder* =

R. canescens *(Michx.) Sweet*

R. canescens *(Michx.) Sweet* **var. candidum** *(Small) Sweet* =
R. canescens *(Michx.) Sweet*

R. cantabile *Balf.f. ex Hutch.* =
R. russatum *Balf.f. & Forrest*

R. capitatum *Franch., non Maxim.* =
R. fastigiatum *Franch.*

R. cardiobasis *Sleumer* =
R. orbiculare *Decne.* subsp.
cardiobasis *(Sleumer) D.F.Chamb.*

R. cardioeides *Balf.f. & Forrest* =
R. oreotrephes *W.W. Sm.*

R. carringtoniae *(F.Muell.) Lane-Poole* =
R. herzogii *Warb.*

R. carringtoniae *F.Muell.* **var. maius** *J.J.Sm.* =
R. maius *(J.J.Sm.) Sleumer*

R. caryophyllum *Hayata* =
R. rubropilosum *Hayata*

R. catanduanense *Merr.* =
R. nortoniae *Merr.*

R. catapastum *Balf.f. & Forrest* =
R. rubiginosum *Franch.* var.
rubiginosum

R. catesbianum *Dum.Cours.* =
R. 'Catesbaei'

R. caucasicum *Pall.* **var. stramineum** *Hook.* =
R. caucasicum *Pall.*

R. cavaleriei *H.Lév.* **var. chaffanjonii** *H.Lév.* =
R. stamineum *Franch.* var.
stamineum

R. cephalanthoides *Balf.f. & W.W.Sm.* =
R. primuliflorum *Bureau & Franch.*

R. cephalanthum *(Franch.) Cowan & Davidian* **var. crebreflorum** *(Hutch.& Kingdon-Ward) Cowan & Davidian* =
R. cephalanthum *Franch.* subsp.
cephalanthum

R. cephalanthum *Franch.* **var. nmaiense** *(Hutch. & Kingdon-Ward) Cowan & Davidian* =
R. cephalanthum *Franch.* subsp.
cephalanthum

R. ceraceum *Balf.f. & W.W.Sm.* =
R. lukiangense *Franch.*

R. cerasiflorum *Kingdon-Ward* =

R. campylogynum *Franch.*

R. cerinum *Balf.f. & Forrest* =
R. sulfureum *Franch.*

R. chaetomallum *Balf.f. & Forrest* =
R. haematodes *Franch.* subsp.
chaetomallum *(Balf.f. & Forrest)*
D.F.Chamb.

R. chaetomallum *Balf.f. & Forrest* **var. chamaephytum** *Cowan* =
R. forrestii *Balf.f. ex Diels*
x haematodes *Franch.*

R. chaetomallum *Balf.f. & Forrest* **var. glaucescens** *Tagg & Forrest* =
R. haematodes *Franch.* subsp.
chaetomallum *(Balf.f. & Forrest)*
D.F.Chamb.

R. chaetomallum *Balf.f. & Forrest* **var. hemigymnum** *Tagg & Forrest* =
R. × hemigymnum *(Tagg & Forrest)*
D.F.Chamb.

R. chaetomallum *Balf.f. & Forrest* **var. xanthanthum** *Tagg & Forrest* =
R. × xanthanthum *(Tagg & Forrest)*
D.F.Chamb.

R. chalarocladum *Balf.f. & Forrest* =
R. selense *Franch.* subsp. selense

R. chamaecystus *L.* =
Rhodothamnus chamaecistus
Rchb.

R. chamaetortum *Balf.f. & Kingdon-Ward* =
R. cephalanthum *Franch.* subsp.
cephalanthum

R. chapaense *Dop* =
R. maddenii *Hook.f.* subsp.
crassum *(Franch.) Cullen*

R. charianthum *Hutch.* =
R. davidsonianum *Rehder &*
E.H.Wilson

R. charidotes *Balf.f. & Farrer* =
R. saluenense *Franch.* subsp.
chameunum *(Balf.f. & Forrest)*
Cullen

R. charitostreptum *Balf.f. & Kingdon-Ward* =
R. brachyanthum *Franch.* subsp.
hypolepidotum *(Franch.) Cullen*

R. charopoeum *Balf.f. & Farrer* =
R. campylogynum *Franch.*

R. chartophyllum *Franch.* =
R. yunnanense *Franch.*

R. chartophyllum *Franch.* **forma**

praecox *Diels* =
R. yunnanense *Franch.*

R. chasmanthoides *Balf.f. & Forrest* =
R. augustinii *Hemsl.* subsp.
chasmanthum *(Diels) Cullen*

R. chasmanthum *Diels* =
R. augustinii *Hemsl.* subsp.
chasmanthum *(Diels) Cullen*

R. chawchiense *Balf.f. & Farrer* =
R. anthosphaerum *Diels*

R. cheilanthum *Balf.f. & Forrest* =
R. cuneatum *W.W Sm.*

R. chengshienianum *W.P.Fang* =
R. ambiguum *Hemsl*

R. chienianum *W.P.Fang* =
R. longipes *Rehder & E.H.Wilson*
var. chienianum *(W.P.Fang)*
D.F.Chamb.

R. chionophyllum *Diels* =
R. argyrophyllum *Franch.* subsp.
argyrophyllum

R. chlanidotum *Balf.f. & Forrest* =
R. citriniflorum *Balf.f. & Forrest*
var. citriniflorum

R. christi *Foerste* =
R. christii *Foerste*

R. christi *Foerste* **var. loniceroides**
Schltr. =
R. christii *Foerste*

R. chrysanthum *Pall.* =
R. aureum *Georgi* var. aureum

R. chrysanthum *Pall.* **var.**
nikomontanum *Komatsu* =
R. × nikomontanum *(Komatsu)*
Nakai

R. chrysopeplon *Sleumer* =
R. beyerinckianum *Koord.*

R. ciliato-pedunculatum *Hayata* =
R. henryi *Hance* var. henryi

R. ciliicalyx *Franch.* **subsp. lyi**
(H.Lév.) R.C.Fang =
R. lyi *H.Lév.*

R. cinereoserratum *P.C.Tam* =
R. farrerae *Tate*

R. cinnabarinum *Hook.f.* **var.**
aestivale *Hutch.* =
R. cinnabarinum *Hook.f.* subsp.
cinnabarinum

R. cinnabarinum *Hook.f.* **var. bland-**
fordiiflorum *(Hook.f.) hort.* =
R. cinnabarinum *Hook.f.* subsp.
cinnabarinum

R. cinnabarinum *Hook.f.* **var.**
pallidum *Hook.f.* =
R. cinnabarinum *Hook.f.* subsp.
xanthocodon *(Hutch.) Cullen*

R. cinnabarinum *Hook.f.* **var.**
purpurellum *Cowan* =
R. cinnabarinum *Hook.f.* subsp.
xanthocodon *(Hutch.) Cullen*

R. cinnabarinum *Hook.f.* **var. roylei**
(Hook.f.) hort. =
R. cinnabarinum *Hook.f.* subsp.
cinnabarinum

R. cinnamomeum *Wall. ex G.Don* =
R. arboreum *Sm.* var.
cinnamomeum *(Wall. ex G.Don)*
Lindl.

R. citriniflorum *Balf.f. & Forrest*
subsp. aureolum *Cowan* =
R. citriniflorum *Balf.f. & Forrest*
var. horaeum *(Balf.f. & Forrest)*
D.F.Chamb.

R. citriniflorum *Balf.f. & Forrest*
subsp. horaeum *(Balf.f. & Forrest)*
Cowan =
R. citriniflorum *Balf.f. & Forrest*
var. horaeum *(Balf.f. & Forrest)*
D.F.Chamb.

R. citriniflorum *Balf.f. & Forrest*
subsp. rubens *Cowan* =
R. citriniflorum *Balf.f. & Forrest*
var. horaeum *(Balf.f. & Forrest)*
D.F.Chamb.

R. citrinum *Miq., non (Hassk.) Hassk.* =
R. citrinum *(Hassk.) Hassk.* var.
discoloratum *Sleumer*

R. citrinum *(Hassk.) Hassk.* **forma**
albiflorum *Miq.* =
R. citrinum *(Hassk.) Hassk.* var.
citrinum

R. clementis *Merr.* =
R. javanicum *(Blume) Benn.* subsp.
schadenbergii *(Warb.) Argent*

R. × clivianum *J.J. Sm.* =
R. 'Clivianum'

R. clivicolum *Balf.f. & W.W.Sm.* =
R. primuliflorum *Bureau & Franch.*

R. cloiophorum *Balf.f. & Forrest* =
R. sanguineum *Franch.* var.
cloiophorum *(Balf.f. & Forrest)*
D.F.Chamb.

R. cloiophorum *Balf.f. & Forrest*
subsp. asmenistum *(Balf.f. &*

Forrest) *Tagg* =
R. sanguineum *Franch.* subsp.
sanguineum var. cloiophorum
(Balf.f. & Forrest) D.F.Chamb.

R. cloiophorum *(Balf.f. & Forrest) Tagg*
subsp. leucopetalum *(Balf.f. &*
Forrest) Tagg =
R. sanguineum *Franch.* subsp.
sanguineum var. cloiophorum
(Balf.f. & Forrest) D.F.Chamb.

R. cloiophorum *Balf.f. & Forrest*
subsp. mannophorum *(Balf.f &*
Forrest) Tagg =
R. sanguineum *Franch.* var.
didymoides *Tagg & Forrest*

R. cloiophorum *Balf.f. & Forrest*
subsp. roseotinctum *(Balf.f &*
Forrest) Tagg =
R. sanguineum *Franch.* subsp.
sanguineum var. didymoides *Tagg*
& Forrest

R. coccinopeplum *Balf.f. & Forrest* =
R. roxieanum *Forrest* var.
cucullatum *(Hand.-Mazz.)*
D.F.Chamb.

R. coenenii *J.J.Sm.* =
R. culminicolum *F.Muell.* var.
nubicola *(Wernham) Sleumer*

R. colletum *Balf.f. & Forrest* =
R. beesianum *Diels*

R. commutatum *Sleumer* =
R. longiflorum *Lindl.* var.
longiflorum

R. concinnum *Hemsl.* **var. bentham-**
ianum *(Hemsl.) Davidian* =
R. concinnum *Hemsl.*

R. concinnum *Hemsl.* **var. pseudo-**
yanthinum *(Hemsl.) Davidian* =
R. concinnum *Hemsl.*

R. confertissimum *Nakai* =
R. lapponicum *(L.) Wahlenb.*

R. coniferum *Wernham* =
R. correoides *J.J. Sm.*

R. convexum *Sleumer* =
R. culminicolum *F.Muell.* var.
culminicolum

R. coombense *Hemsl.* =
R. concinnum *Hemsl.*

R. cooperi *Balf.f.* =
R. camelliiflorum *Hook.f.*

R. copelandii *Merr.* =
R. jasminiflorum *Hook.* var

copelandii *(Merr.) Sleumer*

R. cordatum *H.Lév.* =
R. souliei *Franch.*

R. coreanum *Rehder* =
R. yedoense *Maxim.* var.
poukhanense *(H.Lév.) Nakai*

R. coriifolium *Sleumer*=
R. × coriifolium *(Sleumer) Argent,*
A.L.Lamb & Phillipps

R. corruscum *Ridl.* =
R. wrayi *King & Gamble*

R. coryi *Shinners* =
R. viscosum *(L.) Torr.*

R. coryphaeum *Balf.f. & Forrest* =
R. praestans *Balf.f. & W.W.Sm.*

R. cosmetum *Balf.f. & Forrest* =
R. saluenense *Franch.* subsp.
chameunum *(Balf.f. & Forrest)*
Cullen

R. costulatum *Franch.* =
R. lutescens *Franch.*

R. crassimedium *P.C.Tam* =
R. polyraphidoideum *P.C.Tam* var.
polyraphidoideum

R. crassinervium *Ridl.* =
R. crassifolium *Stapf*

R. crebreflorum *Hutch. & Kingdon-*
Ward =
R. cephalanthum *Franch.* subsp.
cephalanthum

R. cremastum *Balf.f. & Forrest* =
R. campylogynum *Franch.*

R. cremnastes *Balf.f. & Farrer* =
R. lepidotum *Wall. ex G.Don*

R. cremnophilum *Balf.f. & W.W.Sm.* =
R. primuliflorum *Bureau & Franch.*

R. crenatum *H.Lév.* =
R. racemosum *Franch.*

R. crispiflorum *(Hook.f.) Planch.* =
R. 'Crispiflorum'

R. cruentum *H.Lév.* =
R. bureavii *Franch.*

R. cucullatum *Hand.-Mazz.* =
R. roxieanum *Forrest* var. cucullatum *(Hand.-Mazz.) D.F.Chamb.*

R. cuneifolium *Rendle, non Stapf* =
R. quadrasianum *Vidal* var.
rosmarinifolium *(Vidal) Copel.f.*

R. cuneifolium *sensu Ridl., non Stapf* =
R. borneense *(J.J.Sm.) Argent,*
A.L.Lamb & Phillipps subsp.
villosum *(J.J.Sm.) Argent,*

A.L.Lamb & Phillipps

R. cuneifolium *Stapf* **var.
subspathulatum** *Merr., non Ridl.* =
R. borneense *(J.J.Sm.) Argent,
A.L.Lamb & Phillipps* subsp.
villosum *(J.J.Sm.) Argent,
A.L.Lamb & Phillipps*

R. cuneifolium Stapf **var.
subspathulatum** *Ridl.* =
R. bagobonum *Copel.f.*

R. cuprescens *Nitz.* =
R. phaeochrysum *Balf.f. &
W.W.Sm.* var. phaeochrysum

R. curranii *Merr.* =
R. whiteheadii *Rendle*

R. curtisii *T.Moore* =
R. multicolor *Miq.*

R. cuthbertii *Small* =
R. minus *Michx.* var. minus

R. cyanocarpum *(Franch.) W.W.Sm.*
var. eriphyllum *Balf.f. ex Tagg* =
R. cyanocarpum *(Franch.)
W.W.Sm.*

R. cyatheicolum *Sleumer* =
R. spondylophyllum *F.Muell.*

R. cyclium *Balf.f. & Forrest* =
R. callimorphum *Balf.f. & W.W.Sm.*
var. callimorphum

R. cymbomorphum *Balf.f. & Forrest* =
R. × erythrocalyx *Balf.f. & Forrest*

R. daiyuenshanicum *P.C.Tam* =
R. daiyunicum *P.C.Tam*

R. damascenum *Balf.f. & Forrest* =
R. campylogynum *Franch.*

R. danielsianum *(Paxton) Planchon* =
R. 'Danielsianum'

R. daphniflorum *Diels* =
R. rufescens *Franch.*

R. daphnoides *hort.* =
R. 'Daphnoides'

R. dasycladum *Balf.f. & W.W.Sm.* =
R. selense *Franch.* subsp.
dasycladum *(Balf.f. & W.W.Sm.)
D.F.Chamb.*

R. dasylepis *Schltr.* =
R. beyerinckianum *Koord.*

R. dauricum *L.* **subsp. ledebourii**
(Pojark.) Alexandrowa & Schmidt =
R. ledebourii *Pojark.*

R. dauricum *L.* **subsp. sichotense**
(Pojark.) Alexandrowa & Schmidt =
R. sichotense *Pojark.*

R. dauricum *L.* **var. mucronulatum**
(Turcz.) Maxim. =
R. mucronulatum *Turcz.* var.
mucronulatum

R. dauricum *L.* **var. sempervirens**
Sims =
R. ledebourii *Pojark.*

R. davisi *hort. ex Koehne* =
R. 'Daviesi'

R. decandrum *(Makino) Makino* **forma
lasiocarpum** *H.Hara* =
R. decandrum *(Makino) Makino*

R. decandrum *(Makino) Makino* **var.
pilosum** *H.Hara* =
R. decandrum *(Makino) Makino*

R. decandrum *(Makino) Makino* **var.
viscistylum** *(Nakai) Hatus.* =
R. viscistylum *Nakai*

R. decumbens *D.Don ex G.Don* =
R. 'Decumbens'

R. deflexum *Griff.* =
R. triflorum *Hook.f.* subsp.
triflorum

R. degronianum *Carrière* **forma
spontaneum** *Nakai* =
R. degronianum *Carrière* subsp.
degronianum

R. degronianum *Carrière* **forma
variegatum** *Nakai* =
R. degronianum *Carrière* subsp.
degronianum

R. degronianum *Carrière* **var.
amagianum** *(T.Yamaz.) T.Yamaz.* =
R. degronianum *Carrière* forma
amagianum *(T.Yamaz.) H.Hara*

R. degronianum *Carrière* **var. nakaii**
(Komatsu) Nakai =
R. degronianum *Carrière* subsp.
degronianum

R. degronianum *Carrière* **var.
yakushimanum** *(Nakai) Kitam.* =
R. degronianum *Carrière* subsp.
yakushimanum *(Nakai) Kitam.* var.
yakushimanum

R. delavayi *Franch.* **var. peramoenum**
(Balf.f. & Forrest) T.L.Ming =
R. arboreum *Sm.* subsp. delavayi
(Franch.) D.F.Chamb. var.
peramoenum *(Balf.f. & Forrest)
D.F.Chamb.*

R. deleiense *Hutch. & Kingdon-Ward* =
R. tephropeplum *Balf.f. & Farrer*

R. dendritrichum *Balf.f. & Forrest* =
R. uvariifolium *Diels* var.
uvariifolium

R. depile *Balf.f. & Forrest* =
R. oreotrephes *W.W. Sm.*

R. devrieseanum *Koord.* =
R. konori *Becc.* var. konori

R. devriesianum *Koord.* subsp.
astrapiae *Foerste* =
R. konori *Becc.* var. konori

R. dianthiflorum *(Carrière) Millais* =
R. 'Dianthiflorum'

R. dichroanthum *Diels* **subsp.
herpesticum** *(Balf.f. & Kingdon-
Ward) Cowan* =
R. dichroanthum *Diels* **subsp.
scyphocalyx** *(Balf.f. & Forrest)
Cowan*

R. dichroanthum *Diels* **var.
apodectum** *(Balf.f. & W.W.Sm.)
T.L.Ming* =
R. dichroanthum *Diels* subsp.
apodectum *(Balf.f. & W.W.Sm.)
Cowan*

R. dichroanthum *Diels* **var.
scyphocalyx** *(Balf.f. & Forrest)
T.L.Ming* =
R. dichroanthum *Diels* subsp.
scyphocalyx *(Balf.f. & Forrest)
Cowan*

R. dichroanthum *Diels* **var. septentrionale** *(Cowan) T.L.Ming* =
R. dichroanthum *Diels* subsp.
septentrionale *Cowan*

R. dichropeplum *Balf.f. & Forrest* =
R. phaeochrysum *Balf.f. &
W.W.Sm.* var. levistratum *(Balf.f. &
Forrest) D.F.Chamb.*

R. didymum *Balf.f. & Forrest* =
R. sanguineum *Franch.* subsp.
didymum *(Balf.f. & Forrest) Cowan*

R. dilatatum *Miq.* **var. boreale**
Sugim. =
R. hidakanum *H.Hara*

R. dilatatum *Miq.* **var. decandrum**
Makino =
R. decandrum *(Makino) Makino*

R. dilatatum *Miq.* **var. glaucum**
Hatus. =
R. osuzuyamense *T.Yamaz.*

R. dilatatum *Miq.* **var. kiyosumense**
(Makino) Hatus. =

R. kiyosumense *(Makino) Makino*

R. dilatatum **var. lasiocarpum**
(H.Hara) T.Yamaz. =
R. decandrum *(Makino) Makino*

R. dilatatum *Miq.* **var. satsumense**
T.Yamaz. =
R. decandrum *(Makino) Makino*

R. discolor *Warb.* =
R. celebicum *(Blume) DC.*

R. doctersii *J.J.Sm.* =
R. zoelleri *Warb.*

R. dolerum *Balf.f. & Forrest* =
R. selense *Franch.* subsp.
dasycladum *(Balf.f. & W.W.Sm.)
D.F.Chamb.*

R. dryophyllum *Balf.f. & Forrest* =
R. phaeochrysum *Balf.f. &
W.W.Sm.* var. phaeochrysum

R. dubium *King & Gamble* =
R. wrayi *King & Gamble*

R. dunnii *E.H.Wilson* =
R. henryi *Hance* var. dunnii
(E.H.Wilson) M.Y.He

R. durionifolium *Stapf, non Recc.* =
R. fallacinum *Sleumer*

R. duseimatum *Balf.f. & Forrest* =
R. calvescens *Balf.f. & Forrest* var.
duseimatum *(Balf.f. & Forrest)
D.F.Chamb.*

R. eclecteum *Balf.f. & Forrest* **var.
brachyandrum** *(Balf.f. & Forrest)
Cowan & Davidian* =
R. eclecteum *Balf.f. & Forrest* var.
eclecteum

R. edgarii *Gamble* =
R. campanulatum *D.Don*

R. × edinense *Dummer* =
R. 'Edinense'

R. elaeagnoides *Hook.f.* =
R. lepidotum *Wall. ex G.Don*

R. elegans *Ridl.* =
R. pauciflorum *King & Gamble* var.
pauciflorum

R. ellipticum *Maxim.* **var.
leptosanthum** *(Hayata) S.S. Ying* =
R. moulmainense *Hook.f.*

R. elongatum *Blume* =
R. jasminiflorum *Hook.* var.
jasminiflorum

R. emaculatum *Balf.f. & Forrest* =
R. beesianum *Diels*

R. emarginatum *Hemsl. & E.H.Wilson*

var. eriocarpum *K.M.Feng* =
R. euonymifolium *H.Lév.*

R. ericoides *Burtt, non Low ex
Hook.f.* =
R. borneense *(J.J.Sm.) Argent,
A.L.Lamb & Phillipps* subsp.
angustissimum *(Sleumer) Argent*

R. ericoides *Low ex Hook.f.* **var.
silvicolum** *Sleumer* =
R. × silvicolum *(Sleumer) Argent,
A.L.Lamb & Phillipps*

R. erileucum *Balf.f. & Forrest* =
R. zaleucum *Balf.f. & W.W.Sm.* var.
zaleucum

R. eriocarpum *(Hayata) Nakai* **var.
tawadae** *Ohwi* =
R. eriocarpum *(Hayata) Nakai*

R. eriogynum *Balf.f. & W.W.Sm.* =
R. facetum *Balf.f. & Kingdon-Ward*

R. × erythrocalyx *Balf.f. & Forrest*
subsp. beimaense *(Balf.f. &
Forrest) Tagg* =
R. × erythrocalyx *Balf.f. & Forrest*

R. × erythrocalyx *Balf.f. & Forrest*
subsp. docimum *Balf.f. ex Tagg* =
R. × erythrocalyx *Balf.f. & Forrest*

R. × erythrocalyx *Balf.f. & Forrest*
subsp. eucallum *(Balf.f. & Forrest)
Tagg* =
R. × erythrocalyx *Balf.f. & Forrest*

R. × erythrocalyx *Balf.f. & Forrest*
subsp. truncatulum *(Balf.f. &
Forrest) Tagg* =
R. × erythrocalyx *Balf.f. & Forrest*

R. euanthum *Balf.f. & W.W.Sm.* =
R. vernicosum *Franch.*

R. eucallum *Balf.f. & Forrest* =
R. × erythrocalyx *Balf.f. & Forrest*

R. eudoxum *Balf.f. & Forrest* **subsp.
asteium** *(Balf.f. & Forrest) Tagg* =
R. eudoxum *Balf.f. & Forrest* var.
mesopolium *(Balf.f. & Forrest)
D.F.Chamb.*

R. eudoxum *Balf.f. & Forrest* **subsp.
brunneifolium** *(Balf.f. & Forrest)
Tagg* =
R. eudoxum *Balf.f. & Forrest* var.
brunneifolium *(Balf.f. & Forrest)
D.F.Chamb.*

R. eudoxum *Balf.f. & Forrest* **subsp.
epipastum** *(Balf.f. & Forrest)
Tagg* =

R. eudoxum *Balf.f. & Forrest* var.
mesopolium *(Balf.f. & Forrest)
D.F.Chamb.*

R. eudoxum *Balf.f. & Forrest* **subsp.
glaphyrum** *(Balf.f. & Forrest)
Tagg* =
R. temenium *Balf.f. & Forrest* var.
dealbatum *(Cowan) D.F.Chamb.*

R. eudoxum *Balf.f. & Forrest* **subsp.
mesopolium** *(Balf.f. & Forrest)
Tagg* =
R. eudoxum *Balf.f. & Forrest* var.
mesopolium *(Balf.f. & Forrest)
D.F.Chamb.*

R. eudoxum *Balf.f. & Forrest* **subsp.
pothinum** *(Balf.f. & Forrest) Tagg* =
R. temenium *Balf.f. & Forrest* var.
temenium

R. eudoxum *Balf.f. & Forrest* **subsp.
temenium** *(Balf.f. & Forrest) Tagg* =
R. temenium *Balf.f. & Forrest* var.
temenium

R. eudoxum *Balf.f. & Forrest* **subsp.
trichomiscum** *(Balf.f. & Forrest)
Tagg* =
R. eudoxum *Balf.f. & Forrest* var.
eudoxum

R. exquisitum *Hutch.* =
R. oreotrephes *W.W Sm.*

R. exquisitum *T.L.Ming* =
R. sikangense *W.P.Fang* var.
exquisitum *(T.L.Ming) T.L.Ming*

R. falcinellum *P.C.Tam* =
R. rufulum *P.C.Tam*

R. farrerae *Tate* **var. leucotrichum**
Franch. =
R. farrerae *Tate*

R. fauriei *Franch.* =
R. brachycarpum *D.Don ex G.Don*
subsp. fauriei *(Franch.) D.F.Chamb.*

R. ferrugineum *L.* **subsp. kotschyi**
(Simonk.) Hayek =
R. myrtifolium *Schott & Kotschy*

R. ferruginosa *Pall.* =
R. lapponicum *(L.) Wahlenb.*

R. filamentosum *Wernham* =
R. oreadum *Wernham*

R. fissotectum *Balf.f. & Forrest* =
R. aganniphum *Balf.f. & Kingdon-
Ward* var. aganniphum

R. flaviflorum *Elmer ex Merr.* =
R. leytense *Merr.* var. leytense

R. flavorufum *Balf.f. & Forrest* =
R. aganniphum *Balf.f. & Kingdon-Ward* var. flavorufum *(Balf.f. & Forrest) D.F.Chamb.*

R. flavum *Pall.* =
R. aureum *Georgi* var. aureum

R. flavum *G.Don* **var. macranthum**
Bean =
R. luteum *Sweet*

R. floccigerum *Franch.* **var. appropinquans** *Tagg & Forrest* =
R. neriiflorum *Franch.* subsp. phaedropum *(Balf.f. & Farrer)*

R. floccigerum *Franch.* **subsp. appropinquans** *(Tagg & Forrest) D.F.Chamb.* =
R. neriiflorum *Franch.* subsp. phaedropum *(Balf.f. & Farrer)*

R. fongkaiense *C.N.Wu & P.C.Tam* =
R. kwangtungense *Merr. & Chun*

R. fordii *Hemsl.* =
R. simiarum *Hance*

R. formosum *Wall.* **var. johstoneanum** *G.Watt ex Brandis* =
R. johnstoneanum *G.Watt ex Hutch.*

R. formosum *Wall.* **var. salicifolium** *C.B.Clarke* =
R. formosum *Wall.* var. formosum

R. formosum *Wall.* **var. veitchianum** *(Hook.f.) Kurz* =
R. veitchianum *Hook.f.*

R. forrestii *Diels* **var. repens** *(Balf.f. & Forrest) Cowan & Davidian* =
R. forrestii *Balf.f. ex Diels* subsp. forrestii

R. fortunei *Lindl.* **var. kwangfuense** *(Chun & W.P.Fang) G.Z.Li* =
R. fortunei *Lindl.* subsp. discolor *(Franch.) D.F.Chamb.*

R. foveolatum *Rehder & E.H.Wilson* =
R. coriaceum *Franch.*

R. fragrans *Franch., non Maxim.* =
R. trichostomum *Franch.*

R. fragrans *hort.* =
R. maximum *L.*

R. franchetianum *H.Lév.* =
R. decorum *Franch.* subsp. decorum

R. franssenianum *J.J.Sm.* =
R. villosulum *J.J.Sm.*

R. fuchsii *Sleumer* =
R. × fuchsii *(Sleumer) Argent, A.L.Lamb & Phillipps*

R. fuchsiiflorum *H.Lév.* =
R. spinuliferum *Franch.* var. spinuliferum

R. fuchsioides *Schltr.* =
R. lindaueanum *Koord.* var. lindaueanum

R. fulvastrum *Balf.f. & Forrest* **subsp. epipastum** *(Balf.f. & Forrest) Cowan* =
R. eudoxum *Balf.f. & Forrest* var. mesopolium *(Balf.f. & Forrest) D.F.Chamb.*

R. fulvastrum *Balf.f. & Forrest* **subsp. mesopolium** *(Balf.f. & Forrest) Cowan* =
R. eudoxum *Balf.f. & Forrest* var. mesopolium *(Balf.f. & Forrest) D.F.Chamb.*

R. fulvastrum *Balf.f. & Forrest* **subsp. trichomiscum** *(Balf.f. & Forrest) Cowan* =
R. eudoxum *Balf.f. & Forrest* var. eudoxum

R. fulvastrum *Balf.f. & Forrest* **subsp. trichophlebium** *(Balf.f. & Forrest) Cowan* =
R. eudoxum *Balf.f. & Forrest* var. eudoxum

R. fumidum *Balf.f. & W.W.Sm.* =
R. heliolepis *Franch.* var. heliolepis

R. fuscum *Blume* =
R. malayanum *Jack* var. malayanum

R. galioides *J.J.Sm.* =
R. bagobonum *Copel.f.*

R. gaultherioides *Boiss. & Bal.* =
Epigaea gaultherioides *(Boiss. & Bal.) Takht.*

R. germanicum *Tausch* =
R. hirsutum *L.*

R. gibbsiae *J.J.Sm.* =
R. culminicolum *F.Muell.* var. angiense *(J.J.Sm.) Sleumer*

R. gibsonii *Paxton* =
R. formosum *Wall.* var. formosum

R. giganteum *Forrest ex Tagg* **var. seminudum** *Tagg & Forrest* =
R. protistum *Balf.f. & Forrest* var. protistum

R. giraudissii *H.Lév.* =
R. decorum *Franch.* subsp.
decorum

R. glabratum *Hoppe* =
R. hirsutum *L.*

R. glabrifilum *J.J.Sm.* =
R. macgregoriae *F.Muell.* var.
glabrifilum (*J.J.Sm.*) *Sleumer*

R. glabrius (*Regel*) *Nakai* =
R. molle (*Blume*) *G.Don* subsp.
japonicum (*A.Gray*) *Kron*

R. glabrius (*Regel*) *Nakai* **var. aureum**
(*E.H.Wilson*) *Nakai* =
R. molle (*Blume*) *G.Don* subsp.
japonicum (*A.Gray*) *Kron*

R. glandulistylum *Komatsu* =
R. wadanum *Makino*

R. glandulostylum *W.P.Fang &
M.Y.He* =
R. guizhongense *G.Z.Li*

R. glauco-aureum *Balf.f. & Forrest* =
R. campylogynum *Franch.*

R. glaucophyllum *Rehder* **var.
luteiflorum** *Davidian* =
R. luteiflorum (*Davidian*) *Cullen*

R. glaucophyllum *Rehder* **var.
tubiforme** *Cowan & Davidian* =
R. glaucophyllum *Rehder* subsp.
tubiforme (*Cowan & Davidian*)
D.G.Long

R. glaucum *Hook.f., non Sweet* =
R. glaucophyllum *Rehder* subsp.
glaucophyllum var.
glaucophyllum

R. glaucum (*Lam.*) *Sweet* =
R. viscosum (*L.*) *Torr.*

R. glischroides *Tagg & Forrest* **var.
arachnoideum** *Tagg* =
R. aff. glischroides *Tagg & Forrest*

R. glischrum *Balf.f. & W.W.Sm.* **subsp.
glischroides** (*Tagg & Forrest*)
D.F.Chamb. =
R. glischroides *Tagg & Forrest*

R. glischrum *Balf.f. & W.W.Sm.* **var.
adenosum** *Cowan & Davidian* =
R. adenosum *Davidian*

R. gloeoblastum *Balf.f. & Forrest* =
R. wardii *W.W.Sm.* var. wardii

R. gloxinaeflorum *hort.* =
R. arboreum *Sm.* var. album *Wall.*

R. gnaphalocarpum *Hayata* =
R. mariesii *Hemsl. & E.H.Wilson*

R. gorumense *Schltr.* =
R. macgregoriae *F.Muell.* var.
macgregoriae

R. × gowenianum *Sweet* =
R. 'Gowenianum'

R. gracile *Becc., non Low ex Lindl.* =
R. longiflorum *Lindl.* var.
longiflorum

R. gracile *Low ex Lindl.* =
R. brookeanum *Low ex Lindl.*
subsp. gracile (*Lindl.*) *Argent*

R. gracilescens (*Nakai*) *Maekawa* =
R. nudipes *Nakai* var. nudipes

R. gracilipes *Franch.* =
R. argyrophyllum *Franch.* subsp.
hypoglaucum (*Hemsl.*) *D.F.Chamb.*

R. gratum *T.L.Ming* =
R. rex *H.Lév.* subsp. gratum
(*T.L.Ming*) *M.Y.Fang*

R. gregarium *Sleumer* =
R. culminicolum *F.Muell.* var.
culminicolum

R. griffithianum *Wight* **var.
aucklandii** (*Hook.f.*) *Hook.f.* =
R. griffithianum *Wight*

R. gymnanthum *Diels* =
R. lukiangense *Franch.*

R. gymnogynum *Balf.f. & Forrest* =
R. anthosphaerum *Diels*

R. gymnomiscum *Balf.f. & Kingdon-
Ward* =
R. primuliflorum *Bureau & Franch.*

R. haemaleum *Balf.f. & Forrest* =
R. sanguineum *Franch.* subsp.
sanguineum var. haemaleum
(*Balf.f. & Forrest*) *D.F.Chamb.*

R. haematocheilum *Craib* =
R. oreodoxa *Franch.* var. oreodoxa

R. haematodes *Franch.* **var. calycinum**
Franch. =
R. haematodes *Franch.* subsp.
haematodes

R. haematodes *Franch.* **var.
hypoleucum** *Franch.* =
R. haematodes *Franch.* subsp.
haematodes

R. haemonium *Balf.f. & Cooper* =
R. anthopogon *D.Don* subsp.
anthopogon

R. hallaisanense *H.Lév.* =
R. yedoense *Maxim.* var.
poukhanense (*H.Lév.*) *Nakai*

R. hamondi *hort. ex Lavallée* =
R. 'Hammondii'
R. hannoense *Nakai* =
R. indicum *(L.) Sweet*
R. hansemanni *Warb.* =
R. macgregoriae *F.Muell.* var.
macgregoriae
R. harrovianum *Hemsl.* =
R. polylepis *Franch.*
R. hatamense *Sleumer, non Becc.* =
R. culminicolum *F.Muell.* var.
nubicola *(Wernham) Sleumer*
R. hedythamnum *Balf.f. & Forrest* =
R. callimorphum *Balf.f. & W.W.Sm.*
var. callimorphum
R. hedythamnum *Balf.f. & Forrest* **var.
eglandulosum** *Hand.-Mazz.* =
R. cyanocarpum *(Franch.)*
W.W.Sm.
R. heishuiense *W.P.Fang* =
R. tatsienense *Franch.* var.
tatsiense
R. heliolepis *Franch.* **var. fumidum**
(Balf.f. & W.W.Sm.) R.C.Fang =
R. heliolepis *Franch.* var.
heliolepis
R. heliolepis *Franch.* **var. oporinum**
(Balf.f. & Kingdon-Ward)
R.C.Fang =
R. heliolepis *Franch.* var.
heliolepis
R. hellwigii *Koord., non Warb.* =
R. agathodaemonis *J.J.Sm.*
R. helvolum *Balf.f. & Forrest* =
R. phaeochrysum *Balf.f. &*
W.W.Sm. var. levistratum *(Balf.f. &*
Forrest) D.F.Chamb.
R. hepaticum *P.C.Tam* =
R. florulentum *P.C.Tam.*
R. heptamerum *Balf.f.* =
R. anthosphaerum *Diels*
R. heptaster *A.Gilli* =
R. konori *Becc.* var. konori
R. hesperium *Balf.f. & Forrest* =
R. rigidum *Franch.*
R. hexamerum *Hand.-Mazz.* =
R. vernicosum *Franch.*
R. himertum *Balf.f. & Forrest* =
R. sanguineum *Franch.* var.
himertum *(Balf.f. & Forrest)*
D.F.Chamb.
R. hispidum *D.Don* =

R. indicum *(L.) Sweet*
R. hispidum *(Pursh) Torr.* =
R. viscosum *(L.) Torr.*
R. hoi *W.P.Fang* =
R. anthopogonoides *Maxim.*
subsp. hoi *(W.P.Fang) W.P.Fang &*
Xiong
R. honbanianum *A.Ch,v. ex Dop* =
Enkianthus quinqueflorus *Lour.*
R. horaeum *Balf.f. & Forrest* =
R. citriniflorum *Balf.f. & Forrest*
var. horaeum *(Balf.f. & Forrest)*
D.F.Chamb.
R. hortense *Nakai* =
R. stenopetalum *(Hogg) Mabb.*
R. houlstonii *Hemsl. & E.H.Wilson* =
R. fortunei *Lindl.* subsp. discolor
(Franch.) D.F.Chamb.
R. hunanense *Chun ex P.C.Tam* **var.
mangshanicum** *P.C.Tam* =
R. hunanense *Chun ex P.C.Tam*
R. hutchinsonianum *W.P.Fang* =
R. concinnum *Hemsl.*
R. hyacinthiflorum *hort.* =
R. ponticum *L.*
R. hylothreptum *Balf.f. & W.W.Sm.* =
R. anthosphaerum *Diels*
R. hymenanthes *(Blume) Makino* =
R. degronianum *Carrière* subsp.
heptamerum *(Maxim.) H.Hara* var.
heptamerum *(Maxim.) Sealy*
R. hymenanthes *(Blume) Makino* **var.
pentamerum** *Makino* =
R. degronianum *Carrière* subsp.
degronianum
R. hypoblematosum *P.C.Tam* =
R. polyraphidoideum *P.C.Tam* var.
polyraphidoideum
R. hypolepidotum *(Franch.) Balf.f. &*
Forrest =
R. brachyanthum *Franch.* subsp.
hypolepidotum *(Franch.) Cullen*
R. hypopytis *Pojark.* =
R. aureum *Georgi* var. hypopytis
(Pojark.) D.F.Chamb.
R. hypotrichotum *Balf.f. & Forrest* =
R. oreotrephes *W.W.Sm.*
R. indicum *(L.) Sweet* **var. amoenum**
(Lindl.) Maxim. =
R. kiusianum *Makino* 'Amoenum'
R. indicum *(L.) Sweet* **var. amoenum**
(Lindl.) Maxim. **forma japonicum**

Maxim. =
R. kiusianum *Makino* var.
kiusianum

R. indicum *(L.) Sweet* **var. eriocarpum**
Hayata =
R. eriocarpum *(Hayata) Nakai*

R. indicum *(L.) Sweet* **var.
formosanum** *Hayata* =
R. simsii *Planch.* var. simsii

R. indicum *(L.) Sweet* **var. ignescens**
Sweet =
R. 'Ignescens'

R. indicum *(L.) Sweet* **var. japonicum**
(Maxim.) Makino =
R. kiusianum *Makino* var.
kiusianum

R. indicum *(L.) Sweet* **var. kaempferi**
(Planch.) Maxim. =
R. kaempferi *Planch.*

R. indicum *(L.) Sweet* **var.
macranthum** *(G.Don) Maxim.* =
R. 'Macranthum'

R. indicum *(L.) Sweet* **var.
mikawanaum** *Makino* =
R. × transiens *Nakai*

R. indicum *(L.) Sweet* **var. obtusum**
(Lindl.) Maxim. =
R. Obtusum Group

R. indicum *(L.) Sweet* **var. simsii**
(Planch.) Maxim. =
R. simsii *Planch.* var. simsii

R. indicum *(L.) Sweet* **var. sinensis**
Miq. =
R. scabrum *G.Don* subsp. scabrum

R. indicum *(L.) Sweet* **var. smithii**
Sweet =
R. × pulchrum *Sweet*

R. indicum *(L.) Sweet* **var.
sublanceolatum** *(Miq.) Makino* =
R. scabrum *G.Don* subsp. scabrum

R. indicum *(L.) Sweet* **var. tamurai**
Makino =
R. eriocarpum *(Hayata) Nakai*

R. inobeanum *Honda* =
R. decandrum *(Makino) Makino*

R. intortum *Balf.f. & Forrest* =
R. phaeochrysum *Balf.f. &
W.W.Sm.* var. levistratum *(Balf.f. &
Forrest) D.F.Chamb.*

R. invasorium *Sleumer* =
R. inconspicuum *J.J.Sm.*

R. ioanthum *Balf.f.* =

R. siderophyllum *Franch.*

R. ixeunticum *Balf.f. & W.W.Sm.* =
R. crinigerum *Franch.* var.
crinigerum

R. iyoense *Nakai* =
R. kaempferi *Planch.*

R. jahandiezii *H.Lév.* =
R. siderophyllum *Franch.*

R. jangtzowense *Balf.f. & Forrest* =
R. dichroanthum *Diels* subsp.
apodectum *(Balf.f. & W.W.Sm.)
Cowan*

R. japonicum *(A.Gray) J.V.Suringar* =
R. molle *(Blume) G.Don* subsp.
japonicum *(A.Gray) Kron*

R. japonicum *(A.Gray) J.V.Suringar*
forma aureum *E.H.Wilson* =
R. molle *(Blume) G.Don* subsp.
japonicum *(A.Gray) Kron*

R. japonicum *(A.Gray) J.V.Suringar*
forma canescens *(Sugim.)Sugim.* =
R. molle *(Blume) G.Don* subsp.
japonicum *(A.Gray) Kron*

R. japonicum *(A.Gray) J.V.Suringar*
var. canescens *Sugim.* =
R. molle *(Blume) G.Don* subsp.
japonicum *(A.Gray) Kron*

R. japonicum *(Blume) C.K.Schneid.* =
R. degronianum *Carrière* var.
heptamerum *(Maxim.) Sealy*

R. japonicum *(Blume) C.K.Schneid.*
var. pentamerum *(Maxim.)
Hutch.* =
R. degronianum *Carrière* subsp.
degronianum

R. japonoheptamerum *Kitam.* =
R. degronianum *Carrière* var.
heptamerum *(Maxim.) Sealy*

R. japonoheptamerum *Kitam.* **var.
hondoense** *(Nakai) Kitam.* =
R. degronianum *Carrière* var.
hondoense *(Nakai) H.Hara*

R. japonoheptamerum *Kitam.* **var.
kyomaruense** *(T.Yamaz) T.Yamaz* =
R. degronianum *Carrière* var.
kyomaruense *(T.Yamaz.) H.Hara*

R. jasminiflorum *Sarasin, non Hook.* =
R. radians *J.J.Sm.* var. minahasae
Sleumer

R. jasminiflorum *Hook.* **var.
maculatum** *Ridl.* =
R. jasminiflorum *Hook.* var.

punctatum *Ridl.*

R. jasminiflorum *Koord., non Hook.* =
R. citrinum *(Hassk.) Hassk.* var.
citrinum

R. jasminiflorum *Merr., non Hook.* =
R. jasminiflorum *Hook.* var.
oblongifolium *Sleumer*

R. jasminiflorum *Ridl., non Hook.* =
R. pneumonanthum *Sleumer*

R. javanicum *C.B.Clarke, non (Blume)
Benn.* =
R. robinsonii *Ridl.*

R. javanicum *Koord., non (Blume)
Benn.* =
R. celebicum *(Blume) DC.*

R. javanicum *Malm., non (Blume)
Benn.* =
R. renschianum *Sleumer*

R. javanicum *Steenis, non (Blume)
Benn.* =
R. multicolor *Miq.*

R. javanicum *(Blume) Benn.* **subsp.
brookeanum** *(Low ex Lindl.)
Argent & Phillipps* =
R. brookeanum *Low ex Lindl.*
subsp. brookeanum var.
brookeanum

R. javanicum *(Blume) Benn.* **subsp.
cockburnii** *Argent, A.L.Lamb &
Phillipps* =
R. brookeanum *Low ex Lindl.*
subsp. cockburnii *Argent,
A.L.Lamb & Phillipps*

R. javanicum *(Blume) Benn.* **subsp.
kinabaluense** *Argent, A.L.Lamb &
Phillipps* =
R. brookeanum *Low ex Lindl.* var.
kinabaluense *(Argent, A.L.Lamb &
Phillipps) Argent*

R. javanicum *(Blume) Benn.* **subsp.
gracile** *(Lindl.) Argent, A.L.Lamb &
Phillipps* =
R. brookeanum *Low ex Lindl.*
subsp. gracile *(Lindl.) Argent*

R. javanicum *(Blume) Benn.* **subsp.
moultonii** *(Ridl.) Argent* =
R. brookeanum *Low ex Lindl.* var.
moultonii *Ridl.*

R. javanicum *(Blume) Benn.* **var.
schadenbergii** *(Warb.) Sleumer* =
R. javanicum *(Blume) Benn.* subsp.
schadenbergii *(Warb.) Argent*

R. javanicum *(Blume) Benn.* **var.
tubiflorum** *Hook.f.* =
R. longiflorum *Lindl.* var.
longiflorum

R. jenkinsii *Nutt.* =
R. maddenii *Hook.f.* subsp.
maddenii

R. jucundum *Balf.f. & W.W.Sm.* =
R. selense *Franch.* subsp.
jucundum *(Balf.f. & W.W.Sm.)
D.F.Chamb.*

R. kaempferi *Planch.* **var. iyoense**
(Nakai) Sugim. =
R. kaempferi *Planch.*

R. kaempferi *Planch.* **var. japonicum**
(Maxim.) Rehder =
R. kiusianum *Makino* var.
kiusianum

R. kaempferi *Planch.* **var. komatsui**
Nakai =
R. 'Komatsui'

R. kaempferi *Planch.* **var.
lusidusculum** *(Nakai) Sugim.* =
R. kaempferi *Planch.*

R. kaempferi *Planch.* **var.
macrostemon** *(Maxim.) Makino* =
R. 'Macrostemon'

R. kaempferi *Planch.* **var.
mikawanum** *Makino* =
R. × transiens *Nakai*

R. kaempferi *Planch.* **var. plenum**
Nakai =
R. kaempferi *Planch.* 'Plenum'

R. kaempferi *Planch.* **var. purpureum**
Nakai =
R. × komatsui *T.Yamaz.*

R. kaempferi *Planch.* **var. tubidorum**
Komatsu =
R. kaempferi *Planch.*

R. kalmiaefolium *hort. ex Lavallée* =
R. 'Kalmiaefolium'

R. kawakamii *Hayata* **var. flaviflorum**
Liu & Chuang =
R. kawakamii *Hayata*

R. keditii *Sleumer* =
R. × keditii *(Sleumer) Argent,
A.L.Lamb & Phillipps*

R. keleticum *Balf.f. & Forrest* =
R. calostrotum *Balf.f. & Kingdon-
Ward* subsp. keleticum *(Balf.f. &
Forrest) Cullen*

R. × kewense *W.Wats.* =

R. Kewense Group

R. keysii *Hook.f.* **var. unicolor**
Hutch. =
R. keysii *Nutt.*

R. keysseri *Foerster*=
R. culminicolum *F.Muell.* var.
culminicolum

R. kialense *Franch.* =
R. przewalskii *Maxim.*

R. kinabaluense *Merr.* =
R. rugosum *Low ex Hook.f.* var.
laeve *Argent, A.L.Lamb & Phillipps*

R. kingdonii *Merr.* =
R. calostrotum *Balf.f. & Kingdon-*
Ward subsp. riparium *(Kingdon-*
Ward) Cullen

R. kjellbergii *J.J.Sm.* =
R. vanvuurenii *J.J.Sm.*

R. klossii *Ridl.* =
R. moulmainense *Hook.f.*

R. komiyamae *Makino* =
R. tosaense *Makino*

R. kontumense *Sleumer* =
R. irroratum *Franch.* subsp.
kontumense *(Sleumer) D.F.Chamb.*

R. kotschyi *Simonk.* =
R. myrtifolium *Schott & Kotschy*

R. kouytchense *H.Lév.* =
R. chrysocalyx *H.Lév. & Vaniot*

R. kwangsiense *Hu ex P.C.Tam* =
R. mariae *Hance* subsp.
kwangsiense *(P.C.Tam) D.F.Chamb.*
& S.J.Rae

R. kwangsiense *Hu ex P.C.Tam* **var.**
obovatifolium *P.C.Tam* =
R. mariae *Hance* subsp.
kwangsiense *(P.C.Tam) D.F.Chamb.*
& S.J.Rae

R. kwangsiense *Hu ex P.C.Tam* **var.**
salicinum *P.C.Tam* =
R. mariae *Hance* subsp.
kwangsiense *(P.C.Tam) D.F.Chamb.*
& S.J.Rae

R. kwangsiense *Hu ex P.C. Tam* **var.**
subfalcatum *P.C.Tam* =
R. mariae *Hance* subsp.
kwangsiense *(P.C.Tam) D.F.Chamb.*
& S.J.Rae

R. lacteum *Stapf, non Franch.* =
R. stapfianum *Hemsl. ex Prain*

R. lacteum *Franch.* **var.**
macrophyllum *Franch.* =

R. rex *H.Lév.* subsp. fictolacteum
(Balf.f.) D.F.Chamb.

R. × laetevirens *Rehder* =
R. Laetevirens Group

R. laetum *J.J.Sm., non J.J.Sm. 1914* =
R. zoelleri *Warb.*

R. lagopus *Nakai* **var. tokushimense**
(T.Yamaz.) T.Yamaz. =
R. tsurugisanense *(T.Yamaz.)*
T.Yamaz. var. tsurugisanense

R. lagopus *Nakai* **var. tsurugisanense**
(T.Yamaz.) T.Yamaz. =
R. tsurugisanense *(T.Yamaz.)*
T.Yamaz. var. tsurugisanense

R. lamprophyllum *Hayata* =
R. ovatum *(Lindl.) Maxim.*

R. lanatum *Hook.f.* **var. luciferum**
Cowan =
R. luciferum *(Cowan) Cowan*

R. lancifolium *Hook.f.* =
R. barbatum *Wall. ex G.Don*

R. langbianense *A.Chev. ex Dop* =
R. irroratum *Franch.* subsp.
kontumense *(Sleumer)*
D.F.Chamb.

R. lanigerum *Tagg* **var. silvaticum**
(Cowan) Davidian =
R. lanigerum *Tagg*

R. laoticum *Dop* =
R. moulmainense *Hook.f.*

R. lapidosum *T.L.Ming* =
R. araiophyllum *Balf.f. & W.W.Sm.*
subsp. lapidosum *(T.L.Ming)*
M.Y.Fang

R. lapponicum *(L.) Wahlenb.* **subsp.**
parvifolium *(Adams) T.Yamaz.* =
R. lapponicum *(L.) Wahlenb.*

R. lapponicum *(L.) Wahlenb.* **var.**
alpinum *(Glehn) T.Yamaz.* =
R. lapponicum *(L.) Wahlenb.*

R. lateritium *Planch.* =
R. 'Lateritium'

R. lateritium *Planch.* **var.**
brachytrichum *Nakai* =
R. 'Lateritium'

R. laticostum *Ingram* =
R. keiskei *Miq.*

R. latifolium *Hoffmanns.* =
R. maximum *L.*

R. latifolium *Hoppe* =
R. hirsutum *L.*

R. laureola *Schltr.* =

R. dielsianum *Schltr.* var. dielsianum

R. lauterbachianum *Foerster* = R. macgregoriae *F.Muell.* var. macgregoriae

R. leachianum *L.F.Henderson* = R. lapponicum *(L.) Wahlenb.*

R. leclerei *H.Lév.* = R. rubiginosum *Franch.* var. rubiginosum

R. ledifolium *(Hook.f.) G.Don* = R. ripense 'Mucronatum' *(Blume) G.Don*

R. ledoides *Balf.f. & W.W.Sm.* = R. trichostomum *Franch.*

R. leilungense *Balf.f. & Forrest* = R. tatsienense *Franch.* var. tatsienense

R. leiopodum *Hayata* = R. moulmainense *Hook.f.*

R. lemeei *H.Lév.* = R. lutescens *Franch.*

R. lepidanthum *Balf.f. & W.W.Sm.* = R. primuliflorum *Bureau & Franch.*

R. leprosum *Balf.f.* = R. rubiginosum *Franch.* var. rubiginosum

R. leptanthum *Hayata* = R. moulmainense *Hook.f.*

R. leptocladon *Dop* = R. lyi *H.Lév.*

R. leptosanthum *Hayata* = R. moulmainense *Hook.f.*

R. leucandrum *H.Lév.* = R. siderophyllum *Franch.*

R. leucanthum *Bunge* = R. ripense 'Mucronatum' *(Blume) G.Don*

R. leucobotrys *Ridl.* = R. moulmainense *Hook.f.*

R. leucolasium *Diels* = R. hunnewellianum *Rehder & E.H.Wilson* subsp. hunnewellianum

R. leucopetalum *Balf.f. & Forrest* = R. sanguineum *Franch.* var. cloiophorum *(Balf.f. & Forrest) D.F.Chamb.*

R. limprichtii *Diels* = R. oreodoxa *Franch.* var. oreodoxa

R. lindaueanum *Koord.* **var. cyclopicum** *Sleumer* =

R. lindaueanum *Koord.* var. lindaueanum

R. lindaueanum *Koord.* **var. latifolium** *J.J.Sm.* = R. lindaueanum *Koord.* var. lindaueanum

R. lindaueanum *Koord.* **var. psilacrum** *Sleumer* = R. lindaueanum *Koord.* var. lindaueanum

R. linearifolium *Siebold & Zucc.* **var. macrosepalum** *(Maxim.) Makino* = R. stenopetalum *(Hogg) Mabb.*

R. linearifolium *Siebold & Zucc.* **var. macrosepalum** *(Maxim.) Makino* **forma rhodoroides** *(Maxim.) Makino* = R. 'Rhodoroides'

R. linnaeoides *Schltr.* = R. anagalliflorum *Wernham*

R. liratum *Balf.f. & Forrest* = R. dichroanthum *Diels* subsp. apodectum *(Balf.f. & W.W.Sm.) Cowan*

R. liukiuense *Komatsu* = R. scabrum *G.Don* subsp. scabrum

R. lobbii *hort. ex Veitch* = R. longiflorum *Lindl.* var. longiflorum

R. loheri *Copel.f.* = R. leytense *Merr.* var. loheri *(Copel.f.) Sleumer*

R. lompohense *J.J.Sm.* **var. grandifolium** *J.J.Sm.* = R. buruense *J.J Sm.*

R. longiflorum *Lindl.* **var. heusseri** *J.J.Sm.* = R. jasminiflorum *Hook.* var. heusseri *(J.J.Sm.) Sleumer*

R. longifolium *Nutt.* = R. grande *Wight*

R. lophophorum *Balf.f. & Forrest* = R. phaeochrysum *Balf.f. & W.W.Sm.* var. agglutinatum *(Balf.f. & Forrest) D.F.Chamb.*

R. loureirianum *G.Don* = Ardisia loureiriana *(G.Don) Merr.*

R. lowii *(Hook.f.) F.Muell.* = R. englerianum *Koord.*

R. lowii *hort.* = R. ponticum *L.*

R. lucidum *Franch., non Nutt.* =

R. vernicosum *Franch.*
R. lucidum *Nutt.* =
   R. camelliiflorum *Hook.f.*
R. lusidusculum *Nakai* =
   R. kaempferi *Planch.*
R. lussoniense *Rendle* =
   R. vidalii *Rolfe*
R. luteum *(L.) C.K.Schneid.* =
   R. periclymenoides *(Michx.)*
   Shinners
R. luteum *(L.) C.K.Schneid.* **var.
flammeum** *(Michx.) C.K.Schneid.* =
   R. flammeum *(Michx.) Sargent*
R. luteum *Sweet* **var. macranthum**
E.H.Wilson =
   R. luteum *Sweet*
R. maboroense *Schltr.* =
   R. baenitzianum *Lauterb.*
R. mackenzianum *Forrest* =
   R. moulmainense *Hook.f.*
R. macranthum *(Bunge) G.Don* =
   R. indicum *(L.) Sweet*
R. macranthum *Griff.* =
   R. maddenii *Hook.f.* subsp.
   maddenii
R. macrocarpos *Griff.* =
   R. dalhousiae *Hook.f.* var.
   dalhousiae
R. macrosepalum *Maxim.* **var.
linearifolium** *(Siebold & Zucc.)
Makino* =
   R. stenopetalum *(Hogg) Mabb.*
R. macrosepalum *Maxim.* **var.
rhodoroides** *Maxim.* =
   R. 'Rhodoroides'
R. macrostemon *Maxim.* =
   R. 'Macrostemon'
R. maddenii *Hook.f.* **var. longiflora**
Watson =
   R. maddenii *Hook.f.* subsp.
   maddenii
R. maddenii *Hook.f.* **var. obtusifolia**
Hutch. =
   R. maddenii *Hook.f.* subsp.
   crassum *(Franch.) Cullen*
R. magnificum *Sleumer* =
   R. thaumasianthum *Sleumer*
R. mairei *H.Lév.* =
   R. lacteum *Franch.*
R. malayanum *Koord., non Jack* =
   R. zollingeri *J.J.Sm*
R. malindangense *Merr.* =

R. quadrasianum *Vidal* var.
   malindangense *(Merr.) Copel.f.*
R. mandarinorum *Diels* =
   R. fortunei *Lindl.* subsp. discolor
   (Franch.) D.F.Chamb.
R. × manglesii *Veitch* =
   R. 'Manglesii'
R. manipurense *Balf.f. & Watt* =
   R. maddenii *Hook.f.* subsp.
   crassum *(Franch.) Cullen*
R. mannophorum *Balf.f. & Forrest* =
   R. sanguineum *Franch.* var.
   didymoides *Tagg & Forrest*
R. manopeplum *Balf.f. & Forrest* =
   R. esetulosum *Balf.f. & Forrest*
R. maximum *L.* **var. album** *Pursh* =
   R. maximum *L.*
R. maximum *L.* **var. purpureum**
Pursh =
   R. maximum *L.*
R. mayebarae *Nakai* **var. obsumiense**
T.Yamaz. =
   R. mayebarae *Nakai & H.Hara*
R. mayrii *J.J.Sm.* =
   R. macgregoriae *F.Muell.* var.
   mayrii *(J.J.Sm.) Sleumer*
R. medoense *W.P.Fang & M.Y.He* **var.
adenostylum** *W.P.Fang &
M.Y.He* =
   R. ngawchangense *M.N.Philipson
   & Philipson*
R. megalostigma *F.Muell.* =
   R. englerianum *Koord.*
R. megaphyllum *Balf.f. & Forrest* =
   R. basilicum *Balf.f. & W.W.Sm.*
R. mekongense *Franch.* **var.
melinanthum** *(Balf.f. & Kingdon-
Ward) Cullen* =
   R. mekongense *Franch.* var.
   mekongense
R. meridionale *P.C.Tam* **var.
setistylum** *P.C.Tam* =
   R. meridionale *P.C.Tam* var.
   meridionale
R. mesopolium *Balf.f. & Forrest* =
   R. eudoxum *Balf.f. & Forrest* var.
   mesopolium *(Balf.f. & Forrest)
   D.F.Chamb.*
R. metrium *Balf.f. & Forrest* =
   R. selense *Franch.* subsp. selense
R. metternichii *Siebold & Zucc.* **forma
amagianum** *T.Yamaz.* =

R. degronianum *Carrière* var.
kyomaruense *(T.Yamaz.) H.Hara*
forma amagianum *(T.Yamaz.)*
H.Hara

R. metternichii *Siebold & Zucc.* **forma**
angustifolium *Makino* =
R. makinoi *Tagg*

R. metternichii *Siebold & Zucc.* **forma**
latifolium *Sugim.* =
R. degronianum *Carrière* var.
heptamerum *(Maxim.) Sealy*

R. metternichii *Siebold & Zucc.* **subsp.**
pentamerum *(Maxim.) Sugim.* =
R. degronianum *Carrière* subsp.
degronianum

R. metternichii *Siebold & Zucc.* **subsp.**
yakushimanum *(Nakai) Sugim.* =
R. degronianum *Carrière* subsp.
yakushimanum *(Nakai) Kitam.* var.
yakushimanum

R. metternichii *Siebold & Zucc.* **var.**
heptamerum *Maxim.* =
R. degronianum *Carrière* var.
heptamerum *(Maxim.) Sealy*

R. metternichii *Siebold & Zucc.* **var.**
hondoense *Nakai* =
R. degronianum *Carrière* var.
hondoense *(Nakai) H.Hara*

R. metternichii *Siebold & Zucc.* **var.**
intermedium *Sugim.* =
R. degronianum *Carrière* subsp.
yakushimanum *(Nakai) H.Hara*
var. intermedium *(Sugim.) H.Hara*

R. metternichii *Siebold & Zucc.* **var.**
kyomaruense *T.Yamaz.* =
R. degronianum *Carrière* var.
kyomaruense *(T.Yamaz.) H.Hara*

R. metternichii *Siebold & Zucc.* **var.**
micranthum *Nakai* =
R. degronianum *Carrière* var.
heptamerum *(Maxim.) Sealy*

R. metternichii *Siebold & Zucc.* **var.**
yakushimanum *(Nakai) Ohwi* =
R. degronianum *Carrière* subsp.
yakushimanum *(Nakai) Kitam.* var.
yakushimanum

R. microphyton *Franch.* **var.**
trichanthum *A.L.Zhang* =
R. microphyton *Franch.*

R. mirabile *Kingdon-Ward* =
R. genestierianum *Forrest*

R. missionarum *H.Lév.* =

R. ciliicalyx *Franch.*

R. mjobergii *Merr.* =
R. durionifolium *Becc.* var.
durionifolium

R. modestum *Hook.f.* =
R. ciliatum *Hook.f.*

R. molle *(Blume) G.Don* **var.**
japonicum *(A.Gray) Makino* =
R. molle *(Blume) G.Don* subsp.
japonicum *(A.Gray) Kron*

R. mollicomum *Balf.f. & W.W.Sm.* **var.**
rockii *Tagg* =
R. mollicomum *Balf.f. & W.W.Sm.*

R. mollyanum *Cowan & Davidian* =
R. montroseanum *Davidian*

R. mombeigii *Rehder & E.H.Wilson* =
R. uvariifolium *Diels* var.
uvariifolium

R. morsheadianum *Millais* =
R. arboreum *Sm.* var. roseum
Lindl. 'Morsheadianum'

R. moszkowskii *Schltr.* =
R. zoelleri *Warb.*

R. motsouense *H.Lév.* =
R. racemosum *Franch.*

R. moultonii *Ridl.* =
R. brookeanum *Low ex Lindl.* var.
moultonii *(Ridl.) Argent*

R. mucronulatum *Turcz.* **var.**
albiflorum *Nakai* =
R. mucronulatum *Turcz.* var.
mucronulatum

R. mucronulatum *Turcz.* **var.**
chejuense *Davidian* =
R. mucronulatum *Turcz.* var. taquetii
(H. Lév) Nakai

R. mucronulatum *Turcz.* **var. ciliatum**
Nakai =
R. mucronulatum *Turcz.*

R. muliense *Balf.f. & Forrest* =
R. rupicola *W.W.Sm.* var. muliense
(Balf.f. & Forrest) M.N.Philipson &
Philipson

R. multicolor *Miq.* **var. curtisii**
G.Hensl. =
R. multicolor *Miq.*

R. multicolor *Sp.Moore, non Miq.* =
R. citrinum *(Hassk.) Hassk.* var.
discoloratum *Sleumer*

R. murudense *J.J.Sm., non Merr.* =
R. pseudomurudense *Sleumer*

R. murudense *Merr.* =

R. crassifolium *Stapf*
R. × **myrtifolium** *Lodd.* =
R. 'Myrtifolium'
R. myrtilloides *Balf.f. & Kingdon-Ward* =
R. campylogynum *Franch.*
R. nagasakianum *Nakai* =
R. nudipes *Nakai* var. nudipes
R. nagasakianum *Nakai* **var.**
gracilescens *Nakai* =
R. nudipes *Nakai* var. nudipes
R. nakaii *Komatsu* =
R. degronianum *Carrière* subsp. degroniianum
R. nanothamnum *Balf.f. & Forrest* =
R. selense *Franch.* subsp. selense
R. nanum *H.Lév.* =
R. fastigiatum *Franch.*
R. narcissiflorum *Planch.* =
R. mucronatum *(Blume) G.Don* var. mucronatum 'Narcissiflorum'
R. nebrites *Balf.f. & Forrest* =
R. sanguineum *Franch.* var. himertum *(Balf.f. & Forrest) D.F.Chamb.*
R. neglectum *(Ashe) Ashe* =
R. atlanticum *(Ashe) Rehder*
R. nematocalyx *Balf.f. & W.W.Sm.* =
R. moulmainense *Hook.f.*
R. nepalense *hort.* =
R. arboreum *Sm.*
R. neriiflorum *Franch.* **subsp.**
euchaites *(Balf.f. & Forrest) Tagg* =
R. neriiflorum *Franch.* subsp. neriiflorum
R. neriiflorum *Franch.* **subsp.**
phoenicodum *(Balf.f. & Farrer) Tagg* =
R. neriiflorum *Franch.* subsp. neriiflorum
R. neriiflorum *Franch.* **var. agetum**
(Balf.f. & Forrest) T.L.Ming =
R. neriiflorum *Franch.* subsp. agetum *(Balf.f. & Forrest) Tagg*
R. neriiflorum *Franch.* **var.**
phaedropum *(Balf.f. & Farrer) T.L.Ming* =
R. neriiflorum *Franch.* subsp. phaedropum *(Balf.f. & Farrer) Tagg*
R. nervulosum *Sleumer* =
R. × nervulosum *Sleumer*
R. nervulosum *Sleumer* **var.**

exuberans *Sleumer* =
R. exuberans *(Sleumer) Argent*
R. nikoense *(Komatsu) Nakai* =
R. pentaphyllum *Maxim.*
R. nilagiricum *Zenker* =
R. arboreum *Sm.* subsp. nilagiricum *(Zenker) Tagg*
R. ningyuenense sensu *Sleumer, non Hand.-Mazz.* =
R. irroratum *Franch.* subsp. kontumense *(Sleumer) D.F.Chamb.*
R. niphargum *Balf.f. & Kingdon-Ward* =
R. uvariifolium *Diels* var. uvariifolium
R. niphobolum *Balf.f. & Farrer* =
R. stewartianum *Diels*
R. nishiokae *H.Hara* =
R. succothii *Davidian*
R. nitens *Sleumer* =
R. commonae *Foerste*
R. nitidulum *Rehder & E.H.Wilson* **var.**
nubigenum *Rehder & E.H.Wilson* =
R. nitidulum *Rehder & E.H.Wilson* var. nitidulum
R. nitidum *(Pursh) Torr.* =
R. viscosum *(L.) Torr.*
R. nmaiense *(Hutch. & Kingdon-Ward)* = R. cephalanthum *Franch.* subsp. cephalanthum
R. × **nobleanum** *hort. ex Lindl.* =
R. Nobleanum Group
R. nodosum *C.H.Wright* =
R. culminicolum *F.Muell.* var. culminicolum
R. nubicola *Wernham* =
R. culminicolum *F.Muell.* var. nubicola *(Wernham) Sleumer*
R. nudiflorum *(L.) Torr.* **forma album**
Rehder =
R. periclymenoides *(Michx.) Shinners*
R. nudiflorum *(L.) Torr.* **forma**
glanduliferum *(Porter) Fernald* =
R. periclymenoides *(Michx.) Shinners*
R. nudiflorum *(L.) Torr.* **var. album**
(Pursh) C.Mohr =
R. periclymenoides *(Michx.) Shinners*
R. nudiflorum *(L.) Torr.* **var.**
coccineum *(Aiton) Sweet* =

R. flammeum *(Michx.) Sargent*

R. nudiflorum *(L.) Torr.* **var. glanduliferum** *(Porter) Rehder* =
R. periclymenoides *(Michx.) Shinners*

R. nudiflorum *(L.) Torr.* **var. papilionaceum** *(Aiton) Zabel* =
R. periclymenoides *(Michx.) Shinners*

R. nudiflorum *(L.) Torr.* **var. roseum** *(Loisel.) Weigand* =
R. canescens *(Michx.) Sweet*

R. nudipes *Nakai* **subsp. niphophilum** *T.Yamaz.* **var. lagopus** *(Nakai) T.Yamaz.* =
R. lagopus *Nakai* var. lagopus

R. nudipes *Nakai* **subsp. niphophilum** *T.Yamaz.* =
R. lagopus *Nakai* var. niphophilum *(T.Yamaz.) T.Yamaz.*

R. nudipes *Nakai* **subsp. yakumontanum** *T.Yamaz.* =
R. yakumontanum *(T.Yamaz.) T.Yamaz.*

R. nudipes *Nakai* **var. tokushimense** *T.Yamaz.* =
R. lagopus *Nakai* var. tokushimense *(T.Yamaz.) T.Yamaz.*

R. nudipes *Nakai* **var. tsurugisanense** *T.Yamaz.* =
R. tsurugisanense *(T.Yamaz.) T.Yamaz.* var. tsurugisanense

R. nwaiense *hort.* =
R. cephalanthum *Franch.* subsp. cephalanthum

R. oblongum *Griff.* =
R. griffithianum *Wight*

R. obovatum *Hook.f.* =
R. lepidotum *Wall. ex G.Don*

R. obscurinervium *Merr.* =
R. brookeanum *Low ex Lindl.* subsp. gracile *(Lindl.) Argent*

R. obscurum *Franch. ex Balf.f.* =
R. siderophyllum *Franch.*

R. obtusum *hort.* =
R. ponticum *L.*

R. obtusum *(Lindl.) Planch.* **forma amoenum** *(Lindl.) E.H.Wilson* =
R. kiusianum *Makino* 'Amoenum'

R. obtusum *(Lindl.) Planch.* **var. japonicum** *(Maxim.) Kitam.* =
R. kiusianum *Makino* var.

kiusianum

R. obtusum *(Lindl.) Planch.* **var. macrogemmum** *(Nakai) Kitam.* =
R. kaempferi *Planch.*

R. obtusum *(Lindl.) Planch.* **var. mikawanum** *(Makino) T.Yamaz.* =
R. × transiens *Nakai*

R. obtusum *(Lindl.) Planch.* **var. saikaiense** *T.Yamaz.* =
R. kaempferi *Planch.* var. saikaiense *(T.Yamaz.) T,Yamaz.*

R. obtusum *(Lindl.) Planch.* **var. tosaense** *(Makino) Kitam.* =
R. tosaense *Makino*

R. obtusum *(Lindl.) Planch.* **var. tubiflorum** *(Komatsu) Yamazaki* =
R. kaempferi *Planch.* var. tubiflorum *Komatsu*

R. occidentale *(Torr. & A.Gray) A.Gray* **var. paludosum** *Jepson* =
R. occidentale *(Torr. & A.Gray) A.Gray*

R. occidentale *(Torr. & A.Gray) A.Gray* **var. sonomense** *(Greene) Rehder* =
R. occidentale *(Torr. & A.Gray) A.Gray*

R. ochrocalyx *hort.* =
R. × detonsum *Balf.f. & Forrest*

R. oldhamii *Maxim.* **var. glandulosum** *Hayata* =
R. oldhamii *Makino*

R. openshawianum *Rehder & E.H.Wilson* =
R. calophytum *Franch.* var. openshawianum *(Rehder & E.H.Wilson) D.F.Chamb.*

R. oporinum *Balf.f. & Kingdon-Ward* =
R. heliolepis *Franch.* var. heliolepis

R. oranum *J.J.Sm.* =
R. zoelleri *Warb.*

R. oreinum *Balf f.* =
R. nivale *Hook.f.* subsp. boreale *M.N.Philipson & Philipson*

R. oresbium *Balf.f. & Kingdon-Ward* =
R. nivale *Hook.f.* subsp. boreale *M.N.Philipson & Philipson*

R. oresterum *Balf.f. & Forrest* =
R. wardii *W.W.Sm.* var. wardii

R. orion *Ridl.* =
R. scortechinii *King & Gamble*

R. orion *Ridl.* **var. aurantiacum** *Ridl.* =
R. longiflorum *Lindl.* var.
longiflorum

R. × **ornatum** *Sweet* =
R. 'Ornatum'

R. ovatum *(Lindl.) Maxim.* **var.
prismatum** *P.C.Tam* =
R. ovatum *(Lindl.) Makino*

R. pachyphyllum *W.P.Fang* =
R. ziyuanense *P.C.Tam* var.
pachyphyllum *(W.P.Fang) G.Don*

R. pagophilum *Balf.f. & Kingdon-
Ward* =
R. selense *Franch.* subsp. selense

R. palustre *(L.) Kron & Judd* =
R. tomentosum *(Stokes) Harmaja*
var. tomentosum

R. palustre *Turcz.* =
R. lapponicum *(L.) Wahlenb.*

R. pankimense *Cowan & Kingdon-
Ward* =
R. kendrickii *Nutt.*

R. panteumorphum *Balf.f. &
W.W.Sm.* =
R. × erythrocalyx *Balf.f. & Forrest*

R. papuanum *C.H.Wright, non Becc.* =
R. giulianettii *Lauterb.*

R. papyrociliare *P.C.Tam* =
R. mariae *Hance* subsp. mariae

R. partitum *J.J.Sm.* =
R. lanceolatum *Ridl.*

R. parviflorum *F.Schmidt* =
R. lapponicum *(L.) Wahlenb.*

R. parviflorum *Dum.Cours.* =
R. ponticum *L.*

R. parvifolium *Adams* =
R. lapponicum *(L.) Wahlenb.*

R. parvifolium *Adams* **forma alpinum**
Glehn=
R. lapponicum *(L.) Wahlenb.*

R. parvifolium *Adams* **var. alpinum**
(Glehn) Busch =
R. lapponicum *(L.) Wahlenb.*

R. × **pelargoniiflorum** *Van Houtte* =
R. 'Pelargoniaeflorum'

R. pentamerum *(Maxim.) Matsum.* =
R. degronianum *Carrière* var.
degronianum

R. pentaphyllum *Maxim.* **var.
nikoense** *Komatzu* =
R. pentaphyllum *Maxim.*

R. periclymenoides *(Michx.) Shinners*

forma album *(Aiton) C.F.Reed* =
R. periclymenoides *(Michx.)
Shinners*

R. periclymenoides *(Michx.) Shinners*
forma eglandulosum *Seymour* =
R. periclymenoides *(Michx.)
Shinners*

R. periclymenoides *(Michx.) Shinners*
forma glanduliferum *(Porter)
C.F.Reed* =
R. periclymenoides *(Michx.)
Shinners*

R. persicinum *Hand.-Mazz.* =
R. anthosphaerum *Diels*

R. petelotii *Dop* =
R. tanastylum *Balf.f. & Kingdon-
Ward* var. pennivenium *(Balf.f. &
Forrest) D.F.Chamb.*

R. phaedropum *Balf.f. & Farrer* =
R. neriiflorum *Franch.* subsp.
phaedropum *(Balf.f. & Farrer) Tagg*

R. phaeochitum *(F.Muell.) Wright* =
R. rubellum *Sleumer*

R. phaeochlorum *Balf.f. & Forrest* =
R. oreotrephes *W.W.Sm.*

R. phaeopeplum *Sleumer* =
R. konori *Becc.* var. phaeopeplum
(Sleumer) Argent

R. phoeniceum *(Sweet) DC.* =
R. × pulchrum *Sweet*

R. × **phoeniceum** *(Hook.) G.Don* =
R. 'Phoeniceum'

R. phoeniceum *(Sweet) DC.* **forma
smithii** *(Sweet) E.H.Wilson* =
R. × pulchrum *Sweet*

R. piceum *P.C.Tam* =
R. florulentum *P.C.Tam*

R. × **pictum** *Forbes* =
R. 'Pictum'

R. pilicalyx *Hutch.* =
R. pachypodum *Balf.f. & W.W.Sm.*

R. pilovittatum *Balf.f. & W.W.Sm.* =
R. arboreum *Sm.* subsp. delavayi
(Franch.) D.F.Chamb. var. delavayi

R. pittosporaefolium *Hemsl.* =
R. stamineum *Franch.* var.
stamineum

R. planecostatum *Sleumer* =
R. × planecostatum *(Sleumer)
Argent, A.L.Lamb & Phillipps*

R. planifolium *Nutt.* =
R. campanulatum *D.Don*

R. plebeium *Balf.f. & W.W.Sm.* =
R. heliolepis *Franch.* var.
heliolepis

R. podocarpoides *Schltr.* =
R. purpureiflorum *J.J.Sm.*

R. poecilodermum *Balf.f. & Forrest* =
R. roxieanum *Forrest* var.
roxieanum

R. poilanei *Dop* =
R. euonymifolium *H.Lév.*

R. polifolium *(L.) Scopoli* =
Andromeda polifolia *L.*

R. poliopeplum *Balf.f. & Forrest* =
R. sanguineum *Franch.* var.
himertum *(Balf.f. & Forrest)*
D.F.Chamb.

R. polyandrum *Hutch.* =
R. maddenii *Hook.f.* subsp.
maddenii

R. ponticum *(L.) Schreb. ex DC.* =
R. luteum *Sweet*

R. ponticum *L.* **subsp. baeticum**
(Boiss. & Reuter) Hand.-Mazz. =
R. ponticum *L.*

R. ponticum *L.* **var. brachycarpum**
Boiss. =
R. ponticum *L.*

R. ponticum *L.* **var. cheiranthifolium**
hort. ex Millais =
R. ponticum *L.* 'Cheiranthifolium'

R. porphyroblastum *Balf.f. & Forrest* =
R. roxieanum *Forrest* var.
cucullatum *(Hand.-Mazz.)*
D.F.Chamb.

R. porphyrophyllum *Balf.f. &*
Forrest =
R. erastum *Balf.f. & Forrest*

R. porrosquameum *Balf.f. & Forrest* =
R. heliolepis *Franch.* var.
brevistylum *(Franch.) Cullen*

R. pothinum *Balf.f. & Forrest* =
R. temenium *Balf.f. & Forrest* var.
temenium

R. poukhanense *H.Lév.* =
R. yedoense *Maxim.* var.
poukhanense *(H.Lév.) Nakai*

R. poukhanense *H.Lév.* **forma**
acutifolium *Komatsu* =
R. × transiens *Nakai*

R. poukhanense *H.Lév.* **forma**
obtusifolium *Komatsu* =
R. × transiens *Nakai*

R. prasinocalyx *Balf.f. & Forrest* =
R. wardii *W.W.Sm.* var. wardii

R. primuliflorum *Bureau & Franch.*
var. cephalanthoides *(Balf.f. &*
W.W.Sm.) Cowan & Davidian =
R. primuliflorum *Bureau & Franch.*

R. primuliflorum *Bureau & Franch.*
var. lepidanthum *(Balf.f. &*
W.W.Sm.) Cowan & Davidian =
R. primuliflorum *Bureau & Franch.*

R. primulinum *Hemsl.* =
R. flavidum *Franch.* var. flavidum

R. principis *Bureau & Franch.* **var.**
vellereum *(Hutch. ex Tagg)*
T.L.Ming =
R. principis *Bureau & Franch.*

R. pritzelianum *Diels* =
R. micranthum *Turcz.*

R. probum *Balf.f. & Forrest* =
R. selense *Franch.* subsp. selense

R. procumbens *(L.) E.H.L.Krause* =
Loiseleuria procumbens *(L.) Desv.*

R. prophantum *Balf.f. & Forrest* =
R. kyawii *Lace & W.W.Sm.*

R. pseudchrysanthum *Hayata* **forma**
rufovelutinum *T.Yamaz.* =
R. pachysanthum *Hayata*

R. pseudchrysanthum *Hayata* **var.**
rufovelutinum *(T.Yamaz.)*
T.Yamaz. =
R. pachysanthum *Hayata*

R. pseudociliicalyx *Hutch.* =
R. ciliicalyx *Franch.*

R. pseudonitens *Sleumer* =
R. commonae *Foerster*

R. psilostylum *(Rehder & E.H.Wilson)*
Balf.f. =
R. flavidum *Franch.* var.
psilostylum *Rehder & E.H.Wilson*

R. pubigermen *J.J.Sm.* **var.**
banghamiorum *J.J.Sm.* =
R. banghamiorum *(J.J.Sm.)*
Sleumer

R. pubigerum *Balf.f. & Forrest* =
R. oreotrephes *W.W.Sm.*

R. pulchellum *Salib.* =
R. canadense *(L.) Torr.*

R. × pulcherrimum *Lindl.* =
R. 'Pulcherrimum'

R. pumilum *Nutt., non Hook.f.* =
R. leptocarpum *Nutt.*

R. punctatum *Andrews* =

R. minus *Michx.* var. minus

R. puniceum *Roxb.* =
R. arboreum *Sm.* subsp. arboreum

R. purpureum *Komatsu* =
R. × komatsui *T.Yamaz.*

R. purpureum *(Pursh) G.Don* =
R. maximum *L.*

R. purpureum *(Pursh) G.Don* **var.
tigrinum** *Steudel* =
R. maximum *L.*

R. purshii *G.Don* =
R. maximum *L.*

R. pycnocladum *Balf.f. & W.W.Sm.* =
R. telmateium *Balf.f. & W.W.Sm.*

R. quadrasianum *Vidal* **forma
banahaoense** *Copel.f.* =
R. quadrasianum *Vidal* var.
rosmarinifolium *(Vidal) Copel.f.*

R. quadrasianum *Vidal* **forma
davaoense** *Copel.f.* =
R. quadrasianum *Vidal* var.
davaoense *(Copel.f.) Sleumer*

R. quadrasianum *Vidal* **forma
halconense** *Copel.f.* =
R. quadrasianum *Vidal* var.
rosmarinifolium *(Vidal) Copel.f.*

R. quadrasianum *Vidal* **forma
marivelesense** *Copel.f.* =
R. quadrasianum *Vidal* var.
marivelesense *(Copel.f.) Sleumer*

R. quadrasianum *Vidal* **forma
monodii** *H.J.Lam* =
R. quadrasianum *Vidal* var.
selebicum *J.J.Sm.*

R. quadrasianum *Vidal* **forma
negrosense** *Copel.f.* =
R. quadrasianum *Vidal* var.
davaoense *(Copel.f.) Sleumer*

R. quadrasianum *Vidal* **forma
pulogense** *Copel.f.* =
R. quadrasianum *Vidal* var.
rosmarinifolium *(Vidal) Copel.f.*

R. quadrasianum *Vidal* **forma
pulogense** *H.J.Lam, non Copel.f.* =
R. cuneifolium *Stapf* var.
cuneifolium

R. quadrasianum *Vidal* **subsp.
angustissimum** *(Sleumer) Argent* =
R. borneense *(J.J.Sm.) Argent,
A.L.Lamb & Phillipps* subsp.
angustissimum *(Sleumer) Argent*

R. quadrasianum *Vidal* **var.
angustissimum** *Sleumer* =
R. borneense *(J.J.Sm.) Argent,
A.L.Lamb & Phillipps* subsp.
angustissimum *(Sleumer) Argent*

R. quadrasianum *Vidal* **var.
borneense** *J.J.Sm.* =
R. borneense *(J.J.Sm.) Argent,
A.L.Lamb & Phillipps* var.
borneense

R. quadrasianum *Vidal* **var.
cuneifolium** *(Stapf) Copel.f.* =
R. cuneifolium *Stapf* var.
cuneifolium

R. quadrasianum *Vidal* **var. villosum**
J.J.Sm. =
R. borneense *(J.J.Sm.) Argent,
A.L.Lamb & Phillipps* subsp.
villosum *(J.J.Sm.) Argent,
A.L.Lamb & Phillipps*

R. quadrasianum *Vidal* **var. villosum**
J.J.Sm. **forma lutea** *H.J.Lam* =
R. borneense *(J.J.Sm.) Argent,
A.L.Lamb & Phillipps* subsp.
villosum *(J.J.Sm.) Argent,
A.L.Lamb & Phillipps*

R. quadrasianum *Vidal* **var. villosum**
J.J.Sm. **forma rubra** *H.J.Lam* =
R. borneense *(J.J.Sm.) Argent,
A.L.Lamb & Phillipps* subsp.
villosum *(J.J.Sm.) Argent,
A.L.Lamb & Phillipps*

R. quinquefolium *Bisset & S.Moore*
var. roseum *Rehder* =
R. pentaphyllum *Maxim.*

R. racemosum *Franch.* **var. rigidum**
(Franch.) Rehnelt =
R. rigidum *Franch.*

R. radinum *Balf.f. & W.W.Sm.* =
R. trichostomum *Franch.*

R. ramentaceum *(Lindl.) Planch.* =
R. 'Album'

R. randaiense *Hayata* =
R. rubropilosum *Hayata*

R. rarosquameum *Balf.f.* =
R. rigidum *Franch.*

R. rasile *Balf.f. & W.W.Sm.* =
R. decorum *Franch.* subsp.
diaprepes *(Balf.f. & W.W.Sm.)
T.L.Ming*

R. recurvum *Balf.f. & Forrest* =
R. roxieanum *Forrest* var.
roxieanum

R. recurvum *Balf.f. & Forrest* **var.
oreonastes** *Balf.f. & Forrest* =
R. roxieanum *Forrest* var.
oreonastes *(Balf.f. & Forrest)*
T.L.Ming

R. regale *Balf.f. & Kingdon-Ward* =
R. basilicum *Balf.f. & W.W.Sm.*

R. reginaldii *Balf.f.* =
R. oreodoxa *Franch.* var. oreodoxa

R. repens *Balf.f. & Forrest* =
R. forrestii *Balf.f. ex Diels* subsp.
forrestii

R. repens *Balf.f. & Forrest* **var.
chamaedoron** *Tagg & Forrest* =
R. chamaethomsonii *(Tagg &
Forrest) Cowan & Davidian* var.
chamaedoron *(Tagg & Forrest)*
D.F.Chamb.

R. repens *Balf.f. & Forrest* **var.
chamaethauma** *Tagg* =
R. chamaethomsonii *(Tagg &
Forrest) Cowan & Davidian* var.
chamaethauma *(Tagg) Cowan &
Davidian*

R. repens *Balf.f. & Forrest* **var.
chamaethomsonii** *Tagg & Forrest* =
R. chamaethomsonii *(Tagg &
Forrest) Cowan & Davidian* var.
chamaethomsonii

R. reticulatum *D.Don ex G.Don* **var.
bifolium** *T.Yamaz.* =
R. reticulatum *D.Don ex G.Don*

R. reticulatum *D.Don ex G.Don* **var.
lagopus** *(Nakai) Hatus.* =
R. lagopus *Nakai* var. lagopus

R. reticulatum *D.Don ex G.Don* **var.
nudipes** *(Nakai) Hatus.* =
R. nudipes *Nakai* var. nudipes

R. reticulatum *D.Don ex G.Don* **var.
parvifolium** *T.Yamaz.* =
R. reticulatum *D.Don ex G.Don*

R. reticulatum *D.Don ex G.Don* **var.
wadanum** *(Makino) Hatus.* =
R. wadanum *Makino*

R. retusum *Steenis, non (Blume)
Benn.* =
R. jasminiflorum *Hook.* var.
heusseri *(J.J.Sm.) Sleumer*

R. retusum *Wernham, non (Blume)
Benn.* =
R. lindaueanum *Koord.* var.
lindaueanum

R. rhantum *Balf.f. & W.W.Sm.* =
R. vernicosum *Franch.*

R. rhododactylum *Millais* =
R. wasonii *Hemsl. & E.H.Wilson*

R. rhodora *J.F.Gmel.* **forma albiflora**
E.L.Rand & Redf. =
R. canadense *(L.) Torr.*

R. rhombicum *Miq.* =
R. reticulatum *D.Don ex G.Don*

R. rhombicum *Miq.* **var. albiflorum**
Makino =
R. reticulatum *D.Don ex G.Don*

R. ripaecola *P.C.Tam* =
R. naamkwanense *Merr.* var.
naamkwanense

R. riparium *Kingdon-Ward* =
R. calostrotum *Balf.f. & Kingdon-
Ward* subsp. riparium *(Kingdon-
Ward) Cullen*

R. rivulare *Kingdon-Ward* =
R. calostrotum *Balf.f. & Kingdon-
Ward* subsp. riparium *(Kingdon-
Ward) Cullen*

R. rollisonii *Lindl.* =
R. arboreum

R. roseotinctum *Balf.f. & Forrest* =
R. sanguineum *Franch.* var.
didymoides *Tagg & Forrest*

R. roseum *(Loisel.) Rehder* =
R. prinophyllum *(Small) Millais*

R. roseum *(Loisel.) Rehder* **forma
albidum** *Steyerm.* =
R. prinophyllum *(Small) Millais*

R. roseum *(Loisel.) Rehder* **forma
lutescens** *Rehder* =
R. austrinum *(Small) Rehder*

R. roseum *(Loisel.) Rehder* **forma
plenum** *Rehder* =
R. prinophyllum *(Small) Millais*

R. rosmarinifolium *Dippel* =
R. mucronatum *(Blume) G.Don* var.
mucronatum

R. rosmarinifolium *Vidal* =
R. quadrasianum *Vidal* var.
rosmarinifolium *(Vidal) Copel.f.*

R. rosthornii *Diels* =
R. micranthum *Turcz.*

R. rotundifolium *David* =
R. orbiculare *Decne.* subsp.
orbiculare

R. roxieanum *Forrest* **var. globigerum**
(Balf.f. & Forrest) D.F.Chamb. =

R. alutaceum *Balf.f. & W.W.Sm.*
var. alutaceum

R. roylei *Hook.f.* =
R. cinnabarinum *Hook.f.* subsp.
cinnabarinum

R. rubiginosum *Franch.* **var. leclerei**
(H.Lév.) R.C.Fang =
R. rubiginosum *Franch.* var.
rubiginosum

R. rubriflorum *Kingdon-Ward* =
R. campylogynum *Franch.*

R. rubroluteum *Davidian* =
R. viridescens *Hutch.*

R. rubro-punctata *T.L.Ming* =
R. tanastylum *Balf.f. & Kingdon-
Ward* var. lingzhiense *M.Y.Fang*

R. rubro-punctatum *H.Lév. & Vaniot* =
R. siderophyllum *Franch.*

R. rubropunctatum *Hayata* =
R. hyperythrum *Hayata*

R. rufescens *P.C.Tam* =
R. rufulum *P.C.Tam*

R. rufum *Batalin* **var. pachysanthum**
(Hayata) S.S.Ying =
R. pachysanthum *Hayata*

R. rugosum *Sleumer* **var. coriifolium**
(Sleumer) Sleumer =
R. × coriifolium *(Sleumer) Argent,
A.L.Lamb & Phillipps*

R. × russellianum *Sweet* =
R. 'Russellianum'

R. saavedranum *Diels* =
R. beyerinckianum *Koord.*

R. sakawanum *Makino* =
R. reticulatum *D.Don ex G.Don*

R. salicifolium *Blume* =
R. multicolor *Miq.*

R. salignum *Hook.f.* =
R. lepidotum *Wall. ex G.Don*

R. saluenense *Franch.* **var. prostratum**
(W.W.Sm.) R.C.Fang =
R. saluenense *Franch.* subsp.
chameunum *(Balf.f. & Forrest)
Cullen*

R. sanguineum *Franch.* **subsp.
aizoides** *Cowan* =
R. sanguineum *Franch.* var.
himertum *(Balf.f. & Forrest)
D.F.Chamb.*

R. sanguineum *Franch.* **subsp.
atrorubrum** *Cowan* =
R. sanguineum *Franch.* aff. var.

haemaleum *(Balf.f. & Forrest)
D.F.Chamb.*

R. sanguineum *Franch.* **subsp.
cloiophorum** *(Balf.f. & Forrest)
Cowan* =
R. sanguineum *Franch.* var.
cloiophorum *(Balf.f. & Forrest)
D.F.Chamb.*

R. sanguineum *Franch.* **subsp.
consanguineum** *Cowan* =
R. sanguineum *Franch.* var.
didymoides *Tagg & Forrest*

R. sanguineum *Franch.* **subsp.
didymoides** *(Tagg & Forrest)
Cowan* =
R. sanguineum *Franch.* var.
didymoides *Tagg & Forrest*

R. sanguineum *Franch.* **subsp.
haemaleum** *(Balf.f. & Forrest)
Cowan* =
R. sanguineum *Franch.* var.
haemaleum *(Balf.f. & Forrest)
D.F.Chamb.*

R. sanguineum *Franch.* **subsp.
himertum** *(Balf.f. & Forrest)
Cowan* =
R. sanguineum *Franch.* var.
himertum *(Balf.f. & Forrest)
D.F.Chamb.*

R. sanguineum *Franch.* **subsp.
leucopetalum** *(Balf.f. & Forrest)
Cowan* =
R. sanguineum *Franch.* var.
cloiophorum *(Balf.f. & Forrest)
D.F.Chamb.*

R. sanguineum *Franch.* **subsp.
melleum** *Cowan* =
R. sanguineum *Franch.* var.
himertum *(Balf.f. & Forrest)
D.F.Chamb.*

R. sanguineum *Franch.* **subsp.
mesaeum** *Balf.f. ex Cowan* =
R. sanguineum *Franch.* var.
haemaleum *(Balf.f. & Forrest)
D.F.Chamb.*

R. sanguineum *Franch.* **subsp.
roseotinctum** *(Tagg & Forrest)
Cowan* =
R. sanguineum *Franch.* var.
didymoides *Tagg & Forrest*

R. sanguineum *Franch.* **subsp.
sanguineoides** *Cowan* =

R. sanguineum *Franch.* var. sanguineum

R. sanguineum *Franch.* **var. didymum** *(Balf.f. & Forrest) T.L.Ming =* R. sanguineum *Franch.* subsp. didymum *(Balf.f. & Forrest) Cowan*

R. sarasinorum *Warb.* = R. javanicum *(Blume) Benn.* subsp. schadenbergii *(Warb.) Argent*

R. saravanense *Dop* = R. lyi *H.Lév.*

R. saruwagedicum *Foerste* **var. alpinum** *Foerste =* R. saruwagedicum *Foerste*

R. sasakii *E.H.Wilson* = R. lasiostylum *Hayata*

R. sataense *Nakai* = R. kiusianum *Makino* var. sataense *(Nakai) D.F.Chamb. & S.J.Rae*

R. scabrum *G.Don* **forma linearisepalum** *Sugim.* = R. scabrum *G.Don* subsp. scabrum

R. scabrum *G.Don* **var. kaempferi** *(Planch.) Nakai =* R. kaempferi *Planch.*

R. schadenbergii *Merr., non Warb.* = R. williamsii *Merr. ex Copel.f.*

R. schadenbergii *Warb.* = R. javanicum *(Blume) Benn.* subsp. schadenbergii *(Warb.) Argent*

R. schlippenbachii *Maxim.* **forma albiflorum** *Y.N.Lee* = R. schlippenbachii *Makino*

R. schultzei *Schltr.* = R. beyerinckianum *Koord.*

R. sciaphilum *Balf.f. & Kingdon-Ward =* R. edgeworthii *Hook.f.*

R. scintillans *Balf.f. & W.W.Sm.* = R. polycladum *Franch.*

R. sclerocladum *Balf.f. & Forrest* = R. cuneatum *W.W.Sm.*

R. scyphocalyx *Balf.f. & Forrest* **var. septentrionale** *Tagg ex Davidian* = R. dichroanthum *Diels* subsp. septentrionale *Cowan*

R. selense *Franch.* **subsp. axium** *(Balf.f. & Forrest) Tagg =* R. selense *Franch.* subsp. selense

R. selense *Franch.* **subsp. chalarocladum** *(Balf.f. & Forrest) Tagg =*

R. selense *Franch.* subsp. selense

R. selense *Franch.* **subsp. dolerum** *(Balf.f. & Forrest) Tagg =* R. selense *Franch.* subsp. dasycladum *(Balf.f. & W.W.Sm.) D.F.Chamb.*

R. selense *Franch.* **subsp. duseimatum** *(Balf.f. & Forrest) Tagg =* R. calvescens *Balf.f. & Forrest* var. duseimatum *(Balf.f. & Forrest) D.F.Chamb.*

R. selense *Franch.* **subsp. metrium** *(Balf.f. & Forrest) Tagg =* R. selense *Franch.* subsp. selense

R. selense *Franch.* **subsp. nanothamnum** *(Balf.f. & Forrest) Tagg =* R. selense *Franch.* subsp. selense

R. selense *Franch.* **subsp. pagophilum** *(Balf.f. & Kingdon-Ward) Tagg =* R. selense *Franch.* subsp. selense

R. selense *Franch.* **subsp. probum** *(Balf.f. & Forrest) Tagg =* R. selense *Franch.* subsp. selense

R. selense *Franch.* **var. dasycladum** *(Balf.f. & Forrest) T.L.Ming =* R. selense *Franch.* subsp. dasycladum *(Balf.f. & W.W.Sm.) D.F.Chamb.*

R. selense *Franch.* **var. duseimatum** *(Balf.f. & Forrest) Cowan & Davidian =* R. calvescens *Balf.f. & Forrest* var. duseimatum *(Balf.f. & Forrest) D.F.Chamb.*

R. selense *Franch.* **var. jucundum** *(Balf.f. & W.W.Sm.) T.L.Ming =* R. selense *Franch.* subsp. jucundum *(Balf.f. & W.W.Sm.) D.F.Chamb.*

R. selense *Franch.* **var. pagophilum** *(Balf.f. & Kingdon-Ward) Cowan & Davidian =* R. selense *Franch.* subsp. selense

R. selense *Franch.* **var. probum** *(Balf.f. & Forrest) Cowan & Davidian =* R. selense *Franch.* subsp. selense

R. semilunatum *Balf.f. & Forrest* = R. mekongense *Franch.* var. mekongense

R. semnum *Balf.f. & Forrest* = R. praestans *Balf.f. & W.W.Sm.*

R. serpens *Balf.f. & Forrest* =
R. erastum *Balf.f. & Forrest*

R. serpyllifolium *(A.Gray) Miq.* **forma album** *T.Yamaz.* =
R. serpyllifolium *(A.Gray) Miq.*

R. serpyllifolium *(A.Gray) Miq.* **var. albiflorum** *Makino* =
R. serpyllifolium *(A.Gray) Miq.*

R. serrulatum *(Small) Millais* **forma molliculum** *Rehder* =
R. viscosum *(L.) Torr.*

R. serrulatum *(Small) Millais* **var. georgianum** *Rehder* =
R. viscosum *(L.) Torr.*

R. × sesterianum *Nicholson* =
R. 'Sesterianum'

R. setiferum *Balf.f. & Forrest* =
R. selense *Franch.* subsp. setiferum *(Balf.f. & Forrest) D.F.Chamb.*

R. sheilae *Sleumer* =
R. × sheilae *(Sleumer) Argent, A.L.Lamb & Phillipps*

R. sheltoniae *Hemsl. & E.H.Wilson* =
R. vernicosum *Franch.*

R. shimidzuanum *Honda ex Makino* =
R. kiyosumense *(Makino) Makino*

R. shojoense *Hayata* =
R. mariesii *Hemsl. & E.H.Wilson*

R. siamensis *Diels* =
R. moulmainense *Hook.f.*

R. sieboldii *Miq.* =
R. kaempferi *Planch.*

R. sieboldii *Miq.* **var. serrulatum** *Miq.* =
R. indicum *(L.) Sweet*

R. sigillatum *Balf.f. & Forrest* =
R. phaeochrysum *Balf.f. & W.W.Sm.* var. levistratum *(Balf.f. & Forrest) D.F.Chamb.*

R. silvaticum *Cowan* =
R. lanigerum *Tagg*

R. simiarum *Hance* **subsp. youngae** *(W.P.Fang) D.F.Chamb.* =
R. adenopodum *Franch.*

R. simsii *Planch.* **var. yakuinsulare** *(Mazam.) T.Yamaz.* =
R. scabrum *G.Don* subsp. scabrum

R. simulans *(Tagg & Forrest) D.F.Chamb., non Sleumer* =
R. mimetes *Tagg & Forrest* var. simulans *Tagg & Forrest*

R. simulans *J.J.Sm. ex H.J.Lam* =
R. simulans *Sleumer*

R. sinense *(Lodd.) Sweet* =
R. molle *(Blume) G.Don* subsp. japonicum *(A.Gray) Kron*

R. sinense *(Lodd.) Sweet* **var. rosea** *Ito* =
R. molle *(Blume) G.Don* subsp. japonicum *(A.Gray) Kron*

R. sinogrande *Balf.f. & W.W.Sm.* **var. boreale** *Tagg & Forrest* =
R. sinogrande *Balf.f. & W.W.Sm.*

R. sinolepidotum *Balf.f.* =
R. lepidotum *Wall. ex G.Don*

R. sino-vaccinioides *Balf.f. & Forrest* =
R. vaccinioides *Hook.f.*

R. sleumeri *A.Gilli* =
R. blackii *Sleumer*

R. smilesii *Hutch.* =
R. veitchianum *Hook.f.*

R. sonomense *Greene* =
R. occidentale *(Torr. & A.Gray) A.Gray*

R. sordidum *Hutch.* =
R. pruniflorum *Hutch. & Kingdon-Ward*

R. spadiceum *P.C.Tam* =
R. rufulum *P.C.Tam*

R. sparsiflorum *Nutt.* =
R. camelliiflorum *Hook.f.*

R. speciosum *(Willd.) Sweet* **var. major** *Sweet* =
R. calendulaceum *(Michx.) Torr.*

R. spectabile *Merr.* =
R. javanicum *(Blume) Benn.* subsp. schadenbergii *(Warb.) Argent*

R. sphaeranthum *Balf.f. & W.W.Sm.* =
R. trichostomum *Franch.*

R. spiciferum *Franch.* =
R. scabrifolium *Franch.* var. spiciferum *(Franch.) Cullen*

R. spinigerum *H.Lév.* =
R. chrysocalyx *H.Lév. & Vaniot*

R. × spinulosum *hort.* =
R. Spinulosum g. 'Spinulosum'

R. spodopeplum *Balf.f. & Farrer* =
R. tephropeplum *Balf.f. & Farrer*

R. spooneri *Hemsl. & E.H.Wilson* =
R. decorum *Franch.* subsp. decorum

R. × standishii *Paxton* =
R. 'Standishii'

R. stenophyllum *Hook.f. ex Stapf* **var. angustifolium** *J.J.Sm.* =
R. stenophyllum *Hook.f. ex Stapf*
subsp. angustifolium *(J.J.Sm.)*
Argent, A.L.Lamb & Phillipps

R. stenophyllum *Makino* =
R. makinoi

R. stenoplastum *Balf.f. & Forrest* =
R. rubiginosum *Franch.* var.
rubiginosum

R. stereophyllum *Balf.f. & W.W.Sm.* =
R. tatsienense *Franch.* var.
tatsienense

R. stewartianum *Diels* **var. aiolosalpinx** *(Balf.f. & Farrer)*
Cowan & Davidian =
R. stewartianum *Diels*

R. stewartianum *Diels* **var. tantulum**
Cowan & Davidian =
R. stewartianum *Diels*

R. stonori *Sleumer* =
R. commonae *Foerste*

R. subarcticum *Harmaja* =
R. tomentosum *(Stokes) Harmaja*
· var. subarcticum *(Harmaja)*
G.Wallace

R. subcordatum *Becc.* =
R. longiflorum *Lindl.* var.
subcordatum *(Becc.) Argent*

R. subenerve *P.C.Tam* **var. nudistylum** *P.C.Tam* =
R. tsoi *Merr.*

R. suberosum *Balf.f. & Forrest* =
R. yunnanense *Franch.*

R. sublanceolatum *Miq.* =
R. scabrum *G.Don* subsp. scabrum

R. sublateritium *Komatsu* =
R. scabrum *G.Don* subsp. scabrum

R. subnikomontanum *Sato &*
T.Suzuki =
R. keiskei *Miq.*

R. subpacificum *Sleumer* =
R. loranthiflorum *Sleumer*

R. surugaense *Sugim. ex Kurata* =
R. tosaense *Makino*

R. sutchuenense *Franch.* **var. geraldii**
Hutch. =
R. × geraldii *Ivens*

R. sycnanthum *Balf.f. & W.W.Sm.* =
R. rigidum *Franch.*

R. syncollum *Balf.f. & Forrest* =
R. phaeochrysum *Balf.f. &*

W.W.Sm. var. agglutinatum *(Balf.f.*
& Forrest) D.F.Chamb.

R. taiwanianum *S.S.Ying* =
R. kawakamii *Hayata*

R. tamaense *Davidian* =
R. cinnabarinum *Hook.f.* subsp.
tamaense *(Davidian) Cullen*

R. tanakae *(Maxim.) Ohwi* =
R. tsusiophyllum *Sugim.*

R. tanakai *Hayata* =
R. moulmainense *Hook.f.*

R. tapeinum *Balf.f. & Farrer* =
R. megeratum *Balf.f.*

R. tapelouense *H.Lév.* =
R. tatsienense *Franch.* var.
tatsienense

R. taquetii *H.Lév.* =
R. mucronulatum *Turcz.* var.
taquetii *(H.Lév.) Nakai*

R. tawadae *(Ohwi) Ohwi* =
R. eriocarpum *(Hayata) Nakai*

R. tawangense *K.C.Sahni &*
H.B.Naithani =
R. neriiflorum *Franch.* subsp.
phaedropum *(Balf.f. & Farrer) Tagg*

R. taylori *Veitch* =
R. 'Taylorii'

R. × tebotan *Komatzu* =
R. 'Tebotan'

R. tectum *Koidz.* =
R. × transiens *Nakai*

R. tectum *Koidz.* **var. purpureum**
(Komatsu) H.Hara =
R. × komatsui *T.Yamaz.*

R. temenium *Balf.f. & Forrest* **subsp. albipetalum** *Cowan* =
R. eudoxum *Balf.f. & Forrest* var.
eudoxum

R. temenium *Balf.f. & Forrest* **subsp. dealbatum** *Cowan* =
R. temenium *Balf.f. & Forrest* var.
dealbatum *(Cowan) D.F.Chamb.*

R. temenium *Balf.f. & Forrest* **subsp. gilvum** *Cowan* =
R. temenium *Balf.f. & Forrest* var.
gilvum *(Cowan) D.F.Chamb.*

R. temenium *Balf.f. & Forrest* **subsp. glaphyrum** *(Balf.f. & Forrest)*
Cowan =
R. temenium *Balf.f. & Forrest* var.
dealbatum *(Cowan) D.F.Chamb.*

R. temenium *Balf.f. & Forrest* **subsp.**

pothinum *(Balf.f. & Forrest)*
Cowan =
R. temenium *Balf.f. & Forrest* var.
temenium

R. temenium *Balf.f. & Forrest* **subsp.**
rhodanthum *Cowan* =
R. eudoxum *Balf.f. & Forrest* var.
eudoxum

R. tenue *Ching ex W.P.Fang &*
M.Y.He =
R. fuchsiifolium *H.Lév.*

R. tetramerum *(Makino) Nakai* =
R. tschonoskyi *Maxim.* var.
tschonoskyi

R. teysmannii *Henders, non Miq.* =
R. robinsonii *Ridl.*

R. teysmannii *Miq.* =
R. javanicum *(Blume) Benn.* var.
teysmannii *(Miq.) K. & G.*

R. theiochroum *Balf.f. & W.W.Sm.* =
R. sulfureum *Franch.*

R. theiophyllum *Balf.f. & Forrest* =
R. phaeochrysum *Balf.f. &*
W.W.Sm. var. levistratum *(Balf.f. &*
Forrest) D.F.Chamb.

R. thibaudense *hort. ex Dombr.* =
R. cinnabarinum *Hook.f.*

R. thomsonii *Hook.f.* **subsp.**
candelabrum *(Hook.f.)*
D.F.Chamb. =
R. × candelabrum *Hook.f.*

R. thomsonii *Hook.f.* **var.**
candelabrum *(Hook.f.)*
C.B.Clarke =
R. × candelabrum *Hook.f.*

R. thomsonii *Hook.f.* **var.**
cyanocarpum *Franch.* =
R. cyanocarpum *(Franch.)*
W.W.Sm.

R. thomsonii *Hook.f.* **var.**
lopsangianum *(Cowan) T.L.Ming* =
R. thomsonii *Hook.f.* subsp.
lopsangianum *(Cowan) D.F.Chamb.*

R. thomsonii *Hook.f.* **var. pallidum**
Cowan =
R. × candelabrum *Hook.f.*

R. thunbergii *Planch.* =
R. Obtusum Group

R. thyodocum *Balf.f. & Cooper* =
R. baileyi *Balf.f.*

R. timeteum *Balf.f. & Forrest* =
R. oreotrephes *W.W.Sm.*

R. tingwuense *P.C.Tam* =
R. tsoi *Merr.*

R. × torlonianum *hort. ex Lavallée* =
R. 'Torlonianum'

R. torquatum *Balf.f. & Farrer* =
R. dichroanthum *Diels* subsp.
scyphocalyx *(Balf.f. & Forrest)*
Cowan

R. torricellense *Schltr.* =
R. macgregoriae *F.Muell.* var.
glabrifilum *(J.J.Sm.) Sleumer*

R. tovernae *F.Muell.* =
R. konori *Becc.* var. konori

R. trichanthum *Sleumer* =
R. pseudotrichanthum *Sleumer*

R. trichocalyx *Ingram* =
R. keiskei *Miq.*

R. trichocladum *Franch.* **subsp.**
nepalense *H.Hara* [synonym]) =
R. mekongense *Franch.* var.
mekongense

R. trichopodum *Balf.f. & Forrest* =
R. oreotrephes *W.W.Sm.*

R. trichostomum *Franch.* **var.**
hedyosmum *(Balf.f.) Cowan &*
Davidian =
R. hedyosmum *Balf.f.*

R. trichostomum *Franch.* **var.**
ledoides *(Balf.f. & W.W.Sm.)*
Cowan & Davidian =
R. trichostomum *Franch.*

R. trichostomum *Franch.* **var.**
radinum *(Balf.f. & W.W.Sm.)*
Cowan & Davidian =
R. trichostomum *Franch.*

R. triflorum *Hook.f.* **var. mahagoni**
Hutch. =
R. triflorum *Hook.f.* subsp.
triflorum

R. trinerve *Franch.* =
R. tschonoskyi *Maxim.* var
trinerve *(Franch.) Makino*

R. truncatulum *Balf.f. & Forrest* =
R. × erythrocalyx *Balf.f. & Forrest*

R. tsangpoense *Kingdon-Ward* =
R. charitopes *Balf.f. & Farrer*
subsp. tsangpoense *(Kingdon-*
Ward) Cullen

R. tsangpoense *Kingdon-Ward* **var.**
pruniflorum *(Hutch.) Cowan &*
Davidian =
R. pruniflorum *Hutch. & Kingdon-*

Ward

R. tsarongense *Balf.f. & Forrest* =
R. primuliflorum *Bureau & Franch.*

R. tschonoskyi *Maxim.* **forma**
tetramerum *Makino* =
R. tschonoskyi *Maxim.* var.
tschonoskyi

R. tschonoskyi *Maxim.* **var.**
tetramerum *Komatsu* =
R. tschonoskyi *Maxim.* var.
tschonoskyi

R. tubiflorum *DC.* =
R. malayanum *Jack* var.
malayanum

R. tubiflorum *Low ex Lindl.* =
R. longiflorum *Lindl.* var.
longiflorum

R. tubiflorum *Mor., non Blume* =
R. zollingeri *J.J.Sm.*

R. tubiflorum *Reinw.* =
R. malayanum *Jack* var.
malayanum

R. uliginosum *J.J.Sm.* =
R. laetum *J.J.Sm.*

R. umbelliferum *H.Lév.* =
R. mariesii *Hemsl. & E.H.Wilson*

R. undulaticalyx *J.J.Sm.* =
R. arfakianum *Becc.*

R. undulatum *Sweet ex Steudel* =
R. arboreum *Sm.*

R. valentinianum *Forrest ex Hutch.*
var. changii *W.P.Fang* =
R. changii *(W.P.Fang) W.P.Fang*

R. vandeursenii *Sleumer* =
R. vitis-idaea *Sleumer*

R. vaniotii *H.Lév.* =
R. esquirolii *H.Lév.*

R. vaseyi *A.Gray* **forma album** *(Bean)*
Rehder =
R. vaseyi *A.Gray*

R. vaseyi *A.Gray* **var. album** *Bean* =
R. vaseyi *A.Gray*

R. velutinum *Becc.* =
R. verticillatum *Low ex Lindl.*
forma velutinum *(Becc.) Sleumer*

R. venustum *Salisb.* =
R. periclymenoides *(Michx.)*
Shinners

R. versicolor *Chun & W.P.Fang* =
R. simiarum *Hance* var. versicolor
(Chun & W.P.Fang) M.Y.Fang

R. verticillatum *Koord., non Low* =

R. radians *J.J.Sm.* var. minahasae
Sleumer

R. verticillatum *Becc., non Low ex*
Lindl. =
R. jasminiflorum *Hook.* var.
oblongifolium *Sleumer*

R. verticillatum *Low ex Hook.f.* =
R. buxifolium *Low ex Hook.f., non*
Low ex Lindl.

R. verticillatum *Vidal, non Low ex*
Lindl. =
R. vidalii *Rolfe*

R. viburnifolium *W.P.Fang* =
R. simsii *Planch.* var. simsii

R. vicarium *Balf.f.* =
R. nivale *Hook.f.* subsp. boreale
M.N.Philipson & Philipson

R. vicinum *Balf.f. & Forrest* =
R. phaeochrysum *Balf.f. &*
W.W.Sm. var. levistratum *(Balf.f. &*
Forrest) D.F.Chamb.

R. × **victorianum** *Cuvelier* =
R. 'Victorianum'

R. villosum *Hemsl. & E.H.Wilson* =
R. trichanthum *Rehder*

R. viscistylum *Nakai* **var.**
amakusaense *T.Yamaz.* =
R. amakusaense *(Takada ex*
T.Yamaz.) T.Yamaz.

R. viscistylum *Nakai* **var. glaucum**
(Hatus.) Sugim. =
R. osuzuyamense *T.Yamaz.*

R. viscistylum *Nakai* **var. hyugaense**
T.Yamaz. =
R. hyugaense *(T.Yamaz.) T.Yamaz.*

R. × **viscosepalum** *Rehder* =
R. 'Viscosepalum'

R. viscosum *(L.) Torr.* **forma**
coerulescens *Rehder* =
R. viscosum *(L.) Torr.*

R. viscosum *(L.) Torr.* **forma glaucum**
Fernald =
R. viscosum *(L.) Torr.*

R. viscosum *(L.) Torr.* **forma**
hispidum *(Pursh) Voss* =
R. viscosum *(L.) Torr.*

R. viscosum *(L.) Torr.* **forma**
rhodanthum *Rehder* =
R. viscosum *(L.) Torr.*

R. viscosum *(L.) Torr.* **forma roseum**
Hollick =
R. viscosum *(L.) Torr.*

R. viscosum *(L.) Torr.* **forma
rubescens** *(Lodd.) Torr.* =
R. viscosum *(L.) Torr.*

R. viscosum *(L.) Torr.* **var. aemulans**
Rehder =
R. viscosum *(L.) Torr.*

R. viscosum *(L.) Torr.* **var. glaucum**
(Michx.) Torr. =
R. viscosum *(L.) Torr.*

R. viscosum *(L.) Torr.* **var. hispidum**
(Pursh) Rehder =
R. viscosum *(L.) Torr.*

R. viscosum *(L.) Torr.* **var. montanum**
Rehder =
R. viscosum *(L.) Torr.*

R. viscosum *(L.) Torr.* **var. nitidum**
(Pursh) A.Gray =
R. viscosum *(L.) Torr.*

R. viscosum *(L.) Torr.* **var. rubescens**
(Lodd.) Sweet =
R. viscosum *(L.) Torr.*

R. viscosum *(L.) Torr.* **var. serrulatum**
(Small) Ahles =
R. viscosum *(L.) Torr.*

R. viscosum *(L.) Torr.* **var.
tomentosum** *Rehder* =
R. viscosum *(L.) Torr.*

R. **vittatum** *Planch.* =
R. 'Vittatum'

R. **vittatum** *Planch.* **var. punctatum**
Planch. =
R. 'Vittatum'

R. **vonroemeri** *Koord.* =
R. macgregoriae *F.Muell.* var.
macgregoriae

R. **wadanum** *Makino* var. lagopus
(Nakai) H.Hara =
R. lagopus *Nakai* var. lagopus

R. **wadanum** *Makino* var. leucanthum
Makino =
R. wadanum *Makino*

R. **warianum** *Schltr.* =
R. leptanthum *F.Muell.* var.
warianum *(Schltr.) Argent*

R. **warrenii** *(A.Nelson) Macbr.* =
R. albiflorum *Hook.* var. warrenii
(A.Nelson) M.A.Lane

R. **washingtonianum** *hort.* =
R. macrophyllum *D.Don ex G.Don*

R. × **wellesleyanum** *Waterer ex
Rehder* =
R. 'Wellesleyanum'

R. **weyrichii** *Maxim.* **var. amagianum**
(Makino) Hatus. =
R. amagianum *(Makino) Makino ex
H.Hara*

R. **weyrichii** *Maxim.* **var. sanctum**
(Nakai) Hatus. =
R. sanctum *Nakai*

R. **willmottiae** *hort.* =
R. hanceanum *Hemsl.*

R. × **wilsoni** *Nutt. ex Hook.f.* =
R. Wilsoni Group

R. **wilsoniae** *Hemsl. & E.H.Wilson* **var.
ionanthum** *W.P.Fang* =
R. latoucheae *Franch.* var.
ionanthum *(W.P.Fang) G.Z.Li*

R. **wilsoniae** *Hemsl. & E.H.Wilson* **var.
wilsoniae** =
R. latoucheae *Franch.* var.
latoucheae

R. **windsorii** *Nutt.* =
R. arboreum *Sm.* subsp.
arboreum

R. **wollastonii** *Wernham* =
R. wentianum *Koord.*

R. **wrayi** *King & Gamble* **var.
ellipticum** *Ridl.* =
R. wrayi *King & Gamble*

R. **wrayi** *King & Gamble* **var. minor**
Ridl. =
R. wrayi *King & Gamble*

R. **wrightianum** *Koord.* **var. piliferum**
J.J.Sm. =
R. papuanum *Becc.*

R. **xanthinum** *Balf.f. & W.W.Sm.* =
R. trichocladum *Franch.* var.
trichocladum

R. **xanthoneuron** *H.Lév.* =
R. denudatum *H.Lév.*

R. **xiushanense** *W.P.Fang* =
R. chrysocalyx *H.Lév. & Vaniot*
var. xiushanense *(W.P.Fang)
M.Y.He*

R. **yakumontanum** *Masam.* =
R. nudipes *Nakai* var. nudipes

R. **yakushimanum** *Nakai* **var.
intermedium** *(Sugim.)
T.Yamaz.* =
R. degronianum *Carrière* var.
intermedium *(Sugim.)H.Hara*

R. **yanthinum** *Bureau & Franch.* =
R. concinnum *Hemsl.*

R. **yanthinum** *Bureau & Franch.* **var.**

lepidanthum *Rehder &*
E.H.Wilson =
R. concinnum *Hemsl.*

R. yaragongense *Balf.f.* =
R. nivale *Hook.f.* subsp. boreale
M.N.Philipson & Philipson

R. yedoense *Maxim.* **var.**
hallaisanense *(H.Lév.)*
T.Yamaz. =
R. yedoense *Maxim.* var.
poukhanense *(H.Lév.) Nakai*

R. yedoense *Maxim.* **f. poukhanense**
(H.Lév.) Sugim.
R. yedoense *Maxim.* var.
poukhanense *(H.Lév.) Nakai*

R. zippelii *Blume* =
R. citrinum *(Hassk.) Hassk.* var.
citrinum

R. zollingeri *J.J.Sm.* **var. latifolium**
J.J.Sm. =
R. zollingeri *J.J.Sm.*

Rhodora

R. canadensis *L.* =
R. canadense *(L.) Torr.*

R. camschaticus *(Pall.) Lindl.* =
R. camtschaticum *Pall.* subsp.
camtschaticum

Therorhodion

T. camschaticum *(Pall.) Small* =
R. camtschaticum *Pall.* subsp.
camtschaticum

T. glandulosum *Small* =
R. camtschaticum *Pall.* subsp.
glandulosum *(Small) Hultén*

T. redowskianum *(Maxim.) Hutch.* =
R. redowskianum *Maxim.*

Tsusiophyllum

T. tanakae *Maxim.* =
R. tsusiophyllum *Sugim.*

Vireya

V. alba *(Blume) Blume* =
R. album *Blume*

V. celebica *Blume* =
R. celebicum *(Blume)*

V. javanica *Blume* =
R. javanicum *(Blume) Benn.* subsp.
javanicum var. javanicum

V. retusa *Blume* =
R. retusum *(Blume) Benn.* var.
retusum

V. tubiflora *Blume* =
R. malayanum *Jack* var.
malayanum

The Temperate Rhododendrons (excl. Section Vireya)

D.F. Chamberlain

Introduction

Since 1980 there has been a flood of new taxa (species, subspecies and varieties) described in *Rhododendron* by Chinese and Japanese authors, reflecting the considerable amount of material that has been collected recently in the field. The specimens on which these new taxa are based have not always been available for the research on which the accounts presented here are based. As a result, a significant proportion have not been fully assessed. Where there is any doubt the names have been accepted and included under the subsections and sections to which they have been assigned. However, it is not always clear whether any plants that are in cultivation are referable to these new species.

Group Names

The 1980 edition of the *Rhododendron Handbook* marked the transition from the Balfourian classification (based on series and subseries) to the Chamberlain & Cullen classification based on Sleumer's proposals (using subgenera, sections and subsections). As a result, a significant number of species names for entities recognized in cultivation but not maintained for plants in the wild were in danger of being lost. A proposal was therefore made that these could be maintained as group names (now termed cultivar-groups) until such time as they could be assessed and either discarded completely or given formal recognition. Some of these entities represent no more than selections from wild populations that merge with the species under which they are described.

While it is not the intention to provide accounts of cultivars or cultivar-groups in this account, it is nevertheless recognized that some of these entities may be relevant in cultivation. It may therefore be appropriate to provide names for some of these. In a few instances the entities are not known in the wild; provision of formal species, subspecies or varietal names is then inappropriate. In the most extreme cases the name used to refer to plants in cultivation applies to a perfectly distinct and different entity for technical reasons. Continuation of the use of such names (e.g. *R. cubittii*) is actually confusing and is not to be advised.

The list that follows includes those groups that were listed in the 1980 Handbook with a statement, where possible, as to their proposed treatment.

R. annae Laxiflorum Group - the distinctions between *R. annae* and *R. laxiflorum* are very slight. As *R. annae* in the strict sense has been recently introduced into cultivation the validity of these differences should soon become clear.

R. arboreum var. cinnamomeum Campbelliae Group - Plants belonging to this group are distinguished from *R. arboreum* var. *roseum* by the colour of the indumentum on the under surface of the leaves. Wild populations of this taxon are variable, sometimes containing 'Campbelliae' forms next to typical var. *roseum*. If these forms require a name in cultivation then the Campbelliae Group is available.

R. argyrophyllum subsp. argyrophyllum Cupulare Group - the status of the Cupulare Group, with pink cup-shaped flowers requires further study.

R. boothii Mishmiense Group - very little material of *R. boothii* is available, either as preserved or as live specimens. It is therefore not possible to be certain whether or not the range of variation is continuous between *R. boothii*, with unspotted corollas and bristly flower stalks and *R. mishmiense*, in which the flowers are strongly spotted and the flower stalks densely woolly. If a name is required for this group then *R. mishmiense* is available.

R. calostrotum subsp. keleticum Radicans Group - *R. radicans* is no more than an extremely dwarf form of subsp. *keleticum* and does not merit formal taxonomic status.

R. campylocarpum subsp. caloxanthum Telopeum Group - there is no clear cut boundary between *R. telopeum* and subsp. *caloxanthum*, though the former generally has smaller leaves; it is therefore not recognized in this treatment.

R. campylocarpum subsp. campylocarpum Elatum Group - this is an entity that is not known to me.

R. campylogynum Celsum Group, Charopeum Group, Cremastum Group & Myrtilloides Group - these are selections from the forms that make up this variable species; the variation however is not correlated morphologically, or with respect to distribution.

R. cephalanthum subsp. cephalanthum Crebreflorum Group Field observations have shown that the pink-flowered forms with glabrous stamens that are referable to *R. crebreflorum* intergrade with white-flowered forms typical of subsp. *cephalanthum*, and that a very similar variation pattern is exhibited by the closely related *R. primuliflorum*. If a name is required to distinguish these pink-flowered forms of *R. cephalanthum* then the Crebreflorum Group is available.

R. charitopes subsp. tsangpoense Curvistylum Group - is probably a natural hybrid between subsp. *tsangpoense* and *R. campylogynum*. If this is confirmed then *R. × curvistylum* would be the most appropriate nomenclature for this group.

R. cinnabarinum subsp. cinnabarinum Roylei Group & Blandfordiiflorum Group - wild populations of interbreeding individuals of this subspecies exhibit considerable variation in flower colour; those with deep rosy red flowers have been referred to the Roylei Group and those with bicoloured flowers, yellow and orange, to the Blandfordiiflorum Group.

R. cinnabarinum subsp. xanthocodon Concatenans Group, Pallidum Group & Purpurellum Group - this complex of forms requires thorough revision, especially as some exhibit resistance to the rhododendron mildew that can decimate most forms of subsp. *cinnabarinum*. In particular, there does seem to be justification for formal recognition of the Concatenans Group for some plants of wild origin.

R. dauricum Sempervirens Group - the degree to which the leaves over-winter varies from plant to plant; the Sempervirens Group represents no more than an extreme form with more persistent leaves.

R. dendricola Taronense Group - *R. dendricola* is a variable species. The smaller flowered forms (flowers 4.5-5.4cm), with large, widely spaced scales on the leaves have been referred to *R. taronense*. However, there is no correlation with distribution and the variation within *R. dendricola* is more or less continuous. If a name is required for the small-flowered forms in cultivation then the Taronense Group is available.

R. dichroanthum subsp. scyphocalyx Herpesticum Group - this group has been delineated on the basis of its dwarf habit (up to *c*.25cm tall) from the generally larger subsp. *scyphocalyx* (to 1.25m tall). Investigation of herbarium material indicates that there is continuous variation between the 'herpesticum' and 'scyphocalyx' forms and that *R. herpesticum* cannot be distinguished in wild populations.

R. × eythrocalyx Panteumorphum Group - as *R. erythrocalyx* is now recognized as a hybrid, and therefore exhibits a wide range of variation, there is no value in maintaining *R. panteumorphum* as a distinct entity.

R. formosum var. formosum Iteaphyllum Group - this represents no more than a narrow-leaved form of var. *formosum*.

R. forrestii subsp. forrestii Repens Group - in the juvenile state *R. forrestii* almost always have leaves that are purple below. The Repens Group is characterized by the mature leaves that are green below at maturity. This is an unreliable character as it is not always clear whether or not the plants are fully mature.

R. fortunei subsp. discolor Houlstonii Group - those specimens that are referable to this group have the minute calyx more typical of subsp. *fortunei*, but the narrower leaf, with a cuneate base more typical of subsp. *discolor*. There is a more or less continuous variation pattern extending from the more extreme forms of subsp. *discolor* to the extreme forms of Houlstonii Group. If a name is required for plants in cultivation then the Houlstonii Group is available.

R. haematodes subsp. chaetomallum Glaucescens Group - this is a distinctive entity on account of the glaucous upper leaf surfaces that probably requires a cultivar name.

R. hanceanum Nanum Group - if a name is required for the dwarf forms of *R. hanceanum* then the Nanum Group is available.

R. hippophaeoides var. hippophaeoides Fimbriatum Group - the status of this entity, which is distinguished from var. *hippophaeoides* by its longer style (1.3-1.5cm long), is doubtful as the origin the garden plant from which it was described is unknown. *R. hippophaeoides* is a widespread species requiring further study as some of the variation within it is correlated with distribution. However, at this stage it is not clear whether *R. fimbriatum* represents a distinct entity in the wild worthy of formal recognition.

R. johnstoneanum Parryae Group - see note under *R. parryae* (see p.161).

R. lapponicum Parvifolium Group - *R. parvifolium* is no more than a large form

of the generally more dwarf *R. lapponicum*, forming an upright shrub, to 1m and with larger leaves (to 2.5cm long) and larger flowers (to 13mm); it occurs in Soviet Eastern Asia and Alaska. This form is represented in the wild but it is not clear whether there is even a partial discontinuity between it and *R. lapponicum* in the strict sense.

R. mekongense var mekongense Viridescens Group - recent research has indicated that this entity merits specific rank(see p.149).

R. microgynum Gymnocarpum Group - there is no effective dividing line between *R. gymnocarpum* and *R. microgynum* in wild-collected material. As neither form is common in cultivation there is no need to recognize this as a distinct entity.

R. minus var. minus Carolinianum Group - the status of *R. carolinianum* Rehder is the subject of some debate, maintained as a distinct species by some authors, reduced by others to synonymy under *R. minus*. If this entity is to be maintained then the species name is available for use.

R. mollicomum Rockii Group - *R. mollicomum* var. *rockii* is no more than an extreme form with large flowers and not worthy of formal recognition. In any case there is some doubt as to whether this form is in cultivation.

R. neriiflorum subsp. neriiflorum Euchaites Group - the larger, sometimes tree-like forms (to 6m tall) of *R. neriiflorum* have been delimited as subsp. *euchaites*. Some plants from the type locality of *R. neriiflorum* are referable to subsp. *euchaites*, indicating that the latter is not worthy of recognition.

R. pemakoense Patulum Group - this group should be abandoned as at least some of the plants grown as *R. patulum* are referrable to *R. imperator*.

R. polycladum Scintillans Group - plants belonging to *R. scintillans* have a characteristic spreading habit with upright branches but otherwise resemble the more twiggy and compact *R. polycladum* closely. As both *R. polycladum* and *R.*

scintillans were described from the same mountain pass it is probable that they belong to the same entity. Plants in cultivation under the name *R. scintillans* should therefore be referred to *R.polycladum*.

R. roxieanum var. roxieanum Oreonastes Group - recent field studies confirm that the name var. *oreonastes* should be formally retained (see p.173).

R. rubiginosum Desquamatum Group - the larger, more open-flowered forms of *R. rubiginosum*, (flowers 3.5-6cm across) have been referred to *R. desquamatum*. Herbarium material indicates that these two species merge with one another in the wild. Further research will be required to elucidate the problem.

R. saluenense subsp. chameumum Prostratum Group - this group is a selection of high altitude prostrate or spreading forms that are probably no more than ecological variants of subsp. *chameunum*. If a name is required for these forms, some of which are particularly marked in cultivation, then the Prostratum Group is available.

R. smithii Argipeplum Group - the treatment of *R. argipeplum* has been revised as a result of confusion with *R. erosum* (see p. 184).

R. temenium var. gilvum Chrysanthemum Group - *R. temenium* subsp. *chrysanthemum* falls within the natural variation of var. *gilvum*, the boundaries of which are imprecise due to hybridization in the wild with both *R. sanguineum* and *R. citriniflorum*.

R. trichocladum Lophogynum Group - this group falls within the natural variation of *R. trichocladum* and does not merit formal recognition at any level

R. triflorum Mahogani Group - this group of plants is characterized by flowers that are suffused or spotted dark red. As this form occurs sporadically in wild populations among the more typical yellow variants, it is more appropriate that the name be retained under the Cultivated Plant Code.

R. veitchianum Cubittii Group - *R.*

cubittii hort., a name that only applies to plants in cultivation, differs significantly from the wild-collected type of *R. cubittii* Hutch; which is a synonym of *R. veitchianum* . As *R. cubittii* hort. is distinctive but is not known in the wild, it requires a new name under the Cultivated Plant Code.

R. wardii var. wardii Litiense Group - this entity may deserve formal recognition as it has a restricted geographical distribution (see p. 198).

R. yunnanense Hormophorum Group - this includes those forms of *R. yunnanense* with deciduous leaves and probably represents no more than a low altitude form of this widespread species. If a name is required for this group of plants then the Cultivated Plant Code should apply.

Species distributions

The temperate species of *Rhododendron* (excluding Sect. Vireya) extend over the temperate and more humid parts of the Northern Hemisphere but with concentrations in the number of species in

1)The Sino-Himalayan Centre, including SW China, extending Westwards through Burma and along the Indo-Himalayan mountain chain and Eastwards as far as Eastern Sichuan and Guizhou,

2) Southern and & Eastern China,

3) Japan and to a lesser extent in

4) the Eastern part of the United States.

The most significant, the Sino-Himalayan Centre of Distribution, includes N & W Yunnan, W Sichuan, NE Burma and SE Tibet, an area dominated by a markedly monsoonal climate, that has also undergone periods of intense mountain building. This is an area over which there has been a period of active speciation in the recent past, resulting in several species complexes, each containing a number of closely related species that are poorly defined from one another. These complexes are particularly well represented in Subsects. Neriiflora and Taliensia in Subgenus Hymenanthes and Subsects. Lapponica and Maddenia in

Subgenus Rhododendron.

The Southern Chinese and Japanese Centres of Distribution are dominated by members of Subgenus Tsutsusi (the evergreen Azaleas) and the Eastern United States Centre by members of Subgenus Pentanthera.

The list that follows includes those Biological Recording Units (BRUs) in which rhododendrons occur. These BRUs generally follow national, provincial or state boundaries and represent an internationally agreed geographical standard designed for recording plant and animal distributions. The number of species occurring in each BRU is cited. However, these numbers are approximate as they are dependent on species delimitations, and are only as complete as the published plant lists from which they are generated.

The accompanying map covers only the Sino-Himalayan, Southern Chinese and Japanese Centres of Distribution as these account for around 90 per cent of the temperate species.

List of the Number of Rhododendron Species by Biological Recording Unit (BRU)

ASIA

Asia, East (excl. China & India)

BHU-BH	Bhutan	40
BMA-OO	Myanmar (Burma)	93
CBD-OO	Cambodia	1
JAP-OO	Japan	58
KOR-NK	North Korea	9
KOR-SK	South Korea	11
LAO-OO	Laos	8
MON-OO	Mongolia	8
NEP-OO	Nepal	28
PAK-OO	Pakistan	2
SRI-OO	Sri Lanka (Ceylon)	1
TAI-OO	Taiwan	17
THA-OO	Thailand	7
VIE-OO	Vietnam	>25

China

CHC-GU	Guizhou	77
CHC-HU	Hubei	19
CHC-SI	Sichuan	160
CHC-YU	Yunnan	222
CHH-OO	Hainan	2
CHI-NM	Nei Mongol	1
CHM-HE	Heilongjiang	2
CHM-JI	Jilin	3
CHM-LI	Liaoning	2
CHN-GA	Gansu	18
CHN-HB	Hebei	1
CHN-SA	Shaanxi	12
CHN-SD	Shandong	2
CHN-SX	Shanxi	1
CHS-AN	Anhui	9
CHS-FU	Fujian	23
CHS-GD	Guangdong	40
CHS-GX	Guangxi	63
CHS-HA	Hunan	43
CHS-HK	Hong Kong	6
CHS-HN	Henan	2
CHS-JS	Jiangsu	4
CHS-JX	Jiangxi	19
CHS-ZH	Zhejiang	12
CHT-QI	Qinghai	6
CHT-XI	Xizang (Tibet)	165

India

ASS-AP	Arunachal Pradesh	51
ASS-AS	Assam	3
ASS-MA	Manipur	4
ASS-ME	Meghalaya	2
ASS-MI	Mizoram	1
ASS-NA	Nagaland	8
BHU-SI	Sikkim	34
IND-HP	Himachal Pradesh	4
IND-PU	Punjab	1
IND-TN	Tamil Nadu	1
IND-UP	Uttar Pradesh	5
IND-WB	West Bengal	18
JMK-OO	Jammu-Kashmir	4

Asia, West

LBS-OO	Lebanon	1
TCS-AR	Armeniya	3
TCS-AZ	Azerbaijan	1
TCS-GR	Grusiya	5
TUR-OO	Turkey	5

EUROPE

AUT-OO	Austria	3
BUL-OO	Bulgaria	2
CZE-OO	Czechoslovakia	1
FIN-OO	Finland	1

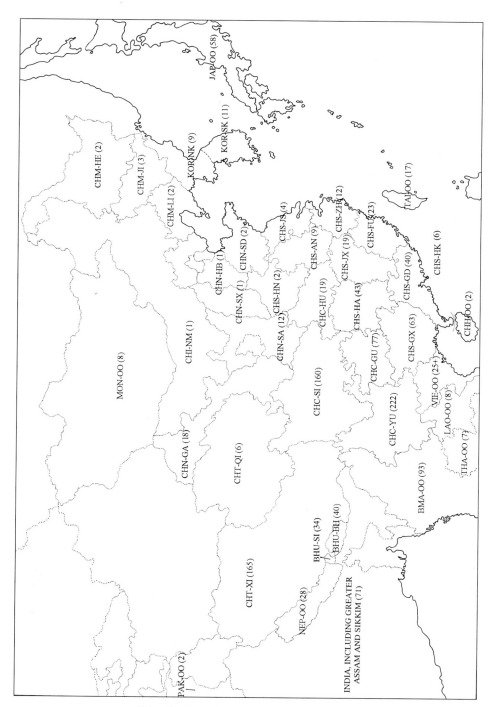

Distribution of temperate rhododendrons
(Key to the abbreviations on pages 78 and 80)

FRA-OO	France	2
GER-OO	Germany	3
ITA-OO	Italy	2
NOR-OO	Norway	2
POL-OO	Poland	2
POR-OO	Portugal	1
SLO-OO	Slovenia	2
SPA-OO	Spain	2
SWE-OO	Sweden	2
SWI-OO	Switzerland	2
UKR-MD	Moldova	1
UKR-UK	Ukraine	2
YUG-OO	Yugoslavia	1

N AMERICA
Canada

ABT-OO	Alberta	2
BRC-OO	British Columbia	6
LAB-OO	Labrador	4
MAN-OO	Manitoba	1
NBR-OO	New Brunswick	3
NSC-OO	Nova Scotia	3
NWT-FR	NW Terr., Franklin	1
NWT-KT	NW Terr., Keewatin	1
NWT-MK	NW Terr., Mackenzie	2
ONT-OO	Ontario	1
QUE-OO	Quebec	3
YUK-OO	Yukon	1

Greenland

GNL-OO	Greenland	3

United States

ALA-OO	Alabama	12
ALU-OO	Aleutian Islands	1
ARK-OO	Arkansas	3
ASK-OO	Alaska	3
CAL-OO	California	4
CNT-OO	Connecticut	3
COL-OO	Colorado	1
DEl-OO	Delaware	1
FLA-OO	Florida	5
GEO-OO	Georgia	14
IDA-OO	Idaho	1
ILL-OO	Illinois	2
KTY-OO	Kentucky	6
LOU-OO	Louisiana	2

MAI-OO	Maine	4
MAS-OO	Massachusetts	3
MIN-OO	Minnesota	1
MON-OO	Montana	2
MSI-OO	Mississippi	4
MSO-OO	Missouri	1
NCA-OO	North Carolina	11
NEV-OO	Nevada	1
NWH-OO	New Hampshire	5
NWJ-OO	New Jersey	3
NWY-OO	New York	6
OHI-OO	Ohio	1
OKL-OO	Oklahoma	3
ORE-OO	Oregon	4
PEN-OO	Pennsylvania	7
SCA-OO	South Carolina	10
TEN-OO	Tennessee	9
TEX-OO	Texas	2
VER-OO	Vermont	4
VRG-OO	Virginia	7
WAS-OO	Washington	3
WVA-OO	West Virginia	5
WYO-OO	Wyoming	1

RUSSIA

ALT-OO	Altay	2
AMU-OO	Amur	9
BRY-OO	Buryatiya	2
CTA-OO	Chita	2
IRK-OO	Irkutsk	4
KAM-OO	Kamchatka	5
KHA-OO	Khabarovsk	4
KRA-OO	Krasnoyarsk	2
KUR-OO	Kuril Islands	2
MAG-OO	Magadan	5
NCS-DA	Dagestan	1
NCS-SO	Severo Ossetya	1
PRM-OO	Primorye	2
RUC-OO	Russia Central	1
RUE-OO	Russia East	1
RUN-OO	Russia North	1
RUW-OO	Russia West	1
SAK-OO	Sakhalin	7
TCS-AB	Abkhasiya	1
YAK-OO	Yakutiya	2

Fig. 1: R. pudorosum

Fig. 2: R. lanigerum

Fig. 3: R. dignabile

Fig. 4: R. calostrotum (left), R. wardii (centre) and R. primuliflorum (right)

Fig. 5: R. complexum

Fig. 6: R. hongkongense

Fig. 7: R. lepidotum

Fig. 8: R. parmulatum pink rimmed

Fig. 9: R. parmulatum white form

Fig. 10: R. neriiflorum subsp. *phaedropum*

Fig. 11: R. fragariiflorum

Fig. 14: R. fragariiflorum, Temo La, SE Tibet

Fig. 12: R. charitopes subsp. *tsangpoense*

Fig. 13: R. leptothrium

Fig.15: R. lowndesii, Marsyandi Valley, Nepal

Fig. 16: R. uniflorum var. *imperator*

Fig. 17: R. laudandum var. *temoense*

Fig. 18: R. glischrum subsp. *rude*

Fig. 19: R. augustinii subsp. *hardyi*   *Fig. 20: R. forrestii*

Fig. 21: R. wadanum

Fig.22: *R. cinnabarinum* subsp.
xanthocodon Concatenans Group

Fig. 23: *R. nivale* subsp. *nivale*

Fig. 24: *R. venator*

Fig. 25: *R. hirtipes*

Fig. 26: *R. primuliflorum*

BARAVALLA GARDENS

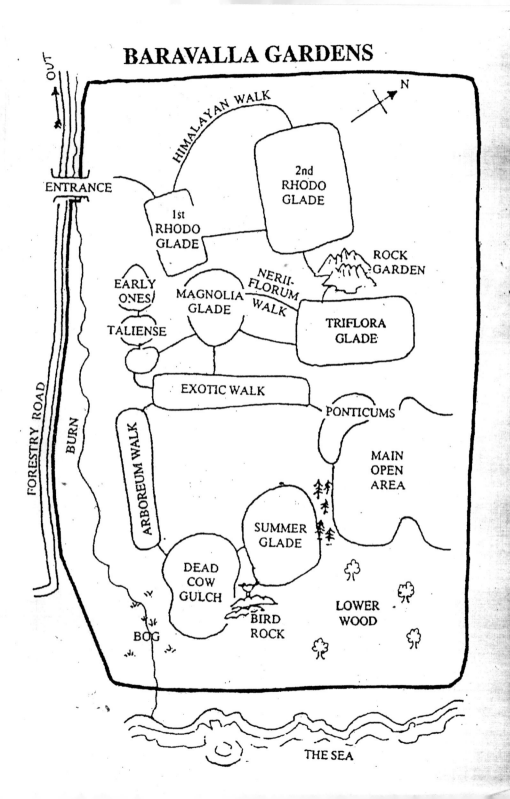

BARAVALLA GARDENS - The Background

If you are visiting Baravalla for the first time, you should perhaps be warned. It is a garden of the W's. It is a wild garden, as far as the gardeners are concerned it is a weekend garden and it is in consequence a somewhat woolly garden. Furthermore there is no house, and all this limits what can sensibly be grown to trees and shrubs; maintenance means keeping the tide of natural encroachment within reasonable limits. As it is a slightly unusual enterprise, it might be helpful to sketch in the background of how it started.

One of the hazards of collecting seed in the wild is that you then have large numbers of seedlings. They are your babies, they grow bigger by the minute and they ultimately need a home. When Peter Cox and Peter Hutchison developed an interest in plant collecting, the idea evolved of a garden in the mild Atlantic climate of Argyll where there would be space to plant generous groups of things they had collected. In addition there would be a chance to grow plants of borderline hardiness that the East coast gardener always envies on the western side of the fence.

And so in 1968 discussions with the Mackie Campbells, whose family estate was Stonefield and who were therefore no strangers to fine rhododendrons, led to a partnership being set up with them. Some 20 acres on the shores of West Loch Tarbert were fenced against rabbits and deer and the first serious planting began in 1969. Recently a strip of land has been acquired to bring the burn into the garden boundary.

The soil is somewhat poor and thin but the garden is sheltered from the worst of the prevailing winds. Natural oak and hazel surround the old crofting fields which are gradually becoming rhododendron glades and there are a few fine beeches and silver firs.

Planting has continued steadily since 1969 with the emphasis on materials collected in the wild by Cox and Hutchison. Early introductions from the Assam Himalayas in 1965 include **Ilex nothofagifolia** for the first time and a new species of rhodendron, **Rh.subansiriense.** The SBEC trip to the Cang Shan range in Yunnan in 1981 produced a rich harvest, including the first introduction of **Rh. sinogrande** since George Forrest and classic plants such as **Rh. lacteum.**

Since that time the seed of 15 expeditions to the Himalayas, Tibet and China has contributed to the garden. A comprehensive collection of big leaved rhododendrons is being planted in the Lower Wood, epiphytes are festooning the moss-covered rocks as in their native habitat, and the Burn Path is home to plants that like as much sun as Argyll can give them.

P.C.H. April 2007

Description of Species in Cultivation

The descriptions presented here are intended to include the diagnostic characters for those entities that are in cultivation and represent species, subspecies or varieties that occur in the wild. These descriptions are similar in format to those provided in the 1980 Handbook. The names are given with the authors to avoid possible confusion. Each is assigned to a subsection, section or subgenus, as appropriate. Relevant synonyms in common use are also included following the names. All other synonyms are listed separately.

Only those species that are known to be in general cultivation are described. All the other recognized names will be found in the section entitled The Classification of Rhododendron (see pps 9-35).

Hardiness ratings only give a rough guide to the hardiness of a particular species and only apply to plants that have reached an age of optimum hardiness (usually 5 years plus). As a consequence, the hardiness ratings of some species only recently introduced into cultivation are uncertain and can only be surmised from the respective geographical distributions. Prolonged, sudden or out of season frosts of a less severe nature than given below may cause damage. In many species the wood and foliage are considerably more hardy than the flower buds, which may be destroyed at temperatures higher than the ratings given. Some species only attain maximum hardiness if grown in regions with warm summers, such as some members of Section Pentanthera and many species in Section Tsutsusi. Ratings for species given in brackets apply to plants grown in areas with cool summers.

H1a   Requiring stove conditions under glass.

H1b   Requiring the protection of a cool glasshouse where the outside temperature drops below -7°C (20°F).

H2   Only hardy in the most favourable sheltered coastal parts of the British Isles, with a winter minimum of -12°C (10°F).

H3   Hardy in sheltered gardens near the coasts, with a winter minimum of -15°C (5°F).

H4a   Hardy at most low elevations in the British Isles provided that there is some shelter, with a winter minimum of -18°C (0°F).

H4b   Hardy throughout the British Isles and most of Western Europe, in areas with a winter minimum of -21 to -24°C (-5 to -10°F).

H4c   Hardy throughout Europe and all but the coldest parts of Eastern North America, in areas with a winter minimum of -29°C (-20°F).

The times of flowering are those appropriate to the British Isles. As with the hardiness ratings some of the more recently introduced species have not been in cultivation long enough to confirm the flowering time reliably; it should be noted that the flowering time in the field often differs significantly from that in cultivation in Britain.

The details of the awards given by the Royal Horticultural Society are given only where these relate to species or cultivars selected within them. The awards quoted are abbreviated as follows:

FCC = First Class Certificate
AM = Award of Merit
PC =   Certificate of Preliminary Commendation
♀ =   the Award of Garden Merit given from 1992 onwards

R. ABERCONWAYI COWAN - SUBSECT. IRRORATA.
Shrub, 1.5-2.5m. Leaves coriaceous, 3-6 × 1.1-2.2cm, elliptic, apex acute, margin strongly recurved, lower surface glabrous though with persistent red punctate hair bases overlying the veins. Flowers 6-12, in a lax truss, white to pale rose, with purple flecks, open-campanulate, lacking nectar pouches, 28-35mm, ovary and style stalked-glandular. H3-4a. April-May. China (N Yunnan, Guizhou), 2,200-2,500m.

A distinctive species allied to *R. annae* and *R. araiophyllum*.

AM 1945 (Crown Estate Commissioners, Windsor) to a clone 'His Lordship', from McLaren T.41; flowers white with crimson dashes.

R. ADENOGYNUM DIELS (INCL. *R. ADENOPHORUM* BALF.F. & W.W.SM.) - SUBSECT. TALIENSIA.
Shrub or small tree, (0.5-)1.3-4m. Leaves 6-11 × 2-4cm, narrowly elliptic to elliptic, apex acute, lower surface usually with a dense spongy to matted (rarely sparse), one-layered tomentum that is composed of ramiform and at least some gland-tipped hairs, and is yellowish at first, maturing to a rich olive brown; petioles glabrescent or tomentose, with at least some stalked glands. Flowers 4-12, generally in a dense truss; calyx (4-)8-15mm, lobes oblong; corolla white flushed pink or pale pink, sometimes with purple flecks, campanulate, nectar pouches lacking, 30-45mm; ovary densely stalked-glandular, style usually glandular in the lower third. H4b. April-May. China (SE Tibet, W Yunnan, SW Sichuan), 3,000-4,250m.

There is a complete range of intermediates between those plants with a more strongly glandular leaf indumentum, that have been called *R. adenophorum*, and those that essentially lack glands, as in *R. adenogynum*. The two are therefore not maintained as separate species.

AM 1976 (R.N.S.Clarke, Borde Hill, Sussex) to *R. adenophorum* 'Kirsty'; flowers

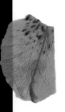

white, lip and reverse suffused red-purple and spotted.

R. adenophorum Balf.f. & W.W. Sm. is a synonym of **R. adenogynum** Diels (Subsect. Taliensia).

R. ADENOPODUM FRANCH. (INCL. *R. YOUNGIAE* FANG) - SUBSECT. ARGYROPHYLLA.
Shrub, to 3m. Leaves 9-16 × 2.5-4cm, oblanceolate, apex acuminate to shortly cuspidate, lower surface with a one-layered dense felted grey to fawn indumentum composed of dendroid hairs, petioles *c.*3cm; flowers 6-8, in a loose inflorescence, pale rose, funnel-campanulate, nectar pouches lacking, 42-50mm; ovary with a dense covering of brownish stalked glands, style glabrous. H4b. April-May. C China (E Sichuan, Hubei), 1,500-2,200m.

The relatively long and narrow leaves with long petioles will usually distinguish this from the remaining species in the subsection.

AM 1926 (G.W.E. Loder, Wakehurst Place, Sussex); flowers rose-pink, paler inside, with a few crimson spots.

R. ADENOSUM DAVIDIAN (INCL. *R. KULUENSE* D.F.CHAMB.) - SUBSECT. GLISCHRA.
Shrub, 2-3m; young shoots densely glandular-setose. Leaves coriaceous, 7-10.5 × 2.4-3cm, ovate to lanceolate or elliptic, apex acuminate, lower surface setose and sparsely evanescent-tomentose. Flowers 6-8, in a lax truss; calyx *c.*7mm; corolla pale pink or white, with purple flecks, funnel-campanulate, nectar pouches lacking, 35-50mm; ovary densely glandular-setose. H4a. May. China (SW Sichuan), *c.*3,500m.

This species is very local in the wild.

R. aeruginosum Hook.f. - is a synonym of **R. campanulatum** D.Don subsp. **aeruginosum** (Hook.f.) D.F.Chamb. (Subsect. Campanulata).

R. AFGHANICUM AITCH. & HEMSL. - SECT. AFGHANICA.

Low shrub, to 0.5m; young growth scaly and sometimes puberulent. Leaves thick, 4.7-8 × 1.3-2.5cm, narrowly elliptic to elliptic, apex more or less obtuse, lower surface pale green, with scales 1-2× their diameter apart, translucent, yellowish, upper surface darker, with midrib puberulent below; petioles puberulent. Pedicels densely scaly. Flowers 12-16, in an elongated raceme with a conspicuous rhachis; calyx lobes 4-6mm; corolla white or greenish white, campanulate, tube 6-8mm, lobes *c*.5mm; stamens 10, regularly arranged; ovary scaly, impressed below the sharply deflexed style. H3. June. Afghanistan/Pakistan Border, 2,000-3,000m.

A distinctive species on account of the characteristic inflorescence.

R. AGANNIPHUM BALF.F. & KINGDON-WARD - SUBSECT. TALIENSIA.
Shrub, 0.3-3m. Leaves 4-12 × 2-5cm, elliptic to broadly ovate-lanceolate, apex more or less acute; lower surface covered with a one-layered compacted to spongy tomentum that is continuous, or splitting and becoming patchy, and composed of ramiform hairs that are whitish or yellowish at first, sometimes turning deep reddish brown; petioles tomentose at first, later glabrescent. Flowers 10-20, in a dense truss; calyx 0.5-1mm, lobes rounded; corolla white, often flushed pink, with purple flecks, campanulate, nectar pouches lacking, 30-35mm; ovary and style glabrous. H4b. April-May. China (SE Tibet, NW Yunnan, SW Sichuan), 3,350-4,550m.

Var. **aganniphum**. (incl. *R. schizopeplum* Balf.f. & Forrest, *R. glaucopeplum* Balf.f. & Forrest & *R. doshongense* Tagg). Indumentum remaining pale and intact at maturity.

Var. **flavorufum** (Balf.f. & Forrest) D.F.Chamb. (*R. flavorufum* Balf.f. & Forrest). Indumentum turning deep brown and splitting, becoming patchy at maturity.

The two varieties merge into one another, even within a single population.

However, those forms occurring at the highest altitudes are generally referable to var. *aganniphum*. Plants from the Western edge of the range of the species have a silvery, more or less agglutinated indumentum and have been referred to *R. doshongense*, an apparently slight difference not meriting formal recognition of this species.

R. aganniphum hybridizes with *R. phaeochrysum* and with *R. proteioides* in the wild. The latter hybrid has been called *R. bathyphyllum*.

R. agapetum Balf.f. & Kingdon-Ward - is a synonym of **R. kyawii** Lace & W.W.Sm. (Subsect. Parishia).

R. × **AGASTUM** BALF.F. & W.W.SM. - is a hybrid between *R.* ARBOREUM SM. SUBSP. *DELAVAYI* (FRANCH.) D.F.CHAMB. AND *R. DECORUM* FRANCH.
Shrub or small tree, 1.5-3(-4)m. Leaves coriaceous, 6-11 × 2.5-5cm, upper surface glabrous, with slightly impressed veins, lower surface with a thin veil of dendroid hairs embedded in a surface film, with numerous red punctate hair bases overlying the veins; petioles glabrous. Flowers 10-15, in a dense inflorescence; calyx 2-3mm; corolla 6-7-lobed, rose-pink, usually with darker margins and at least a few crimson flecks, campanulate or tubular-campanulate, with nectar pouches, 40-50mm; ovary stalked-glandular, style glandular, usually almost to tip. H3. March-April. China (W Yunnan, ?Guizhou), 2,200-3,350m.

This hybrid has been mistakenly placed in Subsect. Irrorata, even though the collector of the type specimen, George Forrest, stated that he considered it to be a hybrid between *R. delavayi* and a species in Subsect. Fortunea. It may be distinguished by the 6-7-lobed corolla and by the leaves that are intermediate between those of the parents. Plants that are undoubtedly referrable to *R.* × *agastum* occur with the parents at or close to the type locality and are clearly of hybrid origin. Some plants in cultivation under the name *R. agastum* belong to *R. papillatum.*

R. agglutinatum Balf.f. & Forrest - is a synonym of **R. phaeochrysum** Balf.f. & Kingdon-Ward var. **agglutinatum** (Balf.f. & Forrest) D.F.Chamb. (Subsect. Taliensia).

R. ALABAMENSE REHDER - SUBSECT. PENTANTHERA.
Deciduous shrub or small tree, 3(-5)m; young twigs densely eglandular-hairy. Leaves 6.1-7.7(-9.4) × 1.9-2.4cm, ovate or obovate to elliptic, lower surface eglandular-hairy. Flower bud scales with outer surface glabrous or with a few unicellular eglandular hairs, margin ciliate. Pedicels sparsely to densely covered with a mixture of eglandular and gland-tipped hairs. Flowers with a sweet delicate fragrance, appearing before or with the leaves, 6-12, in a shortened raceme; calyx 1-2(-10)mm; corolla white with a yellow blotch on upper lobe, funnelform, tube gradually expanding into limb, both surfaces covered in gland-tipped hairs, 25-47mm. Capsules eglandular-hairy. H3-4a. April-May. SE USA, s.l. - 500m.

This species is closely allied to *R. canescens* but may be distinguished by the flower colour.

R. ALBERTSENIANUM FORREST - SUBSECT. NERIIFLORA
Shrub, 1-2m. Leaves 8.5-9.5 × *c.*2.2cm, narrowly elliptic, lower surface with a continuous two-layered indumentum, the upper layer light brown, tomentose, composed of ramiform hairs, the lower felted and more or less compacted. Flowers 5-6, in a loose truss; calyx cupular, 3-4mm; corolla bright crimson-rose, tubular-campanulate, with nectar pouches, *c.*30mm; ovary densely tomentose, tapering into the glabrous style. H4a. April. China (NW Yunnan), *c.*3,000m.

This species, which has affinities with *R. sperabile,* has only been collected once. It may be distinguished from its immediate allies by the two-layered leaf indumentum.

R. ALBIFLORUM HOOK. - SUBGEN. CANDIDASTRUM.
Deciduous shrub, to 2m. Leaves elliptic to oblanceolate, to 8 × 2.5cm, margin minutely toothed, midrib and margin ciliate at first, becoming glabrous. Flowers 1-2, spaced along the previous year's shoots, white, bowl shaped, almost regular, 20mm across, tube short, lobes spreading; stamens 10(-12). H4c June-July. Canada, W USA, 1,200-2,300m.

A distinct species, perhaps distantly related to *R. nipponicum;* it is often difficult in cultivation.

R. ALBRECHTII MAXIM. - SECT. SCIADORHODION.
Deciduous shrub, to 2.5m; young twigs covered with gland-tipped hairs, later glabrescent. Leaves alternate, becoming more closely spaced in pseudowhorls towards apex of stem, 2.1-13.5 × 0.9-6.3cm, obovate to (rarely) elliptic, lower surface glabrous or covered with eglandular or gland-tipped hairs, midrib covered with straight to crisped unicellular hairs. Flowers fragrant, appearing before or with the leaves, 2-5, in an umbellate raceme; calyx 1-3.5mm; corolla pink to reddish purple, broadly rotate to funnelform, the short tube gradually expanding into the longer limb, 18-32mm. Capsule covered with gland-tipped multicellular hairs, occasionally with a few unicellular hairs at apex. H4b. April-May. Japan (Hokkaido, Honshu), 800-2,300m.

A distinctive species not closely related to any other. It is somewhat intermediate between the remaining members of Sect. Sciadorhodion and Sect. Rhodora.

AM 1943 (Lord Aberconway, Bodnant); flowers Phlox Pink.

FCC 1962 (Lord Aberconway and National Trust, Bodnant) to a clone 'Michael McLaren'; flowers Solferino Purple, spotted yellowish green.
♀ 1993

R. alpicola Rehder & E.H.Wilson - is a synonym of **R. nivale** Hook.f. subsp. **boreale**

Philipson & N.M.Philipson (Subsect. Lapponica).

R. ALUTACEUM BALF.F. & W.W.SM. - SUBSECT. TALIENSIA.
Shrub, 0.6-4.5m. Leaves 5-17 × 2-4cm, oblong to oblanceolate, apex apiculate, lower surface covered with a two-layered indumentum, the upper layer more or less continuous, pale brown and lanate or mid- to reddish brown and felted, or partially detersile, then rufous, the lower layer whitish and compacted; petioles usually with a persistent brown tomentum. Flowers 10-20, in a dense truss; calyx 0.5-1mm; corolla white flushed rose, with crimson flecks, campanulate, nectar pouches lacking, 30-35mm; ovary sparsely glandular and tomentose to almost glabrous, style glabrous. H4b. April-May. China (SE Tibet, NW Yunnan, Sichuan), 3,050-4,250m.

Var. **alutaceum** (incl. *R. globigerum* Balf.f. & Forrest). Leaf indumentum usually pale ochraceous brown, lanate, with long fine ramiform hairs, continuous; ovary with a few papillae, otherwise glabrous.

Var. **iodes** (Balf.f. & Forrest) D.F.Chamb. (*R. iodes* Balf.f. & Forrest). Leaf indumentum mid-brown, felted, with short fine hairs, continuous; ovary with a sparse indumentum of rufous hairs and glands.

Var. *iodes* is intermediate between and intergrades with the other two varieties.

AM 1978 (R.N.S. Clarke, Borde Hill, Sussex) to a clone 'White Plains'; flowers white, yellow-green at base externally, spotted red-purple within.

Var. **russotinctum** (Balf.f. & Forrest) D.F.Chamb. (*R. russotinctum* Balf.f. & Forrest, & incl. *R. triplonaevium* Balf.f. and *R. tritifolium* Balf.f. & Forrest). Leaf indumentum with upper layer discontinuous, composed of rufous hairs; ovary with a sparse indumentum of rufous hairs and glands.

AM 1980 (R.N.S. Clarke, Borde Hill, Sussex) to a clone 'Easter Island', from Forrest 20425. Trusses compact, 10-12-flowered; corolla campanulate, white with dorsal red spotting.

This species closely resembles *R. phaeochrysum* but may be distinguished by its narrower leaves, etc. The leaves of some forms emit a characteristic musky odour.

R. AMAGIANUM MAKINO - SECT. BRACHYCALYX.
Tree, to 5m; young shoots covered with dense white hairs, later glabrescent. Leaves in whorls of up to three, at the ends of the branches, 4-9 × 3-9cm, ovate-rhombic, apex acuminate, lower surface with adpressed brown pubescent hairs, especially on the midrib; petioles densely adpressed-brown-pubescent. Pedicels densely pubescent. Flowers solitary or up to 3 per inflorescence, appearing before the leaves; calyx minute; corolla reddish orange, upper lobe with darker flecks, open-campanulate, 25-40mm; ovary densely brown-pubescent, style with white pubescent hairs at base. H4a-b. June-July, Japan (Hondo, Idzu Peninsula), *c*.100m.

This very local species is closely allied to and possibly no more than a variant of *R. sanctum*. The chief difference between the two species is in the flower colour.

AM 1948 (Lord Aberconway, Bodnant); flowers French Rose, suffused Neyron Rose, spotted red.

R. AMBIGUUM HEMSL. - SUBSECT. TRIFLORA.
Shrub, 1.5-5m; young shoots glabrous. Leaves 3-6(-8) × 1.5-3.2cm, narrowly ovate to narrowly elliptic, apex acute, upper surface pubescent for a short distance along midrib, otherwise glabrous, lower surface covered with large dark brown broadly rimmed touching or overlapping scales, midrib pubescent towards base. Flowers 3(-5), in a loose terminal inflorescence; calyx obscurely lobed, sometimes ciliate; corolla yellow, often with greenish or darker yellow spots on upper lobes, openly funnel-shaped, strongly zygomorphic, 20-26mm, outer surface usually scaly, oth-

erwise glabrous; stamens 10; ovary scaly, impressed below the declinate style that is usually glabrous (rarely puberulent) at base. H4b. April-May. China (C Sichuan, Guizhou), 2,600-4,500m.

Superficially similar to *R. triflorum* but differing in its bark, the larger, denser scales, and the lack of indumentum on the corolla.

AM 1976 (W.L. & R.A. Banks, Hergest Croft, Kington) to a clone 'Jane Banks'; flowers yellow-green, with greenish spots.

R. AMESIAE REHDER & E.H.WILSON - SUBSECT. TRIFLORA.
Upright shrub, 2-4m; young shoots densely scaly, setae present or absent. Leaves 2.8-7 × 1.5-3.4cm, ovate to elliptic, apex obtuse, upper surface glabrous or pubescent, midrib pubescent, lower surface pale green, scales unequal, up to their own diameter apart, yellowish brown to dark brown; petioles densely covered with hairs. Flowers 2-5, in a loose terminal inflorescence; calyx to 1mm, sometimes pubescent; corolla purple or dark reddish purple, with or without darker spots, widely funnel-shaped, zygomorphic, 28-40mm, outer surface scaly or not, sometimes hairy; stamens 10; ovary densely scaly, impressed below the declinate glabrous style. H4b. May. China (NW Sichuan), 2,300-3,000m.

This species is closely allied to *R. concinnum* but differs in the more dense indumentum and in the larger corolla.

R. ANNAE FRANCH. (INCL. *R. HARDINGII* TAGG & *R. LAXIFLORUM* BALF.F. & FORREST) - SUBSECT. IRRORATA.
Shrub, 0.5-6m. Leaves coriaceous, 6.5-15 × 2-3.5cm, elliptic to oblanceolate, apex acuminate, lower surface glabrous though with red punctate hair bases persisting on the veins. Flowers 7-12(-17), usually in a lax truss, white, with a rose flush, sometimes with purple flecks, open-campanulate, lacking nectar pouches, 25-40mm; ovary and style stalked-glandular. H3-4a. May-June. China (Guizhou, W Yunnan), NE Burma, 1,500-2,400m.

Both *R. hardingii* and *R. laxiflorum*, from W Yunnan, have larger flowers, c.40mm long, while in *R. annae* (from Guizhou) they are usually 25mm long. However, the type specimens of *R. hardingii* have flowers that span the whole range between these three entities.

AM 1977 (Maj. A.E. Hardy, Sandling Park, Kent) to a clone 'Folks Wood', as *R. laxiflorum*; flowers white.

AM 1979 (R.N.S. Clarke, Borde Hill) to a clone 'Anna Strelow' of *R. laxiflorum*, from Forrest 27706; truss 14-16-flowered, corolla white, shading towards base to a yellowish white, lobes faintly flushed red-purple, stamens 11-12.

R. annamense Rehder - is a synonym of **R. simsii** Planch. var. **simsii** (Subsect. Tsutsusi).

R. ANTHOPOGON D.DON - SECT. POGONANTHUM.
Small shrub, to 1m; leaf bud scales persistent or deciduous. Leaves (1-)1.4-3.5 × 0.8-1.6cm, ovate to elliptic, rarely orbicular, apex rounded, mucronate, lower surface covered with 2-3 tiers of overlapping scales, the upper tier dark brown (rarely pale), those of the lowest tier at least as dark as the rest. Flowers 15-20, in a dense racemose umbel; calyx lobes 3.5-4.5mm; corolla white or pink (rarely yellowish), hypocrateriform, tube 6-12mm, densely pilose within, lobes 4-7.5mm, glabrous; stamens (5-)6-8(-10); ovary scaly. H4a-b. April-May.

Subsp. **anthopogon**. Leaf bud scales deciduous. Nepal, N India (Uttar Pradesh to Arunachal Pradesh), Bhutan, China (S Tibet), 3,350-4,900m.

AM 1955 (Mrs L.C.R. Messel & National Trust, Nymans Garden); flowers Fuchsine Pink.

AM 1969 (E.H.M. & P.A. Cox, Glendoick Gardens, Perth) to a clone 'Betty Graham', from L. & S. 1091; flowers deep pink.

Subsp. **hypenanthum** (Balf.f.) Cullen (*R. hypenanthum* Balf.f.). Leaf bud scales persistent. NW India (Kashmir to Uttar

Pradesh), Nepal, Bhutan, 3,350-4,500m.

AM 1974 (Glendoick Gardens Ltd, Perth) to a clone 'Annapurna', as *R. hypenanthum*, from S., S. & W. 9090; flowers yellow, with darker staining.

Subsp. *hypenanthum* is a western vicariad of subsp. *anthopogon*. Var. *album* Davidian is a white-flowered variant of subsp. *anthopogon*.

R. ANTHOPOGONOIDES MAXIM. - SECT. POGONANTHUM.
Shrub, to 1.6m; leaf bud scales deciduous. Leaves (2-)2.5-4 × 1-2cm, ovate-elliptic, apex rounded, mucronate, lower surface covered with one tier of pale brown overlapping scales that are plastered to the surface and have domed well-developed centres and narrow, scarsely lacerate rims. Flowers many, in a dense racemose umbel; calyx lobes 3-4.5mm, margin erose; corolla white or greenish white, rarely flushed pink, hypocrateriform, tube 5-10mm densely pilose at throat, lobes 1.5-3mm; stamens 5; ovary scaly, sometimes also pubescent. H4a-b. April-May. China (Qinghai, Gansu), 3,050-3,350m.

A distinctive species on account of the form of the scales, the characteristic calyces, etc. Only subsp. *anthpogonoides* has been recorded in cultivation, and then only rarely.

R. ANTHOSPHAERUM DIELS (INCL. *R. ERITIMUM* BALF.F. & W.W.SM.) - SUBSECT. IRRORATA.
Shrub or small tree, 3-12m. Leaves 6-16 × 2-4.5cm, elliptic-oblong to oblong, apex acute to acuminate, lower surface glabrous though with a few red punctate hairs overlying the veins. Flowers 6-7-lobed, 10-15, in a dense truss, rose-magenta to crimson or magenta-blue to pale peach, sometimes with purple flecks and/or a basal blotch, tubular-campanulate, with nectar pouches, 30-45mm; ovary usually glabrous, style glabrous. H2-3. March-April. NE Burma, China (SE Tibet, Yunnan), 2,700-4,000m.

This species differs from all others in the subsection in its 6-7-lobed corollas.

The flower colour is particularly variable. *R. eritimum* is said to differ in its rounded, not acute leaf apex. There is however, gradation from one form to the other, making this an unreliable diagnostic character.

R. ANWHEIENSE E.H.WILSON (*R. MACULIFERUM* FRANCH. SUBSP. *ANWHEIENSE* [E.H.WILSON] D.F.CHAMB.) - SUBSECT. MACULIFERA.
A rounded shrub, 1-3.5m; vegetative buds globose. Leaves 3-8.5 × 1.5-3.5cm, elliptic to oblong-elliptic, apex acute or obtuse, lower surface glabrous or with minute black hairs that sometimes arise from a red punctate base; petioles floccose, with whitish hairs. Flowers 6-12, in a lax truss; calyx *c*.1mm; corolla white tinged pink to pink, sometimes with purple flecks, funnel-campanulate, without nectar pouches, 25-35mm, glabrous or with a few long hairs. H4b. April-May. E China (Anhui), 1,500-1,800m.

♀ 1993

This species has been placed in Subsect. Irrorata where it is anomalous in having a floccose indumentum on the petioles. The globose leaf buds are characteristic and distinguish this species from *R. maculiferum*, with which it has also been allied. This is a geographically isolated species with a very restricted distribution.

R. APERANTUM BALF.F. & KINGDON-WARD - SUBSECT NERIIFLORA.
Dwarf shrub, 0.3-0.6(-1.5)m; bud scales persistent. Leaves 3-6.5 × 1.4-2.4cm, obovate to oblanceolate, lower surface with a glaucous, papillate epidermis, usually glabrous at maturity though sometimes with vestiges of a red-brown or whitish dendroid indumentum that usually persists on the main veins and midrib. Flowers 4-6, in a lax truss; calyx cupular, 3-6mm; corolla thin, white, yellow flushed rose to orange or red to crimson, tubular-campanulate, with nectar pouches, 30-40mm; ovary coarsely rufous-tomentose, with a few gland-tipped setae, abruptly contracted into the glabrous style. H4a. April-May. NE Burma, China (NW

Yunnan), 3,600-4,500m.

AM 1931 (Marquess of Headfort, Kells); flowers crimson.

This high altitude, relatively dwarf species is difficult in cultivation. The persistent bud scales are an unusual feature in this subsection. The wide range in flower colour may have arisen through hybridization with related species in Subsect. *Neriiflora*.

R. ARAIOPHYLLUM BALF.F. & W.W.SM. - SUBSECT. IRRORATA.
Shrub or small tree, 1.5-6.5m. Leaves subcoriaceous, 5.5-13 × 1.8-3.2cm, elliptic to oblanceolate, apex acute to cuspidate, lower surface glabrous, punctate hair bases apparently lacking. Flowers 5-10, in a lax truss, white flushed rose, with a basal blotch, sometimes also with purple flecks, open-campanulate, lacking nectar pouches, 28-35mm; ovary with a sparse covering of short white hairs, style glabrous. H2-3. April-May. NE Burma, China (W Yunnan), 2,300-3,350m.

Closely allied to *R. annae* but distinguished by its glabrous style.

AM 1971 (Royal Botanic Gardens, Kew) to a clone 'George Taylor'; flowers white, with blotch and spots of red-purple.

R. ARBORESCENS (PURSH) TORR. - SUBSECT. PENTANTHERA.
Deciduous shrub or small tree, to 6m; young twigs glabrous or (rarely) very sparsely covered with unicellular hairs. Leaves 4.5-8(-10.5) × 1.6-3cm, ovate or obovate to elliptic, glabrous or nearly so. Flower bud scales with outer surface glabrous or with a few unicellular hairs, margin ciliate. Pedicels covered with gland-tipped hairs. Flowers with a cinnamon-like fragrance, appearing after leaf expansion, 3-7, in a shortened raceme; calyx 1-8mm; corolla funnelform, tube gradually expanding into limb, white, outer surface covered with unicellular and multicellular gland-tipped hairs, 32-50mm; filaments of stamens and style pink to red, contrasting with the corolla.

Capsules covered with sparse unicellular and dense multicellular gland-tipped hairs. H4b. May-August. E USA, 300-1,500m.

This species is closely allied to *R. viscosum*; the latter may be distinguished by its hairy young shoots and whitish filaments and style.

AM 1952 (M. Adams-Acton, London) to a clone 'Ailsa'; flowers white, with yellow blotch.

R. ARBOREUM SM. - SUBSECT. ARBOREA.
Small to large trees, 5-30m, with a well-defined trunk. Leaves leathery, 6.5-19 × 1.8-6cm, narrowly to broadly elliptic or ovate, upper surface with more or less deeply impressed veins, lower surface with a compacted to dense and spongy white to fawn indumentum composed of dendroid hairs, occasionally also with a loose floccose rufous upper layer. Flowers 10-20, in a dense truss, white or pink to deep crimson-red, with dark purple flecks and nectar pouches, fleshy, tubular-campanulate, 30-50mm.

This is one of the most widespread and variable species of *Rhododendron*.

Subsp. **arboreum**. Leaves 10-19 × 2.5-5cm, with a white to silvery compacted indumentum beneath, reticulate above; flowers crimson. H2-3. January-May. N India (Kashmir to Sikkim), Nepal, Bhutan, 1,850-2,550(-3,200)m.

This is the common subspecies across the Indo-Himalayas. In cultivation it is relatively tender.

Subsp. **cinnamomeum** (Wall ex G.Don) Tagg. Leaves 6.5-11 × 2.2-4.5cm, with a white to cinnamon compacted indumentum beneath, sometimes also with an upper layer of rufous hairs, reticulate above; flowers white to crimson. H3-4a. March-May. E Nepal and China (S Tibet) to Bhutan and Arunachal Pradesh, 2,750-3,650m.

This subspecies tends to have a more Easterly distribution than does subsp. *arboreum*, and occurs at higher elevations. It is therefore rather hardier in cultivation.

Var. **cinnamomeum** (Wall ex G.Don)

Lindl. (incl. *R. arboreum* Sm. subsp. *campbelliae* [Hook.f.] Tagg). Leaves with an upper layer of loose rufous hairs.

Var. **roseum** Lindl. Leaves lacking the upper layer of loose hairs.

White-flowered forms from the highest elevations, particularly in Nepal, have been referred to var. **album** Wall.

FCC 1974 (Royal Botanic Gardens, Wakehurst) to a clone *R. arboreum* var. *roseum* 'Tony Schilling'.

♀ 1993

Subsp. **delavayi** (Franch.) D.F.Chamb. Leaves 7-18 × 1.8-3(-4.2)cm, with a thick and spongy white to fawn indumentum beneath, reticulate above; flowers clear red to crimson. H2-3. NE India, Burma, Thailand, SW China, 1,500-3,000m.

This subspecies is tender in cultivation, requiring considerable shelter. It replaces subsp. *arboreum* and subsp. *cinnamomeum* in the Eastern part of the range of the species.

Var. **delavayi** (*R. delavayi* Franch.). Leaves 2.8-4.4× as long as broad.

FCC 1936 (Capt. A.M.T. Fletcher, Port Talbot, Wales), as *R. delavayi*; flowers deep red.

Var. **peramoenum** (Balf.f. & Forrest) D.F.Chamb. (*R. peramoenum* Balf.f. & Forrest). Leaves 4.5-6.5 × as long as broad.

Subsp. **albomentosum** (Davidian) D.F.Chamb. (*R. delavayi* Franch. var. *albomentosum* Davidian). Leaves 4-6 × 2-2.5cm, with a white spongy indumentum beneath, reticulate above; flowers a rich cherry red. H2-3. N Burma (Mt Victoria), 3,000m.

This tender subspecies, which apparently maintains its distinctive features in cultivation, is intermediate between subsp. *arboreum* and subsp. *delavayi*. It is only known in the wild from a single mountain and even then it may be distinguishable from more typical forms of *R. arboreum* that occur on the same mountain at lower altitudes

Subsp. **nilagiricum** (Zenker) Tagg. Leaves 8.5-12 × 3.8-6cm, apex rounded-apiculate, lower surface with a yellowish brown spongy indumentum, upper surface with deeply impressed veins; flowers carmine. H2-3. S India, *c*.2,250m.

This subspecies is intermediate between subsp. *zeylanicum* and subsp. *delavayi*.

Subsp. **zeylanicum** (Booth) Tagg (*R. zeylanicum* Booth). Bark deeply fissured; leaves 8-11 × 3.5-4.5cm, apex blunt to acute, margin strongly recurved; lower surface with a spongy brownish indumentum, upper surface with deeply impressed veins, flowers carmine. H2. Sri Lanka, 1,000-2,500m.

The characteristic leaves and bark will serve to identify this, the most distinctive of the subspecies of *R. arboreum*. It is a plant only for the mildest of British gardens.

AM 1964 (National Trust for Scotland, Brodick Castle Gardens) to a clone *R. arboreum* 'Goat Fell'; flowers Cherry Red, with a few spots in the throat.

AM 1968 (E. de Rothschild, Exbury) to a clone *R. arboreum* 'Rubaiyat'; flowers red, with darker spots.

R. arboreum Sm. subsp. *campbelliae* (Hook.f.) Tagg - is a synonym of **R. arboreum** Sm. var. **cinnamomeum** (Wall ex G.Don) Lindl. (Subsect. Arborea).

R. ARGIPEPLUM NUTTALL EX HOOK.F. (INCL. *R. SMITHII* NUTTALL & *R. MACROSMITHII* DAVIDIAN) - SUBSECT. BARBATA. Large shrub or small tree, 1.5-10m; bark smooth and flaking, reddish brown; young shoots and petioles with long stiff bristles. Leaves 8-13 × 2.7-4cm, elliptic to obovate-lanceolate, apex acute to slightly rounded, base rounded to cordate, upper surface with deeply impressed veins, lower surface with a thin layer of pale brown dendroid hairs that may become whitish with age. Flowers fleshy, 15-20, in a dense truss, scarlet to crimson, with darker nectar pouches, tubular-campanulate, 30-45mm; ovary densely stalked-glandular, also with some hairs, style glabrous. H3-4a. NE India (Sikkim, Arunachal Pradesh), Bhutan, S Tibet (Tibet), 2,700-3,600m.

R. argipeplum is intermediate between the more Easterly *R. erosum* and the more westerly *R. barbatum*, but is sufficiently distinct from either to be maintained as a separate species.

AM 1978 (R.N.S. Clarke, Borde Hill, Sussex) to a clone *R. smithii* 'Fleurie'; trusses to 25-flowered, corolla red.

R. ARGYROPHYLLUM FRANCH. - SUBSECT ARGYROPHYLLA.
Shrub or tree, 2-12m. Leaves 6-16 × 1.8-6cm, narrowly elliptic to oblanceolate, apex acute, upper surface reticulate, lower surface covered with a one-layered thin silvery or fawn compacted indumentum that is usually embedded in a surface film. Pedicels 20-25mm. Flowers 4-10, in a loose inflorescence, white to pink, with purple flecks, open-campanulate, nectar pouches lacking, 30-55mm; ovary with a glandular or eglandular indumentum, style glabrous. H4a-b. May. China (N Yunnan, Sichuan, Shaanxi, Guizhou), 1,600-3,650m.

Subsp. **argyrophyllum**. Leaves 6-12 × 2-3cm, indumentum white or silvery; flowers white to pink, 30-35mm; ovary lacking glands. China (N Yunnan, Sichuan, Shaanxi).

Those forms with more open-campanulate, pink flowers have been referred to var. *cupulare* Rehder & E.H.Wilson. There is however a complete overlap with the more frequent form with funnel-campanulate white flowers.

AM 1934 (G.W.E Loder, Wakehurst Place, Sussex); flowers white flushed rose, with deeper pink spots.

Subsp. **hypoglaucum** (Hemsl.) D.F.Chamb. (*R. hypoglaucum* Hemsl.). Leaves 7-11 × 2.5-4cm, indumentum white; flowers white, 30-35mm; ovary glandular. C China (E Sichuan, Hubei).

1972 (Maj. A.E. Hardy, Sandling Park, Kent) to a clone 'Heane Wood', as *R. hypoglaucum*; flowers pink in bud, opening white, suffused red-purple and spotted red-purple.

This subspecies may be distinguished by the glandular ovaries.

Subsp. **omeiense** (Rehder & E.H.Wilson) D.F.Chamb. Leaves 6-8.5 × 1.5-2cm, indumentum fawn; flowers white; ovary without glands. China (W Sichuan).

This subspecies, which has a restricted distribution in the wild, may be recognised by the relatively small leaves, with a fawn indumentum.

Subsp. **nankingense** (Cowan) D.F.Chamb. Leaves 11-16 × c.4cm, coriaceous, indumentum white; flowers pink, 40-55mm; ovary without glands. China (Guizhou, ?Sichuan).

AM 1957, (Crown Estate Commissioners, Windsor) to a clone 'Chinese Silver'; flowers Persian Rose, with darker flushes.
♀ 1993

This subspecies may be recognised by the large stiff leaves and by the large pink flowers.

R. ARIZELUM BALF.F. & FORREST (*R. REX* H.LÉV. SUBSP. *ARIZELUM* [BALF.F. & FORREST] D.F.CHAMB.) - SUBSECT. FALCONERA.
Large shrub or more commonly a small tree, 2.5-12m; bark rough. Leaves 12-21 × 4.5-11cm, obovate, lower surface densely covered with a two-layered red-brown indumentum, the upper layer composed of strongly fimbriate cup-shaped hairs, the lower compacted; petioles terete. Flowers 12-20, in a tight truss, 7-8-lobed, yellow or cream to (more rarely) pink, with a basal blotch and flecks, obliquely to regularly campanulate, nectar pouches lacking, 30-45mm; stamens 14-16; ovary densely brown-tomentose. H3-4a. April-May. NE Burma, China (SE Tibet, W Yunnan), 3,000-4,000m.

Intermediates (possibly hybrids) between *R. arizelum* and *R. rex* subsp. *ficto-lacteum,* occur where the range of the two taxa meet. Forms, with pink (often relatively intense) flowers have been referred to var. *rubicosum* Cowan & Davidian. The status of this taxon in the wild is, however, uncertain.

AM 1963 (National Trust for Scotland,

Brodick Castle Gardens) to a clone 'Brodick'; flowers Solferino Purple, with a crimson-black blotch.

AM 1963 (Earl of Stair, Stranraer) to var. *rubicosum*; flowers Rose Red, with a more or less black blotch.

R. astrocalyx Balf.f. & Forrest - is a synonym of **R. wardii** var. **wardii** (Subsect. Campylocarpa).

R. ATLANTICUM (ASHE) REHDER - SUBSECT. PENTANTHERA.
Deciduous shrub, 1(-3)m; strongly rhizomatous; young twigs covered in a mixture of eglandular and glandular hairs. Leaves ovate or obovate to elliptic, 3.2-5.2 × 0.8-2cm usually glabrous, lower surface pale to glaucous, with eglandular and/or gland-tipped hairs. Flower bud scales glabrous or covered with unicellular hairs, margin unicellular-ciliate. Pedicels covered gland-tipped or eglandular hairs. Flowers with a sweet musky fragrance, appearing before or with the leaves, 4-13, in a shortened raceme; calyx 1-3(-10)mm; corolla white to pale pink, funnelform, tube gradually expanding into limb, outer surface covered with eglandular and gland-tipped hairs, 25-50mm. Capsules covered with unicellular and multicellular gland-tipped hairs. H4b-c. April-May. Eastern Coastal Plain of the USA, s.l.-150m.

R. atlanticum is allied to *R. viscosum* and *R. arborescens*. It is distinguished from both by the flowers appearing before the leaves and from the former by its generally less dense indumentum.

AM 1964 (Crown Estate Commissioners, Windsor) to a clone 'Seaboard'; flowers white, with pale pink corolla tube.

R. ATROVIRENS FRANCH. - SECT. TSUTSUSI.
Large shrub or small tree; young shoots covered with adpressed flattened brown hairs. Leaves of one kind, persistent, 2-8 × 1-3cm, elliptic, apex acuminate, lower surface covered with adpressed brown hairs, densely so on midrib. Flowers 2-4 per inflorescence; calyx 2-4mm, densely covered with flattened shining brown hairs; corolla red, with darker flecks at base of upper lobes, funnel-campanulate, 15-30mm, glabrous; stamens 10; ovary densely covered with adpressed flattened shining brown hairs; style glabrous. H2-3. China (NE Yunnan, Sichuan, Guizhou), 750-1,800m.

This distinctive species, which has only recently been introduced into cultivation, is almost certainly frost-sensitive

R. AUGUSTINII HEMSL. - SUBSECT. TRIFLORA.
Shrub, to 10m; young shoots scaly and usually pilose. Leaves (4-)5-10(-11) × 1.8-3(-4)cm, narrowly elliptic to elliptic, apex acute to acuminate, upper surface glabrous or with a few hairs overlying the midrib, lower surface sparsely covered with distant golden to brown scales, midrib pilose, the hairs sometimes extending along the petioles. Flowers (2-)3 (-5), in a loose terminal inflorescence; calyx disc-like or with lobes to 3mm, puberulent and often ciliate; corolla blue to purple, or white, with greenish or brown spots, zygomorphic, open-funnel-campanulate, 28-40mm, outer surface with tube sometimes scaly and/or pilose; stamens 10; ovary scaly, apex pilose, impressed below the declinate style. H3-4a. April-May. China (SE Tibet, N Yunnan, Sichuan, Hubei), 1,300-4,000m.

Subsp. **augustinii** (incl. *R. vilmorinianum* Balf.f.). Leaves evergreen, upper surface with hairs overlying the veins, lower surface with indumentum extending along petioles, consisting of filiform acicular hairs; corolla blue or lavender, tube scaly. China (C & E Sichuan, Hubei), 1,300-3,000m.

Subsp. **chasmanthum** (Diels) Cullen (incl. *R. hirsuticostatum* Hand.-Mazz.). Leaves evergreen, upper surface glabrous or hairs restricted to midrib, lower surface with indumentum hardly extending along petioles; corolla blue or lavender, often relatively pale, tube lacking scales usually pilose. China (SE Tibet, N Yunnan, W

Sichuan), 2,200-3,650m.

Subsp. **rubrum** (Davidian) Cullen (*R. augustinii* Hemsl. var. *rubrum* Davidian & incl. *R. bergii* Davidian). Leaves evergreen; petioles with hairs of two kinds, filiform-acicular as well as loriform; corolla reddish purple. China (NW Yunnan), *c.*4,000m.

AM 1978 (R.N.S. Clarke, Borde Hill, Sussex) to a clone *R. bergii* 'Papillon'; flowers red-purple, paler at rim, with darker bars on reverse, spotted.

Subsp. **hardyi** (Davidian) Cullen (*R. hardyi* Davidian). Leaves deciduous, corolla white. China (NW Yunnan), 3,350-3,650m.

This is a variable species; of the four subspecies recognized above, subsp. *augustinii* is only poorly differentiated from subsp. *chasmanthum*. The leaf indumentum will distinguish this species from all but *R. trichanthum*.

AM 1926 (Dame Alice Godman, Horsham); flowers lilac-mauve with greenish dots.

AM 1930 and FCC 1932 (L. de Rothschild, Exbury) to var. *chasmanthum*; flowers bluish purple, with ochraceous spots.

R. AUREUM GEORGI - SUBSECT. PONTICA.
Dwarf shrub, 0.2-1m; young shoots more or less glabrous; bud scales usually persistent. Leaves 2.5-15.5 × 1.2-7cm, ovate to broadly elliptic, apex rounded, upper and lower surface glabrous when mature. Flowers 5-8, in a lax truss; calyx 2-3mm; corolla yellow, usually with a least a few flecks, broadly campanulate, nectar pouches lacking, 25-30mm; ovary rufous-tomentose. H4b-c. April-May. Eastern Russia, Japan, N China (Jilin), 1,500-2,700m.

Var. **aureum**. Leaves 2.5-6.5cm; bud scales persistent.

Var. **hypopitys** (Pojarkova) D.F. Chamb. Leaves 9-15.5cm; bud scales usually deciduous.

The status of var. *hypopitys* is uncertain as it may be no more than a shade form of var. *aureum*. A difficult species in cultivation.

R. AURICULATUM HEMSL. - SUBSECT. AURICULATA.
Small tree, 2-6m; young shoots setose-glandular. Leaves 15-30 × 4.5-10cm, oblong to oblong-lanceolate, apex rounded, apiculate, base auriculate, lower surface glabrous or with scattered villous hairs, especially on the veins and midrib. Flowers fragrant, 6-15, in a loose inflorescence; calyx *c.*2mm; corolla 7-lobed, white or cream to rosy pink, with greenish colouring inside at base, funnel-shaped, nectar pouches lacking, 80-110mm; stamens 14; ovary densely stalked-glandular, style glandular to tip. H4a-b. July-September. China (E Sichuan, W Hubei, E Guizhou), 600-2,000m.

R. auriculatum is late-flowering. It is allied to species in Subsect. Fortunea but is distinguished by the setose-glandular young shoots and by the large auriculate leaves.

AM 1922 (Lord Aberconway, Bodnant); flowers white.

R. AURITUM TAGG - SUBSECT. TEPHROPEPLA.
Shrub, 1-3m; bark flaking, coppery red. Leaves 2.7-6.6 × 1-2.7cm, oblong to lanceolate, apex obtuse to acute, green above, lower surface pale glaucous green, papillose, scales touching or overlapping, unequal, the smaller sunk in pits. Flowers 4-7, in a terminal inflorescence with a 1-2mm rhachis; calyx lobes reflexed, 3-5mm, not ciliate; corolla pale yellow or cream, sometimes with a pale pink flush, tubular-campanulate, 18-25mm, outer surface scaly, glabrous; stamens 10; ovary scaly, impressed below the declinate style that is scaly in the lower half. H2-3. April-May. China (SE Tibet), 2,150-2,600m.

This species is closely allied to *R. xanthostephanum* but differs in the pale flowers and in the reflexed calyx lobes.

AM 1931 (L. de Rothschild, Exbury); flowers sulphur yellow.

R. AUSTRINUM (SMALL) REHDER. - SUBSECT. PENTANTHERA.
Deciduous shrub or small tree, to 5m;

young shoots densely covered with gland-tipped hairs. Leaves 4.7-10 × 2.1-3.9cm, ovate or obovate to elliptic, lower surface densely covered with unicellular hairs sometimes also with multicellular gland-tipped hairs. Flower bud scales with outer surface covered with unicellular hairs, margin glandular. Pedicels covered with unicellular and gland-tipped multicellular hairs. Flowers with a musky-sweet fragrance, appearing before or with the leaves; calyx 1-2mm; corolla yellow to orange with a dark pink, funnelform, tube gradually expanding into limb, both surfaces densely covered in unicellular hairs, outer surface also with gland-tipped multicellular hairs, 28-45mm. Capsules covered with unicellular and multicellular gland-tipped hairs. H3-4b. March-April (-May). S USA, s.l.-100m.

This species resembles *R. canescens* morphologically but differs in its consistently glandular bud scale margins, etc.
♥ 1993

R. bachii H.Lév. - is a synonym of **R. leptothrium** Balf.f. & Forrest (Sect. Azaleastrum).

R. BAILEYI BALF.F. - SECT. BAILEYA.
Shrub, 0.5-2m. Leaves (2-)3-5 × (1-)1.4-1.9(-2.6)cm, narrowly elliptic to elliptic, apex obtuse to rounded, lower surface usually with dark brown overlapping crenulate scales. Pedicels 12-22mm, scaly. Flowers 4-8 per inflorescence, rachis elongate; calyx lobes 1.5-4mm; corolla magenta to purple, often with darker spots, campanulate, 12-15mm; stamens 10, regularly arranged; ovary scaly, style sharply deflexed. H3-4a. April-May. India (Sikkim), Bhutan, China (S Tibet), 3,050-4,250m.

A distinctive species distinguished by a combination of crenulate scales and sharply deflexed style.
AM 1960 (A.C. & J.F.A. Gibson, Glenarn, Dunbartonshire); flowers Doge Purple, with purple spots.

R. BAINBRIDGEANUM TAGG & FORREST - SUBSECT. SELENSIA.

Shrub, sometimes dwarf, 0.6-2m; young shoots covered with glandular setae. Leaves 8-12 × (2.5-)3-4cm, obovate to elliptic, lower surface covered with a continuous felted dark brown indumentum composed of dendroid hairs, also with some stalked glands that are prominent on the midrib towards the base; petioles stalked-glandular. Flowers 4-8, in a lax truss; calyx 3-6mm; corolla white to creamy yellow, usually flushed with pink, with a basal blotch and purple flecks, campanulate, without nectar pouches, 30-35mm; ovary densely stalked-glandular, style usually glandular at base. H4a. April. China (SE Tibet, NW Yunnan), 3,500-4,000m.

An unsatisfactory species close to *R. selense*. Some plants in cultivation as *R. bainbridgeanum* are almost certainly hybrids of *R. selense*.

R. BALANGENSE FANG - SUBSECT. GRANDIA.
Small tree, *c.*3m; bark rough. Leaves thick, 6-10 × 3.5-5cm, obovate to elliptic-obovate, apex acute; lower surface covered with a white or pale yellowish partially floccose indumentum composed of dendroid hairs; petioles thick, more or less flattened. Flowers 13-15, in a dense truss, 5-6-lobed, white, funnel-campanulate, with purple nectar pouches, 35-40mm; stamens 10-12; ovary glabrous. H4a. May. China (W Sichuan), *c.*2,000m.

R. balangense was originally placed in Subsect. Taliensia but is apparently allied to *R. watsonii*. It is restricted to a single mountain (Balang Shan), in W Sichuan.

R. BALFOURIANUM DIELS - SUBSECT. TALIENSIA.
Shrub, 1-4.5m. Leaves 4.5-12 × 2-4cm, ovate-lanceolate to elliptic, apex acute to acuminate, lower surface with a dense compacted to spongy one-layered lanate tomentum composed of ramiform hairs that are silvery white at first, sometimes turning pale pinkish cinnamon at maturity, usually shining and with a surface film; petioles glabrescent. Flowers 6-12, in a

dense truss; calyx 6-10mm, lobes elliptic; corolla pale to deep pink, with purple flecks, campanulate, nectar pouches lacking, 35-40mm; ovary glandular; style glandular in the lower third. H4b. April-May. China (W Yunnan, SW Sichuan), 3,350-4,550m.

Var. **balfourianum**. Leaf indumentum compacted.

Var. **aganniphoides**. Leaf indumentum spongy, thick.

R. balfourianum is allied to *R. adenogynum* but may be distinguished by the leaf indumentum that is generally paler.

R. BARBATUM WALL EX D.DON - SUBSECT. BARBATA.
Large shrub or small tree, 1.5-6m; bark smooth and flaking, reddish brown; young shoots and petioles with long stiff bristles. Leaves 9-19 × 3.5-6.5cm, elliptic to obovate, apex acute to acuminate, upper surface without strongly impressed veins, lower surface glabrous when mature or with scattered dendroid hairs and stalked glands. Flowers fleshy, 10-20, in a tight truss, crimson to blood-red, with darker nectar pouches (rarely pure white), tubular-campanulate, 30-35mm; ovary densely stalked-glandular, also with some hairs, style glabrous. H4a. March-April. N India, Nepal, Bhutan, S Tibet (Tibet), 2,700-3,700m.

Closely allied to *R. argipeplum* (q.v.) but differing in the less hairy leaves.

AM 1934 (C. Armytage Moore, Winterfield House, Cranleigh, Surrey); flowers Turkey Red.

R. BASILICUM BALF.F. & W.W.SM. - SUBSECT. FALCONERA
Shrub or small tree, 3-10m; bark rough. Leaves 17-25 × 8.5-13cm, obovate to oblanceolate, upper surface with deeply impressed veins, lower surface covered with a dense two-layered indumentum, the upper layer greyish at first, usually becoming rufous, composed of only slightly fimbriate cup-shaped hairs, the lower layer compacted; petioles strongly flattened and winged. Flowers 15-25, in a

dense truss, 8-lobed, fleshy, cream or pale yellow, with a crimson blotch, obliquely campanulate, nectar pouches lacking, 35-50mm; stamens 16; ovary densely rufous-tomentose. H3-4a. April-May. NE Burma, China (W Yunnan), 3,000-3,700m.

The flattened petioles and yellow flowers distinguish this from the remaining species in the subsection.

AM 1956 (Col Lord Digby, Minterne, Dorset) from Forrest 24139; flowers pale whitish cream, with a crimson blotch.

R. bathyphyllum Balf.f. & Forrest - is a hybrid between **R. proteoides** Balf.f. & W.W.Sm. and **R. aganniphum** Balf.f. & Kingdon-Ward (Subsect. Taliensia). It is intermediate in stature and in leaf size; it may be distinguished from the latter by its densely tomentose ovaries. It occurs in mixed populations with the parents in the mountains on the border of NW Yunnan and Tibet.

R. bauhiniiflorum Watt ex Hutch. - is a synonym of **R. triflorum** Hook.f. var. **bauhiniiflorum** (Watt ex Hutch.) Cullen. (Subsect. Triflora).

R. BEANIANUM COWAN - SUBSECT. NERIIFLORA.
Straggling shrub, to 3m. Leaves 6-9 × 3.2-4cm, obovate to elliptic, upper surface rugulose, with impressed veins, lower surface with a dense one-layered fulvous tomentum composed of coarse dendroid hairs; petioles setulose to tomentose. Flowers 6-10, in a compact truss; calyx cupular, *c*.5mm; corolla fleshy, carmine to blood-red, tubular-campanulate, with nectar pouches, *c*.35mm; ovary stellate-tomentose, abruptly contracted into the glabrous style. H3-4a. March-May. NE Burma, NE India (Arunachal Pradesh), 3,000-3,350m.

AM 1953 (Col. Lord Dibgy, Minterne, Dorset) from Kingdon-Ward 6805; flowers Cardinal Red.

R. beanianum is closely allied to *R. piercei* but may be distinguished by the coarse leaf indumentum.

R. BEESIANUM DIELS - SUBSECT. TALIENSIA.
Shrub or tree, 1.8-9m. Leaves 9-19 × 2.6-8.2cm, apex apiculate, lower surface with a thin one-layered compacted fawn to brown indumentum composed of stellate hairs; petioles sometimes winged, glabrous or floccose. Flowers 10-25, in a dense truss; calyx 0.5-1mm; corolla white flushed rose to pink, with or without purple flecks and/or a basal blotch, broadly campanulate, nectar pouches lacking; ovary densely white- to brown-tomentose, style glabrous. H4a-b. April-May. NE Burma, China (NW Yunnan, SW Sichuan), 3,350-4,250m.

A distinctive species on account of the size of the leaves. In the wild it usually occurs in the shelter of trees; in cultivation it is prone to leaf snap if planted in an exposed position. It is a difficult subject in cultivation.

R. bergii Davidian - is a synonym of **R. augustinii** Hemsl. subsp. **rubrum** (Davidian) Cullen (Subsect. Triflora).

R. BHUTANENSE LONG & BOWES LYON - SUBSECT. TALIENSIA.
Shrub, 0.6-3m. Leaves 6-12.5 × 3-5cm, elliptic to elliptic-obovate, apex acute, lower surface covered with an adpressed brown one-layered tomentum composed of radiate hairs; petioles greyish-floccose above. Flowers 8-15(-22), in a dense truss; calyx *c.*1mm; corolla pale pink to almost white, with red flecks and a magenta basal blotch, campanulate, nectar pouches lacking; ovary and style glabrous. H4b. May-June. Bhutan, 4,145-4,570m.

A recently described species in Subsect. Taliensia.

R. blepharocalyx Franch. - is a syonym of **R. intricatum** Franch. (Subsect. Lapponica).

R. BOOTHII NUTTALL (INCL. *R. MISHMIENSE* HUTCH. & KINGDON-WARD) - SUBSECT. BOOTHIA.
Usually an epiphytic shrub, to 2m; young growth with a dense indumentum of stiff twisted and matted hairs. Leaves 7.5-11.5 × 3.8-5.5cm, narrowly ovate to ovate-oblong, apex acuminate, upper surface with dense matted stiff hairs overlying the midrib, lower surface with dark brown close, more or less equal scales that are set in pits and have upturned rims. Pedicels stout, to 15mm, indumentum as for young growth. Flowers (3-)4-6(-10) per inflorescence; calyx lobes (7-)10-15mm; corolla dull to bright yellow, sometimes spotted, campanulate, tube *c.*15mm, lobes 10-12mm; stamens 10; ovary scaly, tapering into the declinate style. H1b-2. April-May. NE India (Arunachal Pradesh), China (S Tibet), 1,800-2,450m

This tender species is rare in cultivation.

R. BRACHYANTHUM FRANCH. - SUBSECT. GLAUCA.
Shrub, to 2m; shoots with a shredding coppery bark. Leaves 3.5-5.5 × 1.2-2(-2.3)cm, narrowly elliptic to narrowly obovate, apex acute to rounded, lower surface with scales more than 2× their own diameter apart, the smaller scales clear or milky. Pedicels scaly. Flowers 3-7(-10) per inflorescence; calyx lobes to *c.*8mm, apex rounded; corolla pale to greenish yellow, campanulate, 10-20mm; stamens 10, regular; ovary scaly, style sharply deflexed. H3-4a. May-July. NE Burma, China (Yunnan, SE Tibet), 3,050-4,000m.

Subsp. **brachyanthum**. Scales on mature lower leaf surface distant, sometimes entirely deciduous. China (C Yunnan), 3,050-3,350m.

AM 1966 (Capt. C. Ingram, Benenden, Kent) to a clone 'Jaune'; flowers Primrose Yellow.

Subsp. **hypolepidotum** (Franch.) Cullen. Scales much closer, 1-3× their own diameter apart. NE Burma, China (NW Yunnan, SE Tibet), 3,050-4,000m.

Subsp. *brachyanthum* has a very restricted distribution in the wild.

AM 1951 (Crown Estate Commissioners, Windsor) as *R. brachyanthum,* to a clone 'Blue Light'; flowers Aureolin.

R. BRACHYCARPUM D.DON EX G.DON - SUBSECT. PONTICA
Shrub, 2-3m; young shoots tomentose, soon glabrescent; bud scales deciduous. Leaves 7-11 × 3-4.5cm, oblong to obovate, apex more or less rounded, apiculate, lower surface glabrous or with a thin compacted greyish to fawn indumentum composed of dendroid hairs when mature. Flowers 10-20, in a dense truss; calyx *c*.2mm; corolla white or pale rose-pink, with greenish flecks, broadly funnel-campanulate, nectar pouches lacking, *c*.25mm; ovary densely tomentose. H4b-c. June-July. Japan, Korea, to at least 2,500m.

Subsp. **brachycarpum**. Leaves with a persistent indumentum beneath. Japan, N Korea, *c*.2500m.

Subsp. **fauriei** (Franch.) D.F.Chamb. (*R. fauriei* Franch.). Leaves glabrous beneath when mature. Japan, Eastern Korea.

Apart from the relative persistence or the leaf indumentum there are no significant differences between the two taxa recognized here. A form with leaves 15-25cm long and flowers up to 70mm in diameter has been called var. *tigerstedtii*. Since the only differences between this and subsp. *brachycarpum* are in the size of its leaves and flowers this entity is not formally maintained here.

A very hardy species that will stand winter cold well.

R. brachysiphon Balf.f. ex Hutch. - is a synonym of **R. maddenii** Hook.f. subsp. **maddenii** (Subsect. Maddenia).

R. BRACTEATUM REHDER & E.H.WILSON - SUBSECT. HELIOLEPIDA.
Shrub, to 2m; young shoots purplish, puberulous, leaf bud scales persistent. Leaves to 35 × 15mm, ovate to elliptic, apex more or less acute, lower surface with sparse large golden scales. Pedicels sparsely scaly, puberulous. Flowers 4-6 per inflorescence; calyx minute; corolla white with many reddish flecks, open-funnel-shaped, 15-25mm; stamens 10, declinate; ovary scaly, also puberulent towards apex, style straight, glabrous or sparsely pilose at base. H4a-b. June-July. China (W Sichuan), *c*.3,300m.

This species is allied to *R.heliolepis*.

R. brevistylum Franch. - is a synonym of **R. heliolepis** Franch. var. **brevistylum** (Franch.) Cullen (Subsect. Heliolepida).

R. brunneifolium Balf.f. & Forrest - is a synonym of **R. eudoxum** Balf.f. & Forrest var. **brunneifolium** (Balf.f. & Forrest) D.F.Chamb. (Subsect. Neriiflora).

R. BUREAVII FRANCH. (INCL. *R. CRUENTUM* H.LÉV.) - SUBSECT. TALIENSIA.
Shrub, 1-3(-6)m. Leaves 4.5-12 × 2-7cm, elliptic, apex acuminate, upper surface of leaves often with a thin covering of rusty red hairs, lower surface covered with a dense lanate tomentum composed of ramiform hairs that are salmon-pink when young but soon becoming deep rusty red; petioles densely pilose and glandular. Flowers 10-20, in a dense truss; calyx 5-10mm, lobes sometimes fleshy; corolla white flushed pink to pink, sometimes with purple flecks, tubular-campanulate, 25-40mm; ovary densely stalked-glandular, sometimes also tomentose, style usually glandular, at least near the base. H4b. April-May. China (N Yunnan), 3,350-4,250m.

A distinctive species on account of its attractive foliage. It resembles *R. nigroglandulosum* and *R. bureavioides* (see under those species for the differences). It is also allied to *R. elegantulum*, from which it may be distinguished by its broader leaves.

AM 1939 (L. de Rothschild, Exbury); flowers at first flushed rose, fading to white, with crimson spots.

AM 1972 (Royal Botanic Gardens Wakehurst) as a foliage plant.

AM 1988 (P.A. Cox, Glendoick) to a clone 'Ardrishaig'; trusses 10-11-flowered, corolla white, upper throat densely spotted, sometimes flushed red-purple.

R. BUREAVIOIDES BALF.F. - SUBSECT. TALIENSIA.
Shrub, to 2.5m. Leaves 7-14 × 3.5-6cm,

elliptic to broadly obovate, apex acute to acuminate; lower surface covered with a dense two-layered indumentum, the upper layer white at first, becoming rufous at maturity, composed of ramiform hairs with stiff branches, the lower white and compacted; petioles densely rufous-tomentose. Flowers *c*.10, in a dense truss; calyx 7-12mm; corolla white suffused rose to rose, with crimson flecks and basal blotch, funnel-campanulate, nectar pouches lacking, 40-45mm; ovary and lower half of style stalked-glandular. H4b. May. China (W Sichuan - Kangding), 3,000-?4,770m.

This species clearly differs from *R. bureavii* in its two-layered leaf indumentum, a characteristic that suggests an affinity with *R. rufum* rather than with the former species.

R. BURMANICUM HUTCH. - SUBSECT. MADDENIA.
Shrub, to 2m; young shoots densely covered with setae that are soon deciduous; vegetative bud scales broad and conspicuous. Leaves 5-5.5 × 2-2.5cm, obovate, apex obtuse, margin ciliate when young, more or less crenate above, upper surface with impressed midrib, lower surface with overlapping or touching scales. Flowers 4-6(-10), in a terminal inflorescence, scented; calyx disc-like; corolla greenish yellow, funnel-campanulate, 30-35mm, outer surface scaly throughout, pilose below; stamens 10; ovary densely scaly, impressed below the style that is scaly below. H2-3. March-April. C Burma (Mt Victoria), 2,700-2,900m.

A distinctive species, with characteristic vegetative buds, and with a restricted distribution.

AM 1980 (Mrs E. Mackenzie, Fressingfield, Norfolk) to a clone 'Elizabeth David'; trusses 4-flowered; corolla campanulate, yellow within, outer corolla a deeper shade of yellow.
♀ 1993

R. caeruleum H.Lév. - is a synonym of **R. rigidum** Franch.

R. CAESIUM HUTCH. - SUBSECT. TRICHOCLADA.
Shrub, 1-2m; young shoots sparsely scaly. Leaves more or less deciduous, 3-4.2 × 1.3-1.8cm, oblong-elliptic to (rarely) oblong-ovate, apex subacute to rounded, margin slightly revolute, lower surface white-papillose, scales distant, equal, golden, sparsely covered with straight or slightly curved setae. Flowers (1-)2-3, in a loose terminal inflorescence; calyx lobes to 2mm, ciliate; corolla yellow, funnel-campanulate, *c*.18mm, outer surface scaly, otherwise glabrous; stamens 10; ovary scaly, style impressed, sharply deflexed, glabrous. H3. May-June. China (Yunnan), 2,450-3,050m.

R. calciphilum Hutch. & Kingdon-Ward - is a synonym of **R. calostrotum** Balf.f. & Kingdon-Ward subsp. **riparium** (Kingdon-Ward) Cullen (Subsect. Saluenensia).

R. CALENDULACEUM (MICHX.) TORR. - SUBSECT. PENTANTHERA.
Deciduous shrub or small tree, to 10m; young twigs densely eglandular-hairy. Leaves (4.5-)5.5-7(-9) × (1.3-)1.8-2.6 (-3.3)cm, ovate or obovate to elliptic, with lamina glabrous or covered with eglandular hairs. Flower bud scales with outer surface usually glabrous though rarely sparsely covered with unicellular hairs. Pedicels covered with gland-tipped and/or eglandular hairs. Flowers with an acrid fragrance, appearing before or with the leaves, 5-9, in a shortened raceme; calyx 1-3mm; corolla orange to flame red, funnelform, tube abruptly expanding into the limb, 35-55mm, outer surface of tube covered with unicellular and gland-tipped multicellular hairs. Capsules covered with unicellular hairs and eglandular or (less often) gland-tipped hairs. H4c. May-July. Eastern USA (Appalachians), 180-1,000m.

This species is closely allied to *R. flammeum* but is distinguished by its glandular flower bud scales and more densely glandular corolla tube.

AM 1965 (Crown Estate Commissioners, Windsor) to a clone 'Burning Light'; flowers coral red, with orange throats.

AM 1989 (Crown Estate Commissioners, Windsor) to a clone 'Amber Light'; trusses with up to 10-12 flowers; corolla with shades of orange darkening to red in throat and on lobes.

R. CALLIMORPHUM BALF.F. & W.W.SM. - SUBSECT. CAMPYLOCARPA.
Small shrub, 0.5-3m. Leaves 3.5-7 × 3-5cm, broadly ovate to orbicular, base cordate, glabrous though occasionally glandular on midrib beneath. Flowers 4-8, in a lax truss, white to rose-pink, campanulate, nectar pouches lacking, 30-40mm; ovary stalked-glandular, style glabrous. H3-4a. April-May. China (W Yunnan), 3,000-4,000m.

Var. **callimorphum**. Flowers pink.
AM 1980 (Crown Estate Commissioners, Windsor) to a clone 'Second Attempt'; trusses loosely held, of 4-5 flowers, corolla white with a large dorsal blotch of greyed-purple within, lobes and reverse flushed and rayed with shades of red-purple.

Var. **myiagrum** (Balf.f. & Forrest) D.F.Chamb. (*R. myiagrum* Balf.f. & Forrest). Flowers white.

R. calophyllum Nutt. - is a synonym of **R. maddenii** Hook.f. subsp. **maddenii** (Subsect. Maddenia).

R. CALOPHYTUM FRANCH. - SUBSECT. FORTUNEA.
Tree, (2-)5-12m. Leaves 14-30 × 4-7.2cm, oblong-oblanceolate, base cuneate, glabrous when mature or with vestiges of juvenile indumentum persisting along underside of midrib. Flowers 5-30, usually in a lax truss, 5-7-lobed, pinkish white, with purple flecks and a basal blotch, open-campanulate, nectar pouches lacking; stamens 15-20; ovary and style glabrous, stigma conspicuous, discoid. H4b. March-April. China (Sichuan, NE Yunnan, Guizhou), 1,800-4,000m.

Var. **calophytum**. Leaves 18-30cm long, apex acuminate; flowers 15-30 in a truss.
AM 1920 (G. Reuthe, Keston, Kent); flowers white, heavily flushed pink.
FCC 1933 (Dame Alice Godman, South Lodge, Horsham); flowers pale pink.
✲ 1993

Var. **openshawianum** (Rehder & E.H.Wilson) D.F.Chamb. (*R. openshawianum* Rehder & E.H.Wilson). Leaves 14-18.5cm long, apex cuspidate; flowers 5-10 in a truss.

Plants referable to both varieties occur in cultivation.

From the description, var. *pauciflorum* W.K. Hu, which is said to be in cultivation, is only doubtfully distinct from var. *openshawianum*.

This is an imposing and very distinctive species.

R. CALOSTROTUM BALF.F. & KINGDON-WARD - SUBSECT. SALUENENSIA.
Prostrate, matted or small erect shrub, to 1.5m; young shoots densely scaly, setae, if present, soon deciduous. Leaves 1-3.3 × (0.2-)0.4-2cm, suborbicular, to oblong-ovate, rarely oblong-obovate, margin ciliate, upper surface matt, with persistent dried-up scales, lower surface with dense overlapping scales, the outermost tier of which often have long stalks and cup-shaped discs. Flowers 1-5, in a loose terminal inflorescence; calyx lobes unequal, 3-8mm, ciliate; corolla magenta or pink to purple, often with darker spots on upper lobes, very openly funnel-campanulate, 18-28mm; stamens 10; ovary scaly, glabrous, impressed below the declinate style that lacks both scales and hairs. H4a-b. April-June. N Burma, China (NW Yunnan, S Tibet), 3,850-4,550m.

Subsp. **calostrotum**. Erect or decumbent shrub. Leaves obtuse, 1.2-2.2 × (0.7-)0.9-2cm broad, scales on lower surface in 3-4 clearly defined tiers; flowers 1-2 per inflorescence; pedicels 16-27mm. N Burma, China (W Yunnan), 3,300-4,250m.

Subsp. **riparium** (Kingdon-Ward)

Cullen (incl. *R. nitens* Hutch. & *R. calciphilum* Hutch. & Kingdon-Ward). Erect or decumbent shrub. Leaves obtuse, 1.2-2.2× (0.7-)0.9-2cm broad, scales on lower surface in 3-4 clearly-defined tiers; flowers 2-5 per inflorescence; pedicels 10(-15)mm. India (Arunachal Pradesh), NE Burma, China (NW Yunnan, S Tibet), 3,050-4,550m.

AM 1983 (Glendoick Gardens, Perth)

Subsp. **riparioides** Cullen. Erect or decumbent shrub Leaves obtuse, 2.2-3.3 × (0.7-)0.9-2cm, scales on lower surface flat, tiers indistinct. China (W Yunnan, close to Weixi), 3,650-4,450m.

AM 1935 (Lt-Col L.C.R. Messel, Nymans, Sussex) from Forrest 27065/27497; flowers deep rosy mauve to magenta.

Subsp. **keleticum** (Balf.f. & Forrest) Cullen (*R. keleticum* Balf.f. & Forrest & incl. *R. radicans* Balf.f. & Forrest). Prostrate shrub. Leaves acute, 0.7-2.1 × 0.2-0.7 (-0.9)cm, upper surface lacking scales. NE Burma, China (NW Yunnan, SE Tibet), 4,250-4,550m.

AM 1928 (Messrs Gill, Falmouth) as *R. keleticum*; flowers lilac, darker inside, spotted red.

AM 1926 (J.B. Stevenson, Tower Court, Ascot) as *R. radicans*, from Forrest 19919).

This is a variable species. Subsp. *keleticum*, which is the most dwarf of the four recognized subspecies, apparently intergrades with, and replaces, subsp. *riparium* above 4,200m. It is closely allied to *R. saluenense* but may be distinguished by the totally glabrous ovary and by the shoots, petioles and the lower surface of the midrib that lack bristles.

FCC 1971 (E.H.M. & P.A. Cox, Glendoick Gardens, Perth) to a clone 'Gigha', as *R. calostrotum*; flowers red-purple, paler in throat, upper lobes marked with red-purple.

♀ 1993, to a clone 'Gigha'.

R. caloxanthum Balf.f. & Farrer - is a synonym of **R. campylocarpum** Hook.f. subsp. **caloxanthum** (Balf.f. & Forrest) D.F.Chamb. (Subsect. Campylocarpa).

R. CALVESCENS BALF.F. & FORREST - SUBSECT. SELENSIA.
Shrub, 1-2.5m; young shoots and petioles shortly stalked-glandular, also with a detersile dendroid indumentum. Leaves 6-10 × 2.5-4cm, elliptic to ovate, lower surface with a few stalked glands and a thin detersile indumentum that is sometimes restricted to the vicinity of the midrib at the base. Flowers *c*.5, in a lax truss; calyx 2-3mm; corolla white flushed rose, with a few crimson flecks, funnel-campanulate, without nectar pouches, *c*.35mm; ovary densely glandular, also with a varying proportion of rufous dendroid hairs, style glabrous. H4. China (SE Tibet, NW Yunnan), 3,350-4,550m.

Var. **calvescens.** Leaves 1.5-2.5 × as long as broad; pedicels 15-20mm.

Var. **duseimatum** (Balf.f. & Forrest) D.F.Chamb. Leaves *c*.3x as long as broad; pedicels 20-28mm.

R. calvescens, which may well be a hybrid of *R. selense*, is rare in cultivation.

R. CAMELLIIFLORUM HOOK.F. - SUBSECT CAMELLIIFLORA.
Shrub, often epiphytic, to 2m; young shoots scaly. Leaves (5.3-)6-0-10.5 × (1.6-)2-3(-3.7)cm, narrowly elliptic to oblong-elliptic, apex bluntly acute, lower surface densely covered with almost touching broadly rimmed brown scales, a few of which are darker than the rest. Pedicels densely scaly. Flowers 1-2 per inflorescence; calyx lobes 5-8mm, oblong; corolla white to deep rose, open-campanulate, 14-18(-20)mm, scaly outside, villose within; stamens 11-16; ovary with 5-10 cells, scaly, tapering into the short sharply deflexed style. H3-4a. May-June. Nepal, India (Sikkim) Bhutan, 2,750-3,650m.

This species, the only member of its subsection, is distantly allied to species in Subsect. Boothia but is clearly distinct in its 12-16 stamens and multi-celled ovary, characters that suggest an affinity with Subsect. Maddenia.

R. CAMPANULATUM D.DON - SUBSECT. CAMPANULATA.

Dwarf shrub to a small tree, 0.5-4.5m. Leaves 7-14 × 3.8-7.5cm, ovate to broadly elliptic, upper surface glabrous, with a dense fulvous lanate tomentum composed of capitellate to ramiform hairs. Flowers 8-15 in a truss, white to pale mauve or deep plum purple, with purple flecks, open-campanulate, nectar pouches lacking, 30-50mm; ovary and style glabrous. H3-4b. April-May. N India (Kashmir to Sikkim, Nepal, Bhutan), 2,700-4,500m.

Subsp. **campanulatum**. Shrub or small tree, to 4.5m; flowers white to pale mauve; leaves 9.5-14cm long without a metallic bloom when young. N India (Kashmir to Sikkim), Nepal, Bhutan, 2,700-3,500m.

Plants from NW India, typified by the clone 'Roland Cooper', differ from those from E Nepal, Sikkim and Bhutan in having relatively large leaves.

Subsp. **aeruginosum** (Hook.f.) D.F.Chamb. (*R. aeruginosum* Hook.f.). Dwarf shrub, 0.5-2.5m; flowers pale mauve to plum purple; leaves 7-9.5cm long, with a bluish metallic bloom when young. Sikkim, Bhutan, ?E Nepal, 3,800-4,500m.

Plants from Bhutan, with deep plum purple flowers and a very thick leaf indumentum, which are very slow-growing in cultivation, are perfectly distinct from subsp. *campanulatum*. However, plants from E Nepal, known only to me from photographs, apparently have much paler flowers and are intermediate in stature. *R. campanulatum* is close to *R. wallichii* but can be distinguished by the more dense and paler leaf indumentum.

AM 1925 (L. de Rothschild, Exbury) to a clone 'Knaphill'; flowers a fine lavender blue.

AM 1964 (Royal Botanic Garden, Edinburgh) to a clone 'Roland Cooper'; flowers white, shaded mauve.

AM 1965 (Royal Botanic Garden, Edinburgh) to a clone 'Waxen Bell'; flowers purple, with darker spots.

♧ 1993, to a clone 'Knaphill'

R. CAMPYLOCARPUM HOOK.F. - SUBSECT. CAMPYLOCARPA.

Shrub or small tree, 1-6.5m. Leaves 3.2-10 × 1.5-5 cm, orbicular to elliptic, base cordate, glabrous though rarely with a few glands at base. Flowers 3-10(-15), in a lax to more or less dense truss, pale to sulphur yellow, sometimes tinged with red in bud, with or without a basal blotch, campanulate, nectar pouches lacking, 25-40mm; ovary densely stalked-glandular, style glabrous. H4a. April-May. Nepal, NE India, NE Burma, China (S Tibet, Yunnan), 3,000-4,600m.

Subsp. **campylocarpum**. Leaves elliptic, 1.6-2.5 × as long as broad. Nepal, NE India, China (S Tibet), 3,000-4,600m.

FCC 1892 (Veitch & Sons, Chelsea) as *R. campylocarpum*; flowers Lemon Yellow.

Subsp. **caloxanthum** (Balf.f. & Farrer) D.F.Chamb. (*R. caloxanthum* Balf.f., & Farrer & incl. *R. telopeum* Balf.f. & Forrest). Leaves sub-orbicular, 1.1-1.7 × as long as broad. NE Burma, SW China (SE Tibet, Yunnan), 3,000-4,300m.

AM 1934 (L. de Rothschild, Exbury) as *R. caloxanthum*, from Farrer seed; buds pink, opening deep yellow, suffused red.

Subsp. *caloxanthum* is generally a smaller plant than is subsp. *campylocarpum*; the two apparently intergrade in Southern Tibet.

R. CAMPYLOGYNUM - SUBSECT. CAMPYLOGYNA.

Dwarf prostrate shrub, to 0.6(-1)m; young shoots sparsely scaly, glabrous or pubescent. Leaves (1-)1.4-2.5(-3.5) × (0.4-)0.7-1.2cm, apex obtuse to (rarely) subacute, upper surface pubescent along midrib; lower surface whitish- or silvery-papillose, glabrous but with scattered deciduous vesicular scales. Pedicels 25-50mm, elongating to 75mm in fruit, sparsely scaly and pubescent. Flowers 1-2(-3)-flowered; calyx lobes usually 4-7mm, oblong or obovate; corolla pink to red or purple, pruinose, campanulate, (10-)13-20(-23)mm, tube glabrous outside, sparsely pubescent within; stamens 10; ovary sparsely scaly, impressed below the sharply deflexed style. H3-4b. May-June. India (Arunachal Pradesh), NE Burma, China (S Tibet, Yunnan), 2,750-4,250(-4,900)m.

A distinct species, assigned to its own subsection.

AM 1973 (Capt. C. Ingram, Benenden, Kent) to a clone 'Baby Mouse'; flowers deep plum purple.

AM 1971 (Crown Estate Commissioners, Windsor) to a clone 'Bodnant Red', as var. *cremastum*; flowers greyed-purple.

AM 1966 (Capt. C. Ingram, Benenden, Kent) to a clone 'Thimble', as var. *cremastum*; flowers salmon pink.

AM 1925 (L. de Rothschild, Exbury) as var. *myrtilloides*.

FCC 1943 (E. de Rothschild, Exbury) as var. *myrtilloides*; flowers Magenta Rose.

AMs have been awarded to the clones 'Leucanthum' and 'Beryl Taylor'; both are now considered to be hybrids of *R. campylogynum.*

R. CAMTSCHATICUM PALLAS - SUBGEN. THERORHODION.
Prostrate or low shrub, usually less than 0.2m; bud scales persistent. Leaves 1-6 × 4-2.2cm, obovate or spathulate, apex rounded, with a glandular apiculus, margin toothed and ciliate, lower surface pubescent on veins, otherwise glabrous. Flowers solitary or to 3, in a raceme, the peduncle bearing leafy bracts; calyx 8-18mm, lobes oblong; corolla rose-purple (rarely white), with darker flecks, rotate, divided to the base on the lower side, 20-25mm; stamens 10; ovary pubescent, style pubescent at base. H4b-c. May-June. N Japan, E Russia, USA (Aleutian Islands, Alaska).

Subsp. **camtschaticum.** Corolla lobes pubescent outside, margin ciliate; leaves of vegetative shoots without or with sparse glandular hairs. Japan (N Honshu, Hokkaido), Russia (Kamtschatka, Kuriles), USA (Aleutian Islands, S Alaska).

Subsp. **glandulosum** (Small) Hultèn (*R. glandulosum* Small). Corolla lobes glabrous outside, margins not ciliate; Leaves of vegetative shoots glandular-

hairy. Russia (E Siberia), USA (W Alaska).

This species is very distinctive on account of the leafy peduncles and the form of the corolla. Both subspecies are probably in cultivation.

R. CANADENSE (L.) TORR. - SECT. RHODORA.
Deciduous rhizomatous shrub, to 1m; young twigs sparsely covered with eglandular and gland-tipped hairs. Leaves 1-8.3 × 0.4-3 cm, elliptic or oblong to obovate, often bluish, lower surface covered with eglandular and gland-tipped hairs. Flower bud scales usually covered with unicellular hairs. Pedicels usually sparsely covered with gland-tipped hairs. Flowers not fragrant, usually appearing before, occasionally with, the leaves, 3-9, in a terminal umbellate raceme; calyx 0.5-1.5mm; corolla rose-purple to pink, rarely white, with or without red flecks on upper three lobes, rotate-campanulate, two-lipped, tube lacking, 12-22mm, capsule covered with unicellular and multicellular eglandular and gland-tipped hairs. H4c. April. Eastern Canada, NE USA, s.l.-1,900m.

A distinctive species without close relatives.

R. × candelabrum Hook.f. - is a hybrid between **R. thomsonii** and **R. campylocarpum.** It differs from subsp. **thomsonii,** (which it otherwise resembles), in its pink flowers, glandular ovaries and relatively shorter calyces, 2-8(-15)mm long. H3-4a.

R. CANESCENS (MICHX.) SWEET (INCL. *R. ROSEUM* [LOIS.] REHDER) - SUBSECT. PENTANTHERA.
Deciduous shrub or small tree, to 6m, young twigs sparsely to densely covered with eglandular multicellular hairs, occasionally some gland-tipped, rarely glabrous. Leaves (4.7-)5.9-8.5(-9.8) × (1.4)1.9-2.8(-3.6)cm, ovate or obovate, to elliptic, lower surface covered with a dense covering of eglandular hairs, rarely also with gland-tipped hairs. Flower bud scales with outer surface covered with

unicellular hairs, margin unicellular-ciliate occasionally also with gland-tipped hairs. Flowers with a musky sweet fragrance, appearing with or before the leaves; calyx 1-4mm; corolla pink, or the tube pale to deep pink and the lobes white to pale pink, funnelform, tube gradually expanding into the limb, outer surface covered with unicellular and gland-tipped multicellular hairs, 20-45mm. Capsules eglandular-hairy. H3-4a. March-May. SE USA, s.l.-500m.

This species is closely allied to *R. periclymenoides* and to *R. prinophyllum* but is distinguished from the former by its hairy bud scales and from the latter by its hairy capsules.

R. CAPITATUM MAXIM. - SUBSECT. LAPPONICA.
Upright rounded shrub, to 1.5m. Leaves (0.7)1-1.8(-2.2) × (0.3-)0.5-0.9cm, elliptic or oblong-elliptic, apex rounded without a mucro, lower surface covered with a mixture of touching or discontiguous colourless to straw-coloured scales with golden centres, and tan to dark amber scales with darker centres. Flowers 3-5 per inflorescence; calyx lobes to 6mm, unequal; corolla pale lavender to bluish purple or deep purple, broadly funnel-shaped, 10-15mm; stamens 10, about as long as the corolla, style usually longer than (rarely the same length as) the stamens, glabrous or pubescent towards the base. H4a-b. N China (N Sichuan, Qinghai, Gansu, Shaanxi), 3,000-4,300m.

This species resembles *R. nitidulum*, with which it possibly intergrades.

R. CARNEUM HUTCH. - SUBSECT. MADDENIA.
Shrub, to 1m; young shoots lacking setae. Leaves 5-11 × 3-4cm, usually narrowly elliptic, apex acute, margin not ciliate, upper surface with impressed midrib, lower surface with scales their own diameter apart. Flowers 2-4, in a loose terminal inflorescence, slightly scented; calyx unequally lobed; corolla pink, funnel-shaped, 40-50mm, outer surface scaly throughout, pubescent at base; stamens 10; ovary densely scaly, tapering into the scaly style. H2. April-May. This species is only known in cultivation.

This distinctive species is of uncertain provenance; it is generally grown under glass.

AM 1927 (L. de Rothschild, Exbury); flowers Magenta Rose.

R. carolinianum Rehder - is a synonym of **R. minus** Michx. var. **minus** (Subsect. Caroliniana).

R. CATACOSMUM BALF.F. EX TAGG - SUBSECT. NERIIFLORA.
Shrub, 1.3-3m. Leaves 8-10 × 4.2-5.5.cm, obovate, lower surface covered with a two-layered indumentum, the upper layer loosely fulvous-tomentose, composed of dendroid hairs, the lower whitish and compacted; petioles tomentose. Flowers 6-9, in a tight truss; calyx 16-20mm, cupular; corolla fleshy, crimson, tubular-campanulate, with nectar pouches, *c*.45mm; ovary densely tomentose, abruptly contracted into the glabrous style. H4a. April-May. China (NW Yunnan, SE Tibet), 3,650-4,400m.

This species is closely allied to *R. haematodes*; it may however be distinguished by its larger leaves and calyces.

R. CATAWBIENSE MICHX. - SUBSECT. PONTICA.
Shrub, 2-3m; young shoots tomentose though soon glabrescent; bud scales deciduous. Leaves 6.5-11.5 × 3.5-5cm, broadly elliptic to obovate, apex more or less obtuse, upper and lower surfaces glabrous when mature though with persistent hair bases below. Flowers 15-20, in a dense truss; calyx *c*.1mm; corolla usually lilac-purple, with faint flecks, funnel-campanulate, nectar pouches lacking, 30-45mm; ovary densely rufous-tomentose, style glabrous. H4c. May-June. Eastern N America, 50-1,000m.

This species differs from the closely allied *R. ponticum* in its more or less glabrous ovary. It has been used widely as a parent in breeding programmes.

AM 1990 (Crown Estate Commissioners, Windsor) to a clone 'Catalgla'; trusses full, 15-20-flowered, corolla white, with some yellow-green spotting in upper throat.

R. CAUCASICUM PALLAS - SUBSECT. PONTICA.
Dwarf shrub, 0.3-1m; young shoots sparsely tomentose; bud scales deciduous. Leaves 4-7.5 × 1.3-3cm, obovate to elliptic, apex blunt to apiculate, upper surface glabrous, lower surface covered with a compacted fawn to brownish tomentum composed of dendroid hairs; petioles sparsely velutinous. Flowers 6-15, in a lax to dense truss; pedicels to 30mm in flower, elongating in fruit to 60mm; calyx 2-3mm; corolla whitish to yellow, sometimes flushed with pink, with greenish flecks, broadly campanulate, nectar pouches lacking, 30-35mm; ovary densely dendroid-pilose, style glabrous. H4b. April-May. NE Turkey and adjacent parts of Caucasia, 1,800-2,700m.

The hybrid *R.* × *sochadzeae* Char & Davlianidze (*R. caucasicum* × *R. ponticum*) is occasionally seen in cultivation. It occurs in the wild where the two species grow together.

R. CEPHALANTHUM FRANCH. - SECT. POGONANTHUM.
Dwarf shrub, sometimes prostrate, 0.1-1.2m; leaf bud scales persistent and conspicuous. Leaves 1.2-4.7 × 0.7-2.3cm, broadly elliptic to suborbicular, apex obtuse or rounded; lower surface covered with 2-3 tiers of overlapping scales, the upper tier fawn to brown (rarely dark brown), the lowest tier golden, paler than those of the upper tiers. Flowers many, in a dense racemose umbel; calyx lobes (3-)4-7mm; corolla white to pink, rarely yellowish, tube 6.5-13mm, densely pilose at throat, lobes (3-)4-8mm; stamens 5(-7); ovary scaly. H4a-b. April-May. India (Arunachal Pradesh), N Burma, China (S Tibet, W Yunnan), 3,050-4,500m
Subsp. **cephalanthum**. Leaves 1.2-2.6

× 0.7-1.5cm; corolla tube 6.5-13mm. India (Arunachal Pradesh) N Burma, China (S & SE Tibet, Yunnan), 3,050-4,500m.

AM 1934 (L. de Rothschild, Exbury); flowers white, tinged yellow.

AM 1979 (Mrs K.N. Dryden, Sawbridgeworth) to a clone 'Winifred Murray', as *R. cephalanthum*; flowers usually 8, in loose rounded heads, corolla red, fading white at lip.

Subsp. **platyphyllum** (Franch. ex Balf.f. & W.W.Sm.) Cullen (*R. platyphyllum* Franch. ex Balf.f. & W.W.Sm.). Leaves 2.5-4.7 × 1.8-2.3cm; corolla tube 13-14mm. NE Burma, China (NW & W Yunnan), 3,050-4,000m.

Subsp. *platyphyllum*, which is larger in all its parts than subsp. *cephalanthum*, has been recently introduced to cultivation. It is rare in the wild. *R. cephalanthum* resembles *R. primuliflorum* but may be distinguished by the persistent leaf bud scales.

R. CERASINUM TAGG - SUBSECT. THOMSONIA.
Shrub, 1.2-3.7m; bark rough; young shoots glabrescent. Leaves 4.5-7 × 1.8-4cm, narrowly obovate to elliptic, base rounded, upper and lower surfaces glabrous, lower epidermis shortly papillate, with some red sessile glands; petioles with a sparse covering of rufous dendroid hairs that extend up the midrib on the upper surface of the leaves. Flowers 4-7, in a lax truss; calyx *c.*1.5mm; corolla crimson to scarlet, or white with a crimson border, nectar pouches darker, campanulate, 35-45mm; ovary and style stalked-glandular. H4a. May-June. NE Burma, China (SE Tibet), 3,200-3,800m.

This is a distinctive species unlikely to be confused with any other.

R. cerochitum Balf.f. & Forrest - is a synonym of **R. tanastylum** Balf.f. & Kingdon-Ward var. **tanastylum** (Subsect. Irrorata).

R. CHAMAETHOMSONII (TAGG & FORREST) COWAN & DAVIDIAN - SUBSECT. NERIIFLORA.
Dwarf shrub, 0.1-1m. Leaves 2-6 × 1.5-

3.2cm, broadly obovate to broadly elliptic, lower surface glabrous (in cultivation); petioles tomentose and/or stalked-glandular. Flowers (1-)2-5, in a lax truss; calyx 1-7(-15)mm; corolla fleshy, pink to deep crimson, campanulate, with nectar pouches, 25-45mm; ovary very sparsely to densely rufous-tomentose, sometimes also with at least some glands, abruptly contracted into the glabrous style. H4a-b. March-May. China (S Tibet, NW Yunnan), 4,000-4,600m.

Var. **chamaethomsonii**. Corolla crimson to carmine; calyx lobes to 7(-15)mm; ovary sparsely hairy, sometimes glandular. China (SE Tibet, NW Yunnan).

AM 1932 (Lady Aberconway and Hon H.D. McLaren, Bodnant) as *R. repens* var. *chamaedoxa*; flowers crimson.

Var. **chamaethauma** (Tagg & Forrest) D.F. Chamb. Corolla pale to deep pink; calyx minute, 1mm or less; ovary densely hairy. China (S Tibet).

Var *chamaethomsonii* may be no more than a hybrid of *R. forrestii*. Var. *chamaethauma* is however more distinctive and might be a species in its own right.

R. chameunum Balf.f. & Forrest - is a synonym of **R. saluenense** Franch. subsp. **chameunum** (Balf.f. & Forrest) Cullen (Subsect. Saluenensia).

R. CHAMPIONIAE HOOK.F. - SECT. CHONIASTRUM.
Shrub or small tree, to 8m. Leaves elliptic to obovate, 7-15 × 2.5-5cm, bristly, especially on veins below, apex acuminate. Flowers 4-6, clustered at end of a leafy shoot below the vegetative bud, pink at first, becoming white, with yellow markings, funnel-shaped, tube 12-15mm, lobes 40-45mm; stamens 10. H2. April-May. S China, 500-1,300m.

Only the type variety of this species is in cultivation.

R. chapmanii A.Gray -is a synonym of **R. minus** Michx var. **chapmanii** (A.Gray) Duncan & Pullen (Subsect. Caroliniana).

R. CHARITOPES BALF.F. & FARRER - SUBSECT. GLAUCA.
Dwarf shrub, to 1.5m; shoots with a smooth brown flaking bark. Leaves 3-5.5 × (1.4-)1.8-3cm, elliptic to obovate, apex bluntly rounded to retuse, lower surface with scales of varying density. Pedicels scaly. Flowers (3-)4-5 per inflorescence; calyx (3-)5-7(-9)mm, ovate, rounded at apex; corolla pink to purplish, sometimes with flecks, campanulate, (15-)20-25mm; stamens 10, regular; ovary densely scaly, style sharply deflexed, glabrous. H3-4a. April-May.

Subsp. **charitopes**. Calyx 6-9mm; corolla pink. NE Burma, China (NW Yunnan), 3,200-4,250m.

AM 1979 (Crown Estate Commissioners, Windsor) to a clone 'Parkside'; flowers in clusters of three, red-purple, with upper lobes suffused with darker shades, upper lobes extensively spotted with red-purple.

Subsp. **tsangpoense** (Kingdon-Ward) Cullen (*R. tsangpoense* Kingdon-Ward, & incl. var. *curvistylum* Kingdon-Ward ex Cowan & Davidian). Calyx (3-)5-6mm; corolla pink or purple. China (S Tibet).

There is no clear separation between the two subspecies, the distributions of which do not however overlap.

AM 1972 (Maj. A.E. Hardy, Sandling Park, Kent) to a clone 'Cowtye', probably from Kingdon-Ward 7744; flowers purple, with darker spots and a waxy bloom.

R. chengianum Fang - is a synonym of **R. hemsleyanum** E.H.Wilson (Subsect. Fortunea).

R. CHIONANTHUM TAGG & FORREST - SUBSECT. NERIIFLORA.
Dwarf shrub, 0.6-1m. Leaves 6-7.5 × 2.2-2.8cm, obovate, lower surface with a discontinuous floccose tomentum composed of dendroid hairs; petioles setose. Flowers 4-6, in a tight truss; calyx 2-3mm; corolla white, tubular-campanulate, with nectar pouches, c.35mm; ovary densely rufous-tomentose abruptly contracted into the glabrous style. H4. April-May. NE

Burma, China (W Yunnan), *c.*4,400m.

This species is allied to *R. haematodes* var. *chaetomallum* but differs in its white flowers and discontinuous leaf indumentum.

R. chloranthum Balf.f. & Forrest is a synonym of **R. mekongense** var. **mekongense** (Balf.f. & Kingdon-Ward) Cullen (Subsect. Trichoclada).

R. chlorops Cowan - is almost certainly a hybrid of a species in Subsect. Fortunea. The type of this species was raised at Edinburgh from seed as Forrest 16463 (which is a species of *Acer*). The type sheet is annotated with the remark that it may have been a chance hybrid between *R. wardii* and *R. vernicosum*, a hybrid that does occur in the wild.

AM 1938 (Earl of Stair, Stanraer); from Forrest 16463; flowers pale Primrose to nearly white, with a deep crimson blotch.

R. chryseum Balf.f. & Kingdon-Ward - is a synonym of **R. rupicola** W.W.Sm. var. **chryseum** (Balf.f. & Kingdon-Ward) Philipson & N.M.Philipson.

R. CHRYSODORON Tagg ex Hutch. - Subsect. BOOTHIA.
Dwarf shrub, perhaps epiphytic, to at least 1m in cultivation; young shoots bristly. Leaves to 8.8 × 4.5cm, oblong-elliptic, apex obtuse, lower surface papillose, with close golden-yellow scales slightly sunk in pits. Pedicels very short, densely scaly. Flowers 3-4 per inflorescence; calyx with obscure lobes 2-3mm long; corolla yellow, campanulate, *c.*30mm (to 40mm in cultivation); tube *c.*15mm, outer surface pubescent at base, pilose within; stamens 10, regular; ovary scaly, tapering into the sharply deflexed style. H2-3. March-April.

This is a tender plant, only suitable for gardens with a relatively frost-free climate. It is intermediate between and might be a hybrid of *R. yungchangense* and *R. sulfureum*.

AM 1934 (Lord Aberconway,

Bodnant); flowers clear yellow. This may be a hybrid.

R. CILIATUM Hook.f. - Subsect. MADDENIA.
Shrub, to 2m; young shoots with setae, the bases of which persist to maturity. Leaves 4.5-9 × 2-3.5cm, elliptic to narrowly elliptic, apex acute or obtuse, margin ciliate; upper surface setose, with midrib impressed, lower surface with scattered unequal scales. Flowers 2-5, in a loose terminal inflorescence; calyx conspicuous, lobes to 6-9mm; corolla white, sometimes flushed pink, campanulate to funnel-campanulate, 30-45mm, outer surface glabrous, lacking scales; stamens 10; ovary scaly, style impressed, glabrous. H3-4a. March-May. Nepal, India (Sikkim), Bhutan, China (S Tibet), 2,400-4,000m.

This distinctive species, without close relatives, is one of the most hardy in subsection Maddenia.

AM 1953 (Col Lord Digby, Minterne, Dorset); flowers white, with a tinge of pink on the centre of the corolla lobes.

♀ 1993

R. CILIICALYX Franch. - Subsect. MADDENIA.
Free-growing shrub; young shoots setose. Leaves 7-11 × 2.5-4cm, elliptic to narrowly elliptic, apex acute, margin often slightly ciliate, upper surface with impressed midrib, lower surface brownish, with dense but not touching scales. Flowers (2-)3-5, in a loose inflorescence, slightly scented; calyx lobes to 6mm, ciliate; corolla white or pink, broadly funnel-shaped, 50-60mm, outer surface usually lacking scales, pubescent below; stamens *c.*10; ovary scaly, impressed below the style that is scaly and pubescent towards the base. H2. March-May. SW & C China (Yunnan, Guizhou), *c.*2,400m.

This species is allied to *R. pachypodum* but may be distinguished by the corolla that usually lacks scales on the outer surface.

AM 1923 (Oxford Botanic Garden).

AM 1975 (G. Gorer, Sunte House,

Haywards Heath) to a clone 'Walter Maynard'; flowers white, yellow-green externally, at base mid-ribs of corolla lobes soft red-purple, upper throat flushed yellow-green.

R. CINNABARINUM HOOK.F. - SUBSECT. CINNABARINA.
Straggling shrub, up to 7m; young shoots scaly, often also pruinose. Leaves sometimes deciduous, 3-9 × 2.7-5cm, broadly or narrowly elliptic, apex rounded, lower surface covered in fleshy narrowly rimmed, equal or unequal scales. Pedicels scaly. Flowers 2-7 per inflorescence, yellow or orange, to purple sometimes bicoloured, yellow and orange, usually with a waxy pruinose bloom, tubular to campanulate, 25-36mm; stamens 10; ovary scaly, sometimes also puberulous, style usually glabrous. H3-4a. April-May. India (W Bengal, Sikkim), China (S Tibet), N Burma, 2,750-3,950m.

Subsp. **cinnabarinum** (incl. *R. blandfordiiflorum* Hook. & *R. roylei* Hook.f.). Corolla scaly outside, most leaves evergreen; leaves relatively narrow, more than 2.2 × as long as broad; corolla usually more or less tubular-campanulate. Nepal, India (W Bengal, Sikkim), Bhutan, China (S Tibet), 2,750-3,950m.

AM 1918 (Messrs Reuthe, Keston, Kent) to a clone 'Magnificum', as var. *roylei*; flowers exceptionally large, orange-red.

AM 1953 (Crown Estate Commissioners, Windsor) to a clone 'Vin Rosé', as var. *roylei*; flowers Currant Red outside, Blood Red inside, with a waxy bloom.

AM 1977 (Hydon Nurseries Ltd, Godalming) to a clone 'Nepal', from L., S. & H. 21283; flowers yellow, becoming red at base.

AM 1945 (Lord Aberconway, Bodnant) as var. *blandfordiiflorum*; flowers vermilion at base externally, paler above.

♀ 1993, to a clone 'Conroy'.

Subsp. **xanthocodon** (Hutch.) Cullen (*R. xanthocodon* Hutch. and incl. *R. concatenans* Hutch. & *R. cinnabarinum* Hook.f. var.

purpurellum Cowan). Corolla scaly outside, most leaves evergreen; leaves relatively broad, less than 2.2× as long as broad; corolla usually campanulate. India (Arunachal Pradesh), Bhutan, China (S Tibet), 3,050-3,950m.

AM 1935 (L. de Rothschild, Exbury) from Kingdon-Ward 6026; flowers yellow.

AM 1950 (Capt. C. Ingram, Benenden, Kent) to a clone 'Copper', as *R. concatenans*, from L. & S. 6560; flowers coral coloured, suffused with orange and red.

FCC 1935 (Lt Col L.C.R. Messel, Nymans, Sussex) as *R. concatenans*, from Kingdon-Ward 5874; flowers apricot, flushed rose externally. There is some doubt that this plant is correctly named.

AM 1951 (Capt. C. Ingram, Benenden, Kent) as var. *purpurellum*, from L. & S. 6349A.

♀ 1993

Subsp. **tamaense** (Davidian) Cullen (*R. tamaense* Davidian). Corolla lobes scaly outside; most leaves deciduous; corolla campanulate, purple. N Burma, 2,750-3,200m.

Subsp. *tamaense,* with a more Easterly distribution than the remaining subspecies, represents the end of a geographical cline.

AM 1978 (Maj. A.E. Hardy, Sandling Park, Kent) to a clone 'Triangle' of *R. tamaense*; flowers white in throat, flushed purple, spotted red-purple.

R. CITRINIFLORUM BALF.F. & FORREST - SUBSECT. NERIIFLORA.
Dwarf shrub, 0.2-1.5m. Leaves 4-7.5 × 1.5-2.3cm, obovate to elliptic, lower surface densely covered with a thick grey-brown tomentum composed of ramiform hairs; petioles often winged, glabrous or with a white floccose tomentum when mature. Flowers 2-6, in a tight truss; calyx 2-12mm; when well-developed cupular; corolla not fleshy, yellow or orange to carmine, tubular-campanulate, with nectar pouches, 32-45mm; ovary stalked-glandular, abruptly contracted into the glabrous style. H4a-b. April-May. China (SE Tibet, NW Yunnan), 4,000-4,600m.

Var. **citriniflorum**. Corolla yellow; calyx 2-5(-10)mm; ovary and usually pedicels stalked-glandular.

Var. **horaeum** (Balf.f. & Forrest) D.F.Chamb. (incl. *R. citriniflorum* Balf.f. & Forrest subsp. *aureolum* Cowan). Corolla yellowish red to carmine; calyx (2-)7-12mm, ovary and pedicels lacking glands.

R. citriniflorum hybridizes with *R. sanguineum* and probably also *R. temenium* (q.v.); from both it may be distinguished by its thick tomentose leaf indumentum.

R. citriniflorum Balf.f. & Forrest subsp. *aureolum* Cowan - is a synonym of **R. citriniflorum** Balf.f. & Forrest var. **horaeum** (Balf.f. & Forrest) D.F.Chamb. (Subsect. Neriiflora).

R. CLEMENTINAE FORREST - SUBSECT. TALIENSIA.
Shrub, 1-3m. Leaves (6.5-)9.5-14 × (3-)4.5-8cm, ovate-lanceolate, apex rounded, obtuse, base rounded to cordate, lower surface with a thick whitish to buff two-layered indumentum, the upper layer lanate-tomentose, composed of ramiform hairs, the lower compacted; petioles glabrous when mature. Flowers 10-15, in a dense truss; calyx *c*.1mm; corolla 7-lobed, white to deep rose, with purple flecks, campanulate, nectar pouches lacking, 40-50mm; ovary and style glabrous. H4b. April-May. China (NW Yunnan, SW Sichuan), 3,350-3,950m.

The above description applies to subsp. *clementinae* as this is the only form in cultivation. This is a distinctive species on account of its 7-lobed corolla.

R. COELICUM BALF.F. & FARRER - SUBSECT. NERIIFLORA.
Shrub, 1.3-3m. Leaves 8-10 × 4.2-5.5cm, obovate; lower surface covered with a fulvous tomentum, composed of dendroid hairs; petioles sparsely covered with shortly stalked glands. Flowers *c*.10, in a tight truss; calyx 5-7mm; corolla fleshy, crimson, tubular-campanulate, with nectar pouches, 38-45mm; ovary covered with shortly stalked glands, abruptly con-

tracted into the glabrous style. H4a. April-May. NE Burma, China (W Yunnan), 2,750-4,400m.

Closely allied to *R. pocophorum* but differing in its broader leaves and non-tomentose petioles.

AM 1955 (Col Lord Digby, Minterne, Dorset); flowers a dark shade of Orient Red.

R. COELONEURON DIELS - SUBSECT. TALIENSIA.
Tree 4-8m. Leaves 7.5-12 × 2.5-4cm, oblanceolate, apex acuminate, lower surface covered with a dense two-layered indumentum, the upper layer a persistent or evanescent rufous tomentum, composed of ramiform hairs, the lower compacted, whitish and embedded in a surface film; petioles densely rufous-tomentose. Flowers 6-11, in a lax to more or less dense truss; calyx *c*.0.5mm; corolla white to pale pink, with crimson flecks, campanulate, nectar pouches lacking, 20-32mm; ovary densely reddish tomentose, with a few stalked glands below the style, style glabrous or with a few hairs at base. H4a. China (SE & W Sichuan, Guizhou), 1,200-2,300m.

There are apparently authentic introductions of this species from SE Sichuan.

R. COLLETTIANUM AITCH. & HEMSL. - SECT. POGONANTHUM.
Dwarf shrub, to 1m; leaf bud scales deciduous. Leaves 3-4 × (1-)1.3-1.7cm, more or less elliptic, apex acute, mucronate, lower surface covered with one tier of plastered golden-brown scales. Flowers 16-20, in an elongate, dense, racemose umbel; calyx lobes 5-5.5mm; corolla white (often pink in bud), funnel-hypocrateriform, tube 10-13mm, pilose within, lobes 6-8mm; stamens 8-10; ovary scaly. H4a. May. Afghanistan, Pakistan, 3,050-3,900m.

This species has a very restricted distribution in the wild. It is difficult in cultivation.

PC 1980 (P.A. Cox, Glendoick), from Hedge & Wendelbo seed.

R. commodum Balf.f. & Forrest - is a synonym of **R. sulfureum** Franch. (Subsect. Boothia).

R. compactum Hutch. - is a synonym of **R. polycladum** Franch. (Subsect. Lapponica).

R. COMPLEXUM BALF.F. & W.W.SM. - SUBSECT. LAPPONICA.
Fastigiate or rounded dwarf shrub, 0.1-0.6m. Leaves 0.4-1.1 × 0.2-0.6cm, broadly or narrowly elliptic to ovate, apex obtuse or rounded, mucro small or absent, lower surface covered with uniformly ferruginous, touching scales. Flowers 3-4(-5) per inflorescence; calyx to 1mm, minute; corolla pale lilac to rosy purple, usually narrowly funnel-shaped, 9-13mm; stamens 5-6(-8), included within the tube; ovary scaly, style short or long, glabrous or slightly pubescent at base. H4b. April-May. China (N Yunnan), 3,400-4,600m.
This species may be distinguished from allied species with which it might be confused by the number of stamens.

R. concatenans Hutch. - is a synonym of **R. cinnabarinum** Hook.f. subsp. **xanthocodon** (Hutch.) Cullen (Subsect. Cinnabarina).

R. CONCINNUM HEMSL. (INCL. *R. PSEUDOYANTHINUM* BALF.F. EX HUTCH.) - SUBSECT. TRIFLORA.
Shrub, 0.5-2m; young shoots scaly, otherwise glabrous. Leaves 3.5-6 × 1.8-3.2cm, ovate to elliptic, apex acute to acuminate, upper surface scaly, hairy along midrib; lower surface covered with touching broad-rimmed scales that are golden and brown. Flowers 2-4, in a loose terminal inflorescence; calyx minute, ciliate; corolla rich reddish purple, rarely pale, zygomorphic, funnel-campanulate, 20-30mm; outer surface of tube scaly, otherwise glabrous; stamens 10; ovary scaly, sometimes minutely pubescent at apex, impressed below the declinate style that is glabrous or puberulent. H4a-b. April-May. China (Sichuan, Hubei, Guizhou), 2,300-4,500m.

This species is closely allied to *R. amesiae* (q.v.).
AM 1951 (RHS Garden, Wisley) as *R. pseudoyanthinum*; flowers Lilac Purple.
♀ 1993 as *R. concinnum* Pseudoyanthinum Group.

R. cookeanum Davidian - is a synonym of **R. sikangense** W.P.Fang (Subsect. Maculifera).

R. CORIACEUM FRANCH. - SUBSECT. FALCONERA.
Shrub or small tree, 2-7.5m. Leaves 12-25 × 4.8-6.2cm, oblanceolate, lower surface covered in a dense two-layered indumentum, the upper layer whitish or fawn, composed of scarcely fimbriate broadly cup-shaped hairs, the lower compacted; petioles terete. Flowers 15-20, in a tight truss, usually 7-lobed, white, sometimes flushed rose, with a crimson basal blotch, sometimes also with flecks, funnel-campanulate, nectar pouches lacking, 35-40mm; stamens usually 14; ovary densely rufous-tomentose. H3-4a. April. NE Burma, SW China (SE Tibet, NW Yunnan), 3,000-4,000m.
AM 1953 (Crown Estate Commissioners, Windsor) to a clone 'Morocco'; flowers white, with a crimson blotch and very few spots.

R. CORYANUM TAGG & FORREST - SUBSECT. ARGYROPHYLLA.
Shrub or small tree, 2.5-6m. Leaves 8.5-16 × 2.2-4cm, elliptic to oblanceolate, apex acute, lower surface with a thin compacted silvery to fawn indumentum intermixed with a few glands and embedded in a surface film. Flowers 20-30, in a dense inflorescence, whitish, with crimson flecks, funnel-campanulate, nectar pouches lacking, 25-30mm; ovary glabrous or with a few white simple hairs, style glabrous. H4a. April-May. China (SE Tibet, NW Yunnan), 3,650-4,400m.
The glabrous ovary and many-flowered inflorecence are the distinguishing features of this species.
AM 1979 (R.N.S. Clarke, Borde Hill)

to a clone 'Chelsea Chimes', from Kingdon-Ward 6311. Flowers up to 8-9 per truss; corolla widely funnel-campanulate, white, with sparse red-purple spotting in upper throat.

R. COWANIANUM DAVIDIAN - SUBSECT. LEPIDOTA.
Small shrub, 0.3-2.3m; shoots lacking scales. Leaves deciduous, 4-6.5 × 2.2-3cm, oblong-elliptic to broadly obovate, margin ciliate, lower surface with distant pale brown broad-rimmed scales. Flowers 3-5, in a loose terminal inflorescence; calyx lobes 4-6mm; corolla purplish pink, campanulate, 14-20mm; stamens 10; ovary scaly, style very short, sharply deflexed. H4a. May. Nepal, 3,200-3,950m.

A distinctive species that is included in Subsect. Trichoclada by some authors.

R. COXIANUM DAVIDIAN - SUBSECT. MADDENIA.
Upright shrub, 1-3m; young shoots setose. Leaves 5.5-11.5 × 1.5-3cm, oblanceolate, margin not setose, upper surface bristly (in the type specimen), midrib impressed; lower surface glaucous, the scales unequal, brown, 2-6 × their own diameter apart. Flowers *c.*3, in a loose terminal inflorescence; calyx lobes 4-5mm, ciliate; corolla white, without or with a faint yellow basal blotch, tubular-funnel-shaped, *c.*75mm, outer surface scaly, pubescent towards base; stamens 10; ovary densely scaly, tapering into the style that is scaly below. H2. April-May. India (Arunachal Pradesh), 1,650m.

This species may be a variant of *R. formosum* but is distinguished by the larger calyx, etc. There is some doubt about the status of cultivated plants as the leaves are significantly less setose than those of the type specimen.

R. crassum Franch. - is synonym of **R. maddenii** Hook.f. subsp. **crassum** (Franch.) Cullen.

R. CRINIGERUM FRANCH. - SUBSECT. GLISCHRA.
Shrub or small tree, 1-5m; young shoots with a sparse covering of stalked glands. Leaves subcoriaceous, (7-)10-17 × (2.3-)3-4.2cm, obovate to oblanceolate, apex cuspidate, lower surface with a fawn to red-brown tomentum composed of ramiform hairs. Flowers 8-14 to a truss; calyx 5-10mm; corolla white flushed pink, with purple flecks and a basal blotch, campanulate, nectar pouches lacking, 30-40mm; ovary stalked-glandular. H3-4a. April-May. NE Burma, China (NW Yunnan, SE Tibet), 3,350-4,000m.

Var. **crinigerum**. Leaves sparsely glandular, and with a dense matted tomentum beneath.

Var. **euadenium** Tagg & Forrest. Leaves densely glandular, usually with a sparse indumentum beneath.

R. croceum Balf.f. & W.W.Sm. - is a synonym of **R. wardii** var **wardii** (Subsect. Campylocarpa).

R. cruentum H.Lév. - is a synonym of **R. bureavii** (Subsect. Taliensia).

R. cubittii Hutch. - is a synonym of **R. veitchianum** Hook.f.

R. CUFFEANUM CRAIB EX HUTCH. - SUBSECT. MADDENIA.
Shrub, to 2m; young shoots scaly, stem swollen and tuber-like at base. Leaves 10-12.5 × 3-4cm, narrowly elliptic, apex acuminate, margin not strongly ciliate, upper surface with midrib impressed, lower surface with distant golden scales. Flowers *c.*5, in a loose inflorescence, not scented; calyx lobes unequal, to 7mm, ciliate; corolla white with a yellow blotch within, funnel-campanulate, 55-65mm, outer surface sparsely scaly throughout, pubesent towards base; stamens 10; ovary densely scaly, style impressed, scaly below. H1. April-May. Only known in cultivation, possibly originating in Burma.

Characterized by the swollen stem base, this species remains somewhat obscure as the specimens now in cultivation (as described above) differ significantly from the type description.

R. CUMBERLANDENSE E.L.BRAUN - SUBSECT. PENTANTHERA.
Deciduous shrub, to 2m; young twigs covered with eglandular hairs, rarely glabrous. Leaves (3-)4.5-7(-8.1) × (1.3-)1.8-2.9(-3.5)cm, lower surface glaucous, glabrous or with a few eglandular multicellular hairs. Flower bud scales with outer surface glabrous, margin ciliate at apex, glandular below. Pedicels covered with eglandular hairs rarely with gland-tipped hairs. Flowers with an acrid fragrance, appearing after the leaves have expanded, 3-7, in a shortened raceme; calyx 1-3mm; corolla red, funnelform, tube expanding abruptly into the limb, 28-50mm, outer surface densely covered with unicellular hairs and sparsely covered with gland-tipped hairs. Capsule with eglandular hairs. H4a-b. E USA (Cumberland Mountains), above 900m.

This species is allied to *R. canescens* but may be distinguished by the flowers appearing after the leaves. It has been confused with *R.* × *bakeri*, a hybrid of *R. flammeum* and *R. canescens* (see under *R. flammeum).*

R. CUNEATUM W.W.SM. (INCL. *R. RAVUM* BALF.F. & W.W.SM.) - SUBSECT. LAPPONICA.
Small shrub, 1-2(-4)m. Leaves 1.1-7 × 0.5-2.5cm, narrowly to broadly elliptic; apex acute to rounded, lower surface covered with uniformly fawn or deep rust, touching or overlapping scales. Flowers up to 6 per inflorescence; calyx (2-)5-8 (-12)mm; corolla rose-lavender to deep purple, often with darker flecks, rarely almost white, funnel-shaped, (12-)22-31mm; stamens 10; ovary scaly, style declinate, pubescent towards base. H4a-b. March-May. China (N & W Yunnan, SW Sichuan), 3,000-3,650m

This is an anomalous and distinctive member of Subsect. Lapponica showing some affinities with species in Subsect. Heliolepida.

R. CYANOCARPUM (FRANCH.) W.W.SM. - SUBSECT. THOMSONIA.
Shrub or small tree, 1-3.8m; bark rough; young shoots glabrous. Leaves 6.5-12.5 × 4.2-9cm, broadly elliptic to orbicular, base rounded; upper surface glabrous, lower surface more or less glaucous, with a mamillate epidermis, glabrous or with a few scattered hairs on the midrib towards the base. Flowers 6-11, in a lax truss; calyx (2-)7-15mm, cupular; corolla white or cream, to clear pink, with darker nectar pouches, campanulate to funnel-campanulate, (40-)50-60mm; ovary glabrous or rarely with a few glands, style glabrous. H4a. February-April. China (W Yunnan), 3,000-4,000m.

This species has a very local distribution. It apparently hybridizes in the wild with *R. lacteum.*

AM 1933 (Lady Loder, Leonardslee, Sussex); flowers white, flushed rose.

R. dabanshanense Fang & Wang - is a synonym of **R. przewalskii** Maxim. subsp. **dabanshanense** (W.P.Fang & S.X.Wang) W.P.Fang & S.X.Wang (Subsect. Taliensia).

R. DALHOUSIAE HOOK.F. - SUBSECT. MADDENIA.
Usually an epiphytic shrub (in the wild), in cultivation 1-3m; young shoots setose. Leaves (7.5-)10-17 × 3.5-7cm, usually narrowly elliptic, apex rounded, margins often crenulate, upper surface with raised midrib, lower surface greyish, with small unequal reddish scales that are more than their own diameter apart. Flowers 2-3 in a loose terminal inflorescence, slightly scented, pedicels pubescent and scaly; calyx lobes 10-15mm, pubescent on outer surface; corolla white or cream, often yellowish inside, sometimes with five reddish lines running up lobes, narrowly funnel-campanulate to funnel-campanulate, 85-105mm; stamens 10; ovary scaly, tapering into the style that is scaly below. H2. April-May. India (Sikkim, W Bengal, Arunachal Pradesh), Bhutan, China (S Tibet), 1,800-2,600m.

Var. **dalhousiae**. Corolla lacking

longitudinal lines. Nepal, India (Sikkim, W Bengal), Bhutan, China (S Tibet), 1,800-2,450m.

AM 1930 (Vice Adm. A.W. Heneage-Vivian, Clyne Castle, Swansea); flowers soft yellow, shaded green in tube.

AM 1974 (Maj. A.E. Hardy, Sandling Park, Kent) to a clone 'Tom Spring Smythe'; flowers green, fading to greenish white.

FCC 1974 (Maj. A.E. Hardy, Sandling Park, Kent) to a clone 'Frank Ludlow', from L., S. & T. 6694; flowers white, stained yellow at base internally.

Var. **rhabdotum** (Balf.f. & Cooper) Cullen (*R. rhabdotum* Balf.f. & Cooper). Corolla with five longitudinal red lines. Bhutan, India (Arunachal Pradesh), China (S Tibet), 1,500-2,600m.

AM 1931 (Lady Aberconway & Hon. H.D. McLaren, Bodnant).

FCC 1936 (L. de Rothschild, Exbury). ♔ 1993

This species is closely allied to *R. lindleyi* but may be distinguished by the pubescent pedicels. The small differences between the two varieties do not justify their recognition as separate species.

R. dasycladum Balf.f. & W.W.Sm. - is a synonym of **R. selense** Franch. subsp. **dasycladum** (Balf.f. & W.W.Sm.) D.F.Chamb. (Subsect. Selensia).

R. DASYPETALUM BALF.F. & FORREST - SUBSECT. LAPPONICA.
Much-branched dwarf shrub, to 0.75m. Leaves 0.8-1.5 × 0.3-0.8cm, elliptic to oblong-elliptic, apex obtuse or rounded, mucronate, lower surface covered with uniformly tawny brown touching scales. Flowers 2 per inflorescence; calyx *c*.3mm, lobes broadly strap-shaped; corolla bright purplish rose, broadly funnel-shaped, outer surface pilose, 12-15(-18)mm; stamens 10, about as long as corolla; ovary scaly, style longer than stamens, pubescent at base. H4a-b. April-May. China (NW Yunnan), 3,500m.

This species, which is only known from a single wild collection, may be dis-tinguished from its immediate relatives by the pilose outer surface of the corolla.

R. DAURICUM L. - SUBSECT. RHODORASTRA.
Straggling shrub, 0.5-1.5m; young shoots scaly and puberulous. Leaves thick and leathery, some persisting, 1-3.5 × 0.5-2cm, elliptic to oval, apex rounded, mucronate, upper surface with midrib shortly puberulent, otherwise glabrous, lower surface densely scaly. Flowers solitary, axillary but at the ends of the branches; calyx rim-like; corolla pink or violet pink, openly funnel-shaped, 14-21mm, outer surface pilose towards base; stamens 10; ovary scaly, otherwise glabrous, impressed below the declinate style. H4c. January-March. Russia (Eastern Siberia), Mongolia, N China, Japan (Hokkaido), s.l.-1,600m.

This species is closely allied to *R. mucronulatum* but differs in the partially persistent leaves that are more densely scaly below, and in the smaller flowers.

AM 1990 (Crown Estate Commissioners, Windsor) to a clone 'Hiltingbury'; flowers in clusters of 3-4, corolla purple within, reverse a darker purple.

♔ 1993, to an FCC clone 'Midwinter'.

R. DAVIDSONIANUM REHDER & E.H.WILSON - SUBSECT. TRIFLORA.
Shrub, 0.6-5m; young shoots scaly. Leaves 2.7-6.2 × 1.1-2cm, lanceolate to oblong, apex acute, upper surface scaly, midrib sometimes hairy; lower surface densely covered in small brown, narrow-rimmed scales that are 1-2 × their own diameter apart. Flowers 3-6(-10), in a terminal inflorescence; calyx disc-like, sometimes ciliate; corolla usually pink to lavender, sometimes with darker spots, widely funnel-campanulate, zygomorphic, (19-)23-33mm, stamens 10; ovary densely scaly, impressed below the declinate style that is glabrous or puberulent at base. H(3-)4a. April-May. China (N Yunnan, W Sichuan, Guizhou), 2,000-3,300m.

This species may be recognized from

R. yunnanense and its immediate allies by a combination of the relatively dense narrowly rimmed leaf scales and the size of the flowers.

AM 1935 (Lord Aberconway, Bodnant) and FCC 1953 (Lord Aberconway and National Trust, Bodnant) to a pale rose form.

AM 1993 (David Clulow, Tilgates, Bletchingly, Surrey) to a clone 'Ruth Lyons'; trusses 8-10-flowered, corolla deep purplish pink with light red spotting in upper throat.

♚ 1993

R. DECANDRUM (MAKINO) MAKINO - SECT. BRACHYCALYX.
Shrub or small tree; young shoots soon glabrous. Leaves in whorls of up to three, at the ends of the branches, 2-3(-6) × 2-4cm, broadly rhombic, apex acuminate, lower surface with glands, especially on midrib and veins; petioles sparsely glandular, also with villose hairs. Pedicels villose, densely so at base, also glandular. Flowers solitary or up to 3 per inflorescence, appearing before the leaves; calyx minute; corolla magenta, with flecks, open-funnel-campanulate, 25-28mm; stamens 10; ovary glandular, with a few villose hairs, style glabrous. H4a-b. April-May. Japan (Honshu, Shikoku), *c*.800m.

Distinguished from the apparently allied *R. dilatatum* by the presence of 10 stamens.

R. × decipiens Lacaita - is a naturally occurring hybrid between **R. hodgsonii** and **R. falconeri** (Subsect. Falconera, see under **R. hodgsonii**).

R. DECORUM FRANCH. - SUBSECT FORTUNEA.
Shrub or small tree, 1-14m. Leaves 5.5-19(-30) × 2.2-11cm, elliptic to ovate, base rounded, glabrous. Flowers 5-10, in a lax truss, 6-8-lobed, scented, white, sometimes flushed rose, sometimes also with purple flecks, open- to funnel-campanulate, nectar pouches lacking, 45-100mm; stamens 14-20, hairy below; ovary and

style covered with stalked glands that are usually white. H3-4a. May-June.

Subsp. **decorum**. Flowers 45-60mm; leaves 5.5-15cm. NE Burma, SW China (Yunnan, Sichuan, Guizhou), (1,800-) 2,500-3,600m.

AM 1923 (Lt Col L.C.R. Messel, Nymans, Sussex) to a clone 'Mrs. Messel'; flowers pure white, broad and open, in a truss of *c*.12.

Subsp. **diaprepes** (Balf.f. & W.W.Sm.) T.L.Ming (*R. diaprepes* Balf.f. & W.W.Sm.). Flowers 65-100mm; leaves 12-19(-30)cm long. NE Burma, China (S Yunnan), Laos, *c*.2,000m.

Subsp. *diaprepes* is larger in all its parts than is subsp. *decorum* but otherwise the two are very similar. It comes from the humid part of the range of the species and generally occurs at relatively modest altitudes.

AM 1926 (L. de Rothschild, Exbury) to subsp. *diaprepes*; flowers white, tinged pink externally.

AM 1953 (Mrs R.M. Stevenson, Tower Court, Ascot) and FCC 1974 (Crown Estate Commissioners, Windsor) to a clone 'Gargantua', as *R. diaprepes*, from Forrest 11958; flowers very large, white, with a green basal flush.

R. DEGRONIANUM CARRIÈRE - SUBSECT. PONTICA.
Shrub, 0.5-2.5m; young shoots sparsely tomentose to floccose-tomentose, lacking glands; bud scales generally not persistent. Leaves 6-14 × 2.5-3.5cm, elliptic to oblanceolate, apex acute, upper surface glabrous, lower surface covered with a dense, compacted to lanate, white to fawn or reddish brown indumentum composed of dendroid hairs; petioles usually densely floccose-tomentose. Flowers 9-12, in a tight truss; calyx 2-3mm; corolla 5-7-lobed, pink to soft rose, with conspicuous flecks, widely funnel-campanulate, nectar pouches lacking; ovary white-tomentose, style glabrous. H4a-c. April-May. Japan, 200-1,200m.

Subsp. **degronianum** (incl. *R. metternichii* Sieb & Zucc. var. *pentamerum* Maxim.). Corolla 5-lobed; leaves with a felted fawn to reddish brown indumentum below. C Japan.

AM 1974 (Royal Botanic Gardens, Wakehurst) to a clone 'Gerald Loder'; flowers white, with shades of red-purple and spots.

Subsp. **heptamerum** (Maxim.) H.Hara (incl. *R. metternichii* Sieb. & Zucc. & *R. japonicum* (Blume) Schneider). Corolla 5-7-lobed; leaf indumentum tawny to reddish brown, velutinous to agglutinated below. C & S Japan.

Var. **heptamerum** (Maxim). Leaf indumentum felted, velutinous; corolla 6-7-lobed.

AM 1976, FCC 1982 (R.N.S. Clarke, Borde Hill, Sussex) to a clone 'Ho Emma', as *R. metternichii*; flowers white, flushed red-purple on veins and with spots in throat.

Var. **hondoense** (Nakai) Sealy. Leaf indumentum agglutinated, shining, usually red-brown; corolla 7-lobed.

Var. **kyomaruense** (T.Yamaz.) H.Hara. Leaf indumentum agglutinated; corolla 5-lobed.

Subsp. **yakushimanum** (Nakai) H.Hara. Leaf indumentum whitish to fawn, dense, lanate; corolla 5-lobed. S Japan (Yakushima), 500-2,000m.

Var. **yakushimanum**. (*R. yakushimanum* Nakai). Leaves 5-7cm long; bushes 0.5-1m high.

FCC 1947, (RHS Wisley) to a clone 'Koichiro Wada', as *R. yakushimanum*; flowers pink in bud, opening white.

♀ 1993, to a clone 'Koichiro Wada'.

Var. **intermedium** (Sugim.) H.Hara. Leaves 8-12cm long; bushes to 2.5m high.

The present nomenclature of this species follows that proposed by Hara. The subspecies recognized have essentially different distributions within Japan. Var. *yakushimanum* is distinctive on account of its low stature and the thick leaf indumentum. It is restricted to Yakushima Island, in the south of the Japanese Archipelago; there it is a plant of exposed mountain tops. This is linked with subsp. *degronianum*, with which it

shares a 5-lobed corolla, through var. *intermedium*, which occurs at lower levels on Yakushima and is generally larger, with larger leaves.

R. yakushimanum has been used as a parent to produce a series of garden hybrids that are relatively dwarf and retain its heat tolerance.

Subsp. *heptamerum* has been known as *R. metternichii*, which is an invalid name.

R. delavayi Franch. - is a synonym of **R. arboreum** Sm. subsp. **delavayi** (Franch.) D.F.Chamb. - (Subsect. Arborea).

R. delavayi Franch. var. *albomentosum* Davidian - is a synonym of **R. arboreum** Sm. subsp. **albomentosum** (Davidian) D.F.Chamb. (Subsect. Arborea).

R. DENDRICOLA HUTCH. (INCL. *R. NOTATUM* HUTCH & *R. TARONENSE* HUTCH.). - SUBSECT. MADDENIA.
Epiphytic or free-growing shrub, to 2m; young shoots usually lacking setae. Leaves 7-12 × 3-5cm, narrowly elliptic to narrowly obovate, apex abruptly acute, with a short drip tip, upper surface with impressed midrib, lower surface with a variably dense covering of scales. Flowers *c*.3, in a loose terminal inflorescence, not scented; calyx disc-like, not ciliate; corolla white to white flushed pink, often with yellow, orange or greenish blotch, sometimes flushed pink, 75-80mm, outer surface scaly, pilose at base; stamens 10; ovary scaly, impressed below the style that is scaly below. H1b. April-May. India (Arunachal Pradesh), N Burma, China (SE Tibet, Yunnan), 1,200-1,400m.

This is a variable species, without close allies.

FCC 1935 (L. de Rothschild, Exbury) as *R. taronense*; flowers white, flushed pink, darker externally, especially on lobes.

R. DENDROCHARIS FRANCH. - SUBSECT. MOUPINENSIA.
Shrub, to 0.7m, often epiphytic; young growth setose. Leaves 1.3-1.7 × 0.6-1cm,

elliptic to obovate, apex rounded, margin ciliate, lower surface densely scaly. Flowers 1-2, terminal; calyx lobes to 3mm, pubescent; corolla rose-pink, open-funnel-campanulate, 20-22mm, outer surface glabrous, lacking scales; stamens 10; style longer than stamens, declinate, sometimes pubescent at base. H4a. May. China (W Sichuan), 2,600-3,000m.

This species, which has only recently been introduced to cultivation, is closely allied to, and possibly conspecific with, *R. moupinense*. It is however consistently smaller in all its parts.

R. DENUDATUM H.LÉV. - SUBSECT. ARGYROPHYLLA.

Shrub, 2-3m. Leaves 12.5-20 × 4-7cm, elliptic to oblanceolate, apex apiculate, upper surface with deeply impressed veins, lower surface with a two-layered indumentum, the upper layer of loose woolly yellow to cinnamon ramiform hairs that ultimately rub off, the lower layer whitish, compacted. Flowers 8-10, in a loose inflorescence, rose to wine-red, campanulate, nectar pouches lacking, *c.*40mm; ovary densely whitish-tomentose, style glabrous. H4a?. May. SW China (N Yunnan, S Sichuan, Guizhou), *c.*3,200m.

Only recently introduced to cultivation, this species is closely allied to *R. floribundum* but differs in the impermanent upper layer of the leaf indumentum.

R. desquamatum Balf.f. & Forrest - is a synonym of **R. rubiginosum** Franch. (Subsect. Heliolepida).

R. detonsum Balf.f. & Forrest - is a hybrid of **R. adenogynum** (Subsect. Taliensia). It may be distinguished from the parent species by the broader leaves that have a sparse 1-layered evanescent indumentum.

R. diacritum Balf.f. & W.W.Sm. - is a synonym of **R. telmateium** Balf.f. & W.W.Sm. (Subsect. Lapponica).

R. diaprepes Balf.f & W.W.Sm. - is a synonym of **R. decorum** Franch. subsp. **diaprepes** (Balf.f. & W.W.Sm.) T.L.Ming (Subsect. Fortunea).

R. DICHROANTHUM DIELS - SUBSECT. NERIIFLORA.

Dwarf shrub, 0.3-2.3m. Leaves 4-9.5 × 2-4cm, oblanceolate to elliptic, lower surface with a continuous white to fawn, more or less loose to compacted indumentum composed of rosulate hairs; petioles covered with a white floccose indumentum. Flowers 3-6, in a tight truss; calyx coloured, 3-15mm, cupular when well-developed; corolla fleshy, usually orange-red, occasionally yellow flushed red or carmine, tubular-campanulate, with nectar pouches, 35-50mm; ovary rufous-tomentose, with or without stalked glands, abruptly tapering into the glabrous style. H4a. May-June. NE Burma, China (W Yunnan), 2,750-4,400m.

Subsp. **dichroanthum**. Leaves 2.5-3× as long as broad, indumentum silvery; ovary lacking glands; young shoots not setose. China (W Yunnan).

AM 1923 (Lady Aberconway and Hon. H.D. Mclaren, Bodnant); flowers brick red.

Subsp. **apodectum** (Balf.f. & W.W.Sm.) Cowan. Leaves 1.9-2.5× as long as broad, indumentum silvery to fawn; ovary lacking glands; young shoots not setose. NE Burma, China (W Yunnan).

Subsp. **scyphocalyx** (Balf.f.& Forrest) Cowan. (*R. scyphocalyx* Balf.f. & Forrest, & incl. *R. herpesticum* Balf.f. & Kingdon-Ward). Leaves 1.9-2.7× as long as broad, indumentum fawn; ovary stalked-glandular; young shoots often glandular-setose. NE Burma, China (W Yunnan).

Subsp. **septentrionale** Cowan. (*R. scyphocalyx* Balf.f & Forrest var. *septentrionale* Davidian). Leaves 3-3.3× as long as broad, indumentum whitish to fawn; ovary with or without stalked glands; young shoots not setose.

Some of the variation of this species is correlated with geographical distribution. It is closely allied to *R. sanguineum.*

R. dictyotum Balf.f. ex Tagg - is a synonym

of **R. traillianum** Forrest & W.W.Sm. var. **dictyotum** (Balf.f. ex Tagg) D.F.Chamb. (Subsect. Taliensia).

R. DIGNABILE COWAN - SUBSECT. TALIENSIA.
Shrub or small tree, 0.6-4m. Leaves 7.5-18 × 4-6.5cm, elliptic to obovate-lanceolate, apex acute to apiculate, lower surface with a thin discontinuous one-layered brown indumentum composed of the scattered remains of hairs and glands; petioles sparsely floccose or glabrescent. Flowers 5-15, in a lax to dense truss; calyx 0.5-3mm; corolla white to yellow, sometimes flushed pink, with or without purple flecks and/or a purple basal blotch, campanulate to funnel-campanulate, nectar pouches lacking, 25-45mm; ovary glabrous or with a brownish red floccose indumentum that is sometimes interspersed with glands, style usually glabrous, occasionally glandular below. H4b. China (E Tibet), 3,350-4,550m.

This variable species, which is apparently related to or a hybrid of *R. beesianum*, has been recently reintroduced. Although it has been recorded in living collections for some time there has been some doubt as to the authenticity of the plants.

R. DILATATUM MIQ. - SECT. BRACHYCALYX.
Shrub or small tree, to 2m; young shoots glabrous. Leaves in whorls of up to three, at the ends of the branches, 3-5 × 1.5-3.5cm, rhombic, apex acuminate, lower surface covered with adpressed pilose hairs, eglandular; petioles papillate. Flowers solitary or up to 3, appearing before the leaves; calyx minute; corolla rose-purple (rarely white), open-campanulate, 20-30mm; stamens 5; ovary glandular, style glabrous. H4a-b. May-June. Japan (S Honshu), *c*.1,000m.

Allied to *R. decandrum* (q.v.). Only the type form is in cultivation.

R. dimitrium Balf.f. & Forrest - is intermediate between the species of Subsect. Irrorata and those of Subsect. Neriiflora, with a corolla suggesting the former subsection and the large calyx of the latter. It may be a hybrid between species belonging to the two subsections.

R. DIPHROCALYX BALF.F. - SUBSECT. GLISCHRA.
Shrub, 1-5m; young shoots bristly. Leaves subcoriaceous, 9-14 × 3.5-5cm, elliptic to obovate, apex apiculate, lower surface with a few bristles at base of midrib, otherwise glabrous. Flowers *c*.10, in a lax truss; calyx fleshy, red, 8-20mm; corolla light to deep crimson, with poorly defined nectar pouches, funnel-campanulate, 30-40mm; ovary densely rufous-tomentose, with a few stalked glands. H3. April. China (W Yunnan), 3,000-3,350m.

An anomalous member of Subsect. Glischra on account of its calyx and red corolla. It may have originated as a hybrid between *R. habrotrichum* and a species in Subsect. Neriiflora.

R. discolor Franch. - is a synonym of **R. fortunei** Lindl. subsp. **discolor** (Franch.) D.F.Chamb. (Subsect. Fortunea).

R. doshongense Tagg - is a synonym of **R. aganniphum** Balf.f. & Kingdon-Ward var. **aganniphum** (Subsect. Taliensia).

R. drumonium Balf.f. & W.W.Sm.- is a synonym of **R. telmateium** Balf.f. & W.W.Sm. (Subsect. Lapponica).

R. dryophyllum Balf.f.& Forrest - is a synonym of **R. phaeochrysum** Balf.f. & W.W.Sm. var. **phaeochrysum** (Subsect. Taliensia), but see also note under var. **levistratum**.

R. dumulosum Balf.f. & Forrest - is a synonym of **R. phaeochrysum** Balf.f. & W.W.Sm. var. **agglutinatum** (Balf.f. & Forrest) D.F.Chamb. (Subsect. Taliensia).

R. ECLECTEUM BALF.F. & FORREST - SUBSECT. THOMSONIA.
Shrub, 1-3(-4.5m); bark smooth and peeling; young shoots usually sparsely glan-

dular. Leaves 4-14.5 × 3-5.6cm, obovate-lanceolate (jargonelle-shaped), base acute to rounded, upper surface glabrous, lower epidermis lacking papillae, glabrous though often with some straight simple hairs on either side of the midrib; petioles 4-10mm, narrowly winged, glabrous or with a few stalked glands. Flowers 6-11, in a dense truss; calyx 2-15mm, usually cupular; corolla white or cream, or more usually deep crimson, with darker nectar pouches and sometimes also purple flecks, campanulate to widely funnel-campanulate, (30-)40-50mm; ovary densely stalked-glandular, style glabrous. H3-4a. February to April. NE Burma. China (SE Tibet, NW Yunnan, SW Sichuan), 3,000-4,000m.

AM 1949 (E. de Rothschild, Exbury); flowers Primrose Yellow.

AM 1978 (R.N.S. Clarke, Borde Hill, Sussex) to a clone 'Kingdom Come', Kingdon-Ward 6869; flowers white, flushed yellow green, slightly spotted red-purple.

R. eclecteum Balf.f. & Forrest var. *bellatulum* Balf.f. ex Tagg is a hybrid between var. **eclecteum** and **R. selense.** This natural hybrid may be recognized by its paler flowers, shorter calyces and longer petioles. Plants with yellow flowers, but otherwise resembling *R. eclecteum* occur in the cultivation. It is not clear what status these have.

R. × edgarianum Rehder & E.H.Wilson - is a hybrid of **R. nivale** Hook.f. subsp. **boreale** M.N.Pilipson & Philipson (Subsect. Lapponica). It is occasionally seen in cultivation.

R. EDGEWORTHII HOOK.F. - SUBSECT. EDGEWORTHIA.
Shrub, to 2.5m, sometimes epiphytic. Leaves 6-15 × 2.5-5cm, oblong-ovate to (rarely) elliptic, apex acuminate, upper surface strongly bullate, lower surface with the small distant golden scales completely obscured by a dense indumentum. Pedicels densely tomentose. Flowers usu-

ally fragrant, 2-3 per inflorescence; calyx lobes conspicuous; corolla white, sometimes flushed pink and/or with a yellow blotch at base, funnel-campanulate, (35-)45-65mm; stamens 10, declinate; ovary densely tomentose; style declinate. H2-3. April-May. India (Sikkim, W Bengal, Arunachal Pradesh), Bhutan, NE Burma, China (S Tibet, Yunnan), 2,100-3,300m.

This is a distinctive and attractive species that requires protection from frost.

AM 1923 (T.H. Lowinsky, Sunninghill) as *R. bullatum*, from Farrer 842; flowers white.

AM 1946 (Lord Aberconway, Bodnant as *R. bullatum*; flowers bluish pink, flushed rose externally.

FCC 1933 (Lt Col L.C.R. Messel, Nymans); flowers white.

FCC 1937 (L. de Rothschild, Exbury) as *R. bullatum*; flowers white.

FCC 1981 (Sir Giles Loder, Leonardslee, Horsham, Sussex) to a clone 'Red Collar', from Kingdon-Ward 20840; trusses 3-5-flowered, corolla white, suffused pink, usually on three upper lobes and most strongly on reverse as a diffused central band, some light to faint yellow-orange spotting deep in upper throat.
♀ 1993

R. ELEGANTULUM TAGG & FORREST - SUBSECT. TALIENSIA.
Shrub 1-1.6m. Leaves 7-13 × 2.5-3.5cm, elliptic-oblong, apex acute; lower surface covered with a dense one-layered lanate indumentum composed of ramiform hairs that are deep pink when young, maturing to a rich rufous brown; petioles tomentose at first, later glabrescent. Flowers 10-20, in a dense truss; calyx c.12mm, lobes oblong; corolla pale purplish pink, with crimson flecks, campanulate, nectar pouches lacking, 30-40mm; ovary densely stalked-glandular, style with a few glands at base. H4b. May. China (border of Sichuan and Yunnan, near Yungning), 3,650-3,950m.

This species, which has a very limited

distribution in the wild, is allied to *R. bureavii* and R. *adenogynum.*

R. ELLIOTTII WATT - SUBSECT. PARISHIA. Small straggling shrub or small tree, to 4.5m; young shoots and petioles reddish stellate-tomentose, also with stalked glands. Leaves 8.5-10 × 2.5-5.1cm, oblanceolate to elliptic, both surfaces glabrous and shining when mature. Flowers 6-10, in a lax truss; calyx 3-4mm; corolla rose-purple, with darker flecks, funnel-campanulate, with nectar pouches, 40-50mm; ovary densely rufous-stellate-tomentose, style tomentose and glandular to tip. H2-3. May-July. NE India (Nagaland), 2,700-3,000m.

This species is allied to *R. facetum* and to *R. kyawii* but differs from both in the corolla shape and in its smaller leaves.

AM 1934 (J.J. Crosfield, Embley Park, Romsey) from Kingdon-Ward 7725; flowers deep blood red, faintly spotted.

FCC 1937 (Adm. A.W. Heneage-Vivian, Clyne Castle, Swansea) from Kingdon-Ward 7725; flowers deep scarlet, with light chocolate spots.

R. ellipticum Maxim. - is a synonym of **R. moulmainense** Hook.f. (Sect. Choniastrum).

R. epapillatum Balf.f. & Cooper - is a synonym of **R. papillatum** Balf.f. & Cooper (Subsect. Irrorata).

R. epipastum Balf.f. & Forrest - is a synonym of **R. eudoxum** Balf.f. & Forrest var. **mesopolium** (Balf.f. & Forrest) D.F. Chamb. (Subsect. Neriiflora).

R. eriandrum H.Lév. - is a synonym of **R. rigidum** Franch. (Subsect. Triflora).

R. ERIOCARPUM (HAYATA) NAKAI (INCL. *R. TAMURAE* [MAKINO] MASAMUNE) - SECT. TSUTSUSI.
Dwarf shrub, to 0.4m or more; young shoots and petioles densely covered with broad flattened brown adpressed hairs. Leaves of one kind, persistent, 1.7-2.5 × 1-

1.5cm, obovate to elliptic, apex bluntly mucronate, both surfaces stiffly hairy, especially on the midrib. Pedicels densely and stiffly adpressed-hairy. Flowers 1-2 per inflorescence; calyx 2-3mm; corolla white to purplish-pink, with darker flecks, broadly funnel-campanulate, *c.*30mm; stamens 9-10; ovary stiffly hairy, style glabrous. H2-3. S Japan, (Kyushu, Ryukyu Islands), *c.*300m.

This is a tender species that is affected by frosts. It rarely flowers in Britain when grown outside.

R. eritimum Balf.f. & W.W.Sm. - is a synonym of **R. anthosphaerum** Diels (Subsect. Fortunea).

R. EROSUM COWAN - SUBSECT. BARBATA. Large shrub or small tree, 3.5-6.5m; bark smooth and flaking, reddish brown; young shoots and petioles with long stiff bristles. Leaves 8-12.5 × 3.5-6.5cm, broadly elliptic to oblong, apex rounded, apiculate, base cordate, upper surface with strongly impressed veins, lower surface with a floccose dendroid indumentum. Flowers fleshy, 10-15, in a tight truss, crimson to blood-red, with darker nectar pouches, tubular-campanulate, 30-35mm; ovary densely stalked-glandular, style glabrous. H3-4a. March-April. China (SE Tibet), 3,000-3,800m.

R. erosum is the most Easterly of a complex of three closely allied species, also including *R. barbatum* and *R. argipeplum.* Some cultivated plants of this species have been called *R. argipeplum*, but it may be distinguished from that species by the relatively broader (1.5-2× as long as broad) and more rounded leaves.

R. erubescens Hutch. - is a synonym of **R. oreodoxa** Franch. var. **fargesii** (Franch.) D.F.Chamb. (Subsect. Fortunea).

R. × **ERYTHROCALYX** BALF.F. & FORREST - IS A NATURAL HYBRID BETWEEN *R. SELENSE* AND *R. WARDII.*
Shrub, 1-2.5m; young shoots stalked-glandular. Leaves 6-10 × 3.6-5cm, obovate to

oblong, upper surface glabrous, lower surface punctulate, otherwise glabrous. Flowers 4-10, in a lax truss; calyx 3-7mm; corolla pale yellow or white flushed rose, with or without purple flecks and a basal blotch, campanulate to open-campanulate, 35-45mm; ovary stalked-glandular, style glabrous or stalked-glandular for half its length. H4a. April-May. China (SE Tibet, NW Yunnan), 3,350-3,950m.

This hybrid is seen occasionally in gardens and is morphologically intermediate between the parents. It occurs with them in NW Yunnan, especially around the type locality (Beima Shan).

R. ESETULOSUM BALF.F. & FORREST - SUBSECT. SELENSIA.
Shrub, 1.5-2m; young shoots and petioles glabrous or with minute stalked glands. Leaves thick, 6-12 × 3-4cm, ovate to elliptic, lower surface with a thin adpressed indumentum of scattered dendroid hairs. Flowers 8-10, in a lax truss; calyx (1-)4-10mm; corolla white flushed rose, with or without purple flecks, funnel-campanulate, nectar pouches lacking, 30-35mm; ovary densely stalked-glandular, style glandular, at least near the base. H4a. April-May. China (SE Tibet, NW Yunnan), 3,000-4,250m.

As there is no direct connection between the few plants in cultivation and wild-collected herbarium specimens, there is some doubt as to their status. In any case *R. esetulosum* may be a hybrid between *R. selense* and *R. vernicosum*.

R. euchaites Balf.f. & Forrest - is a synonym of **R. neriiflorum** Franch. subsp. **neriiflorum** (Subsect. Neriiflora).

R. EUDOXUM BALFF. & FORREST - SUBSECT. NERIIFLORA.
Dwarf shrub, 0.3-1.2m. Leaves 3.5-9 × 1-3cm, elliptic, lower surface with a green epidermis and a thin discontinuous whitish to brown indumentum; petioles usually tomentose, sometimes also weakly setose. Flowers 2-6, in a tight truss; calyx 2-7mm, cupular when well-devel-

oped; corolla not fleshy, pink to rose-carmine, tubular-campanulate to campanulate, 25-40mm; ovary predominantly glandular to predominantly tomentose, abruptly contracted into the glabrous style. H4a. April-May. China border (between Tibet & Yunnan), 3,350-4,250m.

Var. **eudoxum**. (incl. *R. trichomiscum* Balf.f & Forrest & *R. trichophlebium* Balf.f. & Forrest). Ovary predominantly glandular.

AM 1960 (E.H.M. & P.A. Cox, Glendoick, Perth); flowers Solferino Purple with a basal crimson fringe.

Var. **brunneifolium** (Balf.f. & Forrest) D.F.Chamb. (*R. brunneifolium* Balf.f. & Forrest) Ovary predominantly tomentose; leaves 7-9cm, indumentum brownish; corolla *c.*40mm.

Var. **mesopolium** (Balf.f. & Forrest) D.F.Chamb. (incl. *R. epipastum* Balf.f. & Forrest). Ovary predominantly tomentose; leaves 3.5-7cm, indumentum whitish; corolla 30-35mm.

A variable species that may have arisen as a hybrid of *R. sanguineum*. It is also allied to *R. temenium* (q.v.).

R. EURYSIPHON TAGG & FORREST - SUBSECT. THOMSONIA.
Dwarf shrub, 1-1.8m; bark rough; young shoots minutely stalked-glandular. Leaves 3.5-5.5 × 1.8-2.1cm, elliptic to oblanceolate, base rounded, upper and lower surfaces glabrous, lower epidermis glaucous but not papillate; petioles glabrous or stalked-glandular at maturity. Flowers solitary or up to 3, in a lax truss; calyx *c.*3mm; corolla creamy white flushed pale rose, with conspicuous flecks, campanulate, with nectar pouches, 30-40mm; ovary and most of style densely stalked-glandular. H4. May. China (SE Tibet), 4,000m.

This is a rare species, both in the wild and in cultivation, that may prove to be a hybrid of *R. stewartianum.*

R. EXASPERATUM TAGG - SUBSECT. BARBATA.
Shrub or small tree, 2-5m; bark smooth,

reddish brown; young shoots and petioles densely covered with gland-tipped bristles. Leaves 11-13.5 × 6-7.5cm, broadly elliptic to obovate, apex and base rounded, upper surface with impressed veins, lower surface with gland-tipped stiff hairs or bristles. Flowers 10-15, in a dense truss, brick-red, with darker nectar pouches, tubular-campanulate, 35-45mm; ovary densely stalked-glandular, style glabrous. H4a. April-May. Upper Burma and adjacent parts of NE India and SW China (Tibet), 3,000-3,700m.

A rare species that is difficult to cultivate. The newly flushed leaves are an attractive plum purple colour.

R. EXCELLENS HEMSL. & E.H.WILSON - SUBSECT. MADDENIA.
Shrub, to at least 3m; young shoots scaly. Leaves 15-19 × 4-5.5cm, oblong-elliptic, apex obtuse, margin not ciliate, upper surface with raised midrib, lower surface glaucous, with the scales their own diameter apart. Flowers 3-4, in a loose inflorescence; calyx conspicuous, lobes 5-15mm, glabrous; corolla white to cream, funnel-campanulate, 100-110mm, outer surface scaly; stamens 10(-15); ovary densely scaly, tapering into the style which is scaly at base. H1b-2. May. China (S Yunnan, Guizhou), Northern Vietnam, 1,800-2,500m.

While plants in cultivation and herbarium specimens recently collected in Vietnam generally have 10-11 stamens, the type has 15, suggesting an affinity with *R. maddenii*. Vegetatively there is a similarity with *R. nuttallii*, with which it grows in the wild, but the leaves are narrower than those of the latter species.

R. eximium Nuttall - is a synonym of **R. falconeri** Hook.f. subsp. **eximium** (Nuttall) D.F.Chamb. (Subsect. Falconera).

R. FABERI HEMSL. (INCL. *R. FABERIOIDES* BALF.F. & *R. WUENSE* BALF.F.) - SUBSECT. TALIENSIA.
Shrub, 2-3m. Leaves 6-11 × 2.8-4.5cm,

oblanceolate to elliptic, apex acuminate to apiculate, lower surface covered with a two-layered indumentum, the upper layer loose, composed of brown to rust-red detersile ramiform hairs, the lower compacted, whitish; petioles 0.5-2cm, densely tomentose. Flowers 7-20, in a more or less dense truss; calyx 7-10mm, lobes broad; corolla white, occasionally flushed pink, sometimes with crimson flecks, campanulate or funnel-campanulate, nectar pouches lacking, 30-40mm; ovary densely stalked-glandular, style glabrous or glandular at base. H4b. April-May. China (C Sichuan), 2,650-3,350m.

This species is allied to *R. prattii* (q.v.).

R. faberi Hemsl. subsp. *prattii* (Franch.) D.F.Chamb. - is a synonym of **R. prattii** Franch. (Subsect. Taliensia).

R. faberioides Balf.f. - is a synonym of **R. faberi** Hemsl. (Subsect. Taliensia).

R. FACETUM BALF.F. & KINGDON-WARD - SUBSECT. PARISHIA.
Shrub or tree, 2-10m; young shoots and petioles rufous stellate-tomentose. Leaves 10-18.5 × 3-7.2cm, oblanceolate to elliptic, both surfaces glabrous and shining when mature, or with vestiges of indumentum, especially on the midrib towards the base. Flowers *c*.10, in a lax truss; calyx 3-5mm; corolla deep rose to scarlet, tubular-campanulate, with nectar pouches, 40-50mm; ovary rufous stellate-tomentose; style with floccose stellate hairs and glands. H2-3. June-July. NE Burma, China (W Yunnan), 2,700-3,350m.

This species is allied to *R. kyawii* but lacks the setose glands on the young shoots that characterize the latter species.

AM 1924 (T.H. Lowinsky, Sunninghill); flowers reddish salmon, with darker spots.

FCC 1980 (R.N.S. Clarke, Borde Hill, Sussex) to a clone 'Eric Rudd', from Forrest 26045; truss loose, rounded, comprising up to 13 flowers, corolla red, with overall red mottling.

R. FALCONERI HOOK.F. - SUBSECT.
FALCONERA.
Tree, 6-12m; old branches with a smooth
cinnamon bark. Leaves 18-35 × 8-17cm,
broadly elliptic to obovate, upper surface
rugulose with deeply impressed veins,
lower surface densely covered with a two-
layered indumentum, the upper layer
rufous, composed of strongly fimbriate
cup-shaped hairs, the lower compacted;
petioles terete. Flowers 15-20, in a dense
truss, 8(-10)-lobed, fleshy, whitish to
cream or pale pink, with a purple basal
blotch, obliquely campanulate, nectar
pouches lacking, 40-50mm; stamens usually 16; ovary densely sticky-glandular.
H3-4a. April-May. NE India (Bengal to
Arunachal Pradesh), E Nepal, Bhutan,
2,700-3,750m
    Subsp. **falconeri**. Flowers white to
cream; leaves glabrous above at maturity.
E Nepal, NE India (Bengal to Arunachal
Pradesh), Bhutan.
    AM 1922 (Messrs Gill, Falmouth);
flowers yellowish white, with a dark purple blotch.
    ♚ 1993
    Subsp. **eximium** (Nuttall) D.F.Chamb.
(*R. eximium* Nuttall). Flowers pale pink
with darker tips; leaves with a rufous
scurfy indumentum above when mature.
NE India (Arunachal Pradesh).
    R. falconeri hybridizes with *R. hodg-
sonii* in the wild (q.v.).
    AM 1973 (Royal Botanic Gardens,
Wakehurst) as a foliage plant, as *R. eximium*.

R. fargesii Franch. - is a synonym of **R. oreodoxa** Franch. var. **fargesii** (Franch.)
D.F.Chamb. (Subsect. Fortunea).

R. FARRERAE TAIT - SECT. BRACHYCALYX.
Dwarf shrub; young shoots glabrescent.
Leaves in whorls of up to three, at the
ends of the branches, thick, 1.5-3 × 1-2cm,
ovate, apex acute, lower surface covered
with long brown simple hairs; petioles
densely villose. Pedicels villose. Flowers
1-2, appearing before the leaves; calyx
minute; corolla pale purple or lilac, upper

lobe spotted, open-campanulate, 20-
30mm; stamens 10; ovary densely hairy,
eglandular, style glabrous. H1b-2. June. S
China, 600m.
    R. farrerae is closely allied to *R. mariesii*
but differs in its small thick leaves and
densely villose petioles. As this is a very
tender species it is very rare in cultivation.

R. FASTIGIATUM FRANCH. - SUBSECT.
LAPPONICA.
Prostrate or cushion-forming shrub, to
1.5m. Leaves often bluish, (0.5-)0.7-1.6 ×
0.3-0.6(-0.9)cm, broadly elliptic or oblong
to ovate, apex rounded to subacute,
mucronate, lower surface covered with
white or pinkish milky scales that are
touching in groups or more scattered.
Flowers 1-3(-4) per inflorescence; calyx 3-
6mm, lobes oblong to bluntly triangular;
corolla bright lavender-blue to rich purple, funnel-shaped, 10-16(-18)mm; stamens (6-)10, as long as the corolla; ovary
scaly, style longer than the stamens,
glabrous (rarely scaly and pubescent at
base). H4a-b. April-May. China (N & C
Yunnan), 3,400-4,400m.
    R. fastigiatum may be distinguished by
the milky scales on the lower surface of
the leaves.
    AM 1914 (G. Reuthe, Keston, Kent);
flowers bluish lilac.
    ♚ 1994

R. FAUCIUM D.F.CHAMB. - SUBSECT.
THOMSONIA.
Shrub or small tree, 1.5-6.5m; bark
smooth; young shoots glabrous. Leaves 7-
12 × 2.5-3cm, oblanceolate, base cuneate,
upper surface glabrous, lower surface
with a greenish epidermis, papillae lacking, also with a few weak fasciculate hairs
near the midrib, and with persistent red
punctate hair bases overlying the veins;
petioles often winged, 7-15mm, stalked-
glandular. Flowers 5-10, in a lax truss;
calyx 3-5mm; corolla pink, white tinged
pink or (rarely) sulphur yellow, with purple flecks, campanulate, with nectar
pouches, 37-40mm; ovary densely stalked-
glandular, style glabrous. H3-4a. April-

May. China (SE Tibet), 2,600-3,350m.

This species is allied to *R. hylaeum* but differs in the smaller leaves that taper below, in the shorter petioles and in the glandular ovary.

R. fauriei Franch. - is a synonym of **R. brachycarpum** D.Don ex D.Don subsp. **fauriei** (Franch.) D.F.Chamb. (Subsect. Pontica).

R. FERRUGINEUM L. - SUBSECT. RHODODENDRON.
Small shrub, to 1.5m; young shoots densely scaly, sometimes with a few hairs. Leaves 2.8-4 × 0.8-1.6cm, narrowly elliptic to elliptic, apex acute or mucronate, margin not ciliate, upper surface dark shining green, lower surface reddish brown, with dense overlapping scales. Flowers many, in a dense inflorescence; rhachis 10-20mm; calyx lobes to 1.5mm, scaly, ciliate; corolla deep pink, rarely pale pink or white, tubular-campanulate, 12-15(-17)mm, outer surface scaly and usually pubescent; stamens 10; style glabrous, up to 2× as long as ovary. H4b. June-July. Europe (Austria, France, Germany, Italy, Switzerland), 1,700-2,500m.

This, and the related *R. hirsutum* are known as the Alpenrose. It is also closely allied to *R. myrtifolium* (q.v.).

AM 1969 (Crown Estate Commissioners, Windsor) as var. *album*; flowers White.

AM 1990 (Valerie Finnis, Kettering, Northants); trusses 12-14-flowered, corolla red-purple, inner surface red-purple.

R. fictolacteum Balf.f. - is a synonym of **R. rex** H.Lév. subsp. **fictolacteum** (Balf.f.) D.F.Chamb. (Subsect. Falconera).

R. fimbriatum Hutch. - is a synonym of **R. hippophaeoides** Balf.f. & W.W.Sm. var **hippophaeoides** (Subsect. Lapponica).

R. FLAMMEUM (MICHX.) SARGENT - SUBSECT. PENTANTHERA.
Deciduous shrub, to 2.5m; young twigs densely covered with eglandular hairs.

Leaves (3-)3.9-6.3(-8.2) × 1.5-2.4(-2.7)cm, ovate or obovate to elliptic, lower surface densely eglandular-hairy or glabrous. Flower bud scales with outer surface covered with unicellular hairs, rarely glabrous. Flowers with an acrid fragrance, appearing before or with the leaves, 6-11, in a shortened raceme; calyx 1-3(-5)mm; corolla scarlet to orange, funnelform, tube abruptly expanding into the limb, outer surface of corolla covered with eglandular hairs, 27-45mm. Capsule with eglandular-hairs. H4a-b. April. SE USA, s.l.-500m.

R. flammeum differs from the allied *R. prunifolium* and *R. cumberlandense* in the precocious flowers that appear before the leaves.

R. FLAVIDUM FRANCH. - SUBSECT. LAPPONICA.
Erect shrub, to 2.5m. Leaves 0.7-1.5 × 0.3-0.7cm, broadly elliptic to oblong, apex rounded, shortly mucronate, lower surface with brown to dark brown scales that are 0.5-2× their own diameter apart. Flowers 1-3 per inflorescence; calyx 2-4 (-7)mm, lobes strap-shaped or deltoid; corolla yellow, broadly funnel-shaped, pubescent outside and inside, scaly outside, 12-18mm; stamens 8-10, as long as corolla; ovary scaly, style longer than stamens, pubescent towards the base. H4a-b. April-May. China (NW Sichuan), 3,000-4,000m.

Var. *psilostylum* Rehder & E.H.Wilson, which differs from var. *flavidum* in having leaf scales of two kinds, some dark, the rest golden, is probably not in cultivation.

R. flavorufum Balf.f. & Forrest - is a synonym of **R. aganniphum** Balf.f. & Kingdon-Ward var. **flavorufum** Balf.f. & Forrest (Subsect. Taliensia).

R. FLETCHERIANUM DAVIDIAN - SUBSECT. MADDENIA.
Compact shrub 0.6-1.2m; young shoots covered with setae. Leaves 2.3-5.5 × 1-2.8cm, elliptic to oblong-lanceolate, apex obtuse or acute, mucronate, margin dis-

tinctly crenate, upper surface with impressed midrib, lower surface with distant scales. Flowers 2-4(-5), in a loose inflorescence, not scented; calyx lobes 8-10mm, ciliate; corolla pale yellow, broadly funnel-shaped, 35-42mm, outer surface scaly or not, base glabrous; stamens 10; ovary scaly, conspicuously setose towards apex. H4a. March-May. China (SE Tibet), 4,000-4,300m.

Closely allied to *R. valentinianum* but differing in the partially setose ovary and in the leaves that are crenulate, with distant scales below.

AM 1964 (E.H.M. & P.A. Cox, Glendoick Gardens, Perth) from Rock 22302, to a clone 'Yellow Bunting'; flowers Primrose Yellow

R. FLINCKII DAVIDIAN - SUBSECT. LANATA.
Shrub, 1.5-2.5m. Leaves thin, 4-10 × 2-4.5cm, oblong-lanceolate to elliptic, apex rounded, apiculate, lower surface covered in a dense rufous, somewhat matted indumentum composed of dendroid hairs. Flowers 3-8, in a lax truss, pale yellow (to pink?), with purple flecks, campanulate, lacking nectar pouches, 35-50mm; ovary densely covered with a whitish to brown tomentum, without glands, style glabrous. H4a-b. April-May. E Bhutan., c.3,000m.

This species apparently hybridizes with *R. wallichii* and/or *R. campanulatum*. This may be the origin of the pink-flowered forms that have been reported from the wild and have been named *R. poluninii* Davidian.

R. FLOCCIGERUM FRANCH. - SUBSECT. NERIIFLORA.
Shrub, 0.6-3m. Leaves 3.5-11 × 1-2.7cm, narrowly oblong to narrowly elliptic, lower surface with a glaucous papillate epidermis, and with varying amounts of a rufous floccose, usually patchy, tomentum composed of ramiform hairs; petioles floccose-tomentose, rarely also setulose-glandular. Flowers 4-7 per truss; calyx 1-4mm; corolla fleshy, crimson to scarlet, rarely yellowish to pink, tubular-campanulate,

with nectar pouches, 30-40mm; ovary densely stellate-tomentose, lacking glands, tapering into the glabrous style. H3-4a. March-May. China (SE Tibet, NW Yunnan), 2,750-3,950m.

Allied to *R. neriiflorum, R. sperabile* and *R. sperabiloides* but distinguished from all three by the characteristic patchy leaf indumentum.

AM 1957 (Col Lord Digby, Minterne, Dorset); flowers pale cream, edged very pale Cherry, with pale greenish spots.

R. FLORIBUNDUM FRANCH. - SUBSECT. ARGYROPHYLLA.
Shrub or small tree, 2-5m. Leaves 10-18 × 3.2-5.5cm, elliptic to oblanceolate, apex apiculate, upper surface with deeply impressed veins, lower surface with a two-layered indumentum, the upper layer loose, woolly, persistent, yellowish at first but soon becoming white or greyish, composed of ramiform hairs, the lower layer white and compacted. Flowers 7-12, in a loose inflorescence, magenta-rose fading pale pink, with crimson flecks and a basal blotch, broadly campanulate, nectar pouches lacking, c.40mm; ovary densely tomentose, style glabrous. H4a. March-April. China (W Sichuan, Guizhou), 1,300-2,600m.

Allied to *R. denudatum* (q.v.). It is susceptible to bark-split in cold winters in Britain.

AM 1963 (E. de Rothschild, Exbury) to a clone 'Swinhoe'; flowers Roseine Purple, with a dark crimson blotch.

R. FLUMINEUM W.P.FANG & M.Y.HE - SECTION TSUTSUSI.
Shrub, 2-3m; young shoots densely adpressed-bristly. Leaves of two kinds; spring leaves deciduous, 5.7-9 × 2.3-3cm, elliptic, apex acute to cuspidate, both surfaces with scattered adpressed hairs; summer leaves persistent, (1.2)-2.5-3 × 0.8-1.5cm. Flowers 3-7 per inflorescence; calyx c.1mm, bristly; corolla pinkish white to red, with darker flecks, funnel-campanulate, c.18mm, outer surface glabrous; stamens 5; ovary densely bristly, style bristly

towards base. H?. China (S Yunnan), 1,400-1,750m.

This recently introduced species will almost certainly prove frost-sensitive.

R. fokiense Franch. - is a synonym of **R. simiarum** Hance (Subsect. Argyrophylla).

R. FORMOSANUM HEMSL. - SUBSECT. ARGYROPHYLLA.
Shrub or small tree, 2-5.5m. Leaves 7-13 × 1.5-3cm, elliptic to oblanceolate, apex cuspidate, upper surface reticulate, lower surface with a one-layered compacted fawn indumentum intermixed with a few glands; petioles 1-2cm. Flowers 10-20, in an open inflorescence, white to pink, with purplish flecks, widely funnel-shaped, nectar pouches lacking, 30-40mm; ovary densely reddish-tomentose, style glabrous. H3-4a. April. China (Taiwan), 800-2,000m.

The relatively narrow leaves with a one-layered indumentum and short petioles will distinguish this from the remaining species in Subsect. Argyrophylla. It is little grown as some forms are tender.

R. FORMOSUM WALL. - SUBSECT. MADDENIA.
Erect free-growing shrub, to 2m; young shoots covered with setae. Leaves (2.5-)4-7.2 × 1-2cm, elliptic to linear-obovate, apex acute or acuminate, margin fringed with long white hairs, upper surface with midrib impressed, lower surface with unequal scales their own diameter apart. Flowers 2-3, in a loose inflorescence, not scented; calyx disc-like, weakly ciliate; corolla white, sometimes flushed pink, often with a yellow blotch, openly-funnel-campanulate, 40-55mm, outer surface pilose at base and variably scaly; stamens 10; ovary scaly, impressed below the style that is scaly below. H2-3. April-May. NE India, 1,450-2,300m.

Var. **formosum** (incl. *R. iteaphyllum* Hutch.). Leaves 10-16mm broad. India (Meghalaya).

AM 1960 (Royal Botanic Garden, Edinburgh); flowers white, pale orange in throat internally, slightly pink-stained externally.

AM 1979 (Mrs E. Mackenzie, Fressingfield, Norfolk) to a clone 'Lucy Elizabeth', as *R. iteaphyllum*. Flowers in trusses of 2-3; corolla white, flushed yellow, white in upper throat.

AM 1988 (P.A. Cox, Glendoick) to a clone 'Khasia', from Cox and Hutchison 320; trusses 3-4-flowered, corolla white, with slight flush of greyed yellow in throat, strongly fragrant.

♀ 1993

Those forms with linear leaves have been referred to *R. iteaphyllum*. However, in the wild there is a complete gradation between these forms and those that match the type of *R. formosum*.

Var. **inaequale** C.B. Clarke (*R. inaequale* Hutch.). Leaves 15-21mm broad. India (Meghalaya, Manipur, Arunachal Pradesh).

The broad-leaved var. *inaequale* is more widespread in the wild than var. *formosum*.

AM 1947 (Lord Aberconway, Bodnant) as *R. inaequale*; flowers white, with a yellow band on posterior lobe, sweetly scented.

FCC 1981 (Mrs E. Mackenzie, Fressingfield, Norfolk) as *R. inaequale* to a clone 'Elizabeth Bennet', from Cox & Hutchison 301; truss 3-5-flowered, corolla white with a blotch of yellow-green in the upper throat.

R. FORRESTII BALF.F. EX DIELS - SUBSECT. NERIIFLORA.
Dwarf creeping shrub; stems up to 60cm long though rarely more than 10cm high; bud scales persistent. Leaves 1-2.8 × 0.9-1.8cm, obovate to orbicular, lower surface glabrous or with a few stalked glands and branched hairs towards base. Flowers solitary or rarely up to 3 per truss; calyx c.1mm; corolla fleshy, crimson, tubular-campanulate, with nectar pouches, 30-35mm; ovary densely stalked-glandular and rufous-tomentose, abruptly contracted into the glabrous style. H4. April-May. China (S Tibet, NW Yunnan), NE Burma,

3,050-4,500m.

Subsp. **forrestii**. Leaves 1.1-1.5(-2.2) × as long as broad, lower epidermis purple or green, not papillate, stalked glands absent. China (SE Tibet, NW Yunnan), NE Burma.

FCC 1935 (J.B. Stevenson, Tower Court, Ascot) as *R. repens* from KW 6832; flowers deep scarlet crimson.

AM 1957 (Mrs R.M. Stevenson, Tower Court, Ascot) as var. *tumescens*, from Rock 11169 (= USDA 59174); flowers Cherry.

Subsp. **papillatum** D.F.Chamb. Leaves 2.2-2.6(-3.2)× as long as broad, lower epidermis glaucous, papillate, with conspicuous stalked glands. China (S Tibet).

Subsp. *papillatum* apparently intergrades with *R. chamaethomsonii* in S Tibet. *R. forrestii* Diels var. *tumescens* Cowan & Davidian is one of the intermediate forms.

♀ 1994, to a clone 'Seinghku'.

R. FORTUNEI LINDL. - SUBSECT. FORTUNEA.
Shrub or tree, 3-10m. Leaves 8-18 × 2.5-6cm, broadly oblanceolate to obovate, base rounded, lower surface glabrous except for persistent punctulate hair bases. Flowers scented, 5-12, in a lax truss; calyx 1-3mm; corolla 7-lobed, pale rose, sometimes fading white, open- to funnel-campanulate, nectar pouches lacking, 55-70mm; stamens 14-16, filaments glabrous; ovary and entire style stalked-glandular. H4a-b. May-July. C, S & E China, 600-2,300m.

Subsp. **fortunei**. Leaves obovate, 1.8-2.5× as long as broad.

Subsp. **discolor** (Franch.) D.F.Chamb. (*R. discolor* Franch., & incl. *R. houlstonii* Hemsl. & E.H. Wilson & *R. kwangfuense* Chun & Fang). Leaves oblanceolate, 2.8-4× as long as broad.

AM 1921 (Messrs Wallace, Tunbridge Wells) as *R. discolor*; flowers white, tinted pink externally.

AM 1922 (Hon. H.D. McLaren, Bodnant) as *R. discolor*; flowers pale pink, with a dull crimson blotch.

AM 1974 (Crown Estate Commis-

sioners, Windsor) to a clone 'John R. Elcock', as *R. houlstonii*; flowers purple, yellow in throat, with some spots in upper part.

FCC 1922 (Royal Botanic Gardens, Kew) as *R. discolor*; flowers white, tinted pink externally.

AM 1981 (R.N.S. Clarke, Borde Hill) to a clone 'Random Harvest', as *R. houlstonii*, from an E.H. Wilson collection; flowers in trusses of 10-12, corolla white, tinged pink, with some yellow-green in upper throat.

♀ 1993

The two subspecies have partially overlapping distributions and apparently also overlap morphologically. *R. fortunei* can be confused with *R. decorum* but may be distinguished by the glabrous stamens. In cultivation it often has reddish petioles. *R. fortunei* has been much used as a parent in the generation of garden hybrids.

R. FRAGARIIFLORUM KINGDON-WARD - SUBSECT. FRAGARIIFLORA.
Dwarf shrub, to 40 cm; young shoots scaly and puberulent. Leaves 1-1.7 × 0.5-1cm, oblong-elliptic, rounded at base and apex, margin bluntly toothed, ciliate, lower surface with distant golden vesicular scales. Flowers 2-3, in a loose terminal inflorescence; calyx lobes 5-7mm, reddish, apex rounded; corolla red to purple, open-campanulate, 13-18mm; ovary scaly, style declinate, glabrous. H4a-b. Bhutan, China (SE Tibet), 3,650-4,500m.

This species may be distantly related to *R. setosum* but is sufficiently distinctive to be placed in its own subsection.

R. FULGENS HOOK.F. - SUBSECT. FULGENSIA.
Shrub, 1.5-4.5m. Leaves (7-)9-11 × (4-)5-7cm, broadly ovate to obovate, apex and base rounded, lower surface with dense fulvous lanate indumentum composed of fasciculate hairs. Flowers 8-14, in a dense truss; calyx 1-2mm; corolla scarlet to blood-red, with darker nectar pouches, tubular-campanulate, 20-35mm; ovary glabrous. H4a. March-April. E Nepal,

Bhutan, NE India (Sikkim, Bengal, Arunachal Pradesh) China (S Tibet), 3,200-4,300m.

A distinctive species unlikely to be confused with any other.

AM 1933 (G.W.E. Loder, Wakehurst Place, Sussex); flowers blood red.

R. fulvastrum Balf.f. & Forrest - is intermediate between and probably a hybrid of **R. temenium** and **R. sanguineum** (Subsect. Neriiflora).

R. fulvastrum Balf.f. & Forrest var. *albipetalum* Cowan - is an albino form of **R. eudoxum** Balf.f. & Forrest var. **eudoxum** (Subsect. Neriiflora).

R. fulvoides Balf.f. & Forrest - is a synonym of **R. fulvum** Balf.f. & W.W.Sm. subsp. **fulvoides** (Balf.f. & Forrest) D.F.Chamb. (Subsect. Fulva).

R. FULVUM BALF.F. & W.W.SM. - SUBSECT. FULVA.
Shrub or small tree, 2-8mm. Leaves 8-22 × 3.6-8cm, oblanceolate to elliptic, lower surface covered with a two-layered indumentum, the upper layer reddish brown to fulvous, largely composed of capitellate hairs, giving the surface a granular appearance. Flowers 10-20, in a dense truss, white to pink, with a basal blotch, with or without purple flecks, campanulate, nectar pouches lacking, 25-45mm; ovary glabrous. H4a. March-May. NE Burma, China (SE Tibet, W Yunnan, SW Sichuan), 3,000-4,000m.

Subsp. **fulvum**. Leaves 1.8-2.5× as long as broad, indumentum rich reddish brown. NE Burma, China (W Yunnan), 3,000-3,700m.

AM 1933 (Hon. R.H. McLaren, Bodnant); flowers pink, with a crimson blotch.

FCC 1981 (R.N.S. Clarke, Borde Hill); trusses tight, rounded, up to 20-flowered, inner corolla rich creamy white, suffused towards the rim with shades of red-purple, and with a red-purple blotch deep in throat, reverse white to red-purple, veined with a darker red-purple.

Subsp. **fulvoides** (Balf.f. & Forrest) D.F. Chamb. (*R. fulvoides* Balf.f & Forrest). Leaves (2.5-)2.8-3× as long as broad, indumentum fulvous to brown. NE Burma, China (SE Tibet, NW Yunnan, SW Sichuan), 3,350-4,000m.

The two subspecies apparently intergrade though there is at least partial geographical separation between them.
♀ 1993

R. fumidum Balf.f. & W.W.Sm. - is a synonym of **R. heliolepis** Franch. var. **heliolepis** (Subsect. Heliolepida).

R. GALACTINUM BALF.F. EX TAGG - SUBSECT. FALCONERA.
Tree, 5-6m; bark rough. Leaves 14-20 × 5-6.5cm, ovate-lanceolate, upper surface reticulate, lower surface covered with a two-layered indumentum, the upper layer dense, cinnamon, composed of strongly fimbriate narrowly cup-shaped hairs, the lower compacted; petioles terete. Flowers 9-15 in a truss, 7-lobed, pale rose with a crimson blotch, campanulate, nectar pouches lacking, (30-)40-50mm; stamens 14; ovary glabrous or with a few rufous hairs. H4a-b. April-May. China (Sichuan), *c*.2,000m.

This species may be distinguished from the remaining members of the subsection by the almost glabrous ovary.

R. GENESTIERIANUM FORREST - SUBSECT. GENESTIERIANA.
Shrub, to 5m; bark of older branches smooth, purplish; young shoots glabrous. Leaves 6.5-12 × 2.5-4cm, narrowly elliptic to narrowly elliptic-oblanceolate, apex abruptly acuminate; lower surface with a white papillate epidermis, the scales distant, equal, golden-yellow to brown. Pedicels thin. Flowers *c*.12, in a lax raceme; calyx to 2mm; corolla fleshy, reddish purple, pruinose, campanulate, 12-17mm; stamens (8-)10, regular; ovary scaly, style sharply deflexed, glabrous. H2-3. April-May. NE Burma, China (NW Yunnan, SE Tibet), 2,450-4,250m.

This is a distinctive species that is

probably distantly allied to *R. campylogynum*. It is generally tender in cultivation and is only suitable for relatively frost-free sites.

R. × GERALDII (HUTCH.) IVENS - ?*R. PRAEVERNUM* HUTCH. X *R. SUTCHUENENSE* FRANCH. (SUBSECT. FORTUNEA). Resembling *R. sutchuenense* in the leaf characters and flower shape but the corolla has a marked basal blotch. H4b. February-April.

While it is presumed to be the above mentioned hybrid, further fieldwork is required to confirm the status of this taxon.

AM 1945 (The Misses Godman, Horsham); flowers Amaranth Rose, with a Beetroot Purple blotch.

AM 1971 (G. Gorer, Sunte House, Haywards Heath) to a clone 'Sunte Rose'; flowers red-purple in bud, paling on opening, with red-purple basal blotch and some spotting.

R. giganteum Tagg - is a synonym of **R. protistum** Balf.f. & Forrest var. **giganteum** (Tagg) D.F.Chamb. (Subsect. Grandia).

R. GLANDULIFERUM FRANCH. - SUBSECT. FORTUNEA.
Shrub; young shoots sparsely stalked-glandular. Leaves 12-16 × 2-4cm, oblong-lanceolate, glabrous below. Rhachis elongate. Flowers 5-6 in a truss; pedicels densely covered with long-stalked glands; calyx *c*.3mm; corolla 7-8-lobed, white, funnel-campanulate, 50-60mm, outer surface densely long-stalked-glandular; stamens 14-16; ovary and style stalked-glandular. H4a? China (NE Yunnan), 2,300-2,400m.

This species, which may be distinguished by the stalked glands on the corollas and flower stalks, has only recently been introduced into cultivation.

R. glandulosum Small - is a synonym of *R. camtschaticum* Pall. var. *glandulosum* (Small) Hultèn (subgen. Therorhodion).

R. glaphyrum Balf.f. & Forrest - is a synonym of **R. temenium** Balf.f. & Forrest var. **dealbatum** Cowan (Subsect. Neriiflora).

R. glaucopeplum Balf.f. & Forrest - is a synonym of **R. aganniphum** Balf.f. & Kingdon-Ward var. **aganniphum** (Subsect. Taliensia).

R. GLAUCOPHYLLUM REHDER - SUBSECT. GLAUCA.
Low shrub, to 1.5m; shoots with a peeling reddish brown bark. Leaves (3.5-)4-6 × (1.3-)1.5-2.5cm, narrowly elliptic to elliptic, lower surface with a glaucous papillate epidermis, the scales 1-3× their own diameter apart, unequal, the smaller golden, the larger brown. Pedicels scaly. Flowers (2-)4-6 per inflorescence; calyx lobes 6-9(-11)mm, acuminate, with a tuft of hairs inside at the apex; corolla pink or white flushed pink, rarely white, sometimes also with flecks; campanulate to tubular-campanulate, (18-)20-27(-32)mm; stamens 10, regular; ovary scaly, style sharply deflexed or declinate, glabrous. H(3-)4a?. April-May. India (Sikkim, Arunachal Pradesh), Bhutan, China (S Tibet), 2,750-3,650m.

Subsp. **glaucophyllum**. Corolla campanulate; style sharply deflexed. Nepal, India (Sikkim) Bhutan, 3,050-3,350m

Subsp. **tubiforme** (Cowan & Davidian) D. G. Long (*R. tubiforme* [Cowan & Davidian] Davidian). Corolla tubular-campanulate; style declinate. India (Arunachal Pradesh), Bhutan, China (S Tibet), 2,750-3,650m.

Subsp. *tubiforme* has a more Easterly distribution than subsp. *glaucophyllum*.

This species closely resembles *R. luteiflorum* (q.v.). White-flowered forms have been referred to var. **album** Davidian.

R. GLISCHROIDES TAGG & FORREST (*R. GLISCHRUM* BALF.F. & FORREST SUBSP. *GLISCHROIDES* (TAGG & FORREST) D.F.CHAMB.) - SUBSECT. GLISCHRA.
Shrub, 1.3-4.5m; young shoots setose-glandular. Leaves herbaceous, 8-11 × 2.8-5cm, elliptic to oblanceolate, apex cuspi-

date, upper surface rugulose, with deeply impressed veins, lower surface setose, especially on the veins, usually also with a thin whitish arachnoid tomentum on the veins. Flowers 7-12, in a lax truss; calyx 5-10mm; corolla white or pale rose, with purple flecks and a basal blotch, campanulate, nectar pouches lacking, 30-40mm; ovary densely covered with stalked glands. H3-4a. April-May. NE Burma, China (W Yunnan), 2,700-3,350m.

R. *glischroides* is allied to *R. vesiculiferum*, with which it shares rugulose leaves. It can however be distinguished by the lack of vesiculate leaf hairs.

AM 1990 (E. de Rothschild, Exbury) to a clone 'Glister'; trusses loosely borne with up to 12 flowers, corolla white with central part and lobe of each section flushed red-purple with a darker chocolate purple blotch in upper throat.

R. GLISCHRUM BALF.F. & W.W.SM. - SUBSECT. GLISCHRA.
Shrub or small tree, 2-8m; young shoots densely glandular-setose. Leaves herbaceous, 11.5-30 × 3.3-8cm, obovate to elliptic, apex cuspidate, upper surface smooth, lower surface covered with glandular setae, especially on veins and midrib. Flowers 10-14 in a truss; calyx 5-10mm; corolla rose-pink to scarlet, with purple flecks and usually also a purple basal blotch, campanulate, 30-50mm; ovary densely stalked-glandular. H3-4a. April-May. China (S Tibet, NW Yunnan), 2,100-4,000m.

Subsp. **glischrum**. Leaves glabrous above at maturity though sometimes with a few setae above midrib at base. NE Burma, China (S Tibet, NW Yunnan).

Subsp. **rude** (Tagg & Forrest) D.F.Chamb. (*R. rude* Tagg & Forrest). Leaves with persistent setae on upper surface, even when mature. China (NW Yunnan).

AM 1968 (Crown Estate Commissioners, Windsor) to a clone 'High Flier', as *R. rude*; flowers red-purple in bud, opening white, flushed red-purple up centre of lobes.

AM 1969 (A.C. & J.F.A. Gibson, Glenarn, Dunbartonshire) to a clone 'Frank Kingdon-Ward', as *R. rude*; flowers pinkish purple, spotted.

R. *glischrum* is allied to *R. habrotrichum*, from which it may be distinguished by the leaf shape, and to *R. glischroides*, from which it differs in its smooth upper leaf surface.

R. *glischrum* Balf.f. & W.W.Sm. subsp. *glischroides* (Tagg & Forrest) D.F. Chamb. - is a synonym of **R. glischroides** Tagg & Forrest - Subsect. Glischra.

R. *globigerum* Balf.f. & Forrest - is a synonym of **R. alutaceum** Balf.f. & W.W.Sm. var. **alutaceum** (Subsect. Taliensia).

R. *glomerulatum* Hutch. - is a synonym of **R. yungningense** Balf.f. (Subsect. Lapponica).

R. GORERI DAVIDIAN - SUBSECT. MADDENIA.
Differs from the closely allied *R. nuttallii* in its leaves with lower surface greenish (not glaucous), the veins less prominent, and with the upper surface not or only slightly bullate. H1-2. China (S Tibet - Tsangpo Valley), 2,150-2,300m.

The status of this species is uncertain. As it grows with the related *R. nuttallii*, it could be a natural hybrid of the latter species. It does however have a distinctive appearance.

R. GRANDE WIGHT - SUBSECT. GRANDIA.
Tree, 5-12m. Leaves 15-27 × 5-9.5cm, elliptic to oblanceolate, lower surface with a thin silvery compacted indumentum. Flowers 15-25, in a dense truss, 8-lobed, cream to pale yellow, rarely with a purplish tinge, with purple nectar pouches, ventricose-campanulate, 50-70mm; stamens 16; ovary covered with stalked glands, sometimes also with a dense pale brown tomentum. H2-3. February-April. E Nepal, NE India, Bhutan, China (S Tibet), 2,500-3,000m.

The glandular ovary will distinguish

this from the remaining species in Subsect. Grandia.

FCC 1901 (F.D. Godman, South Lodge, Horsham); flowers creamy white, with a purple blotch.

R. GRIERSONIANUM BALF.F. & FORREST - SUBSECT. GRIERSONIANA.

Shrub, 1.5-3m. Leaves 10-20 × 2-5cm, elliptic, apex acute to acuminate, lower surface covered with a dense whitish to pale brown lanate tomentum composed of dendroid hairs; petioles densely setulose-glandular. Flowers 5-12, in a lax truss; corolla deep rose to scarlet, tubular- to funnel-campanulate, 55-80mm, outer surface of tube densely hairy; ovary densely covered with dendroid hairs. H3. May-June. China (W Yunnan), NE Burma, 2,150-2,700m.

A distinctive species that has been often used as a parent in garden hybrids.

FCC 1924 (T.H. Lowinsky, Sunninghill and L. de Rothschild, Exbury); flowers fiery salmon, with striking red filaments.

R. GRIFFITHIANUM WIGHT - SUBSECT. FORTUNEA.

Shrub or tree, 1.3-10m. Leaves 10-19(-30) × 4-7.5(-10)cm, oblong, base rounded, glabrous. Flowers 4-5, in a lax truss; calyx 7-20mm long, lobes rounded; corolla 5-lobed, pale pink at first, soon fading white, open-campanulate, nectar pouches lacking, 55-80mm; stamens 12-18; ovary and entire style glandular. H2-3. April-May. E Nepal, NE India (Bengal, Sikkim, Arunachal Pradesh), Bhutan, 2,100-2,850m

A distinctive species that requires a mild climate in Britain and is thus rare in cultivation. It has been used widely to produce many worthy garden hybrids.

FCC 1866 (J. Standish, Ascot) as *R. griffithii*.

R. GROENLANDICUM (OEDER) KRON & JUDD (*LEDUM GROENLANDICUM* OEDER) - SUBSECT. LEDUM.

Erect shrub, 0.5-2m; young shoots ferruginous-lanate. Leaves 1.2-6 × 0.5-1.5cm, linear-elliptic, margins revolute, upper surface dark green, lower surface with a thickly ferrugineous lanate indumentum that usually conceals the midrib, epidermis papillose covered with short white setulose hairs, scales dense, rimless, golden, intermixed with red-brown glands; petioles 1-5mm. Flowers numerous, in a loose terminal umbellate corymb; calyx minute; corolla white, rotate, 4-8mm; stamens 7-10; ovary glandular, style glabrous. H4. May-June. Greenland, Canada, Northern USA, s.l.-1,800m.

R. GROTHAUSII DAVIDIAN - SUBSECT. MADDENIA.

Differs from *R. lindleyi* in its smaller flowers, 5-7.5cm long, and perhaps also in the bullate upper surfaces of the leaves. H2-3. China (S Tibet), Bhutan?

The status of this species is uncertain as at least some of the material cited in the type description falls outside the limits of the species as defined. The type itself is extreme but does not have the bullate leaves as described. It is treated as a synonym of *R. lindleyi* by some recent authors.

R. gymnocarpum Balf.f. ex Tagg - is a synonym of **R. microgynum** Balf.f. & Forrest (Subsect. Neriiflora).

R. HABROTRICHUM BALF.F. & W.W.SM. - SUBSECT. GLISCHRA.

Shrub, 1-4m; young shoots densely glandular-setose. Leaves subcoriaceous, 7-16 × 3-7.5cm, ovate to obovate, apex acute, lower surface with midrib and main veins glandular-setose. Flowers c.10 in a truss; calyx red, 10-15mm; corolla white flushed rose to pink, with or without purple flecks and a basal blotch, campanulate, nectar pouches absent, 40-50mm; ovary densely glandular-setose. H3-4a. April-May. NE Burma, China (W Yunnan), 2,700-3,350m.

Allied to *R. glischrum* but with broader leaves.

AM 1933 (R. White, Sunningdale); flowers pink.

R. HAEMATODES FRANCH. - SUBSECT. NERIIFLORA.
Small shrub, 0.6-1.8m. Leaves 4.5-10 × 1.8-5.5cm, obovate to oblong, lower surface with a two-layered indumentum, the upper layer a fawn to red-brown densely matted tomentum, composed of dendroid hairs, the lower whitish, compacted; petioles densely tomentose or setose and tomentose. Flowers 4-8, in a tight truss; calyx 1-15mm, when well-developed cupular, but with irregular lobes; corolla fleshy, scarlet to deep crimson, tubular-campanulate, with nectar pouches, 35-45 (-50) mm; ovary densely rufous-tomentose, abruptly contracted into the glabrous style. H4a-b. March-June. China (SE Tibet, W Yunnan), 3,350-4,450m.

Subsp. **haematodes**. Petioles and young shoots predominantly tomentose, setae, when present, few and slender. China (W Yunnan).

FCC 1926 (A.M. Williams, Launceston, Cornwall); flowers bright scarlet.

Subsp. **chaetomallum** (Balf.f. & Forrest) D.F.Chamb. (*R. chaetomallum* Balf.f. & Forrest). Petioles and young shoots predominantly setose, setae stout. NE Burma, China (SE Tibet, NW Yunnan).

AM 1959 (E. de Rothschild, Exbury) as *R. chaetomallum*, from Forrest 25601; flowers Turkey Red.

The two subspecies merge in NW Yunnan where the ranges of the two overlap, perhaps as a result of hybridization. However, only subsp. *haematodes* occurs in the Dali region of W Yunnan, and some populations in NW Yunnan contain only subsp. *chaetomallum*.

R. HANCEANUM HEMSL. - SUBSECT. TEPHROPEPLA.
Shrub, to 2m; bark smooth, bronze. Leaves 7-11.5 × 3.5-5.7cm, oblong-elliptic to narrowly ovate, apex acuminate, upper surface green, lower surface pale green, scales flat, golden-brown, distant. Flowers 5-15, in a loose or dense terminal inflorescence with a rhachis up to 12mm long; calyx lobes *c*.5mm, not ciliate but fringed with scales; corolla white to yellow, nar-rowly funnel-campanulate, *c*.20mm, outer surface scaly, glabrous; stamens 10; ovary scaly, style impressed, declinate, glabrous. H3-4b. April-June. China (C Sichuan), 1,200-1,500m.

A dwarf form, no more than 0.2m high, with small leaves 2-3.5cm long is grown under the name Nanum Group.

This species is considered by some authors to belong to Subsect. Triflora.

AM 1957 (Crown Estate Commissioners, Windsor) to a clone 'Canton Consul', as var. *nanum*; habit rather dwarf, flowers creamish green in bud, opening cream.

R. HAOFUI CHUN & W.P.FANG - SUBSECT. ARGYROPHYLLA.
Shrub, 4-6m. Leaves leathery, 7-22 × 3-7cm, elliptic, upper surface shining, lower surface covered with a thick cinnamon tomentum that becomes greyish-white and thinner on maturity. Flowers 5-9 per inflorescence; calyx *c*.1mm; corolla white, sometimes flushed with rose and/or with a red basal blotch, broadly campanulate, without nectar pouches; stamens 18-21; ovary covered with a dense whitish to pale brown tomentum, style glabrous. H4a. May. C & S China (Guizhou, Guangxi, Hunan), 1,500m.

The large number of stamens and characteristic leaves make this a very distinctive species. It has only recently been introduced into cultivation but appears to be relatively hardy despite its provenance.

R. hardingii Tagg - is a synonym of **R. annae** (Subsect. Irrorata).

R. hardyi Davidian - is a synonym of **R. augustinii** Hemsl. subsp. **hardyi** (Davidian) Cullen (Subsect. Triflora).

R. headfortianum Hutch. - is a synonym of **R. taggianum** Hutch. (Subsect. Maddenia).

R. hedyosmum Balf.f. - is probably a hybrid

of **R. trichostomum** Franch. (Sect. Pogonanthum; see note under the latter species).

R. heftii Davidian - is a form of **R. wallichii** Hook.f. (Subsect. Campanulata).

R. HELIOLEPIS FRANCH. - SUBSECT. HELIOLEPIDA.
Shrub, to 3m; young growth scaly, purplish. Leaves strongly aromatic when crushed, (5-)5.7-10.5 × (1.8-)2-4cm, oblong-ovate to oblong-elliptic, apex acute, upper surface dark green and shining, lower surface with close but not touching conspicuous brownish scales. Flowers (4-)6-10 per inflorescence; calyx minute to 3mm; corolla white to pink or purple, usually with greenish or brownish flecks on upper lobes, funnel-shaped, (22-)24-34mm; stamens 10; ovary densely scaly, usually pubescent above, style straight, pubescent below. H4a. June-July.
Var. **heliolepis** (incl. *R. fumidum* Balf.f. & W.W.Sm.). Leaves with base truncate or rounded, 2.2-2.8(-3.3)× as long as broad; inflorescence (4-)5-8-flowered. NE Burma, China (Yunnan, SE Tibet), 2,500-3,700m.
AM 1954 (Mrs R.M. Stevenson, Tower Court, Ascot) from Forrest 26961; flowers white, spotted with green and brown.
Var. **brevistylum** (Franch.) Cullen (*R. brevistylum* Franch. & incl. *R. pholidotum* Balf.f. & W.W.Sm.). Leaves cuneate at base, (2.2-)2.7-3.3(-3.6)× as long as broad; inflorescence (5-)6-10-flowered. China (SE Tibet, Yunnan, SW Sichuan), 3,000-3,700m.
AM 1933 (J.J. Crosfield, Kensington, London) from Kingdon-Ward 7108; flowers pink externally, white inside, with pink spots.

R. hemidartum Tagg - is a synonym of **R. pocophorum** Balf.f. ex Tagg var. **hemidartum** (Tagg) D.F.Chamb. (Subsect. Neriiflora).

R. HEMITRICHOTUM BALF.F. & FORREST - SUBSECT. SCABRIFOLIA.
Shrub, 0.6-2m; young shoots scaly, also covered with filiform hairs. Leaves 2.5-4 ×

0.7-1.3cm, narrowly elliptic, upper surface covered with filiform hairs only, lower surface shining, white-papillose, glabrous except for a few hairs along the midrib, scales scattered, rimless. Flowers 2-3, in an axillary inflorescence; calyx rim-like, scaly, ciliate; corolla pink or white edged with pink, openly funnel-shaped, 10-15mm, outer surface glabrous and lacking scales; stamens 10; ovary densely scaly, sparsely pilose, style impressed, declinate. H4a. April-May. China (N Yunnan, SW Sichuan), 2,900-4,300m.
This species is closely allied to *R. mollicomum* but differs in its smaller flowers and in the less densely hairy leaf lower surfaces.

R. HEMSLEYANUM E.H.WILSON (INCL. *R. CHENGIANUM* FANG) - SUBSECT. FORTUNEA.
Shrub to tree, 2-8m; Leaves 10-20 × 4-10cm, ovate to ovate-elliptic, base cordate, margin undulate, lower surface with scattered punctulate hair bases and a few stalked glands at base, otherwise glabrous. Flowers 5-8, in lax trusses; calyx *c*.1mm; corolla 6-7-lobed, white, without flecks, campanulate, nectar pouches lacking, 45-60cm; stamens *c*.14; ovary and style glandular. H4a. May-June. China (W Sichuan), 1,100-2,000m.
A distinctive species with a very restricted distribution in the wild.

R. herpesticum Balf.f. & Kingdon-Ward - is a synonym of **R. dichroanthum** Diels subsp. **scyphocalyx** (Balf.f. & Forrest) Cowan (Subsect. Neriiflora).

R. HIDAKANUM H.HARA - SECT. BRACHYCALYX.
Shrub, to 3m; young shoots more or less glandular, later glabrescent. Leaves in whorls of up to three, at the ends of the branches, 2.5-6 × 1.5-5cm, broadly rhombic-ovate, apex shortly cuspidate, lower surface pale, with adpressed hairs or glabrous except for minute papillate glands and long hairs on midrib; petioles glandular. Pedicels glandular, pilose

below. Flowers 1-3 per inflorescence, appearing with the leaves; calyx *c*.3mm, lobes purple, ribbon-like; corolla magenta, funnel-campanulate, 25-30mm; stamens 10; ovary shortly stalked-glandular, with scattered pilose hairs, style glabrous. H4a-b. April-May. Japan (S Hokkaido), mountains, *c*.175m.

This species is probably allied to *R. decandrum* but it is distinguished from it and all the remaining members of the section by the conspicuous calyx. It is isolated from the related species and has a very restricted distribution.

R. × *hillieri* Davidian - is a hybrid of **R. temenium** Balf.f. & Forrest.

R. HIPPOPHAEOIDES BALF.F. & W.W.SM. - SUBSECT. LAPPONICA.
Erect shrub, to 1.7m. Leaves (0.6-)1.2-2.5 (-3) × 0.4-1.1cm, elliptic to oblong, apex obtuse to rounded, lower surface covered with uniformly yellowish buff overlapping scales. Flowers 4-7 per inflorescence, calyx to 2mm, the lobes often unequal; corolla bright rose to lavender blue, rarely white, broadly funnel-shaped, 11-15mm; stamens 10, shorter than corolla; ovary scaly, style glabrous. H4b-c. March-May.

Var. **hippophaeoides** Balf.f. & W.W.Sm. (incl. *R. fimbriatum* Hutch.). Style 4-11mm.

AM 1927 (Lady Aberconway and Hon. H.D. McLaren, Bodnant); flowers lavender blue.

Var. **occidentale** Philipson & N.M.Philipson. Style 13-16mm.

The pale leaf scales and several-flowered inflorescence are distinguishing features of this species.

♀ 1993, to a clone 'Haba Shan'.

R. hirsuticostatum Hand.-Mazz. - is a synonym of **R. augustinii** Hemsl. subsp. **chasmanthum** (Diels) Cullen (Subsect. Triflora).

R. HIRSUTUM L. - SUBSECT. RHODODENDRON.
Small shrub, to 1m; young shoots sparsely scaly, pubescent and setose. Leaves 1.3-3 × 0.7-1.4cm, narrowly obovate to obovate-orbicular, apex acute, margin ciliate, glabrous above, lower surface with well-spaced golden scales. Flowers many, rhachis to 10mm; pedicels scaly and puberulent; calyx lobes 2-4mm, scaly, ciliate; corolla pink, tubular-campanulate, outer surface scaly and sparsely pubescent; stamens 10; style as long as ovary, sparsely pubescent at base. H4b. June-July. European Alps (Austria, France, Italy, Yugoslavia, Switzerland, mountainous regions, 400-1,900m.

Along with *R. ferrugineum*, this is known as the Alpenrose.

R. HIRTIPES TAGG - SUBSECT. SELENSIA.
Low shrub or tree, 0.5-8m; young shoots and petioles covered with glandular bristles. Leaves 5-11 × 3.5-6cm, broadly obovate, lower surface with scattered stalked glands and a sparse floccose indumentum. Flowers 3-5, in a lax truss; calyx 4-10mm; corolla white to pink, usually with a few purple flecks, campanulate, nectar pouches lacking, *c*.40mm; ovary and style base densely stalked-glandular. H4a. April. China (SE Tibet), 3,000-4,000m.

A distinctive species, more closely allied to *R. selense* subsp. *dasycladum* than to *R. glischrum*, with which it has been traditionally allied.

AM 1965 (A.C. & J.F.A. Gibson, Glenarn, Dunbartonshire) to a clone 'Ita'; flowers Phlox Pink, stained and striped.

R. HODGSONII HOOK.F. - SUBSECT. FALCONERA.
Tree, 3-11mm; bark smooth, peeling, reddish brown. Leaves 17-24 × 6.5-10cm, obovate to oblanceolate, upper surface smooth, reticulate, lower surface with a dense two-layered indumentum, the upper layer silvery to cinnamon, composed of slightly fimbriate, broadly cupshaped hairs, the lower compacted; petioles terete. Flowers 15-25, in a dense truss, 7-10-lobed, pink to magenta or purple, with a darker blotch, tubular-campanulate, nectar pouches lacking; stamens 15-

18; ovary tomentose. H4a. April-May. E Nepal, N India (Sikkim, Bengal, Arunachal Pradesh), Bhutan, China (S Tibet), 3,000-4,000m.

The hybrid with *R. falconeri* (known as *R.* Hodconeri Group [or *R.* × *decipiens* Lacaita] which also occurs in the wild) may be distinguished by its paler flowers and often darker brown leaf indumentum.

AM 1964 (Crown Estate Commissioners, Windsor) to a clone 'Poet's Lawn'; flowers white, shaded Rhodamine Purple.

R. HONGKONGENSE HUTCH. - SECT. AZALEASTRUM.
Shrub, to 5m. Leaves 3-6.5 × 1.5-3.5 cm, elliptic to narrowly elliptic, apex blunt or notched. Flowers slightly scented, single, borne laterally below vegetative buds, white with purple spots on upper lobes, rotate, tube short, lobes spreading, *c.*50mm across; stamens 5. H1b-2?. March-April. S China (Hong Kong, Guangdong), *c.*1,000m.

Closely allied to *R. ovatum* and only doubtfully distinct.

R. HOOKERI NUTT. - SUBSECT. THOMSONIA.
Shrub or small tree, *c.*4m; bark smooth; young shoots glabrous. Leaves 8-14 × 3-5cm, broadly oblanceolate, base rounded; upper surface glabrous, lower surface with epidermis lacking papillae, glabrous except for large fasciculate hairs overlying the veins; petioles slightly winged, glabrous. Flowers 8-15, in a dense truss; calyx (5-)10-20mm, cupular; corolla deep rose to crimson, with darker nectar pouches and a few flecks, tubular-campanulate, 35-45mm; ovary and style glabrous. H3 (-4a). March-April. NE India (Arunachal Pradesh), 2,500-3,700m.

The large fasciculate hairs on the veins of the lower surface of the leaves characterize this species. In cultivation the flowers are either a clear crimson or a muddy deep rose pink.

FCC 1933 (Hon. H.D. McLaren, Bodnant); flowers of the darkest red, with a large, similarly coloured calyx.

R. HORLICKIANUM DAVIDIAN - SUBSECT. MADDENIA.
Epiphytic or free-growing shrub, to 3m; young shoots setose. Leaves 8.5-10 × *c.*3cm, narrowly elliptic, apex long-acuminate, margin ciliate, upper surface with midrib impressed, lower surface covered with lax dark scales. Flowers 2-3, in a lax terminal inflorescence; calyx more or less disc-like, fringed with setae; corolla white flushed pink, with a yellow blotch inside, funnel-campanulate, 60-70mm, outer surface pubescent, especially on tube, scaly, more densely so on lobes; stamens 10; ovary densely scaly, tapering into the scaly style. H1b-2. April. N Burma, 1,200-2,150m.

A distinctive species on account of its hairy corolla and long-acuminate leaves.

R. hormophorum Balf.f. & Forrest - is a synonym of **R. yunnanense** Franch. (Subsect. Triflora).

R. houlstonii Hemsl. & E.H.Wilson - is a synonym of **R. fortunei** Lindl. subsp. **discolor** (Franch.) D.F.Chamb.(Subsect. Fortunea).

R. HUIANUM FANG - SUBSECT. FORTUNEA.
Shrub or small tree, 2-9m; shoots soon becoming glabrous. Leaves 10-12.5 × 2-3cm, oblanceolate, apex cuspidate to acuminate, lower surface glabrous. Flowers 6-10, borne on a 3-6cm rhachis; pedicels glabrous; calyx 5-10mm, lobes rounded; corolla 7-lobed, pale red to purplish or lilac, open-campanulate, 35-50mm, glabrous; stamens 12-14; ovary and style glandular. H4a. China (NE Yunnan & adjacent parts of Sichuan), 1,000-2,700m.

This species is allied to *R. davidii* but differs in the larger calyx. It has only recently been introduced into cultivation from seed collected in NE Yunnan.

R. HUNNEWELLIANUM REHDER & E.H.WILSON - SUBSECT. ARGYROPHYLLA.
Shrub or small tree, 2-6m. Leaves 7-15 × 1.6-2.8cm, narrowly oblanceolate, apex

acuminate, upper surface reticulate; lower surface with a two-layered indumentum, the upper layer loose, white, persisting or rubbing off, composed of ramiform hairs, the lower compacted and whitish. Flowers 6-10, in a loose truss, white to pale rose or purple, with purple flecks, widely campanulate, nectar pouches lacking, 40-50mm; ovary densely and coarsely yellowish-tomentose, style glabrous. H4a-b. March-April. China (Sichuan, Gansu), 2,000-3,000m.

Subsp. **hunnewellianum**. Leaves (7-) 10-15cm long, upper layer of leaf indumentum remaining whitish. China (C Sichuan), 2,000-3,000m.

Subsp. **rockii** (E.H.Wilson) D.F. Chamb. (*R. rockii* E.H.Wilson). Leaves 7-12cm long, upper layer of leaf indumentum turning yellow. China (N Sichuan, S Gansu), 2,000-2,400m.

R. HYLAEUM BALF.F. & FARRER - SUBSECT. THOMSONIA.
Shrub or tree, 2.5-12m; bark smooth, peeling; young shoots more or less glabrous. Leaves 8.5-14.5 × 3.3-5.7cm, base rounded, upper surface glabrous, lower surface with epidermis greenish and lacking papillae, with scattered fasciculate hairs arising from red persistent hair bases on the veins, otherwise glabrous; petioles 1.5-2cm, narrowly winged, stalked-glandular when young, soon glabrous. Flowers 10-12, in a dense truss; calyx 2-8mm, cupular when well-developed; corolla fleshy, rose-pink, with dark flecks, tubular-campanulate, with nectar pouches; ovary and style glabrous. H3. May. NE Burma, China (SE Tibet), 2,700-3,700m.

This species is allied to *R. faucium* (q.v.).

R. hypenanthum Balf.f. - is a synonym of **R. anthopogon** D.Don subsp. **hypenanthum** (Balf.f.) Cullen (Sect. Pogonanthon).

R. HYPERYTHRUM HAYATA - SUBSECT. PONTICA.
Shrub, to 2.5m; young shoots and petioles with a floccose indumentum though soon glabrescent; bud scales deciduous. Leaves 8-12 × 2.5-3.5cm, elliptic, apex more or less cuspidate, upper surface glabrous, lower surface with persistent punctate hair bases, otherwise glabrous, or with some persistent dendroid hairs, especially towards base and on midrib. Flowers *c*.10, in a lax truss; calyx *c*.3mm; corolla white, with reddish flecks, funnel-campanulate, without nectar pouches, 35-45mm; ovary densely glandular, style glandular below. H4b. April-May. Taiwan, 1,000-1,300m.

R. hyperythrum is a distinctive species without close allies.

AM 1976 (Capt. C. Ingram, Benenden, Kent) to a clone 'Omo'; flowers white.

R. hypoglaucum Hemsl. - is a synonym of **R. argyrophyllum** Franch. subsp. **hypoglaucum** (Hemsl.) D.F.Chamb.

R. HYPOLEUCUM (KOM.) HARMAJA (*LEDUM HYPOLEUCUM* KOM., *L. PALUSTRE L.* VAR. *DIVERSIPILOSUM* NAKAI) - SUBSECT. LEDUM.
Erect shrub, 0.5-1.1m; young shoots covered with a ferrugineous tomentum. Leaves 1.7-8 × 0.5-2cm, oblong-elliptic, apex acuminate, margins revolute, ciliate with long brown crisped hairs, upper surface dark green, with ferrugineous hairs, lower surface glaucous, more or less papillate, densely white-pubescent, scales rimless, golden, 1-3× their own diameter apart, midrib with long crisped ferrugineous hairs; petioles 2-7mm. Flowers numerous, in a loose terminal umbellate corymb; calyx lobes 1-2mm, orbicular; corolla white, rotate, 5-7mm; stamens 9-12; ovary ovoid, densely pubescent and scaly, style glabrous. H4. June-July. NE Russia, Japan.

R. hypoleucum may be distinguished from the remaining species in Subsect. Ledum by the pubescent undersurfaces of the leaves, on which the longer ferrugineous hairs are restricted to the midrib.

R. hypophaeum Balf.f. & Forrest - is a synonym of **R. tatsienense** Franch. (Subsect. Triflora).

R. idoneum Balf.f. & W.W.Sm. - is a synonym of **R. telmateium** Balf.f. & W.W.Sm. (Subsect. Lapponica).

R. igneum Cowan - is a synonym of **R. keysii** Nuttall (Subsect. Cinnabarina).

R. imberbe Hutch. - is probably a hybrid between **R. barbatum** Wall. ex G.Don and **R. arboreum** Sm.

R. IMPEDITUM BALF.F. & W.W.SM. (INCL. *R. LITANGENSE* BALF.F. EX HUTCH.) - SUBSECT. LAPPONICA.
Compact, much-branched shrub, to 0.9 (-1.2)m. Leaves (0.4-)0.5-1.5 × 0.3-0.7cm, broadly elliptic to ovate or oblong, apex obtuse or acute, mucronulate, lower surface covered with uniformly rusty, markedly to slightly spaced scales. Flowers to 4 per inflorescence; calyx 2.5-4mm, lobes strap-shaped; corolla violet or purple to rose-lavender, rarely white, broadly funnel-shaped, 7-15mm; stamens usually 10, about as long as the corolla; ovary scaly, style variable in length shorter or longer than the stamens, glabrous or pubescent towards base. H3-4b. April-May. China (N Yunnan, SW Sichuan), 3,300-4,600m

This species is similar to *R. polycladum* but differs in the longer calyx, etc.

AM 1944 (Sunningdale Nurseries, Windlesham, Surrey) from Rock 11469 (= USDA 59263); flowers violet.

♛ 1993

R. imperator Kingdon-Ward - is a synonym of **R. uniflorum** Kingdon-Ward var. **imperator** (Kingdon-Ward) Cullen (Subsect. Uniflora).

R. inaequale Hutch. - is a synonym of **R. formosum** Wall. var. **inaequale** C.B. Clarke (Subsect. Maddenia).

R. INDICUM SWEET - SECT. TSUTSUSI.
Much-branched shrub, usually low and prostrate though sometimes to 2m; young shoots and petioles covered with adpressed flattened chestnut brown bristles. Leaves of two kinds; spring leaves deciduous, 2-3 × 0.8-1cm, narrowly lanceolate to oblanceolate, apex acute, upper surface with scattered bristles, lower surface paler, with bristles restricted to midrib, summer leaves persistent, 1-1.8 × 0.3-0.5cm. Pedicels covered with stiff brown hairs. Flowers 1-2 per inflorescence; calyx c.1mm; corolla bright red to scarlet, occasionally rose-red, broadly funnel-shaped, 30-50mm; stamens 5; ovary densely covered with adpressed shining brown hairs, style glabrous. H3-4a. June-July. Japan (Honshu, Kyushu), 60-1,100m.

This is a widely cultivated species in its native Japan; selected forms are also to be found in gardens in Britain. It is closely allied to *R. kaempferi* (q.v.).

AM 1975 (RHS Garden, Wisley) to a very free-flowering form, with flowers red speckled crimson.

R. inopinum Balf.f. - is a chance hybrid of *R. wasonii* (Subsect. Taliensia). It was raised at Edinburgh, along with typical *R. wasonii*, from seed as Wilson 1866.

R. INSIGNE HEMSL. & E.H.WILSON - SUBSECT. ARGYROPHYLLA.
Shrub, 1.5-3.5m. Leaves 7-13 × 2-4.5cm, stiff, elliptic, apex acuminate, lower surface with a compacted fawn indumentum embedded in a shining surface film. Flowers c.8, in a lax truss, pink with a darker median stripe down each lobe, widely campanulate, nectar pouches lacking, c.40mm; ovary densely hairy, without glands, style glabrous. H4b. May-June. China (Sichuan), 2,300-3,000m.

The stiff leaves and shining fawn indumentum will distinguish this species. It has not been seen in the wild since it was originally collected by Wilson.

AM 1923 (Lady Aberconway and Hon. H.D. McLaren, Bodnant); flowers pink.

AM 1990 (E. de Rothschild, Exbury) to a clone 'Annie Darling'; trusses 14-16-flowered, white, strongly marked along the centre of each lobe and lip with red-purple, and with numerous small spots of red in upper throat. ♀ 1993

R. INTRICATUM FRANCH. (INCL. *R. BLE-PHAROCALYX* FRANCH. & *R. PERAMABILE* HUTCH.) - SUBSECT. LAPPONICA.
Compact shrub, to 1.5m. Leaves (0.4-)0.6-1.4 × 0.3-0.8cm, oblong or elliptic to rotund, apex rounded, usually mucronate, lower surface covered with uniformly buff to straw-coloured touching or overlapping scales. Flowers (1-)2-6(-8) per inflorescence; calyx 0.5-2mm; corolla pale lavender to dark blue, rarely yellowish, hypocrateriform, 8-12(-14)mm; stamens 10, included within tube; ovary scaly, style short, glabrous. H4a-b. March-May. China (N Yunnan, W Sichuan), 2,800-4,900m

The short stamens included within the corolla tube characterize this distinctive species.
FCC 1907 (Messrs J. Veitch, Chelsea); flowers rosy lilac.

R. iodes Balf.f. & Forrest - is a synonym of **R. alutaceum** Balf.f. & W.W.Sm. var. **iodes** (Balf.f. & Forrest) D.F.Chamb. (Subsect. Taliensia).

R. IRRORATUM FRANCH. - SUBSECT. IRRORATA.
Shrub or small tree, 1.5-9m. Leaves coriaceous, 7-14 × 2-3.7cm, oblanceolate to elliptic, apex acuminate, lower surface glabrous though with persistent red punctate hair bases overlying the veins. Flowers 12-17, in a dense truss, white or cream to deep pink (in cultivation), with at least a few greenish or more commonly purple flecks, campanulate or tubular-campanulate, with nectar pouches, 35-50mm; ovary and style stalked-glandular. H3-4a. March-May. Extending from SW China to Tropical Malesia.
Subsp. **irroratum** (?incl. *R. ningyuenense* Hand.-Mazz.). Ovary and calyx stalked-glandular, not tomentose. China (W & C Yunnan, SW Sichuan, Guizhou), 2,500-3,350m.
AM 1957 (Col Lord Digby, Minterne); flowers white, faintly tinged pink.

R. ningyuenense is said to differ from subsp. *irroratum* in its more hairy leaf stalks and in the more open, unspotted corollas. Plants under that name have been introduced into cultivation recently; this should allow its status to be checked.
AM 1957 (E. de Rothschild, Exbury) to a clone 'Polka Dot'; flowers white, heavily spotted deep purple, suffused pink.
Subsp. **pogonostylum** (Balf.f. & W.W.Sm..) D.F.Chamb. (*R. pogonostylum* Balf.f. & W.W.Sm.*).* Ovary and calyx tomentose and glandular. China (Yunnan, SW Sichuan), 2,100-3,000m.

There is a complete range of variation from the white to cream-flowered forms with strong flecks and exclusively glandular ovaries and calyces that occur in the north of the range of the species to forms with pink flowers, with few flecks and ovaries that are glandular and tomentose, that occur further south. Some populations contain both forms.

R. iteaphyllum Hutch. - is a synonym of **R. formosum** Wall. var. **formosum** (Subsect. Maddenia).

R. japonicum (A.Gray) Valcken - is a synonym of **R. molle** (Blume) G.Don subsp. **japonicum** (A.Gray) K.Kron (sect. Pentanthera).

R. japonicum (Blume) Schneider - is a synonym of **R. degronianum** Carrière var. **heptamerum** (Maxim.) H.Hara (Subsect. Pontica).

R. JOHNSTONEANUM WATT EX HUTCH. - SUBSECT. MADDENIA.
Shrub, 1.2-3.7m; young shoots setose. Leaves 5.5-7.5 × 2.4-3cm, broadly elliptic, apex obtuse or subacute, margins variably ciliate, upper surface with impressed midrib, lower surface brownish, with touching or overlapping scales. Flowers 3-4, in a loose terminal inflorescence, not scented; calyx disc-like, ciliate; corolla white or cream, often with a yellowish blotch and pink or purplish flush, funnel-shaped, 48-55mm, outer surface pilose

only at base, scaly; stamens 10; ovary scaly, impressed below the style that is scaly below. H2-3. April-May. India (Manipur, Mizoram), 1,850-3,100m.

This is a distinctive species.

AM 1934 (Col S. Clay, Lingfield, Surrey and Lt Col L.C.R. Messell, Nymans); flowers creamy white, with a yellow blotch.

AM 1941 (Lt Col E.H.W. Bolitho, Penzance) to a probable hybrid clone 'Rubeotinctum' from Kingdon-Ward 7732; flowers white, with a deep pink stripe on each corolla lobe and a pink or yellow blotch.

AM 1975 (Sir Giles Loder, Leonardslee, Sussex) to a clone 'Demijohn'; flowers white, throat flushed yellow-green.

♀ 1993

R. jucundum Balf.f. & W.W.Sm. - is a synonym of **R. selense** Franch. subsp. **jucundum** (Balf.f. & W.W. Sm.) D.F. Chamb. (Subsect. Selensia).

R. KAEMPFERI PLANCH. - SECT. TSUTSUSI.
Shrub, 1-3m; young shoots and petioles densely covered with adpressed flattened red-brown hairs. Leaves of two kinds; spring leaves deciduous, 2-4(-5) × 1-2.5cm, lanceolate to elliptic, apex acute or obtuse, both surfaces covered with stiff hairs especially on midrib; summer leaves persistent or deciduous, 1-2 × 0.5-1cm. Pedicels densely covered with adpressed brown stiff hairs. Flowers 2-3 per inflorescence; calyx 3-5mm; corolla red (in cultivated forms from pink to salmon-red), funnel-shaped, 20-30mm; stamens 5(-6); ovary densely covered with stiff red-brown hairs, style glabrous. H4a-b. May-June. Japan (Hokkaido to Yakushima), 600-1,000m.

Var. **kaempferi**. Flowers usually red; the smaller summer leaves usually deciduous

AM 1953, FCC 1955 (Crown Estate Commissioners, Windsor) to a clone 'Eastern Fire'; flowers Camellia Rose, darker at tips

AM 1988 (Crown Estate Commissioners, Windsor) to a clone 'Mikado'; flowers red, with some darker spotting in throat

Var. **macrogemma** Nakai. Flowers usually light purple, only occasionally red; the smaller summer leaves usually persistent.

Var. *macrogemma* is much less common in cultivation than is var. *kaempferi*.

R. kaempferi is only doubtfully distinct from *R. indicum*; it may be distinguished by its broader leaves and greater stature. In the wild it hybridizes with *R. kiusianum* where the ranges of the two species overlap (q.v.).

♀ 1993

R. KANEHIRAE E.H.WILSON - SECT. TSUTSUSI.
Much-branched shrub, 1-2.5m; young shoots and petioles densely covered with adpressed stiff broad flattened chestnut-brown hairs. Leaves of two kinds; spring leaves deciduous, 2-5 × 0.5-1.5cm, oblanceolate to narrowly obovate, apex acute, gland-tipped, both surfaces sparsely covered with stiff hairs, especially on midrib; summer leaves persistent, 1.5-3 × 0.2-0.6cm. Pedicels densely covered with stiff chestnut-brown hairs. Flowers 1(-2) per inflorescence; calyx *c*.1mm; corolla pink or carmine to scarlet, funnel-campanulate, 25-40mm; stamens 10; ovary densely covered with stiff grey or chestnut-brown hairs, style usually glabrous. H2?. March. N Taiwan, *c*.400m.

This species is apparently closely allied to *R. tashiroi*.

R. KEISKEI MIQ. - SUBSECT. TRIFLORA.
Small shrub, (0.1-)0.3-3m; young shoots scaly, sometimes also puberulent. Leaves (2.5-)3.5-7.5 × (0.8-)1.1-2.8cm, lanceolate to narrowly elliptic, apex acute or acuminate, upper surface with midrib puberulent, also hairy towards base of lamina, lower surface with large distant brown scales. Flowers 2-3(-4), in a loose terminal inflorescence; calyx with lobes absent or to 2.5mm, frequently ciliate; corolla pale yellow, unspotted, zygomorphic, funnel-

campanulate, 18-24mm, outer surface scaly, somtimes also puberulent; stamens 10; ovary scaly, impressed below the declinate, glabrous style. H4a-b. April-May. Japan, 600-1,850m.

Var. **keiskei**. Shrub, 1-2m; leaves 3-9 × 1.1-2.8cm; flowers yellow.

AM 1929 (H. White, Windlesham); flowers pale yellow.

Var. **hypoglaucum** Suto & Suzuki. Dwarf shrubs 0.3-0.5m; leaves 2-4 × 1-1.5cm, glaucous beneath; flowers white tinged yellow.

Var. **ozawae** T.Yamaz. Dwarf shrubs, 10-15cm tall; leaves 1.5-2.5 × 1-1.5cm; flowers yellow.

AM 1970 (B.N. Starling, Epping Upland, Essex) to a clone of var. *ozawae*, 'Yaku Fairy'; habit very dwarf, flowers yellow.

♀ 1993, to a clone of var. *ozawae*, 'Yaku Fairy'.

The dwarf forms of this distinctive species, especially those of var. *ozawae* from Yakushima, are good rock garden subjects.

R. keleticum Balf.f. & Forrest - is a synonym of **R. calostrotum** Balf.f. & Kingdon-Ward subsp. **keleticum** (Balf.f. & Forrest) Cullen (Subsect. Saluenensia).

R. KENDRICKII NUTTALL (?INCL. *R. SHEPHERDII* NUTTALL) - SUBSECT. IRRORATA. Shrub or small tree, 3-8m. Leaves subcoriaceous, 10-13.5 × 2-3.5cm, narrowly elliptic to narrowly oblanceolate, apex acuminate, margin usually strongly undulate, lower surface with hairs on midrib, otherwise glabrous, punctate hair bases not persisting. Flowers fleshy, 10-20, in a dense truss, deep rose to scarlet, with darker flecks, tubular-campanulate, with nectar pouches, 30-40mm; ovary with a few dendroid hairs, eglandular, style glabrous. H2-3. April-May. Bhutan, NE India (Arunachal Pradesh), China (S Tibet), 2,300-2,800m.

Closely allied to *R. ramsdenianum*, which may be distinguished by its broader leaves.

R. shepherdii, which is not now in cultivation, is probably a form of *R. kendrickii* but material is not available to confirm this.

R. KESANGIAE D.G.LONG & RUSHFORTH - SUBSECT. GRANDIA. Large shrub or tree, 3-12m; bark rough. Leaves (15-)20-30 × (7-)10-16cm, broadly elliptic to obovate, apex rounded to more or less truncate and mucronate, lower surface covered with a dense white to silvery matted floccose indumentum composed of dendroid hairs; petioles terete. Flowers 7-8-lobed, 20-25, in a dense truss, pale to deep pink, with a large purple basal blotch and nectar pouches, funnel-campanulate, 30-47mm; stamens 14-16; ovary densely glandular, with or without a sparse eglandular tomentum. H4a. April-May. Bhutan, 2,750-3,500m.

Var. **kesangiae**. Flowers rich purple.

Var. **album** D.G.Long. Flowers white.

A recently described species that is apparently quite common in C Bhutan.

R. KEYSII NUTTALL (INCL. VAR. *UNICOLOR* HUTCH. & *R. IGNEUM* COWAN) - SUBSECT. CINNABARINA. Straggling shrub, 1-3.5m; young shoots scaly. Leaves 6-10(-15) × 1.9-3(-3.6)cm, elliptic, apex acute, lower surface densely covered with close to distant unequal flat broad-rimmed scales. Flowers pendulous, 2-5 per inflorescence, the individual inflorescences often fusing together; calyx minute; corolla tubular, deep red to salmon pink, lobes usually yellow, (14-)20-25mm; stamens 10, declinate; ovary scaly, slightly pubescent at top, style declinate, pubescent towards base. H3-4a. June-July. India (Sikkim, Arunachal Pradesh), Bhutan, China (S Tibet), 2,440-3,650m.

A distinctive species without close allies.

AM 1933 (L. de Rothschild, Exbury) as var. *unicolor*, from Kingdon-Ward 6257; flowers Carthamus Red, tips of corolla lobes slightly yellowish.

R. KIUSIANUM MAKINO - SECT. TSUTSUSI.

Dwarf, much-branched shrub, 0.6-1m; young shoots covered with adpressed flattened red-brown hairs. Leaves of one kind, deciduous, 0.5-3 × 0.2-1.5cm, oval-obovate, apex acute, both surfaces, and petioles, covered with stiff red-brown hairs. Pedicels covered with stiff red-brown hairs. Flowers 2-3 per inflorescence; calyx 2-3mm; corolla usually rose-pink, occasionally rose to deep purple, funnel-shaped, 15-20mm; stamens 5; ovary densely covered with stiff red-brown hairs, style glabrous. H4a-b. May-June. Japan (Kyushu), 600-800m.

Var. **kiusianum.** Leaves 0.5-2 × 0.2-1cm, oval to obovate.

AM 1977 (Capt. C. Ingram, Benenden, Kent) to a clone 'Chidori'; flowers white.

AM 1981 (Crown Estate Commissioners, Windsor) to a clone 'Mountain Gem'; flowers in clusters of 2-3, corolla red-purple.

♀ 1993

Var **sataense** (Nakai) D.F.Chamb. Leaves 1-3 × 0.5-1.5cm, ovate-elliptic.

Var. *sataense* is intermediate between var. *kiusianum* and *R. kaempferi* and may have arisen as a hybrid. Hybrids with this parentage occurs in the wild and selected forms have almost certainly been cultivated for several hundred years, giving rise to at least some of the cultivars described under *R. obtusum* and also those known as the 'Kurume' azaleas.

R. stenopetalum and *R. ripense* are also involved as parents in some of these cultivars.

R. saisiuense Nakai is apparently a dwarf form of *R. kiusianum* that originated in Korea.

R. KIYOSUMENSE (MAKINO) MAKINO - SECT. BRACHYCALYX.
Shrub or small tree; young shoots glabrous. Leaves in whorls of up to three, at the ends of the branches, 3-5 × 2.5-3cm, rhombic, apex acuminate, lower surface sparsely covered with brown simple hairs, at least when young, midrib glabrous or shortly pilose; petioles glabrous or with scattered brown hairs near base of lamina.

Flowers 1-2 per inflorescence, appearing before the leaves; calyx minute; corolla purple, open-campanulate, 20-30mm; stamens 10; ovary densely and stiffly hairy, style glabrous H4a-b. Japan (E Honshu), *c.* 650m.

This species is probably allied to *R. maybarae* and *R. nudipes* but differs in the shape of the leaf apex.

R. KONGBOENSE HUTCH. - SECT. POGONANTHUM.
Spindly much-branched low shrub, to 1m; leaf bud scales deciduous. Leaves 1.3-2.8 × 0.6-1.2cm, oblong or elliptic-oblong, apex subacute, lower surface with 1 tier of plastered pale brown more or less overlapping scales, most with well-developed domed centres. Flowers many, in a dense racemose umbel; calyx lobes 3-4mm; corolla pink to red, rarely pinkish white, hypercrateriform, tube 6-8mm, pilose on outer surface, densely so within, especially at mouth, lobes 2.5-4mm; stamens 5; ovary scaly. H4a-b. March-May. China (S Tibet), 3,200-4,700m.

Closely resembling *R. primuliflorum*, but differing in the form of the scales, the leaf shape, habit and flower colour.

R. kuluense D.F.Chamb. - is a synonym of **R. adenosum** Davidian (Subsect. Glischra).

R. kwangfuense Chun & Fang - is a synonym of **R. fortunei** Lindl. subsp. **discolor** (Franch.) D.F.Chamb. (Subsect. Fortunea).

R. KYAWII LACE & W.W.SM. (INCL. *R. AGAPETUM* BALF.F. & KINGDON-WARD) - SUBSECT. PARISHIA.
Shrub or small tree, 3-9m; young shoots densely stellate-tomentose and glandular-setose. Leaves 9-22(-30) × 4-9(-10)cm, elliptic to oblong, upper surface glabrous, lower surface glabrescent or with a more or less persistent stellate tomentum intermixed with a few glands. Flowers 10-15, in a lax truss; calyx 1-2mm; corolla bright crimson to scarlet, without flecks, tubular-

campanulate, with nectar pouches, 45-60mm; ovary densely stellate-tomentose, also with setose glands, style floccose and stalked-glandular, at least in the lower half. H2(-3). July. NE Burma, China (W Yunnan), 1,800-3,650m.

This species may be distinguished from the allied *R. facetum* and *R. elliottii* by its setose hairs.

R. LACTEUM FRANCH. - SUBSECT. TALIENSIA.
Shrub or small tree, 2-7.5m. Leaves 8-17 × 4.5-7cm, elliptic to obovate, apex rounded, apiculate, lower surface covered with a thin one-layered compacted indumentum composed of grey-brown radiate hairs; petioles glabrescent. Flowers 15-30, in a dense truss; calyx *c*.1mm; corolla pure yellow, without flecks though a purple blotch is sometimes present, widely campanulate, nectar pouches lacking, 40-50mm; ovary densely tomentose, style glabrous. H4a-b. April-May. China (W & N Yunnan), 3,700-4,000m.

A distinctive species on account of its yellow flowers and stellate indumentum. In cultivation there are forms with a pink flush to the corolla. These may be hybrids with *R. cyanocarpum*.
FCC 1926 (A.M. Williams, Werrington Park, Cornwall); flowers Sulphur White, with a dark crimson blotch.
FCC 1965 (S.F. Christie, Blackhills, Elgin) to a clone 'Blackhills'; flowers yellow, without a blotch or spots.

R. LAGOPUS NAKAI - SECT. BRACHYCALYX.
Shrub or small tree; young shoots glabrous. Leaves in whorls of up to three, at the ends of the branches, 3.5-5 × 2.5-4cm, rhombic, apex acute, lower surface sparsely pilose, more densely so over lower part of midrib; petioles densely lanate. Pedicels covered with brown pubescent hairs. Flowers 1-2, appearing before or with the leaves; calyx minute; corolla rose-purple, funnel-campanulate, 20-30mm; stamens 8-10; ovary densely pale brown villose, style glabrous. H4. May.

Var. *lagopus* differs from the closely allied *R. nudipes* in the densely lanate petioles, etc. and is the only form of this species in cultivation.

R. lampropeplum Balf.f. & Forrest - is a synonym of **R. proteoides** Balf.f. & W.W.Sm. (Subsect. Taliensia).

R. LANATOIDES D.F.CHAMB. - SUBSECT. LANATA.
Shrub, 2-4m. Leaves coriaceous, 9-11 × 2-3.2cm, lanceolate, apex acuminate, lower surface covered with a dense thick dark fawn to light brown indumentum composed of dendroid hairs with long straight branches. Flowers 10-15, in a dense truss, white flushed pink, with a few flecks, campanulate, lacking nectar pouches, 35-40mm; ovary densely brown-tomentose, style glabrous. H4a-b?. February-April. China (SE Tibet), 3,200-3,650m.

This species is apparently quite distinct from all the remaining members of the subsection, though it is probably allied to *R. luciferum*.

R. LANATUM HOOK.F. - SUBSECT. LANATA.
Shrub, 0.5-3m. Leaves coriaceous, leathery, 6-12 × 1.8-5cm, elliptic to obovate, apex rounded, apiculate, lower surface covered with a dense thick, coffee-brown indumentum composed of dendroid more or less crisped hairs. Flowers 5-10, in a lax truss, creamy yellow, with crimson flecks, campanulate, without nectar pouches, 32-50mm; ovary densely tomentose, style glabrous. H4a-b. April-May. NE India (Sikkim), W Bhutan, China (S Tibet), 3,000-4,500m.

A difficult species to cultivate, apparently liking relatively dry sites. It is closely allied to *R. flinckii* but it is distinguished by the darker and thicker leaf indumentum.

R. LANIGERUM TAGG (INCL. *R. SILVATICUM* COWAN) - SUBSECT. ARBOREA.
Shrub or small multi-stemmed tree, 2.7-6m. Leaves 16-22 × 5-7cm, elliptic to

oblanceolate, lower surface with a two-layered white to fawn indumentum, the upper layer dense and woolly, composed of dendroid hairs, the lower compacted. Flowers 20-25(-50), in a dense inflorescence, deep rose-pink to reddish purple, with darker nectar pouches, campanulate, *c*.35mm. H3-4a. March-April. China (S Tibet), NE India, 2,550-3,350m.

The red-flowered forms of this species have been referred to *R. silvaticum.*

AM 1949 (Col E.H.W. Bolitho, Trengwainton, Cornwall); flowers Carmine.

AM 1951 (Mrs R.M.Stevenson, Tower Court, Ascot) as *R. silvaticum,* from Kingdon-Ward 6258.

AM 1951 (Crown Estate Commissioners, Windsor) to a clone 'Round Wood', as *R. silvaticum,* from Kingdon-Ward 6258; flowers crimson.

AM 1954 (R.O. Hambro, Logan House, Stranraer) to a clone 'Sylvia', as *R. silvaticum*; flowers pale crimson, suffused white, with a dark crimson ring in the throat.

AM 1961 (R. Strauss, Stonehurst, Ardingly, Sussex) to a clone 'Stonehurst'; flowers a light shade of Cherry, in clusters of *c*.35.

AM 1961 and FCC 1967 (Crown Estate Commissioners, Windsor) to a clone 'Chapel Wood'; flowers Neyron Rose, in trusses of up to 50.

R. LAPPONICUM (L.) WAHLENB. (INCL. *R. PARVIFOLIUM* ADAMS) - SUBSECT. LAPPONICA.
Prostrate to erect shrub, to 1m. Leaves 0.4-2(-2.5) × 0.2-0.7(-0.9)cm, oblong-elliptic to elliptic-ovate, apex obtuse or rounded, mucronate, lower surface covered with a mixture of touching, straw-coloured to fawn and ferrugineous scales. Flowers 3-6; calyx lobes 1-2mm, deltoid; corolla violet-rose to purple or sometimes white, broadly funnel-shaped, 7-15mm; stamens 5-10, about as long as the corolla; ovary scaly, style longer than the stamens, glabrous. H4b-c. March-April. Circumpolar, USA (Alaska), Canada, Greenland, Scandinavia, Arctic Russia.

A distinctive and widespread species that is difficult in cultivation.

PC 1993 (A.J. Richards, Newcastle upon Tyne) to a clone 'Brian Davidson', from seed collected in Norway by Brian Davidson.

R. lasiopodum Hutch. - is a synonym of **R. rosseatum** Hutch. (Subsect. Maddenia).

R. LATOUCHEAE FRANCH. (INCL. *R. WILSONIAE* HEMSL. & E.H.WILSON) - SECT. CHONIASTRUM.
Shrub, to 7m. Leaves 5-10 × 1.8-5cm, broadly obovate to elliptic-lanceolate, glabrous when mature, apex acuminate. Flowers single, axillary below terminal vegetative bud, pink to purple, with darker spots on upper lobe, funnel-shaped; tube *c*.10mm; lobes *c*.25mm, spreading; stamens 10. H1b-3. April-May. C, S & E China, Japan, 1,000-2,000m.

Rare in cultivation and tender.

AM 1971 (Crown Estate Commissioners, Windsor) as *R. wilsoniae*; flowers purple, red-purple at base, with brown mottling in throat.

R. LAUDANDUM COWAN - SECT. POGONANTHUM.
Small shrub, usually to 0.6m; leaf bud scales persistent but not conspicuous. Leaves 1.1-1.7 × 0.6-0.9cm, oblong to ovate or almost orbicular, apex rounded, slightly mucronate; lower surface covered with 2-3 tiers of overlapping chocolate-brown scales, the lowest tier as dark as or darker than the upper tiers. Flowers many, in a dense racemose umbel; calyx lobes 5-6mm; corolla white or pink, rarely yellowish, hypocrateriform, tube 4.5-11.5mm, outer surface pilose, inner surface densely pilose at mouth, lobes 3.5-6mm; stamens 5-6; ovary scaly, sometimes also sparsely puberulent. H4a-b. April-May. China (SE Tibet), 2,900-4,700m.

Var. **laudandum**. Leaves 2 or more times as long as broad; corolla usually pink, tube densely pilose outside.

Var. **temoense** Kingdon-Ward ex

Cowan & Davidian. Leaves less than 2× as long as broad; corolla usually white, tube laxly pilose outside.

The two varieties intergrade; it is therefore not always possible to assign individual plants to a variety.

R. laxiflorum Balf.f. & Forrest - is a synonym of **R. annae** Franch. (Subsect. Irrorata).

R. leei Fang - is a synonym of **R. prattii** Franch. (Subsect. Taliensia).

R. LEPIDOSTYLUM BALF.F & FORREST - SUBSECT. TRICHOCLADA.

Shrub, 0.5-1.5m; young shoots scaly and densely setose. Leaves evergreen, thick, with a persistent bluish bloom, 3-3.5 × 1.5-1.8cm, obovate to obovate-elliptic, apex rounded, margin revolute, lower surface with equal golden scales. Flowers 2(-3) in a loose terminal inflorescence; calyx lobes 1-7mm, ciliate; corolla clear yellow, sometimes with orange spots, funnel-campanulate, 20-33mm, outer surface scaly and sparsely setose; stamens 10; ovary scaly and densely setose, impressed below the style that is strongly deflexed and usually glabrous, though rarely with a few scales at base. H4a-b. May-June. China (SW Yunnan), 3,050-3,650m.

The thick bluish leaves make this a distinctive species.

AM 1969 (Capt. C. Ingram, Benenden, Kent); flowers green-yellow.

♀ 1993

R. LEPIDOTUM WALL. EX D.DON - SUBSECT. LEPIDOTA.

Small shrub, to 2m; young shoots densely scaly. Leaves semi-persistent or persistent, thick, 0.6-2.5(-3) × 0.3-1.2(-1.6)cm, narrowly elliptic to obovate, margin not ciliate, lower surface with distant to overlapping large brownish scales with translucent rims. Flowers 1-2, in a loose terminal inflorescence; calyx lobes 2-4mm; flowers white, yellow or pink to purple, often with darker spots, campanulate, 10-17mm; stamens 10; ovary scaly, style very

short, deflexed. H3-4b. April-May. N India (Kashmir to Arunachal Pradesh), Nepal, Bhutan, N Burma, China (S Tibet, NW Yunnan), 2,450-4,550m.

A widespread and variable species, especially in respect to flower colour and leaf shape.

R. LEPTOCARPUM NUTT. (INCL. *R. MICROMERES* TAGG) - SUBSECT. BOOTHIA.

Usually an epiphytic shrub, to 2m; young shoots scaly, glabrous. Leaves 5.5-7.5 × 1.8-2.5cm, elliptic or narrowly elliptic, apex rounded, mucronate, lower surface papillose, scales close, yellow, unequal, the smaller sunk in pits, their rims upturned. Pedicels thin, 25-35mm, scaly; Flowers 4-10 per inflorescence; calyx lobes 2-5mm, well-developed, spreading or reflexed; corolla yellow, campanulate, 9-13mm; tube 4-6mm, scaly outside, hairy within; stamens 10, regular; ovary scaly, tapering into the declinate style. H3-4a. April-May. NE India (Arunachal Pradesh), Bhutan, NE Burma, China (NW Yunnan, S Tibet), 2,450-3,350(-4,300)m.

A distinctive species, without close relatives.

R. LEPTOTHRIUM BALF.F. & FORREST (INCL. *R. BACHII* H.LÉV.) - SECT. AZALEASTRUM.

Shrub, to 8m. Bark red-brown, peeling. Leaves 3.5-12 × 1.5-3.5cm, narrowly elliptic to lanceolate, apex acute to blunt. Flowers single, borne laterally below vegetative buds, rose to purple, with darker markings, rotate, *c.*50mm across, tube short, lobes spreading; stamens 5. H2-3. April-May. NE Burma, SW China, 2,150-3,300m.

This species is usually frost sensitive and hence difficult to grow outside in Britain.

R. LEUCASPIS TAGG - SUBSECT. BOOTHIA.

Small shrub, to 1m; young shoots densely covered with straight bristles. Leaves 3-4.5 × 1.8-2.2cm, broadly elliptic, apex obtuse, upper surface densely covered with setae, lower surface with vesicular scales sunk in pits. Flowers 1-2 per inflorescence; calyx lobes 7-8mm, obovate; corolla white, often tinged pink, broadly campanulate to rotate, 25-30mm; tube scaly outside, pilose within; stamens 10; ovary scaly, tapering into the sharply deflexed style. H3. March-April. China (S Tibet), 2,450-3,050m.

AM 1929 (L. de Rothschild, Exbury) from Kingdon-Ward 6273; flowers with a touch of Sulphur Yellow at the base of the corolla internally.

♀ 1994

R. LEVINEI MERR. - SUBSECT. MADDENIA. Shrub, 3-4m; young shoots with or without setae. Leaves thick and coriaceous, 6-6.5 × c.3cm, oblong-obovate, apex rounded, mucronate; margin setose, upper surface with an impressed midrib, lower surface covered with slightly unequal golden scales. Flowers solitary or up to 3, in a loose terminal inflorescence, scented; calyx lobes c.8mm, scaly; corolla white, funnel-campanulate, c.45mm, outer surface scaly; stamens 10; ovary scaly, tapering into the style that is scaly at base. H1b?. China (Guizhou, Guangdong), c.950m.

It is not clear whether any of the plants in cultivation fit the above description; material collected in S China by Walder differs in its significantly larger (8-9cm) flowers.

R. levistratum Balf.f. & Forrest - is a synonum of **R. phaeochrysum** Balf.f. & W.W.Sm. var. **levistratum** (Balf.f. & Forrest) D.F.Chamb. (Subsect. Taliensia).

R. LINDLEYI T.MOORE - SUBSECT. MADDENIA.
A straggly upright usually epiphytic shrub, 1-4m; young shoots lacking setae. Leaves 8.5-13 × 3-4.5cm, narrowly elliptic to oblong-elliptic, apex obtuse or rounded, margin not setose, upper surface with raised midrib, lower surface greyish green, with distant unequal reddish brown scales. Flowers 2-3(-5), in a loose terminal inflorescence, scented; calyx conspicuous, lobes 11-18 × 5-8(-10)mm, ciliate;

corolla white or cream with an orange-yellow blotch at base, openly funnel-campanulate, 65-95mm, outer surface without or with a few scales, glabrous or pubescent at base; stamens 10; ovary densely scaly, tapering into the style that is scaly in the lower half. H2-3. Nepal, India (W Bengal, Arunachal Pradesh, Manipur), Bhutan, China (S Tibet), 2,000-2,750m.

This species is close to *R. dalhousiae* (q.v.).

AM 1935 (L. de Rothschild, Exbury); flowers flushed rose magenta.

AM 1965 (G. Gorer, Sunte House, Haywards Heath) to a clone 'Dame Edith Sitwell'; flowers white, tinged pale pink. This may be a hybrid.

AM 1969 (A.C. & J.F.A. Gibson, Glenarn, Dunbartonshire) to a clone 'Geordie Sherriff'; flowers strongly flushed externally with red-purple.

FCC 1937 (Vice Adm. A.W. Heneage-Vivian, Clyne Castle, Swansea); flowers with a tinge of pink at the ends of the corolla lobes.

♀ 1993

R. linearifolium Sieb & Zucc. - is a synonym of **R. stenopetalum** (Sect. Tsutsusi).

R. litangense Balf.f. ex Hutch. is a synonym of **R. impeditum** Balf.f. & W.W.Sm. (Subsect. Lapponica).

R. lithophilum Balf.f. & Kingdon-Ward - is a synonym of **R. trichocladum** Franch. var. **trichocladum** (Subsect. Trichoclada).

R. litiense Balf.f. & Forrest - is a synonym of **R. wardii** W.W.Sm. var. **wardii** (Subsect. Campylocarpa).

R. LONGESQUAMATUM SCHNEIDER - SUBSECT. MACULIFERA.
Shrub, 3-4m; young shoots and petioles densely rufous tomentose. Leaves 6-11 × 2-3.5cm, elliptic to oblanceolate, apex shortly cuspidate, upper surface shortly stalked-glandular and rufous-tomentose when young; lower surface ultimately with lamina glabrous though with a

rufous tomentum composed of flagellate hairs covering the midrib. Flowers 4-6, in a lax truss; calyx 6-10mm, lobes lingulate; corolla rose-pink, with a basal blotch, open-campanulate, without nectar pouches, 40-45mm; ovary and lower half of style stalked-glandular. H4b. May. China (Sichuan, Guizhou), 2,300-3,350m.

A distinctive species without close allies.

R. LONGIPES REHDER & E.H.WILSON - SUBSECT. ARGYROPHYLLA.
Shrub or small tree, 1-10m; young shoots pubescent. Leaves 5-11 × 1.5-3cm, oblanceolate, apex cuspidate, lower surface covered with a felted to compacted fawn or brownish indumentum that is intermixed with a few glands. Flowers 8-15, in a lax truss; calyx 1-2mm; corolla pinkish to pale purple, with darker flecks, funnel-campanulate, 30-35mm; ovary rufous-tomentose and glandular, style glabrous. H4a-b. China (Sichuan, Guizhou), 2,000-2,900m.

This species has only recently been introduced into cultivation.

R. LONGISTYLUM REHDER & E.H.WILSON - SUBSECT. TEPHROPEPLA.
Shrub, 0.5-2m. Leaves 3.5-5.2 × 1-1.5cm, apex acute, upper surface persistently scaly, lower surface pale green, papillose, scales distant, unequal, golden and brown, with broad rims. Flowers (1-)2-3, in a loose terminal inflorescence that has a 3-12mm rhachis; calyx lobes narrowly triangular, to 4mm, not ciliate but fringed with scales; corolla white, narrowly funnel-shaped, c.20mm, outer surface lacking scales, glabrous; stamens 10; ovary impressed below the declinate, glabrous style. H3. April-May. China (C Sichuan), 1,300-2,300m.

This species has a restricted distribution in the wild and is rare in cultivation.

R. lopohogynum Balf.f. & Forrest ex Hutch. - is a synonym of **R. trichocladum** Franch. var. **trichocladum** (Subsect. Trichoclada).

R. lopsangianum Cowan - is a synonym of **R. thomsonii** Hook.f. subsp. **lopsangianum** (Cowan) D.F.Chamb. (Subsect. Thomsonia).

R. LOWNDESII DAVIDIAN - SUBSECT. LEPIDOTA.
Creeping shrub, to 0.25m; young shoots glabrous. Leaves deciduous, thin, 1.5-2.5 × 0.6-1.1cm, narrowly elliptic to oblanceolate, margin slightly crenulate, ciliate, lower surface with distant yellow scales with broad translucent margins. Flowers 1-2, in a terminal inflorescence; calyx lobes c.3mm; corolla yellow, sometimes spotted or streaked with red, campanulate, 13-15mm, outer surface usually densely scaly; stamens 10; ovary scaly, style short, deflexed. H3-4a. May-June. Nepal, 3,800-4,550m.

R. LUCIFERUM (COWAN) COWAN - SUBSECT. LANATA.
Shrub or small tree, 1.5-7.5m. Leaves coriaceous, 8.5-11 × 3-4.5 cm, elliptic to ovate, apex acute to acuminate, lower surface covered with a thick rusty brown indumentum composed of dendroid hairs. Flowers 8-10, in a dense truss, pale yellow, with at least a few red flecks, funnel-campanulate, without nectar pouches, 30-45mm; ovary densely covered with a pale brown tomentum; style glabrous. H4a-b. April-May. China (SE Tibet), 3,350-4,000m.

This species is closely allied to *R. lanatum* but it is usually a larger plant, with a reddish brown leaf indumentum. It also has a more Easterly distribution.

R. LUDLOWII COWAN - SUBSECT. UNIFLORA
Small spreading shrub, to 0.3m; young shoots scaly, glabrous. Leaves c.1.5 × 1cm, broadly obovate or oblong-obovate, apex obtuse, margin crenate, lower surface with distant narrowly rimmed brown scales. Flowers solitary, terminal; calyx lobes c.7mm, ciliate, corolla yellow, drying greenish yellow, sometimes with red spots, broadly funnel-campanulate, 20-

23mm, tube *c*.14mm, outer surface densely scaly and pubescent; stamens 10; ovary scaly, impressed below the declinate, glabrous style that is longer than the stamens. H4a. April-May. China (S Tibet), *c*.4,000m.

This is a distinctive species that is rare in the wild.

R. LUDWIGIANUM HOSSEUS - SUBSECT. MADDENIA.
Free-growing shrub, to 1.5m; young shoots lacking setae. Leaves 3-7 × 1.5-3.5cm, obovate, apex rounded, margin not ciliate, upper surface with midrib impressed; lower surface covered with dense but not overlapping brownish scales. Flowers 2-3, in a loose terminal inflorescence, not scented; calyx disc-like, ciliate; corolla white and pink, funnel-campanulate, *c*.65mm, outer surface pubescent, with scales restricted to the lobes; stamens 10; ovary scaly, tapering into the style that is scaly and pubescent below. H1b. March-April. Thailand, 1,600-2,180m.

R. LUKIANGENSE FRANCH. - SUBSECT. IRRORATA.
Shrub or small tree, 1-7.5m. Leaves coriaceous, 8-16.5 × 3-5.2cm, elliptic to oblanceolate, apex acuminate, lower surface of leaves glabrous though with persistent red punctate hairs bases overlying the veins. Flowers 6-15, in a truss, pale to deep magenta rose, darker on the lobe margins, with darker flecks and usually also a basal blotch; tubular-campanulate; ovary glabrous to sparsely rufous-tomentose, style glabrous. H2-3. March-April. China (SE Tibet, NW Yunnan, SW Sichuan), 2,100-3,350m.

This species is closely allied to *R. irroratum* but may be distinguished from the latter species by its glabrous style. The subspecies that have been recognized in the past intergrade to such an extent that their maintenance is not justified.

R. LUTEIFLORUM (DAVIDIAN) CULLEN - SUBSECT. GLAUCA.

Shrub, to 1m; shoots with a peeling brown bark. Leaves (4-)6.8 × 1.5-2.6cm, elliptic, apex obtuse, lower surface with a glaucous papillate epidermis, scales 3-8× their own diameter apart, unequal, the smaller golden, the larger brown. Pedicels scaly. Flowers 3-6 per inflorescence; calyx lobes 6-8mm, lacking a tuft of hairs at the obtuse apex; corolla bright yellow, campanulate, 20-22mm; stamens 10, regular; ovary scaly, style sharply deflexed, glabrous. H3. April-May. NE Burma, 3,050-3,350m.

Closely allied to *R. glaucophyllum* but differing in the obtuse elliptic leaves, the calyx lobes lacking a tuft of hairs at the apex, and in the bright yellow flowers.

AM 1960 and FCC 1966 (National Trust for Scotland, Brodick Castle Gardens) to a clone 'Glen Cloy', from Kingdon-Ward 21556; flowers Dresden Yellow.

R. LUTESCENS FRANCH. - SUBSECT. TRIFLORA.
Straggling shrub, to 6m; bark brown, flaking; young shoots scaly, otherwise glabrous. Leaves 5-9 × 1.3-2.6(-3.7)cm, lanceolate to oblong, apex acuminate, with a long drip-tip, margins crenulate, upper surface scaly, usually glabrous; lower surface with large distant broad-rimmed golden scales. Flowers 1-3, in a loose, usually axillary inflorescence; calyx minute, ciliate; corolla pale yellow with greenish spots, zygomorphic, widely funnel-campanulate, 18-25mm, outer surface with tube pubescent, the hairs retrorse; stamens 10; ovary scaly, style impressed below the declinate, glabrous style. H3-4a. February-April. China (Yunnan, W Sichuan, Guizhou), (550-)1,750-3,000m.

This species is distinctive on account of its well-developed leaf drip-tip.

AM 1953 (Mrs R.M. Stevenson, Tower Court, Ascot) to a clone 'Bagshot Sands'; flowers Primrose Yellow with darker spots.

FCC 1938 (L. de Rothschild, Exbury) to a clone 'Exbury'; flowers clear Lemon Yellow.

♀ 1993, to a clone 'Bagshot Sands'.

R. LUTEUM SWEET - SUBSECT. PENTANTHERA.
Deciduous shrub, to 2m; young twigs densely covered with gland-tipped and/or eglandular multicellular hairs. Leaves 6.5-12(-14.5) × 1.6-3.4(-4.2)cm, ovate or obovate to elliptic, lower surface sometimes glaucous, covered with glandular or eglandular hairs. Flower bud scales glabrous to (occasionally) covered with unicellular hairs, margins glandular. Pedicels densely covered with gland-tipped hairs. Flowers with a sweet fragrance, appearing before or with the leaves, 9-17, in a shortened raceme; calyx 1-4(-7)mm; corolla yellow, with a darker yellow blotch on the upper lobe, funnelform, tube gradually expanding into the limb, outer surface covered with unicellular and gland-tipped hairs, 25-50mm. Capsule covered with unicellular and gland-tipped hairs. H4b. May-June. Eastern Europe, Turkey, Caucasia, s.l.-2,300m.

R. luteum may be distinguished from the allied *R. austrinum* by the yellow flowers with a darker blotch and by the less hairy capsules.

♀ 1993.

R. LYI H.LÉV. - SUBSECT. MADDENIA.
Shrub, to 2m; young shoots with persistent setae. Leaves 7-8 × 2.5-3cm, narrowly obovate, apex bluntly acute, margin with or without bristles, upper surface with impressed midrib, lower surface brown, with dense, but not touching, scales. Flowers (2-)3-4, in a loose terminal inflorescence, scented; calyx lobes 1-2mm, usually fringed with setae; corolla white, funnel-campanulate, 45-60mm, outer surface scaly throughout; stamens 10; ovary densely scaly, tapering into the style which is scaly below. H1b-2. China (Guizhou), Vietnam, Laos, 1,400-2,200m.

This species, which is rare in cultivation, is allied to *R. ciliicalyx* and to *R. roseatum*, but differs in the more persistent setae on the young stems.

R. lysolepis Hutch. - is a hybrid of **R. flavidum** Franch. (Subsect. Lapponica).

R. MACABEANUM WATT EX BALF.F. - SUBSECT. GRANDIA.
Tree, to 15m; bark rough. Leaves 14-25 × 9-18.5cm, broadly ovate to broadly elliptic, apex rounded, often apiculate, lower surface with a dense two-layered indumentum, the upper layer lanate-tomentose, composed of rosulate and ramiform hairs, the lower compacted; petioles terete. Flowers 15-25, in a dense truss, 8-lobed, lemon yellow, with a purple blotch in the throat, tubular- to narrowly funnel-campanulate, with nectar pouches, *c*.50 mm; stamens 16; ovary densely rufous-tomentose. H3-4a. March-May. NE India (Manipur, Nagaland), 2,500-3,000m.

In cultivation the hybrids with *R. sinogrande* are often difficult to distinguish from this species, but usually can be separated by the floccose leaf indumentum that tends to rub off.

AM 1937 and FCC 1938 (Lt Col E.H.W. Bolitho, Trengwainton, Cornwall); flowers yellowish white, with a bright red stigma.

♀ 1993

R. MACROPHYLLUM D.DON EX G.DON - SUBSECT. PONTICA.
Shrub, 2-4m; young shoots and petioles soon more or less glabrous. Leaves (6.5-)8.5-12(-17) × 3-5.2(-7.5cm), broadly elliptic, apex acute to minutely apiculate, upper and lower surfaces glabrous when mature. Flowers 10-20, in a dense truss; calyx *c*.1mm; corolla white to pink, with yellowish flecks, broadly campanulate, without nectar pouches, 30-40mm; ovary densely rufous-pilose, style glabrous. H4a-b. May-June. Western seaboard of America, s.l.-150m.

Closely allied to *R. maximum* though with relatively broader leaves, 2.5-2.8× as long as broad.

R. macrosepalum Maxim. - is a synonym of **R. stenopetalum** (Hogg) Mabb. (sect. Tsutsusi).

145

R. macrosmithii Davidian - is a synonym of **R. argipeplum** Balf.f. & Cooper.

R. MACULIFERUM FRANCH. - SUBSECT. MACULIFERA.
Shrub or small tree, 1-10m; young shoots and petioles with an evanescent tomentum. Leaves 5-10 × 2.7-4.2cm, oblong to obovate, apex rounded, apiculate, lower surface with lamina glabrous at maturity though with a thick tomentum composed of folioliferous hairs overlying the midrib. Flowers 5-10, in a lax truss; calyx *c*.1mm; corolla white, sometimes suffused with pale pink, with a purple blotch and a few flecks, open-campanulate, nectar pouches lacking, 25-30mm; ovary densely rufous-tomentose, style glabrous. H4b. April. N, C & S China, 1,200-3,000m.

A rare species in cultivation. It is probably allied to *R. anwheiense*.

R. maculiferum Franch. var. *anwheiense* (E.H.Wilson) D.F. Chamb. - is a synonym of **R. anwheiense** E.H.Wilson (Subsect. Maculifera).

R. MADDENII HOOK.F. - SUBSECT. MADDENIA.
Free-growing or epiphytic shrub, to 2.5m; young shoots lacking setae. Leaves 6-16 (-18) × 2.8-6(-8)cm, elliptic to broadly obovate, apex acute or obtuse, margin not ciliate, upper surface with midrib impressed; lower surface often brownish, the scales overlapping. Flowers (1-)2-5 (-7), in a loose terminal inflorescence, scented; calyx lobes (3-)5-12(-16)mm; corolla white, often flushed pink or purplish, rarely totally pink, usually with a yellow blotch at base, at first narrowly funnel-campanulate, later funnel-campanulate, (35-)60-85(-100)mm, outer surface scaly from base to middle of lobes; stamens (15-)17-27; ovary divided into (8-)10(-12) chambers, densely scaly, tapering into the scaly style. H2-3. May-June. N India, Bhutan, N Burma, SW China, N Vietnam.
Subsp. **maddenii** (incl. *R. calophyllum* Nuttall, *R. brachysiphon* Balf.f. ex Hutch. &

R. polyandrum Hutch.). Leaves 6-11(-15) × 2.8-4(-5.5)cm, often obovate; filaments of stamens often glabrous; capsule ovoid-globose, apex rounded. India (Sikkim, Arunachal Pradesh), Bhutan, China (SE Tibet), 1,900-2,600m.

R. brachysiphon is distinctive, with small flowers, 45-48mm long, but is no more than an extreme among a series of forms that do not have clear morphological boundaries.
AM 1933 (Lt Col L.C.R. Messel, Nymans) as *R. polyandrum*; flowers white, with a yellow blotch.
AM 1938 (Lt Col L.C.R. Messel, Nymans) as *R. polyandrum*; flowers white, flushed pink.
AM 1938 (Lt Col E.H.W. Bolitho, Trengwainton, Cornwall); buds greenish yellow, flushed pink, opening white, greenish within.
AM 1978 (Maj. A.E. Hardy, Sandling Park, Kent) to a clone 'Ascreavie', from L. & S. 1141; flowers white, flushed red-purple externally.
♀ 1993
Subsp. **crassum** (Franch.) Cullen (*R. crassum* Franch., and incl. *R. manipurense* Balf.f. & Watt & *R. odoriferum* Hutch.). Leaves 9-15(-18) × (4-)5.5-8cm, usually elliptic; stamen filaments usually pubescent; capsule oblong-cylindrical, apex abruptly rounded to truncate. India (Manipur), Burma, China (SE Tibet, Yunnan), Vietnam, 2,400-3,650m.

This is a very variable species as the synonymy quoted indicates. However, *R. maddenii* is consistently characterized by the large number of stamens and by the number of ovary chambers.
AM 1924 (T.H. Lowinsky, Sunninghill) to subsp. *crassum*; buds tinted pink, flowers white.
♀ 1993

R. MAGNIFICUM KINGDON-WARD - SUBSECT. GRANDIA.
Tree, 13-18m; bark rough. Leaves 20-32 × 10-14 (-17)cm, broadly obovate, apex rounded, lower surface with a thin continuous, apparently two-layered indumen-

tum, the upper arachnoid, buff, the lower compacted; petioles slightly flattened and winged. Flowers *c.*30, in a dense truss, *c.*8-lobed, rosy purple, with darker nectar pouches, funnel-campanulate, 45-60mm; stamens 16; ovary densely rufous-tomentose. H2-3. February-April. NE Burma, China (W Yunnan), 1,800-2,500m.

This species is rare in cultivation; as it is relatively tender; it is only to be found in the mildest gardens in Britain.

AM 1950 (Lt Col D.R. Carrick-Buchanan, Corsewell, Stranraer) from Kingdon-Ward 9200; flowers Fuchsine Pink, with darker veins.

FCC 1966 (National Trust for Scotland, Brodick Castle Gardens) to a clone 'Kildonan', from Kingdon-Ward 9200; flowers Fuchsine Pink.

R. MAKINOI TAGG (*R. YAKUSHIMANUM* NAKAI SUBSP. *MAKINOI* (TAGG) D.F.CHAMB.). - SUBSECT. PONTICA.
Shrub, 1-2.5m; young shoots floccose-tomentose; bud scales persistent. Leaves 7-18 × 1-2.5cm, narrowly lanceolate, apex acute, upper surface glabrous, lower surface with a thick white to fulvous tomentum composed of dendroid hairs; petioles tomentose at first, usually soon glabrescent. Flowers 5-10, in a tight truss; calyx 2-5mm; corolla 5-lobed, pale rose, with or without flecks, funnel-campanulate, nectar pouches lacking, 30-40mm; ovary densely whitish to brown-tomentose, style glabrous. H4b. May-June. C Japan (Honshu), to 2,000m.

Allied to *R. degronianum* but differing in the persistent bud scales and narrower leaves, 7.5-10× as long as broad.
♀ 1993

R. MALLOTUM BALF.F. & KINGDON-WARD - SUBSECT. NERIIFLORA.
Shrub or small tree, 1.5-6.5m. Leaves 10-13 × 4.5-6.3cm, broadly oblanceolate to obovate, lower surface covered with a dense rufous lanate tomentum composed of dendroid hairs; petioles densely tomentose. Flowers 7-14, in a dense truss; calyx 2-3mm; corolla fleshy, crimson, tubular-campanulate, with nectar pouches, 40-45mm; ovary densely rufous-tomentose, abruptly contracted into the glabrous style. H3-4a. March-April. NE Burma, China (W Yunnan), 3,350-3,650m.

A distinctive and fine species in cultivation.

AM 1933 (Col S.R. Clarke, Borde Hill, Sussex); flowers crimson.

AM 1973 (Crown Estate Commissioners, Windsor), as a foliage plant.

R. manipurense Balf.f. & Watt. - is synonym of **R. maddenii** Hook.f. subsp. **crassum** (Franch.) Cullen (Subsect. Maddenia).

R. MARIESII HEMSL. & E.H.WILSON - SECT. BRACHYCALYX.
Shrub or small tree, 1-3m; young shoots covered at first with adpressed yellowish hairs, later glabrescent. Leaves in whorls of up to three, at the ends of the branches, 3-7.5 × 2-4.5cm, ovate-lanceolate, apex acute, lower surface glabrescent; petioles glabrous. Pedicels villose. Flowers 1-2 per inflorescence, appearing before the leaves; calyx minute; corolla rose-purple, upper lobe with flecks, funnelform, 25-30mm; stamens 10; ovary yellowish grey-villose, style glabrous. H3?. April-May. C, S & E China, incl. Taiwan, 200-1,300m
Closely allied to *R. farrerae* (q.v.).

R. MARTINIANUM BALF.F. & FORREST - SUBSECT. SELENSIA.
Much-branched shrub, 0.8-3.5m; young shoots usually stalked- or setose-glandular. Leaves 4.5-5 × 1.4-2.4cm, elliptic to obovate, lower surface punctulate, otherwise glabrous; or (rarely) with a few tufts of hairs, even at maturity; petioles with a few setulose glands or more or less glabrous at maturity. Flowers solitary or up to 4, in a lax truss; calyx 1-3mm; corolla pale yellow, or white flushed rose to pink, with or without purple flecks, funnel-campanulate, nectar pouches lacking, *c.*30mm; ovary and style base densely stalked-glandular. H4a. April-May. China (SE Tibet, NW Yunnan), 3,000-4,250m.

Closely allied to *R. selense* but distinguished by its smaller leaves and fewer flowers per truss. In the wild it apparently has a narrower corolla but it is not certain whether this is a consistent diagnostic character.

R. MAXIMUM L. - SUBSECT. PONTICA.
Shrub or small tree, 1.3-3.5m; young shoots tomentose and stalked-glandular though soon glabrescent; bud scales deciduous. Leaves 10-16 × 3-5cm, oblanceolate to elliptic, upper surface glabrous, lower surface with a thin fugaceous indumentum that is embedded in a surface film that usually persists towards the leaf base, especially near the midrib; petioles usually sparsely tomentose, even when mature. Flowers 14-25, in a dense truss; calyx 3-5mm; corolla white to rose-purple, with yellowish green flecks, campanulate, nectar pouches lacking, 25-30mm; ovary pilose and stalked-glandular, style glabrous. H4c. July. Eastern USA & adjacent Canada, 300-1,700m.

Closely allied to *R. macrophyllum* but with narrower leaves, 3.3-4× as long as broad.

AM 1974 (Crown Estate Commissioners, Windsor) to a clone 'Summertime'; flowers white, suffused at tip with shades of red-purple, throat with yellow-green spots.

R. MAYBARAE NAKAI & H.HARA - SECT. BRACHYCALYX.
Shrub; young shoots glabrous. Leaves in whorls of up to three, at the ends of the branches, 2.5-3 × 1.5-1.7cm, apex acute, lower surface with lamina glabrous, veins and midrib with brown hairs, especially towards base. Pedicels densely and stiffly brownish-pubescent. Flowers solitary, appearing before the leaves; calyx minute; corolla deep magenta, upper lobe with darker flecks, open-campanulate, c.25mm; stamens 10; ovary densely covered with brownish bristles, style glabrous. H4a-b. Japan (S Kyushu), 600-1,000m.

Closely allied to *R. nudipes* but differing in the less hairy leaf under surfaces

and in the densely pubescent pedicels.

R. MEDDIANUM FORREST - SUBSECT. THOMSONIA.
Shrub, 1-2.3m; bark slightly rough; young shoots glabrous. Leaves 8-11(-15) × 4.5-5.2(-8.2)cm, obovate to broadly elliptic, base rounded to more or less cuneate, entirely glabrous, lower epidermis green and lacking papillae; petioles glabrous. Flowers 6-10, in a lax truss; calyx fleshy, 3-12(-18)mm, cupular, reddish; corolla fleshy, deep rose to deep blackish crimson, tubular-campanulate, with nectar pouches, 40-65mm; ovary glabrous to densely glandular and viscid, style glabrous. H3-4a. April. NE Burma, China (W Yunnan), 2,700-3,600m.

Var. **meddianum**. Ovary more or less glabrous. NE Burma, China (W Yunnan).

Var. **atrokermesinum** Tagg. Ovary densely glandular and viscid. NE Burma.

AM 1954 (R.O. Hambro, Logan House, Stranraer); flowers light red, with a little dark spotting on upper lobes.

AM 1965 (National Trust for Scotland, Brodick Castle Gardens) to a clone 'Machrie'; this is now regarded as a hybrid of *R. meddianum*..

AM 1977 (National Trust for Scotland, Brodick Castle Gardens) to a clone 'Bennan'; flowers red, with darker markings.

This species resembles *R. thomsonii* but may be distinguished by characters of the lower leaf epidermis.

R. MEGACALYX BALF.F. & KINGDON-WARD - SUBSECT. MADDENIA.
Shrub, 1-3.5m; young shoots not setose. Leaves 10-16 × 4.5-7.5mm, elliptic to obovate, apex rounded, margin not ciliate, upper surface usually bullate with midrib impressed, lower surface brownish, with unequal more or less touching golden or brownish scales, the smaller of which are rimless. Flowers 2-6, in a loose terminal inflorescence, strongly scented; calyx lobes 22-30mm, whitish-pruinose, becoming papery in fruit, glabrous and lacking scales; corolla white or cream, rarely

flushed pinkish purple, funnel-campanulate, with an oblique mouth, 65-95mm, outer surface sparsely scaly; stamens 10; ovary densely scaly, tapering into the style that is scaly at base. H2-3. April-June. India (Arunachal Pradesh), NE Burma, China Yunnan, SE Tibet), 2,000-3,350m.

This is a very distinctive species.

AM 1937 (Vice Adm. A.W. Heneage-Vivian, Clyne Castle, Swansea); flowers pure white.

R. MEGERATUM BALF.F. & FORREST - SUBSECT. BOOTHIA.
Small shrub, sometimes epiphytic, 0.3-1m; young shoots with setae persisting for at least one year. Leaves 2-3.5 × 1.2-2cm, elliptic to more or less orbicular, apex obtuse, upper surface glabrous except for a few setae at the base of the midrib, lower surface whitish-papillose, with vesicular scales sunk into pits. Pedicels short, more or less lacking scales, covered with setae. Flowers 1-3 per inflorescence; calyx lobes 6-10mm, obovate; corolla yellow or (rarely) cream, broadly campanulate, 16-23 mm; stamens 10; ovary scaly, tapering into the strongly deflexed style. H3. March-April. India (Arunachal Pradesh), NE Burma, China (SE Tibet, NW Yunnan), 3,050-4,150m.

R. megeratum is probably allied to *R. leucaspis*.

AM 1935 (Lord Swaythling, Townhill Park, Southampton); flowers deep yellow.

AM 1970 (Lord Aberconway and the National Trust, Bodnant); flowers yellow-green.

R. MEKONGENSE FRANCH. - SUBSECT. TRICHOCLADA.
Shrub, to 2m; young shoots scaly and variably setose. Leaves deciduous, obovate to obovate-elliptic, 2.5-4.5(6.5) × 1.4-2.1(-2.7)cm, apex rounded, margin ciliate, upper surface usually lacking setae at maturity, lower surface with a varying number of setae that are sometimes restricted to the base of the midrib and the margins, the scales of two kinds, the smaller tend to become greyish to purple or even black and are half the size of the larger. Flowers precocious, 2-4, in a terminal and sometimes also axillary inflorescence; calyx small; corolla yellow to greenish, 17-23mm; stamens 10; ovary scaly, style sometimes puberulent at base. H4a-b. May. Nepal, China (S Tibet, W Yunnan), NE Burma, 2,900-4,400m.

Var. **mekongense**. (incl. var. *melinanthum* (Balf.f. & Kingdon-Ward) Cullen, *R. melinanthum* Balf.f. & Kingdon-Ward & *R. chloranthum* Balf.f. & Forrest). Corolla yellow or greenish-yellow, scales polymorphic in size and colour. Nepal, NE Burma, China S Tibet, NW Yunnan), 2,900-4,400m.

Var. *mekongense* has a surprisingly disjunct range, extending from SW China to Nepal.

AM 1979 (R.N.S. Clarke, Borde Hill) to a clone 'Yellow Fellow'; flowers in trusses of 3-5, yellow, with yellow-green spotting in throat on upper 3 lobes.

Var. **rubrolineatum** (Balf.f. & Forrest) Cullen (*R. rubrolineatum* Balf.f. & Forrest). Corolla reddish yellow, scales varying in size but uniformly golden. China (SE Tibet, W Yunnan), 3,200-4,500m.

R. mekongense is closely allied to *R. trichocladum* (q.v.).

R. mekongense Franch. var. *longipilosum* (Cowan) Cullen - is a synonym of **R. trichocladum** Franch. var. **longipilosum** Cowan (Subsect. Trichoclada).

R. melinanthum Balf.f. & Kingdon-Ward - is a synonym of **R. mekongense** Franch. var. **mekongense** - Subsect. Trichoclada.

R. metternichii Sieb. & Zucc. - is a synonym of **R. degronianum** Carrière var. **heptamerum** (Maxim.) H.Hara (Subsect. Pontica).

R. metternichii Sieb. & Zucc. var. *pentamerum* Maxim. - is a synonym of **R. degronianum** Carrière subsp. **degronianum** (Subsect. Pontica).

R. MICRANTHUM TURCZ. - SUBSECT. MICRANTHA.

Shrub, to 2.5m; young shoots scaly and puberulent. Leaves (1.6-)3-4(-5.6) × (0.5-)1-2.5cm, oblong-elliptic, sometimes narrowly so, apex acute, midrib sparsely puberulent above, lower surface with brown broad-rimmed touching or overlapping scales. Flowers usually more than 20, in a dense terminal inflorescence with a conspicuous rhachis; pedicels puberulent; calyx lobes 1-2mm, triangular, ciliate; corolla white, unspotted, funnel-campanulate, 5-8mm, outer surface densely scaly; stamens 10, longer than corolla; ovary scaly, impressed, below the straight style that is shorter than the stamens, and glabrous or with a few hairs at base. H4a-b. May-July. N & C China (Heilongjiang, Jilin, Hebei, Hubei, Gansu, Shanxi, Shandong, Sichuan), Korea, 1,600-2,600m.

A distinct species, though in some respects resembling members of Subsect. Ledum.

R. MICROGYNUM BALF.F. & FORREST (INCL. *R. GYMNOCARPUM* BALF.F. EX TAGG & *R. PERULATUM* BALF.F. & FORREST) - SUBSECT. NERIIFLORA.

Shrub, usually dwarf, 0.6-2m. Leaves 5.5-7.5 × 1.5-2(-3)cm, elliptic, lower surface covered with a dense felted, cinnamon to buff indumentum composed of rosulate hairs; petioles glabrescent. Flowers 3-7, in a tight truss; calyx 2-10mm; corolla fleshy, pale rose to deep crimson, sometimes with faint flecks, 30-35mm; ovary brown-tomentose and glandular, abruptly contracted into the glabrous style. H4a. April-May. China (SE Tibet, NW Yunnan), 3,650-4,250m.

Allied to *R. sanguineum* but generally a larger plant, with a thicker leaf indumentum.

AM 1940 (L. de Rothschild, Exbury) as *R. gymnocarpum*; flowers deep rich crimson.

R. microleucum Hutch. - is a synonym of **R. orthocladum** Balf.f. & Forrest var. **microleucum** (Balf.f. & Forrest) N.M.Philipson & Philipson (Subsect. Lapponica).

R. micromeres Tagg - is a synonym of **R. leptocarpum** Nuttal (Subsect. Boothia).

R. MICROPHYTON FRANCH. - SECT. TSUTSUSI.

Upright, usually dwarf shrub, 1.3-2m; young shoots covered with adpressed flattened brown hairs. Leaves of one kind, persistent, 1-4 × 0.5-1.5cm, apex obtuse to acute, mucronulate, both surfaces with adpressed red-brown hairs, lower surface paler; petioles covered with brown bristles. Pedicels covered with shining chestnut-brown hairs. Flowers 3-6 per inflorescence; calyx 1-2mm; corolla usually purple-rose, occasionally white flushed pink, with crimson flecks, funnel-campanulate, 10-15(-22)mm; stamens 5; ovary densely covered with shining chestnut-brown hairs, style glabrous. H2-3. April-May. NE Burma, China (Yunnan,SW Sichuan, Guizhou), ?Thailand, 1,800-3,050m.

This species has no obvious allies. It is frost sensitive in Britain.

R. MIMETES TAGG & FORREST. - SUBSECT. TALIENSIA.

Shrub, 1-2.2m. Leaves 8.5-11 × 3-4.5cm, lanceolate to oblanceolate, apex acute to apiculate, lower surface covered with a two-layered indumentum, the upper layer fulvous, lanate-tomentose and often detersile by maturity, or cinnamon, persistent, composed of ramiform hairs, the lower whitish, compacted and persistent; petioles glabrescent by maturity. Flowers 6-10 in a lax to dense truss; calyx 3-10mm, lobes broad, rounded, or narrow and reflexed, irregular; corolla white to rose, with crimson flecks, funnel-campanulate, nectar pouches lacking, 35-45mm; ovary densely rufous-tomentose and stalked-glandular, style glabrous. H4b. May. China (SW Sichuan), 3,350-4,450m.

Var. **mimetes**. Leaf indumentum with upper layer often detersile, fulvous; calyx with broad lobes.

Var. **simulans** Tagg & Forrest (*R. sim-*

ulans [Tagg & Forrest] D.F.Chamb.). Leaf indumentum persistent, cinnamon; calyx with narrow reflexed lobes.

Both varieties may have a hybrid origin with *R. adenogynum* as one parent. The other parent of var. *simulans* could be *R. sphaeroblastum*.

R. MINUS MICHX. - SUBSECT. CAROLINIANA.
Shrub, 2(-5)m; young shoots sparsely scaly. Leaves (1-)5.5-8(-11) × (1.8-)2.5-3.5 (-5)cm, elliptic to broadly elliptic, lower surface densely covered with small-rimmed brownish scales. Pedicels scaly. Flowers 5-8, in a dense inflorescence; calyx lobes 1-2mm; corolla white to pink, usually with greenish flecks, (21-)25-30(-35)mm, tube scaly, occasionally also hairy on outside, pubescent within; stamens 10; ovary scaly, style more or less glabrous. H3-4a. May-June. E & S USA.

Var. **minus** (incl. *R. carolinianum* Rehder). Leaf apex acute or acuminate; branches usually not erect and rigid. E & S USA (Tennessee to Alabama).

AM 1968 (Col N.R. Colville, Launceston, Cornwall) as *R. carolinianum*; flowers Red-Purple.

Var. **chapmanii** (A.Gray) Duncan & Pullen (*R. chapmanii* A.Gray). Leaf apex obtuse or retuse; branches erect and rigid. SE USA (Florida).

R. mishmiense Hutch. & Kingdon-Ward - is a synonym of **R. boothii** Nuttall (Subsect. Boothia).

R. miyazawae Nakai & Hara - is a synonym of **R. tosaense** Makino (sect. Tsutsusi).

R. MOLLE (BLUME) G.DON. - SUBSECT. SINENSIA.
Deciduous shrub, to 2m; young twigs with eglandular hairs. Leaves (4-)5-9.5 (-13.2) × 1.7-2.9(-4.3)cm, ovate or obovate to elliptic, sparsely covered with eglandular hairs. Flower bud scales with outer surface covered with unicellular hairs, margin ciliate. Pedicels densely covered with eglandular and gland-tipped hairs. Flowers with a sweet fragrance, appearing before or with the leaves, 3-13, in a shortened raceme; calyx to 1-4mm; corolla yellow to red, with flecks on the upper corolla lobe, broadly funnelform, tube broadly expanding into limb, both surfaces usually covered with eglandular hairs, 30-70mm. Capsules eglandular-hairy. H3-4a. May. China, Japan, s.l.-2,500m.

Subsp. **molle**. Flowers yellow; capsules sparsely hairy. C, S & E China.

Subsp. **japonicum** (A.Gray) K.Kron. (*R. japonicum* (A.Gray) Valcken. & incl. *R. sinense* (Lodd.) Sweet). Flowers yellow to red; capsules more densely hairy. Japan.

This is the most distinctive of the species in Sect. Pentanthera.

R. MOLLICOMUM BALF.F. & W.W.SM. - SUBSECT. SCABRIFOLIA.
Small shrub, 0.5-2m; young shoots scaly, pubescent, with or without setae. Leaves 1.2-3.5 × 0.3-1.5cm, lanceolate or rarely oblong, upper surface covered with filiform hairs, usually without setae; lower surface green, not shining, lamina densely pubescent, the setae restricted to midrib, the scales their own diameter apart. Flowers 1-3, in an axillary inflorescence; calyx rim-like, ciliate; corolla pale to deep pink, narrowly funnel-shaped, 19-30mm; outer surface glabrous and lacking scales; stamens 10; ovary scaly and sparsely pilose, style impressed, often slightly pilose at base. H3-4a. April-May. China (N Yunnan, SW Sichuan), 2800-3800m.

This species is closely allied to *R. hemitrichotum* (q.v.).

AM 1931 (Lady Aberconway and Hon. H.D. McLaren, Bodnant); flowers bright rose.

R. monosematum Hutch. - is a synonym of **R. pachytrichum** Franch var. **monosematum** (Hutch.) D.F.Chamb. (Subsect. Maculifera).

R. MONTROSEANUM COWAN & DAVIDIAN - SUBSECT. GRANDIA.

Tree 12-15m; bark rough. Leaves 20-30 (-50) × 5.5-10(-20)cm, oblanceolate, apex rounded, apiculate, lower surface covered with a thin one-layered silvery compacted indumentum; petioles terete. Flowers *c*.20, 8-lobed, in a dense truss, rose-pink, with a crimson blotch at base, ventricose-campanulate, nectar pouches lacking, *c*.50mm; stamens 16; ovary densely rufous-tomentose. H3. March-May. ?NE Burma, China (S Tibet), *c*.2,600m.

This species may be distinguished by the pink flowers and the silvery leaf indumentum.

FCC 1957 (Younger Botanic Garden, Argyll) to a clone 'Benmore' from Kingdon-Ward 6261a; flowers Fuchsine Pink, with deep pink staining and a crimson blotch.

R. MORII HAYATA - SUBSECT. MACULIFERA.
Shrub or small tree, 4-8m; young shoots with a dense blackish floccose indumentum, soon becoming glabrous. Leaves 7-14 × 2.8-3.5cm, lanceolate to elliptic, apex acuminate, lower surface with lamina glabrous though with a floccose tomentum composed of folioliferous hairs overlying the midrib; petioles finely hirsute and glandular. Flowers 5-12, in a lax truss; calyx *c*.2mm; corolla white, sometimes tinged pink, with a red basal blotch and flecks, widely campanulate, lacking nectar pouches, 30-50mm; ovary densely tomentose, also with a few stalked glands, style tomentose at base, otherwise glabrous. H3-4a. April-May, Taiwan, 2,000-2,200m.

Closely allied to *R. pseudochrysanthum*, the two apparently merge with one another in some wild populations. It is therefore treated by some as a synonym of the latter species, but the differences in leaf shape and general size of plant are maintained in cultivation.

AM 1956 (Capt. C. Ingram, Benenden, Kent); flowers white, blotched and spotted crimson.

♔ 1993

R. MOULMAINENSE HOOK.F. (INCL. *R. ELLIPTICUM* MAXIM., *R. OXYPHYLLUM* FRANCH., *R. PECTINATUM* HUTCH., *R. STENAULUM* BALF.F. & FORREST & *R. WESTLANDII* HEMSL.) - SECT. CHONIASTRUM.
Shrub or tree, to 15m. Leaves 6-17 × 2-5cm, narrowly elliptic to elliptic, glabrous when mature, apex acuminate. Flowers 3-5 (rarely solitary), clustered at end of a leafy shoot below the vegetative buds, white or pink to magenta, with a yellow blotch, funnel-shaped; tube 16-22mm; lobes 30-40mm, broad, spreading; stamens 10. H1b-2. March-April. Widespread in SE Asia, from E India to Cambodia, China and Malaya, 100-3,000m.

A cool glasshouse subject in temperate regions. A widespread and variable species in the wild.

AM 1937 (L. de Rothschild, Exbury & Earl of Stair, Stranraer) as *R. stenaulum*; flowers silvery lilac, with violet tinge, dark on lobes, spotted pale brown, tube pale crimson externally.

R. MOUPINENSE FRANCH. - SUBSECT. MOUPINENSIA.
Shrub, 1-1.3m, often epiphytic; young shoots setose. Leaves 3-4 × 1.6-2.2cm, narrowly ovate to elliptic or obovate, apex rounded, margin ciliate, lower surface densely scaly. Flowers 1-2, terminal; calyx lobes *c*.2mm, pubescent; corolla white, often flushed pink, usually with dark red spots, open-funnel-campanulate, 30-35mm, outer surface glabrous, lacking scales; stamens 10; style longer than stamens, declinate. H3-4a. February-March. China (W Sichuan, Guizhou), 2,000-4,000m.

This species is closely allied to *R. dendrocharis* (q.v.) and one of the earliest species to flower in cultivation.

FCC 1994 (Crown Estate Commissioners, Windsor) to a clone 'Ice Cool'; truss 1-3-flowered, greenish white, with two small clusters of moderate red spots in the dorsal throat.

♔ 1993

R. mucronatum (Blume) G.Don - is presumed to be an artificial hybrid of **R. ripense** Makino and **R. stenopetalum** (Sect. Tsutsusi).

R. MUCRONULATUM Turcz. - Subsect. Rhodorastra
Straggling shrub, to 2m; young shoots scaly and puberulous. Leaves thin, completely deciduous, 4-6 × 1.5-3cm, elliptic to lanceolate, apex mucronate, upper surface puberulent on midrib, with strigose hairs towards the margin, lower surface sparsely scaly. Flowers solitary, axillary, but at the tips of the branches, opening before the leaves; calyx rim-like; corolla bright mauve pink, rarely white, very openly funnel-shaped, 21-26mm, outer surface pilose near base; stamens 10; ovary scaly, style impressed, declinate. H4b-c. January-March. Russia (E Siberia), China (Hubei, Shandong), Mongolia, Korea, Japan (Honshu, Kyushu), 300m upwards.

This species is closely allied to *R. dauricum* (q.v.).

A dwarf form, 10-50cm high, from Cheju Island & the mainland of S Korea, has been given the name var. **taquetii** (H.Lév.) Nakai (syn. var. *chejuense* Davidian).

AM 1924 (Royal Botanic Gardens, Kew); flowers rich purplish rose.

AM 1935 (Royal Botanic Gardens, Kew) to a clone 'Roseum'; flowers bright rose.

AM 1965 (Crown Estate Commissioners, Windsor) to a clone 'Winter Brightness'; flowers a rich purplish rose.

♀ 1993, to a clone 'Cornell Pink.

♀ 1993 to a clone 'Winter Brightness'.

R. myiagrum Balf.f. & Forrest - is a synonym of **R. callimorphum** Balf.f. & W.W.Sm. subsp. **myiagrum** (Balf.f.& Forrest) D.F.Chamb.

R. MYRTIFOLIUM Schott & Kotschy - Subsect. Rhododendron.
Small shrub, to 0.5m; young shoots densely scaly, sometimes with a few hairs.

Leaves 1.4-2.3 × 0.5-0.8cm, narrowly obovate, apex obtuse; margin not ciliate, obscurely crenulate, upper surface dark green, shining, lower surface scaly but not densely so. Flowers many, in a dense inflorescence; rhachis 10-20mm; pedicels scaly and pubescent; calyx lobes to 2mm, narrowly triangular, usually fringed with scales and a few hairs; corolla pink, tubular-campanulate, 15-17mm, outer surface sparsely scaly, densely pubescent; stamens 10; style shorter than to as long as the ovary. H4a-b. Mountains of E Europe (Bulgaria, Yugoslavia, Romania, W Russia), 1,200-2,400m.

This species is closely allied to *R. ferrugineum*, replacing it in the East. It differs in its hairy pedicels, paler flowers and shorter style.

R. NAKAHARAE Hayata - Sect. Tsutsusi.
Much-branched prostrate shrub, rarely more than 0.3m high; young shoots covered with adpressed flattened shining brown hairs. Leaves of one kind, persistent, 0.5-1.2 × 0.2-1cm, elliptic to elliptic-obovate, apex acute or mucronulate, upper surface with scattered pilose hairs borne on raised pustules, lower surface paler, with scattered adpressed shining brown hairs; petioles densely bristly. Pedicels covered with flattened brown shining hairs. Flowers 2-3 per inflorescence; calyx *c*.2mm; corolla dark red, funnel-campanulate, 20-25mm; stamens 10; ovary densely bristly, style glabrous. H4a. June-August. N Taiwan, 350-2,300m.

This is a distinctive species on account of its dwarf, creeping habit.

AM 1970 (Hydon Nurseries, Godalming) to a clone 'Mariko'; flowers red, flushed deeper in centre of upper throat.

R. NAKOTILTUM Balf.f. & Forrest - Subsect. Taliensia.
Shrub, 1-3.5m. Leaves 8-11 × 3-4.3cm, elliptic, apex acute, lower surface covered with a two-layered indumentum, the upper layer loose and fawn, composed of long-

rayed stellate hairs, the lower compacted; petioles glabrescent. Flowers 12-15, in a dense truss; calyx *c*.1mm; corolla white flushed rose to pale pink, with purple flecks and sometimes also a basal blotch, funnel-campanulate, nectar pouches lacking, 30-35mm; ovary densely rufous-tomentose, style glabrous. H4. May. China (NW Yunnan), 3,350-4,000m.

This is a rare species, both in the wild and in cultivation. There is some doubt as to the authenticity of cultivated plants as none can be linked for certain with any of the available preserved material.

R. nankotaisanense Hayata - is a synonym of **R. pseudochrysanthum** Hayata var. **nankotaisanense** (Hayata) T.Yamaz. (Subsect. Maculifera).

R. NEOGLANDULOSUM HARMAJA (*LEDUM GLANDULOSUM* MURR.) - SUBSECT. LEDUM.
Erect shrub, 0.5-2.0m; young shoots puberulent, gland-dotted. Leaves 1.5-3.5 (-4) × 0.5-2cm, broadly elliptic-oval, apex acuminate, margins flat or slightly incurved, upper surface dark green, lower surface lighter green, papillate, glabrous or more or less pubescent, scales rimless, golden, 1-2× their own diameter apart; petioles 4-10mm. Flowers many, in a loose terminal umbellate corymb; calyx small, lobes rounded, margins ciliate; corolla white, rotate, *c*.6mm; pedicels 1.5-4cm, often glandular; stamens 8-12; ovary densely glandular and scaly, style sparsely glandular. H4. May-August. NW USA.

Intermediates (that occasionally occur in cultivation) between this species and *R. groenlandicum*, with leaves 4-6 × 1-2cm, slightly revolute and sometimes with a few ferrugineous hairs on the lower surfaces, have been called *R.* × *columbianum* (Piper) Harmaja (*Ledum columbianum* Piper).

R. NERIIFLORUM FRANCH. - SUBSECT. NERIIFLORA.
Shrub or small tree, 1-6m. Leaves 4-11 ×

1.9-3.2cm, elliptic to oblong or oblanceolate, lower surface glabrous with a glaucous, strongly papillate epidermis; petioles sparsely floccose-tomentose or glabrescent, rarely setose-glandular. Flowers 5-8(-12), in a tight truss; calyx 2-15mm, cupular when well-developed; corolla fleshy, crimson to light red, occasionally straw yellow, tubular-campanulate, with nectar pouches, 35-45mm; ovary densely tomentose, sometimes also with at least some glands, tapering into the glabrous style. H3-4a. April-May. Bhutan, NE India, China (S Tibet, W Yunnan), NE Burma, 275-3,350m.

Subsp. **neriiflorum** (incl. *R. euchaites* Balf.f. & Forrest & *R. phoenicodum* Balf.f. & Farrer). Pedicels, calyx and ovary lacking glands; leaves 4-9cm, 1.7-3× as long as broad, plane below, lacking reticulations. NE Burma, China (SE Tibet, W Yunnan).

AM 1929 (Lady Aberconway and Hon. H.D. McLaren, Bodnant) as subsp. *euchaites*; flowers a rich ruby red.

Subsp. **agetum** (Balf.f. & Forrest) Tagg. As for subsp. *neriiflorum* but with lower leaf surface reticulate, forming alveoli with some papillae horizontal. China (W Yunnan).

Subsp. **phaedropum** (Balf.f. & Farrer) Tagg. Pedicels, calyx and ovary with at least some glands; leaves 8-11cm, 3-5(-7)× as long as broad, plane below. Bhutan, NE India (Arunachal Pradesh), China (S Tibet, W Yunnan).

The status of subsp. *agetum* is uncertain, even though the cited difference is striking. Subsp. *neriiflorum* merges with the more Westerly subsp. *phaedropum* where the distributions of the two meet.

R. NIGROGLANDULOSUM NITZELIUS - SUBSECT. TALIENSIA.
Shrub or small tree, 3-5m; young shoots tomentose and with blackish purple stalked glands. Leaves 12-17 × 4-5cm, lanceolate to oblong, apex apiculate, lower surface with a light reddish brown, loosely lanate, one-layered indumentum composed of ramiform hairs; petioles floccose-tomentose, and with black glands.

Flowers 8-10 in a dense truss; calyx *c.*1mm; corolla deep pink at first, later yellowish pink, with conspicuous purple flecks, campanulate, nectar pouches lacking; ovary stipitate-glandular and tomentose, style glabrous. H4b. May. China (Sichuan), *c.*3,500m.

A rare species in cultivation that may be distinguished from its immediate relatives, *R. bureavii* and *R. elegantulum*, by its small calyx. The black glands on the young shoots and petioles are also diagnostic.

R. nigropunctatum Franch. - is a synonym of **R. nivale** subsp. **boreale** Philipson & N.M.Philipson (Subsect. Lapponica).

R. ninguenense Hand.-Mazz. - is a synonym of **R. irroratum** Franch. subsp. **irroratum** (Subsect. Irrorata).

R. NIPPONICUM MATSUM. - SECT. VISCIDULA.
Deciduous shrub, to 2m. Leaves 4-18 × 1.5-8.5cm, obovate, often broadly so, to broadly elliptic, lower surface with scattered eglandular and gland-tipped hairs, the midrib fringed with straight to crisped unicellular hairs. Flowers appearing with or after the leaves, 6-15, in an umbellate raceme; calyx 1-6mm; corolla white, lacking spots, regular, tubular-campanulate, tube broadly expanding into the shorter limb, 15-25mm. Capsule covered with gland-tipped hairs. H4a-b. May-June, S Japan, 1,000-1,850m.

This is a very distinctive species on account of its regular tubular-campanulate flowers. It may be distantly allied to *R. albiflorum*. It is considered to be one of the most primitive species in the genus.

R. nitens Hutch. - is a synonym of **R. calostrotum** Balf.f. & Kingdon-Ward subsp. **riparium** (Kingdon-Ward) Cullen (Subsect. Saluenensia).

R. NITIDULUM REHDER & E.H.WILSON - SUBSECT. LAPPONICA.
Erect or ascending much-branched low shrub, to 1.3m. Leaves 0.5-1.1 × 0.3-0.7cm, ovate to elliptic, apex obtuse or rounded, mucro absent or obscure, base widening abruptly from the petiole, lower surface covered with uniformly fawn, golden-centred touching scales sometimes also with scattered darker scales. Flowers 1-2 per inflorescence; calyx (1.5-)2.5-3mm, lobes strap-shaped, rounded; corolla rosy-lilac to violet-purple, funnel-shaped, outer surface without scales, 12-15mm; stamens (8-)10, more or less equalling the corolla; ovary lepidote, style exceeding the stamens, sometimes pubescent at base. H4a-b. April-May. China (Sichuan), 3,200-5,000m.

Var. **nitidulum**. Leaves covered with uniformly pale scales beneath. China (NW Sichuan), 3,300-5,000m.

Var. **omeiense** Philipson & N.M.Philipson. Leaf scales predominantly pale (though with a few dark) beneath. China (C Sichuan - Mt Emei), 3,200-3,500m.

This species is allied to *R. websterianum* but may be distinguished by the golden-centred leaf scales.

R. NIVALE HOOK.F. - SUBSECT. LAPPONICA.
Prostrate or compact shrub, 0.6-0.9(-1.2)m. Leaves 0.4-0.9(-1.2) × 2-6cm, elliptic to broadly elliptic, apex rounded to subacute, with at most a very short mucro, lower surface covered with more or less touching scales, the majority usually pale gold but with a few darker. Flowers 1-2 (-3) per inflorescence; calyx minute or lobes 2-5mm and oblong or oblong-deltoid; corolla rich purple to lilac or pink, broadly funnel-shaped, (7-)9-13(-16)mm; stamens usually 10, longer or shorter than the corolla; ovary scaly, style usually longer than stamens, glabrous or slightly pubescent at base. H4a-b. April-May. Nepal, India (Sikkim), China (S Tibet, Yunnan, W Sichuan), 3,100-5,800m.

Subsp. **nivale** (incl. *R. paludosum* Hutch. & *R. ramosissimum* Franch.). Calyx lobes 2-5mm, margins with scales; leaf apex rounded. Nepal, India (Sikkim),

China (S Tibet), to 5,800m.

Subsp. **australe** Philipson & N.M.Philipson. Calyx lobes 2-5mm, ciliate; leaf apex more or less acute. China (NW & C Yunnan), 3,100-4,300m.

Subsp. **boreale** Philipson & N.M.Philipson (incl. *R. alpicola* Rehder & E.H.Wilson, *R. nigropunctatum* Franch., *R. oresbium* Balf.f. & Kingdon-Ward, *R. ramosissimum* Franch., *R. stictopyllum* Balf.f. & *R. violaceum* Rehder & E.H.Wilson). Calyx more or less obsolete; leaf apex more or less acute. China (SE Tibet, NW Yunnan, W Sichuan), 3,200-5,000m.

This is a variable and widespread species.

R. NIVEUM HOOK.F. - SUBSECT. ARBOREA. Multi-stemmed tree, to 6m. Leaves 11.5-17 × 4-4.5cm, elliptic to oblanceolate, lower surface with a compacted fawn dendroid indumentum. Flowers 15-20, in a dense inflorescence, deep magenta to deep lilac, with darker nectar pouches, tubular-campanulate, 30-35mm. H3-4a. April-May. N India (Sikkim), W Bhutan, 2,900-3,650m.

This distinctive species is rare and threatened in the wild.

AM 1951 (Mrs R.M. Stevenson, Tower Court, Ascot); flowers Imperial Purple, with darker staining.

FCC 1979 (Crown Estate Commissioners, Windsor) to a clone 'Crown Equerry'; trusses containing up to 32 flowers, corolla purple-violet, with darker lip and deeper veining.

♀ 1993

R. NORIAKIANUM SUZUKI - SECT. TSUTSUSI. Low shrub; young shoots densely covered with adpressed bristles. Leaves of one kind, deciduous, 0.7-1.5 × 0.4-0.6cm, ovate to ovate-oblong, apex obtuse, apiculate; upper surface glabrescent; petioles covered with bristles. Pedicels densely pilose. Flowers 3-4 per inflorescence; calyx small; corolla red, funnel-shaped, *c*.15mm; stamens 7-10; ovary pubescent, style glabrous. H4a?. May. N Taiwan, 2,000-3,000m.

This species is allied to *R. nakaharae* but is said to differ in its smaller corolla and slightly exserted stamens. It may no longer be in cultivation.

R. notatum Hutch. - is a synonym of **R. dendricola** Hutch.

R. nudiflorum (L.) Torr. - is a synonym of **R. periclymenoides** (Michx.) Shinners (Subsect. Pentanthera).

R. NUDIPES NAKAI - SECT. BRACHYCALYX. Shrub or small tree; young shoots glabrous. Leaves in whorls of up to three, at the ends of the branches, 2-8 × 1-6.5cm, broadly rhombic, apex acute with tip blunt, lower surface covered with long brown hairs; petioles densely brown-villose above, glabrous below. Pedicels covered with brown pubescent hairs. Flowers 1-2 per inflorescence, appearing before the leaves; calyx minute; corolla rose-purple, funnel-campanulate, 20-30mm; stamens 8-10; ovary densely pale brown villose, style glabrous. H4a-b. May. Japan (Honshu, Kyushu), 200-1,000m.

Var. *kirishimense* T.Yamaz., which is said to differ in its pubescent young shoots and smaller leaves (1.5-4.5 × 1.2-3cm) with apex obtuse, may be in cultivation.

R. nudipes is allied to *R. reticulatum* (q.v.).

R. NUTTALLII BOOTH (INCL. *R. SINONUTTALLII* BALF.F. & FORREST - SUBSECT. MADDENIA. Shrub or small tree, sometimes epiphytic, 2-10m; young shoots not bristly. Leaves 17-26 × 7.5-13cm, oblong-elliptic to oblong-obovate, apex bluntly acute or obtuse, margin not ciliate, upper surface rugose, midrib raised; lower surface glaucous, with a conspicuous reticulum of secondary veins, scales brown, unequal, up to 2× their own diameter apart. Flowers 2-5, in a loose terminal inflorescence, not scented; calyx 15-25mm, without or with a few scales, sometimes with a few hairs;

corolla white with a yellow blotch, funnel-campanulate, with an oblique mouth, (75-)100-125mm, outer surface sparsely scaly; stamens 10; ovary densely scaly, tapering into the style that is scaly below. H1b(-2). April-May. India (Arunachal Pradesh), China (NW Yunnan, SE Tibet, Vietnam), 1,200-3,650m.

AM 1936 (L. de Rothschild, Exbury) as var. *stellatum*, from Kingdon-Ward 6333; flowers small, scented.

AM 1955 (Sunningdale Nurseries, Windlesham, Surrey) as *R. sinonuttallii*.

FCC 1864 (Victoria Nursery, Highgate).

♀ 1993

R. oblongifolium (Small) Millais - is a synonym of **R. viscosum** (L.) Torr. (Subsect. Pentanthera).

R. obtusum (Lindl.) Planchon - and the many of the forms and varieties described under that name are cultivated selections of *R. kiusianum*, or hybrids between it and *R. kaempferi* (see note under the former species).

AM 1898 (W. Nicholson, Basing Park, Alton); flowers clear orange-scarlet.

AM 1965 (Knaphill Nursery, Woking) to a clone 'Splendens'; flowers Rose Bengal.

R. occidentale (Torr. & A.Gray) A.Gray - Subsect. Pentanthera.
Deciduous shrub or small tree, to 8(-10)m; young twigs glabrous to densely covered with gland-tipped and/or eglandular hairs. Leaves (2.5-)3.5-8.2(-10.8) × (0.8)1.2-2.9(-3.6)cm, ovate to obovate or elliptic, lower surface usually covered with unicellular and gland-tipped multicellular hairs. Flower bud scales with outer surface covered with unicellular and eglandular or gland-tipped multicellular hairs, margin ciliate with gland-tipped or eglandular hairs. Pedicels covered with hairs that are usually gland-tipped. Flowers with a sweet fragrance, appearing with the leaves or after they have expanded; calyx 1-4(-9)mm; corolla white and pink to salmon or pink, with an orange blotch on the upper corolla lobe, funnelform, with tube gradually expanding into the limb, 30-60mm. Capsule sparsely covered with eglandular or gland-tipped hairs. H4a-b. June-July. W USA (Oregon & California), s.l.-2,700m.

R. occidentale may be distinguished from the allied *R. austrinum* and *R. luteum* by the colour of the corolla.

AM 1944 (Royal Botanic Gardens, Kew); flowers white, heavily flushed rose pink, with a yellow blotch.

♀ 1993

R. ochraceum Rehder & E.H.Wilson - Subsect. Maculifera.
Small tree, c.3m; young shoots covered with glandular setae. Leaves 5.5-10 × 1.3-2cm, apex cuspidate, lower surface covered with a dense matted yellow-brown indumentum composed of flagellate hairs. Flowers 8-12, in a dense inflorescence; calyx c.1mm; corolla dark red, with nectar pouches, tubular-campanulate, c.35mm; ovary densely covered with small gland-tipped bristles, style glabrous. H4a?. China (Sichuan), 2,600-3,000m.

This distinctive species is probably allied to *R. strigillosum* but differs in the characteristic leaf indumentum. As it has only recently been introduced, it is not known how it will perform in cultivation.

R. odoriferum Hutch. - is synonym of **R. maddenii** Hook.f. subsp. **crassum** (Franch.) Cullen.

R. oldhamii Maxim. (incl. *R. ovatosepalum* Yamamoto) - Sect. Tsutsusi.
Much-branched shrub, to 3m; young shoots densely covered with spreading red-brown gland-tipped hairs intermixed with scattered more or less spreading flattened hairs. Leaves of two kinds; spring leaves deciduous, 3.5-6 × 1.8-2.5cm, ovate-lanceolate, apex acute to mucronate, both surfaces covered with light brown pilose hairs that are longer on the midrib; summer leaves 1.5-2 × 0.8-1cm; petioles cov-

ered with spreading pilose hairs. Pedicels covered with spreading gland-tipped red-brown hairs. Flowers 1-3 per inflorescence; calyx *c*.2mm; corolla orange-red to coral-pink, funnel-shaped, 25-35mm; stamens (8-)10; ovary densely covered with gland-tipped bristles, style glabrous. H2-3. May-August. Taiwan, s.l.-2,450m.

This is a distinctive species, with no close allies.

R. oleifolium Franch. - is a synonym of **R. virgatum** Hook.f. subsp. **oleifolium** (Franch.) Cullen (Subsect. Virgata).

R. ombrochares Balf.f. & Kingdon-Ward - is a synonym of **R. tanastylum** Balf.f. & Kingdon-Ward var. **tanastylum** (Subsect. Irrorata).

R. openshawianum Rehder & E.H.Wilson - is a synonym of **R. calophytum** Franch. var. **openshawianum** (Rehder & E.H.Wilson) D.F.Chamb. (Subsect. Fortunea).

R. ORBICULARE DECNE. - SUBSECT. FORTUNEA.
Shrub or tree, 1.5-15m. Leaves 7-12.5 × 5.6-7.7cm, orbicular to ovate-orbicular, base cordate, lower surface glabrous. Flowers 10-17 in a truss; calyx *c*.0.5mm; corolla 7-lobed, deep rose-pink, campanulate to open-campanulate, nectar pouches lacking, 35-40mm; stamens 14; ovary stalked-glandular, style glabrous. H4a-b. April-May. China (Sichuan, Guangxi), 2,500-4,000m.

Only subsp. *orbiculare*, with orbicular leaves, is known in cultivation.

AM 1922 (Hon. H.D. McLaren, Bodnant); flowers rose pink.

R. OREODOXA FRANCH. - SUBSECT. FORTUNEA.
Shrub or small tree, 1.3-5m. Leaves 6-8.5 × 2.2-4cm, obovate-elliptic to elliptic, base rounded, lower surface with persistent punctulate hair bases, otherwise glabrous. Flowers 6-8, in a lax truss; calyx 2-3mm; corolla 5-7-lobed, pink, campanulate, nec-

tar pouches lacking, 35-40mm; stamens 10-14; ovary glabrous or with stalked glands, style glabrous. H4b. March-April. China (NW Yunnan, Sichuan, S Gansu, W Hubei, Shaanxi), 2,650-4,100m.

Var. **oreodoxa**. Ovary glabrous; corolla 6-7-lobed; pedicels glandular. China (Sichuan).

AM 1937 (L. de Rothschild, Exbury); flowers pale rose, with darker stripes.

Var. **fargesii** (Franch.) D.F.Chamb. (*R. fargesii* Franch. & incl. *R. erubescens* Hutch.). Ovary stalked-glandular; corolla (5-)6-7-lobed; pedicels glandular. China (NW Yunnan, Sichuan, Gansu, Hubei).

AM 1926 (G.W.E. Loder, Wakehurst Place, Sussex) as *R. fargesii*; flowers rose pink, with crimson spots.

AM 1969 (Lord Aberconway and National Trust, Bodnant) to a clone 'Budget Farthing', as *R. fargesii* ; flowers white, suffused Red-Purple.

♀ 1993

Var. **shensiense** D.F.Chamb. Ovary stalked-glandular; pedicels sparsely rufous-tomentose; corolla 5-lobed. China (Shaanxi).

Plants now referred to var. *shensiense* have in the past been grown as *R. purdomii* Rehder & E.H.Wilson, the type specimen of which is too poorly preserved to be sure that it is the same as the former. The affinities of var. *shensiense* are unclear but it seems that the plants in cultivation have a close affinity with *R. oreodoxa*.

R. OREOTREPHES W.W.SM. - SUBSECT. TRIFLORA.
Shrub or small tree, 1-8m; young shoots scaly. Leaves evergreen or semi-deciduous, often bluish, 2.1-6.3(-8.7) × 1.8-3.1 (-4)cm, orbicular to oblong or obovate, apex rounded to acute, upper surface often slightly hairy along midrib, lower surface with dense (but not touching) reddish brown to grey, opaque narrow-rimmed scales, often puberulent below. Flowers 1-3(-4), in a loose terminal inflorescence; calyx minute, sometimes ciliate; corolla rose-pink to rose-lavender, with darker spots, rarely white, funnel-shaped

to funnel-campanulate, 21-34mm, outer surface lacking scales, glabrous; stamens 10; ovary scaly, impressed below the declinate, glabrous style. H4a. April-May. China (S Tibet, N Yunnan, SW Sichuan), 2,750-4,250m.

This is a distinctive species, with no close allies.

AM 1932 (L. de Rothschild, Exbury) as *R.timetum*; flowers rosy purple.

AM 1935 (J.J. Crosfield, Embley Park, Hants) as *R. siderophylloides*; flowers bright pinkish mauve, with darker spots.

AM 1937 (L. de Rothschild, Exbury) as *R. exquisitum*, from Forrest 20489; flowers light mauve pink, spotted red.

AM 1990 (P.A. Cox, Glendoick) to a clone 'Pentland'; trusses compound, containing up to 21 flowers, corolla purple, paling in throat, with sparse green and red-brown spotting in upper throat.

R. oresbium Balf.f. & Kingdon-Ward - is a synonym of **R. nivale** Hook.f. subsp. **boreale** Philipson & N.M.Philipson (Subsect. Lapponica).

R. ORTHOCLADUM BALF.F. & FORREST - SUBSECT. LAPPONICA.
Much-branched erect low shrub, to 1.3m. Leaves 0.8-1.6 × 0.3-0.6cm, narrowly elliptic to lanceolate, apex obtuse, obscurely mucronate, lower surface covered with more or less touching yellow-brown scales, intermixed with few to many that are dark brown. Flowers (1-)2-5 per inflorescence; calyx 0.5-1.5mm, lobes rounded to deltoid, unequal; corolla pale to deep lavender-blue to purple or whitish pink, funnel-shaped, 7-14mm; stamens 8-10, shorter than to equalling corolla; ovary scaly, style short or long, glabrous or sparsely scaly. H4a-b. April-May. China (N Yunnan, SW Sichuan), 2,500-4,500m.

Var. **orthocladum**. Corolla blue or purple; style 3.5-5mm. China (N Yunnan, SW Sichuan), 2,500-4,500m.

Var. **longistylum** Philipson & N.M.Philipson. Corolla blue or purple; style 15-16mm. China (N & NW Yunnan), 3,500m.

Var. **microleucum** (Hutch.) Philipson & N.M.Philipson (*R. microleucum* Hutch.). Corolla white; style 3.5-5mm. Only known in cultivation.

FCC 1939 (L. de Rothschild, Exbury); flowers white.

♀ 1994

This is a variable species; var. *microleucum* may be no more than an albino form of var. *orthocladum*.

R. oulotrichum Balf.f. & Forrest - is a synonym of **R. trichocladum** Franch. var. **trichocladum** (Subsect. Trichoclada).

R. ovatosepalum Yamamoto - is a synonym of **R. oldhamii** Maxim. (sect. Tsutsusi).

R. OVATUM (LINDL.) MAXIM. - SECT. AZALEASTRUM.
Shrub, to 4m. Leaves 3-6 × 1.5-2.5cm, broadly ovate to broadly elliptic, apex acute or obtuse. Flowers single, borne laterally below vegetative buds, white to pale purple, upper lobes with darker spots, rotate; tube short; lobes spreading, 40-50mm across; stamens 5. H3-4a. May-June. C, S & E China, Taiwan, *c.* 1,000m.

This species is rare in cultivation and somewhat tender.

R. oxyphyllum Franch. - is a synonym of **R. moulmainense** Hook.f. (Sect. Choniastrum).

R. PACHYPODUM BALF.F. & W.W.SM. (INCL. *R. SCOTTIANUM* HUTCH. & *R. SUPRANUBIUM* HUTCH.) - SUBSECT. MADDENIA.
Shrub or small tree, 0.6-7.5m; young shoots lacking bristles. Leaves 5-10 × 2-4cm, obovate, apex abruptly acute, margin not ciliate, upper surface with midrib impressed, lower surface with the brown unequal scales touching or to a half their own diameter apart. Flowers 1-5, in a loose terminal inflorescence, not scented; calyx lobes 1-3mm, usually setose; corolla white with a yellowish basal blotch, sometimes tinged pink, funnel-shaped, 45-65mm, outer surface scaly throughout,

pubescent at base; stamens 10; ovary scaly, tapering into the glabrous style. H2-3. March-April. N Burma, China (Yunnan), 1,800-4,000m.

This species is closely allied to *R. ciliicalyx* (q.v.).

FCC 1936 (L. de Rothschild, Exbury); flowers white, with a pale yellow streak.

R. PACHYSANTHUM HAYATA (SYN. *R. PSEUDOCHRYSANTHUM* HAYATA VAR. *RUFOVELUTINUM* (T.YAMAZ.) T.YAMAZ. - SUBSECT. MACULIFERA.

Shrub, young shoots tomentose, later glabrous. Leaves 6-9 × 2.5-3.5cm, oblong, apex acute to apiculate, lower surface with a whitish brown to rufous tomentum that usually persists, occasionally only over the midrib; petioles tomentose. Flowers 10-20, in a dense truss; calyx *c.*1mm; corolla white to pale pink, with or without purple flecks, blotch apparently absent, 40mm, widely campanulate, without nectar pouches; ovary densely stalked-glandular, style glabrous. H4a-b. April-May. Taiwan,

Cultivated plants are distinctive on account of their usually persistent leaf indumentum. However, recent Japanense authors treat this as a variety of *R. pseudochrysanthum*.

In the wild this taxon has an extremely restricted distribution.

AM 1989 (P.A. Cox, Glendoick, Perthshire), from Rhododendron Venture, Taiwan, RV 72/001; corolla white and densely spotted.

♛ 1993

R. PACHYTRICHUM FRANCH. - SUBSECT. MACULIFERA.

Shrub or small tree, 1-6m; young shoots and petioles tomentose or stalked-glandular. Leaves 9-15 × 2-4.2cm, elliptic to obovate, apex more or less cuspidate, lower surface with lamina glabrous though with short folioliferous hairs on or near the midrib. Flowers 7-10, in a lax truss; calyx *c.*1.5mm; corolla white suffused pink to pink, with a purple blotch and flecks, narrowly campanulate, lacking nectar pouch-

es, 35-50mm; ovary densely tomentose or stalked-glandular, style glabrous or glandular at base. H4a. March-April. China (NE Yunnan, SW Sichuan), 2,500-3,600m.

Var. **pachytrichum**. Petioles, pedicels, calyx and ovary tomentose, eglandular.

AM 1963 (Lord Aberconway and National Trust, Bodnant) to a clone 'Sesame'; flowers white, tinged purple.

Var. **monosematum** (Hutch.) D.F.Chamb. (*R. monosematum* Hutch.). Petioles, pedicels, calyx and ovary stalked-glandular.

Var. *monosematum* is only known for certain from Emei Shan in W Sichuan, and has apparently arisen as a stabilized backcross from the hybrid swarms of var. *pachytrichum* and *R. strigillosum* that occur close by. It was originally described from cultivated material that resembled var. *pachytrichum*. It is therefore more appropriate to treat it as a variety of *R. pachytrichum* rather than of *R. strigillosum* as do some Chinese authors.

R. paludosum Hutch. - is a synonym of **R. nivale** Hook.f. var. **nivale** (Subsect. Lapponica).

R. PAPILLATUM BALF.F & COOPER (INCL. *R. EPAPILLATUM* BALF.F. & COOPER) - SUBSECT. IRRORATA.

Shrub or small tree, 2-5m. Leaves subcoriaceous, 9-14 × 3-5cm, oblanceolate to oblong, apex acuminate, lower surface usually with a papillate cuticle and a thin persistent or detersile stellate indumentum, lacking punctate glands. Flowers 5-10, in lax truss, pale cream to pink, with purple flecks and a basal blotch, campanulate, nectar pouches lacking, 40-55mm; ovary with a dense dendroid tomentum intermixed with stalked glands. H3-4. April-May. Bhutan, NE India (Arunachal Pradesh), 1,800-3,300m.

Rarely grown; plants in cultivation are sometimes wrongly named *R. agastum*, a species that may be distinguished by its 6-7-lobed corolla, etc.

R. paradoxum Balf.f. - is probably a chance

hybrid of *R. wiltonii* (Subsect. Taliensia). It was raised at Edinburgh from seed as Wilson 1353, herbarium specimens of which are referrable to *R. wiltonii*.

R. PARMULATUM COWAN - SUBSECT. NERIIFLORA.
Dwarf shrub, 0.6-3m. Leaves 4.5-8 × 2-3.5cm, obovate to elliptic, lower surface glabrous except for a few white hairs on the midrib and main veins; petioles glabrescent. Flowers 4-6, in a tight truss; calyx *c*.5mm; corolla white or pale yellow flushed pink, occasionally red, with red flecks, tubular-campanulate, with nectar pouches, 40-50mm; ovary with a few scattered hairs, abruptly contracted into the glabrous style. H4a. March-May. China (S Tibet), 3,000-3,700m.

The conspicuous red flecks on the corolla are an unusual feature in Subsect. Neriiflora. This is a rare species, both in cultivation, and in the wild.

AM 1977 (Maj.Gen. E.G.W.W. Harrison, Tremeer, Cornwall) to a clone 'Ocelot'; flowers yellow-green, lobes with a darker central band, upper throat heavily spotted with greyed purple.

AM 1983 (Lord Aberconway and National Trust, Bodnant) to a clone 'Palma'; trusses loose, 3-7-flowered, corolla green-white, each lobe having a slightly deeper coloured central band, with heavy spotting of greyed purple in upper throat.

R. PARRYAE HUTCH. - SUBSECT. MADDENIA.
Shrub, 1.5-3m, sometimes epiphytic; young shoots with or without setae. Leaves 6-14 × 3-6cm, elliptic to oblong-elliptic, apex acuminate to rounded, margin lacking setae, upper surface with impressed midrib; lower surface with unequal brown scales that are 1-2× their own diameter apart. Flowers 3-5, in a loose terminal inflorescence, scented; calyx minute, ciliate; corolla white with a yellowish blotch at base, funnel-shaped, 70-85mm, outer surface with scales throughout, pilose at base; ovary scaly, tapering into the style that is scaly below.

H1-2. May. India (Arunachal Pradesh), 1,750-2,150m.

Material introduced from the Apa Tani Valley suggests an affinity with *R. walongense*, not with *R. johnstoneanum*, as has been proposed by some authors.

AM 1957 (Royal Botanic Garden, Edinburgh); flowers white, with a yellow-orange blotch.

FCC 1973 (G. Gorer, Sunte House, Haywards Heath).

♀ 1993

R. parvifolium Adams - is a synonym of **R. lapponicum** (L.) Wahlenb. (Subsect. Lapponica).

R. patulum Kingdon-Ward - is a synonym of **R. pemakoense** Kingdon-Ward (Subsect. Uniflora).

R. pectinatum Hutch. - is a synonym of **R. moulmainense** Hook.f. (sect. Choniastrum).

R. PEMAKOENSE KINGDON-WARD (INCL. *R. PATULUM* KINGDON-WARD) - SUBSECT. UNIFLORA.
Prostrate or erect dwarf shrub, to 0.3m; young growth scaly and pubescent. Leaves 1.7-2.6 × 0.6-1.3cm, obovate or obovate-elliptic, apex rounded, margin revolute, entire, lower surface densely covered with unequal scales that are golden when young, becoming brown, the larger of which have undulate rims. Flowers 1-2, in a terminal inflorescence; calyx lobes oblong, 2.5-4mm, not ciliate; corolla pink to pale purplish mauve, funnel-campanulate, 24-30mm, tube 13-18mm, outer surface densely pilose and sparsely scaly; stamens 10; ovary scaly, style impressed, declinate, pubescent, scaly or glabrous at base, longer than stamens. H3-4a. March-April. India (Arunachal Pradesh), China (SE Tibet), 2,900-3,050m.

The markedly unequal leaf scales and the larger corolla will distinguish this species from the allied *R. uniflorum*.

AM 1933 (Sir John Ramsden, Bulstrode, Gerrards Cross) from Kingdon-

Ward 6301; flowers white, suffused mauve externally.

R. PENDULUM HOOK.F. - SUBSECT. EDGEWORTHIA.
Straggling epiphytic shrub, 0.3-1.3m. Leaves 3.5-5 × 1.5-2.5cm, oblong-elliptic, apex obtuse, upper surface smooth; lower surface with a glaucous papillate epidermis, scales small, distant, golden, also with a dense woolly cinnamon tomentum. Pedicels densely tomentose. Flowers 2-3 per inflorescence; calyx lobes *c*.6mm; corolla white, sometimes flushed pink, or cream, open-funnel-campanulate, 15-22mm; stamens 10, regular; ovary scaly and densely tomentose, style sharply deflexed, usually with a few scales at base. H3-4a. April-May. Nepal, India (Sikkim) Bhutan, China (S Tibet), 2,270-3,630m.
This species is allied to *R. seinghkuense* (q.v.).

R. pennivenium Balf.f. & Forrest - is a synonym of **R. tanastylum** Balf.f. & Kingdon-Ward var. **pennivenium** (Balf.f. & Forrest) D.F.Chamb. (Subsect. Irrorata).

R. PENTAPHYLLUM MAXIM. - SECT. SCIADORHODION.
Deciduous shrub or small tree, to 4(-8)m; vegetative shoots arising from buds in the axils of the previous year's leaves; young twigs glabrous or sparsely covered with eglandular and gland-tipped hairs. Leaves turning red in autumn, arranged in pseudowhorls of 5(-7) at the apices of the branches, 2.1-6.3 × 1.1-3.8cm, elliptic to obovate, apex acuminate to acute, base cuneate, lower surface glabrous to very sparsely unicellular-pubescent towards base, veins and midrib sometimes covered with straight or crisped eglandular or glandular hairs. Pedicels glabrous or covered with gland-tipped hairs. Flowers fragrant, appearing before or with the leaves, 1-2, in a contracted raceme; calyx 0.5-5mm; corolla pink to deep rose, usually with red-brown flecks on upper three lobes, rotate-campanulate, the short tube gradually expanding into the longer limb,

15-35mm. Capsule glabrous. H4a-b. March-April. Japan (Honshu, Shikoku, Kyushu), 500-1,700m.
This species is most closely allied to *R. quinquefolium* (q.v.).
AM 1942 (Lord Aberconway, Bodnant); flowers Rose Bengal, paler with age.

R. peramabile Hutch. – is a synonym of **R. intricatum** Franch. (Subsect. Lapponica)

R. peramoenum Balf.f. & Forrest - is a synonym of **R. arboreum** Sm. var. **peramoenum** (Balf.f. & Forrest) D.F.Chamb.

R. peregrinum Tagg - is almost certainly a rogue hybrid of *R. galactinum* (Subsect. Falconera) that was raised from seed of that species as Wilson 4254, by Mr Magor at Lamellan in Cornwall. It differs in the leaf indumentum that lacks the cup-shaped hairs of *R. galactinum*.

R. PERICLYMENOIDES (MICHX.) SHINNERS (INCL. *R. NUDIFLORUM* (L.) TORR.) - SUBSECT. PENTANTHERA.
Deciduous shrub or small tree, to 5m; young twigs eglandular-hairy. Leaves 5.2-9(-11) × 1.5-3(-3.5)cm, ovate or obovate to elliptic, lower surface eglandular-hairy, or glabrous. Flower bud scales with outer surface glabrous or occasionally covered with unicellular hairs; margin unicellular-ciliate, rarely also glandular. Pedicels covered with unicellular and/or multi-cellular eglandular hairs. Flowers with a sweet fragrance, appearing before or with the leaves, 6-15, in a shortened raceme; calyx 1-2(-4)mm; corolla deep pink, sometimes with a dark pink to crimson tube, funnelform, tube gradually expanding into limb, outer surface covered in a mixture of eglandular and gland-tipped hairs, 20-47mm. Capsules eglandular-hairy. H4b-c. May-June. E USA, 100-1,000m.
Allied to *R. canescens* but differing in the usually glabrous flower bud scales and the more gradually tapering corolla tube. The name *R. nudiflorum*, used in the past for this plant, is illegitimate.

R. perulatum Balf.f. & Forrest - is a synonym of **R. microgynum** Balf.f. & Forrest (Subsect. Neriiflora).

R. phaeochrysum Balf.f. & W.W.Sm. - Subsect. Taliensia.
Shrub, 1.2-4.5m. Leaves 4-14.5 × 1-6.5cm, elliptic to ovate-oblong, apex acute to apiculate, lower surface covered with a one-layered compacted or felted, sometimes agglutinated, brown indumentum composed of radiate to sub-ramiform hairs; petioles floccose. Flowers 8-15, in a dense truss; calyx *c*.1mm; corolla white flushed pink, with crimson flecks, funnel-campanulate, nectar pouches lacking; ovary glabrous or with a few papillate hairs, style glabrous. H4b. April-May. China (S Tibet, NW Yunnan, SW & C Sichuan), 3,350-4,200m.

Var. **phaeochrysum**. (incl. *R. dryophyllum* Balf.f. & Forrest). Leaves 8-14.5cm, indumentum felted, not splitting; corolla 32-50mm.

Var. **agglutinatum** (Balf.f. & Forrest) D.F.Chamb. (*R. agglutinatum* Balf.f. & Forrest & incl. *R. dumulosum* Balf.f. & Forrest). Leaves 4-9cm, indumentum agglutinated, sometimes splitting; corolla 20-35mm.

Var. **levistratum** (Balf.f. & Forrest) D.F.Chamb. (*R. levistratum* Balf.f. & Forrest). Leaves 4-9cm, indumentum felted, continuous; corolla 20-35mm

This species shows considerable variation in the leaf indumentum. It apparently merges with *R. przewalskii* in C Sichuan (q.v.) and hybridizes with *R. aganniphum* and perhaps other species in Subsect. Taliensia. Most cultivated plants named *R. dryophyllum* should be referred to var. *levistratum;* the type of *R. dryophyllum* is however referrable to var. *phaeochrysum.*

AM 1977 (R.N.S. Clarke, Borde Hill, Sussex) to a clone 'Greenmantle', Rock 11325 (=USDA 59229); flowers white, with a small red blotch.

R. phoenicodum Balf.f. & Farrer - is a synonym of **R. neriiflorum** Franch. subsp. **neriiflorum** (Subsect. Neriiflora).

R. pholidotum Balf.f. & W.W.Sm. - is a synonym of **R. heliolepis** Franch. (Subsect. Heliolepida).

R. piercei Davidian - Subsect. Neriiflora.
Straggling shrub, 1.5-2.5m. Leaves 6-11 × 2.7-5.2cm, ovate to elliptic, upper surface rugulose; lower surface with a two-layered indumentum, the upper layer a thick fulvous tomentum composed of dendroid hairs, the lower layer white and adpressed; petioles tomentose. Flowers 6-8, in a tight truss; calyx 3-6mm, irregular; corolla fleshy, crimson with darker nectar pouches, tubular-campanulate, 28-35mm; ovary densely tomentose, abruptly contracted into the glabrous style. H3-4a. March-May. China (S Tibet).

This species is closely allied to *R. beanianum*, with which it shares the rugulose upper surface of the leaves. It does however differ in the form of the leaf indumentum that is thicker and lighter in colour.

R. pingianum Fang - Subsect. Argyrophylla.
Shrub or small tree, 4-8m. Leaves 8-13.5 × 3-4.2cm, lanceolate to oblanceolate, apex acute, upper surface reticulate, lower surface with a white compacted indumentum embedded in a surface film. Pedicels 30-40mm. Flowers 8-20, in a loose to dense truss, pinkish to pale purple, funnel-campanulate, nectar pouches lacking, 28-35mm; ovary rufous (or white?)-tomentose, eglandular, style glabrous. H4b. May-June. China (W Sichuan), 2,000-2,750m.

Closely allied to *R. argyrophyllum* but it may generally be distinguished by the rufous-tomentose ovary and the longer pedicels.

R. planetum Balf.f. - is probably a hybrid of **R. decorum** (Subsect. Fortunea). The type of this species was raised from Wilson seed number 1882 (perhaps a mistake for

1782) at Caerhays. the seed is supposed to have originated near Tatsienlu (Kangding) in W Sichuan though no matching wild collected specimens are known. This species should not therefore be accorded any formal status.

R. platyphyllum Franch. ex Balf.f. & W.W.Sm. - is a synonym of **R. cephalanthum** Franch. subsp. **platyphyllum** (Franch. ex Balf.f. & W.W.Sm.) Cullen (sect. Pogonanthum).

R. PLEISTANTHUM BALF.F. EX WILDING - SUBSECT. TRIFLORA.
Differs from *R. yunnanense* in the absence of setose hairs on the leaf margins and upper surface, and the puberulent petioles that also lack setae. H3-4a. May. China (N Yunnan, W Sichuan), 2,000-4,500m.

This species is very closely allied to *R. yunnanense* and may prove to be synonymous with it. Its wild distribution is however more northerly.

R. pogonostylum Balf.f & W.W.Sm. - is a synonym of **R. irroratum** Franch. subsp. **pogonostylum** (Balf.f. & W.W.Sm) D.F.Chamb. (Subsect. Irrorata).

R. POCOPHORUM BALF.F. EX TAGG - SUBSECT. NERIIFLORA.
Shrub, 0.6-3m. Leaves 8-15 × 3.2-5.2cm, oblong to obovate, lower surface covered with a thick, continuous or patchy rufous tomentum composed of dendroid hairs; petioles tomentose and stalked-glandular. at least when young. Flowers 10(-20), in a tight truss; calyx 5-10mm, lobes irregular; corolla fleshy, light to deep crimson, tubular-campanulate, 40-50mm; ovary densely stalked-glandular. H3-4a. NE India (Arunachal Pradesh), China (S Tibet, NW Yunnan), 3,650-4,600m.

Var. **pocophorum**. Leaves with a continuous indumentum beneath.

AM 1971 (National Trust and Countess of Rosse, Nymans); to a clone 'Cecil Nice' from Kingdon-Ward 8289; flowers uniform deep red above, with dark markings in throat.

Var. **hemidartum** (Tagg) D.F.Chamb. (*R. hemidartum* Tagg). Leaves with a patchy discontinuous indumentum beneath.

This species is closely allied to *R. coelicum* but differs in the narrower leaves and non-tomentose petioles.

R. polifolium Franch. - is a synonym of **R. thymifolium** Maxim. (Subsect. Lapponica).

R. poluninii Davidian (incl. *R. tsariense* Cowan var. *magnum* Davidian) - Subsect. Lanata; probably a hybrid of *R. flinckii* and *R. wallichii* or *R. campanulatum*. It differs from *R. flinckii* in the ivory-white to pink flowers but otherwise resembles it closely.

R. polyandrum Hutch. is a synonym of **R. maddenii** Hook.f. subsp. **maddenii** (Subsect. Maddenia).

R. POLYCLADUM FRANCH. (INCL. *R. COMPACTUM* HUTCH. & *R. SCINTILLANS* BALF.F. & W.W.SM.) - SUBSECT. LAPPONICA.
Erect low shrub, to 1.2m. Leaves (0.4-)0.8-2 × 0.2-0.6(-0.8)cm, narrowly elliptic to elliptic, acute or obtuse, obscurely mucronulate, lower surface covered with uniformly reddish brown scales that are either, not touching, or in groups touching one another. Flowers to 5 per inflorescence; calyx obsolete to 2.5mm, lobes sometimes unequal, deltoid to rounded; corolla lavender to rich purple-blue, rarely white, broadly funnel-shaped, 8-13mm; stamens 10, as long as the corolla; ovary scaly, style longer than the stamens, glabrous or pubescent towards the base. H4a-b. April-May. China (Yunnan), 3,000-4,300m.

R. polycladum is probably allied to *R. impeditum* but differs in the shorter calyx, etc.

AM 1924 (Lady Aberconway and Hon. H.D. McLaren, Bodnant); flowers purplish rose.

FCC 1934 (L. de Rothschild, Exbury) to a clone 'Policy'; flowers lavender blue.

♈ 1993, to a clone 'Policy'.

R. POLYLEPIS FRANCH. - SUBSECT. TRIFLORA.
Shrub or small tree, 1-6m; young growth scaly. Leaves 5-10 × 1.5-3cm, narrowly elliptic, apex acute to rounded, upper surface scaly or not, glabrous, lower surface covered with dark to yellowish brown overlapping large flaky scales. Flowers 3-4, in a loose terminal inflorescence; calyx minute, usually not ciliate; corolla purple, zygomorphic, widely funnel-shaped, 25-30mm, outer surface scaly; stamens 10; ovary scaly, pubescent at apex, impressed below the declinate, glabrous style. H3-4a. April-June. China (W Sichuan), 2,000-3,000m.

This is a distinctive species.

R. PONTICUM L. - SUBSECT. PONTICA.
Shrub or small tree, 2-5(-8)m; young shoots glabrous; bud scales deciduous. Leaves 6-18 × 2.4-5.5cm, oblanceolate to broadly elliptic, apex acute to acuminate; upper and lower surfaces glabrous when mature; petioles glabrous or with a few stalked glands and a sparse floccose tomentum. Flowers 8-20, in a dense truss; calyx 1-2mm; corolla lilac-pink to purple, usually with greenish yellow flecks, campanulate, nectar pouches lacking, 35-50mm; ovary and style glabrous. H4a-b. June-July. Spain, Portugal, Bulgaria, N Turkey, Georgia, Armeniya, Lebanon, s.l.-1,800m.

R. ponticum is closely allied to *R.catawbiense* (q.v.). It has become naturalized in Britain where it is extremely invasive and difficult to eradicate, once established. It hybridizes with *R. caucasicum* (q.v.), and with other members of the subsection where the ranges overlap.

R. PRAESTANS BALF.F. & W.W.SM. - SUBSECT. GRANDIA.
Shrub or small tree, 3-10m; bark rough. Leaves 14-40 × 5.2-12cm, oblong-obovate to oblanceolate, apex rounded, base cuneate, lower surface covered in a one-layered silvery compacted agglutinated indumentum; petioles strongly flattened and winged. Flowers 12-20, in a dense truss, 7-8-lobed, pale yellow or white flushed pink, to pink, with crimson flecks and a basal blotch, obliquely campanulate, nectar pouches lacking, 35-50mm; stamens c.16; ovary covered with a dense buff tomentum. H4a. April-May. China (SE Tibet, NW Yunnan), 3,350-4,250m.

R. praestans may be distinguished by the strongly flattened petiole and the shining silvery compacted leaf indumentum. This species apparently hybridizes with several other species in the wild, including *R. arizelum*, and perhaps also *R. fulvum*.

AM 1963 (E. de Rothschild, Exbury) to a clone 'Exbury', as *R. coryphaeum*; flowers white, tinged pale yellow, with a crimson blotch.

R. PRAETERITUM HUTCH. - SUBSECT. FORTUNEA.
Shrub. Leaves 6-8 × 2.5-3.2cm, obovate-elliptic, base rounded, lower surface glabrous. Flowers 5-lobed, c.7, in a lax truss; calyx 1-2mm; corolla white flushed pink to pale pink, with purple flecks, open-campanulate, with nectar pouches, 30-40mm; stamens 10; ovary and style glabrous. H4. March-April. China (W Hubei).

This species was described from plants in cultivation that were supposed to have been raised from Wilson seed, apparently collected in W Hubei. *R. praeteritum* is the only member of Subsect. Fortunea with nectar pouches; in view of its origins its status is uncertain.

R. PRAEVERNUM HUTCH. - SUBSECT. FORTUNEA.
Shrub, 1.5-5m. Leaves 10-18 × 2.5-6cm, elliptic-oblanceolate, base broadly cuneate, lower surface entirely glabrous. Flowers c.10 in a truss; calyx 1-2mm; corolla 5-lobed, white, sometimes suffused with pink, with flecks and a conspicuous basal blotch, campanulate, nectar pouches lacking; stamens 10; ovary and style glabrous. H4b. February-April.

China (Sichuan, Hubei), 1,500-2,500m.

R. praevernum is closely allied to *R. sutchuenense* and apparently hybridizes with it in the wild.

AM 1954 (Col Lord Digby, Minterne, Dorset); flowers white, with a pinkish blue flush and crimson chocolate blotch.

R. PRATTII FRANCH. (*R. FABERI* FRANCH. SUBSP. *PRATTII* (FRANCH.) D.F.CHAMB. & INCL. *R. LEEI* FANG) - SUBSECT. TALIENSIA.
Shrub, 1.5-5m. Leaves 10-17 × 4.2-8cm, elliptic to broadly ovate, apex acuminate, lower surface covered with a thin two-layered indumentum, the upper layer more or less detersile, brown, composed of ramiform hairs, the lower whitish, compacted; petioles 1-2.5cm, covered with an arachnoid tomentum that is intermixed with glands. Flowers 12-20, in a dense truss; calyx 8-10mm, lobes broad, apex rounded; corolla white or (rarely) creamish, often flushed pink, crimson flecks and a basal blotch often present; ovary rufous-tomentose, style glabrous or glandular below. H4b. April-May. China (W Sichuan), 3,100-4,450m.

This species is allied to *R. faberi* but differs in its larger leaves and in the leaf indumentum. It is also allied to *R. bureavioides* (q.v.).

AM 1967 (Maj. A.E. Hardy, Sandling Park, Kent) to a clone 'Perry Wood'; flowers white, flushed red-purple in throat.

R. PREPTUM BALF.F. - SUBSECT. FALCONERA.
Shrub or small tree, 2.5-9m; bark rough. Leaves 13.5-15 × 5.5-6.2cm, upper surface with impressed veins, lower surface with a two-layered indumentum, the upper layer buff, composed of strongly fimbriate cup-shaped hairs, the lower compacted; petioles terete. Flowers 10-20, in a dense truss, 6-7-lobed, white with a purple basal blotch, ventricose-campanulate, nectar pouches lacking, 35-45mm; stamens (10-)12-14; ovary densely tomentose. H3-4a. April-May. NE Burma, *c*.3,350m.

R. preptum may be a hybrid of *R. rex*

and *R. coriaceum*.

R. PRIMULIFLORUM BUREAU & FRANCH. - SECT POGONANTHUM.
Small shrub, to 1(-1.5)m; leaf bud-scales quickly deciduous. Leaves 1.1-3.5 × 0.5-1 (-1.5)cm, narrowly elliptic to elliptic, apex rounded or tapered, lower surface with 2-3 tiers of dense overlapping scales, the lowest tier, golden yellow, the upper tiers pale brown to brown. Flowers several, in a dense racemose umbel; calyx lobes 2.5-6mm; corolla white flushed pink to pink, often yellowish orange towards base of tube, hypocrateriform, tube 6-12mm, outer surface usually glabrous, more rarely sparsely pilose or scaly, densely pilose within at throat; stamens 5(-6); capsule scaly. H4a-b. April-May, China (N Yunnan, S Tibet, SW Sichuan), 3,350-4,600m.

This widespread species resembles *R. cephalanthum* but it may be distinguished by the deciduous leaf bud scales, etc.

AM 1980 (P.A. Cox, Glendoick) to a clone 'Doker-la', as *R. primuliflorum* var. *cephalanthoides*; truss compact, 10-12-flowered, corolla red-purple, paling to near white at rim.

R. PRINCIPIS BUREAU & FRANCH. (INCL. *R. VELLEREUM* HUTCH.) - SUBSECT. TALIENSIA.
Shrub, 2-6m. Leaves 6-12 × 1.8-5cm, oblong to ovate-lanceolate, apex more or less acute, lower surface covered with a white to fawn two-layered indumentum, the upper layer spongy, lanate-tomentose, composed of ramiform hairs, the lower compacted; petioles tomentose. Flowers 10-20, in a dense truss; calyx *c*.1mm; corolla white to pink, with purple flecks, campanulate, nectar pouches lacking, 25-37mm; ovary and style usually glabrous. H4b. March-April. China (E Tibet), 2,900-3,950m.

This species is allied to *R. aganniphum* but the leaves are relatively narrower.

AM 1976 (R.N.S. Clarke, Borde Hill, Sussex) to a clone 'Lost Horizon', as *R. vellereum*, from Kingdon-Ward 5656; flowers white suffused red-purple, spotted red.

AM 1979 (R.N.S. Clarke, Borde Hill, Sussex) to a clone 'Far Horizon', as *R. vellereum*, from Kingdon-Ward 5656.

R. PRINOPHYLLUM (SMALL) MILLAIS - SUBSECT. PENTANTHERA.
Deciduous shrub, to 3m; young twigs densely covered with eglandular (rarely gland-tipped) hairs. Leaves (4-)5-7.4(-8.7) × (1.2-)1.8-3(-3.7)cm, ovate or obovate to elliptic, lower surface covered with eglandular hairs, rarely glabrous. Flower bud scales densely covered with unicellular hairs, rarely glabrous. Pedicels with a mixture of eglandular and gland-tipped multicellular hairs. Flowers with a spicy fragrance, appearing before or with the leaves, 4-13, in a shortened raceme; calyx 1-3mm; corolla deep to rose pink, rarely white, funnelform, tube gradually expanding into the limb, 23-42mm. Capsule covered with unicellular and gland-tipped multicellular hairs. H4b. April-May. NE & C USA, 150-1,500m.

Resembling *R. periclymenoides* and *R. canescens* but differing from both in its more gradually tapered corolla tube and the gland-tipped hairs on the pedicels and capsules.

AM 1955 (Mrs R.M. Stevenson, Tower Court, Ascot) as *R. roseum*; flowers Phlox Pink, with darker tube and buds.

FCC 1981 (Anne, Countess of Rosse and the National Trust, Nymans) to a clone 'Philip Holmes'; flowers in trusses of 6-9, corolla white flushed pink, deepening in throat to red-purple.

R. PRONUM TAGG & FORREST - SUBSECT. TALIENSIA.
Creeping shrub, 0.15-0.6m; perulae persistent. Leaves (4-)6-7.5 × 1.8-2.8cm, elliptic, apex acuminate, lower surface with a dense greyish to fawn two-layered indumentum, the upper layer loosely lanate-tomentose, composed of ramiform hairs, the lower compacted; petioles glabrescent. Flowers 6-10, in a tight truss; calyx 1-2mm; corolla white or cream to pink, with pur-

ple flecks, funnel-campanulate, nectar pouches lacking, 35-45mm; ovary and style glabrous. H4b. May. China (W Yunnan), 3,650-4,400m.

This is a rare species in the wild that rarely flowers in cultivation. Its dwarf habit and a greyish leaf indumentum make this a distinctive species that has no close allies.

R. prostratum W.W.Sm. - is a synonym of **R. saluenense** Franch. subsp. **chameunum** (Balf.f. & Forrest) Cullen (Subsect. Saluenensia).

R. PROTEOIDES BALF.F. & W.W.SM. (INCL. *R. LAMPROPEPLUM* BALF.F. & FORREST) - SUBSECT. TALIENSIA.
Dwarf shrub, 0.15-1m. Leaves 2-4 × 0.7-1cm, elliptic, apex cucullate, lower surface with a dense two-layered indumentum, the upper layer brown to rufous, bleaching with age, loosely lanate-tomentose, composed of ramiform hairs, the lower radiate, compacted; petioles densely tomentose. Flowers 5-10, in a tight truss, white or pale cream, flushed rose, with purple flecks, 25-35mm, campanulate, nectar pouches lacking; ovary rufoustomentose, eglandular, style glabrous. H4b. April-May. China (SE Tibet, NW Yunnan, SW Sichuan), 3,650-4,550m.

This species is allied to *R. roxieanum*, especially var. *cucullatum*, but differs in its smaller leaves and lower stature. It hybridizes with *R. roxieanum* (see under that species)and with *R. aganniphum* (see *R. bathythyllum*). This dwarf alpine is very slow-growing in cultivation.

R. PROTISTUM BALF.F. & FORREST - SUBSECT. GRANDIA.
Tree, 6-30m; bark rough. Leaves (12-)20-37 × (4-)8.8-16cm, obovate to elliptic, apex rounded, sometimes apiculate, lower surface glabrous in the juvenile state though sometimes developing a continuous buff adpressed tomentum, at least along a marginal band; petioles terete. Flowers *c*.25, in a dense truss, 8-lobed, rose, sometimes whitish at base, with a dark basal blotch

and nectar pouches, sometimes also with a few purple flecks, funnel-campanulate, 50-75mm; stamens *c*.16; ovary densely rufous-tomentose. H2-3. February-March. NE Burma, China (W Yunnan), Northern Vietnam, 2,450-3,350m.

Var. **protistum**. Mature leaves with a sparse discontinuous indumentum below though sometimes denser along a marginal band.

AM 1983 (Maj. S.E. Bolitho and the National Trust, Trengwainton), from Kingdon-Ward 8609; truss averaging 25 flowers, corolla creamy white flushed rose.

Var. **giganteum** (Tagg) D.F.Chamb. (*R. giganteum* Tagg). Mature leaves with a continuous indumentum beneath.

FCC 1953 (Duchess of Montrose, Brodick Castle) as *R. giganteum*, from Forrest 19335; flowers heavily veined and streaked Magenta Rose, with dark nectaries.

Var. *protistum* may represent an arrested juvenile stage of development that is retained into maturity in some plants, especially those from higher altitudes in NW Yunnan. This species requires a relatively frost-free climate and is therefore rare in cultivation. It is one of the first species to flower.

R. PRUNIFLORUM HUTCH. & KINGDON-WARD - SUBSECT. GLAUCA.
Dwarf shrub, to 1m; shoots with a shredding brownish bark. Leaves 3-4.2 × 1.4-2.5cm, obovate to narrowly obovate, apex rounded, lower surface covered with pale yellow, clouded or milky scales, the smaller more or less touching. Pedicels scaly. Flowers 4-6 per inflorescence; calyx lobes 3.5-5mm, rounded at apex; corolla dull crimson to plum purple, campanulate, 10-13mm; stamens 10, regular; ovary scaly, style sharply deflexed, glabrous. H3-4a. July-August. India (Arunachal Pradesh, NE Burma), 3,050-3,950m.

This is a distinctive species.

R. PRUNIFOLIUM (SMALL.) MILLAIS - SUBSECT. PENTANTHERA.
Deciduous shrub or small tree, to 5m; young twigs glabrous. Leaves (5.5-)6-11.5(-15.2) × (2.5-)2.8-4.2cm, ovate or obovate to elliptic, lower surface glabrous except for unicellular hairs on midrib and main veins. Flower bud scales with outer surface glabrous, margin uncellular-ciliate. Pedicels covered with eglandular hairs, occasionally glabrous. Flowers not fragrant, appearing after the leaves have fully expanded, 4-7, in a shortened raceme; calyx 1-4mm; corolla coral-orange to deep red, with a darker red blotch on the upper lobe, funnelform, tube abruptly expanding into limb, outer surface usually glabrous though occasionally sparsely covered with eglandular hairs, 38-52mm. Capsule sparsely covered with eglandular hairs. H3-4a. June-August. SE USA, 90-200m.

Allied to *R. flammeum*, *R. cumberlandense* and *R. calendulaceum* but generally less hairy and differing from all three in the indistinctly blotched corolla. This species has an extremely restricted distribution, along the border of Georgia and Alabama.

AM 1950 (Crown Estate Commissioners, Windsor) to a clone 'Summer Sunset'; flowers Vermilion.

R. PRZEWALSKII MAXIM. - SUBSECT. TALIENSIA.
Shrub, 1-2.7m. Leaves (4.5-) 6-10 × 2-4.5cm, broadly elliptic, apex apiculate, lower surface covered with a compacted, more or less agglutinated, one-layered, whitish to pale brown indumentum composed of long-rayed stellate hairs, or glabrous at maturity; petioles glabrous, yellow. Flowers 10-15, in a dense truss; calyx *c*.0.5mm; corolla white to pale pink, with purple flecks, campanulate, nectar pouches lacking, 25-35mm; ovary and style glabrous. H4b. April-May. China (Qinghai, Gansu, N & C Sichuan), 3,050-4,250m.

Subsp. **przewalskii**. Lower surface of leaves covered with a whitish to pale brown, thin indumentum at maturity.

Subsp. **dabanshanense** (W.P.Fang &

S.X.Wang) W.P.Fang & S.X.Wang (*R. dabanshanense* Fang & Wang). Lower surface of leaves glabrous at maturity.

Subsp. *dabanshanense* apparently only differs from subsp. *przewalskii* in its glabrous leaves. The latter closely resembles *R. phaeochrysum*. While material from the north of the range of *R. przewalskii* is generally distinct, it apparently merges with the latter species in C Sichuan. When there is any doubt *R. przewalskii* may be distinguished by its bright yellow petioles.

R. PSEUDOCHRYSANTHUM HAYATA - SUBSECT. MACULIFERA.
Low shrub, 0.5-2m; young shoots and petioles covered with a rufous to grey floccose tomentum. Leaves 3-8 × 1.5-5cm, ovate to elliptic, apex acuminate, lower surface with a floccose indumentum when young, with a few scattered hair remains on the lamina at maturity, though with a more persistent tomentum of folioliferous hairs overlying the midrib. Flowers 5-12, in a tight truss; calyx *c*.2mm; corolla white, sometimes tinged pink, usually with a red basal blotch and flecks, widely campanulate, nectar pouches lacking, 30-50mm; ovary densely tomentose, also with a few stalked glands, style tomentose at base. H4a-b. April-May. Taiwan, to 4,000m.

Var. **pseudochrysanthum.** Ovary densely rufous-tomentose or more or less glabrous; pedicels 13-20mm.

AM 1956 (E. de Rothschild, Exbury); flowers white flushed pink, spotted crimson.

Var. **nankotaisanense** (Hayata) T.Yamaz. (*R. nankotaisanenese* Hayata). Ovary stalked-glandular; pedicels 25-30mm.

The status of var. *nankotaisanense* is somewhat problematical as there is very little material available. *R. pseudochrysanthum* apparently merges with *R. morii* in the wild but generally occurs at higher altitudes. In cultivation the two are generally distinct; the present species is a smaller plant, with smaller leaves.
♀ 1993

R. pseudoyanthinum Balf.f. ex Hutch. - is a synonym of **R. concinnum** (Subsect. Triflora).

R. PUBESCENS BALF.F. & FORREST - SUBSECT. SCABRIFOLIA.
Small shrub, to 1.3m; young shoots scaly, and with an indumentum of filiform hairs. Leaves 1.8-2.4 × 0.3-0.6cm, narrowly elliptic to narrowly lanceolate, margin strongly revolute, both surfaces with a persistent indumentum of filiform hairs, the upper surface also with ultimately deciduous setae that lack swollen bases. Flowers 2-3, in a loose terminal inflorescence; calyx rim-like, ciliate; corolla rose-pink, funnel-shaped, 6-11mm, outer surface not scaly, glabrous; stamens 10; ovary scaly and pilose, impressed below the declinate style. H3-4a. March-April. China (Yunnan, Sichuan), 2,800-3,000m.

AM 1955 (Crown Estate Commissioners, Windsor) to a clone 'Fine Bristles'; flowers white, suffused with shades of Persian Rose, buds a deep shade of pink.

R. PUDOROSUM COWAN - SUBSECT. GRANDIA.
Tree, 6-15m; bark rough; bud scales persistent on the apical shoots. Leaves 14-20 × 5-7cm, oblanceolate, apex more or less acute, apiculate, lower surface with a thin whitish compacted and agglutinated indumentum; petioles terete. Flowers 15-25, in a dense truss, 6-8-lobed, rose pink, with a darker blotch, ventricose-campanulate, nectar pouches absent, 30-35mm; stamens 12-16; ovary whitish-tomentose. H4a. March-April. China (S Tibet), 3,600-3,800m.

This is a rare species in cultivation; it is vulnerable to late frosts.

R. pulchrum Sweet - is one of the 'Indica' Azalea garden hybrids.

R. PUMILUM HOOK.F. - SUBSECT. UNIFLORA.
Creeping shrub, to 0.1m; young shoots scaly and puberulent. Leaves 0.9-1.9 × 0.5-

1.2cm, elliptic to broadly elliptic, apex acute to rounded, margin entire, lower surface with distant small equal golden scales. Flowers 1-3, in a loose terminal inflorescence; calyx lobes oblong, 2-4mm, not ciliate; corolla pink or purple, campanulate, slightly oblique, 11-21mm, tube 7-14mm, outer surface densely pilose, scales few, mostly on lobes; stamens 10; ovary scaly, impressed below the straight, glabrous style that is shorter than the stamens. H3-4a. April-June. Nepal, India (Sikkim, Arunachal Pradesh), Bhutan, N Burma, China (S Tibet), 3,500-4,250m.

This species differs from the remaining species in the subsection in its small campanulate corolla and short style.

AM 1935 (Lord Swaythling, Townhill Park, Southampton) from Kingdon-Ward 6961; flowers pinkish mauve.

R. puralbum Balf.f. & W.W.Sm. - is a synonym of **R. wardii** W.W.Sm. var. **puralbum** (Balf.f. & W.W.Sm.) D.F.Chamb. (Subsect. Campylocarpa).

R. purdomii Rehder & E.H. Wilson - may be the same entity as *R. oreodoxa* subsp. *shensiense* (Subsect. Fortunea, q.v.).

R. QUINQUEFOLIUM BISSET & S.MOORE - SUBSECT. SCIADORHODION.
Shrub or small tree, to 6(-8)m; vegetative shoots arising from axillary buds associated with the lowest scaly leaves of the present year's shoots; young twigs glabrous. Leaves turning red in autumn, arranged in pseudowhorls of 3(-5) at the apices of the branches, 1-5.8 × 0.6-3.6cm rhombic-elliptic to obovate, apex acute to rounded, base cuneate, lower surface glabrous or unicellular-pubescent, the midrib usually with long straight or crisped unicellular hairs, especially towards base. Pedicels glabrous or with eglandular or gland-tipped hairs. Flowers not scented, appearing with the leaves, solitary or up to 3, in a contracted raceme; calyx 1-3mm; corolla white, with greenish spots on upper lobes, rotate-funnelform, the short tube abruptly contracted into the longer limb, 17-32mm.

Capsule glabrous to sparsely unicellular-pubescent, especially at apex. H4a-b. April-May. Japan (Honshu, Shikoku), 300-1,700m.

This species is probably closely allied to *R. pentaphyllum* but may be distinguished by the position of the vegetative buds and by the flower colour.

AM 1931 (Dowager Countess Cawdor, Haslemere); flowers white, spotted pale green.

AM 1958 (E. de Rothschild, Exbury) to a clone 'Five Arrows' flowers white, with olive green spots.
♀ 1993

R. RACEMOSUM FRANCH. - SUBSECT. SCABRIFOLIA.
Small shrub, 0.2-3m; young shoots scaly, glabrous or finely puberulent. Leaves 1.5-5 × 0.7-3cm, broadly obovate to oblong-elliptic, apex usually rounded and mucronate, upper surface with a few filiform hairs overlying the midrib, otherwise glabrous, lower surface with epidermis white-papillose, densely covered with rimless scales, glabrous. Flowers 2-3, in a loose axillary terminal inflorescence; calyx rim-like, not ciliate; corolla pale to deep pink, occasionally white, openly funnel-shaped, 7-17mm; stamens 10; ovary densely scaly, glabrous, impressed below the declinate, glabrous style. H3-4b(-4c). March-May. China (Yunnan, SW Sichuan, Guizhou), (800-)2,750-4,300m.

This is a common species with distinctive leaves.

AM 1970 (Hydon Nurseries, Godalming) to a clone 'Rock Rose', from Rock 11265 (=USDA 59578); flowers red-purple.

AM 1974 (Glendoick Gardens, Perth) to a clone 'White Lace'; flowers white.

FCC 1892 (J. Veitch and Sons, Chelsea).
♀ 1993, to a clone 'Rock Rose'.

R. radicans Balf.f. & Forrest - is a synonym of **R. calostrotum** Balf.f. & Kingdon-Ward subsp. **keleticum** (Balf.f. & Forrest) Cullen (Subsect. Saluenensia).

R. ramosissimum Franch. - is a synonym of **R. nivale** Hook.f. subsp. **boreale** N.M. Philipson & Philipson (Subsect. Lapponica).

R. RAMSDENIANUM COWAN - SUBSECT. IRRORATA.
Shrub or tree, 1.5-12m. Leaves coriaceous, 8.5-14 × 3-4.5cm, oblanceolate to elliptic, apex acute to acuminate, lower surface glabrous or with the vestiges of a brown indumentum, with persistent red punctate hair bases overlying the veins. Flowers 15-20, in a dense truss, scarlet to deep crimson, tubular-campanulate, with prominent nectar pouches, 35-40mm; ovary glabrous or with a few rufous hairs (rarely densely tomentose and glandular), style glabrous. H2-3. China (SE Tibet), 2,100-2,700m.
Closely allied to *R. kendrickii* but with broader leaves.

R. ravum Balf.f. & W.W.Sm.- is a synonym of **R. cuneatum** W.W.Sm. (Subsect. Lapponica).

R. RECURVOIDES TAGG & KINGDON-WARD - SUBSECT. GLISCHRA.
Generally a dwarf shrub, 1-1.5m; young shoots glandular-setose; bud scales persistent. Leaves coriaceous, 3-7 × 1-2cm, lanceolate to oblanceolate, apex blunt, margins strongly inrolled, lower surface with a dense cinnamon tomentum composed of ramiform hairs. Flowers 4-7 to a truss; calyx 8-10mm; corolla white flushed pink to rose, lacking a basal blotch though with crimson spots, campanulate, nectar pouches absent, *c.*30mm; ovary densely glandular-setose. H4a-b. April-May. NE Burma, 3,350m.
R. recurvoides superficially resembles *R. roxieanum* in Subsect. Taliensia, but the glandular-setose young shoots indicate a closer affinity with species in Subsect. Glischra.
AM 1941 (Col E.H.W. Bolitho, Trengwainton, Cornwall); flowers pale Rose Bengal, flushed with deeper shades.

R. RETICULATUM D.DON - SECT. BRACHYCALYX.
Shrub or small tree, 1-8m; young shoots soon glabrous. Leaves in whorls of up to three, at the ends of the branches, 3-6 × 1.5-4cm, rhombic-ovate, apex acute, lower surface with short brown hairs, mainly on the midrib and veins; petioles covered with bristle-like hairs. Pedicels covered with adpressed brown hairs. Flowers 1-2(-3) per inflorescence, appearing before the leaves; calyx minute; corolla rose-purple (rarely white), funnel-campanulate, 25-30mm; stamens 10; ovary villose, style glabrous. H4a-b. April-May. Japan (S Honshu, Shikoku, Kyushu), 400-700m.
R. reticulatum is allied to *R. nudipes* but differs in the pilose petioles and leaf midrib.
FCC 1982 (Hydon Nurseries, Godalming) to a clone 'Sea King', raised from seed from Japan; corolla solitary, red-purple, with upper lobe slightly paler and sparingly spotted.
♀ 1993

R. REX LÉVL. - SUBSECT. FALCONERA.
Large shrub or small tree, 2.5-12m; bark rough; leaves 8-37 × 5.5-13.5cm, obovate to oblanceolate; upper surface reticulate, lower surface covered with a dense fawn to rufous indumentum composed of slightly to moderately fimbriate cup-shaped hairs; petioles terete. Flowers 12-20, in a dense truss, fleshy, 7-8-lobed, white, with a crimson basal blotch and flecks, more or less regularly campanulate, nectar pouches lacking; stamens 14-16; ovary densely brown-tomentose. H4a-b. April-May. China (Tibet, W Yunnan, S Sichuan), 3,000-4,000m.
Subsp. **rex**. Leaf indumentum fawn, composed of only slightly fimbriate cup-shaped hairs. China (S Sichuan, NE Yunnan), *c.*3,500m.
AM 1946 (Lord Aberconway, Bodnant) to a clone 'Roseum', as *R. ficto-lacteum* var. *roseum*, from Kingdon-Ward 4509; flowers pale rose, with deeper coloured buds and with a small blotch.
AM 1955 (Crown Estate

Commissioners, Windsor) to a clone 'Quartz', from Rock 18234 (=USDA 3800); flowers pale pink, with a dull crimson blotch and spots.

FCC 1935 (J.J. Crosfield, Embley Park, Romsey) as *R. fictolacteum*, Ward's var., from Kingdon-Ward 4509; flowers white, with a crimson blotch.

♀ 1993, to a clone 'Quartz'.

Subsp. **fictolacteum** (Balf.f.) D.F.Chamb. (*R. fictolacteum* Balf.f.). Leaf indumentum rufous to dark brown, composed of moderately fimbriate cup-shaped hairs. China (W Yunnan, SE Tibet), 3,000-4,000m.

AM 1923 (G. Reuthe, Keston, Kent); flowers white, blotched crimson, with a few crimson spots.

AM 1953 (Col. Lord Digby, Minterne, Dorset) to a clone 'Cherry Tip', as *R. fictolacteum*, from Rock 11385 (= USDA 59255); flowers white, margined pink, with a deep crimson blotch and numerous spots.

A variable subspecies in respect of the size of the leaves and the colour of the leaf indumentum; those forms with small leaves, 8-14cm long, and small flowers, have been referred to *R. fictolacteum* Balf.f. var. *miniforme* Davidian, here treated as a synonym of subsp. *fictolacteum*.

The morphological boundary between the two subspecies is not clear-cut. It does however seem that those plants that equate with subsp. *rex*, with a paler leaf indumentum and large leaves, occur in the NE of the distribution of the species. These are replaced by typical subsp. *fictolacteum* in the West. In parts of SE Tibet subsp. *fictolacteum* apparently hybridizes with *R. arizelum* to produce mixed populations in which it is not possible to assign some individuals to either taxon.

R. rex Lévl. subsp. *arizelum* (Balf.f. & Forrest) D.F.Chamb. - is a synonym of **R. arizelum** Balf.f. & Forrest (Subsect. Falconera).

R. rhabdotum Balf.f & Cooper - is a synonym of **R. dalhousiae** Hook.f. var. **rhab-dotum** Balf.f. & Cooper (Subsect. Maddenia).

R. rhaibocarpum Balf.f. & W.W.Sm. - is a synonym of **R. selense** Franch. subsp. **dasycladum** (Balf.f. & W.W.Sm.) D.F.Chamb. (Subsect. Selensia).

R. RIGIDUM FRANCH. (INCL. *R. CAERULEUM* H.LÉV. & *R. ERIANDRUM* H.LÉV.) - SUBSECT. TRIFLORA.
Shrub, 1-10m; young shoots sparsely scaly, with a bloom. Leaves 3-6.5 × 1.3-2.5cm, elliptic to narrowly elliptic, apex acute, upper surface glabrous, lower surface with narrowly rimmed golden or brown scales 5-8× their own diameter apart; petioles glabrous. Flowers 2-6, in a loose terminal inflorescence; calyx minute, usually glabrous; corolla white to rose-pink or lilac, sometimes with red flecks, widely funnel-shaped, (21-)24-27(-30)mm, outer surface usually lacking scales, glabrous; stamens 10; ovary scaly, impressed below the declinate, glabrous style. H3-4a. April-May. China (N Yunnan, SW Sichuan, Guizhou), 2,000-3,350m.

This species differs from the closely allied *R. pleistanthum* in its more distant leaf scales and glabrous petioles.

AM 1933 (H. White, Sunningdale Nurseries) as *R. eriandrum*, from Rock 11288 (=USDA 59207); flowers white, slightly pink-flushed.

AM 1939 (L. de Rothschild, Exbury) as *R. caeruleum*, from Rock 11288 (=USDA 59207); flowers white, spotted red.

R. RIPENSE MAKINO - SUBSECT. TSUTSUSI
Shrub, 1-2m; young shoots and petioles densely covered with loosely adpressed flattened bristles that are intermixed with softer grey-brown, sometimes gland-tipped hairs. Leaves of two kinds; spring leaves deciduous, 3.5-5 × 1.5-2cm, ovate-lanceolate, apex mucronate, both surfaces covered with adpressed reddish grey pilose hairs, especially on the midrib; summer leaves 1.5-3 × 0.5-1cm, oblanceo-

late. Pedicels covered with soft spreading pilose hairs, sometimes with glandular and flattened bristles. Flowers 1-3 per inflorescence; calyx to 15mm; corolla white or rose-pink to red, widely funnel-shaped, 25-50mm; stamens 10; ovary covered with bristles, style glabrous. H3-4a. April-May. Japan (Honshu, Shikoku, Kyushu), 50-500m.

This species is closely allied to *R. stenopetalum* but differs in the smaller leaves and adpressed-hairy shoots, etc.

R. mucronatum, with white flowers, is presumed to be an artificial hybrid derived from *R. ripense* and *R. stenopetalum*.

AM 1933 (Hon. H.D. McLaren, Bodnant); flowers delicate pink.

R. RIRIEI HEMSL. & E.H.WILSON - SUBSECT. ARGYROPHYLLA.
Tree, 3.5-16m. Leaves 9.5-17 × 3-5.5cm, elliptic to oblanceolate, apex acute, upper surface reticulate, lower surface with a white, thin, compacted indumentum embedded in a surface film. Flowers 4-10, in a lax truss, purplish to violet, with darker nectar pouches, campanulate, 40-50mm; ovary covered with a grey felted tomentum, style glabrous. H4a-b. February-April. China (W Sichuan, Guizhou), *c*.2,000m.

This is the only species in Subsect. Argyrophylla that has nectar pouches.

AM 1931 (Lady Aberconway and Hon. H.D. McLaren, Bodnant); flowers light magenta, with darker nectaries.

R. rockii E.H.Wilson - is a synonym of **R. hunnewellianum** Rehder & E.H.Wilson subsp. **rockii** (E.H.Wilson) D.F.Chamb. (Subsect. Argyrophylla).

R. ROSEATUM HUTCH. (INCL. *R. LASIOPO-DUM* HUTCH.) - SUBSECT. MADDENIA.
Shrub, 1-4m; young shoots sparsely setose, the setae soon deciduous. Leaves 7-12 × 3.5-6cm, obovate, apex abruptly acute, margin ciliate, upper surface with midrib impressed, lower surface brownish with scales up to their own diameter

apart. Flowers (2-)3-5, in a loose terminal inflorescence, scented; calyx obscurely lobed, ciliate; corolla white, sometimes flushed pink, with a yellow basal blotch, funnel-shaped, (50-)55-75mm, outer surface scaly throughout, pubescent at base; stamens 10; ovary scaly, tapering into the style that is scaly below. H1b-2. April-May. China (W Yunnan), 1,800-2,750m.

This species is closely allied to *R. pachypodum* but differs in its broader leaves, with less densely spaced scales.

R. roseum (Lois.) Rehder is a synonym of **R. prinophyllum** (Small) Millais.

R. ROTHSCHILDII DAVIDIAN - SUBSECT. FALCONERA.
Large shrub or small tree, 5-6m; bark rough. Leaves 26.5-35 × 10-14cm, obovate-oblanceolate, upper surface reticulate, lower surface with a dense two-layered indumentum, the upper layer agglutinated, patchy, often red-brown, composed of strongly fimbriate cup-shaped hairs, the lower compacted; petioles flattened and with a marked wing. Flowers 12-17, in a dense truss, 8-lobed, pale yellow, with a purple blotch, obliquely campanulate, nectar pouches lacking, 35-45mm; stamens 16; ovary densely tomentose. H4a. April-May. China (NW Yunnan), 3,700-4,000m.

R. rothschildii may have originated as a hybrid. It has a very restricted distribution in the wild.

R. ROXIEANUM FORREST - SUBSECT. TALIENSIA.
Shrub, sometimes dwarf, 0.15-2.5(-4)m. Leaves 5-12 × 0.6-4cm, apex acute to cucullate, margins strongly recurved, lower surface covered with a thick two-layered indumentum, the upper layer rufous, loose, lanate-tomentose, composed of ramiform hairs, the lower radiate, compacted; petioles rufous-tomentose to glabrescent. Flowers 6-15, in tight truss; calyx 0.5-2mm; corolla white to (rarely) pale yellow, sometimes flushed with pink, with purple flecks, funnel-campanulate,

nectar pouches lacking; ovary densely rufous-tomentose and/or glandular, style glabrous. H4b. April-May. China (SE Tibet, NW Yunnan, SW Sichuan), 3,050-4,250m.

Var. **roxieanum** (incl. *R. recurvum* Balf.f. & Forrest). Leaves linear, 4-8× as long as broad; ovary and pedicels tomentose, with or without glands.

Var. **cucullatum** (Hand.-Mazz.) D.F.Chamb. Leaves elliptic, 2.2-4× as long as broad; ovary and pedicels glandular and/or tomentose.

Var. **oreonastes** (Balf.f. & Forrest) Davidian. Leaves linear, 8-15× as long as broad; ovary and pedicels glandular.

AM 1973 (Crown Estate Commissioners, Windsor); flowers white, corolla lobes tipped red-purple, with darker spots in throat.

♀ 1993

R. roxieanum hybridizes in the wild with *R. proteoides* and probably also with several other species, thus blurring the distinctions between the taxa. Var. *oreonastes* is a marked form with short, extremely narrow leaves. The variable var. *cucullatum* is morphologically intermediate between var. *roxieanum* and *R. proteoides* and is probably of hybrid origin. *R. aganniphum, R. alutaceum* and perhaps *R. phaeochrysum* may also be involved as parents in this hybrid complex.

R. roxieanum Forrest var. *parvum* Davidian - is either a synonym of **R. proteoides** or a hybrid of it (see under **R. proteoides**).

R. RUBIGINOSUM FRANCH. (INCL. *R. DESQUAMATUM* BALF.F. & FORREST) - SUBSECT. HELIOLEPIDA.
Shrub or small tree, to 10m; young growth purplish, scaly. Leaves (4-)6-11.5 × (1.2-)2-4.5cm, narrowly elliptic to elliptic or lanceolate, apex acute to acuminate, lower surface pale or dark brown as a result of the dense overlapping or touching, unequal scales, the larger of which are usually darker than the smaller. Pedicels scaly. Flowers to 10 per inflorescence; calyx very small; corolla pink, rarely white

flushed pink, openly funnel-shaped, (15-)20-30(-38)mm; stamens 10; ovary densely scaly, style declinate, glabrous. H4a-b. April-May. NE Burma, China (SE Tibet, Yunnan, SW Sichuan), 2,500-3,500m.

A variable and widespread species.

AM 1938 (Capt. A.W.T. Fletcher, Port Talbot, Wales) from Forrest 24535, as *R. desquamatum*; flowers ranging from pale mauve to reddish mauve, with reddish spots.

AM 1960 (Sir Henry Price, Wakehurst, Sussex) to a clone 'Wakehurst'; flowers Mallow Purple with prominent purple spots. This clone may be a hybrid.

R. rubrolineatum Balf.f. & Forrest) - is a synonym of **R. mekongense** Franch. var. **rubrolineatum** (Balf.f. & Forrest) Cullen (Subsect. Trichoclada).

R. RUBROPILOSUM HAYATA - SECT. TSUTSUSI.
Shrub, to 3m; young shoots densely covered with adpressed flattened grey to reddish brown hairs. Leaves of one kind, persistent, 1-3(-5.5) × 0.5-1(-2.5)cm, oblong-lanceolate to elliptic, apex acute, with a glandular mucro, upper surface with pale grey adpressed hairs, lower surface covered with flattened adpressed red-brown hairs, especially on the midrib; petioles densely covered with adpressed flattened red-brown hairs. Pedicels densely bristly. Flowers 2-4 per inflorescence; calyx minute; corolla pink, with rose flecks, funnel-shaped, 10-15(-25)mm; stamens 7-10; ovary covered with pale grey soft hairs, style more or less glabrous. H3-4a. May. Taiwan, 2,400-3,000m.

Var. **rubropilosum**. Stamens not appendiculate.

Var. **breviperulatum** (Hayata) T.Yamaz. Stamens appendiculate.

The only significant difference between these two varieties, both of which are rare in cultivation and frost-sensitive, is in the form of the stamens.

R. rude Tagg & Forrest - is a synonym of **R. glischrum** Balf.f. & W.W.Sm. subsp. **rude**

(Tagg & Forrest) D.F.Chamb. - Subsect. Glischra.

R. RUFUM BATALIN (INCL. *R. WELDIANUM* REHDER & E.H.WILSON) - SUBSECT. TALIENSIA.
Shrub, 1.3-4.5m. Leaves 6.5-11 × 2.5-5cm, obovate to elliptic, apex apiculate, lower surface covered with a two-layered indumentum, the upper layer a thin to dense reddish brown tomentum composed of ramiform hairs, the lower compacted, whitish, embedded in a surface film; petioles tomentose. Flowers 6-11, in a tight truss; calyx *c*.0.5mm; corolla white to pale pink, with crimson flecks, campanulate, nectar pouches lacking; ovary densely reddish-tomentose, with a few stalked glands below the more or less glabrous style. H4b. April-May. China (N Sichuan, Gansu), 3,050-3,650m.

R. rufum is allied to *R. bureavioides* (q.v.), and perhaps also to *R. przewalskii*.

AM 1980 (National Trust for Scotland, Brodick). Trusses 10-flowered; corolla widely funnel-campanulate, white with red dorsal spotting.

R. RUPICOLA W.W.SM. - SUBSECT. LAPPONICA.
Much-branched dwarf shrub, to 0.6 (-1.2)m. Leaves 0.7-2 × 0.3-1.3cm, broadly elliptic to ovate, apex rounded, mucronate, lower surface covered with overlapping to slightly separated, predominantly dark brown (though with some amber to pale golden) scales. Flowers to 6 per inflorescence; calyx lobes 3-6mm, oblong or broadly ovate, with a central band of scales; corolla usually an intense purple or yellow, occasionally deep crimson, magenta, or even white, broadly funnel-shaped, (8-)10-16(-18)mm; stamens 5-10, about as long as the corolla; ovary entirely pubescent or with scales on the upper half and a tuft of hairs at the apex, style longer than the stamens, glabrous or pubescent at base. H4a-b. April-May. N Burma, China (SE Tibet, W Yunnan, SW Sichuan), 3,000-4,875m.

Var. **rupicola** (incl. *R. achroanthum*

Balf.f. & W.W.Sm). Corolla purple to crimson, rarely white. N Burma, China (SE Tibet, Yunnan, SW Sichuan), to at least 4,000m.

Var. **chryseum** (Balf.f. & Kingdon-Ward) N.M.Philipson & Philipson (*R. chryseum* Balf.f. & Kingdon-Ward). Corolla yellow; calyx lobes margined with scales and hairs. NE Burma, China (SE Tibet, NW Yunnan), 3,300-4,750m.

Var. **muliense** (Balf.f. & Forrest) N.M.Philipson & Philipson. Corolla yellow; calyx lobes margined with hairs only. China (SW Sichuan), 3,050-4,875m.

This species is closely allied to *R. russatum* but may be distinguished by the presence of a central band of scales on the corolla lobes. It usually also has rather smaller leaves.

R. RUSSATUM BALF.F. & FORREST - SUBSECT. LAPPONICA.
Low shrub, 0.3-1.5m. Leaves 1.6-4 × 0.7-1.7cm, narrowly to broadly elliptic or oblong, apex obtuse or rounded, mucronate, lower surface covered with more or less touching scales that vary in colour from pale to dark brown, sometimes on a single leaf. Flowers up to 6 per inflorescence; calyx lobes up to 6mm, broadly oblong, without a central band of scales; corolla deep indigo purple to pink or rose, broadly funnel-shaped, 10-20mm; stamens 10, about as long as corolla; ovary scaly; style longer than stamens. H4a-b. April-May. China (N Yunnan, SW Sichuan), 3,400-4,300m.

This species is allied to *R. rupicola* (q.v.).

AM 1927 (A.M. Williams, Launceston); flowers an intense violet-blue.

FCC 1933 (L. de Rothschild, Exbury); flowers intense purple.

♀ 1993.

R. russotinctum Balf.f. & Forrest - is a synonym of **R. alutaceum** Balf.f. & W.W.Sm. var. **russotinctum** (Balf.f. & Forrest) D.F.Chamb. (Subsect. Taliensia).

R. saisiuense Nakai - is apparently a dwarf

form of **R. kiusianum** Makino (q.v., Sect. Tsutsusi).

R. SALUENENSE FRANCH. - SUBSECT. SALUENENSIA.

Prostrate or upright shrubs, 0.05-1.5m; young shoots setose, the setae persistent. Leaves 0.8-3 × 0.5-1.5cm, oblong-orbicular to oblong-elliptic, apex rounded, mucronate, upper surface usually glossy, and lacking scales, lower surface with dense overlapping brownish scales in several tiers, midrib usually with some setae. Flowers 1-3, terminal; calyx lobes 4.5-8mm, oblong-orbicular, scaly, ciliate and puberulent; corolla magenta to purple, rarely bluish purple, very openly funnel-campanulate, 17-28mm, outer surface pilose, with a few scales; stamens 10; ovary scaly, usually puberulent impressed below the usually glabrous style. H4a-b. April-June. NE Burma, China (SE Tibet, N Yunnan, SW Sichuan), 3,300-4,500m.

Subsp. **saluenense**. Erect shrub, to 1.5m; upper surface of leaves persistently scaly and usually setose. NE Burma, China (NW Yunnan, SE Tibet), 3,300-4,400m.

Subsp. *saluenense* is intermediate between subsp. *chameunum* and *R. calostrotum* subsp. *riparium* and occupies a restricted area where their ranges overlap.

AM 1965 (L. de Rothschild, Exbury); flowers Rhodamine Purple.

Subsp. **chameunum** (Balf.f. & Forrest) Cullen (*R. chameunum* Balf.f. & Forrest & incl. *R. prostratum* W.W.Sm.). Prostrate or decumbent shrub, rarely to 1m; upper surface of leaves usually glossy and lacking scales, without setae. NE Burma, China (N & NW Yunnan, SE Tibet, SW Sichuan), 3,500-4,500m.

R. saluenense is closely allied to *R. calostrotum* (q.v.).

♀ 1993

R. SANCTUM NAKAI - SECT. BRACHYCALYX.

Tree, to 5m; young shoots becoming glabrous. Leaves in whorls of up to three,

at the ends of the branches, 3-8 × 2.5-6cm, broadly rhombic, apex acuminate, lower surface glabrous except for a few hairs persisting on the midrib; petioles densely covered with red-brown hairs. Pedicels densely pilose. Flowers 3-4 per inflorescence, appearing before the leaves; calyx minute; corolla rose-pink (rarely white), with darker flecks on upper lobe, funnel-campanulate, 25-35mm; stamens 10; ovary densely pilose, style pilose in lower half. H4a-b. May-June. Japan (Hondo), mountains, 300-500m.

This species is closely allied to *R. amagianum* (q.v.).

R. SANGUINEUM FRANCH. - SUBSECT. NERIIFLORA.

Dwarf shrub, 0.3-1.5m. Leaves 3-8 × 1.5-3.2cm, elliptic to obovate, lower surface covered with a continuous compacted silvery to greyish indumentum composed of rosulate hairs; petioles floccose when young, rarely also glandular, soon glabrescent. Flowers 3-6, in a tight truss; calyx 3-10mm, coloured, cupular when well-developed; corolla fleshy, white or yellow to pink or crimson to blackish red, shortly tubular-campanulate, with nectar pouches, 25-35mm; ovary tomentose to stalked-glandular, abruptly contracted into the glabrous style. H4a-b. China (SE Tibet, NW Yunnan), 3,000-4,500m.

Subsp. **sanguineum**. Ovary tomentose, with or without glands; bud scales usually deciduous; leaves usually more than 5cm. March-May.

Var. **sanguineum**. Corolla bright crimson; ovary lacking glands.

AM 1973 (Countess of Rosse & National Trust, Nymans) from Rock (USDA 59453); flowers red.

Var. **cloiophorum** (Balf.f. & Forrest) D.F.Chamb. Corolla white or yellow suffused pink to pink; ovary lacking glands.

Var. **didymoides** (incl. *R. sanguineum* Franch. subsp. *roseotinctum* [Balf.f. & Forrest] Cowan & subsp. *consanguineum* Cowan). Corolla yellow flushed pink to pink; ovary at least partly glandular.

Var. **haemaleum** (Balf.f. & Forrest)

D.F.Chamb. Corolla blackish crimson; ovary lacking glands.

FCC 1981 (R.N.S. Clarke, Borde Hill, Sussex) to a clone 'Phantom Rock', as *R. sanguineum* subsp. *haemaleum*; trusses 4-6-flowered, corolla red-purple.

Subsp. **didymum** (Balf.f. & Forrest) Cowan. Corolla deep blackish crimson; ovary at least partly glandular; leaves 3-5cm. June.

Subsp. *didymum* is the most distinct of the taxa recognized within *R. sanguineum*. It is generally a dwarf shrub with tiny leaves, a blackish red corolla and an at least partly glandular corolla. In some respects var. *didymoides* is intermediate between subsp. *didymum* and the remaining varieties in subsp. *sanguineum*. While the most obvious differences between the varieties involve the colour of the corolla, there is some variation in the colour and texture of the leaf indumentum. This complex variation pattern has arisen, at least in part, through hybridization with both *R. temenium* and *R. citriniflorum*; hybrid populations involving all three parents occur in the wild in NW Yunnan.

R. SARGENTIANUM REHDER & E.H.WILSON - SECT. POGONANTHUM.
Dwarf shrub, to 0.6m; leaf bud scales persistent. Leaves 0.9-1.5 × 0.5-0.8cm, elliptic, apex rounded with a conspicuous mucro, lower surface with 2-3 tiers of dense overlapping scales the upper tiers brown or pale brown, the lowest pale, golden yellow. Flowers 5-12, in a dense racemose umbel; calyx lobes *c*.3mm; corolla whitish to yellow, hypocrateriform, tube *c*.8mm, scaly and puberulent outside, densely pilose within, lobes *c*.6mm; stamens 5; ovary scaly. H4b. April-June. China (Sichuan), 3,000-3,600m.

A distinctive species that apparently has a restricted distribution in the wild.

AM 1923 (Lady Aberconway and Hon. H.D. McLaren, Bodnant); flowers pale yellow.

AM 1966 (E.H.M. & P.A. Cox, Glendoick Gardens Ltd, Perth) to a clone 'Whitebait'; flowers pale Primrose Yellow. ♀ 1993

R. SAXICOLUM SLEUMER - SECT. TSUTSUSI.
Shrub, 3-6m; young shoots at first covered with adpressed red-brown bristles, soon glabrescent. Leaves of two kinds; spring leaves deciduous, 4-7.5 × 2-3.5cm, ovate to ovate-oblong, apex acuminate, upper surface glabrescent, lower surface with scattered bristles that persist on the lamina; summer leaves persistent, 1.5-2 × 0.5-1cm; petioles densely covered with adpressed bristles. Pedicels densely covered with rufous bristles. Flowers 3-4(-5) per inflorescence; calyx *c*.2mm; corolla white tinged rose, funnel-shaped, 15-20mm; stamens 5; ovary densely covered with rufous bristles, style hairy at base. H3?. March-April. Vietnam, 400-1,800m.

Seed of this species has been recently introduced from the wild. Its performance in cultivation is not yet known.

R. SCABRIFOLIUM FRANCH. - SUBSECT. SCABRIFOLIA.
Shrub, to 3m; young shoots with dimorphic indumentum composed of filiform hairs and setae with swollen bases. Leaves 1.5-9 × 0.4-2.5cm, narrowly elliptic to oblanceolate, upper surface with indumentum as for young shoots, bullate, lower surface scaly and densely covered with setae with swollen bases. Flowers 2-3(-5), in a loose axillary terminal inflorescence; calyx rim-like or with lobes 2-3mm, ciliate; corolla white to deep pink, 9-23mm; stamens 10; ovary scaly and densely pilose, impressed below the declinate style that is pilose at base. H2-3. March-May. China (Yunnan, Guizhou), 1,800-3,000m.

Var. **scabrifolium**. Leaves 4-9 × 1-1.8cm; corolla openly funnel-shaped, 9-15mm, tube 3-7mm. China (N Yunnan), 1,800-3,000m.

Var. **spiciferum** (Franch.) Cullen. Leaves 1.5-3.0 × 0.4-1cm; Corolla narrowly funnel-shaped, 13-15mm, tube 6-8mm. China (C & S Yunnan, Guizhou), 2,000-

2,500m.

The bullate leaves will distinguish this species from its immediate relatives. Var. *pauciflorum*, which is probably not in cultivation, differs in its larger flowers, 16-23mm long, and larger leaves, 25-90 × 8-25mm.

R. SCABRUM G.DON - SECT. TSUTSUSI.
Loosely branched shrub, 1-2m; young shoots and petioles covered with adpressed grey-brown hairs. Leaves of two kinds; spring leaves deciduous, 3-9 × 2-3.5cm, elliptic to lanceolate, apex acute, both surfaces with scattered adpressed pilose hairs, lower surface paler than upper; summer leaves persistent, 3-4 × 1-1.5cm. Pedicels densely covered with fulvous eglandular or gland-tipped bristles. Flowers 2-6 per inflorescence; calyx *c*.5mm; corolla rose-red to scarlet, with dark flecks on upper lobes, broadly funnel-shaped, 45-60mm; stamens 10; ovary covered with eglandular or gland-tipped hairs. H2. April-May. Japan (Ryukyu Islands), s.l.-400m.

Subsp. **scabrum** (incl. *R. yakuinsulare* Masamune). Pedicels, calyx and ovary eglandular.

Subsp. **amanoi** (Ohwi) D.F.Chamb. Pedicels, calyx and ovary glandular.

R. schizopeplum Balf.f. & Forrest - is a synonym of **R. aganniphum** Balf.f. & Kingdon-Ward var. **aganniphum** (Subsect. Taliensia).

R. SCHLIPPENBACHII MAXIM. - SECT. SCIADORHODION.
Deciduous shrub or small tree, to 2.5(-5)m; vegetative shoots arising from buds in the axils of the lowest scale-like leaves; young twigs usually covered with unicellular and a few gland-tipped hairs. Leaves turning yellow, orange or red in autumn, arranged in pseudowhorls of (4-)5(-9) at the apices of the branches, 2.5-11.7 × 0.9-7.2cm, orbicular to broadly obovate or elliptic, apex obtuse or rounded and mucronate, base cuneate, lower surface glabrous to sparsely unicellular-pubes-cent, mibrib with short curled hairs and fringed with longer straight or crisped hairs. Pedicels usually covered with eglandular hairs or occasionally with unicellular hairs only. Flowers not scented, appearing before or with the leaves, 3-6, in an umbellate raceme; calyx 1.5-7mm; corolla light to deep pink, with red-brown spots on upper lobes, broadly rotate to funnelform, the short tube expanding gradually into the longer limb, 23-47mm. Capsule covered with gland-tipped hairs. H4c. April-May. Korea and adjacent parts of Eastern Russia, 400-1,500m.

This species is distantly related to *R. pentaphyllum* and *R. quinquefolium* on account of its whorled leaves but is very different from either.

AM 1896 (Messrs J. Veitch & Sons, Chelsea); flowers soft pink.

FCC 1944 (Lord Aberconway, Bodnant); flowers Rhodamine Pink.

FCC 1965 (Sir Giles Loder, Leonardslee, Sussex) to a clone 'Prince Charming'; flowers Rhodamine Pink, with darker tinges, spotted deep crimson. ❦ 1993

R. scintillans Balf.f. & W.W.Sm. - is a synonym of **R. polycladum** Franch. (Subsect. Lapponica).

R. SCOPULORUM HUTCH. - SUBSECT. MADDENIA.
Shrub, to 2.6m; young growth setose. Leaves pale, 4.7-7.5 × 1.8-3.2mm, elliptic to obovate-elliptic, apex obtuse to rounded, margin not setose, upper surface with impressed midrib, lower surface with well-spaced unequal golden scales. Flowers 2-4, in a loose terminal inflorescence, scented; calyx lobes *c*.3mm, not ciliate; corolla white or white flushed pink, with a yellow or golden blotch, funnel-campanulate, 50-55mm, outer surface with scales restricted to lobes, sparsely pilose over tube; stamens 10; ovary densely scaly, impressed below the style that is scaly at extreme base. H1b-2. April-May. China (SE Tibet), 1,950-2,450m.

The pale leaf colour (especially in

dried specimens) is a distinctive feature of this species.

AM 1936 (L. de Rothschild, Exbury); flowers pale pink.

R. scottianum Hutch. - is a synonym of **R. pachypodum** Balf.f. & W.W.Sm. (Subsect. Maddenia).

R. scyphocalyx Balf.f. & Forrest - is a synonym of **R. dichroanthum** Diels subsp. **scyphocalyx** (Balf.f. & Forrest) Cowan - (Subsect. Neriiflora).

R. scyphocalyx Balf.f. & Forrest var. *septentrionale* Davidian - is a synonym of **R. dichroanthum** Diels subsp. **septentrionale** Cowan - (Subsect. Neriiflora).

R. SEARSIAE REHDER & E.H.WILSON - SUBSECT. TRIFLORA.
Shrub, 1.5-3m; young shoots scaly. Leaves 2.5-8 × 1-2.6cm, narrowly elliptic, apex acuminate or acute, upper surface usually with midrib puberulent, lower surface silvery, covered with touching polymorphic scales that are small or large and milky to golden. Flowers 3-8, in a terminal inflorescence; calyx minute to (rarely) 5mm, rarely ciliate; corolla white to pale purple, with greenish flecks, zygomorphic, widely funnel-shaped, 20-35mm, outer surface usually glabrous, rarely scaly on tube; stamens 10; ovary scaly, impressed below the declinate style that is usually glabrous, rarely puberulous at base. H4a-b. April-May. China (W Sichuan), 2,300-2,800m.

This species differs from the closely allied *R. concinnum* in its paler corolla and narrower leaves, with characteristic scales.

R. SEINGHKUENSE KINGDON-WARD - SUBSECT. EDGEWORTHIA.
Straggling epiphytic shrub, 0.3-1m. Leaves 2.5-5.5 × 1.5-2.8cm, ovate to elliptic, apex acuminate, upper surface bullate; lower surface with a glaucous papillate epidermis, scales dense, golden, also with a brown woolly tomentum. Pedicels densely tomentose. Flowers solitary; calyx lobes to 8mm; corolla bright yellow,

campanulate, 18-25mm; stamens 10, regular; ovary scaly and densely tomentose, especially towards apex, style glabrous. H2-3?. April. NE Burma, China (NW Yunnan, SE Tibet), 1,800-3,000m.

R. seinghkuense resembles *R. pendulum* but may be distinguished by the flower colour and the acuminate leaves.

AM 1953 (Crown Estate Commissioners, Windsor); flowers Sulphur Yellow.

R. SELENSE FRANCH. - SUBSECT. SELENSIA.
Shrub or small tree, 1-5m; young shoots and petioles stalked- to setose-glandular. Leaves 3.5-9 × 1.8-4cm, ovate or obovate to elliptic, lower surface occasionally with a few persistent hairs towards the base otherwise glabrous. Flowers 3-8, in a lax truss; calyx 1-10mm; corolla white or pale cream to deep pink, with or without purple flecks, funnel-campanulate, nectar pouches lacking, 25-40mm; ovary densely stalked-glandular, style glabrous. H4a. April-May. China (SE Tibet, NW Yunnan, SW Sichuan), 3,200-4,500m.

Subsp. **selense.** Young shoots with shortly stalked glands; leaves without a persistent indumentum and with a non-glaucous epidermis beneath; longest calyx lobes 2(-5)mm. China (NW Yunnan, SW Sichuan), 3,350-4,550m.

The naturally occurring hybrid between subsp. *selense* and *R. wardii* is grown as *R. × erythrocalyx*. This subspecies also hybridizes in the wild with *R. eclecteum* (q.v.), and probably also with subsp. *dasycladum* and *R. vernicosum*

Subsp. **dasycladum** (Balf.f. & W.W.Sm.) D.F.Chamb. (*R. dasycladum* Balf.f. & W.W.Sm. & incl. *R. rhaibocarpum* Balf.f. & W.W.Sm.). Young shoots with setose glands; leaves without a persistent indumentum beneath; longest calyx lobes 1-2(-5)mm. China (W Yunnan, SW Sichuan), 3,350-4,000m.

Subsp. *dasycladum* generally occurs at a lower altitude than does subsp. *selense*, even though the two do occur at the same localities. Subsp. *dasycladum* tends to have slightly larger leaves, darker pink flowers and a dense setose-glandular indumentum on the young shoots. However, there are intermediate forms that have in the past been referred to *R. rhaibocarpum.*

Subsp. **setiferum** (Balf.f. & Forrest) D.F.Chamb. (*R. setiferum* Balf.f. & Forrest & incl. *R. vestitum* Tagg & Forrest). Young shoots with setose glands, leaves with a persistent or discontinuous indumentum beneath; longest calyx lobes (2-)4-10mm. China (SE Tibet, NW Yunnan), 3,650-4,500m.

Intermediate between subsp. *selense* and *R. bainbridgeanum,* and possibly of hybrid origin.

Subsp. **jucundum** (Balf.f. & W.W.Sm.) D.F.Chamb. (*R. jucundum* Balf.f. & W.W.Sm.). Young shoots with long-stalked glands; leaves glabrous and glaucous beneath; longest calyx lobes (2-)4-6mm. China (W Yunnan - Dali), 3,200-3,900m.

This subspecies has a very restricted distribution.

R. selense is a variable species, the boundaries of which are ill-defined owing to widespread hybridization.

R. SEMIBARBATUM MAXIM. - SUBGEN MUMEAZALEA.
Deciduous shrub, to 2(-3)m; young shoots puberulous and with gland-tipped hairs. leaves turning wine-red in autumn, clustered at the end of short-growing branches, 2-6 × 1-2.6cm, elliptic or ovate, apex apiculate to obtuse, base rounded or cuneate, margin serrulate and sometimes ciliate, lower surface glabrous except for the puberulous midrib and ciliate veins. Flowers borne laterally, below the vegetative buds, solitary; calyx *c.*2mm, lobes rounded; corolla white, with a pink flush and rose-purple flecks, rotate, with a short wide tube and spreading lobes, *c.*20mm across; stamens 5, strongly dimorphic; ovary setose and densely glandular, style glabrous. H4a. June. S Japan (Honshu, Shikoku, Kyushu), in the mountains.

A distinctive species on account of its strongly dimorphic stamens. The arrangement of the one-flowered inflorescence is similar to that of Subgen. Azaleastrum but it is very diffeent in other characters.

R. SEMNOIDES TAGG & FORREST - SUBSECT. FALCONERA.
Shrub, 4-6m; bark rough. Leaves up to 24 × 11.5cm, obovate-lanceolate, upper surface reticulate, lower surface covered with a two-layered undumentum, the upper layer loosely tomentose, whitish to buff, composed of strongly fimbriate, narrowly cup-shaped hairs, the lower compacted; petioles more or less flattened. Flowers *c.*15, in a dense truss, white flushed rose, obliquely campanulate, nectar pouches lacking, 40-50mm; stamens 16; ovary densely brownish-tomentose. H3-4a. March-April. China (SE Tibet, NW Yunnan), 3,700-4,000m.

R. semnoides may have been derived as a hybrid between *R. praestans* and *R. arizelum*; plants in the wild presumed to be of that parentage are a good match.

R. SEROTINUM HUTCH. - SUBSECT. FORTUNEA.
Straggling shrub, to 3m. Leaves 10-15 × 6-7cm, oblong-elliptic, base unequally cordate, lower surface glabrous, with a glaucous papillate epidermis. Flowers 7-8, in a loose fragrant truss; calyx *c.*8mm; corolla 7-8-lobed, white flushed pink, with a crimson blotch breaking into flecks within, open- to funnel-campanulate, nectar pouches lacking, 55-65mm; ovary and entire style clothed with white stalked glands. H3-4a. July-September. China (S Yunnan), Northern Vietnam?, Northern Laos.

This species was grown at Kew from seed thought to have originated in Southern Yunnan. It may however no longer be in cultivation. It is allied to *R. decorum* but differs in the blotched corolla and in the habit of the plant. The occurrence of this species in the wild has now been confirmed by recent collections though it is still not clear as to how distinct it is from *R. decorum.* It is notable for its very late flowering period.

AM 1925 (Royal Botanic Gardens, Kew); flowers white, flushed rose externally, blotched and tinged internally.

R. serpyllifolium (A.Gray) Miq. - Sect. Tsutsusi.
Low, much-branched shrub; young shoots covered with adpressed flattened chestnut-brown hairs. Leaves of one kind, 0.3-1 × 0.3-0.5cm, obovate-oblong to elliptic, apex obtuse or acute, upper surface with scattered brown bristles, lower surface with hairs mainly on midrib, arising from pustules; petioles and pedicels covered with bristles. Flowers 1(-2) per inflorescence; calyx small; corolla rose-pink or occasionally white, funnelform, *c.*17mm; stamens 5; ovary densely covered with pale flattened hairs, style glabrous H3-4b. April-May. C & S Japan, 300-900m.

This species does not have any close allies.

R. serrulatum (Small) Millais - is a synonym of **R. viscosum** (L.) Torr. (Sect. Pentanthera).

R. setiferum Balf.f. & Forrest - is a synonym of **R. selense** Franch. subsp. **setiferum** (Balf.f. & Forrest) D.F.Chamb. (Subsect. Selensia).

R. setosum D.Don - Subsect. Lapponica.
Dwarf intricate shrublet, to 0.3m; young shoots densely scaly, and with conspicuous loriform setae. Leaves 1-1.5 × 0.6-0.8cm, elliptic to obovate, apex rounded, mucronate, margins ciliate, lower surface covered with vesicular and golden, or flat, broadly rimmed and pale to dark brown dimorphic scales. Flowers 1-3 per inflorescence; calyx lobes 5-8mm, oblong-orbicular; corolla purple or pinkish, open-funnel-shaped, 15-18mm; stamens 10, about as long as corolla; ovary scaly and pubescent towards apex, style longer than stamens, glabrous. H4a-b. May. Nepal, India (Sikkim, W Bengal), Bhutan, China (S Tibet - Chumbi Valley), 3,650-4,550m.

Its general appearance places *R. setosum* in Subsect. Lapponica, but it is anomalous in respect of the setose indumentum.

R. shepherdii Nuttall - is probably a synonym of **R. kendrickii** Nuttall (Subsect. Irrorata).

R. sherriffii Cowan - Subsect. Thomsonia.
Large shrub or small tree; bark smooth, peeling; young shoots with a mealy tomentum, also stalked-glandular. Leaves *c.*7.5 × 4cm, broadly obovate, base rounded, upper surface glabrous, lower surface with a dense fulvous tomentum composed of fasciculate hairs; petioles glabrous when mature. Flowers 4-5, in a lax truss; calyx 3-5mm; corolla deep carmine, with darker nectar pouches, campanulate, 35-40mm; ovary glabrous. H4a. March-April. China (S Tibet), *c.*4,000m.

This species has been traditionally placed in Subsect. Fulgensia on account of its dense leaf indumentum. However, it resembles *R. thomsonii* in its flower characters and is therefore better placed in Subsect. Thomsonia.

AM 1966 (Crown Estate Commissioners, Windsor) from L. & S. 2751; flowers Cardinal Red at tip, darker below.

R. shweliense Balf.f. & Forrest - Subsect. Glauca.
Compact shrub, 0.3-0.8m; shoots with a flaking brownish bark. Leaves 3.2-4 × *c.*1.5cm, narrowly elliptic to narrowly obovate, apex rounded, mucronate, lower surface with a glaucous papillate epidermis, scales 3-4× their own diameter apart, unequal, the smaller pale yellow, the larger brown. Pedicels scaly. Flowers yellowish flushed pink, campanulate, outer surface lacking scales, 11mm; stamens regular; ovary scaly, style sharply deflexed, puberulent over its whole length. H3-4a. April-June. China (SW Yunnan), 3,050-3,350m.

Most cultivated plants referred to this species are forms of *R. glaucophyllum* or hybrids of it. Its status in cultivation therefore remains doubtful. This species closely resembles *R. charitopes* but differs in the narrower leaves and puberulent style.

R. SIDEREUM BALF.F. - SUBSECT. GRANDIA.

Shrub or small tree, 3-9m; bark rough. Leaves (9-)16-23 × 4-6.3cm, narrowly elliptic to oblanceolate, apex acute to rounded and apiculate, lower surface covered with a one-layered buff to silvery, sometimes shining compacted and agglutinated indumentum composed of rosulate hairs; petioles terete. Flowers 12-20 to a truss, cream to clear yellow, sometimes with a red basal blotch, ventricose-campanulate, with nectar pouches, 30-40mm; stamens *c.*16; ovary densely rufous-tomentose. H2-3. April-May. NE Burma, China (W Yunnan), 2,500-3,700m.

This is a tender species that is only occasionally grown in Britain.

AM 1964 (National Trust for Scotland, Bridock Castle Gardens) to a clone 'Glen Rosa'; flowers Primrose Yellow, with a dark crimson blotch.

R. SIDEROPHYLLUM FRANCH. - SUBSECT. TRIFLORA.

Shrub, 1-7m; young shoots brownish, scaly. Leaves 4.8-8.4 × (1.6-)2.4-3.2cm, broadly elliptic to elliptic, rarely ovate, apex acute, upper surface lacking scales, lower surface with a dense covering of large flat broadly rimmed scales that are 1-2× their own diameter apart. Flowers 3-6, in a dense coalesced compound inflorescence; calyx minute, usually not ciliate; corolla white or pinkish violet, zygomorphic, widely funnel-shaped, 18-22 (-25)mm, outer surface lacking scales, glabrous; stamens 10; ovary scaly, impressed below the declinate, usually glabrous style. H3(-4a). May. China (C & S Yunnan, Guizhou), 840-2,100 (-2,600)m.

This somewhat tender species differs from the allied *R. tatsienense* in the form of the leaf scales, and in its coalescing inflorescences.

AM 1945 (E. de Rothschild, Exbury).

R. SIKANGENSE FANG - SUBSECT. MACULIFERA.

Shrub or tree, 1.8m; young shoots more or less densely rufous- to white-stellate-tomentose though often soon becoming glabrous. Leaves 7-15 × 2.8-6cm, elliptic to oblanceolate, lower surface glabrous when mature, or with a rufous stellate indumentum persisting towards the base; petioles more or less glabrous when mature. Flowers 5-15 in a truss, white to pink, with or without a purple blotch, campanulate, nectar pouches lacking, 35-50mm; ovary densely to very sparsely brownish stellate-tomentose, style glabrous. H4a-b. May-June. China (W Sichuan, NE Yunnan), 3,500-4,500m.

Var. **sikangense** (incl. *R. cookeanum* Davidian). Lower surface of leaves more or less glabrous when mature. China (W Sichuan, ?Yunnan), 3,700-4,500m.

Var. **exquisitum** (T.L.Ming) T.L.Ming. Lower surface of leaves with a persistent rufous stellate tomentum towards the base. China (NE Yunnan), 3,500-4,500m.

Var. *exquisitum* has recently come into cultivation so it should soon be possible to confirm the apparently small differences between the two varieties.

R. silvaticum Cowan - is a synonym of **R. lanigerum** Tagg (Subsect. Arborea).

R. SIMIARUM HANCE (INCL. *R. FOKIENSE* FRANCH.) - SUBSECT. ARGYROPHYLLA.

Shrub, 2-6m. Leaves 7-14.5 × 1.8-4.5cm, narrowly elliptic to broadly oblanceolate, apex rounded to acuminate, upper surface reticulate, lower surface with a one-layered white thin compacted indumentum embedded in a surface film. Flowers 4-7, in a lax truss, pink, with a few darker flecks, open-campanulate, nectar pouches lacking, 25-35mm; ovary rufous-stellate-tomentose, and with shortly stalked glands, style glabrous or with a few glands at base. H2-3. April-May. S & E

China, 600-1,000m.

Rare in cultivation as it is susceptible to frost damage; only the type variety is in cultivation.

R. SIMSII PLANCH. - SECT. TSUTSUSI.
Much-branched twiggy shrub, 1-3mm; young shoots densely covered with adpressed flattened shining brown bristles. Leaves of two kinds; spring leaves deciduous, 3-7 × (0.6-)1-2cm, ovate-lanceolate to linear-elliptic, apex acute, upper surface sparingly covered with adpressed bristles, lower surface paler, more densely covered with bristles, especially on midrib and veins; summer leaves persistent, 1-2 × 0.5-1cm, elliptic to oblong-elliptic; petioles covered with adpressed red-brown bristles. Pedicels densely covered with bristles. Flowers 2-6 per inflorescence; calyx 3-7mm, lobes ovate-lanceolate; corolla white to dark red, upper lobes with darker flecks, broadly funnel-shaped, 25-60mm; stamens (8-)10; ovary densely covered with bristles, style with bristles at base, otherwise glabrous. H1-2. May. NE Burma, China, Taiwan, Laos, Thailand, S Japan, 600-2,700m.

Var. **simsii**. Corolla red to rich carmine, 35-60mm. NE Burma, China (except the N), Hong Kong, Taiwan, Laos, Thailand, S Japan (Ryukyu Islands), 600-2,700m.

FCC 1933 (G.W.E. Loder, Wakehurst Place, Sussex); flowers bright rose.

Var. **mesembrinum** Balf.f. & Forrest ex Rehder. Corolla white to rose-pink, 25-40mm. NE Burma, China (Yunnan), 1,800-2,700m.

R. simsii is cultivated widely in the warm temperate parts of the world and many cultivars are known. It has been used as a parent to produce the popular 'Pot Azaleas' that are sold for display indoors.

R. simulans (Tagg & Forrest) D.F.Chamb. - is a synonym of **R. mimetes** Tagg & Forrest var. **simulans** Tagg & Forrest (Subsect. Taliensia).

R. SINOFALCONERI BALF.F. - SUBSECT. FALCONERA.
Tree, to 7m, bark rough. Leaves 17-28 × 11.8-16cm, broadly obovate; upper surface rugulose, with deeply impressed veins, lower surface with a 1-2 layered indumentum, the upper layer dense, light brown, composed of moderately fimbriate broadly cup-shaped hairs, the lower layer, when present, compacted; petioles terete. Flowers pale yellow, 8-lobed, obliquely campanulate, nectar pouches lacking, 50-60mm; stamens 16; ovary densely fulvous-lanate-tomentose. H2-3. April-May. China (S Yunnan), 2,700-3,000m.

This species, which has been recently introduced into cultivation, is closely allied to *R. falconeri*. It differs however in the ovaries and pedicels that lack the glands that are characteristic of the latter species. It is likely to require a reasonably frost-free climate.

R. SINOGRANDE BALF.F. & W.W.SM. - SUBSECT. GRANDIA.
Tree, 6-12m; bark rough. Leaves 20-70 × 8-30cm, oblanceolate to broadly elliptic, apex rounded or retuse, minutely apiculate, lower surface with a silvery compacted and agglutinated indumentum, that is largely composed of rosulate hairs; petioles terete. Flowers 8-10-lobed, pale creamy white, with a purple basal blotch, ventricose-campanulate, with nectar-pouches, 40-60mm; stamens 18-20; ovary densely rufous-tomentose. H3. April-May. NE Burma, China (SE Tibet, Yunnan), 2,450-4,250m.

The very large leaves with an agglutinated indumentum will distinguish this tender species. Hybrids between *R. sinogrande* and *R. macabeanum* occur in cultivation.

AM 1922 (Dame Alice Godman, Horsham); flowers creamy white, with a crimson blotch.

FCC 1926 (G.H. Johnstone, Trewithian, Cornwall); flowers ivory white, with a big crimson blotch.

♀ 1993

R. sinonuttallii Balf.f. & Forrest - is a synonym of **R. nuttallii** Booth.

R. SMIRNOWII TRAUTV. - SUBSECT. PONTICA.
Shrub or small tree, 1-4m; young shoots and petioles densely whitish-lanate-tomentose, sometimes also with a few scattered glands; bud scales deciduous. Leaves 7.5-11.5(-14) × 2.5-3.2cm, oblanceolate to elliptic; apex usually rounded, upper surface glabrous, lower surface covered with a dense white to cinnamon lanate indumentum composed of dendroid hairs. Flowers 7-15, in a dense truss; calyx 2-3mm; corolla pink, with yellowish flecks, funnel-campanulate, nectar pouches lacking, 35-40mm; ovary densely white-strigillose, eglandular, style glabrous. H4b-c. May-June. NE Turkey, Georgia, (500-)1,500-2,300m.

Allied to *R. ungernii* but distinguished by the non-glandular ovary.

AM 1991 (E. de Rothschild, Exbury) to a clone 'Vodka'; trusses with 16-18 flowers, corolla shading from white deep in throat to red-purple along lip and strongly down each lobe, upper throat heavily marked with yellow-green.

R. smithii Nuttall - is a synonym of **R. argipeplum** Balf.f. & Cooper.

R. × sochadzeae Char & Davlianidze - is a hybrid of **R. caucasicum** Pallas and **R. ponticum** L.

R. SOULIEI FRANCH. - SUBSECT. CAMPYLOCARPA.
Shrub. 1-2-5m. Leaves 5.5-8 × 3.5-4cm, broadly ovate, base rounded to cordate, glabrous. Flowers 3-5, in lax trusses, pale purplish pink (? rarely white), open-campanulate (saucer-shaped), nectar pouches lacking, 25-40mm; ovary and style densely stalked-glandular. H4a-b. May-June. China (Sichuan), 3,000-3,800m.

This species may be distinguished from *R. callimorphum* by the generally larger leaves, the more open flowers and the glandular style.

FCC 1909 (Messrs J. Veitch, Chelsea); flowers pale rose, deeper towards margin.

FCC 1936 (L. de Rothschild, Exbury) to a clone 'Exbury Pink'; flowers a deeper shade of pink.

FCC 1951 (Crown Estate Commissioners, Windsor) to a clone 'Windsor Park'; flowers white, with pink flush, deepening at margins, three upper lobes stained at base with a small crimson blotch.

R. SPERABILE BALF.F. & FARRER - SUBSECT. NERIIFLORA.
Shrub, 1-2m. Leaves 5-9.5 × 1-2.6cm, elliptic, sometimes narrowly so; lower surface covered with a dense but loose continuous whitish to cinnamon indumentum composed of ramiform hairs, also with glandular setae overlying the midrib, epidermis glaucous-papillate; petioles densely tomentose, with some glandular setae. Flowers 4-5, in a dense truss; calyx 2-3mm, coloured; corolla fleshy, crimson, tubular-campanulate, 35-40mm; ovary densely rufous-tomentose and stalked-glandular, tapering into the glabrous style. H3-4a. April-May. NE Burma, China (NW Yunnan), 3,000-3,650m.

Var. **sperabile**. Leaf indumentum cinnamon when mature; leaves 2.5-3.5× as long as broad.

AM 1925 (L. de Rothschild, Exbury) from Farrer 888; flowers scarlet.

Var. **weihsiense** Tagg & Forrest. Leaf indumentum whitish when mature; leaves 3-4(-8)× as long as broad.

AM 1985 (R.N.S. Clarke, Borde Hill) to a clone 'Rouge et Noir', from Kingdon-Ward 7124; trusses loose, up to 11 flowers, corolla deep crimson, with darker spotting in throat.

This species is allied to *R. sperabiloides* (q.v.) and to *R. floccigerum*; from the latter it differs in its thicker, more persistent leaf indumentum.

R. SPERABILOIDES TAGG & FORREST - SUBSECT. NERIIFLORA.
Dwarf shrub, 1-1.5m. Leaves 5.5.-6.5 × 1.8-2.5cm, elliptic, lower surface with a floc-

cose discontinuous rufous tomentum composed of ramiform to sub-rosulate hairs, epidermis green, not papillate; petioles slightly winged, floccose-tomentose. Flowers 4-5, in a tight truss; calyx 4-7mm, cupular; corolla fleshy, crimson to deep red, tubular-campanulate, 25-35mm; ovary more or less abruptly contracted to tapering into the glabrous style. H3-4a. April-May. China (SE Tibet), 3,650-3,950m.

This species is intermediate between *R. sperabile* and related species, with the ovary tapering into the style, and the remaining species in the subsection, with the ovary abruptly contracted into the style. This may indicate a hybrid origin for *R. sperabiloides*.

AM 1933 (L. de Rothschild, Exbury); flowers lustrous deep crimson.

R. SPHAEROBLASTUM BALF.F. & FORREST - SUBSECT. TALIENSIA.
Shrub 1-3(-7)m. Leaves (6-)9-12 × 3.6-6.2cm, broadly ovate-lanceolate, apex acute to apiculate, lower surface covered with a dense two-layered indumentum, the upper layer usually rust-red, lanate-tomentose, composed of ramiform hairs, the lower compacted; petioles glabrescent. Flowers 10-20, in a dense truss; calyx 1.5-2mm; corolla white to pink, with purple flecks, funnel-campanulate, nectar pouches lacking, 35-40mm; ovary and style glabrous. H4b. April-May. China (N Yunnan, SW Sichuan), 3,350-4,550m.

This species is closely allied to *R. taliense* and to *R. mimetes*. Plants from NE Yunnan have been referred to var. *wumengense* K.M.Feng. These are said to differ in the thinly coriaceous leaves with a fulvous-cinereous-indumentum.

R. spilanthum Hutch.- is a synonym of **R. thymifolium** Maxim. (Subsect. Lapponica).

R. SPILOTUM BALF.F. & FARRER - SUBSECT. GLISCHRA?
Shrub or small tree; young shoots glandular-setose. Leaves coriaceous, 7-11 × 3-4.2cm, elliptic, apex acuminate, lower surface with punctate hair bases persistent over the veins, with scattered setose glands towards the base and a thin indumentum, especially near the midrib, Flowers *c*.8 in a truss; calyx *c*.10mm; corolla pink, with a basal blotch, funnel-campanulate, *c*.30mm; ovary densely stalked-glandular. H3-4a. April-May. NE Burma.

The origin of the plants in cultivation is uncertain though they are a good match with the type specimen. *R. spilotum* may be a hybrid of a species in Subsect. Glischra.

R. SPINULIFERUM FRANCH. - SUBSECT. SPICIFERA.
An upright shrub, 0.6-4.5m; young shoots covered with filiform hairs, also with setae with swollen bases. Leaves 2.5-9.5 × 0.6-4.5cm, lanceolate to elliptic, upper surface bullate, with filiform hairs that persist only along midrib, lower surface scaly and with setae that are soon deciduous though with swollen bases persisting around the margins. Flowers (1-)2-5, in a loose axillary terminal inflorescence; calyx disc-like, densely pubescent; corolla crimson to yellowish, tubular, 17-23mm; stamens 10, exserted; ovary scaly, densely tomentose, impressed below the declinate style. H2-3. April-May. China (C & S Yunnan, Guizhou), (800-)1,800-2,500m.

This is a somewhat tender species that is generally distinctive on account of its tubular flowers, though some forms of *R. scabrifolium* do approach it. Only var. *spinuliferum* is known in cultivation.

AM 1974 (N.T. Holman, Chyverton, Truro) to a clone 'Jack Hext'; flowers red, paler below.

AM 1977 (National Trust for Scotland, Brodick Castle Gardens) to a clone 'Blackwater'; flowers red, greenish white at base.

R. STAMINEUM FRANCH. - SECTION CHONIASTRUM.
Shrub or small tree, to 13m. Leaves 6-14 × 2-4.5cm, elliptic to oblanceolate, apex acuminate. Flowers 3-5 (occasionally to 8),

clustered at end of a leafy shoot below a vegetative bud, white or pink, with yellow blotch, funnel-shaped; tube narrow, 10-15mm; lobes narrowly oblong, spreading to reflexed; stamens 10, long-exserted. H2-3. April-May. NE Burma, SW, S & C China, 400-1,450m.

Rare in cultivation, this species is distinguished from the allied R. *moulmainense* by the long-exserted stamens and the reflexed corolla lobes.

AM 1971 (Crown Estate Commissioners, Windsor); flowers white, upper lobe flushed yellow-orange.

R. *stenaulum* Balf.f. & Forrest - is a synonym of **R. moulmainense** Hook.f. (sect. Choniastrum).

R. STENOPETALUM (HOGG) MABB. (INCL. R. *MACROSEPALUM* MAXIM.) - SECT. TSUTSUSI.
Low shrub, 0.3-1m; young shoots covered with greyish spreading-pilose, sometimes gland-tipped, hairs, also with a few bristles. Leaves of two kinds; spring leaves deciduous, 2.5-7 × 1.5-2.5cm, ovate-elliptic, apex acute, lower surface with gland-tipped hairs, with a few bristles on the midrib and main veins; summer leaves persistent, 1.2-2 × 0.3-0.6cm; petioles densely pilose, also with a few flattened setae. Pedicels covered with long spreading pilose, partly gland-tipped hairs. Flowers 2-10 per inflorescence; calyx 15-30mm, lobes lanceolate to broadly oblong; corolla lilac-pink to rose-purple, with purple flecks on upper lobe, broadly funnel-shaped, 35-50mm; stamens 5(-7); ovary covered with gland-tipped bristles, style glabrous. H3. May-June. Japan (Honshu, Shikoku), 150-400m.

This species is closely allied to R. *ripense* (q.v.). It may hybridize with R. *kaempferi* in the wild. R. *linearifolium* Sieb. & Zucc., which is equivalent to the type of R. *stenopetalum*, is an aberrant plant with very narrow leaves and linear corolla lobes that is only known in cultivation. Plants from the wild correspond to R. *macrosepalum* and conform to the descrip-

tion given above.

AM 1984 (E. de Rothschild, Exbury) as R. *macrosepalum* 'Linearifolium'; trusses 3-5-flowered, corolla divided almost to base, with segments widely deflexed, red-purple with some darker marking.

R. STEWARTIANUM DIELS - SUBSECT. THOMSONIA.
Shrub, 0.5-2.5m; bark smooth or rough, peeling on smaller branches; young shoots often glandular. Leaves 4-12 × 2-6.5cm, obovate to elliptic, base rounded, upper surface glabrous, lower surface with a mammillate epidermis and a thin more or less persistent to evanescent indumentum interspersed with sessile glands; petioles usually glabrous occasionally with a few glands. Flowers 3-7, in lax truss; calyx (2-)5-15mm, cupular; corolla white or cream to pale (rarely deep) rose, with or without purple flecks, campanulate to tubular-campanulate, with nectar pouches, 35-55mm; ovary usually densely glandular, style glabrous. H3-4a. February-April. NE Burma, China (SE Tibet, NW Yunnan), 3,000-4,250m.

This is a variable species, especially with respect to the flower colour. It is allied to R. *eurysiphon* and perhaps also R.*eclecteum*, though the presence of a more or less persistent leaf indumentum will distinguish it from these two species.

AM 1934 (L. de Rothschild, Exbury).

R. *stictophyllum* Balf.f. - is a synonym of **R. nivale** Hook.f. subsp. **boreale** Philipson & N.M.Philipson (Subsect. Lapponica).

R. STRIGILLOSUM FRANCH. - SUBSECT. MACULIFERA.
Shrub or small tree, 1.5-6m; young shoots densely long-stalked-glandular. Leaves 7.5-14 × 1.8-3.8cm, elliptic to oblanceolate, apex cuspidate, lower surface with varying amounts of crisped setae with glandular or branched tips that usually persist; petioles glandular-setose. Flowers 8-12 in a truss; calyx *c*.1mm; corolla deep red,

tubular-campanulate, with nectar pouches, 40-60mm; ovary with a dense covering of long weak glandular hairs, style glabrous. H4a. February-April. China (NE Yunnan, W Sichuan), 2,200-3,350m.

A distinctive species, that hybridizes in the wild with *R. pachytrichum* (q.v.).

AM 1923 (Lady Aberconway & Hon. H.D. McLaren, Bodnant); flowers a rich blood red.

R. SUBANSIRIENSE D.F.CHAMB. & P.A. COX - SUBSECT. THOMSONIA.
Shrub or tree, up to 14m; bark smooth and peeling; young shoots apparently tomentose. Leaves 7-10.5 × 2-3.5cm, oblong, base more or less rounded, upper surface glabrous, lower surface with epidermis lacking papillae, with numerous red punctate hair bases on the veins, each with the vestige of fasciculate hairs, otherwise glabrous; petioles glabrous. Flowers up to 15, in a dense truss; calyx 4-5mm, cupular; corolla fleshy, scarlet, with a few purple flecks, tubular-campanulate, with nectar pouches, up to 40mm; ovary densely tomentose, lacking glands, style glabrous. H3(-4a). April. NE India (Arunachal Pradesh), 2,600-2,800m.

This species is at present only known from the Subansiri district in NE India. In cultivation it produces a very early leaf flush that is often affected by late frosts. While it will grow outside in Britain it rarely flowers.

R. SUBSESSILE RENDLE - SECT. TSUTSUSI.
Much-branched shrub; shoots densely covered with adpressed flattened brown hairs. Leaves of two kinds; spring leaves deciduous, 2.5-4 × 0.9-1.2cm, elliptic-lanceolate, apex acute and mucronate, both surfaces at first covered with rufous-grey hairs, upper surface also with adpressed white hairs; summer leaves persistent, *c.*1.5 × 0.7cm; petioles covered with adpressed chestnut-brown hairs. Pedicels covered with adpressed ferrugineous hairs. Flowers 2-4 per inflorescence; calyx small; corolla lilac-purple, funnel-campanulate, 15-20mm; stamens 6-10; ovary

densely covered with flattened ferruginous hairs, style with a few hairs at base. H2?. May. Philippines (Luzon), 2,100-2,600m.

This is a glasshouse subject in Britain that has no close allies.

R. SUCCOTHII DAVIDIAN - SUBSECT. BARBATA.
Shrub or small tree, 1-6m; bark smooth, reddish brown; young shoots glabrous. Leaves 5-13.5 × 2.5-5.5cm, apex rounded, base cordate, upper surface without deeply impressed veins, both surfaces glabrous; petioles very short, 1-5mm. Flowers fleshy, 10-15, in a tight truss, crimson, with conspicuous nectar pouches, tubular-campanulate, 28-35mm; ovary and style glabrous. H4a. March-April. Bhutan, 3,400-4,200m.

An anomalous species in that it lacks the bristles that characterize the remaining species in the subsection. It was originally considered to be an ally of *R. fulgens* but it differs in its glabrous leaves.

R. SULFUREUM FRANCH. (INCL. *R. COMMODUM* BALF.F. & FORREST) - SUBSECT. BOOTHIA.
Low shrub, 0.6-1.6m, sometimes epiphytic; young shoots often setose. leaves 3.5-8.5 × 2-4.5cm, broadly obovate to (more rarely) narrowly elliptic, apex rounded to subacute, upper surface glabrous, lower surface with close unequal scales with upturned rims that are sunk in pits. Pedicels stout, to 15mm, scaly, sometimes also setose or stiffly pubescent. Flowers 3-6 per inflorescence; calyx lobes 5-6mm, ovate to oblong; corolla greenish to bright yellow, campanulate, 15-20mm, tube scaly and sometimes also pubescent outside, pilose within; stamens 10; ovary scaly, tapering into the strongly deflexed style. H2-3. March-April. NE Burma, China (W Yunnan, SE Tibet), 2,500-3,650(-4,000)m.

This species is allied to (or a parent of) *R. chrysodoron* but differs in its smaller flowers with obscure calyx lobes, etc.

AM 1937 (Earl of Stair, Stranraer) as *R. commodum*; flowers Sulphur Yellow.

R. *supranubium* Hutch. - is a synonym of **R. pachypodum** Balf.f. & W.W.Sm. (Subsect. Maddenia).

R. SUTCHUENENSE FRANCH. - SUBSECT. FORTUNEA.
Shrub or small tree, 1-5m. Leaves 11-25 × 3.5-5cm, oblong-lanceolate, base broadly cuneate, lower surface glabrous except for a floccose indumentum along the midrib. Flowers *c*.10, in a lax truss, rose-pink, with darker flecks, widely campanulate, nectar pouches lacking, 50-75mm; stamens 12-15; ovary and style glabrous. H4b. February-April. C & S China, 2,400m.

Closely allied to R. *praevernum* and apparently hybridizing with it where the ranges overlap (see under R. × *geraldii*). It may be distinguished from the latter by the absence of a blotch on the corolla and by the persistent floccose indumentum along the midrib on the lower surface.

AM 1978, FCC 1987 (R.N.S. Clarke, Borde Hill, Sussex) to a clone 'Seventh Heaven', from Wilson 1232; flowers white in throat, suffused red-purple, with numerous small spots.

R. TAGGIANUM HUTCH. (INCL. R. *HEAD-FORTIANUM* HUTCH.) - SUBSECT. MADDENIA.
Very similar to R. *lindleyi*, differing in the larger calyx lobes, 17-19 × *c*.11mm, that are not ciliate, though often margined with quickly deciduous scales. H2. April-May. N Burma, China (NW Yunnan), 1,800-3,700m.

R. *taggianum* occurs in an area to the east of the range of the allied R. *lindleyi*.

AM 1932 (Marquess of Headfort, Kells); flowers white, with a yellow blotch.

AM 1992 (Millais Nurseries, Churt) to a clone 'Cliff Hanger', from Kingdon-Ward 8546; trusses 5 or 6-flowered, corolla white, with a small blotch of yellow-orange in upper throat.

FCC 1943 (M. Adams-Acton, London); flowers white, buds tinged salmon pink.

R. TALIENSE FRANCH. - SUBSECT. TALIENSIA.
Shrub, 0.8-4m. Leaves emitting a musky odour, broadly ovate-lanceolate, 5-11 × 2-4cm, oblong-ovate to broadly lanceolate, apex acute; lower surface covered with a dense two-layered indumentum, the upper layer fulvous, lanate to tomentose, composed of ramiform hairs, the lower compacted; petioles glabrescent. Flowers 10-20, in a dense truss; calyx 0.5-2mm; corolla white or (rarely) pale yellow, sometimes flushed with pink, with crimson flecks, funnel-campanulate, nectar pouches lacking, 30-35mm; ovary and style glabrous. H4b. April-May. China (W Yunnan), 3,050-4,000m.

Some cultivated plants have a leaf indumentum that is speckled and very shortly tomentose; in the wild the most common form has a more densely lanate indumentum.

This species is allied to R. *alutaceum*, from which it may be distinguished by its glabrous ovary, and to R. *sphaeroblastum*. It apparently has a very restricted distribution, occurring only around Dali in W Yunnan.

R. *tamurae* (Makino) Masamune - is a synonym of **R. eriocarpum** (Hayata) Nakai (sect. Tsutsusi).

R. TANASTYLUM BALF.F. & KINGDON-WARD - SUBSECT. IRRORATA.
Shrub or small tree, 1-4(-10)m. Leaves coriaceous, 7.5-15 × 3-5cm, elliptic to oblanceolate, apex acuminate, lower surface glabrous or with a thin veil of indumentum, also with persistent red punctate hair bases overlying the veins. Flowers 4-8, in a lax truss, deep pink to deep crimson, with black nectar pouches and few to many flecks, tubular-campanulate, 45-55mm; ovary glabrous to rufous-tomentose and glandular, style glabrous. H2. April-May. NE India (Arunachal Pradesh, NE Burma, China (W Yunnan), 1,850-3,350m.

Var. **tanastylum** (incl. R. *cerochitum* Balf.f. & Forrest & R. *ombrochares* Balf.f. &

Kingdon-Ward). Leaves at maturity more or less glabrous beneath; pedicels eglandular.

Var. **pennivenium** (Balf.f. & Forrest) D.F.Chamb. (*R. pennivenium* Balf.f. & Forrest). Leaves with a persistent indumentum beneath; pedicels glandular.

Both varieties have been reported as being in cultivation though neither is at all common.

R. TAPETIFORME BALF.F. & KINGDON-WARD - SUBSECT. LAPPONICA.
A low matted, prostrate or rounded shrub, to 0.9m. Leaves 0.4-1.2(-1.7) × (0.2-)0.3-1cm, broadly elliptic to rotund, apex obtuse or rounded, mucro absent or minute, lower surface covered with uniformly rufous touching scales. Flowers 1-3(-4) per inflorescence; calyx to 2mm, lobes, when present, rounded or deltoid; corolla purplish or violet to rose, exceptionally yellow, broadly funnel-shaped, 9-16mm; stamens 10, rarely 5-6, about as long corolla; ovary scaly, style usually longer than stamens, glabrous or (rarely) puberulous at base. H4a-b. April. NE Burma, China (NW Yunnan, SE Tibet), 3,500-4,600m.

This species is allied to *R. orthocladum* but may be distinguished by the relatively broader leaves.

R. taronense Hutch. - is a synonym of **R. dendricola** Hutch. (Subsect. Maddenia).

R. TASHIROI MAXIM. - SECT. TSUTSUSI.
Branched shrub, 2-6m; young shoots covered with more or less flattened weak brown hairs. Leaves apparently of one kind, persistent, apparently in clusters of 2-3 at the tips of the branches, 4.5-7 × 1.5-2.5cm, apex acute, both surfaces at first covered with adpressed grey-brown hairs, glabrescent though with some hairs remaining on midrib; petioles covered with adpressed brown hairs. Pedicels densely clothed with brown bristles. Flowers 2-5 per inflorescence; calyx *c*.1mm; corolla pale rose-purple, with a few flecks, broadly funnel-campanulate,

25-40mm; stamens (4-)5; ovary densely covered with adpressed flattened shining brown hairs, style glabrous. H2-3. May. S Japan, ?S Taiwan, s.l.-500m.

This distinctive species shows features of both Sect. Brachycalyx and Sect. Tsutsusi; in the past it has been placed in its own section.

R. TATSIENENSE FRANCH. (INCL. *R. HYPOPHAEUM* BALF.F. & FORREST) - SUBSECT. TRIFLORA.
Shrub, 0.3-5m; young shoots scaly, deep crimson. Leaves 2.2-4.2(-5.2) × 1.2-2.3 (2.7)cm, broadly to narrowly elliptic, apex acute, upper surface usually persistently scaly and with midrib puberulent, lower surface covered with unequal brown narrowly rimmed scales that are 1-2× their own diameter apart. Flowers 3-6, in a loose terminal inflorescence; calyx disc-like, usually ciliate; corolla whitish to rose-pink or lavender, with or without red flecks, zygomorphic, widely funnel-shaped, 16-21mm, outer surface lacking scales; stamens 10; ovary scaly, impressed below the declinate style that is glabrous or puberulous at base. H3-4a. April-May. China (N Yunnan, W Sichuan, Guizhou), 2,100-4,250m.

This species resembles both *R. siderophyllum* (q.v.) and *R. davidsonianum*. It differs from the former in its broader leaves and smaller corolla, and from the latter in its narrowly rimmed leaf scales.

R. TELMATEIUM BALF.F. & W.W.SM. (INCL. *R. DIACRITUM* BALF.F. & W.W.SM., *R. DRUMONIUM* BALF.F. & W.W.SM. & *R. IDONEUM* BALF.F. & W.W.SM.) - SUBSECT. LAPPONICA.
Much-branched, prostrate or erect shrub, to 1m. Leaves 0.3-1.2(-1.4) × 0.2-0.7cm, narrowly elliptic to rotund, apex acute to rounded, strongly mucronate, lower surface covered with overlapping scales, the majority of which are pale gold to reddish brown, usually with few to many darker scales. Flowers 1-3 per inflorescence; calyx 0.5-3mm, lobes often unequal deltoid to rounded; corolla lavender or rose-

pink to purple, broadly funnel-shaped, scaly outside, 6-14mm; stamens 10× as long as corolla; ovary scaly, style of varying length, glabrous or pubescent towards base. H4a-b. China (Yunnan, SW Sichuan), 2,500-5,000m.

R. *telmateium* is allied to R. *nivale* but differs in the sparse covering of darker scales on the leaf undersurface.

R. *telopeum* Balf.f. & Forrest - is a synonym of **R. campylocarpum** Hook.f. subsp. **caloxanthum** (Balf.f. & Farrer) D.F.Chamb. (Subsect. Campylocarpa).

R. TEMENIUM BALF.F. & FORREST - SUBSECT. NERIIFLORA.
Dwarf shrub, 0.3-1.5m. Leaves 3.5-5(-8) × 1.2(-3)cm, elliptic, lower surface glabrous or with the remains of a whitish floccose indumentum persisting, especially on the midrib and main veins, lower epidermis glaucous-papillate; petioles tomentose, usually also setose. Flowers 2-6, in a lax to dense truss; calyx 2-5mm; corolla fleshy, white to pink or carmine, or yellow, campanulate to tubular-campanulate, 35-45mm; with nectar pouches; ovary tomentose, sometimes also with a few glands, abruptly contracted into the style. H4a-b. April-May. China (Border of Yunnan & Tibet), (3,650-)4,250-4,550m.

Var. **temenium**. Corolla carmine to crimson; inflorescence dense; young shoots and pedicels always setose, usually strongly so.

Var. **gilvum** (Cowan) D.F. Chamb. (incl. R. *temenium* Balf.f. & Forrest subsp. *chrysanthum* Cowan). Corolla yellow, otherwise as for var. *temenium*.

AM 1958 amd FCC 1964 (Mrs K.L. Kenneth, Ardrishaig) to a clone 'Cruachan', as R. *temenium* var. *chrysanthum*; flowers Sulphur Yellow.

Var. **dealbatum** (Cowan) D.F.Chamb. (incl. R. *glaphyrum* Balf.f. & Forrest). Corolla white to deep rose-pink; inflorescence lax; young shoots and pedicels weakly setose, occasionally lacking setae.

This species is closely allied to R.

eudoxum and to R. *sanguineum*, and almost certainly hybridizes with both. R. *temenium* may also hybridize with R. *citriniflorum* and R. *catacosmum*.

R. *temenium* Balf.f. & Forrest subsp. *chrysanthum* Cowan - is a synonym of **R. temenium** Balf.f. var. **gilvum** (Cowan) D.F.Chamb. (Subsect. Neriiflora).

R. TEPHROPEPLUM BALF.F. & FARRER - SUBSECT. TEPHROPEPLA.
Shrub, 0.5-1.3m; bark flaking, brownish. Leaves 4.2-7.5(-10) × (1.1-)1.6-3(-4)cm, apex rounded, dark green above, lower surface greyish-papillose, scales unequal, soon becoming dark brown, in shallow pits, touching, to their own diameter apart. Flowers 3-9, in a terminal inflorescence that usually has a conspicuous rhachis; calyx lobes spreading, 5-8mm, ciliate; corolla pink to red, campanulate (17-)20-24mm, outer surface scaly, glabrous; stamens 10; ovary scaly, style impressed, declinate, scaly in lower half. H3(-4a). April-May. India (Arunachal Pradesh), N Burma, China (SE Tibet, NW Yunnan), 2,450-4,300m.

AM 1929 (Lady Aberconway & Hon. H.D. McLaren, Bodnant); flowers pale pink.

AM 1935 (Lord Swaythling, Townhill Park, Southampton); flowers magenta pink.

AM 1975 (Maj. A.E. Hardy, Sandling Park, Kent) to a clone 'Butcher Wood', from Kingdon-Ward 20844.

⚜ 1993

R. THAYERIANUM REHDER & E.H.WILSON - SUBSECT. ARGYROPHYLLA.
Shrub, 3-4m; bud scales persistent, at least on young shoots. Leaves stiff, 8-13 × 1.5-3cm, narrowly oblanceolate, apex cuspidate, upper surface reticulate, lower surface with a dense one-layered fawn compacted indumentum composed of ramiform hairs. Flowers 10-15 in a truss, white tinged pink, lobes sometimes with a darker median line and purple flecks, funnel-shaped, nectar pouches lacking, 25-30mm,

ovary covered with rufous stalked glands, sometimes also with a rufous tomentum, style glandular to tip. H4b. June-July. China (W Sichuan), *c*.2,700m.

The persistent bud scales and glandular style will distinguish this from the remaining species in the subsection.

AM 1990 (Crown Estate Commissioners, Windsor); trusses 14-16-flowered, corolla white, faintly tinged pink when fully open, colour stronger in bud stage.

R. THOMSONII HOOK.f. - SUBSECT. THOMSONIA.
Shrub or small tree, 0.6-3.5(-6)m; bark smooth, reddish, peeling; young shoots glabrous or sparsely glandular. Leaves 3-7.5(-11) × 2-5.5(-7.5)cm, orbicular to obovate or elliptic, base rounded to cordate, entirely glabrous (occasionally with a few hairs below), lower epidermis, strongly glaucous-papillate, with some red-stalked glands; petioles glabrous or sparsely glandular. Flowers 3-10, in a lax truss; calyx 2-20mm, irregular to cupular, often coloured; corolla fleshy, deep crimson, campanulate, with nectar pouches, 35-50mm; ovary glabrous or glandular, style glabrous. H3-4a. April-May. N India (Sikkim, Arunachal Pradesh), Bhutan, China (S Tibet).

Subsp. **thomsonii**. Leaves 5-11cm long, calyx (6-)10-18, shrubs 1.3-6m. Nepal, N India (Sikkim, Arunachal Pradesh), Bhutan, 3,000-4,000m.

AM 1973 (Crown Estate Commissioners, Windsor); flowers red in throat, darkening at rim.

Subsp. **lopsangianum** (Cowan) D.F.Chamb. (*R. lopsangianum* Cowan). Leaves 3-4.5cm long; calyx 2-4mm; shrubs 0.6-1.8m. China (S Tibet), 2,500-4,300m.

Subsp. *lopsangianum* is in some respects intermediate between subsp. *thomsonii* and *R. sherriffii*; some plants in cultivation have a few scattered hairs on the lower leaf surface.

R. thomsonii hybridizes in the wild with *R. campylocarpum* (see under *R.* × *candelabrum*).

R. THYMIFOLIUM MAXIM. (INCL. *R. POLIFOLIUM* FRANCH. & *R. SPILANTHUM* HUTCH.) - SUBSECT. LAPPONICA.
Erect, shrub, to 1.2m. Leaves (0.3-)0.5-1.4 × 2-6mm, narrowly ovate or elliptic to oblanceolate, apex obtuse, usually shortly mucronate, lower surface covered with uniformly straw-coloured, touching to overlapping scales. Flowers 1(-2) per inflorescence; calyx *c*.1mm, rim-like or with rounded to deltoid lobes; corolla pale lavender blue to purplish, broadly funnel-shaped, 7-11mm; stamens 10, exceeding the corolla; ovary scaly, style long or short, glabrous or (rarely) with a few hairs or scales at base. H4a-b. April-May. China (N Sichuan, Qinghai, Gansu), 2,600-4,600m.

This species is probably allied to *R. websterianum* and *R. nitidulum*, but it may be distinguished from both by its short calyx.

R. TOLMACHEVII HARMAJA (*LEDUM MACROPHYLLUM* TOLM.) - SUBSECT. LEDUM.
Erect shrub, *c*.0.5m; young shoots ferruginous-tomentose. Leaves 2.5-8.5 × 0.5-2cm, oblong-lanceolate, more or less acuminate, margins revolute, upper surface dark green, lower surface white-pubescent, also with long crisped ferruginous hairs on midrib and lamina, scales rimless, golden, 1-2× their own diameter apart, intermixed with red-brown glands; petioles 3-6mm. Flowers many, in a loose terminal umbellate corymb; calyx lobes obsolete; corolla rotate, white, *c*.7mm; stamens *c*.11; ovary densely glandular and pubescent, style glabrous. H4. June-July. E Russia (Sachalin).

This species may be distinguished from the allied *R. hypoleucum* by the ferruginous hairs on the lamina of the lower surface of the leaves.

R. TOMENTOSUM HARMAJA - SUBSECT. LEDUM.
Small, erect or decumbent shrub, 0.3-1.2m; young shoots ferruginous-lanate, glandular. Leaves 0.6-5 × 0.1-0.5(-1.2)cm, linear to narrowly elliptic-oblong, margin strongly

revolute, upper surface dark green, dull, lower surface densely ferrugineous-lanate, epidermis with or without short setulose hairs, sometimes also with reddish glands, scales rimless, golden. Flowers many, in a loose terminal umbellate corymb; calyx minute; corolla white, rotate, 4-8mm; stamens 7-10; ovary glandular, style glabrous. H4. June-July. Holarctic, s.l.-2,000m.

Subsp. **tomentosum.** (*Ledum palustre* L.). Leaves 1.2-5 × 0.2-0.5(-1.2)cm, lower epidermis covered with short setulose hairs. N & C Europe, Russia (European part, extending to S Siberia), s.l.-2,000m.

Subsp. **subarcticum** (Harmaja) G.Wallace (*Ledum* minus hort., *L. palustre* L. var. *decumbens* Aiton, *R. subarcticum* Harmaja). Leaves 0.6-2 × 0.1-0.3cm, lower epidermis with few or no setulose hairs. Arctic regions of Europe, America and Russia, also Japan (Hokkaido) and Korea.

R. TOSAENSE MAKINO (INCL. *R. MIYAZA-WAE* NAKAI & H.HARA) - SECT. TSUTSUSI. Much-branched shrub, 1.5-2m; young shoots clothed with adpressed flattened grey-brown strigose hairs. Leaves of two kinds, deciduous or persistent, spring leaves 0.7-4 × 0.2-1cm, oblanceolate to oblanceolate-spathulate, apex acute, both surfaces with scattered adpressed grey hairs; summer leaves 0.3-0.7cm long, otherwise as for spring leaves. Pedicels adpressed-strigose. Flowers 1-6 per inflorescence; calyx *c*.2mm; corolla purplish pink, with or without darker flecks, rarely white with a faint pink flush, funnel-shaped, 18-25mm; stamens 5(-10); ovary densely strigose, style glabrous. H3-4a. April-May. Japan (Kyushu, Shikoku, Honshu), *c*.100m.

AM 1978 (Countess of Rosse and National Trust, Nymans Garden) to a clone 'Ralph Clarke'; flowers red-purple, fading to white at base externally.

R. TRAILLIANUM FORREST & W.W.SM. - SUBSECT. TALIENSIA.
Shrub or small tree, 0.6-8m. Leaves 7-13 ×

3-6.5cm, obovate to elliptic, apex apiculate to acuminate, lower surface covered in a one-layered indumentum composed of radiate hairs that is either rust-red and powdery or brown and matted; petioles floccose. Flowers 6-15, in a dense truss; calyx *c*.1mm; corolla white, sometimes flushed rose, with crimson flecks, funnel-campanulate, nectar pouches lacking, 25-45mm; ovary glabrous or sparsely red-brown-tomentose, style glabrous. H4b. April-May. China (SE Tibet, W Yunnan, SW Sichuan), 3,350-4,550m.

Var. **traillianum.** Leaf indumentum composed of radiate hairs with short pyriform arms; corolla 25-35mm. China (W Yunnan, SW Sichuan).

Var. **dictyotum** (Balf.f. ex Tagg) D.F.Chamb. (*R. dictyotum* Balf.f. ex Tagg). Leaf indumentum composed of radiate hairs with long ribbon-like arms; corolla (35-)45mm. China (SE Tibet, NW Yunnan).

This species is closely allied to *R. phaeochrysum* but may be distinguished by the leaf indumentum.

AM 1965 (E. de Rothschild, Exbury) to a clone 'Kathmandu', as *R. dictyotum*; flowers white, with a crimson blotch and crimson spots.

R. TRICHANTHUM REHDER - SUBSECT. TRIFLORA.
Shrub, 1-3(-6)m; young shoots scaly and densely setose. Leaves 5.5-8 × 2.3-3.5cm, ovate-elliptic to narrowly elliptic, apex acute, upper surface with or without scales, glabrous or setose, lower surface pilose, at least on midrib, scales unequal, brown, 1-4× their own diameter apart; petioles densely pilose. Flowers 2-3, in a loose terminal inflorescence; calyx lobes 1-2mm, setose; corolla light to dark purple, zygomorphic, widely funnel-shaped, 30-36mm, outer surface scaly and variably setose; stamens 10; ovary scaly, pilose and setose, style impressed, declinate, usually glabrous. H4a. May-June. China (W Sichuan), 2,300-3,300m.

This species apparently has affinities with *R. concinnum* but is more hairy.

AM 1971 (Maj. A.E. Hardy, Sandling

Park, Kent) to a clone 'Honey Wood'; flowers purple-violet, paler in throat, with green mottling, becoming red-purple at base externally.

R. TRICHOCLADUM FRANCH. - SUBSECT. TRICHOCLADA.

Shrub, to 1.5m; young shoots usually with at least some twisted or curled setae. Leaves deciduous, 2.4-4 × 1-2cm, obovate or obovate-elliptic, margin ciliate, upper surface often with some setae persisting to maturity, sometimes also puberulent, lower surface with few to many twisted setae, scales uniform or of differing sizes, usually uniformly golden though occasionally with some discoloured, purplish scales. Flowers precocious, 1-3, in a terminal inflorescense; calyx 2-5mm; corolla yellow or greenish yellow, funnel-campanulate; stamens 10; ovary scaly, rarely with a few setae at apex, style sometimes puberulent at base. H(3-)4a-b. April-May. NE Burma, China (S Tibet, NW Yunnan).

Var. **trichocladum.** (incl. *R. lithophilum* Balf.f. & Kingdon-Ward, *R. lophogynum* Balf.f. & Forrest ex Hutch. & *R. oulotrichum* Balf.f. & Forrest). Upper surface of leaves with a sparse covering of setae. NE Burma, China (W Yunnan), 2,450-3,350m.

AM 1971 (Crown Estate Commissioners, Windsor) as *R. lophogynum*; flowers yellow, with darker, greenish yellow mottling.

Var. **longipilosum** Cowan (*R. mekongense* Franch. var. *longipilosum* (Cowan) Cullen). Upper surface of leaves with a dense covering of setae. NE Burma, China (S Tibet, NW Yunnan), 3,050-4,000m.

R. trichocladum has been traditionally delineated from the closely allied *R. mekongense* by the presence of uniform scales. While some forms of the present species do have uniform scales, the type of *R. trichocladum* does not. The relative abundance of twisted or curled setae on the leaves does however seem to be a reliable character.

R. trichomiscum Balf.f. & Forrest - is a synonym of **R. eudoxum** Balf.f. & Forrest var. **eudoxum** (Subsect. Neriiflora).

R. trichophlebium Balf.f. & Forrest - is a synonym of **R. eudoxum** Balf.f. & Forrest var. **eudoxum** (Subsect. Neriiflora).

R. TRICHOSTOMUM FRANCH. - SECT. POGONANTHUM.

Dwarf shrub, 0.3-1(-1.5)m; leaf bud scales usually deciduous. Leaves 1.2-3 × 0.3-0.6cm, linear to oblanceolate, apex rounded, slightly mucronate to emarginate, margins usually strongly revolute, lower surface covered with 2-3 tiers of dense overlapping scales, the upper tiers usually pale brown, the lowest paler, golden yellow. Flowers many, in a racemose umbel; calyx lobes 1-2.5mm; corolla white or pink, hypocrateriform, tube 4.5-8(-10)mm, glabrous outside, hairy within; stamens 5(-6); ovary scaly. H(3-)4a. May-June. China (Yunnan, Sichuan), 3,400-4,600m.

This species is allied to *R. primuliflorum* but may be distinguished by the narrower leaves. *R. hedyosmum* Balf.f., which differs in its larger flowers, and is only known in cultivation, is probably a hybrid of *R. trichostomum*.

AM 1925 (A.K. Bulley, Neston).

AM 1971 (M. Simmons, Quarry Wood, Newbury) to a clone 'Quarry Wood', as var. *ledoides*; flowers white, flushed with a shade of red-purple.

AM 1960 (Crown Estate Commissioners, Windsor) to a clone 'Sweet Bay', as var. *radinum*; flowers Tyrian Rose, suffused white to appear soft pink.

AM 1972 (Crown Estate Commissioners, Windsor) to a clone 'Lakeside'; flowers white, flushed red-purple.

AM 1972 (Mr & Mrs M. Simmons, Quarry wood, Newbury), as var. *radianum*; flowers red-purple.

FCC 1976 (Lady Anne Palmer, Rosemoor Garden Charitable Trust, Torrington) to a clone 'Collingwood Ingram'; flowers red-purple, paler in throat.

♀ 1993

193

R. TRIFLORUM HOOK.F. - SUBSECT. TRIFLORA.
Straggling shrub, (0.5-)1-5(-7)m; young shoots scaly, mature bark smooth and peeling, reddish brown. Leaves usually evergreen, 3.8-6.5 × 2-3.2cm, ovate to lanceolate or elliptic, apex acute, upper surface lacking scales, glabrous, lower surface greyish brown, densely covered with small almost rimless brown scales. Flowers 2-4, in a loose terminal inflorescence; calyx small, scaly, not ciliate; corolla pale yellow, sometimes suffused with red, sometimes with greenish to red flecks, zygomorphic, funnel-shaped to widely funnel-shaped, 21-30mm, outer surface densely scaly, pubescent at sinuses; stamens 10; ovary scaly, impressed below the declinate, glabrous or (rarely) puberulent at base, style. H3-4a. May-June. N India (Bengal, Manipur), Bhutan, N Burma, China (S Tibet), 2,300-3,650m.

Var. **triflorum**. (incl. *R. triflorum* Hook.f. var. *mahogani* Hutch.). Corolla funnel-shaped to widely funnel-shaped. Nepal, India (Sikkim, W Bengal, Arunachal Pradesh), Bhutan, N Burma, China (S Tibet), 2,300-3,650m.

Var. **bauhiniiflorum** (Watt ex Hutch.) Cullen (*R. bauhiniiflorum* Watt ex Hutch.). Corolla very openly funnel-shaped to almost flat. India (Manipur), 2,450-2,750m.

The two varieties recognized here are distinguished only by the shape of the corolla. They apparently have different geographical distributions.

R. triplonaevium Balf.f. & Forrest - is a synonym of **R. alutaceum** Balf.f. & W.W.Sm. var. **iodes** (Balf.f. & Forrest) D.F.Chamb. (Subsect. Taliensia).

R. tritifolium Balf.f. & Forrest - is a synonym of **R. alutaceum** Balf.f. & W.W.Sm. var. **iodes** (Balf.f. & Forrest) D.F.Chamb. (Subsect. Taliensia).

R. tsangpoense Kingdon-Ward var. *tsangpoense* and var. *curvistylum* Kingdon-Ward ex Cowan & Davidian - are synonyms of

R. charitopes Balf.f. & Farrer subsp. **tsangpoense** (Kingdon-Ward) Cullen (Subsect. Glauca).

R. TSARIENSE COWAN - SUBSECT. LANATA.
Shrub, 1-3m. Leaves coriaceous, 3.5-5.5 × 1.5-3cm, obovate to oblong, apex bluntly apiculate to acute, lower surface covered with a dense reddish brown or pale fawn tomentum composed of ramiform hairs. Flowers 3-5, in a lax truss, cream, with a pink flush or white to pale pink, open-campanulate, nectar pouches lacking, 25-35mm; ovary densely tomentose, style glabrous. H4a. March-May. NE India (Arunachal Pradesh), China (S Tibet), ?E Bhutan, 3,500-4,500m.

Var. **tsariense**. Leaves with a reddish brown indumentum beneath.

AM 1964 (Maj.Gen. and Mrs E.G.W.W. Harrison, Tremeer, Cornwall) to a clone 'Yum-Yum'; flowers white flushed Phlox Pink, with Carmine buds.

Var. **trimoense** Davidian. Leaves with a whitish to pale fawn indumentum beneath.

R. TSCHONOSKYI MAXIM. - SECT. TSUTSUSI.
Much-branched shrub, 0.3-1.5m; young shoots and petioles densely covered with adpressed flattened rufous hairs. Leaves of one kind, 1-3.5 × 0.3-1cm, lanceolate to elliptic, apex acute, both surfaces with scattered adpressed whitish to pale brown villose hairs, especially on the midrib. Pedicels covered with adpressed whitish hairs. Flowers 3-6 per inflorescence; calyx minute; corolla white, funnel-shaped, 7-9mm; stamens 4-5; ovary densely covered with pale brown bristles, style glabrous. H4b. May. S Korea, Japan, Russia (Kamschatka), 700-1,800m.

Var. **tschonoskyi**. Leaves 4-5-nerved, 1-2cm. S Korea, Japan, Russia (Kamschatka), 1,500-1,800m.

Var. **trinerve** (Franch.) Makino. Leaves 3-nerved, 2-3.5cm. Japan (Honshu), 700-1,000m.

Both varieties of this distinctive

species are cultivated.

R. TSUSIOPHYLLUM SUGIM. (*TSUSIOPHYLLUM TANAKAE* MAXIM.) - SECT. TSUTSUSI.
Dwarf shrub, to *c*.0.3m; young shoots covered with adpressed flattened bristles. Leaves of one kind, 1-1.2 × 0.5-0.7cm, obovate, apex acute, upper surface glabrous when mature, lower surface with a few bristles on the midrib, otherwise glabrous; petioles covered with bristles. Pedicels apparently hairy. Flowers 1-4 per inflorescence; calyx minute; corolla pink in bud, fading to white, tubular-campanulate, *c*.10mm; stamens (4-)5; ovary covered with bristles, style glabrous. H4a-b. July. Japan (S Honshu and adjacent Islands), *c*.500m.

A distinctive species on account of its tubular-campanulate corolla with short lobes, half as long as tube.

R. tubiforme (Cowan & Davidian) Davidian - is a synonym of **R. glaucophyllum** Rehder subsp. **tubiforme** (Cowan & Davidian) D.G.Long (Subsect. Glauca).

R. UNGERNII TRAUTV. - SUBSECT. PONTICA
Shrub or small tree, 1-7m; young shoots densely whitish-lanate-tomentose, bud scales deciduous. Leaves 11.5-21 × 3.5-6cm, oblanceolate to obovate, apex usually rounded, acuminate, upper surface glabrous, lower surface covered with a dense whitish to fawn lanate tomentum composed of dendroid hairs; petioles lanate-tomentose and stalked-glandular at first, later glabrescent. Flowers 12-25, in a lax truss; calyx 5-9mm; corolla white, sometimes flushed pink, with greenish flecks, funnel-campanulate, nectar pouches lacking, *c*.35mm; ovary covered with brownish stipitate glands, also with a few whitish non-glandular hairs, style glabrous. H4b. June-July, 1,200-1,850m.

Allied to *R. smirnowii* but differing in its glandular ovary.

AM 1973 (Lord Aberconway and National Trust, Bodnant); flowers white inside, edged pale pink, pink outside, spotted green.

R. UNIFLORUM KINGDON-WARD - SUBSECT. UNIFLORA.
Dwarf prostrate shrub, the ends of the branches ascending to 0.5m; young growth scaly. Leaves 1.3-2.5 × 0.5-1cm, oblong-elliptic, apex acute or rounded, margin entire, lower surface with very distant scales that are equal, golden at first, soon turning brown, and have narrow rims. Flowers 1-2, in a terminal inflorescence; calyx lobes oblong, 1.5-2.5mm; corolla purple, funnel-campanulate, 21-25mm, tube 12-14mm, outer surface densely pilose, sparsely scaly; stamens 10; ovary scaly, impressed below the declinate style that is glabrous and longer than the stamens. H(3-)4a. April-May. China (SE Tibet), NE Burma, 3,050-3,650m.

Var. **uniflorum.** Leaf apex rounded. China (SE Tibet), 3,350-3,650m.

Var. **imperator** (Hutch. & Kingdon-Ward) Cullen (*R. imperator* Hutch. & Kingdon-Ward). Leaf apex acute. NE Burma, 3,050-3,350m.

This species is allied to *R. pemakoense* (q.v.).

AM 1934 (Lord Swaythling, Townhill Park, Southampton) as *R. imperator*, from Kingdon-Ward 6884; flowers rosy purple.

R. UVARIIFOLIUM DIELS - SUBSECT. FULVA.
Large shrub or small tree, 2-10m. Leaves 8-22 × 3.3-6.5cm, oblanceolate to oblong, lower surface with a 1-2 layered silvery indumentum, the upper layer (when present) composed of more or less floccose dendroid hairs, the lower layer compacted. Flowers 6-30, in a dense truss, white to pale pink, with crimson flecks and a purple basal blotch, campanulate, nectar pouches lacking, 30-35mm; ovary glabrous. H3-4a. March-April. China (S Tibet, NW Yunnan, SW Sichuan), (2,100)-3,000-4,000m.

Var. **uvariifolium.** Leaves oblanceolate, cuneate at base, indumentum floccose. China (S Tibet, NW Yunnan, SW Sichuan).

AM 1965 (Royal Botanic Garden, Edinburgh) to a clone 'Yangtze Bend'; flowers rose-pink, spotted and blotched Indian Lake.

AM 1976 (Royal Botanic Gardens, Wakehurst) to a clone 'Reginald Childs'; flowers white, suffused red-purple and with a red blotch.

Var. **griseum** Cowan. Leaf base rounded, indumentum compacted. China (S Tibet).

These two varieties are poorly delineated from one another though there is some correlation between the morphological differences and the geographical distributions of the two taxa.

R. VALENTINIANUM FORREST EX HUTCH. - SUBSECT. MADDENIA.
Small shrub, 0.3-1.3m; young growth densely setose. Leaves 2.6-3.8(-5) × 1.6-2.2(-3.1)cm, elliptic, apex obtuse, margin entire, ciliate, upper surface with midrib impressed, lower surface brown, with dense overlapping unequal scales. Flowers (1-)2-6, in a loose terminal inflorescence, not scented; calyx 5-7mm, ciliate; corolla bright yellow, funnel-campanulate, 20-32mm, outer surface with tube pubescent and scales restricted to the lobes; stamens 10; ovary densely scaly, impressed below the style that is variably scaly towards the base. H2-3. March-April. N Burma, China (SW Yunnan, Guizhou), 2,700-3,600m.

This yellow-flowered species is allied to *R. fletcherianum* but differs in the entire leaves, with a dense brown covering of scales on the undersurface. It is one of the hardier members of Subsect. Maddenia that can be grown successfully outside in the more sheltered gardens of the S & W of Britain.

The recently described var. *oblongilobatum* R.C.Fang is reported to be in cultivation. It differs from the type variety (as described above) in its shorter (4-5mm), oblong calyx lobes that are glandular-scaly, not ciliate.

AM 1933 (Hon. H.D. McLaren, Bodnant); flowers yellow.

R. VASEYI A.GRAY - SECT. RHODORA.
Deciduous shrub or small tree, 2.5(-5.5)m; young twigs covered with eglandular and gland-tipped hairs. Leaves 2.3-17 × 0.8-5.5cm, elliptic to obovate, lower surface with scattered gland-tipped hairs also with larger eglandular hairs on main veins. Flower bud scales unicellular-pubescent, margin usually glandular. Pedicels pubescent, also with gland-tipped hairs. Flowers fragrant, appearing before the leaves, 5-15, in an umbellate raceme; calyx 0.5-8.5mm; corolla pink or occasionally white, with brown to red flecks on the upper three lobes, broadly rotate-funnelform, two-lipped, tube short, gradually expanding into the limb, 20-35mm. Capsule covered with gland-tipped hairs. H4b. April-May. E USA (N Carolina), 900-1,830m.

This is a distinctive species with no close relatives. It is rare in the wild and considered to be threatened.

AM 1969 (E. de Rothschild, Exbury) to a clone 'Suva'; flowers red-purple, becoming paler, throat more or less white, with sparse, dark red-purple spots.

♔ 1993

R. VEITCHIANUM HOOK.F. (INCL. *R. CUBITTII* HUTCH.) - SUBSECT. MADDENIA.
Epiphytic or free-growing shrub, to 2m; young shoots sparsely setose. Leaves 6.5-10 × 2.8-4cm, obovate or narrowly elliptic, apex shortly acuminate, margin ciliate, at least when young, upper surface with impressed midrib, lower surface pale, with distant unequal golden scales. Flowers (1-)2-5, in a loose inflorescence, not scented; calyx disc-like, ciliate; corolla white, often with a yellow blotch, openly funnel-campanulate, 50-60(-65)mm; outer surface scaly only on adaxial (inner) side, pubescent at base, lobes usually crisped; stamens 10; ovary scaly, tapering into the style which is scaly well above the base. H1b-2. May-June. Burma, Thailand, Laos, Vietnam, 1,200-2,400m.

R. cubittii, as known in cultivation, does not match the type specimen and is of uncertain provenance. It is therefore not formally recognized here. The name technically applies to a plant that is clearly referrable to *R. veitchianum*.

AM 1935 (Lt Col E.H.W. Bolitho, Penzance) to *R. cubittii* hort.; flowers white deeply flushed rose.

AM 1978 (G.Gorer, Sunte House, Haywards Heath) to a clone 'Margaret Mead'; truss 2-3-flowered, corolla white with faint orange flush in upper throat.

FCC 1962 (Crown Estate Commissioners, Windsor), as *R. cubittii* hort. 'Ashcombe'; flowers white with an orange-yellow blotch.

♀ 1993 to *R. veitchianum*
♀ 1993 to *R. cubittii* hort.

R. vellereum Hutch. - is a synonym of **R. principis** Bureau & Franch. (Subsect. Taliensia).

R. VENATOR TAGG - SUBSECT. VENATORA. Straggly shrub, 1-3m; young shoots and petioles with an evanescent stellate tomentum intermixed with setose glands. Leaves 8.5-14 × 2-2.4cm, elliptic to lanceolate, apex acute to acuminate, upper and lower surfaces glabrous except for a thin stellate indumentum that is intermixed with folioliferous hairs on the midrib below. Flowers 7-10, in a tight truss; calyx 3-5mm; corolla fleshy, crimson, with darker nectar pouches, tubular-campanulate, 30-35mm; ovary with a dense tomentum intermixed with stalked glands, style glabrous. H3(-4a). May-June. China (SE Tibet), 2,500m.

A distinctive species with no close allies. It has a restricted distribution in the wild and is only occasionally seen in cultivation.

AM 1933 (Hon. H.D. McLaren, Bodnant) from Kingdon-Ward 6285; flowers reddish orange.

R. VERNICOSUM FRANCH. - SUBSECT. FORTUNEA.
Shrub or tree, 1.3-8m. Leaves 7-10 × 2.7-5cm, elliptic to ovate- or obovate-elliptic, base rounded, lower surface with persistent punctulate hair bases, otherwise glabrous when mature. Flowers 6-10 to a truss; calyx *c.*2mm; corolla 6-7-lobed, pale rose to pinkish purple, with crimson flecks, broadly funnel-campanulate, nectar pouches lacking, 35-50mm; stamens *c.*14, filaments glabrous; ovary and style covered with red stalked glands. H4a-b. May. SW & C China (N Yunnan, SW Sichuan, Guizhou), 2,600-3,650m.

This species can be confused with *R. decorum* but may be distinguished by the glabrous stamen filaments and usually by the red stylar glands and broader leaves. *R. vernicosum* usually occurs at higher altitudes than *R. decorum* and is more hardy than many forms of the latter species.

AM 1964 (Younger Botanic Garden, Benmore, Argyll) to a clone 'Loch Eck'; flowers pure white.

AM 1976 (Lord Aberconway and National Trust, Bodnant) to a clone 'Spring Sonnet', from Rock 11408 (=USDA 59625); flowers white, flushed red-purple, spotted.

R. verruculosum Rehder & E.H.Wilson - is a hybrid of **R. flavidum** Franch. (Subsect. Lapponica).

AM 1932 (Col S.R. Clarke, Borde Hill, Sussex); flowers purple.

R. VESICULIFERUM TAGG - SUBSECT. GLISCHRA.
Large shrub or small tree; young shoots densely glandular-setose. Leaves 12-14.5 × 3.5-5cm, obovate to oblanceoate; upper surface rugulose, with deeply impressed veins, lower surface with veins and midrib covered with glandular setae and with white vesiculate hairs. Flowers 10-15 in a truss; calyx 8-10mm; corolla white to rose-purple, with flecks and a small basal blotch, funnel-campanulate, nectar pouches lacking, 25-35mm; ovary densely covered with rufous stalked glands, with an understorey of white vesiculate hairs. H3-4a. April-May. NE Burma, China (W Yunnan, SE Tibet), 2,500-3,350m.

This species is closely allied to *R. glischroides* but may be distinguished from that species by the presence of vesiculate hairs.

R. vestitum Tagg & Forrest - is a synonym of **R. selense** Franch. subsp. **setiferum** (Balf.f. & Forrest) D.F.Chamb. (Subsect. Selensia).

R. VIALII DELAVAY & FRANCH. - SECT. AZALEASTRUM.
Shrub, to 3m. Leaves 4-7 × 1.5-3cm, elliptic to obovate, apex obtuse or notched. Flowers single, borne laterally below vegetative buds, crimson broadly funnel-shaped; tube *c*.15mm; lobes rotund, *c*.10mm; stamens 5. H1-2. April-May. China (S Yunnan), adjacent parts of Laos and Vietnam, *c*.1,700m.

Some plants in cultivation under this name are referrable to *R. leptothrium*, from which it may be distinguished by the shape of the corolla. Its status in cultivation is therefore doubtful.

R. vilmorinianum Balf.f. - is a synonym of **R. augustinii** Hemsl. var. **augustinii** (Subsect. Triflora).

R. violaceum Rehder & E.H.Wilson - is a synonym of **R. nivale** Hook.f. var. **boreale** Philipson & M.N. Philipson (Subsect. Lapponica).

R. VIRGATUM HOOK.F. - SUBSECT. VIRGATA.
Small shrub, 0.3-2.5m; young shoots scaly. Leaves 1.8-8 × 0.5-2cm, narrowly oblong or oblong-elliptic, apex acute to rounded, upper surface with scales, especially on midrib and at base, lower surface densely covered with brown to dark brown peltate scales. Flowers 1(-2), in an inflorescence borne in the axils of the upper leaves; calyx lobes 2-3mm, sometimes ciliate; corolla white to deep pink or mauve, funnel-shaped, 15-37mm, outer surface of tube sparsely scaly and pubescent; stamens 10; ovary densely scaly, impressed below the declinate style that is scaly

and/or pilose towards base. H2-3. April-May. India (Sikkim, Arunachal Pradesh), Bhutan, China (S Tibet, Yunnan), 2,000-4,000m.

Subsp. **virgatum**. Corolla 25-37mm, tube 11-20mm, pale or deep pink to mauve. Nepal, India (Sikkim, Arunachal Pradesh), Bhutan, China (S & SE Tibet), 2,500-3,800m.
AM 1973 (Maj. A.E. Hardy, Sandling Park, Kent); flowers white.
Subsp. **oleifolium** (Franch.) Cullen (*R. oleifolium* Franch.). Corolla 15-25mm, tube 8-15mm, white or pink. China (SE Tibet, W & N Yunnan), 2,000-4,000m.
This is a distinctive species on account of the axillary inflorescences.

R. VIRIDESCENS HUTCH. (INCL. *R. RUBROLUTEUM* DAVIDIAN) - SUBSECT. TRICHOCLADA.
Small shrub, 0.3-1.5m; young shoots scaly, setose, sometimes also puberulous. Leaves evergreen, 2.3-6.7 × 1.3-3cm, obovate, to elliptic, usually lacking setae, though occasionally with midrib puberulent or with a few setae, lower surface pale green, covered with large to medium-sized scales, 1-3× their own diameter apart. Flowers 3-6, in a loose inflorescence; calyx small; corolla yellowish green, yellow or reddish yellow, funnel-campanulate, zygomorphic, 15-25mm; stamens 10; ovary densely scaly, style straight or sharply bent. H4a-b. May-June. China (S Tibet), 2,850-3,300m.
Recent field observations (P. & K. Cox) have confirmed the distinctness of this species. It may be distinguished from the closely allied *R. mekongense* by its evergreen leaves.
AM 1972 (E.H.M. and P.A. Cox, Perth) to a clone 'Doshong La', from Kingdon-Ward 5829; flowers yellow, flushed rose at corolla lobe tip externally, with Olive Green flecking.

R. VISCIDIFOLIUM DAVIDIAN - SUBSECT. THOMSONIA.
Shrub, 0.6-2.4m; bark smooth; young shoots glabrous or glandular. Leaves 4-9.7

× 2.8-6.6.cm, oval to orbicular, base rounded to sub-cordate, entirely glabrous, lower epidermis strongly glaucous-papillate, with scattered viscid glands; petioles glabrous. Flowers 1-2; calyx 4-9mm, cupular; corolla coppery red, with dark nectar pouches and flecks, tubular-campanulate, 35-45mm; ovary densely tomentose and stalked-glandular, style glabrous. H3-4a. April-May. China (SE Tibet), 2,700-3,350m.

This species is allied to *R. thomsonii* but differs in the flower colour, etc. The whole plant is viscid, as the name implies.

R. viscosum (L.) Torr. (incl. *R. oblongifolium* [Small] Millais & *R. serrulatum* [Small] Millais) - subsect Pentanthera.
Deciduous shrub or small tree, to 6m; young twigs usually eglandular-hairy, occasionally with gland-tipped hairs. Leaves (3-)4-6(-8) × 1.3-2.3(-3.1)cm ovate or obovate to elliptic, lower surface glabrous, sometimes glaucous, occasionally with eglandular and/or gland-tipped hairs. Flower bud scales with outer surface sparsely to densely covered with unicellular hairs or glabrous, margin unicellular-ciliate, occasionally glandular below. Flowers with a sweet fragrance, appearing after the leaves have expanded, 3-14, in a shortened raceme; calyx 1-2(-5)mm; corolla white, occasionally with a pink or purplish tinge, rarely completely pink, funnelform, tube gradually expanding into limb, outer surface usually covered with unicellular and gland-tipped hairs, 20-57mm. Capsule covered with eglandular or gland-tipped hairs. H4b-c. May-July. E & S USA, s.l.-1,500m.

This is a variable and widespread species.

AM 1921 (F.G. Strover, South Norwood, London) as *Azalea viscosa glauca*; flowers white.

♀ 1993.

R. wadanum Makino - Sect. Brachycalyx.
Shrub or small tree; young shoots villose.

Leaves in whorls of up to three, at the ends of the branches, 3-5 × 2-4cm, rhombic, apex acute, tip blunt, lower surface sparsely villose, more densely so on the midrib; petioles densely villose. Pedicels with eglandular or glandular hairs. Flowers 1-2 per inflorescence, appearing before the leaves; calyx minute; corolla rich rose-pink, funnel-campanulate, 22-30mm; stamens 10; ovary densely villose; style stalked-glandular in lower half. H4a-b. April-May. Japan (SE Honshu), 950-1,500m.

A distinctive species on account of its glandular style.

R. wallichii Hook.f. (incl. *R. heftii* Davidian) - Subsect. Campanulata.
Shrub, 1-4.5m. Leaves 7-14 × 3.5-6.5cm, elliptic to ovate, glabrous above, with a sparse discontinuous indumentum of dark brown fasciculate hairs, to more or less glabrous. Flowers 5-8, in a lax truss, white to pale mauve or lilac, with or without flecks, funnel-campanulate, nectar pouches lacking, 25-50mm; ovary almost glabrous, style glabrous. H4a. April-May. E Nepal, N India (Sikkim, Bengal), Bhutan, China (S Tibet), 3,000-4,000m.

White-flowered forms with leaves more or less glabrous beneath have been referred to *R. heftii* Davidian. This species is closely allied to *R. campanulatum* and treated by some as a variety of that species. Natural hybrids between *R. wallichii* and *R. arboreum* are found in cultivation.

R. walongense Kingdon-Ward - Subsect. Maddenia.
Shrub, 2-3m; young shoots not setose. Leaves 10-11 × 3.8-4.5cm, elliptic, apex slightly acute, sometimes with a short drip-tip, margin not ciliate; upper surface with midrib impressed, lower surface brownish, covered with large scales 1-3× their own diameter apart. Flowers 3-6, in a lax terminal inflorescence, scented; calyx disc-like, ciliate; corolla creamy white, with a greenish blotch, funnel-shaped, *c*.60mm, outer surface pubescent and

scaly throughout; stamens 10; ovary densely scaly, tapering into the style that is scaly in the lower half. H2?. April-May. India (Arunachal Pradesh), China (SE Tibet), 1,500-2,150m.

This species may be distinguished from the allied *R. dendricola* by the calyx that is not ciliate.

R. WARDII W.W.SM. - SUBSECT. CAMPYLOCARPA.
Shrub or small tree, 0.6-8m. Leaves 6-11 × 2.3-6cm, often glaucous when young, base cordate, glabrous. Flowers 5-15, in a lax to dense truss, white to sulphur yellow, buds often strongly tinged pink, with or without a basal blotch, open-campanulate (saucer-shaped), nectar pouches lacking, 25-40mm; ovary and style stalked-glandular. H4a-b. May-June. China (SE Tibet, NW Yunnan, SW Sichuan), 3,000-4,300m.

Var. **wardii**. (incl. *R. litiense* Balf.f. & Forrest and *R. croceum* Balf.f. & W.W.Sm.) Flowers clear yellow.

Forms with relatively narrow leaves that are more glaucous than the type, from a restricted zone around the Li-ti-ping in W Yunnan, have been referred to *R. litiense*. This taxon is not maintained as it merges with the type form that has broader leaves. There are no significant differences in the flower characters.

AM 1926 (A.M. Williams, Launceston) as *R. croceum*; flowers bright yellow, touched with crimson internally.

AM 1926 (A.M. Williams, Launceston) as *R. astrocalyx*; flowers flat, clear lemon yellow.

AM 1931 (L. de Rothschild, Exbury) from Kingdon-Ward 4170; flowers bright yellow, flushed green.

AM 1931 (L. de Rothschild, Exbury) as *R. litiense*; flowers yellow.

AM 1959 (Capt. C. Ingram, Benenden, Kent) to a clone 'Ellestee', from L., S. & T. 5679; flowers clear Lemon Yellow, with a crimson blotch.

AM 1963 (Crown Estate Commissioners, Windsor) to a clone 'Meadow Pond', from L., S. & T. 15764; flowers Primrose Yellow, with a crimson blotch.

FCC 1953 (Col Lord Digby, Minterne, Dorset).

Var. **puralbum** (Balf.f. & W.W.Sm.) D.F.Chamb. (*R. puralbum* Balf.f. & W.W.Sm.) Flowers pure white.

This may be no more than an albino form of the much more common var. *wardii*.

R. wardii hybridizes in the wild with *R. selense* (see under *R.* × *erythrocalyx*) and with *R. vernicosum*. Where its range overlaps with *R. campylocarpum* (in S Tibet) the two species apparently intergrade, probably due to local hybridization. These two are sometimes confused but *R. wardii* can always be distinguished by its glandular style.

R. WASONII HEMSL. & E.H.WILSON - SUBSECT. TALIENSIA.
Sprawling shrub, 0.6-1.5m. Leaves 4-8 × 2.5-4cm, ovate-lanceolate, apex apiculate to shortly acuminate, lower surface with a sparse to dense one-layered reddish brown indumentum composed of long-rayed hairs, also with a few glands; petioles tomentose and sparsely glandular. Flowers 8-15, in a dense truss; calyx *c.*0.5mm; corolla open-campanulate, yellow or white to pink, with purple flecks, open-campanulate, nectar pouches lacking, 25-40mm; ovary densely reddish hairy, glands lacking, style glabrous. H4b. April-May. China (C Sichuan), 2,300-3,800m.

Var. **wasonii**. Flowers pale yellow, 35-40mm.

Var. **wenchuanense** L.C.Hu. Flowers white to pink, 25-35mm.

The application of the varietal names within this species is problematical as it is not clear whether Hemsley & Wilson intended the name 'wasonii' to apply to the yellow- or white to pink-flowered forms. Var. *wenchuanense* is at one extreme of the variation exhibited by this species while the yellow-flowered forms are at the other. Intermediates, with the white to pink flowers of the former but the flower size of the latter, have been referred to '*R. rhododactylum*' hort., the basionym of var.

'*rhododactylum*' (hort.) Davidian, a name that is probably invalid. In any case var. *rhododactylum* may be no more than a larger-flowered form of var. *wenchuanense*.

AM 1974 (Crown Estate Commissioners, Windsor) as var. *rhododactylum*.

R. WATSONII HEMSL. & E.H.WILSON - SUBSECT. GRANDIA.
Shrub or small tree, 2-6m. Leaves 10-23 × 4.3-10cm, obovate to oblanceolate, apex acute to acuminate, lower surface covered with a whitish thin compacted and agglutinated indumentum; petioles to 5mm, stout and flattened. Flowers 12-15, in dense truss, *c*.7-lobed, white, with a crimson basal blotch, campanulate, nectar pouches lacking, 35-40mm; stamens 14; ovary glabrous. H4a-b. March-April. China (Gansu, Sichuan), 2,600-3,300m.

A distinctive species on account of its short flattened petioles. It is allied to *R. balangense*.

R. WEBSTERIANUM REHDER & E.H.WILSON - SUBSECT. LAPPONICA.
Erect much-branched shub, to 1.5m. Leaves 0.6-1.5 × 0.3-0.9cm, ovate to oblong-elliptic, apex obtuse, base widening gradually from petiole, lower surface covered with uniformly straw-coloured or golden brown touching scales the centres of which are pale. Flowers 1(-2) per inflorescence; calyx 3-5mm, lobes broadly rounded; corolla pale purple or yellow, funnel-shaped, 14-19mm; stamens 10, equalling the corolla; ovary scaly, style exceeding the stamens, slightly pubescent and with some scales at base. H4a-b. April-May. China (NW Sichuan), 3,300-4,900m.

The yellow-flowered var. **yulongense** N.M.Philipson & Philipson is probably not in cultivation.

This species is allied to *R. nitidulum* (q.v.) and *R. hippophaeoides*.

R. weldianum Rehder & E.H.Wilson - is a synonym of **R. rufum** Batalin (Subsect. Taliensia).

R. westlandii Hemsl. - a synonym of **R. moulmainense** Hook.f. (Sect. Choniastrum).

R. WEYRICHII MAXIM. - SECT. BRACHYCALYX.
Shrub or small tree; young shoots soon becoming glabrous. Leaves in whorls of up to three, at the ends of the branches, 3.5-8 × 1.5-6cm, broadly rhombic, apex acute, lower surface with scattered brown hairs, especially on the midrib; petioles covered with brown pilose hairs at first, soon glabrescent. Pedicels densely covered with brown pilose hairs. Flowers 2-4 per inflorescence, appearing before or with the leaves; calyx minute; corolla pink to brick-red, with darker flecks on upper lobes, open-funnel-campanulate, 30-40mm; stamens 10; ovary densely pilose, style glabrous or pilose below, sometimes also papillate. H4a-b. April-May. Japan (Kyushu, Shikoku, SE Honshu), Korea, 20-1,200m.

R. weyrichii may be distinguished from the allied *R. sanctum* and *R. amagianum* by the larger flowers, to 40mm long, and the more numerous flowers per inflorescence.

R. WIGHTII HOOK.F. - SUBSECT TALIENSIA.
Shrub, 2-4.5m. Leaves 5-14 × 3.5-6cm, broadly elliptic to obovate, apex apiculate, lower surface covered with a dense one-layered rust-brown indumentum composed of ramiform hairs; petioles sparsely tomentose to glabrescent. Flowers 10-20, in a tight or loose truss; calyx *c*.0.5mm; corolla 5-lobed, pale to lemon yellow, with brown or purple flecks, campanulate, necter pouches lacking, 35-45mm; ovary densely red-brown-tomentose, style glabrous. H4b. April-May. Nepal, NE India (Assam, Arunachal Pradesh), Bhutan, China (S Tibet), 3,350-4,550m.

The above description applies to plants of wild origin that have been introduced recently. The most commonly grown plant under this name is straggly and differs in its 7-lobed, mortar-shaped corolla. This may be a hybrid between *R. wightii* and *R. grande*; it is sufficiently different from plants of wild origin to suggest that it should not be referred to *R. wightii*.

AM 1913 (Miss C. Mangles, Littleworth, Seale, Surrey); flowers pale Sulphur Yellow, with crimson markings at base.

R. WILLIAMSIANUM REHDER & E.H.WILSON - SUBSECT. WILLIAMSIANA.
A spreading dwarf shrub, 0.6-1.5m; young shoots setose-glandular; young growth coppery-coloured. Leaves 2-4.5 × 1.4-3.5cm, ovate-orbicular, base cordate, upper and lower surfaces glabrous though with red sessile glands below; petioles glabrous or setose-glandular. Flowers 2-3(-5) in a lax truss; calyx *c*.1mm; corolla pale rose, with darker flecks, campanulate, lacking nectar pouches, 30-40mm; ovary and style glandular. H4a-b. April-May. China (Sichuan, Guizhou), 1,800-2,800m.

This is a distinctive species without close allies that is local and rare in the wild.

AM 1938 (Lord Aberconway, Bodnant); flowers pink.

♀ 1993

R. wilsonaie Hemsl. & E.H.Wilson - a synonym of **R. latoucheae** Franch. (sect. Choniastrum).

R. WILTONII HEMSL. & E.H.WILSON - SUBSECT. TALIENSIA.
Shrub, 1.4.5m. Leaves 5-12 × 1.5-4cm, oblanceolate to broadly elliptic, apex apiculate, upper surface with deeply impressed veins so appearing bullate, lower surface with dense one-layered brown to rust-red indumentum composed of fasciculate to ramiform hairs; petioles tomentose at first, soon glabrescent. Flowers *c*.10, in a dense truss; calyx *c*.1mm; corolla white to pink, with red flecks, campanulate, nectar pouches absent, 30-40mm; ovary densely rust-red lanate tomentose, eglandular, style

glabrous or hairy at base. H4b. April-May, China (C Sichuan, Guizhou), 2,250-3,500m.

A distinctive species on account of its bullate leaves.

AM 1957 (E. de Rothschild, Exbury); flowers white, with a dark crimson blotch in throat, flushed pink externally.

R. wongii Hemsl. & E.H.Wilson- is doubtfully distinct from and may be the correct name for **R. ambiguum**. Plants under this name are in cultivation but it is not known how these relate to the original very poor dried specimen. Cultivated plants are hybrids of **R. ambiguum** and **R. flavidum**.

R. wuense Balf.f. - is a synonym of **R. faberi** Hemsl. (Subsect. Taliensia).

R. xanthocodon Hutch - is a synonym of **R. cinnabarinum** Hook.f. var. **xanthocodon** (Hutch.) Cullen (Subsect. Cinnabarina).

R. XANTHOSTEPHANUM MERR. - SUBSECT. TEPHROPEPLA.
Shrub, 0.6-2m; mature bark smooth, reddish brown. Leaves 5-8(-10.5) × 1.5-2.5(-3)cm, narrowly elliptic to oblong, apex acute, upper surface brownish green, lower surface silvery-papillose, scales unequal, their own diameter apart, borne in pits, the larger stalked. Flowers (3-)4-5, in a terminal inflorescence that has a rhachis 1-5mm long; calyx lobes (2-)5-7mm, erect or spreading, not ciliate; corolla deep yellow, sometimes almost yellow-orange, narrowly campanulate, 18-28mm; outer surface scaly, sometimes slightly pubescent; stamens 10; ovary scaly, tapering into the declinate style that is scaly at base. H2-3. April-May. India (Arunachal Pradesh), N Burma, China (Yunnan, SE Tibet), 1,600-3,000(-3,900)m.

This is a rare species in cultivation as it is tender. It is closely allied to *R. auritum* (q.v.).

AM 1961 (Crown Estate Commissioners, Windsor) to a clone 'Yellow Garland', from Forrest 21707/

22652; flowers Aureolin.

R. yakuinsulare Masamune - is probably a synonym of **R. scabrum** G.Don subsp. **scabrum** (Sect. Tsutsusi).

R. yakushimanum Nakai - is a synonoym of **R. degronianum** Carrière var. **yakushimanum** (Nakai) H.Hara (Subsect. Pontica).

R. yakushimanum Nakai subsp. *makinoi* (Tagg) D.F. Chamb. - is a synonym of **R. makinoi** Tagg (Subsect. Pontica).

R. YEDOENSE MAXIM. - SECT. TSUTSUSI.
Compact densely branched shrub, 1-2m; young shoots covered with adpressed flattened bristles. Leaves of two kinds; spring leaves deciduous, 3-8 × 1-2.5cm, elliptic-lanceolate to oblanceolate, apex acute, mucronate; both surfaces with scattered adpressed shining brown bristles, lower surface pale; summer leaves as for the spring leaves; petioles and pedicels covered with loosely adpressed bristles. Pedicel indumentum as for petioles. Flowers fragant; calyx 5-8mm, lobes ovate; corolla rose to pale lilac-purple, with flecks, broadly funnel-shaped, 35-40mm; ovary densely covered with adpressed hairs, style glabrous or pilose towards base. H4a-b. May. Korea, Japan (Tsushima), to *c*.1,100m.
　Var. **yedoense**. Flowers double; calyx to 15mm. Only known in cultivation.
　Var. **poukhanense** (H.Lév.) Nakai. Flowers single; calyx 5-8mm. Korea, Japan (Tsushima), 50-1,100m.
　This species is probably most closely allied to *R. ripense*, but it differs in the indumentum of the young shoots, etc.

R. youngiae Fang - is a synonym of **R. adenopodum** Franch. (Subsect. Argyrophylla).

R. YUNGNINGENSE BALF.F. (INCL. *R. GLOMERULATUM* HUTCH.) - SUBSECT. LAPPONICA.

Erect shrub, 1(-1.3)m. Leaves (0.6-)0.8-2 × (2-)4-8mm, elliptic to broadly elliptic or oblong, apex acute to obtuse, clearly or obscurely mucronate, lower surface covered with uniformly fawn to ferrugineous touching scales. Flowers 3-4(-6) per inflorescence; calyx 2-3mm, lobes sometimes irregular, strap-shaped or deltoid; corolla deep purplish blue, rose-lavender or rarely white, broadly funnel-shaped, outer surface glabrous or minutely puberulous, 11-14(-17)mm; stamens (8-)10, about as long as corolla; style about as long as stamens, glabrous or hairy at base. H4a-b. April-May. China (W Yunnan, SW Sichuan), 3,200-4,300m.
　R. yungningense may be distinguished from the allied *R. orthocladum* by its broader leaves.

R. YUNNANENSE FRANCH. (INCL. *R. HORMOPHORUM* BALF.F. & FORREST) - SUBSECT. TRIFLORA.
Shrub, (0.3-)1-6m; young shoots scaly, sometimes also setose. Leaves evergreen to deciduous, 3-7 × 1.2-2cm, narrowly elliptic to elliptic, apex acute, margin ciliate, at least when young, upper surface usually lacking scales, setose when young, the setae variably deciduous, midrib puberulent, lower surface with flat brown scales that are 3-5× their own diameter apart. Flowers 3-5, in a loose terminal inflorescence; calyx disc-like, usually ciliate; corolla white or pink to lavender, usually with dense red or yellow flecks, zygomorphic, widely funnel-shaped, 20-35mm, outer surface usually lacking scales, glabrous; stamens 10; ovary densely scaly, occasionally puberulent at apex, style depressed, declinate, glabrous. H3-4a. May. N Burma, China (N & W Yunnan, W Sichuan, Guizhou), 2,100-3,950m.
　This variable species is common in the wild. It is closely allied to *R. pleistanthum* (q.v.) and to *R. davidsonianum* (q.v.).
　AM 1903 (F.W. Moore, Glasnevin, Dublin); flowers Pink, with brown spots.
　AM 1943 (Col Lord Digby, Minterne, Dorset) as *R. hormophorum*; flowers white,

with a few buff spots.

♀ 1993, to a clone 'Openwood'.

R. ZALEUCUM BALF.F. & W.W.SM. - SUBSECT. TRIFLORA.

Shrub, (0.6-)2-8(-11)m; young shoots scaly. Leaves 3.8-6.2(-8.8) × (1.6-)2-2.8cm, lanceolate to oblong-lanceolate, rarely elliptic, apex acute to acuminate, margin ciliate, at least when young, upper surface usually lacking scales, midrib usually puberulent, lower surface shining, white-papillose, scales large, rimless, golden, distant. Flowers 1-4, in a loose terminal inflorescence; calyx very small, often ciliate; corolla white, white flushed pink or lavender, zygomorphic, funnel-shaped, 27-45mm, outer surface scaly and usually puberulent at base of tube; stamens 10; ovary densely scaly, impressed below the declinate style that is glabrous or (rarely) pubescent at base. H3-4a. April-May. N Burma, China (W Yunnan, Guizhou), 1,800-3,500m.

Var. **zaleucum**. Flowers white or white flushed pink, to lavender; leaves generally to 8cm long. N Burma, China (W Yunnan, Guizhou), 1,800-3,500m.

AM 1932 (Col S.R. Clarke, Borde Hill, Sussex); flowers mauve-pink, spotted.

Var. **flaviflorum** Davidian. Flowers yellow; leaves to 10cm long. N Burma (Uring Bum).

The white-papillose leaf under-surface will distinguish this from the species with which it might be confused.

R. zeylanicum Booth - is a synonym of **R. arboreum** Sm. subsp. **zeylanicum** (Booth) Tagg.

The Vireya Rhododendrons

G Argent

Vireya rhododendrons are those in Section Vireya, part of Subgenus *Rhododendron*, the scaly rhododendrons. It is a large and fairly well marked group (*c.*300 species) both in form and geographical distribution. In form they usually have seeds with long tails at both ends, an ovary with the upper end tapering to the style and no junction or abscission layer between the two. In many other respects such as flower shape and colour they are the most variable group of rhododendrons but recognition can be aided by a number of negative characteristics. They are never spotted with colour (although they can be with scales) and are never truly blue. They are never very strongly zygomorphic (bilaterally symmetrical) and they never have a rhachis in the inflorescence. Species of this section are generally confined to the SE Asian archipelago of tropical islands but occur from India in the west to the Solomon Islands in the east, Tibet and Taiwan in the north and Queensland, Australia in the south. The largest number of species (over half) occur in New Guinea.

The subsectional groupings given here follow Sleumer's account (1966), the best known and still the only work which more or less covers the whole group. Despite being highly artificial in parts it is a reasonably workable system. The provisional revision of Bornean sections (Argent 1988) still requires finalization in its extention to Vireyas of other areas.

Vireyas are a predominantly epiphytic group of plants occurring in pockets of humus in the crooks of tree branches in the cool montane forests particularly at intermediate altitudes that tend to be shrouded for long periods in cloud. At higher altitude many species grow terrestrially in open situations on peaty ridges or banks and they are sometimes among the first colonists of open situations such as land slips or road embankments. A few species occur down to sea level and may truly be regarded as tropical but generally the designation 'tropical' is misleading from the grower's point of view as they do best in cool but light situations with open acid compost. In temperate cultivation few will stand much frost and they are best regarded as intolerant despite the fact that in the wild many of the high altitude species are frequently exposed to frost.

This puzzles many people but is not difficult to understand in comparing the natural conditions on a tropical mountain with those in gardens in temperate latitudes. On the tropical mountain the temperature is high by day very often rising rapidly as the very powerful sun shines on a clear morning. As convection currents build up, cloud forms and thickens, and typically it rains in the afternoon and early evening. After the sun sets the convection currents die, the cloud disperses and the sky clears. When this happens the temperature drops fast and above 2,000m frosts can be common although they vary greatly depending on the surrounding topography. As soon as the sun rises the following morning temperatures increase again. Thus there is a situation of growing temperatures and high light regimes by day followed by resting temperatures at night the whole year round. Rainy seasons which may be wetter and cooler by day are, because of the more persistent cloud cover, warmer by night.

In contrast in temperate situations our plants go into a long period of winter gloom, with both low temperatures and poor light. Also, due to changing weather patterns the change to long hours of light can be very sudden and may cause unsightly leaf burn on plants that, in the wild, would normally take much higher light levels but for shorter periods and continuously over the year. Often plants need shade in late spring and early summer to avoid this burning. Higher temperatures persist for much longer in the temperate summer as a result of which the plants become prone to soil pathogens and may collapse and die for no apparent reason. Cool temperate summers suit these plants much better than Mediterranean heat.

Unlike rhododendron hunting in the Himalayas, which are sufficiently far north to have temperate type growing and resting periods, collecting Vireya species from high altitudes is no guarantee of hardiness in temperate regions. In fact those that grow at the highest altitudes in the tropics have generally proved the most difficult to cultivate. The easiest are probably those from about 1,200-2,400m in the wild, those species coming from below this band requiring more heat while those from above becoming progressively more difficult to grow successfully. In practice most of the species listed here are remarkably tolerant and easy to grow. Hardiness ratings follow those given for temperate rhododendrons (see p. 81).

They will provide flowers throughout the year if a range of species are grown and the wide variety means there are plants to suit virtually any taste from the large blowsy and flamboyant to the most delicate of alpines. Many are exquisitely and powerfully perfumed and a single plant can fill a room with scent. There are now some superb modern hybrids which are even easier to grow well, more vigorous and often much more floriferous than the species.

Given that most of the species like cool but frost-free conditions, they make ideal greenhouse or conservatory plants and require little heating to keep them happy. Most species like high humidity but not airless conditions and a free flow of air round the plants is important. Watering correctly is most crucial and an open, well draining, acid compost, comprising 2 parts coarse peat, 1 part fine peat, 1 part bark plus magnesian limestone to balance the pH to around 5.5 will be a good start. These plants, like all rhododendrons, have very fine roots which do not like to dry out completely but equally will not stand waterlogging. Never soak a plant which has dried out as such wild fluctuations in watering often cause fungal infections of the roots. If a plant becomes overdry, and shows dulling of the leaves (often a prelude to death), the best course of action is to spray it overhead, keep it in a very humid atmosphere and slowly moisten the compost. The plants can be liquid fed in the growing season and will respond to most proprietary feeds.

These rhododendrons are sometimes criticized for being ungainly and rather 'leggy'. The small delicate, alpine species like *R. anagalliflorum*, *R. gracilentum*, and *R. saxifragoides* are never subject to this drawback and produce compact hybrids. For many of the other species a little understanding of the way the plants grow might save some disappointment. It is usual for the plants to grow one or a few stems to perhaps over half the height of the mature plants. If these are left with plenty of space round them they eventually fill out from the base and almost all species will, with time, grow into conventional 'rhododendron-shaped' bushes. An exception may be *R. lowii* which even in the wild is a lanky shrub of sometimes very long unbranched canes. Pruning to encourage bushiness does not always work and cutting the plants back hard can be enough to kill them, so prune with caution and if reducing the amount of foliage drastically keep the plants very much on the dry side until new growth is evident.

Another criticism is that the vegetative buds break from below a flower bud before the flowers have opened and the flowers may be obscured by the new leafy stems. This is usually true only of young vigorous plants which are growing strongly but once established the flowers

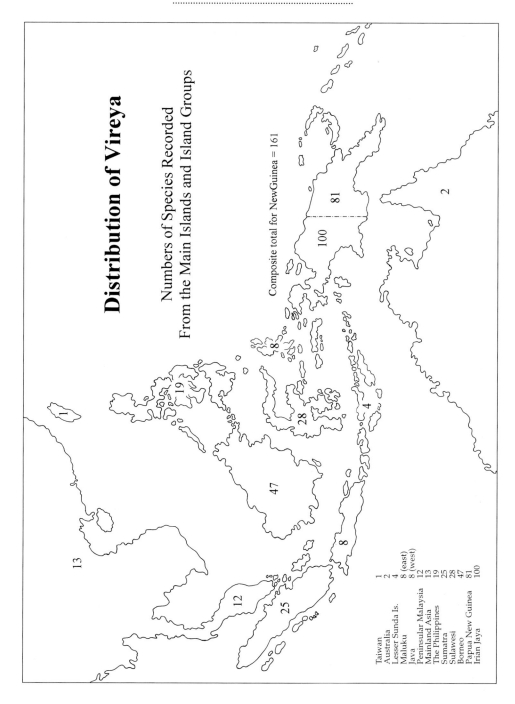

Distribution of Vireya

Numbers of Species Recorded
From the Main Islands and Island Groups

Composite total for NewGuinea = 161

Taiwan	1
Australia	2
Lesser Sunda Is.	4
Maluku	8 (east)
Java	8 (west)
Peninsular Malaysia	12
Mainland Asia	13
The Philippines	19
Sumatra	25
Sulawesi	28
Borneo	47
Papua New Guinea	81
Irian Jaya	100

are thrown well clear of the leaves.

There are few very special pests and diseases but a number of common problems will often afflict the plants if they become neglected. Mildew is common particularly when temperatures are high. Spraying with conventional fungicides will control this problem. Small orange-brown pustules on the leaves indicate rust. Infected leaves should be picked off and burnt and a proprietary spray used. Aphids, mealy bug and scale, will build up if left and will distort and disfigure the plants. Vine weevil larvae can cause the collapse of small plants by eating away at the roots. They can usually be discovered as white grubs if the pots are knocked out and the soil examined. The adults will also eat the parts above ground and are not easy to deal with but a night time search with a torch will reveal them. Cockroaches can be a problem and will often wait to chew off pristine unfolding flowers although they will also eat young leaves and stems. Surprisingly bees can be a pest when they discover that they can reach the nectar of long flowered species by chewing through the base of the flower but this does not often happen. It is as well to realize, as with many plants, that the life of the flower is greatly reduced if it is pollinated and removal of the stamens within a day or two of the flower opening is a means of avoiding this.

The descriptions below are of necessity short, they are all plants in cultivation at the present time although some will not be easy to find. The full list of species in cultivation is given under The Classification of Rhododendron (p.9), which contains some species currently found only at the RBG, Edinburgh and not in general cultivation. These species are not described below.

Vireya growers, like most plant enthusiasts, have established a network and the best way of linking in to this is to subscribe to the *Vireya Vine* which is edited and distributed by E White Smith from PO Box 3798, Federal Way, Washington, 98063, USA. Another useful source of information is *The Rhododendron* - Journal of the Australian Rhododendron Society, which has published over the years a large number of articles, many illustrated with colour plates. A selected bibliography is appended (p. 351) but literature on Vireyas is mostly not freely available. These descriptions are new in the sense that as far as possible they have been drawn up from living plants in cultivation at the RBG, Edinburgh, supplemented by measurements from herbarium specimens and reports from the literature. They are not verbatim repetition of older accounts most of which repeat Professor Sleumer's descriptions which, though meticulously accurate for scientific work, were largely from dried material and rarely represented living flower sizes. A very useful computer database of Vireya Names has been compiled by Robert Murray. It has a wealth of information, particularly on hybrids, which is not readily available elsewhere and is currently available from Clover Springs Computer Services, 21 Squire Terrace, Colts Neck, New Jersey 07722, USA.

For those that wish to see Vireyas in the wild the easiest place to do so is Mt Kinabalu in Sabah, East Malaysia. Sabah is a delightful part of Malaysia offering a range of accommodation. There is a good tarmac road to the Kinabalu Park Headquarters at 1,500m and the trail up the mountain is no more than a steep walk to the huts at just over 3,000m where one can have a heated room and hot meals. The mountain boasts 25 species of Vireya and although it would be almost impossible to see them all on one visit, there are several species that flower throughout the year and at the right time one might see as many as 15 species in flower. It is a nature reserve however and collecting is forbidden except by permit. The only other place where relatively large numbers of species can be seen at one place is New Guinea but this is not an easy place to visit at the present time. While on most mountains in SE Asia there are only one or two species and it can be hard work finding them.

Fig. 27: R. javanicum

Fig. 28: R. longiflorum

Fig. 29: R. rarilepidotum

Fig. 30: R. himantodes

Fig. 31: R. phaeochitum

Fig. 32: R. christi

Fig. 33: R. herzogii

Fig. 34: R. aurigeranum

Fig. 35: R. citrinum

Fig. 36: R. album

Fig. 37: R. leucogigas

Fig. 38: R. goodenoughii

Fig. 39: R. burttii

Fig. 40: R. rarum

Fig. 41: R. anagalliflorum

Fig. 42: R. herzogii × R. aurigeranum

Fig. 43: R. fallacinum

Fig. 44: R. konori

Fig. 45: R. brookeanum

Fig. 46: R. polyanthemum

Fig. 47: R. culminicolum

Fig. 48: R. macgregoriae

Fig. 49: R. zoelleri

Fig. 50: R. orbiculatum

Description of Species in Cultivation: Vireya

....

R. ACUMINATUM HOOK.F. - SUBSECT
MALAYOVIREYA
Shrub to 3m, mostly terrestrial; young
stems rough, completely covered in
brown scales. Leaves 7-9 × 2.5-5cm, ovate-
acuminate to broadly elliptic-acuminate,
the apex bluntly pointed, the margin
entire, flat or slightly recurved, the base
rounded or broadly tapering; upper surface at first densely scaly, becoming
glabrous with very deeply impressed
veins; lower surface with strongly raised
veins, completely and persistently brown-
scaly with variably sized scales, the largest
of which have dark swollen centres.
Flowers 12-20 hanging, half hanging or
horizontal in a loose umbel; calyx a low
scaly ring; corolla bright orange or red,
narrowly funnel shaped, 2.5-3.1 × 1.5-2cm,
outer surface usually with sparse scales
sometimes almost glabrous; stamens 10,
scattered all round the mouth of the
flower; ovary densely scaly, style scaly in
the basal half. H1b. Malaysia (Sabah, Mt
Kinabalu), 2,800-3,400m.

Commonly confused with *R. rugosum*
which has totally different leaf scales and
differently coloured flowers. This species
has so far proved difficult to cultivate and
most records of it in cultivation are attributable to *R. rugosum*.

R. AEQUABILE J.J.SM. - SUBSECT.
ALBOVIREYA
Tree or large shrub to 4m, mostly terrestrial; young stems densely dark scaly.
Leaves 4.5-10 × 2.5-5cm, elliptic, the apex
shortly acuminate or apiculate to obtuse,
the edge somewhat revolute, the base long
attenuate; upper surface at first brown-
scaly, later white-scaly and finally,
glabrous at maturity, with impressed

midrib and distinct (5-6 pairs) of laterals,
underneath the midrib only strongly
raised; densely dark brown and persistently scaly underneath although sometimes shedding scales irregularly, scales
well developed variable in size with small
centres, often overlapping. Flowers 2-12
per umbel, rigidly disposed half hanging
to semi-erect; calyx a low scaly ring; corolla mostly orange but also reported red,
campanulate, 1.7-2.5 × 3-4cm, laxly scaly
on the tube and lower part of the lobes
outside but these scales often obscure; stamens 10, distributed round the mouth of
the flower; ovary densely silvery scaly,
style glabrous. H1b. Indonesia (Sumatra,
Mts Singgalang, Kerintji and Pesagi),
1,200-2,870m.

Easily grown although rather slow,
the foliage is very handsome when young
and covered in bronze scales. The flowers
are attractive although in young specimens may be poorly displayed on the
plants.

R. ALBUM BLUME - SUBSECT. ALBOVIREYA
Epiphytic shrub to 1.5m, young stems at
first densely brown-scaly, later becoming
pale green as the scales become translucent, sometimes smelling lightly of lemon.
Leaves 7-10 × 2-3.5cm, elliptic, the apex
acute, the edge slightly revolute, the base
tapering; upper surface green, at first
slightly scaly with silvery scales, later
glabrous the midrib very slightly
impressed, the lateral veins slightly raised
rather indistinct, underside with strongly
raised midrib and indistinct secondary
veins; at first brown-scaly with many of
the scales touching, later more spaced
with few scales touching, the scales almost
circular, with pale margin and a small

point-like brown centre. Flowers 7-16 in an umbel, semi-erect to hanging; calyx with broadly obtuse lobes 1-1.5mm appressed to the corolla; corolla cream or pale yellow in cultivation rarely described as yellowish pinkish, campanulate, 1.7-2.5 × 1.5-2.0cm, laxly scaly outside; stamens 10, arranged round the mouth of the flower; ovary densely scaly, style scaly in the lower half. H1b. Indonesia (Java, Mts Salak and Gedeh), 1,200-1,700m.

Flowered in cultivation in England in 1856 and figured in *Curtis's Botanical Magazine* the following year, it was lost to cultivation soon after. It has recently been reintroduced to cultivation and although delicate is not particularly showy.

R. ALTICOLUM SLEUMER - SUBSECT. VIREYA
Small tree to 5m, terrestrial; young stems smooth, green, at first covered with flat pale brown, star-shaped scales. Leaves 6-10 × 2.5-4.5cm, obovate to elliptic, apex obtuse to rounded, the edge flat, the base broadly to narrowly tapering; upper surface smooth, the midrib, very slightly depressed, about 5-7 pairs of lateral veins distinct but not depressed, at first obscurely covered with a fine silvery covering of scales, quickly becoming glabrous; lower surface with raised midrib almost throughout its length, the laterals distinct but not raised, the indumentum of fine well spaced silvery, star-shaped scales which are small and rather inconspicuous. Flowers 1-5 in an umbel, half hanging to hanging; calyx an irregular 5-dented slightly scaly ring; corolla dark red, tubular-cylindrical, a little curved and slightly dilated distally, 5-6 × 2-3cm, laxly scaly outside; stamens 10, grouped together on the upper side of the flower; ovary densely scaly, style scaly only at the base glabrous above. H1b. Papua New Guinea (Morobe and Central Districts), 2,200-3,600m.

Close to *R. culminicolum* but said to differ in having larger flowers and ovaries without simple hairs. One of the handsome bird pollinated species from the high mountains of New Guinea.

R. ANAGALLIFLORUM WERNHAM - SUBSECT. VIREYA
Dwarf shrub to 0.2m, epiphytic; young stems distinctly scaly the scales standing on small projections which remain after the scales are shed. Leaves 0.3-0.7 × 0.2-0.3cm, elliptic, the apex acute to rounded, margin plain, base cuneate; upper surface with a few silvery scales which quickly disappear, venation totally obscure; lower surface with scattered brown scales only the midrib barely visible in the lower half, scales disc-shaped or with incised margins and small centres. Flowers solitary, half hanging to hanging, calyx a low slightly lobed scaly ring; corolla white variably flushed pink or purple, cylindrical to narrowly funnel-shaped, 1.2-1.8 × 1.3-1.8cm, laxly and obscurely scaly on the tube outside; stamens 10, scattered round the mouth of the flower; ovary covered in semi-erect, white hairs and silvery scales, style with simple hairs in the basal half, glabrous above. H1b. New Guinea (main range from Irian Jaya to Papua New Guinea), also in New Britain (Mt Lululua), 1,100-3,000m.

A very delicate and pretty species which has been used for hybridizing, several of the resultant progeny have been registered and make attractive hanging basket plants. Confused in the past with *R. rubineiflorum* Craven, see *Notes RBG Edinb.* **38(1)** pp 141-144, 1980, but easily distinguished by its paler, narrower, flowers.

R. ARFAKIANUM BECC. - SUBSECT. VIREYA
Shrub to 2.5m, epiphytic or terrestrial, young stems sparsely scaly and papillose pubescent. Leaves 5-10 × 2-3.5cm, oblong to obovate-elliptic, the apex obtuse to almost rounded, the margin slightly revolute, the base tapering; upper surface sparsely silvery scaly at first but soon becoming glabrous with minute papillose spreading hairs on the midrib which is weakly depressed in the basal part, lateral veins 6-8 pairs moderately conspicuous,

very slightly raised; lower surface with the veins slightly raised beneath, laxly scaly, the scales small, irregularly lobed and with small dark brown centres. Flowers in 4-10 flowered umbels, hanging diagonally to vertically downwards, calyx a low wavy ring; corolla deep pink, tubular straight or slightly curved expanded towards the mouth 2.5-3.5 × 2-3cm, glabrous outside; stamens 10, clustered on the upper side of the flower; ovary densely short pubescent and inconspicuously scaly, style glabrous except for a few hairs at the base. H1b. New Guinea (Irian Jaya [Arfak and Nettoti Mts]), 1,200-2,100m.

R. ARMITII F.M.BAILEY - SUBSECT. SOLENOVIREYA

Shrub to 2m, terrestrial, young twigs slightly scaly at first with stellate scales Leaves 7-10 × 4-6cm, broadly elliptic to sub-obovate, the apex obtuse or very shortly attenuate in a deflexed glandular mucro, the margin flat or slightly revolute, the base broadly attenuate, rounded or slightly cordate; the upper surface at first scaly, quickly glabrescent, the midrib impressed, lateral veins 8-10 pairs, slightly impressed; lower surface with the midrib strongly raised, the laterals slightly prominent; scales moderately dense, rusty brown, and deeply incised. Flowers 3-7 per umbel, horizontal to half-hanging; calyx with 5 distinct but low lobes, both hairy and scaly; corolla white flushed with pink, beautifully scented, trumpet-shaped but with the tube slightly curved, 6-8 × 3-4cm, slightly scaly outside; stamens 10, clustered in the mouth of the flower; ovary densely covered in yellowish to whitish, subappressed hairs which tend to obscure the presence of the scales, style hairy and scaly in the lower half, glabrous above. H1b. Papua New Guinea (Owen Stanley Mountains [Mt Simpson and Mt Dayman]), 2,400-2,700m.

A lovely and free flowering plant introduced by P. Woods close to *R. tuba* but with larger leaves. See also remarks under that species.

R. ATROPURPUREUM SLEUMER - SUBSECT. VIREYA

Shrub to 3m, terrestrial, young stems densely covered with substellate, short-stalked rusty coloured scales and short papillose hairs. Leaves 1.7-3 × 1.5-2.2cm, broadly elliptic to ovate-elliptic, apex obtuse to rounded sometimes with a protruding apical gland, margin slightly cartilaginous, and crenulate, flat, base rounded to slightly cordate; upper surface silvery scaly when young, quickly becoming glabrescent, midrib impressed often reddish brown and more persistently scaly than the lamina, lateral veins 3-4 pairs slightly impressed; lower surface with the midrib strongly raised beneath for the whole of the length of the leaf, lateral veins slightly raised, scales small with an irregular membranous marginal zone which quickly disappears leaving the thick, blackish red, impressed central portions. Flowers 2-3 per umbel half-hanging to hanging, calyx a low scaly, 5-lobed ring; corolla dark red, tubular-funnel-shaped, curved, 3.5-5 × 3-4cm, densely covered with substellate scales outside; stamens 10, grouped on the upper side of the flower; ovary densely substellate scaly, the style scaly in the lower third, glabrous above. H1b. Papua New Guinea (Eastern and Western Highlands Provinces), 3,500-3,800m.

A characteristic species on the upper slopes of Mt Wilhelm and frequently collected there. It is doubtful if it persists long in cultivation although it quite commonly appears on lists of species.

R. AURIGERANUM SLEUMER - SUBSECT. VIREYA

Shrub or small tree to 4m, mostly terrestrial; young stems green at first rather densely covered in flat brown scales; Leaves 8-16 × 4-7cm, elliptic to oblong, the apex short acuminate to acute, sometimes deflexed, the margin smooth and flat, the base broadly or narrowly tapering; upper surface very lightly puckered, the small silvery scales disappearing early, the midrib grooved near the base, very slightly impressed, later veins 6-8 pairs, very slightly impressed; lower surface finely covered with small deeply lobed brown scales with small centres, midrib strongly raised almost the total length of the leaf, lateral veins only slightly raised in the basal half. Flowers with 8-14 flowers per umbel, semi-erect to horizontal; calyx a low inconspicuous ring; corolla bright yellow or orange or yellow with orange flushing, funnel-shaped, 5-7 × 5.5-7.5cm, with scattered small brown scales outside; stamens 10, loosely arranged on the lower side of the corolla sometimes in two groups, sometimes all round the mouth; ovary covered in silvery hairs and scales, the style hairy and scaly in the lower ¾ the scales rising beyond the hairs but totally glabrous in the upper 1cm. H1b. New Guinea (Morobe Province mainly in the Bulolo-Wau area), 900-1,800m.

The very showy flowers and the accessible locality from which it comes, mean this has long been a popular species in cultivation and has been used extensively as a parent in hybridizing. It is also one of the easiest although it needs space to reach its full potential.

R. BAENITZIANUM LAUTERB. - SUBSECT. VIREYA
Shrub to 2m, terrestrial, young stems at first with a red-brown substellate tomentum. Leaves 15-25 × 3.5-9cm, oblong, broadly elliptic to ovate-elliptic, the apex long drawn out, acute, caudate-acuminate, the margin flat, the base broadly tapering, occasionally rounded; upper surface at first finely scaly, quickly becoming completely glabrous, midrib narrow and impressed above, the lateral veins 8-12 pairs slightly raised or impressed; the lower surface laxly scaly, the scales small, flat, irregularly but not deeply lobed or dented, the centres small, midrib broadly prominent, lateral veins distinctly prominent. Flowers 4-12 per umbel, erect to horizontal; calyx a low scaly ring; corolla with a yellow tube and orange lobes, funnel-shaped, 8-10 × 8-10cm, finely scaly on the tube outside; stamens 10, scattered irregu-

larly but mostly on the lower side of the flower; ovary covered with semi-appressed, forward pointed, white hairs and silvery scales, style both hairy and scaly to near the top. H1a-b. Papua New Guinea (the western part, Torricelli Mts and Ok Tedi area), 200-1,200m.

A plant of this species was rescued from the collection made by Paul Kores at Wau by the Rev. Canon Norman Cruttwell who grew it and distributed it for general cultivation. It is a very handsome species with a large truss of golden flowers. It may be distinguished from *R. zoelleri* by its much more sharply attenuate leaves and finer pattern of lateral veins.

R. BAGOBONUM COPEL.F. - SUBSECT. VIREYA
Small shrub to 0.6m, usually epiphytic occasionally terrestrial on landslides; young stems, green, smooth but minutely covered in brown scales. Leaves 1.2-2 × 0.4-0.7cm, narrowly obovate, the apex broadly acute, the margin flat and minutely crenulate, the base narrowly cuneate, the upper surface at first sparsely scaly, smooth, midrib slightly impressed above, disappearing before the apex, lateral veins not visible; lower surface with the midrib flat and distinct to the leaf tip, the scales, small, well spaced, brown, disc-shaped or deeply lobed. Flowers solitary or occasionally in pairs, held horizontally or diagonally angled downwards; calyx a low angled disc; corolla orange on opening becoming a rich glossy red with age, cylindrical, 1.4-2 × 0.6-1cm, with a few pale scales on the tube; stamens 10, in a regular pattern of alternating long and short, curved towards the centre of the flower so that it self pollinates; ovary both scaly and hairy in the lower half, hairy only in the upper part, style glabrous. H1b. Philippines, Indonesia (Kalimantan, Seram), Malaysia (Sabah, Sarawak), 1,200-1,900m.

Often confused with *R. quadrasianum* and its allies but apart from the different scale types *R. bagobonum* has the ovary longer than the style whereas in *R.*

quadrasianum it is always much shorter. Surprisingly for its rather small flowers it is the parent of some spectacular hybrids.

R. BEYERINCKIANUM KOORD. - SUBSECT. PHAEOVIREYA
Tree or shrub mostly 1-2m, but recorded up to 4m, terrestrial or epiphytic, young branches at first densely covered with a rusty coloured, stellate-dendroid tomentum. Leaves 3-6 × 1-3.5cm, variable in shape from broadly elliptic to ovate, obovate to sub-orbicular, apex narrowly to broadly obtuse or rounded, the margin usually strongly revolute, the base broadly tapering to rounded; upper surface at first densely red-brown, stellate-scaly, becoming silvery scaly and rather tardily glabrescent, midrib slightly impressed above, lateral veins 4-7 pairs, slightly impressed; below, the midrib strongly prominent, the laterals slightly to strongly prominent, scales dendroid, deeply stellate incised, dense and overlapping, growing from pronounced, persistent, epidermal tubercles, the scales themselves disappearing easily with any abrasion and often then only found in protected corners. Flowers 2-6 per umbel, half-hanging to hanging; calyx a low stellate-scaly ring; corolla, white, yellow, greenish, pink, purplish pink but most commonly dark red, tubular funnel-shaped, curved, zygomorphic, 3-4.5 × 2-2.5cm, densely stellate-scaly outside; stamens 10, clustered in the upper mouth of the flower; ovary densely brown-stellate-scaly, style stellate-scaly throughout its length. H1b. New Guinea (east to west, mostly on the main range), 1,500-4,000m.

A very common and wide ranging species in the wild in both area and altitude. It is very closely related to *R. phaeochitum* but differs in its glabrous disc and glabrous or only sparsely hairy filaments. The lower altitude forms tend to be the easiest to cultivate.

R. BLACKII SLEUMER - SUBSECT. VIREYA
Large shrub to 5m, mostly terrestrial occasionally epiphytic; young stems smooth with a moderate covering of flat brown scales. Leaves 6-8 × 5-7cm, ovate to orbicular, apex obtuse to rounded, edge smooth or very slightly recurved, base rounded to auriculate, the leaves being virtually sessile; upper surface at first scurfy-scaly, quickly becoming glabrous, the midrib prominently raised above for the basal 1cm, lateral veins about 4 pairs, moderately conspicuous smooth; underneath the midrib raised for about ¾ of its length, the laterals distinct but only slightly raised, scales, brown well spaced, very variable in size, disc-shaped, sometimes lobed and with small centres. Flowers 4-7 per umbel, horizontal to half hanging; calyx a slightly swollen lobed ring, more or less glabrous; corolla red, slightly curved and narrowly tubular-funnel-shaped, 5.5-6 × 3-4cm, finely white-scaly on the tube and lobes; stamens 10, grouped on the upper side of the mouth of the flower; ovary silvery scaly and hairy, style with a few simple hairs at the base otherwise glabrous. H1b. Papua New Guinea (Western and Southern Highlands), 2,500-3,400m.

Similar in floral characters to *R. culminicolum* but differing in its cordate to auriculate leaves. Named after Michael Black of Grasmere in whose garden Sleumer reported this species growing in 1973. It includes *R. sleumeri* A.Gilli.

R. BROOKEANUM LOW EX LINDL. - SUBSECT. VIREYA
Epiphytic or terrestrial shrub or small tree, up to 2m, rarely 5m, young stems green with fine stellate scales but quickly becoming glabrescent or (var. *cladotrichum* Sleumer) with fine simple hairs. Leaves 10-30 × 3-9cm, narrowly elliptic or elliptic, the apex acute to obtuse, often shortly acuminate, the margin entire and flat, the base broadly to narrowly tapering; the upper surface at first with a fine silvery appressed covering of scales but quickly becoming glabrous, or minutely hairy (var. *cladotrichum*), often characteristically puckered with hollows between the lateral veins, midrib slightly raised in the lower half, lateral veins 8-12 pairs distinct

but not raised; lower surface with the midrib raised for about ⅔ of its length, the laterals hardly raised, scales, lobed discs with small centres, small and widely spaced and with small white hairs, especially on the veins in var. *cladotrichum*. Flowers 3-12 per umbel, erect to horizontal; calyx a low scaly ring; corolla pale yellow through orange to red, sometimes strikingly bicoloured with a yellow throat and orange lobes, funnel-shaped, 4-6 × 4-5cm, glabrous outside, reported as having a delicate lemon-like fragrance but usually scentless; stamens 10, irregular or somewhat placed into two lateral groups; ovary with simple hairs and scales (glabrous in subsp. *moultonii* [Ridl.]Argent), style glabrous. H1a-b. Borneo (widespread), Sumatra (west and north), s.l. to 1,800m.

FCC 1869 (J. Veitch, Chelsea, London); flowers clear yellow.

FCC 1970 (Mr & Mrs E.F. Allen, Felcourt, Copdock, Suffolk) to a clone 'Mandarin'; flowers Red Group 40C, fading to 40D, throat bright yellow (between Yellow-Orange Group 18A and 17D).

This species is common in Borneo and has occasionally been found in Sumatra, it is very variable and still poorly understood as a species despite having been cultivated in various forms for a long time. The bicoloured forms from Mt Kinabalu produce exceptional flowers and it was one of these that was registered as 'Mandarin'. This species is of easy cultivation and it has the advantage that the flowers are most commonly produced in the depths of winter.

Subsp. **gracile** (Lindl.)Argent (syn. *R. brookeanum* var. *gracile* [Low ex Lindl.] G. Henslow), with narrower leaves rarely more than 3cm wide.

FCC 1972 (Mr and Mrs E.F. Allen, Felcourt, Copdock, Suffolk) to a clone 'Raja'; flowers Yellow Group 13A.

R. BRYOPHILUM SLEUMER - SUBSECT. PHAEOVIREYA
Shrub to 2m epiphytic often high in trees, young stems brown with the stellate-dendroid tomentum when very young.

Leaves 3.5-5.5 × 1.2-2cm, elliptic or broadly elliptic, the apex obtuse to rounded, the margin flat or slightly revolute, the base broadly to narrowly tapering, upper surface brown-scaly when young, flat, the midrib very slightly impressed, lateral veins obscure about 3-5 pairs; lower surface with midrib a little raised throughout its length, lateral veins obscure, at first with a rather sparse covering of dendroid scales which are easily removed leaving the pale tubercles from which the scales arise. Flowers in 2-3 flowered umbels half hanging to hanging; calyx a low scaly disc; corolla pink, cylindrical, very slightly curved 2-2.7 × 1.7-2.5cm, glabrous outside; stamens 10, loosely clustered in the upper half of the mouth of the flower; ovary densely stellate-scaly, style covered with sub-patent simple hairs nearly to the top. H1b. New Guinea, (Irian Jaya, Cycloop Mts), 1,000-1,800m.

A delicate species that has been in cultivation for some time, similar to *R. dielsianum* and differing in the hairy style, *R. dielsianum* having a scaly or glabrous style.

R. BURTTII P.WOODS - SUBSECT. VIREYA
Shrub to 0.8m, epiphytic, young stems green or reddish, both finely hairy and scaly. Leaves 1.8-2.8 × 0.9-1.2cm, obovate, the apex broadly pointed to rounded, the margin entire and slightly recurved, the base tapering; upper side minutely scaly at first but quickly becoming glabrescent with the midrib impressed above, the lateral veins not visible; underside with the midrib raised below, the lateral veins faint, 2-3 pairs, scales lobed, substellate with small centres. Flowers 1-2, rarely 4 per umbel, hanging vertically down; calyx a low ring with a ciliate margin, corolla red, cylindrical with a straight tube, 2-2.5 × 2.4-2.8cm, finely hairy outside; stamens 10, spreading round the mouth of the tube; ovary densely hairy with white semi-appressed hairs which tend to obscure the presence of brown scales which are also present, style glabrous except for a few hairs near the base. H1b. Borneo, Sabah and Northern Sarawak,

1,500-1,600m.

A very pretty and easily grown species which tends to flower in bursts which may be as often as six times a year.

R. BUXIFOLIUM LOW EX HOOK.F. - SUBSECT. PSEUDOVIREYA
Shrub or tree to 10m, terrestrial, young stems covered in brown scales and very finely hairy. Leaves 1.3-3.7 × 0.6-2.8cm, almost circular to broadly elliptic, the apex obtuse, rounded or retuse, the margin slightly recurved, crenulate, the base cordate, rounded or broadly tapering; upper side sparsely scaly with the small scales sunk into pits, the midrib slightly impressed, lateral veins 3-5 pairs, inconspicuous; lower surface with the midrib raised, lateral veins very slightly or not raised, the scales small and rather sparse, circular to irregular, with relatively large cushion-like centres and a narrow flange. Flowers 5-10 per umbel, more or less horizontally held; calyx a low scaly ring; corolla red, strongly honey-scented, funnel shaped to almost campanulate, 2-2.6 × 3-4cm, finely golden scaly outside; stamens 10, arranged evenly around the mouth of the flower; ovary densely scaly, style scaly at the base, glabrous above. H1b. Borneo, Sabah, Mt Kinabalu endemic, 3,100-3,900m.

One of the most magnificent sights of Kinabalu when in flower but it tends to be slow and feeble in cultivation with the flowers smaller and less rich in colour. It is anomalous as to subsection combining characters from Pseudovireya with those of Vireya.

R. CALIGINIS KORES - SUBSECT. PHAEOVIREYA
Straggling shrub to 1m, terrestrial or epiphytic, young stems densely covered with brown, scurfy scales. Leaves 1-5 × 0.1-1cm, linear to elliptic, the apex narrowly to broadly acute, the margin slightly revolute, base narrowly to broadly tapering; upper surface at first densely covered in the brown dendroid scales but quickly becoming glabrous, midrib impressed above lateral veins obscure; lower surface densely brown scaly the dendroid scales forming a complete and rather persistent felt, midrib raised throughout the length of the leaf, other veins obscure. Flowers mostly solitary occasionally 2-3 in a small umbel, hanging more or less vertically downwards; calyx a low scaly ring; corolla, white to pink, cylindrical, 3-3.5 × 2-2.5cm, densely pale brown-scaly on the tube and lobes outside; stamens 10, clustered on the upper side of the mouth of the flower; ovary densely dendroid-scaly, style scaly in the basal half, glabrous in the upper part. H1b. North-western Papua New Guinea (West Sepik and Enga Provinces), 2,400-2,500m.

Described in 1984 by Paul Kores, various forms of this species have come into cultivation some with much broader leaves than the plant which was originally described. Said to be close to *R. hooglandii* and differing in the less revolute, more patent leaves and darker scales. It might also be confused with *R. rarum* but is more scaly and lacks the simple hairs on stamens and style of that species.

R. CARRII SLEUMER - SUBSECT. SOLENOVIREYA
Shrub to 2m, mostly epiphytic, twigs green, only finely silvery scaly. Leaves 4.5-7 × 4-6cm, broadly ovate to rounded, the apex obtuse to almost rounded, sometimes shortly apiculate, the margin, entire and flat, the base cordate to auriculate; upper surface minutely silvery scaly at first, quickly glabrescent, broad and raised in the basal part, fine and impressed distally, the lateral veins very slightly raised, conspicuous, 6-8 pairs; lower surface with the midrib slightly raised, lateral veins smooth, the scales well spaced, inconspicuous with lobed to substellate pale margin and small centres. Flowers 3-6 per umbel, horizontal to half-hanging; calyx a low 5-lobed ring with a short fringe; corolla white, 6-8 × 3-4cm, trumpet-shaped, the tube slightly curved and dilated gradually upwards, substellate scaly outside; stamens 10, a little exserted and clustered at

the centre of the flower mouth; ovary densely covered in appressed yellowish hairs and silvery scales, the style hairy and scaly at the base for c.5mm and then glabrous. H1b. Papua New Guinea (Mt Victoria), 2,440m.

The distinctive sessile leaves look reminiscent of *R. blackii* but the flowers of that species are red, and the veins are fewer and bolder.

R. CARRINGTONIAE F.MUELL. - SUBSECT. SOLENOVIREYA
Shrub or small tree up to 5m, terrestrial, young stems rather densely covered in thin scales. Leaves 3.5-9 × 2.5-5.5cm, obovate to broadly elliptic, the apex obtuse to rounded, the margin entire, revolute, the base broadly tapering, rounded or truncate; upper surface finely covered in small scales, quickly glabrescent, midrib impressed above, lateral veins 6-8 pairs somewhat raised; lower surface with the midrib strongly prominent beneath, the lateral veins obscure almost smooth, subdensely but minutely scaly the scales shallowly and irregularly lobed, impressed and with small centres. Flowers 3-9 per umbel, held erect or semi-erect; calyx a low fringed ring; corolla white, fragrant, trumpet-shaped with the tube slightly curved, 5-7 × 1.8-2.5cm, subdensely scaly outside; stamens 10, slightly exserted from the mouth of the flower; ovary covered with semi-appressed hairs which tend to obscure an additional covering of scales. H1b. New Guinea (the eastern part, Mts Obree, Victoria, Suckling and Dayman), 1,830-2,950m.

Superficially somewhat like *R. herzogii* but the scales have small centres unlike that species and the foliage is not aromatic.

R. CHRISTIANAE SLEUMER - SUBSECT. VIREYA
Shrub to 3m, terrestrial, twigs with a very fine covering of scales. Leaves 4-7.5 × 3-4.5cm, elliptic, broadly elliptic or sub-obovate, apex obtuse to rounded, sometimes shortly acuminate, margin entire and flat, base broadly wedge-shaped; upper surface at first minutely scaly, quickly becoming glabrous, midrib slightly impressed otherwise the surface smooth, the laterals 5-7 pairs but obscure; lower surface with the midrib slightly raised, the lateral not raised almost as obscure as on the upper side, scales well spaced, brown, rounded to lobed and with small, darker brown centres. Flowers 2-7 per umbel, semi-erect, horizontal or half-hanging; calyx a lobed scaly ring; corolla yellow or greenish yellow with orange lobes, cylindrical with a straight but deeply fluted tube, 2.5-3.5 × 2.5-3.5cm, minutely scaly on the tube outside; stamens 10, spreading irregularly from the mouth of the flower sometimes somewhat upturned; ovary white-hairy and obscurely scaly, the style, hairy and scaly for about ¾ of its length. H1b. SE Papua New Guinea (Milne Bay District), 600-1,500m.

Quite variable and very free flowering in cultivation and the parent of some delightful hybrids.

R. CHRISTI FOERSTER - SUBSECT. VIREYA
Shrub to 1.2m, usually epiphytic, twigs at first with a covering of brown scales which quickly fall off. Leaves 4-9 × 2-6cm, ovate, the apex acute and sometimes shortly attenuate, the margin flat or slightly revolute, the base rounded to cordate; upper surface very quickly glabrous, clearly reticulate, the midrib impressed, lateral veins 4-6 pairs only minutely impressed; underneath the midrib strongly raised and often coloured red, the laterals distinct but hardly raised, scales well spaced, disc-shaped or irregularly lobed with small centres. Flowers 1-4 per umbel, hanging diagonally to vertically downwards; calyx a low lobed ring; corolla bicoloured with a yellow tube and orange lobes, cylindrical, the tube slightly curved, 3-3.5 × 3.5-4cm, with distinct white hairs outside; stamens 10, spread round the upper half of the mouth of the flower, ovary hairy, the style hairy nearly to the top. H1b. New Guinea (widespread from Irian Jaya to Papua New Guinea), 1,200-

3,000m.

This delightful and easily grown species occurs in two forms in cultivation, one with large leaves and the other more delicate and smaller, the flowers of both however are very similar, forms with pink flowers are usually considered hybrids particularly with *R. beyerinckianum*.

R. christii Foerster Orthographic variant = **R. christi** Foerster.

R. COMMONAE FOERSTER - SUBSECT. VIREYA
Shrub to 6m (in cultivation rarely more than 0.8m), terrestrial, the young stems with stellate scales and rough below the leaves from the raised leaf scars. Leaves 1.2-4.5 × 0.8-2cm, elliptic to obovate-elliptic, apex obtuse to rounded, with a small thick protruding apical gland, margin cartilaginous, flat or slightly revolute and distinctly serrulate-crenulate in the upper half, base broadly tapering; the upper surface sparsely scaly at first, quickly glabrescent the scales leaving minute pits, midrib impressed above, the laterals 4-6 pairs, slightly impressed; lower surface with the midrib broadly raised in the lower half, laterals smooth or only very slightly raised, scales rather distant, silvery, rather deeply substellately lobed and impressed in small pits. Flowers 3-8 per umbel, semi-erect to half-hanging; calyx scaly, deeply 5-lobed; corolla deep red, orange-red or pale yellow, 2-4 × 1.3-2.8cm, finely, laxly to subdensely scaly outside; stamens 10, in a rather irregular group in the mouth of the flower; ovary densely hairy and scaly, style with a few hairs near the base, otherwise glabrous. H1b. Papua New Guinea (Western, Eastern and Southern Highlands and Morobe Provinces), 2,600-4,000m.

Generally growing in open ground in the wild, this is one of the hardiest of the New Guinea Vireyas in cultivation. Described by Sleumer (*Flora Malesiana* I [6] 587, 1966) as 'stiff', in cultivation it is often 'floppy' but cheerful with brightly coloured flowers in 3 distinct colour forms.

R. CRASSIFOLIUM STAPF - SUBSECT. VIREYA
Shrub to 2.5m, young stems smooth, inconspicuously covered in brown scales. Leaves 8-14 × 4-8cm, ovate, obovate or oblong with a broad blunt to rounded apex, the margin smooth somewhat irregular, flat or slightly revolute, the base cordate, rounded or more rarely wedge-shaped. Upper surface when young silvery scaly, the scales turning brown before quickly falling off, the mature surface characteristically puckered, the midrib very large and conspicuous, very strongly raised, lateral veins 8-12 pairs hardly raised, spreading at a wide angle; underneath the midrib only slightly raised, lateral veins smooth, the scales small, well spaced, disc-shaped and irregularly lobed with small centres. Flowers 6-30 in each umbel, semi-erect to half-hanging; calyx a low ring; corolla mostly pink to red but rarely recorded as orange and white, funnel-shaped, sometimes with the lobe sides attractively reflexed, 2.3-3.5 × 4-5.2cm, glabrous outside; stamens 10, conspicuously alternating long and short and regularly distributed around the mouth of the flower; ovary glabrous, style glabrous. H1b. Borneo, widespread (Sabah, Brunei, Sarawak and Kalimantan), 1,200-2,200m.

Distinctive with its broad blunt leaves and clearly dimorphic stamens. It is an easily grown species but rarely looks happy confined to a pot.

R. CRUTTWELLII SLEUMER - SUBSECT. SOLENOVIREYA
Shrub or small tree up to 6m, young stems laxly scaly, Leaves 6-12.5 × 3-6cm, obovate to elliptic or broadly elliptic, the apex mostly obtuse, sometimes rounded or acute, the margin plain and flat, the base tapering to broadly tapering; upper surface at first finely and minutely silvery scaly with the midrib impressed, lateral veins 6-8 pairs. narrowly but distinctly impressed above to give conspicuous reticulation; under surface with the midrib strongly raised, the laterals not

raised but distinctively darker than the pale lamina surface and so showing up as a very distinctive reticulation, scales small brown, rather irregular, circular to lobed, well spaced and with small centres. Flowers 4-9 per umbel, erect or semi-erect; calyx a lobed, almost glabrous but laxly ciliate ring; corolla white, trumpet-shaped, the tube slightly curved, 5-7 × 2.5-3cm, finely scaly outside; stamens 10, exserted from the mouth of the flower and distributed evenly; ovary covered with semi-erect, whitish hairs but no scales, style hairy at the very base otherwise glabrous. H1b. South-east Papua New Guinea, 1,800-2,600m.

A beautiful and easily cultivated species named after the Rev. Canon Norman Cruttwell who after taking First Class honours in botany at Oxford went on to pursue a career as a missionary in New Guinea but sent a great many plants for description and cultivation from the remote areas in which he worked.

R. CULMINICOLUM F.MUELL. - SUBSECT. VIREYA

Shrub or small tree up to 8m high, terrestrial, young stems sparsely covered in substellate scales. Leaves 2-9 × 1-1.5cm, elliptic, broadly elliptic or occasionally obovate, the apex broadly acute to obtuse or rounded, the margin flat or slightly revolute, the base broadly tapering to rounded; upper surface sparsely scaly at first, quickly glabrescent, the midrib impressed above, lateral veins 4-8 pairs slightly impressed; below the midrib prominently raised, the laterals slightly raised, the scales well spaced, rather small, irregularly lobed to substellate, with small dark centres. Flowers 3-12 per umbel, horizontal to hanging vertically; calyx a lobed, scaly disc; corolla bright red or purplish, more rarely pink, 2.5-6 × 1.6-4cm, laxly to subdensely scaly outside; stamens 10, clustered on the upper side of the flower; ovary covered with yellowish hairs and obscurely scaly, style hairy and scaly in the lower third, glabrous above. H1b. New Guinea (from east to west), one

record from the island of New Ireland (Papua New Guinea), 900-4,000m.

One of the most widespread of the New Guinea rhododendrons and very variable as a consequence.

R. DIANTHOSMUM SLEUMER - SUBSECT. PHAEOVIREYA

Shrub up to 2m, epiphytic, young stems densely stellate-dendroid scaly at first but quickly rather glaucous, glabrescent. Leaves 9-14 × 3-6cm, elliptic or broadly elliptic, the apex obtuse or shortly sub-acuminate-attenuate, margin slightly recurved, the base broadly tapering to rounded; upper surface at first brown-scaly, later rough with persistent epidermal tubercles, midrib slightly raised; lower surface with the midrib and lateral veins somewhat raised, scales deeply divided, dendroid, from pronounced and persistent epidermal tubercles. Flowers 4-6 per umbel, more or less horizontal; calyx a scaly ring; corolla white with 6-7 lobes, strongly smelling of carnations, tubular to tubular-funnel-shaped, conspicuously pouched at the base, 5-7 × 2.5-4cm, glabrous outside; stamens 12-14, irregularly exserted from the mouth; ovary covered with forward pointing hairs and (obscurely) with scales, style hairy in the lower ¾, glabrous towards the top. H1b. New Guinea, (Irian Jaya, Cycloop Mts), 500-1,400m.

Close to *R. hyacinthosmum* but that species has larger flowers with 6-7-lobed corollas.

R. DIELSIANUM SCHLTR. - SUBSECT. PHAEOVIREYA

Erect shrub to 2m, epiphytic or terrestrial; young stems densely covered at first with brown stellate-dendroid scales, soon glabrescent. Leaves 4-7 × 1.5-3cm, elliptic or narrowly elliptic, the apex acute to obtuse, the margin flat or very slightly recurved; base broadly to narrowly wedge-shaped; upper surface at first brown-scaly but quickly glabrescent, the surface left somewhat rough by the persistent raised scale bases, midrib impressed, lateral veins 4-6 pairs, obscure or feint; lower surface with the midrib strongly raised, particularly in the basal half, lateral veins only slightly raised and only slightly more distinct than when viewed from above, scales fairly well spaced, brown, dendroid and from prominent epidermal tubercles, easily rubbed off. Flowers 2-4 per umbel, horizontal to hanging, calyx a low scaly ring; corolla pink, tubular, curved 2.5-3.5 × 2-3cm, slightly scaly outside; stamens 10, loosely to tightly grouped on the upper side of the corolla mouth; ovary silvery or silvery and brown-scaly, the style scaly up to half way, glabrous above (the var. *stylotrichum* Sleumer with short spreading hairs in the lower part). H1b. New Guinea (widespread in the eastern half of the island), 1,200-2,000m.

A pretty and freely growing species in cultivation.

R. ERICOIDES LOW EX HOOK.F. - SUBSECT. PSEUDOVIREYA
Shrub erect or prostrate, to 1.5m, rarely to 3m, terrestrial; young stems scaly and sometimes minutely hairy, distinctly rough with raised leaf scars for some distance below the leaves. Leaves 0.4-0.8 × 0.08-0.16cm, linear or very narrowly elliptic, the apex acute, with the extreme point rounded, margin not revolute, entire or somewhat indented with irregular crenulations, the base tapering; upper surface smooth with a few minute scales which quickly disappear, midrib faint, minutely impressed near the base, no lateral veins visible; lower surface paler than the upper, with a trace of the midrib only, with well spaced small disc-shaped scales with indistinct centres. Flowers 1-4 per umbel, hanging diagonally to vertically downwards; calyx of 5 well developed lobes each 2-3mm long; corolla red, cylindrical 13-15 × 10-12mm, finely scaly on the tube and lobes; stamens 10, on the lower side of the mouth of the flower; ovary densely scaly, style glabrous. H1b. Malaysia (Sabah - Mt Kinabalu only), 2,700-4,000m.

This, the most alpine species on Kinabalu is a real plantsman's challenge, various introductions have grown and flowered in cultivation but it seems prone to soil borne diseases and does not persist well. It is well named with its narrow foliage looking very ericoid. The consistently long calyx lobes will distinguish it from other species which may approach it in general appearance.

R. FALLACINUM SLEUMER - SUBSECT. MALAYOVIREYA
Shrub to 5m, epiphytic or terrestrial, the young stems with a dense and persistent covering of dark brown scales. Leaves 9-16 × 3-5.5cm, ovate, lanceolate or elliptic, the apex acute and often acuminate, the margin irregularly wavy but flat, the base rounded to auriculate; the upper surface at first densely silvery scaly with overlapping scales, only gradually becoming glabrescent, midrib slightly impressed in the basal half, smooth above, the laterals 8-12 pairs, smooth; the lower surface with the midrib strongly raised for most of its length, the laterals very slightly so, scales: brown, dense and overlapping, variable in size and very persistent. Flowers 15-35 per umbel, erect to horizontal; calyx a low densely scaly ring; corolla bright orange, shortly cylindrical to narrowly funnel-shaped, 1.8-2.5 × 3-3.7cm, densely and conspicuously brown-scaly outside on the tube and up onto the lobes; stamens 10, arranged fairly regularly around the mouth of the flower; ovary densely brown-scaly; style densely scaly for 2-3mm at the base, glabrous in the remaining part. H1b. Malaysia, (Sabah, Mt Kinabalu and Crocker Range to Mt Mulu and Mt Murud in Northern Sarawak), 1,200-2,500m.

A variable species distinguished from the closely related *R. durionifolium* Becc. by its shorter, much more scaly flowers. One of the more challenging species in cultivation, tending to be rather slow.

R. GARDENIA SCHLTR. - SUBSECT. PHAEOVIREYA

An imperfectly understood species similar to *R. konori* and differing in the nearly completely glabrous style. Most if not all plants of this species are now referable to cultivar 'Gardenia Odyssey' a plant introduced into Australia from The Netherlands and now widely distributed. See: Craven L. *The Rhododendron*, Spring 1993, **Vol. 33** pp 11-12, Bringing a conclusion to confusion: *Rhododendron* 'Gardenia Odyssey'.

R. GIULIANETTII LAUTERB. - SUBSECT. ALBOVIREYA
Shrub to 3m, terrestrial, young stems moderately densely covered with shortly stalked scales. Leaves 0.7-2.8 × 0.5-1.8cm, broadly elliptic, obovate-elliptic to subcircular, the apex obtuse to rounded, rarely retuse, the margin slightly revolute, the base broadly tapering to rounded but often decurrent in a wing on the petiole; upper surface densely scaly with flat scales, soon becoming glabrous, the scales leaving shallow pits, midrib slightly impressed, lateral veins 4-5 pairs, slightly depressed; lower surface with the midrib only slightly raised, the laterals obscure, the scales dense, overlapping, broadly lobed and some darker in colour giving a spotted appearance to the surface. Flowers 3-4 per umbel, horizontally spreading; calyx a densely scaly and wavy disc; corolla bright red, cylindrical to narrowly funnel-shaped, 2.8-3.5 × 1.8-2.4cm, completely glabrous outside; stamens 10, rather irregularly centrally disposed; ovary hairy and scaly, style scaly at the base, glabrous above. H1b. Papua New Guinea (Mt Scratchley, Mt Victoria), 3,000-3,900m.

R. GOODENOUGHII SLEUMER - SUBSECT. SOLENOVIREYA
Shrub to 2m, terrestrial or epiphytic; young stems at first finely brown-scaly, quickly becoming glabrescent. Leaves 5.5-10 × 3-6cm, mostly obovate but some elliptic or broadly elliptic, the apex broadly obtuse to rounded, the margin almost flat, the base broadly tapering; upper surface finely scaly at first but very quickly becoming glabrous, the midrib broad and grooved in the lower part, hardly raised at the base, slightly impressed in the upper part, lateral veins 5-8 pairs hardly raised; the lower surface with the midrib raised almost throughout its length, the laterals distant but almost smooth, finely scaly with small disc-shaped scales impressed in shallow pits. Flowers 7-16 per umbel, mostly semi-erect; calyx a low scaly ring; corolla white, scented, trumpet-shaped but curved and saccate at the base, 6-8 × 2-4cm, slightly scaly on the tube outside; stamens 10, irregularly arranged around and somewhat protruding from the mouth of the flower; ovary covered with scales and appressed hairs, style similarly covered in scales and hairs for the basal ⅔, glabrous near the top. H1b. Papua New Guinea (endemic to Goodenough Island, Mt Goodenough), 800-1,500m.

A beautiful species, the flowers at first held in a 'collar' of bud scales but this does not persist long.

R. GRACILENTUM F.MUELL. - SUBSECT. VIREYA
Small usually spreading much branched shrub to 0.5m, mostly considerably less, terrestrial or epiphytic; young stems finely scaly with dark brown scales. Leaves 0.8-1.5 × 0.2-0.7 narrowly to broadly elliptic, apex acute rarely sub-obtuse, margin flat, base narrowly to broadly tapering; upper surface glossy green with only very inconspicuous scale remnants, the midrib faint, lateral veins obscure; lower surface with small dark brown disc-shaped to stellate, well spaced scales which clearly show up as darker dots, midrib distinct but lateral veins obscure. Flowers mostly solitary, rarely in pairs, hanging vertically down; calyx a low scaly lobed disc; corolla red or deep pink cylindrical to narrowly funnel-shaped, 2-3 × 1.5-2cm, with a few inconspicuous scales on the tube; stamens 10, rather irregularly on the upper side of the mouth of the flower; ovary densely scaly, style with simple hairs at least in the basal half. H1b. Papua New Guinea (east-

ern end), 2,000-2,800m.

A delightful, small, bushy plant in cultivation, that covers itself in flowers in the spring. It is unlikely to be confused with other species. The nearest relation in cultivation is possibly *R. womersleyi* which has a very different habit with few branches and simple white hairs on the ovary.

R. HELLWIGII WARB. - SUBSECT. PHAEOVIREYA

Shrub to 3m, mostly epiphytic, young stems at first densely brown-scaly, quickly glabrescent and then characteristically pale whitish or yellowish cream. Leaves 8-12.5 × 4.5-8cm, broadly elliptic, ovate or obovate, the apex obtuse to rounded, the margin flat or very slightly recurved and narrowly cartilaginous, the base rounded or cordate; upper surface at first densely dark-brown scaly, later glabrescent green but slightly rough with scale bases, midrib strongly raised at the base but becoming slightly impressed in the upper part, lateral veins 5-7 pairs, very slightly impressed; lower surface with the midrib raised throughout its length, laterals smooth, at first densely brown-scaly with very unequally sized dendroid scales which quickly fall or become eroded and ultimately leave a rough green surface of scale bases. Flowers 2-5 per umbel, horizontal to half-hanging, calyx of 6-7 short (2mm), brown-scaly lobes; corolla deep pink to dark blood red, with 6 or 7 lobes, tubular funnel-shaped, slightly curved. 7-8 × 8-9cm, glabrous outside but flecked with indistinct paler marks; stamens 12-14, grouped on the lower side of the mouth of the flower; ovary densely scaly, the style glabrous, at first curving upwards away from the stamens, later moving to the centre of the flower. H1b. Papua New Guinea (Finisterre and Saruwaged Mts) 1,100-2,500m.

Well described in the wild as 'a glorious species with petals a very dark blood red and so thick and fleshy that one can easily squeeze them so that the red sap runs out through the fingers'. In cultiva-

tion it is rather slow but certainly very handsome when in flower.

R. HERZOGII WARB. - SUBSECT. SIPHONOVIREYA

Erect shrub to 2m, mostly epiphytic, young stems finely brown-scaly. Leaves 5-8 × 2.5-4.5cm, broadly elliptic to obovate, the apex broadly obtuse to rounded, margin revolute, base broadly tapering to rounded; upper surface at first covered with rounded silvery scales, quickly glabrous, midrib broad and raised at the very base, quickly tapering so that it is narrow and slightly impressed, for most of its length, lateral veins 4-6 pairs, very slightly impressed; undersurface with the midrib broadly raised throughout, lateral veins smooth, scales moderately spaced, disc-shaped with variable sized centres and impressed into the leaf surface. Flowers 5-14 per umbel, held stiffly sub-erect; calyx a low scaly ring; corolla white to pale pink, most commonly white with the tube suffused pink from the base, strongly and sweetly scented, slender trumpet-shaped with a curved tube, 6-11 × 1.5-2.5cm, densely mealy-scaly on the tube outside; stamens 10, rather irregularly grouped in the mouth of the flower but falling to the lower side as the stigma matures; ovary densely scaly, the style densely scaly for most of its length. H1b. New Guinea, a common and widespread species on the main range, 1,500-2,500m.

A very attractive and easily grown species with aromatic foliage as well as the beautifully scented flowers.

R. HIMANTODES SLEUMER - SUBSECT. MALAYOVIREYA

Shrub up to 2m, usually epiphytic but also terrestrial on deep peat of some summit ridges; young stems densely brown-scaly. Leaves 2-9 × 0.3-0.6cm, linear, acute or sometimes rounded at the apex, margin entire, somewhat irregular and slightly reflexed, the base wedge-shaped; upper surface silvery scaly becoming glabrous, with an impressed midrib but no visible lateral veins; lower surface with the midrib raised throughout its length, completely covered in variably sized brown scales, the largest with dark brown swollen centres. Flowers 8-15 per umbel, horizontal or semi-erect; calyx a low rounded, scaly disc; corolla white but with a prominent and attractive pattern of brown scales outside on the tube and lobes, saucer-shaped 1.1.4 × 2.-2.7cm; ovary densely brown-scaly, style glabrous or scaly near the base. H1b. Borneo (Sabah, Brunei, Sarawak and Kalimantan [Mt Kemul]), 1,300-2,000m.

One of the most attractive species in this section. When in flower it rarely escapes comment even from non rhododendron lovers. Its densely scaly, strap-shaped leaves and dainty, short, white flowers will not allow confusion with any other species.

R. HOOGLANDII SLEUMER - SUBSECT. PHAEOVIREYA

Shrub to 2.5m, terrestrial or epiphytic; young stems densely set with golden brown, stalked scales, warty and rough to the touch. Leaves 3-5.5 × 0.2-0.6cm, linear, the apex sub-acute to obtuse, the margin very strongly revolute, the base narrowly tapering; the upper surface densely covered with golden brown scales initially, becoming glabrescent but remaining scabrous with the persistent scale bases, midrib impressed, lateral veins obscure; lower surface with the midrib prominently raised, lateral veins obscure, the surface covered in the rather persistent stellate scales. Flowers 1-2 per umbel, horizontal or semi-erect; calyx a densely scaly, 5-lobed disc; corolla pinkish red or cream, cylindrical, 2.8-3.5 × 1.2-1.6cm, densely golden brown-scaly outside; stamens 10, held on the upper side of the mouth of the flower; ovary densely scaly, the style mostly glabrous but with just a few scales at the base. H1b. Widespread on the main range of New Guinea (Irian Jaya to Papua New Guinea), 3,000-3,400m.

An odd looking but attractive plant now doubtfully still in cultivation.

R. HYACINTHOSMUM SLEUMER - SUBSECT. PHAEOVIREYA

Shrub to 3m, epiphytic or terrestrial; young stems at first stellate-scaly, the scales from epidermal tubercles which make the stems rough to the touch. Leaves 6-9 × 3.5-5cm, broadly elliptic to ovate, the apex broadly obtuse to rounded, the margin flat or slightly recurved, narrowly cartilaginous, the base rounded to cordate; the upper surface at first finely brown-scaly, becoming glabrescent but remaining rather rough, midrib raised at the very base, impressed above, lateral veins 3-7 pairs slightly raised; lower surface with the midrib prominent and raised, the laterals mostly obscure, hardly raised, scales brown-stellate to dendroid from pronounced epidermal tubercles, moderately densely set. Flowers 2-5 per umbel, horizontal to half hanging; calyx a 5-lobed, hairy and scaly disc, corolla white with a pink flush in bud and pink patches at the base of the lobes in the mouth, powerfully scented like hyacinths, glabrous outside; stamens 10, irregularly disposed on the lower side of the mouth; ovary white-hairy, style hairy only for about ⅓ of its length, glabrous at the top. H1b. Papua New Guinea (Milne Bay Province), 1,800-2,300m.

An attractive species discovered by the Rev. Canon N.E.G. Cruttwell in the Daga country where he worked as a missionary and distributed via the Australian Rhododendron Society.

R. INCONSPICUUM J.J. SM. - SUBSECT. VIREYA

Shrubs to 3m or more rarely trees to 10m, mostly terrestrial; young stems densely covered with scurfy brown scales some of these from epidermal tubercles. Leaves 1.5-2.5 × 0.8-1.7cm, ovate to elliptic or broadly elliptic, the apex obtuse to rounded, the margin entire and flat, the base broadly tapering to rounded; the upper surface at first silvery-scaly, quickly glabrescent, midrib slightly impressed, lateral veins 3-6 pairs very slightly impressed; lower surface with the midrib slightly raised, lateral veins not raised but quite distinct in being darker in colour than the surrounding tissue, scales pale silvery brown rounded to deeply lobed and with small centres and each impressed in a low pit. Flowers in 1-7 flowered umbels, horizontal to half-hanging; calyx a densely scaly lobed disc; corolla pink to red, campanulate or short-ly cylindrical, 1.3-1.8 × 0.8-1.7cm, quite densely pale brown-scaly outside; stamens 10, spreading all round the mouth of the flower; ovary densely silvery scaly, the scales stopping rather abruptly at the junction with the glabrous style. H1b. Widespread throughout the highlands of New Guinea, 1,800-3,400m.

Often confused with *R. yelliotii* Warburg a species which is generally much more difficult to cultivate but the flowers of that species are usually darker in colour, the scales on the undersides of the leaves denser (usually touching each other) and the flower buds are scaly and minutely hairy (in this species they are glabrous or scaly only).

R. INTRANERVATUM SLEUMER - SUBSECT. VIREYA
Shrub to 1m, usually epiphytic, also on cliffs; minutely scaly at first quickly becoming smooth and glabrescent. Leaves 9-15 × 6-11cm, broadly elliptic, sub-ovate occasionally subcircular or sub-obovate, the apex broadly obtuse, rounded or retuse, often with a small hard recurved apiculus, margin recurved, the base cordate to auriculate; upper surface minutely and obscurely pale brown stellate-scaly, the midrib strongly raised for ½-⅔ of the length, lateral veins 10-16 pairs, strongly raised and with the lamina deeply sulcate between so that the leaves are more distinctively 'ribbed' than any other species; lower surface with the midrib strongly raised and the laterals deeply impressed, scales rather dense, brown-lobed to stellate with small centres. Flowers 1-5 per umbel, semi erect to horizontal; calyx a low scaly disc, corolla pale yellow, broadly funnel-shaped, glabrous outside; sta-

mens 10, spreading all round the mouth of the flower; ovary softly white-hairy, the style glabrous. H1a-b. Borneo (S Sarawak and W Kalimantan), 60-1,100m.

This species is grown as much for its bizarre looking leaves as for the flowers. If grown in full sun the leaves become very pale yellowish in colour often with a bronze tinge which makes it either wonderfully exciting or sick-looking depending on the viewpoint of the observer. If grown in shade the plants are quite acceptably green and growth better.

R. JASMINIFLORUM HOOK. - SUBSECT. SOLENOVIREYA
Shrub to 2.5m, epiphytic or terrestrial; young stems finely brown-scaly and slightly rough to the touch. Leaves 2.5-6 × 1-3.6cm, mostly elliptic, occasionally sub-obovate or sub-circular, the apex mostly obtuse to rounded, occasionally sub-acute, the margin strongly and broadly recurved, the base rounded or truncate; upper surface initially and laxly stellate-scaly, quickly glabrescent, midrib impressed, the lateral veins rather obscure; lower surface with the midrib strongly raised in the lower half, almost smooth above, lateral veins obscure, scales well spaced, small, dark brown and irregularly stellate, each raised on a minute epidermal tubercle. Flowers 3-20 per umbel, semi-erect to half-hanging; calyx a low scaly and hairy disc; corolla often at first pink, becoming white, usually lightly scented, trumpet-shaped, 4-5.5 × 2-2.5cm, distinctly but minutely brown-scaly out-side and obscurely white-hairy; stamens 10, scattered irregularly in the mouth of the flower; ovary scaly and hairy, style scaly in the lower ⅓, hairy to near the top. H1b. West Malaysia (Sarawak, Sumatra) and Philippines (Mindanao), recorded from s.l. to 3,100m, most commonly at about 1,000m.

In cultivation since Victorian times and still one of the best Vireyas to grow, most plants in cultivation are the West Malaysian form.

R. javanicum (Blume) Benn. - Subsect. Vireya

Shrub or small tree to 5m, terrestrial or epiphytic; young stems finely brown-scaly, becoming smooth and glabrous. Leaves 10-20 × 3-6cm, elliptic or elliptic-lanceolate, the apex acute, the margin flat, sometimes slightly irregular, the base broadly to narrowly tapering; upper surface, finely and indistinctly scaly at first, quickly glabrescent, midrib raised in the lower half, somewhat impressed in the upper half of the leaf, lateral veins 7-10 pairs, minutely impressed; lower surface with the midrib raised throughout its length, laterals more or less smooth but distinct, scales brown, scattered and well spaced, lobed to substellate with small centres. Flowers 4-12 per umbel, erect to horizontal; calyx a low glabrous ring; corolla usually orange often with a pink-ish violet throat, occasionally reported as yellow or red, funnel-shaped, 3-5 × 5-7.5cm, glabrous or almost so outside; stamens 10, irregularly scattered mostly on the lower side of the mouth; ovary glabrous or very sparsely scaly, (hairy in var. *teysmannii* [Miq.] King & Gamble), style glabrous. H1a-b. Indonesia (Sumatra, Java, to Bali), Malaysia (West) (as var. *teysmannii*), Philippines and Celebes as subsp. *schadenbergii* (Warb.) Argent, 300-2,600m.

AM 1933 (L. de Rothschild, Exbury); flowers deep orange, with pink throat.

The Javan form with bright orange flowers has long been grown and admired but some Philippine forms with bright scarlet and bicoloured flowers show considerable potential.

R. kawakamii Hayata - Subsect. Pseudovireya

Shrub to 1.5m, epiphytic or terrestrial; young stems laxly covered with brown scales at first. Leaves 2.5-5 × 1-1.8cm, elliptic or obovate-elliptic, the apex acute to obtuse with the midrib protruding as a short glandular point, margin entire, narrowly cartilaginous, the base broadly to narrowly tapering; upper surface at first with minute brown scales, quickly becoming glabrescent, midrib impressed, lateral veins 3-5 pairs, smooth, often somewhat obscure; lower surface with the midrib raised for most of its length, the laterals rather obscure, scales well spaced, rounded, brown, impressed in shallow pits. Flowers 4-7 per umbel, semi-erect to half-hanging; calyx of 5 unequal lobes both hairy and scaly; corolla yellow or pink or red, campanulate, 1-1.5 × 1.3-1.8cm, covered in translucent scales, stamens 10, dimorphic and arranged all round the corolla; ovary silvery scaly, style glabrous. H2-3. Taiwan (Central Mts), 1,800-2,200m.

Only the yellow form of this species, sometimes designated var. *flaviflorum* Lin & Chuang, appears to be in cultivation and there is still some mystery surrounding the pink form. The original description does not mention flower colour although it was reputed to be pink or red. *R taiwanianum* Ying is considered synonymous with this species at present.

This is reported to be the hardiest of the Vireyas withstanding several degrees of frost and having a winter resting period in America.

R. konori Becc. - Subsect. Phaeovireya

Shrub up to 4m, epiphytic or terrestrial; young stems at first densely brown-scaly with easily detached scales. Leaves 8-14 × 5-7.5, broadly elliptic or occasionally obovate, the apex obtusely pointed to rounded, the margin flat and entire, the base broadly tapering; upper surface at first densely brown-scaly, the scales becoming silvery as the leaf expands and quickly becoming glabrescent, with the midrib raised above near the base, becoming slightly impressed in the distal part, lateral veins 7-10 pairs, smooth, rather fine; lower surface with the midrib strongly raised throughout its length, the laterals smooth, densely brown-scaly with dendroid, unevenly sized scales, each from a small epidermal tubercle. Flowers 3-12 per umbel, more or less horizontally disposed; calyx stellate-scaly, a lobed oblique disc;

corolla white to pink, often marked with darker pink spots at the base of the lobes, powerfully and sweetly scented, funnel-shaped, 8-19 × 9-15cm, sparsely scaly or glabrous outside, mostly with 7 lobes; stamens 14, more or less clustered on the lower side of the mouth, ovary silvery scaly and densely hairy, style hairy and scaly in the lower half, becoming less hairy in the upper half and finally glabrous near the top. H1b. Widespread in New Guinea from west to east, 750-2,500m.

AM 1969 (M. Black, Grasmere, Westmorland) to a clone 'Eleanor Black'; flowers white flushed red.

A very attractive species in cultivation with handsome foliage and its beautiful and powerfully scented flowers. *R. phaeopeplum* Sleumer now reduced to a variety of *R. konori* is generally smaller in all its parts and more suited to pot culture. The spelling 'konorii' is sometimes used but because Beccari named this plant after a Papuan deity not a person there is no requirement under the existing Code of Botanical Nomenclature to adopt this.

R. LAETUM J.J.SM. - SUBSECT. VIREYA
Shrub to 3m, terrestrial; young stems laxly scaly. Leaves 7-10 × 3-6cm, broadly elliptic to obovate, the apex mostly shortly acuminate to an acute point, sometimes obtuse and mucronate, the margin flat and entire, the base broadly tapering; upper surface at first brown-scaly, the scales quickly becoming silvery and obscure or the surface becoming glabrescent, midrib slightly raised in the basal half and grooved, then smooth, lateral veins 5-8 pairs, slightly raised; lower surface with the midrib raised for most of its length, the laterals smooth, often obscure, the scales pale brown, lobed to substellate, well scattered and slightly impressed. Flowers 5-9 per umbel, semi-erect to horizontal, calyx a scaly and shortly hairy 5-lobed disc; corolla yellow or yellow suffused with red or orange, often fragrant, funnel-shaped, sometimes with a few hairs at the base outside and laxly stellate-scaly, 6-7 × 4.5-

6cm; stamens 10, rather irregularly arranged in the mouth of the flower; ovary densely white-hairy and inconspicuously scaly, style hairy to just over half way, glabrous in the upper part. H1b. New Guinea (Irian Jaya, Arfak Mts), 1,800-2,300m.

A lovely and well established species closely related to *R. zoelleri*. It differs in the shortly petiolate leaves, the petioles rarely more than 7mm, the flowers generally opening yellow, even when they change with age and the anthers being short, up to 5mm long, while in *R. zoelleri* the petioles are usually more than 7mm, the flowers orange at the lobes from the beginning, and anthers usually more than 5mm long.

R. LANCEOLATUM RIDL. - SUBSECT VIREYA
Shrub up to 1.2m, mostly epiphytic, sometimes terrestrial; young stems green, smooth with a fine covering of minute scales. Leaves 7-12 × 2.5-4.5cm, lanceolate to elliptic, the apex acute, the margin entire, flat or weakly revolute, the base tapering to rounded and characteristically wrinkled; upper surface green, smooth but often with puckers alongside the midrib, the scales hardly visible, the midrib broad and raised for most of its length often coloured red towards the base, lateral veins 7-12 pairs rather obscure; lower surface with minute, widely spaced, lobed scales which are difficult to see, the midrib smooth or slightly raised, the laterals fine and obscure. Flowers 4-10 per umbel, horizontal or slightly nodding, calyx a low ring; corolla white, very widely funnel-shaped, 2.2-2.5 × 2-2.4cm, with very small brown scales outside; ovary covered with white hairs but no scales, style hairy in the lower half, glabrous above. H1a-b. Borneo (Sabah, Sarawak and Kalimantan), 1,000-1,500m.

Unlike most rhododendrons this is a plant of shaded habitats within the montane forest, it requires high humidity and a little more heat than most others of section Vireya but the clear white flowers are very pretty.

R. LEPTANTHUM F.MUELL. - SUBSECT
PHAEOVIREYA
A small bush or straggling shrub reported up to 3m but rarely more than 1m high; young stems at first rough with dark brown dendroid scales which easily detach. Leaves, 3-6.5 × 2-3.5cm ovate or oblong-ovate, the apex broadly and bluntly pointed, the margin flat or slightly revolute, the base rounded to cordate; the upper surface smooth, at first silvery scaly but quickly becoming glabrous, midrib impressed, three to four pairs of laterals somewhat impressed and the reticulation distinct; lower surface moderately densely covered in the rusty brown dendroid scales of different sizes and each mounted on a small white tubercle which remains after the scales have gone, midrib raised and distinct throughout its length the laterals slightly raised but less prominent than on the upper side. Flowers 2-5 per umbel, hanging; calyx a low scaly ring; corolla pink, shortly cylindrical with a curved tube and rather large lobes, 2.5-3.5 × 3.5-4cm, with rather inconspicuous brown scales on the tube and lobes outside; ovary densely stellate-scaly, style stellate-scaly almost to the top. H1b. Eastern Papua New Guinea (from Morobe Province to Milne Bay Province), 1,300-2,300m.

This lovely and easily grown species now includes *R. warianum* Schltr. Various forms are in cultivation, some of them very compact which makes them excellent pot plants.

R. LEUCOGIGAS SLEUMER - SUBSECT.
VIREYA
Shrub 1-3m, epiphytic; young twigs finely scaly, quickly glabrescent. Leaves 12-30 × 3.5-10.5cm, elliptic or sub-obovate-elliptic, the apex broadly acute to obtuse, sub-acuminate or mucronate, the margin entire, flat or weakly revolute, the base rounded to cordate; the upper surface at first silvery scaly, quickly glabrescent, midrib raised in the lower half and often grooved, impressed in the upper part, lateral veins 7-12 pairs, finely impressed; lower surface with the midrib strongly raised for most of its length, lateral veins smooth and sometimes obscure, scales variable from flat silvery stellate incised to tall brown and dendroid but these not mounted on prominent epidermal tubercles. Flowers 5-8 per umbel, stiffly semi-erect to horizontal; calyx a low slightly scaly lobed ring; corolla deep pink to white, often with darker pink marks at the corners of the lobes, powerfully carnation-scented, tubular-funnel-shaped, with a straight tube, 13.5-16 × 12-15cm, finely scaly outside on the tube; stamens 14, clustered on the lower side of the tube; ovary densely hairy and obscurely scaly, style hairy to about half way, scaly to within about 1cm of the stigma. H1b. New Guinea (Irian Jaya [Cycloop Mts] and Papua New Guinea [Huntstein Mts]), 1,200-1,400m.

Introduced into cultivation by Professor Sleumer from the Cycloop Mts. and subsequently from Mt Huntstein from which was named 'Hunsteins Secret'. It is a superb plant although of rather slow growth.

R. LINDAUEANUM KOORD. - SUBSECT.
PSEUDOVIREYA
Shrub up to 2m, terrestrial or epiphytic; young twigs densely covered with stalked scales which leave a rough verruculose surface from the persistent stalks. Leaves 0.8-2.5 × 0.5-1.8cm, obovate to spathulate, the apex rounded or slightly retuse, the margin strongly revolute, the base tapering; the upper surface at first laxly scaly, quickly glabrescent, often convex, midrib impressed above, lateral veins 3-5 pairs slightly impressed; lower surface with the midrib and laterals raised beneath, the scales well spaced, red-brown, disc-shaped with a narrow marginal flange, slightly impressed. Flowers solitary, hanging; calyx a low scaly and sometimes ciliate, obtusely 5-toothed disc; corolla deep red to pink, tubular, straight but slightly zygomorphic by the lateral flattening, 1.7-2.5 × 1.2-1.6cm, laxly scaly outside on the tube; stamens 10, exserted on the upper

side of the flower; ovary densely scaly, style glabrous. H1b. New Guinea: (Arfak Mts to Saruwaged Mts), commonly collected from the wild, 1,200-3,200m.

The var. *bantaengense* J.J.Smith from Selebes differs by the 1mm long calyx lobes and probably represents a different species. This is not as yet in cultivation.

R. lochiae orthographic error = **R. lochiae**

R. LOCHIAE F. MUELL. NAME CONSERVED - SUBSECT. VIREYA
Shrub or tree to 3m, epiphytic or terrestrial; young twigs usually dark red and finely scaly. Leaves 4-9 × 2.5-4.5cm, elliptic to broadly elliptic or obovate, the apex acute, acuminate, sometimes mucronate, the margin entire, flat or weakly revolute, the base broadly tapering to rounded; the upper surface at first minutely brown-scaly, quickly glabrescent, midrib impressed throughout its length, lateral veins 4-10 pairs, fine, minutely impressed; lower surface with the midrib strongly raised at the base, less so above, lateral veins smooth, distinct to obscure, scales well spaced, lobed to rounded and very slightly impressed. Flowers 2-7 per umbel, half-hanging to hanging; calyx an undulate, scaly, disc; corolla mostly deep red, sometimes pink, campanulate to funnel-shaped with a straight tube, 4-5.5 × 4-6cm, minutely scaly outside; stamens 10, disposed all round the mouth of the flower; ovary both hairy and scaly, style hairy and scaly in the basal ⅔, glabrous above. H1b. Australia (N Queensland, Mt Finnigan, Thornton Peak, Mt Windsor Tableland and main Coast Range), 900-1,330m.

AM 1957 (Crown Estate Commissioners, Windsor); flowers Geranium Lake (HCC 20).

This attractive and floriferous species has been in cultivation at least since 1939 and is the parent of many hybrids. It was for these reasons that the name has recently been conserved and the original plant described under this name is now *R. notiale* (see L.A. Craven & R.M. Withers: *A second species of* Rhododendron *(Ericaceae)*

from Australia, Edinb. J. Bot. **53(1)**: 27-37, 1996).

R. LONGIFLORUM LINDL. - SUBSECT. VIREYA
Shrub or tree to 3m, epiphytic or terrestrial; young twigs initially covered in brown scales. Leaves 5-12 × 2-5.5cm, narrowly to broadly elliptic, sometimes obovate, the apex obtuse or acute and often acuminate, the margin entire and flat, the base rounded to broadly or narrowly tapering; the upper surface at first brown-scaly, quickly glabrescent, the midrib smooth or slightly depressed, lateral veins 5-8 pairs, slender, hardly raised; the lower surface with the midrib slightly raised, the lateral veins more or less smooth, the surface moderately covered with lobed to substellate scales. Flowers 3-13 per umbel, erect or semi-erect; calyx a low scaly ring; corolla orange, pink or red, often with a yellow throat, cylindrical, straight or curved, 4-5.5 × 3-6cm, laxly scaly outside; stamens 10, spreading around the mouth of the flower; ovary densely hairy and scaly, style hairy in the lower half, glabrous towards the top. H1a. West Malaysia; Sumatra; Borneo (widespread) and Karimata Archipelago, s.l.-1,000m.

This is very much a lowland species although it still usually occurs on hills, and it requires more heat than most Vireyas to do well. It was confused with *R. praetervisum* but the leaves of this species are much more revolute, the flowers purplish pink and hanging rather than semi-erect.

R. LORANTHIFLORUM SLEUMER - SUBSECT. SOLENOVIREYA
Shrub to 2m, epiphytic; young twigs initially finely brown-scaly, quickly glabrescent. Leaves 5-7 × 2.3-4.5cm, elliptic to slightly obovate, the apex obtuse, rounded or occasionally retuse, the margin entire, slightly revolute, the base broadly tapering; the upper surface at first minutely brown-scaly, quickly becoming glabrescent, glossy green, the midrib grooved near the base and slightly impressed, the

laterals 3-5 pairs, smooth; the lower surface with the midrib slightly raised in the basal half, the laterals smooth and rather obscure, the surface with well spaced circular to deeply lobed scales rather impressed into the surface. Flowers 2-7 per umbel, erect to hanging; calyx a low scaly ring; corolla white, delicately perfumed, trumpet-shaped, 2.5-3.2 × 4-5 cm, laxly scaly on the tube outside; stamens 10, irregularly exserted from the mouth of the flower; ovary densely silvery scaly and laxly and shortly hairy, the style with hairs and stalked scales at the base, hairy in the central part and finally glabrous in the upper third. H1b. Papua New Guinea (New Britain, Manus and Bougainville Islands only, not on the mainland), Solomon Islands (Malaita; New Georgia Group [Kolumbangara Islands]), 180-1,000m.

A delicate and very floriferous species which is easily grown.

R. LOWII HOOK.F. - SUBSECT. VIREYA
Shrub up to 10m, terrestrial; young stems, green covered in brown lobed scales. Leaves 10-20 × 4.5-10cm, broadly elliptic to ovate or slightly obovate, the apex obtuse to rounded or sometimes shortly acuminate, the margin entire, flat, sometimes somewhat wavy, the base broadly rounded to cordate; upper surface at first brown-scaly, quickly glabrescent, with the midrib strongly raised in the lower half, lateral veins 9-15 pairs not raised; lower surface with the veins not or hardly raised at all, scales rather widely spaced, lobed to substellate, with small centres. Flowers 8-15 per umbel, erect to horizontal; calyx a low scaly ring; corolla yellow to orange, often delicately scented, broadly funnel-shaped, 6-11 × 7-8cm, glabrous outside; stamens 10, usually all on the lower side of the mouth; ovary hairy and inconspicuously scaly, style glabrous. H1b. Sabah (Mt Kinabalu, Trus Madi and possibly Monkobo), 2,700-3,650m.

One of Kinabalu's most remarkable plants which never fails to impress people with its enormous trusses of flowers pro-duced throughout the year often on long vigorous unbranched canes which may be 6m in length. In cultivation it is very different being slow and often rather contorted and rather shy to flower.

R. LURALUENSE SLEUMER - SUBSECT. VIREYA
Shrub or small tree up to 9m, epiphytic or terrestrial; young stems at first with fine brown scales, quickly glabrescent. Leaves 4-6.5 × 1.8-2.8cm, elliptic to elliptic-spathulate, the apex obtuse or broadly acute sometimes submucronate, the margin flat and smooth, the base tapering; the upper surface smooth with only very fine scales at first, the midrib very slightly impressed, the lateral veins 3-5 pairs, smooth or minutely raised; the lower surface with the midrib raised below in the lower half, the laterals faint and often obscure, the scales well spaced, rounded to somewhat lobed and impressed in small pits. Flowers 3-6 per umbel, semi-erect; calyx a low slightly scaly disc; corolla white, funnel-shaped, 3-4.5 × 2.5-3cm, slightly scaly on the tube outside; stamens 10, scattered round the mouth of the flower; ovary hairy and obscurely scaly, style hairy and scaly in the lower ¼, glabrous above. H1b. Papua New Guinea (Bougainville Islands only), Solomon Islands (Guadalcanal [Mt Gallego]), 900-1,500m.

A species which tends to cover itself in flowers once a year, rather similar to *R. loranthiflorum* but with a much broader funnel-shaped tube and without scent.

R. MACGREGORIAE F. MUELL. - SUBSECT. VIREYA
Mostly a shrub rarely a small tree and recorded possibly erroneously up to 15m, terrestrial; young stems, smooth, green with small inconspicuous scales. Leaves 5-8 × 2-5cm, elliptic, broadly elliptic to ovate, the apex shortly acuminate to rounded, the margin usually distinctly recurved, the base broadly tapering or rounded; the upper surface smooth with only very indistinct scales, the midrib very slightly

impressed; the lower surface with distinctly raised midrib for almost its whole length, lateral veins 6-10 pairs distinct but not raised, scales small, brown, stellate to disc-shaped well spaced. Flowers 7-15 in an umbel, erect to horizontal; calyx a low ring; corolla varying from yellow to orange and pink to red, shortly tubular with relatively large and well expanded lobes, 1.5-2.5 × 2-3cm minutely scaly on the tube and base of the lobes; stamens 10, prominent and scattered round the mouth of the flower; ovary covered with subappressed hairs and silvery scales, style both hairy and scaly in the lower half, glabrous above. H1b. Widespread over the whole of New Guinea, 500-3,300m.

AM 1977 (G. Gorer, Sunte House, Haywards Heath) to a clone 'Elsie Louisa'; flowers Orange Group 29A, shading through 29B to Yellow-Orange Group 23B in throat.

Probably the easiest species to cultivate and certainly most attractive with very brightly coloured and freely produced flowers. It is often considered a weed in its native country since it grows at low enough altitudes to occur in pastures and is well known as being poisonous to stock. The red and pink forms seem to be more common in Irian Jaya at the western end of the island and rare in Papua New Guinea.

R. MAIUS (J.J. SMITH) SLEUMER - SUBSECT. SOLENOVIREYA
Shrub up to 3m, terrestrial or epiphytic, young stems laxly scaly. Leaves 4.7-8.7 × 2.5-4cm, elliptic, broadly elliptic to elliptic-ovate, the apex broadly attenuate to obtuse, the margin slightly revolute, the base broadly tapering to rounded; the upper surface at first finely silvery scaly, quickly glabrescent, midrib slightly impressed above, laterals 9-10 pairs, also slightly impressed; underneath the midrib very prominent but tapering markedly from the base, lateral veins and even the finer veins slightly prominent. Flowers 5-15 in an umbel, horizontal to half hanging; calyx laxly scaly, an almost entire disc or

irregularly 5-toothed; corolla white or a little pink on the tube, trumpet-shaped but slightly curved and broadest in the middle, beautifully scented, 7-9 × 2.2-2.8cm, laxly scaly outside; stamens 10, irregular in the mouth; ovary densely hairy and scaly, the style densely hairy and scaly near the base, the indumentum thinning until the top third is entirely glabrous. H1b. New Guinea (Hubrecht Mts near Lake Habbema and in Papua New Guinea, widespread but rather infrequent from Mt Capella to the Bulldog Road), 2,700-3,200m.

A lovely and easily grown species.

R. MALAYANUM JACK - SUBSECT. MALAYOVIREYA
Epiphytic or terrestrial shrub to 2m, young stems densely dark brown, scaly. Leaves 8.5-15 × 3.5-5.5cm, elliptic or broadly elliptic, the apex acute, often acuminate, sometimes shortly and broadly pointed, the edge entire and flat except near the base it may be somewhat revolute, the base broadly or narrowly tapering; the upper surface densely scaly but becoming glabrescent, the midrib slightly impressed, lateral veins up to 8 pairs, slightly impressed; underneath the midrib strongly raised, the laterals raised near the midrib, completely and persistently scaly with variable scales, the largest of which have swollen dark centres. Flowers terminal or lateral in 1-5 flowered umbels, the flowers hanging vertically downwards; calyx a low densely scaly ring; corolla reddish purple, purplish pink or greenish white, cylindrical, the tube often compressed laterally 2.5-3 × 1.4-2.4cm, laxly scaly on the tube outside; stamens 10, irregularly grouped on the lower side of the mouth; ovary densely covered in brown scales, style scaly at the base otherwise glabrous. H1a-b. Thailand, Malaysia (Peninsula, Sarawak, and Sabah), Indonesia (Sumatra, Java, Kalimantan, Sulawesi & Seram), 200-3,000m.

A widespread and variable species that has been in cultivation since Victorian times, the best forms are the higher altitude ones with smaller leaves and darker coloured flowers, lowland forms are difficult to cultivate and much less attractive.

R. MICROMALAYANUM SLEUMER - SUBSECT. MALAYOVIREYA

Shrub to 1.2m, epiphytic, the young stems at first completely covered with dark brown overlapping scales. Leaves 2.5-4 × 0.7-1.2cm, narrowly elliptic, the apex shortly obtuse to rounded, the margin entire but slightly wavy, the base tapering; upper surface at first silvery brown-scaly but becoming glabrescent, the midrib impressed above, the lateral veins 3-4 pairs, slightly impressed; the lower surface with the midrib very prominent, the lateral veins almost smooth, densely scaly, the scales variable in size, often overlapping, the largest dark sooty brown with prominent large centres. Flowers 1-4 per umbel, hanging vertically downwards; calyx a low brown-scaly disc, corolla purplish pink or greenish white 2.5-3 × 1.5-2cm, cylindrical with a fluted and slightly swollen base and scattered orange-brown scales outside; stamens 10, irregularly disposed, mostly on the lower side of the mouth; ovary densely brown-scaly, style scaly in the basal ¼, then glabrous. H1b. Borneo (N Sarawak and Sabah), 800-2,000m.

A neat free flowering species which is probably the easiest to grow of the very scaly malayovireyas.

R. MULTICOLOR MIQ. - SUBSECT. VIREYA

Shrub to 1.5m, terrestrial or epiphytic, young twigs very smooth with a few small scales. Leaves 3-7 × 0.7-2cm, narrowly elliptic to narrowly oblanceolate, the apex acute or acuminate, sometimes with the extreme tip rounded, margin flat, the base narrowly tapering; upper surface with fine scattered brown scales at first, soon glabrescent, the midrib raised in the lower half, smooth above, the laterals obscure; the lower surface with the midrib almost completely smooth, the laterals obscure, the scales rather sparse and small, brown, lobed to substellate with small centres.

Flowers 3-6 per umbel, horizontal to half-hanging; calyx a low disc; corolla whitish cream, yellow or red, sometimes sweetly scented, broadly funnel-shaped, glabrous outside; stamens 10, arranged all round the mouth of the flower; ovary and style glabrous. H1b. Indonesia (Sumatra), 900-2,100m.

One of the parents of some of the old Veitch hybrids but not one of the more flamboyant species.

R. MULTINERVIUM SLEUMER - SUBSECT. SOLENOVIREYA

Shrub or small tree to 3m, terrestrial or epiphytic, the young stems at first with scattered brown scales. Leaves 5-8 × 3.5-6cm, narrowly obovate, obovate or elliptic, the apex obtuse or obtusely acuminate, the margin flat or minutely turned down, very narrowly cartilaginous, the base broadly to narrowly tapering; the upper surface minutely scaly but quickly glabrous, the midrib slightly impressed, the laterals finely raised 10-14 pairs, rather regularly parallel with each other; underside with the midrib strongly raised to just over half way, the laterals obscure, not raised, scales well spaced, circular to lobed, small and impressed in shallow pits in the surface. Flowers 3-7 per umbel, semi-erect to horizontal; calyx a low scaly ring; corolla white, powerfully scented of clove pinks, trumpet-shaped but rather compressed laterally, with the tube strongly angled, 5-6.5 × 3-3.5cm, finely substellate-scaly on the outside; stamens 10, protruding from the mouth of the flower and bending downwards as a group as the flower ages; ovary densely scaly, the style glabrous, becoming well exserted from the mouth of the flower. H1b. Papua New Guinea (Western Highlands Province, Eastern Highland Province and Sepik River area), 1,300-2,000m.

An attractive and easily grown species with beautifully scented flowers.

R. NERVULOSUM SLEUMER - SUBSECT. VIREYA

Shrub to 1.5m, mostly terrestrial; young

twigs only very finely scaly, quickly glabrescent. Leaves 5.5-8 × 0.7-1.5, narrowly elliptic to almost linear, the apex acute, the margin entire, slightly revolute in the basal half, the base narrowly tapering; the upper surface at first finely pale brown-scaly, quickly glabrescent, midrib slightly impressed in the basal half, smooth in the upper part, lateral veins 4-6 pairs, smooth; lower surface with the midrib very slightly raised throughout its length, the laterals smooth, the scales small, lobed and sparse. Flowers 1-6 per umbel, horizontal to half hanging; calyx a low minutely scaly ring; corolla opening orange and darkening to reddish with age, funnel-shaped, 2.5-4 × 2-3cm, glabrous outside; stamens 10, slightly dimorphic, arranged regularly around the mouth of the flower; ovary densely white-hairy and with small brown scales, style glabrous. H1b. Borneo (Sabah, Kinabalu to Mt Lotung), 2,500-3,000m.

This is closely allied to *R. stenophyllum* but may be distinguished by its broader leaves.

R. NOTIALE CRAVEN - SUBSECT. VIREYA
Similar in most respects to *R. lochiae* but the leaf apex sometimes retuse in this species, the corolla curved and the stamens clustered on the upper side of the flower. Described in 1996, material of this species is already in the trade and it should quickly be widely available. H1b. Australia (N Queensland, Bellenden Ker Range and Bell Peak in the Malbon Thompson Range), 1,200-1,500m.

R. ORBICULATUM RIDL. - SUBSECT. SOLENOVIREYA
Shrub or small tree up to 4m, usually epiphytic; young twigs thinly covered in small scales. Leaves 3-6.5 × 3.5-6cm, broadly ovate to sub-circular, the apex obtusely pointed or rounded, the margin entire, flat with a narrow cartilaginous edge, the base rounded to cordate; upper surface minutely and obscurely scaly at first, then glabrescent, midrib slightly impressed above, lateral veins 5-7 pairs also very

slightly impressed; lower surface with the midrib slightly raised, the laterals rather indistinct, scales very small, widely spaced, rounded to lobed and with a relatively large central area. Flowers 2-6 per umbel, horizontal to half-hanging; calyx a low circular or 5-angled disc; corolla pale pink or white, sometimes slightly scented, trumpet-shaped but with enormous lobes compared with most species of this flower type, 7-8 × 7-8cm, finely and indistinctly scaly outside; stamens 10, in a group on the lower side of the mouth of the corolla; ovary with silvery scales and very short, white hairs, style shortly hairy and with a few scales in the lower half, glabrous in the upper part. H1b. Borneo (Sabah, Brunei and Northern Sarawak), 800-1,800m.

This species was confused with *R. suaveolens* but it is clearly distinct with its shorter leaves and much broader flowers (see D.R. Hunt, *The Botanical Magazine* 1970, **178** tab. 575).

R. PAUCIFLORUM KING & GAMBLE - SUBSECT. VIREYA
Shrub to 1m, epiphytic; young stems finely scaly and hairy. Leaves 1.5-3 × 1-2.5cm, obovate to sub-circular, the apex obtuse, rounded or retuse, the margin slightly revolute, narrowly cartilaginous, minutely crenulate, the base broadly tapering; upper surface finely and sparsely scaly and hairy, soon glabrescent, midrib slightly impressed, laterals 1-3 pairs rather obscure; lower surface with the midrib raised at the base, soon becoming smooth or even impressed near the apex, lateral veins obscure, scales widely scattered, brown, rounded or irregularly lobed, from shallow pits in the epidermis. Flowers solitary or in pairs, horizontal to half-hanging; calyx somewhat five-lobed, hairy and scaly; corolla deep pink, shortly cylindrical or campanulate, 1.7-2.4 × 1.5-2cm, sparsely scaly and hairy outside; stamens 10, slightly dimorphic, arranged regularly around the mouth; ovary with long silvery hairs and scales, style glabrous except with a few hairs and

scales at the very base. H1b. West Malaysia, 1,400-1,800m.

A very pretty species, not especially flamboyant but flowering over a long period.

R. PERAKENSE KING & GAMBLE - SUBSECT. PSEUDOVIREYA
Shrub to 2m, epiphytic, young stems fairly densely covered in golden brown scales on long epidermal tubercles. Leaves 1.3-1.7 × 0.7-1cm, elliptic, broadly elliptic or obovate, the apex rounded or often slightly retuse the margin strongly revolute, the whole leaf being convex, the base tapering; upper surface finely but rather conspicuously brown-scaly at first becoming glabrescent with age, the midrib impressed throughout its length as are the 1-3 pairs of lateral veins; lower surface with the midrib strongly raised throughout its length as are the laterals, the scales well spaced, disc- or funnel-shaped, pale brown and slightly sunken in small pits. Flowers 2-5 per umbel, horizontal to hanging; calyx a densely scaly, 5-lobed ring; corolla yellow or white, tubular or tubular-campanulate, 10-15 × 0.6-0.8cm, with scattered scales outside; stamens 10, regularly arranged inside the mouth of the flower; ovary densely scaly, the style glabrous. H1b. West Malaysia, 1,700-1,900m.

A pretty species only known with yellow flowers in cultivation, it appears to habitually self pollinate and to be an inbreeding species. It grows weakly on its own roots but more strongly when grafted onto *R. fragrantissimum*. It is reported to be incompatible when grafted with Subsection Vireya stock.

R. PHAEOCHITUM F. MUELL. - SUBSECT. PHAEOVIREYA
Shrub to 2.5m, epiphytic, young stems densely covered in dark brown stellate-dendroid scales. Leaves 4-9 × 2.5-4.5cm, elliptic to sub-obovate, the apex obtusely pointed to rounded occasionally mucronate, the margin slightly reflexed, the base broadly tapering to rounded; upper surface light brown- to silvery scaly but very quickly glabrescent, the midrib slender and slightly impressed, lateral veins 3-7 pairs very slightly impressed; lower surface with the midrib very strongly raised, the laterals slightly raised, the scales dense to rather sparse, dendroid, and very unevenly sized each from a small epidermal tubercle. Flowers 2-5(-11) per umbel, more or less half hanging; calyx a low densely scaly ring; corolla usually pink, sometimes red or cream, somewhat curved-cylindrical, 4.5-5.5 × 3-4cm, densely brown-scaly outside; stamens 10, grouped on the upper side of the corolla mouth; ovary densely covered in brown, stellate-dendroid scales, the style scaly to nearly the top. H1b. New Guinea (widespread on the main ranges), 2,100-2,600m.

This variable species grows well in cultivation, the form with cream flowers looks most exciting, owing to the strong contrast with the dense rusty brown scales.

R. phaeopeplum Sleumer - is a synonym of **R. konori** Becc. var. **phaeopeplum** (Sleumer)Argent

R. × **PLANECOSTATUM** (SLEUMER)ARGENT A.L.LAMB & PHILLIPPS - SUBSECT. VIREYA
Shrub to 1m, epiphytic or terrestrial, young stems smooth with fine scales at first. Leaves 4-5 × 1.5-1.8cm, elliptic to obovate, the apex acute, often acuminate, the margin entire, flat, the base tapering, upper surface at first minutely scaly, quickly glabrescent and shiny, main vein slightly raised, laterals 5-7 pairs, smooth, rather obscure; lower surface with the midrib more or less flat and the laterals obscure, scales rather sparse, lobed with small centres. Flowers 3-6 per umbel, horizontal to half hanging; calyx a low scaly ring; corolla red, cylindrical to narrowly funnel-shaped, 2-2.5 × 1.3-1.8cm, glabrous; stamens 10 arranged around the mouth of the flower, ovary glabrous, style glabrous. H1b. Sabah (E Malaysia), Kinabalu and

Crocker Range, 1,300-1,700m.

A hybrid originally described as a species and often sold as such. It is cheerful, vigorous and free flowering.

R. PLEIANTHUM SLEUMER - SUBSECT. SOLENOVIREYA

Shrub or tree to 6m, terrestrial; young stems laxly stellate-lepidote. Leaves 6.5-14 × 4-9cm, elliptic to obovate-elliptic, the apex rounded or broadly obtuse, the margin entire and flat, the base cordate, to rounded; upper surface at first finely stellate-scaly, later glabrescent, midrib impressed to the apex, lateral veins about 8 pairs finely impressed; lower surface with the midrib broad and strongly raised, the laterals also well raised, the scales well spaced broadly lobed to stellate, rather fine. Flowers 6-20 per umbel, half hanging; calyx with short, or sometimes long, lobes, scaly; corolla white suffused with pink or entirely pink, trumpet-shaped with a curved tube, 7-9 × 3-4cm, slightly scaly outside; stamens 10, rather irregularly exserted from the mouth of the flower; ovary densely hairy and obscurely scaly, the style hairy and scaly in the basal 1cm, above this glabrous. H1b. New Guinea (widespread in the eastern half of the island), 2,600-3,300m.

R. POLYANTHEMUM SLEUMER - SUBSECT. VIREYA

Shrub or small tree to 7m, epiphytic or terrestrial; young stems at first with a covering of rusty brown dendroid scales, later smooth. Leaves 8-13 × 5-8cm, broadly elliptic, the apex obtuse, rounded or apiculate, the margin entire and flat, the base broadly tapering to rounded; upper surface at first white-scaly, then brown but quickly becoming glabrous, the midrib flat, 6-8 pairs of lateral veins not raised or impressed; the lower surface with the midrib slightly raised, lateral veins not raised, the scales brown, dendroid, easily removed but not standing on raised epidermal tubercles. Flowers 25-30 per umbel, held semi-erect to horizontal; calyx a low scaly ring; corolla bright orange or

pinkish orange with a yellow eye, very powerfully and sweetly scented, narrowly funnel-shaped, 3-3.5 × 4-5cm, laxly covered in scales outside; stamens 10, roughly arranged in two groups on either side of the flower; ovary hairy, the style hairy near the base, glabrous in the upper part. H1b. Malaysia (Sabah and Northern Sarawak), 1,300-2,300m.

A delightful species which can make a magnificent visual display but is so powerfully scented that in forests in the wild it is often the nose which discovers it before the eye.

R. PRAETERVISUM SLEUMER - SUBSECT. VIREYA

Shrub to 2m, usually epiphytic; young twigs covered in small brown or transparent scales but soon smooth. Leaves 5-7 × 2-3cm, elliptic or ovate, the apex rounded or retuse, the margin entire, broadly recurved, the base broadly to narrowly tapering; upper surface at first with small silvery scales, quickly glabrescent, the midrib impressed, lateral veins 3-4 pairs rather obscure, lower surface with the midrib raised throughout its length, the laterals smooth, scales rather sparse and small, deeply lobed and with small centres. Flowers 3-7 per umbel, hanging vertically or nearly vertically down; calyx a low angular slightly scaly disc; corolla pink or pinkish violet, long cylindrical, only slightly curved 5-7.5 × 2.7-3.5cm, minutely scaly outside; stamens 10, spreading in the mouth of the flower on the lower side; ovary hairy and with rather obscure scales, style glabrous. H1b. Borneo (Sabah, Kinabalu and the Crocker Range), 1,100-1,800m.

A beautiful and easily grown species with the longest pendent flowers of any Vireya. Previously confused with *R. longiflorum* (see notes under that species for distinctions).

R. PURPUREIFLORUM J.J.SM. - SUBSECT. VIREYA

Shrub to 0.5m, epiphytic; young stems moderately covered with brown stellate scales at first. Leaves 2.7-7 × 0.4-1cm, linear-lanceolate, the apex obtuse to subacute, the margin flat, the base narrowly tapering; upper surface at first scaly but quickly glabrescent, the midrib impressed above, lateral veins obscure; lower surface with the midrib strongly raised beneath, lateral veins obscure, scales moderately to deeply lobed, moderately dense and slightly impressed. Flowers 2-4 per umbel, hanging; calyx a low scaly, slightly lobed disc; corolla reddish purple to pale pink, tubular, somewhat zygomorphic, 2.7-3.2 × 2-2.4cm, glabrous or slightly scaly outside; stamens 10, rather unequal and grouped on the upper side of the flower; ovary densely scaly, style glabrous. H1b. West New Guinea (Perameles and Schrader Mts), 1,100-2,200m.

Introduced by Professor Sleumer and one of his narrow leafed species in series *Stenophylla* but doubtfully still in cultivation.

R. QUADRASIANUM VIDAL - SUBSECT. PSEUDOVIREYA
Shrub or small tree to 6m, terrestrial, sometimes epiphytic; young stems finely scaly and minutely white-hairy. Leaves 1.5-3.5 × 0.5-1.3cm, narrowly elliptic, elliptic, obovate or spathulate, the apex obtuse, rounded, often retuse, the margin strongly reflexed sometimes almost revolute, the base narrowly to broadly tapering; upper surface finely silvery or brown-scaly, the midrib impressed, the laterals 1-3 pairs mostly obscure; lower surface with the midrib strongly, weakly or hardly raised, the laterals smooth, the scales well spaced, circular or slightly lobed with small to large centres. Flowers 1-4 per umbel, half hanging to vertically hanging; calyx a low scaly and/or hairy disc; corolla red, cylindrical, 1.3-2.5 × 0.8-1.4cm, usually scaly and laxly hairy outside, sometimes scaly only; stamens 10, mostly irregularly arranged in the mouth of the flower sometimes roughly grouped on the lower side; ovary scaly only, the style glabrous. H1b. Philippines (widespread) possibly also in Selebes, 1,000-2,500m.

Bornean specimens are now all attributable to other species (see *Rhododendrons of Sabah* 1988, G. Argent, A. Lamb, A. Phillipps & S. Collenette, Sabah Parks Publication No. 8). A variable species with different forms coming from the different mountain groups in the Philippines, the most commonly cultivated form is var. *rosmarinifolium* (Vidal) Copel.f. with elongate-obovate leaves, with pedicels pubescent and scaly and corolla up to 1.5cm long.

R. RARILEPIDOTUM J.J.SM. - SUBSECT. VIREYA
Tree or shrub to 4m, terrestrial; young stems at first covered in brown scales later glabrous. Leaves 5-9 × 1.8-3.5cm, elliptic, the apex narrowly to broadly acute, the margin flat, the base narrowly tapering; upper surface, sparsely scaly initially, soon glabrous, midrib slightly raised above, lateral veins 6-12 pairs raised, rather obscure; lower surface with the midrib slightly raised, the laterals very obscure, scales fairly dense, brown, circular to lobed and with small centres. Flowers 10-18 per umbel, more or less horizontal; calyx a low scaly ring; corolla bright orange to red often with a darker red centre, sweetly scented, shortly funnel-shaped, 2.5-3.5 × 4-5cm, glabrous or very sparsely scaly outside; stamens 10, rather irregular, generally distributed around the lower 2/3 of the mouth of the flower; ovary glabrous or with a very few scales, style glabrous. H1b. Indonesia (Northern Sumatra), 1000-2500m.

A lovely and vigorous species in cultivation.

R. RARUM SCHLTR. - SUBSECT. PHAEOVIREYA
Delicate shrub up to 1m, epiphytic, young stems densely brown-scaly at first, quickly glabrescent. Leaves 2-5.5 × 0.5-1.2cm, narrowly elliptic to sublinear, the apex acute although with the very tip rounded, margin narrowly cartilaginous, slightly irregular, flat to slightly recurved, the base broadly tapering to rounded; upper sur-

face minutely brown-scaly at first, quickly glabrous, midrib impressed, lateral veins obscure; lower surface with the midrib raised, lateral veins obscure, scales brown, well spaced at maturity, dendroid and easily removed but leaving the protruding epidermal bases. Flowers 1-4 per umbel, half hanging to hanging; calyx a low brown-scaly ring; corolla red, curved-cylindrical, 2.5-3.5 × 2-2.7cm, finely but densely scaly outside; stamens 10, grouped in the upper side of the mouth of the flower; ovary densely stellate-scaly, style scaly in the lower third or half, above this with simple hairs and finally near the top glabrous. H1b. Papua New Guinea (Western and Eastern Highlands Provinces), 1,500-3,400m.

Its prostrate to hanging habit make it an ideal species for hanging baskets and it is the parent of a number of lovely hybrids which can similarly be displayed.

R. RETIVENIUM SLEUMER - SUBSECT. VIREYA
Shrub to 3m, usually terrestrial; young stems green or reddish, covered in flat substellate scales. Leaves 11-16 × 3-5cm, narrowly elliptic, the apex acute, the margin more or less flat, the base narrowly tapering; upper surface at first silvery scaly, quickly glabrescent, the midrib raised near the base and impressed in the upper part, lateral veins 12-18 pairs, slightly raised; lower surface with the midrib raised below, lateral veins somewhat raised, with small, widely distributed, lobed, scales with small centres. Flowers 4-7 per umbel, more or less horizontally held; calyx a low scaly ring; corolla yellow or yellow flushed orange, usually sweetly scented, funnel-shaped, 3-6.5 × 3.5-7.5cm, with a few scattered scales outside; stamens 10, loosely and irregularly arranged on the lower side of the mouth; ovary very finely hairy (when viewed with a strong lens) and with a very few scales, style glabrous or hairy at the very base. H1b. Sabah (Mt Kinabalu and Mt Alab), 2,000-2,700m.

R. RETUSUM (BLUME) BENN. - SUBSECT. PSEUDOVIREYA
Shrub or small tree, generally to 2m, exceptionally to 7m, usually terrestrial, young stems at first covered in raised discoid scales, later rough with the persistent tubercular scale bases. Leaves 2-4 × 1-2cm, elliptic, broadly elliptic or obovate, the apex broadly pointed, rounded or retuse, the margin slightly recurved to strongly and broadly turned down to give the leaf a reverse channelled appearance, the base broadly tapering; upper surface at first finely set with golden discoid scales, later glabrous, midrib narrowly impressed, lateral veins 2-4 pairs hardly impressed, often obscure; lower surface with the midrib slightly raised, lateral veins very slightly raised, rather obscure, scales well spaced, discoid with broad centres. Flowers 2-10 per umbel, from terminal and lateral buds, erect to half hanging; calyx a low scaly and hairy ring; corolla red, cylindrical to narrowly funnel-shaped, 1.6-2.5 × 1-1.5cm, sparsely scaly and hairy outside; stamens 10, more or less evenly distributed around the mouth; ovary densely scaly but without simple hairs, style with a few scales at the very base but otherwise glabrous. H1b. Indonesia (Sumatra and Java), 1,300-3,400m.

This species has rather small but attractive bright red flowers produced in profusion over quite a long season as the apical buds tend to open first, followed by laterals.

R. RHODOLEUCUM SLEUMER - SUBSECT. SOLENOVIREYA
Erect shrub to 4m usually terrestrial, young stems with scattered scales at first. Leaves 3-7 × 2-6cm, elliptic, broadly elliptic or slightly obovate-elliptic, the apex shortly and broadly attenuate to a mostly obtuse point, occasionally rounded, the margin entire and flat, the base strongly to weakly cordate; the upper surface at first with rather smooth silvery scales, quickly glabrescent, the midrib slightly impressed above, widening abruptly to the petiole

near the base, the laterals 6-8 irregular pairs with other smaller but distinct ones between, all slightly raised; the lower surface with the midrib only very slightly raised but the laterals finely but distinctly so, scales rather widely spaced, small, flat and irregularly lobed. Flowers 4-6 per umbel, half hanging; calyx indistinctly five-lobed, slightly scaly; corolla mostly red at the base, fading to pink upwards and with white lobes but quite variable in the intensity of the pigmentation, beautifully scented, long-tubular, with a straight or more usually slightly curved tube, 6-8 × 2.5-3.5cm, slightly scaly outside; stamens 10, rather irregularly exserted from the mouth; ovary densely covered with appressed hairs and scales, the style also hairy and scaly in the lower ⅔. H1b. Papua New Guinea (Maneau Range in the Milne Bay Province), 2,200-2,800m.

See remarks under *R. tuba* for differences between this species and the most closely related ones.

R. ROBINSONII RIDL. - SUBSECT. VIREYA
Shrub to 2.5m, usually epiphytic, young stems at first finely scaly, quickly glabrescent. Leaves 8-16 × 4-6.5cm, elliptic or broadly elliptic occasionally lanceolate, the apex acute, often acuminate, the margin entire, slightly revolute, the base broadly to narrowly tapering, sometimes slightly asymmetric; the upper surface with a strongly raised midrib in the basal half, the laterals 5-10 pairs only slightly raised or smooth, very finely scaly at first, quickly glabrescent; the lower surface with the midrib raised throughout its length, the laterals rather obscure, scales very small, brown, rounded to lobed. Umbels 4-12 flowered, erect to half-hanging; calyx disc-shaped sometimes with low lobes, almost glabrous; corolla yellow variably and sometimes heavily flushed orange, funnel-shaped, 3-3.5 × 3-3.5cm, glabrous outside; stamens 10, somewhat irregularly arranged in the mouth of the flower; ovary glabrous, or with a few scales, the style completely glabrous. H1b.

West Malaysia (from Perak to Selangor and in the Taiping Hills), 1,000-1,800m.

Distinguished from most forms of the very similar *R. brookeanum* by its almost glabrous ovary and glabrous filaments.

R. RUBINEIFLORUM CRAVEN - SUBSECT. VIREYA
Shrub to 0.2m, epiphytic or creeping on peaty banks, young stems densely rough scaly the scales fairly persistent. Leaves 0.5-1 × 0.2-0.5cm, ovate to elliptic, broadly elliptic, to occasionally subcircular the apex acute to obtuse, rarely rounded, often sub-acuminate, the margin recurved, rather cartilaginous, often erose, subserrate in the upper part, the base tapering to rounded; upper surface with a slightly impressed midrib near the base, or quite smooth, the laterals obscure, with a few small scales on the upper surfaces at first but quickly glabrescent; below the midrib slightly raised near the base, the laterals obscure, scales well spaced, brown, irregularly lobed to sub-entire. Flowers solitary, hanging; calyx a low scaly ring; corolla red, campanulate, 2-2.5 × 2.5-3cm, conspicuously scaly on the tube outside; stamens 10, evenly arranged around the mouth of the flower; ovary densely hairy and scaly, style at the base hairy and scaly, glabrous in the upper half. H1b. Widespread in Papua New Guinea, not yet recorded from Irian Jaya, 2,600-3,400m.

A pretty species which since its recognition and introduction into cultivation has been used a great deal as a parent for hybridizing. Previously included within *R. anagalliflorum* q.v. but *R. rubineiflorum* may be distinguished by its much broader more open flowers which are solidly coloured red or pink.

R. RUGOSUM LOW EX HOOK.F. - SUBSECT. VIREYA
Shrub or small tree to 8m, mostly terrestrial but also found epiphytically; young stems rather scabrid at first with brown scales that quickly fall. Leaves 6-10 × 3-5.5cm, ovate or broadly to narrowly ellip-

tic often strongly concave, the apex broadly pointed or shortly acuminate, the margin entire and slightly reflexed, the base broadly cuneate to rounded; upper surface with strongly impressed midrib throughout its length and about 8 pairs of strongly impressed laterals, at first brown-scaly above but very quickly glabrescent; below all veins distinct and strongly raised, with a moderately dense covering of dendroid brown scales which fall off at a touch and in old leaves may only be found in protected corners. Umbels 8-14 flowered, the flowers hanging or half hanging; calyx a low scaly and hairy ring; corolla pink to purplish pink (rarely reported as red), tubular campanulate, 2.5-3.5 × 2.5-3cm, with fine white hairs on the tube and hairs and scales on the lobes, the scales sometimes grouped at the base of the lobes; stamens 10, irregularly arranged but predominantly on the lower side of the mouth; ovary densely white-hairy and with some silvery scales, style glabrous. H1b. Malaysia (Sabah and N Sarawak?), 2,000-3,500m.

Often confused with *R. acuminatum* q.v. It is a most attractive plant with glowing pink flowers.

R. SANTAPAUI SASTRY ET AL. - SUBSECT. PSEUDOVIREYA
Shrub to 1.5m, epiphytic; young stems moderately densely brown-scaly, becoming glabrescent. Leaves 2.5-4.5 × 1-1.8cm, narrowly obovate to elliptic, the apex acute to obtuse, somewhat downturned and minutely mucronate by a small protruding gland, margin flat or slightly revolute, the base narrowly tapering, upper surface with the midrib impressed to the apex, laterals 2-4 pairs, slightly impressed, the scales sparse, brown, the older surfaces glabrescent; lower surface with the midrib shallowly raised, the laterals obscure, scales moderately spaced, circular to slightly lobed, with a fairly broad flange and rather small centres. Flowers 1-4 per umbel, horizontal to half-hanging; calyx a low somewhat lobed, scaly disc; corolla white, short campanulate, 1-1.5 ×

1.5-2cm, sparsely scaly outside; stamens 10, protruding in a more or less regular group from the mouth; ovary densely silvery scaly, style glabrous. H2-3? India (NEFA, Subansiri District), 1,500-2,300m.

A pretty species now well established and widespread in cultivation.

R. SAXIFRAGOIDES J.J.SM. - SUBSECT. VIREYA
Dense cushion forming shrub to 0.25m, terrestrial; young stems with a few scales. Leaves 1.6-5.5 × 0.5-1cm, linear-lanceolate or oblanceolate, the apex acute to obtuse, often shortly acuminate or apiculate, the margin flat or revolute, the base narrowly tapering; upper surface with the midrib impressed above, laterals 2-3 pairs, slightly impressed, often obscure, with a few sparse scales at first, quickly glabrescent; lower surface with the midrib slightly raised, laterals mostly obscure, scales small, well spaced, deeply or shallowly lobed and slightly impressed. Flowers mostly solitary, occasionally in pairs, semi-erect to half-hanging (the ovaries becoming erect after the corollas wither); calyx a low wavy disc often fringed with hairs; corolla red to pink, tubular-cylindrical, somewhat curved and expanded near the mouth, 2.5-3 × 1.5-2.5cm, scaly on the tube outside; stamens 10, clustered on the upper side of the mouth; ovary hairy and obscurely scaly, style hairy at the base, glabrous above. H1b. New Guinea (widespread along the Main Range), 3,200-4,000m.

The dense cushion-forming habit of this species will distinguish it from all others but it is slow and difficult to cultivate although it can be found in collections in various parts of the world. Os Blumhardt working in New Zealand has produced some wonderful hybrids using this species to compact plants with a rather straggly habit and these are also now very widespread.

R. SAYERI SLEUMER - SUBSECT. VIREYA
Shrub to 2m, terrestrial or epiphytic, young stems at first densely brown-scaly,

becoming smooth. Leaves 4-7 × 2-4cm, elliptic, broadly elliptic or obovate-elliptic, the apex obtuse or rounded, the margin entire and revolute, the base broadly to narrowly tapering; the upper surface at first scaly, quickly glabrescent, the midrib narrowly impressed the lateral veins 6-8 pairs smooth, often rather obscure; underside densely to sparsely red-brown scaly, the scales deeply to finely lobed with small dark centres. Flowers 1-4 per umbel, horizontal to hanging; calyx an irregularly 5-lobed scaly disc; corolla pink to red, tubular-funnel-shaped, curved, 4-6 × 1.5-2.5cm, finely stellate-scaly outside; stamens 10, on the upper side of the mouth, ovary densely stellate-scaly, the style scaly in the lower ⅓, glabrous above. H1b. Papua New Guinea (Central and Enga Provinces), 1,700-2,200m.

R. SCABRIDIBRACTEUM SLEUMER - SUBSECT. VIREYA
Shrub or tree reported up to 12m, young stems at first quite densely brown-scaly but quickly becoming glabrescent. Leaves 6.5-12 × 2-5cm, elliptic to sub-obovate, the apex obtuse, rounded or emarginate, sometimes acute by a short somewhat deflexed mucro, the margin flat to slightly revolute, the base broadly tapering to almost rounded; the upper surface at first finely brown-scaly, the scales becoming silver before disappearing, the midrib impressed throughout its length and grooved in the basal part, lateral veins 9-12 pairs, very slightly impressed; underside with the midrib strongly raised throughout its length, the laterals only slightly raised; scales fairly dense, mostly silvery or pale brown, with a few dark brown ones, scattered rather evenly among them, lobed to substellate and slightly impressed. Flowers 6-12 per umbel at first semi-erect, later horizontal or hanging; calyx brown-scaly, a 5-lobed disc; corolla red or dark pink, tubular-funnel-shaped but distinctly curved, 6-7.5 × 4-5cm, finely but distinctly brown-scaly on the tube outside; stamens 10, clustered on the upper side of the mouth of the flower;

ovary covered with white or yellowish hairs which tend to obscure scales on the surface, style both hairy and scaly almost to the stigma. H1b. Papua New Guinea, 1,900-2,400m.

A striking species named from the covering of scabrid yellowish subappressed hairs on the floral bracts which tend to persist around the pedicels when the flowers first open.

R. SCHODDEI SLEUMER - SUBSECT. PHAEOVIREYA
Shrub to 2m, terrestrial, young stems at first densely covered with bright brown stellate scales. Leaves 3-6 × 1.5-2.3cm, ovate to ovate-elliptic, the apex acute, the margin entire, narrowly but distinctly revolute, the base broadly tapering to rounded; upper surface densely scaly at first but quickly glabrescent, midrib impressed, lateral veins 6-8 pairs slightly impressed or obscure; underside with the midrib strongly raised throughout its length, the laterals obscure, scales brown, stellate-dendroid, moderately dense, from small epidermal tubercles. Flowers 1-3 per umbel, half-hanging to hanging; calyx a low lobed, densely scaly disc; corolla deep pink, broadly tubular, slightly curved, 2.6-3 × 1.5-2.5cm, densely scaly outside; stamens 10, clustered on the upper side of the mouth; ovary densely scaly and hairy, the style hairy in the basal ½, glabrous above. H1b. Papua New Guinea (Western Highlands Province), 2,600m.

R. SEARLEANUM SLEUMER - SUBSECT. SOLENOVIREYA
Shrub to 4m, terrestrial, young stems densely scaly at first. Leaves 8-11 × 5-8cm, broadly elliptic, the apex obtusely pointed to rounded, the margin entire, flat or slightly revolute, the base broadly tapering to rounded; upper surface finely scaly at first, quickly glabrescent, the midrib raised for about half its length and grooved, laterals 5-6 pairs very slightly raised or smooth, the largest of them grooved; underside with the midrib raised for most of its length. the laterals slightly

raised, the scales well spaced almost circular, quite variable in size with small centres and impressed. Flowers 11-16 per umbel, more or less horizontally disposed; calyx a low slightly scaly ring; corolla pale pink, slightly darker at the mouth, beautifully and powerfully scented, trumpet-shaped with a straight tube, 10-12.5 × 4.5-6cm, laxly scaly outside; stamens 10, rather loosely clustered on the lower side of the mouth; ovary densely scaly and with yellowish hairs, style densely hairy and scaly at the base, gradually becoming less so until the ultimate 1.5cm is glabrous. H1b. Papua New Guinea (Eastern Highlands Province near Gumine, also reported from Mt Digini in the Kubor Range), 2,100-2,200m.

A magnificent species which is very poorly known in the wild but well known in cultivation since its original and only introduction by Mr L.K. Searle in 1973.

R. SESSILIFOLIUM J.J.SM. - SUBSECT. VIREYA
Shrub to 3m, usually terrestrial, young stems finely and smoothly, stellate-brown-scaly, becoming glabrescent. Leaves 8-16 × 2.5-5cm, lanceolate to elliptic, the apex broadly to narrowly acute, sometimes abruptly acuminate, the margin mostly flat but rather wavy, the base truncate to subauriculate strongly rugose from the very short petiole; upper surface very finely scaly at first, soon glabrous, the midrib strongly raised for just over half its length, laterals 10-13 pairs, smooth or with the lamina sulcate between the veins near the middle of the leaf; underside with the midrib flat or only slightly raised, the laterals rather obscure, not raised at all; scales rather pale brown to translucent, lobed and impressed. Flowers 4-10 per umbel, erect to half hanging; calyx a low slightly angled disc; corolla bright yellow, broadly funnel-shaped, 2.5-3 × 3.5-5.5cm, glabrous outside; stamens 10, rather irregular but mostly disposed in the lower ⅔ of the mouth of the flower; ovary with a few obscure scales, minutely papillose, style glabrous. H1a-b. Indonesia, (Sumatra),

1,100-2,000m.

Delightful bright yellow flowers, very freely produced, the forms in cultivation appreciate a little more heat than most of the Vireyas.

R. × SHEILAE (SLEUMER)ARGENT (*R. ABI-ETIFOLIUM* SLEUMER × *R. BUXIFOLIUM* LOW EX HOOKER F.) - SUBSECT. VIREYA
Shrub to 2m, terrestrial; stems finely scaly at first. Leaves 1.5-4 × 0.4-1.3cm, narrowly elliptic, the apex rounded or slightly retuse, the margin reflexed and minutely crenulate, the base narrowly tapering; upper surface finely scaly at first but quickly glabrescent, midrib impressed, lateral veins 4-5 pairs, inconspicuous; lower surface with the midrib raised, lateral veins inconspicuous. Flowers 3-6 per umbel, horizontal to half-hanging; calyx a low scaly ring; corolla reddish purple, 2.5-3.2 × 1.7-2.4cm, sparsely scaly and finely white-hairy outside; stamens 10 distributed around the mouth of the flower; ovary densely white-hairy and obscurely scaly, style glabrous. H1b. Sabah (E Malaysia) Kinabalu, east ridge, 3,200-3,700m.

Sometimes seen in lists as a species this natural hybrid is quite variable. It is a very attractive plant with the young leaves flushing red and is far more vigorous and easy to cultivate than either of its parents.

R. sleumeri A. Gilli is a synonym of **R. blackii** Sleumer Subsect. Vireya.

R. SOLITARIUM SLEUMER - SUBSECT. PHAEOVIREYA
Shrub to 2m, mostly terrestrial, young stems at first densely brown-scaly and minutely hairy. Leaves 8-11 × 3-5.5cm, elliptic or slightly obovate-elliptic, the apex rounded to broadly obtuse, sometimes with a very slightly protruding apical gland, margin slightly revolute and narrowly cartilaginous, the base broadly tapering to rounded; upper surface at first densely brown-scaly but quickly becoming glabrescent, midrib slightly raised in

the basal half, impressed above, lateral veins 7-10 pairs markedly impressed as also the finer veins to give a bullate surface with clear reticulation; under surface with the midrib and laterals very strongly raised, densely brown-scaly at first with very varied dendroid scales from epidermal tubercles but the scales all easily removed at a touch. Flowers 4-6 per umbel, horizontal to half-hanging; calyx a low angled somewhat scaly disc but sometimes with elongate lobes; corolla pure white, scented, trumpet-shaped with a slightly curved tube, 5-7 × 2-3cm, slightly scaly outside; stamens 10, exserted from the mouth in a central group but falling to the lower side of the mouth as the corolla ages; ovary densely covered with hairs and scales, style hairy and scaly in the basal ¾, glabrous above. H1b. Papua New Guinea (Morobe Province, Mt Kaindi), 1,700-2,000m.

This species with its bullate, strongly reticulate leaves and dark brown dendroid scales is very distinct and most attractive. It is unlikely to be confused with any other although the flowers might suggest affinities in Subsect. Solenovireya.

R. SOROR IUM SLEUMER - SUBSECT. PSEUDOVIREYA
Shrub to 2m, terrestrial, young stems covered in small stalkless scales, quickly glabrescent, sometimes rough from raised leaf scars but not from scale bases. Leaves 2.5-4.5 × 1-2cm, obovate with an emarginate apex in which lies a distinct apical gland, margin slightly recurved, somewhat cartilaginous, the base narrowly tapering; upper surface finely scaly at first, quickly glabrescent, the midrib impressed, laterals 1-3 pairs, slightly impressed; underside with the midrib slightly raised, the laterals slightly raised or obscure, the scales widely spaced, variable, slightly depressed, the smaller circular and pale brown, the larger darker brown and clearly lobed. Flowers solitary or occasionally paired, horizontal to half-hanging; calyx a low ring; corolla yellow, campanulate 1-1.5 × 0.8-1.4cm, densely

scaly outside; stamens 10, dimorphic, arranged all round the mouth of the corolla; ovary densely scaly, style glabrous. H1b. Tonkin, Lao Kay, 1,400-1,700m.

Widely distributed and in many collections from recent wild seed exchanges but not yet well known as most plants have yet to reach flowering size.

R. STAPFIANUM HEMSL. EX PRAIN - SUBSECT. SOLENOVIREYA
Shrub to 1m, usually epiphytic; young twigs rounded with white spreading hairs and brown scales. Leaves 4.5-5.8 × 1.2-2cm, elliptic or narrowly elliptic, the apex obtuse to rounded, the margin entire and strongly revolute, the base rounded or broadly tapering; the upper surface hairy or scaly becoming glabrescent, the midrib raised above at the base of the leaf but then impressed for the reminder of its length, lateral veins hardly visible; the lower surface with the midrib slightly raised, the laterals obscure, with a distinct indumentum of erect, simple, white hairs and brown stellate to subdendroid scales from a smooth surface. Flowers 7-18 per umbel, erect to horizontal; calyx a low hairy ring; corolla white, sometimes sweetly scented, trumpet-shaped, 4.5-5.5 × 2-2.5cm, rather densely hairy outside; stamens 10, irregularly spreading round the mouth of the flower; ovary densely hairy and with silvery scales, the style hairy and with silvery scales to near the top. H1b. Borneo (Sabah, N Sarawak and Kalimantan), 900-1,550m.

First described as *R. lacteum* Stapf but this name was already in use for the Chinese species of this name.

R. STENOPHYLLUM HOOK.F. EX STAPF - SUBSECT. VIREYA
Shrub to 3m, usually terrestrial; young stems smooth and very finely scaly. Leaves 4-7 × 0.14-0.5cm, linear, the apex acute, the margin entire and flat, the base narrowly tapering; upper surface with small fine scales at first quickly becoming glabrescent, midrib a little impressed above, the lateral veins up to 7 pairs but

obscure; lower surface with the midrib smooth and laterals obscure, the scales sparsely distributed, substellate with small centres. Flowers 1-5 per umbel, held horizontally or half hanging; calyx a low scaly ring; corolla opening orange but turning red with age, campanulate, 2.5-3.5 × 3-4.5cm, glabrous outside; stamens 10, slightly dimorphic, arranged all round the mouth of the flower; ovary densely white hairy, style glabrous. H1b. Sabah, Brunei and Northern Sarawak, 1,500-2,400m.

This species with its bizarre leaves is relatively easy to cultivate, it occurs in two distinct subspecific forms: subsp. *stenophyllum* is endemic to Mt Kinabalu and has leaves less than 25× as long as wide (2.5-6mm wide); subsp. *angustifolium* is of much wider distribution in the wild and has leaves more than 30× as long as wide (1.4-2.2mm wide).

R. STEVENSIANUM SLEUMER - SUBSECT. VIREYA

Shrub to 0.75m, epiphytic; young stems at first rather densely covered in pale brown scales, some distinctly stalked and also with a fine indumentum of short hairs. Leaves 3-4.5 × 2-3.5cm, ovate or broadly-ovate, the apex obtuse, somewhat decurved, the margin slightly recurved, the base cordate; upper surface at first silvery scaly, quickly glabrescent, the midrib finely impressed for most of its length, laterals 4-6 pairs smooth or very slightly raised or impressed; the lower surface with the midrib strongly raised in the lower half, the laterals smooth, scales moderately dense, brown, irregularly lobed and in shallow depressions. Flowers 2-3 per umbel, semi-erect to half-hanging; calyx a hairy and scaly irregularly lobed disc; corolla pink sometimes with a bluish purple tinge, cylindrical, straight or slightly curved, 2-2.5 × 2.5-3cm, rather sparsely scaly and hairy outside; stamens 10, slightly dimorphic at first clustered in the centre of the flower, later spreading back against the lobes; ovary silvery hairy and scaly, style hairy in the lower half, glabrous above. H1b. Papua New Guinea

(Eastern Highlands Province, Mt Michael, and near Obura, Simbu [Chimbu] Province, Porul Range), 2,000-2,100m.

R. SUAVEOLENS SLEUMER - SUBSECT. SOLENOVIREYA

Shrub to 3m, terrestrial or epiphytic; young stems smooth with only very inconspicuous scales. Leaves 6-10 × 3.5-7cm, elliptic, the apex rounded or sometimes broadly pointed, margin flat with a translucent edge, base cordate to rounded; upper surface green with inconspicuous scales, the midrib weakly channelled for most of its length otherwise smooth, with a red pigmented triangular area at the base, the 5-7 pairs of lateral veins rather indistinct; the lower surface with the midrib weakly raised in the lower third, all other veins obscure, scales minute, widely spaced, brown and deeply lobed. Flowers 14-20 per umbel, erect to horizontal in disposition; calyx circular with a red edge; corolla white or pink (forma *roseum*) often but not always sweetly scented, trumpet-shaped, 4.5-5.5 × 1.5-2.5cm glabrous outside; stamens 10, clustered in the mouth; ovary densely covered in silvery scales and erect white hairs, style with scattered scales at the base and white hairs in approximately the basal half. H1b. Malaysia (Sabah, Kinabalu and the Crocker Range south to Mt Lotung), 1,200-1,700m.

This very attractive species although described by Professor Sleumer was later reduced by him to synonymy with *R. orbiculatum*. David Hunt at Kew clearly established their distinctness, this species having leaves about twice as long as wide and much narrower flowers.

R. SUMATRANUM MERR. - SUBSECT. VIREYA

Shrub to 3m, terrestrial or occasionally epiphytic; young stems covered with substellate scales but quickly glabrescent. Leaves 2.5-8.5 × 1.5-4cm, mostly elliptic or obovate-elliptic, the apex obtuse to rounded, margin flat or slightly recurved, the base broadly tapering; upper surface at first finely brown-scaly, quickly glabrescent, midrib impressed, laterals 4-7 pairs more or less smooth; lower surface with the midrib raised for most of its length, the laterals flat, moderately densely covered in small brown mostly circular scales which are slightly impressed in shallow pits. Flowers 1-6 per umbel, horizontal to half-hanging; calyx a densely scaly and sparsely hairy disc; corolla red or reddish orange, narrowly funnel-shaped, 2-3 × 1.5-2cm, sparsely scaly and hairy outside; stamens 10, evenly distributed around the mouth; ovary densely scaly, style glabrous. H1b. Northern Sumatra, 1,800-2,700m.

This species hybridizes in the wild with *R. rarilepidotum* and *R. retusum* to give larger and smaller flowered forms respectively.

R. SUPERBUM SLEUMER - SUBSECT. PHAEOVIREYA

Shrub or small tree to 6m, mostly epiphytic but terrestrial in open situations; young stems densely brown-stellate-scaly but quickly glabrescent. Leaves 8-12 × 4.5-8cm, broadly elliptic to sub-ovate or sub-obovate, the apex broadly acute to obtuse, occasionally shortly acuminate, the margin slightly recurved, the base broadly tapering, rounded to rarely subcordate; the upper surface at first with brown dendroid scales, quickly glabrescent leaving an almost smooth surface, midrib raised in the lower half to one third and grooved, slightly impressed in the upper part, lateral veins 5-8 pairs, smooth and rather obscure; lower surface with the midrib raised for most of its length, the laterals smooth and often obscure, at first fairly densely covered in brown dendroid scales from rather low epidermal tubercles. Flowers 3-5 per umbel, horizontal to half-hanging; calyx a low, lobed, densely scaly disc; corolla white, cream, or various shades of pink, often with darker pink marks at the base of the lobes, deliciously and powerfully carnation scented, funnel-shaped or very broadly trumpet-shaped, the lobes usually 6-7, occasionally 5, 5-14 ×

9-12cm, sparsely scaly outside; stamens twice the number of corolla lobes, mostly scattered round the basal ⅔ of the mouth of the flower; ovary densely covered with reddish brown deeply lobed scales, the style scaly in the basal ¼ or completely glabrous. H1b. Papua New Guinea (widespread on the main ranges), 1,500-3,000m.

One of the most attractive species in the section, it is very close to *R. hellwigii* with which it probably hybridizes in the wild and the darker pink forms may be this hybrid. This species generally has a straight corolla tube and the stamens are less densely clustered than in *R hellwigii*, the nearly glabrous style separates this species from *R. konori*.

R. taiwanianum Ying - is considered a synonym of **R. kawakamii** Hayata (Subsect. Pseudovireya).

R. TUBA SLEUMER - SUBSECT. SOLENOVIREYA

Shrub to 5m, usually terrestrial, young stems sparsely scaly. Leaves 4-9 × 2.5-5cm, elliptic to broadly elliptic, the apex broadly acute often somewhat acuminate, the margin flat, narrowly cartilaginous in the upper part, the base truncate or rounded occasionally weakly cordate; the upper surface at first scaly but quickly becoming glabrescent, the midrib depressed above, grooved near the base, lateral veins 6-8 pairs slightly depressed; lower surface with the midrib broadly raised beneath, the laterals smooth or very slightly raised, scales moderately dense and persistent, substellately lobed, brown, the centres somewhat impressed. Flowers 4-7 per umbel, horizontal to half-hanging; calyx variable from a low almost glabrous disc to occasionally having long laciniate lobes; corolla white with a pink tube, trumpet-shaped but somewhat curved, 6.5-9 × 2-3cm, obscurely scaly outside; stamens 10, rather unequal and grouped in the mouth of the flower; ovary both hairy and scaly, style hairy and scaly in the lower half. H1b. Papua New Guinea, SE, (Mt Dayman), 2,500-2,700m.

Very similar to *R. rhodoleucum* from which it is distinguished by its non or hardly cordate leaves, a longer petiole and smaller anthers (petioles 2-4mm instead of 0-1mm in *R. rhodoleucum* and anthers up to 2.5 v. more than 3.5mm in *R. rhodoleucum*). It is also very similar to *R. armitii* which is distinguished by its larger leaves and much longer petioles, more than 6mm long.

R. VACCINIOIDES HOOK.F. - SUBSECT. PSEUDOVIREYA
Shrub to 1m, terrestrial or epiphytic, young stems densely covered with brown scales on prominent stalks, later scabrid by the persistent stalks alone. Leaves 1.2-2.2 × 0.4-1cm, spathulate to elliptic, the apex obtuse, rounded or emarginate with a prominent yellowish apical gland, the margin flat or very slightly reflexed the base narrowly to broadly wedge-shaped; the upper surface with well spaced pale brown scales, midrib strongly impressed above, lateral veins obscure or traces of 1-3 pairs; lower surface with the midrib slightly raised, the laterals obscure, scales disk-shaped to lobed, dark brown, distinct and well spaced. Flowers solitary, rarely up to 4 together, more or less horizontal; calyx of 5 rather long scaly lobes; corolla white with a tinge of pink, sub-urceolate or shortly cylindrical with the long lobes reflexing back against the tube, 0.7-8 × 0.9-1.1cm, scaly outside; stamens 10, protruding in a rather irregular mass from the mouth; ovary densely silvery scaly, style glabrous, pink. H1b-2. Nepal, India (Sikkim and Assam Sirhoi), China (Yunnan, Tibet [Eastern]), Bhutan, Burma (upper), 1,700-4,200m.

A delicate species disliking the high temperatures of summer which makes it a temperamental plant to keep on a long term basis. *R. vaccinoides* includes *R. sino-vaccinioides* Balf.f. which only differs in having larger leaves and a range of inter-mediates occur.

R. vandeursenii Sleumer - is a synonym of **R. vitis-idaea** Sleumer (Subsect. Vireya).

R. VERSTEEGII J.J.SM. - SUBSECT. ALBOVIREYA
Shrub to 1m, terrestrial; young stems densely scaly but quickly becoming glabrescent and smooth. Leaves 1-4 × 0.6-2cm, obovate to elliptic, the apex obtuse to rounded, the margin flat, often minutely crenulate especially towards the apex, base tapering; upper surface densely silvery scaly, only slowly glabrescent, midrib slightly impressed above, lateral veins 3-4 pairs also slightly impressed or obscure; lower surface with the midrib broad and strongly raised at the base, disappearing upwards before the apex, lateral veins rather obscure, densely scaly with over-lapping silvery scales. Flowers 2-5 per umbel, mostly half-hanging; calyx a densely scaly, lobed disc; corolla red and yellow in an irregular pattern, funnel-shaped, 2.5-4 × 3-4cm, rather densely scaly outside; stamens 10, scattered around the mouth of the flower; ovary densely scaly and hairy, the style densely scaly and hairy in the lower ⅕ to ¾, glabrous near the top. H1b. New Guinea (Irian Jaya Mt Trikora [Wilhelmina] and Lake Habbema region), 3,200-4,000m.

Recorded as being in cultivation but undoubtedly difficult and probably misidentified. The extraordinary bicoloured flowers would make it unmistakable when in flower.

R. VITIS-IDAEA SLEUMER - SUBSECT. VIREYA
Erect shrub up to 2m, mostly terrestrial; young stems at first covered with stalked stellate scales which soon disappear to leave a rough warty surface. Leaves 0.8-5 × 0.5-2.5cm, obovate to elliptic, the apex obtuse, rounded to retuse, the margin strongly recurved, the base tapering; upper surface at first with small silvery scales, quickly glabrescent, the midrib impressed, the laterals 3-5 pairs smooth or very slightly impressed; lower surface with the midrib raised throughout its length, laterals slightly raised or obscure, scales well spaced, brown, circular to sub-stellate, conspicuous against the pale sur-

face of the leaf. Flowers mostly solitary occasionally in pairs, pendent; calyx a low scaly and slightly hairy ring; corolla red, cylindrical, sometimes slightly curved, 2-5 × 1.8-2.5cm, finely silvery scaly and inconspicuously white-hairy outside; stamens 10, clustered on the lower side of the mouth; ovary densely white-hairy and scaly, style hairy in the basal half, glabrous above. H1b. Papua New Guinea (main range around Mt Wilhelm, Saruwakets, Rawlinson Range, vicinity of Bulolo and Owen Stanley Mts), 2,100-3,500m.

Now including *R. vandeursenii* Sleumer originally distinguished by its larger flowers but all intermediates have been shown to occur; these large-flowered forms are the best in cultivation.

R. warianum Schltr. is a synonym of **R. leptanthum** F. Muell.

R. WILLIAMSII MERR. EX COPEL.F. - SUBSECT. VIREYA
Small tree to 7m, terrestrial; young stems at first sparsely scaly but quickly glabrescent, pale and slightly glaucous or flushed with red. Leaves 8-11 × 3-6cm, elliptic, broadly elliptic or sub-ovate, the apex acute and shortly and sharply acuminate, the margin entire, flat or very slightly revolute, the base tapering, cuneate; the upper surface at first silvery-scaly, quickly glabrescent, the midrib raised in the lower third, impressed above, lateral veins 6-12 pairs distinct, either impressed or raised; the lower surface with the midrib strongly prominent, the lateral veins distinct but smooth, the scales rather sparse, small, flat and variously lobed with dark centres and tending to leave shallow dark pits after they have fallen. Flowers 5-8 per umbel, erect or semi-erect; calyx disc shaped or irregularly 5-lobed, tinged red; corolla white, funnel-shaped, 2.5-4 × 3-5.5cm, sparsely scaly or glabrous outside; stamens 10 distributed around the mouth of the flower; ovary densely silvery scaly, style with a few scales near the base, otherwise glabrous. H1b. Philippines (Mountain and Zambeles Provinces),

1,500-2,200m.

R. WOMERSLEYI SLEUMER - SUBSECT. VIREYA
Erect shrub to 2m, mostly terrestrial; young stems at first covered with dark brown scales raised on stalks and minutely hairy, later scabrid. Leaves 0.6-1 × 0.4-0.5cm, elliptic or broadly elliptic to subspherical, the apex acute, obtuse and sometimes mucronate, the margin flat, slightly cartilaginous and sometimes minutely crenulate, the base broadly tapering to rounded; the upper surface with a few scales initially but quickly glabrous, midrib impressed, laterals obsolete; the lower surface with the midrib almost flat, the laterals obsolete, the scales widely spaced, dark brown and irregularly but not deeply lobed, not impressed or raised. Flowers 1-3 per umbel, hanging vertically down; calyx a low scaly and hairy ring; corolla red, cylindrical, mostly with 5 but sometimes up to 7 lobes, 2-2.5 × 2-2.5cm, finely and obscurely scaly and hairy outside; stamens mostly 10, sometimes up to 14, distributed irregularly all round the mouth of the flower; ovary densely white-hairy, style covered in white hairs for the basal ¾, glabrous above. H1b. Widespread on the main range in Papua New Guinea, 3,200-4,000m.

A pretty species of stiffly erect growth in the wild but inclined to be straggly in cultivation.

R. WRIGHTIANUM KOORD. - SUBSECT. VIREYA
Shrub to 2m, epiphytic or terrestrial; young stems finely brown-scaly from low epidermal tubercles which make the twigs slightly rough to the touch. Leaves 2-4 × 1-2cm, obovate, the apex broadly obtuse to rounded, more rarely retuse and mucronate, the margin revolute, entire, the base broadly tapering; the upper side at first sparsely scaly with silvery scales, quickly glabrescent, midrib impressed for most of its length, lateral veins up to 5 pairs obscure or not at all visible; the

lower side with the midrib raised for most of its length, the laterals flat and obscure, the scales small, well spaced, brown, discoid or lobed and in shallow depressions. Flowers mostly in 2-3 flowered umbels, hanging or half-hanging; calyx a low scaly ring; corolla most commonly red or very dark blackish red, rarely white with pink lobes or red with white lobes, cylindrical to narrowly funnel-shaped, 3-3.5 × 1.5-2.5cm, finely scaly on the tube outside; stamens 10, clustered on the lower side of the mouth of the flower; ovary densely silvery scaly, the style glabrous apart from a few scales at the very base. H1b. New Guinea (widespread from east to west), 1,400-3,200m

R. YELLIOTII WARB. - SUBSECT. ALBOVIREYA

Shrub to 8m in the wild, terrestrial, young stems densely covered with shortly stalked scales. Leaves 0.7-4 × 0.5-2cm, ovate, elliptic, broadly elliptic to subcircular, the apex broadly acute, abruptly acuminate or more rarely obtuse, the margin slightly revolute and minutely crenulate with impressed scales, the base rounded; the upper surface at first densely scaly but weathering and only leaving impressed scale bases, midrib slightly impressed above, the laterals 2-4 pairs, very slightly impressed; underside with the midrib strongly raised, the laterals slightly so, densely and persistently scaly with touching or overlapping stellate to almost rounded silvery brown scales. Flowers 3-5 per umbel, horizontal to hanging; calyx disk-shaped, densely scaly; corolla dark red, rarely white, cylindrical, slightly curved, 0.8-1.5 × 0.5-0.7cm, densely scaly outside; stamens 10, rather unequal and irregularly grouped in the mouth; ovary densely brown-scaly, the style glabrous. H1b. Papua New Guinea (widespread on the main ranges), 1,300-3,700m.

Commonly mistaken for *R. inconspicuum* which is an easier species to grow and much more common in collections. *R. yelliotii* is more densely scaly with the scales touching or overlapping on the undersides of the leaves; the flower buds are hairy and scaly with ciliated edges to the bracts and the flowers are generally darker in colour than in *R. inconspicuum*.

R. YONGII ARGENT - SUBSECT. VIREYA

Shrub to 3m, predominantly terrestrial but occasionally epiphytic, young stems sparsely covered with pale brown scales. Leaves 6-11 × 2-5.5cm, elliptic to broadly elliptic, the apex rounded to slightly retuse, the margin entire and broadly recurved, the base broadly tapering; the upper surface at first minutely scaly, quickly glabrescent and shiny, the midrib impressed above, the laterals 5-8 pairs, very slightly impressed; underside with the midrib very strongly raised, the laterals only slightly so, rather sparsely covered in pale brown, deeply lobed scales. Flowers 5-12 per umbel, semi-erect to half-hanging; calyx a shallowly 5-lobed scaly disc; corolla dark red, strongly curved, cylindrical or narrowly funnel-shaped, 2-3.2 × 1-2cm, with a few scattered brown scales but numerous and more conspicuous white hairs outside; stamens 10, clustered on the upper side of the mouth; ovary densely white-hairy and scaly, the style glabrous. H1b. Malaysia (Sabah and Northern Sarawak from Mt Kinabalu to Mt Mulu), 1,500-2,100m.

A lovely species with intense, blood red flowers which shine brilliantly when the sun is behind them. There are two distinct forms in cultivation at present: one tall and straggly with good foliage from Mt Mulu; the other from Mt Alab is much more compact but subject to leaf burn.

R. ZOELLERI WARB. - SUBSECT. VIREYA

Shrub or tree up to 10m, terrestrial; young stems finely scaly at first. Leaves 7-17 × 3-9cm, elliptic, broadly elliptic to sub-obovate, the apex shortly acuminate, broadly acute or obtuse, the margin flat and entire, the base broadly tapering, sometimes rather unequal; the upper surface at first with pale brown scales, these becoming silvery and soon disappearing, the midrib slightly raised in the basal half, distinctly grooved to over half way, the lateral veins 9-14 pairs very slightly raised; lower surface with the midrib strongly raised for most of its length, the laterals very slightly raised, scales rather sparse, pale brown, lobed and with small darker centres. Flowers 4-8 per umbel, semi-erect to half hanging; calyx a low scaly and hairy disc; corolla orange to pink with a yellow throat, sometimes scented, funnel-shaped, 4-10 × 5-6cm, sometimes with a few hairs at the base and generally laxly scaly outside; stamens 10, rather irregularly scattered usually on the lower side of the mouth; ovary hairy and obscurely scaly,

the style hairy and often scaly as well for about ¾ of its length, glabrous at the top. H1a-b. Throughout New Guinea and west to the Moluccas (W Seram), almost from s.l.-2,000m.

AM 1973 (Royal Botanic Gardens, Kew) to a clone 'Decimus'; flowers Orange-Red Group 31B at tip, Yellow-Orange Group 21A at base.

This widespread species is one of the boldest of the Vireyas with its flamboyant orange and yellow flowers. It is the parent of many hybrids both cultivated and in the wild. It is most likely to be confused with *R. laetum* or *R. baenitzianum* and may be distinguished as noted under those species.

Collectors' Numbers

Introduction

Since 1980 travel within China has become possible and there have been a number of Chinese expeditions since then. Lists from these expeditions comprise a significant proportion of those included here for the first time. It should be noted that there are restrictions on the export of live material from both Bhutan and China (including seed) and that publication of these lists does not imply that live material is or ever has been available from expeditions to these countries.

Some corrections have been made to the determinations published in previous editions of the Handbook to bring this account up to date.

Lists for the Malesian rhododendrons of Sect. Vireya are not included though a number of those for plants raised at Edinburgh have been published in Chamberlain et al. (1996).

These lists are arranged in alphabetical order by collectors' names. The nomenclature used follows that to be found in the text; no attempt has been made to include the names originally used. Where the name is not known for an individual number, the number is cited as 'sp.' Where a number can only be identified to a subsection then that subsection is cited against the appropriate number. When an identification is tentative, the number is followed by the abbreviation 'aff.' (affinity). Where more than one entity has been raised under a single number, or the resultant plant is different from the parent then that number is supplied with a lower case alphabetic suffix. An '=' sign is used in the text to denote alternative numbers for a single collection. Some of Rock's collections have been introduced into cultivation under US Department of Agriculture numbers; these are cited with the corresponding field numbers.

Alpine Garden Society

SIKKIM EXP. (1983)

418	anthopogon
547	hodgsonii
561	anthopogon
637	lepidotum

JAPAN EXP. (1988)

43	brachycarpum
64	degronianum subsp. degronianum
69	brachycarpum subsp. brachycarpum
139	aureum
163	albrechtii
177	kaempferi
282	camtschaticum
366	aureum
441	dauricum

CHINA EXPS. (1994)

1183	phaeochrysum aff.
1275	nivale aff.
1423	primuliflorum aff.
1481	campylogynum aff.
1485	nivale aff.
1506	rupicola var. chryseum
1513	nivale subsp. boreale aff.
1515	primuliflorum aff.
1549	Subsect. Lapponica
1572	primuliflorum
1619	hippophaeoides var. hippophaeoides
1637	racemosum
1664	rubiginosum aff.
1670	sp.
1706	primuliflorum
1756	sp.
1775	sp.
1776	saluenense subsp. chameunum
1777	phaeochrysum aff.

1779   Sect. Pogonanthum
1787   Subsect. Lapponica
1824   Subsect. Taliensia
1864   russatum aff.
1879   beesianum
1928   rubiginosum aff.
2011   yunnanense aff.
2069   sp.
2071   sp.
2083   sp.
2086   sp.
2087   Subsect. Taliensia
2088   Subsect. Taliensia
2089   Subsect. Taliensia
2090   beesianum aff.
2091   rex subsp. fictolaceum
2096   decorum subsp. decorum
2097   yunnanense
2100   sp.
2102   russatum
2103   Subsect. Taliensia
2115   sp.
2116   Subsect.Taliensia
2118   roxieanum
2130   Subsect. Lapponica
2143   saluenense subsp.
          chameunum
2152   sp.
2154b sp.
2155   Subsect. Lapponica
2161   roxieanum
2192   decorum subsp. decorum
2255   phaeochrysum aff.
2256   sp.
2257   wardii aff.
2258   rupicola var. chryseum
2259   Subsect. Lapponica
2384   sp.
2441   Subsect. Lapponica
2496   fastigiatum
2499   campylogynum
2518   sp.

Apold, Cox and Hutchison (ACH)
NE TURKEY EXP. (1962)

102   × sochadzeae White (hybrid)
103   × sochadzeae Pink (hybrid)

114   caucasicum
118   smirnowii
119   ungernii
120   ungernii × smirnowii (hybrid)
121   ungernii × smirnowii (hybrid)
121b   ungernii
129   smirnowii
130   × sochadzeae (hybrid)
131   × sochadzeae (hybrid)
147   caucasicum
204   luteum
205   ponticum
206   caucasicum

Bartholomew, B.
BHUTAN EXP. (1974)

141   keysii
147   barbatum
150   barbatum
151   barbatum
185a   succothii
185b   lanatum
207   hodgsonii
259   barbatum

Beer, L.
NEPAL EXP. (1975)

620   lepidotum
633   setosum
643   campanulatum subsp.
          campanulatum
652   cinnabarinum subsp.
          cinnabarinum
653   hodgsonii
655   barbatum × campanulatum
          (hybrid)
662   camelliiflorum
670   grande
703   arboreum var.
          cinnamomeum

Beer, L., Lancaster, R. & Morris (BLM)
E NEPAL EXP. (1971)

26   ciliatum

92	wightii		151	hodgsonii
153	camelliiflorum		152	barbatum
217	setosum		153	thomsonii subsp. thomsonii
220	cinnabarinum subsp. cinnabarinum		172	arboreum var. cinnamomeum

92 wightii
153 camelliiflorum
217 setosum
220 cinnabarinum subsp.
       cinnabarinum
228 thomsonii subsp.
       thomsonii
231 anthopogon
233 cinnabarinum subsp.
       cinnabarinum
234 cinnabarinum subsp.
       cinnabarinum
239 triflorum subsp.
       triflorum
279 lepidotum
280 cinnabarinum subsp.
       cinnabarinum
283 campanulatum subsp.
       campanulatum
314 ciliatum
315 glaucophyllum subsp.
       glaucophyllum
323 hodgsonii
324 ciliatum
325 barbatum
330 fulgens
332 anthopogon subsp.
       anthopogon
344 campanulatum subsp.
       campanulatum
10094 thomsonii subsp. thomsonii
10637 camelliiflorum
12288 dalhousiae var. dalhousiae

Beyer, R., Erskine, C. & Cowley, J.
KOREA EXP. (1982)

28 weyrichii
45 mucronulatum var.
       mucronulatum
139 schlippenbachii
271 yedoense var. poukhanense

Binns, Mason & Wright
NEPAL EXP. (1978)

66 falconeri subsp. falconeri
107 campanulatum forma

151 hodgsonii
152 barbatum
153 thomsonii subsp. thomsonii
172 arboreum var. cinnamomeum

Bowes-Lyon, S.
NEPAL EXP. (1962)

48 arboreum subsp. cinnamomeum
84 campanulatum subsp.
       campanulatum
88 barbatum
142 lepidotum

NEPAL EXP. (1964)

2031 cinnabarinum subsp.
       cinnabarinum
2072 lepidotum
2098 nivale subsp. nivale

BHUTAN-SIKKIM EXP. (1966)

3011 lindleyi
3012 barbatum
3013 barbatum
3024 pendulum
3040 virgatum subsp. virgatum
3047 triflorum
3068 virgatum subsp. virgatum
3069 cinnabarinum subsp.
       xanthocodon
3071 cinnabarinum subsp.
       xanthocodon
3098 pendulum
3124 nivale subsp. nivale
3149 anthopogon subsp. anthopogon
3152 lanatum
3155 campanulatum subsp.
       aeruginosum
3173 cinnabarinum subsp.
       xanthocodon
3189 keysii
3193 edgeworthii
3194 ciliatum
3197 griffithianum
3214 dalhousiae var. rhabdotum
3225 campanulatum
3226 wallichii
3231 anthopogon subsp. anthopogon

3232	lanatum
3241	wightii
3255	thomsonii subsp. thomsonii
3260	fulgens
3268	campylocarpum × thomsonii (hybrid)
3286	× candelabrum (hybrid)
3355	baileyi
3462	lepidotum
3491	maddenii subsp. maddenii
3493	maddenii ssp, maddenii

BHUTAN EXP. (1967)

5089	wightii
5089a	campanulatum subsp. aeruginosum
5194	maddenii subsp. maddenii
5194a	grande
5795	grande

BHUTAN EXP. (1969)

15005	maddenii subsp. maddenii
15006	maddenii subsp. maddenii
15018	camelliiflorum
15020	dalhousiae var. rhabdotum
15027	campanulatum
15040	campanulatum
15040a	lanatum
15041	wightii
15042	succothii
15043	cinnabarinum subsp. xanthocodon
15051	campanulatum
15073	argipeplum
15150	maddenii subsp. maddenii

BHUTAN EXP. (1970)

6003	niveum
6004	× candelabrum (hybrid)
6005	glaucophyllum
6006	argipeplum
6007	pendulum
6008	niveum
6016	argipeplum
6020	glaucophyllum
6025	lindleyi
6026	dalhousiae var. dalhousiae
6035	succothii

6037	maddenii subsp. maddenii
6038	maddenii subsp. maddenii
6074	argipeplum
6075	argipeplum
6076	ciliatum
6077	cinnabarinum subsp. xanthocodon
6078	succothii
6086	kendrickii
6092	maddenii subsp. maddenii

BHUTAN EXP. (1987-89)

1	dalhousiae var. rhabdotum
2	maddenii subsp. maddenii
4	wightii
6	camelliiflorum
7	glaucophyllum
12	barbatum
13	cinnabarinum
16	lindleyi
18	campylocarpum subsp. campylocarpum
19	cinnabarinum
22	grande
23	thomsonii subsp. thomsonii
25	sp.
31	griffithianum
32	maddenii subsp. maddenii
33	vaccinioides (Sect. Vireya)
425	kesangiae var. kesangiae

BHUTAN EXP. (1994)

10133	edgworthii
10134	maddenii subsp. maddenii
10138	falconeri subsp. falconeri
10139	kesangiae var. kesangiae
10140	succothii
10141	flinckii
10142	sp.
10143	sp.
10144	sp.
10145	sp.
10146	sp.
10147	sp.
10148	sp.
10149	sp.
10150	sp.

Cave, G.
SIKKIM, W BENGAL, N INDIA
(C. 1914)

6712	falconeri subsp. falconeri
6714	argipeplum
6715	arboreum var. cinnamomeum

Chamberlain, D., Cox, P.A. & Hutchison, P.C. (CCH)
SICHUAN, CHINA EXP. (1989)

3902	pachytrichum var. monosematum
3903	pachytrichum var. pachytrichum
3904	faberi
3905	pingianum
3906	wiltonii
3907	pachytrichum var. pachytrichum
3908	calophytum var. calophytum
3909	strigillosum
3910	pachytrichum var. pachytrichum
3911	calophytum var. calophytum
3912	pingianum
3914	strigillosum
3915	dendrocharis
3917	davidii
3919	pachytrichum var. pachytrichum
3920	longesquamatum
3921	augustinii var. augustinii
3922	lutescens
3923	calophytum var. calophytum
3924	prattii
3925	concinnum
3926	wasonii
3927	vernicosum
3928	nivale subsp. boreale
3929	przewalskii
3930	aganniphum?
3932	aganniphum var. aganniphum
3933	rufum
3938	aganniphum var. aganniphum
3939	watsonii
3944	przewalskii
3946	aganniphum var. aganniphum
3951	oreodoxa var. oreodoxa
3952	rufum
4012	dendrocharis
4016	orbiculare subsp. orbiculare
4020	augustinii var. augustinii

4021	balangense
4023	galactinum
4026	watsonii
4029	concinnum
4030	nivale subsp. boreale
4034	primuliflorum
4054	phaeochrysum var. phaeochrysum
4064	aganniphum var. aganniphum
4065	phaeochrysum var. phaeochrysum
4066	rufum
4089	rufum
4103	primuliflorum
4104	rufum
4105	capitatum
4107	aganniphum var. aganniphum

Chengdu Edinburgh Exp. (CEE)
SICHUAN, CHINA (1991)

102	concinnum
133	strigillosum
140	moupinense
141	wiltonii
142	argyrophyllum subsp. argyrophyllum
160	argyrophyllum subsp. argyrophyllum
171	pachytrichum var. pachytrichum
172	sutchuenense?
174	trichanthum
191	strigillosum
200	stigillosum
209	calophytum var. calophytum
217	prattii
227	wiltonii
228	wiltonii aff.
229	pachytrichum var. pachytrichum
230	orbiculare subsp. orbiculare
231	sikangense
232	faberi
233	prattii aff.
242	trichanthum
245	faberi
246	sikangense
257	sp.
284	rubiginosum

285	ririei ?
299	prattii
311	argyrophyllum subsp. argyophyllum
313	rubiginosum
318	floribundum
334	tatsienense
335	decorum subsp. decorum
336	nitidulum aff.
344	bureavioides
345	sp.
348	oreodoxa var. fargesii
355	decorum subsp. decorum
364	intricatum
365	nitidulum ?
369	phaeochrysum var. agglutinatum
370	phaeochrysum var. agglutinatum
371	souliei
391	nitidulum ?
392	nivale subsp. boreale
393	intricatum
394	websterianum
407	websterianum
429	websterianum
430	nivale subsp. boreale
432	phaeochrysum var. agglutinatum
450	galactinum
455	Subsect. Triflora
459	balangense
468	trichostomum ?
477	nivale
479	augustinii aff.
480	sp.
483	sp.
485	heliolepis aff.
500	argyrophyllum subsp. argyrophyllum
501	lutescens
502	strigillosum
511	calophytum var. calophytum
518	concinnum aff.
524	trichanthum
525	sp.
526	prattii
531	concinnum
532	pachytrichum var. pachytrichum
554	sp.
556	sp.
557	hippophaeoides
559	websterianum
565	phaeochrysum var. agglutinatum

Chungdien-Lijiang-Dali (CLD)

CHINA EXP. (OCT. 1990)

129	rubiginosum
130	decorum subsp. decorum
144	racemosum
211	decorum aff.
214	oreotrephes
245	sp.
302	hippophaeoides var. hippophaeoides
412	rubiginosum aff.
511	hippophaeoides var. hippophaeoides
512	rubiginosum
513	primuliflorum aff.
514	decorum aff.
515	hippophaeoides var. hippophaeoides
516	rubiginosum
539	sp.
558	racemosum
652	yunnanense
715	telmateium
719	rubiginosum
787	cuneatum
795	adenogynum
807	cuneatum
857	primuliflorum
868	cuneatum aff.
928	yunnanense
935	lepidotum
1016	trichostomum
1019	hippophaeoides var. hippophaeoides
1057	lepidotum
1095	adenogynum
1096	sp.
1097	rupicola var. rupicola
1275	cyanocarpum
1281	sp.
1282	lacteum
1283	haematodes subsp. haematodes
1285	fastigiatum
1287	taliense
1295	rex subsp. fictolacteum
1297	cyanocarpum aff.
1300	selense subsp. jucundum
1334	fastigiatum
1347	trichocladum var.trichocladum

1357	sp.	1584	thomsonii subsp. thomsonii
1427	haematodes subsp. haematodes	1590	wightii
1430	edgeworthii	1591	cinnabarinum subsp.
1444	× agastum ? (hybrid)		xanthocodon
1455	rex subsp. fictolacteum aff.	1592	hodgsonii aff.
1464	arboreum var. delavayi	1594	flinckii
1471	rubiginosum aff.	1595	succothii
1473	decorum subsp. decorum	1596	hodgsonii
1490	sp.	1597	cinnabarinum var.
1497	sp.		cinnabarinum
1507	cyanocarpum	1599	succothii
1511	sp.	1602	camelliiflorum
1512	yunnanense	1608	kesangiae
1514	trichocladum var. trichocladum	1609	falconeri subsp. falconeri
1522	haematodes subsp. haematodes	1614	virgatum subsp. virgatum
1526	sp.	1615	maddenii subsp. maddenii
1529	sp.	1618	kesangiae var. kesangiae
1533	haematodes subsp. haematodes	1623	kendrickii
1538	fastigiatum	1624	grande
1539	sp.	1632	kesangiae var. kesangiae
1541	racemosum	1633	glaucophyllum var. tubiforme
1544	dichroanthum subsp.	1634	wallichii
	dichroanthum	1635	thomsonii subsp. thomsonii
1547	sp.	1637	wallichii
1553	sp.	1638	thomsonii subsp. thomsonii
1564	sp.	1639	flinckii
1575	sp.	1640	wightii
		1642	nivale subsp. nivale
		1643	bhutanense

Clark, A. & Sinclair, I.
BHUTAN EXP. (1994)

		1644	sp.
		1645	bhutanense
		1646	sp.
		1647	flinckii
1514	kesangiae var. kesangiae	1648	bhutanense
1515	arboreum var. delavayi	1652	campylocarpum subsp.
1516	kesangiae var. kesangiae		campylocarpum
1517	kesangiae var. kesangiae	1655	keysii
1523	arboreum	1656	glaucophyllum
1528	virgatum subsp. virgatum	1658	cinnabarinum
1531	triflorum	1659	neriiflorum subsp. phaedropum
1532	arboreum	1662	kesangiae var. kesangiae
1561	arboreum	1664	lepidotum
1562	kesangiae var. kesangiae	1666	flinckii aff.
1563	kesangiae var. kesangiae	1667	succothii
1568	barbatum	1682	falconeri subsp. falconeri
1572	argipeplum	1683	kendrickii
1573	kesangiae var. kesangiae	1692	campylocarpum subsp.
1576	hodgsonii		campylocarpum
1581	camelliiflorum	1693	cinnabarinum
1582	argipeplum	1694	hodgsonii
1583	thomsonii subsp. thomsonii	1695	arboreum

1696	keysii
1697	falconeri subsp. falconeri
1698	hodgsonii
1699	argipeplum
1703	griffithianum
1708	lindleyi
1715	campylocarpum subsp. campylocarpum
1759	fulgens

Cooper, R.E.
BHUTAN EXP. (1914)

1	cinnabarinum subsp. cinnabarinum
15	campylocarpum subsp. campylocarpum
46	setosum
47	lepidotum
91	lepidotum
155	campanulatum subsp. aeruginosum
237	lepidotum
295	lepidotum
743	lepidotum
744	lepidotum
745	cinnabarinum subsp. cinnabarinum
747	cinnabarinum subsp. cinnabarinum
749	campylocarpum subsp. campylocarpum
1282	maddenii subsp. maddenii
1291	arboreum subsp. arboreum
1292	maddenii subsp. maddenii
1454	maddenii subsp. maddenii
1456	keysii
1545	arboreum subsp. arboreum
1575	arboreum subsp. arboreum
1741	lepidotum
1805	lepidotum
1937	cinnabarinum subsp. cinnabarinum
2040	grande
2088	hodgsonii
2088a	hodgsonii × falconeri (hybrid)
2089	arboreum
2146	cinnabarinunm subsp. xanthocodon

2147	wallichii
2148	lanatum
2149	wallichii
2154	cinnabarinum subsp. xanthocodon
2217	campanulatum subsp. aeruginosum
2217a	wightii
2223	lepidotum
2224	baileyi
2233	hodgsonii
2315	griffithianum
2475	arboreum var. roseum
2487	succothii
2489	succothii
2490	setosum
2503	setosum
2504	campylocarpum subsp. campylocarpum
2505	hodgsonii
2523	lepidotum
2552	lepidotum
2581	cinnabarinum subsp. cinnabarinum
2590	wightii
2592	campanulatum
2648	cinnabarinum
2756	edgeworthii
2760	arboreum subsp. arboreum
2819	virgatum subsp. virgatum
2843	arboreum subsp. arboreum
2903	arboreum subsp. arboreum
2922	cinnabarinum subsp. cinnabarinum
2922a	camelliiflorum
2924	arboreum var. roseum
2928	thomsonii subsp. thomsonii
3064	virgatum subsp. virgatum
3151	virgatum subsp. virgatum
3233	campanulatum subsp. aeruginosum
3234	wightii
3235	anthopogon subsp. anthopogon
3236	lepidotum
3238	wallichii
3256	cinnabarinum
3257	argipeplum
3383	keysii
3287	barbatum
3423	maddenii subsp. maddenii
3479	lepidotum

3480	campanulatum		4009	baileyi
3482	setosum		4083	camelliiflorum
3483	nivale subsp. nivale		4084	hodgsonii
3484	lanatum		4086	kendrickii
3485	anthopogon subsp. anthopogon		4101	succothii
3487	sp.		4115	argipeplum
3490	lanatum		4128	lepidotum
3491	campylocarpum subsp. campylocarpum		4160	kendrickii
			4285	baileyi
3492	wallichii		4804	cinnabarinum subsp. cinnabarinum
3493	cinnabarinum subsp. cinnabarinum		4830	barbatum
3498	wightii		4978	kendrickii
3503	arboreum subsp. arboreum		4979	cinnabarinum
3507	barbatum		4980	maddenii subsp. maddenii
3527	wightii		4981	arboreum var. roseum
3528	campanulatum subsp. aeruginosum		4982	cinnabarinum subsp. cinnabarinum
3540	arboreum var. roseum			
3541	triflorum subsp. triflorum			

PUNJAB, N INDIA EXP. 1916

3469	lepidotum
3588	virgatum subsp. virgatum
3593	arboreum var. roseum
3601	maddenii subsp. maddenii
3615	griffithianum
3698	wightii

5738	anthopogon subsp. hypenanthum
5768	campanulatum subsp. campanulatum
5926	campanulatum subsp. campanulatum
5928	lepidotum

BHUTAN EXP. (1915)

NE BURMA EXP.

5975	burmanicum

3786	arboreum subsp. arboreum
3806	dalhousiae var. dalhousiae
3815	virgatum subsp. virgatum
3819	cinnabarinum subsp. cinnabarinum
3831	triflorum var. triflorum
3838	nivale subsp. nivale
3873	cinnabarinum
3876	pendulum
3879	edgeworthii
3903	anthopogon subsp. anthopogon
3913	keysii
3935	dalhousiae var. dalhousiae
3939	griffithianum
3940	grande
3957	maddenii subsp. maddenii
3959	camelliiflorum
3990	lanatum
3991	thomsonii subsp. thomsonii
3998	cinnabarinum subsp. xanthocodon
4003	setosum

Cox, K.N.E. & Vergera, S. (CV)

SE TIBET, CHINA EXP. (1995)

9501	primuliflorum
9503	bulu
9504	cerasinum
9506	wardii var. wardii
9508	faucium
9513	cephalanthum subsp. cephalanthum
9514	aganniphum var. aganniphum
9515	charitopes subsp. tsangpoense
9516	forrestii subsp. forrestii
9517	forrestii subsp. forrestii
9519	fragariiflorum
9522	viridescens

9523 cinnabarinum subsp. xanthocodon 'Concatenans'
9524 glischrum subsp. rude aff.
9526 lanigerum (red)
9527 arizelum aff.
9530 lanigerum (red)
9532 sinogrande
9533 arizelum aff.
9535 glischrum subsp. rude aff.
9540 kongboense
9541 aganniphum var. aganniphum
9544 chamaethomsonii var. chamaethomsonii
9546 hirtipes
9547 principis
9548 wardii var. wardii
9552 phaeochrysum var. agglutinatum
9557 oreotrephes aff.
9558 wardii var. wardii
9561 phaeochrysum var. phaeochrysum
9564 fragariiflorum
9565 laudandum var. temoense
9567 wardii var. wardii
9569 dignabile
9574 phaeochrysum var. agglutinatum
9575 triflorum subsp. triflorum

Cox, P.A.

SICHUAN, CHINA EXP. (1990)

5000 wiltonii
5001 pachytrichum var. pachytricum
5003 decorum subsp. decorum
5005 racemosum
5008 lutescens
5009 davidsonianum
5011 concinnum
5012 sikangense var. sikangense
5013 watsonii
5014 faberi
5015 orbiculare subsp. orbiculare
5016 dendrocharis
5020 floribundum
5021 calophytum var. calophytum
5022 lutescens
5025 polylepis
5028b prattii
5029 longesquamatum
5030 prattii
5031 nitidulum var. nitidulum
5035 davidsonianum
5039 bureavioides
5040 davidsonianum
5043 nitidulum var. nitidulum
5044 thymifolium
5045 intricatum
5046 wasonii aff.
5056 souliei
5057 phaeochrysum var. levistratum
5058 phaeochrysum var. agglutinatum
5059 Subsect. Lapponica
5060 intricatum
5061 prattii
5062 concinnum
5063 oreodoxa var. fargesii
5064 Subsect. Lapponica
5066 bureavii × prattii
5069 nivale subsp. boreale
5070 concinnum
5071 primuliflorum
5072 bureavioides
5073 przewalskii
5075 watsonii
5076 bureavioides
5080 websterianum
5081 phaeochrysum var. agglutinatum
5085 concinnum
5089 trichanthum
5090 floribundum aff.
5091 davidsonianum
5092 lutescens
5099 racemosum
5100 lutescens
5101 galactinum
5105 sikangense var. sikangense
5110 wiltonii
5118 phaeochrysum var. phaeochrysum
5121 intricatum
5123 websterianum
5132 phaeochrysum var. levistratum
5133 prattii

NW YUNNAN & SICHUAN (1992)

6000 Subsect. Lapponica
6001 Subsect. Lapponica
6012 rupicola var. chryseum

6016	aganniphum var. flavorufum	6514	rubiginosum
6021	edgeworthii	6515	rupicola var. chryseum
6024	selense subsp. selense	6516	aganniphum var. flavorufum
6025	praestans	6517	saluenense subsp. saluenense
6026	fulvum	6519	uvariifolium var. uvariifolium
6035	saluenense	6521	sanguineum var. sanguineum
6036	eudoxum var. eudoxum	6529	saluenense var. saluenense
6037a	temenium	6530	heliolepis
6038	temenium aff.	6531	coriaceum
6047	selense subsp. selense	6532	fulvum subsp. fulvoides
6048	arizelum hybrids	6534	eclecteum
6051	brachyanthum subsp. hypolepidotum	6539	citriniflorum var. citriniflorum aff.
6053	cephalanthum subsp. cephalanthum	6540	sanguineum var. didymoides aff.
6054	eclecteum	6541	× bathyphyllum (hybrid)
6055	mekongense var. mekongense	6542a	proteoides
6056	sanguineum	6542b	× bathyphyllum (hybrid)
6067	selense subsp. selense	6543	citriniflorum var. citriniflorum
6070	aganniphum var. flavorufum	6544	mekongense var. mekongense
6094	tapetiforme aff.	6548	decorum subsp.decorum
6095	campylogynum aff.		
6096	campylogynum aff.		

Cox, P.A. & Cox, K.N.E. (CC)
SE TIBET EXP. (SPRING 1996)

6099	forrestii × aganniphum		
6100	forrestii subsp. forrestii		
6101	sanguineum	7500	nivale subsp. nivale
6108	wardii	7501	bulu
6111	sanguineum aff.	7502	triflorum var. triflorum
6112	saluenense subsp. chameunum	7503	viridescens
6117	uvariifolium var. uvariifolium	7504	cephalanthum subsp. cephalanthum
6119	wardii	7506	uvariifolium var. griseum
6124	augustinii subsp. chasmanthum	7508	hirtipes
6130	Subsect. Lapponica	7509	dignabile
6132	intricatum	7510	cerasinum
6136	primuliflorum	7514	wardii var. wardii
6143	flavidum	7516	forrestii subsp.forrestii
6144	souliei	7517	cinnabarinum subsp. xanthocodon 'Concatenans'
6145a	radendum?		
6146	phaeochrysum var.agglutinatum	7518	parmulatum
6148	bureavii	7519	mekongense var. mekongense
6149	trichanthum	7520	viridescens
6150	wiltonii	7521	cephalanthum subsp. cephalanthum
6157	calostrotum subsp. riparium	7522	arizelum aff.

NW YUNNAN, CHINA (1994)

		7523	exasperatum
6502	adenogynum	7524	glischrum subsp. rude aff.
6507	edgeworthii	7525	glischrum subsp. rude aff.
6511	praestans		× campylocarpum (hybrid)
6512	arizelum		
6513	eclecteum		

7526	lanigerum (red)
7527	megeratum
7530	uniflorum var. imperator
7531	viridescens
7536	fulvum subsp.fulvoides
7537	cerasinum
7538	parmulatum
7541	campylocarpum subsp. campylocarpum
7542	calostrotum subsp. riparium
7545	laudandum var. laudandum
7546	laudandum var. temoense
7547	lepidotum
7549	hirtipes
7550	oreotrephes aff.
7553	lepidotum
7554	scopulorum
7556	uvariifolium var. griseum
7557	viridescens
7558	lepidotum
7559	primuliflorum
7561	pemakoense
7562	sanguineum var. sanguineum
7563	calostrotum subsp. riparium
7565	charitopes subsp. tsangpoense
7566	faucium
7567	ramsdenianum
7570	nuttallii
7571	scopulorum
7574	lanatoides
7575	kongboense
7577	lanatoides
7578	hirtipes
7580	fragariiflorum
7581	laudandum var. temoense
7584	wardii var. wardii
7585	lepidotum
7591	nivale subsp. nivale

Cox, P.A. & Hutchison, P.C. (C&H)
KHASIA, ARUNACHAL PRADESH & BENGAL N INDIA EXP. (1965)

301	formosum var. inaequale
302	formosum var. formosum
305	arboreum var. delavayi

320	formosum var. formosum
373	walongense aff.
389	griffithianum
396	coxianum
399	lindleyi
416	kendrickii
418	subansiriense
420	leptocarpum
421	edgeworthii
422	neriiflorum subsp. phaedropum
427	falconeri subsp. eximium
431	grande
438	maddenii subsp. maddenii
459	santapauii (Sect. Vireya)
579	cinnabarinum subsp. cinnabarinum
580	barbatum
581	hodgsonii
584	falconeri subsp. falconeri

SICHUAN & YUNNAN, EXP. (1995)

(see also Millais, E.G. *et al* Sichuan and Yunnan Exp. 1995)

7003	rex subsp. rex
7008	augustinii subsp. augustinii
7009	vernicosum
7010	racemosum
7012	denudatum
7022	Subsect. Lapponica
7025	ambiguum
7027	vernicosum
7032	argyrophyllum subsp. argyrophyllum
7033	argyrophyllum subsp. argyrophyllum
7034	rex subsp. rex
7035	strigillosum
7037	racemosum
7040	augustinii subsp. augustinii
7041	rubiginosum
7045	argyrophyllum subsp. argyrophyllum
7047	strigillosum
7049	huianum
7050	sp.
7051	asterochnoum
7052	ochraceum
7053	tatsienense aff.
7055	calophytum var. openshawianum

7072	longipes var. longipes		2652	tatsienense var. tatsienense
7073	huianum			
7085	denudatum		**BHUTAN EXP. (1988)**	
7100	irroratum 'Ningyuenense'			
7108	strigillosum		3006	kesangiae
7111	calophytum var. calophytum		3007	barbatum
7124	lutescens		3008	camelliiflorum
7131	glanduliferum		3009	keysii
7132	vernicosum		3017	falconeri subsp. falconeri
7145	yunnanense		3020	grande
7150	vernicosum aff.		3024	campylocarpum subsp.
7157	sphaeroblastum var.			campylocarpum
	wumengense		3025	succothii
7158	bureavii		3026	argipeplum
7159	Subsect. Lapponica		3030	thomsonii subsp.
7164	lacteum			thomsonii
7166	sikangense var.		3036	triflorum var. triflorum
	exquisetum		3050	camelliiflorum
7179	arboreum var. delavayi		3056	hodgsonii
7183	sinofalconeri		3058	kesangiae
7185	Subsect. Irrorata		3060	griffithianum
7186	valentinianum var.		3062	falconeri subsp. falconeri
	oblongilobatum ?		3070	argipeplum
7189	hemlseyanum aff.		3076	camelliiflorum
			3077	hodgsonii
			3079	succothii

Cox, P.A., Hutchison, P.C. & Maxwell McDonald, D. (CHM)

SICHUAN & YUNNAN, CHINA EXP. (1986)

			3080	flinckii
			3082	setosum
			3088	thomsonii subsp.
				thomsonii
2500	polylepis		3089	wallichii
2517	phaeochrysum var.		3090	campanulatum subsp.
	levistratum			aeruginosum
2523	capitatum		3091	bhutanense
2531	rufum		3093	hodgsonii aff.
2545	przewalskii		3094	pendulum
2568	Subsect. Triflora		3099	kesangiae aff.
2578	watsonii		3105	succothii
2591	rufum		3106	campylocarpum subsp.
2604	yunnanense			campylocarpum
2619	decorum subsp. decorum		3108	cinnabarinum subsp.
2620	vernicosum			cinnabarinum
2630	primuliflorum		3109	succothii
2636	cuneatum		3113	argipeplum
2638	adenogynum		3114	glaucophyllum subsp.
2639	traillianum var. traillianum			glaucophyllum
2646	uvariifolium var.		3115	kesangiae
	uvariiflorum		3116	camelliiflorum
			3130	wightii
			3132	fulgens
			3136	flinckii

Dingle, H.R.
NEPAL EXP. (1984)

1	arboreum
5	arboreum
8	lepidotum
9	lepidotum
13	hodgsonii
18	thomsonii subsp. thomsonii
21	ciliatum
22	glaucophyllum
23	ciliatum

Doleshy, F.
HONSHU, JAPAN EXP. (1965)

1	makinoi
2	makinoi
3	makinoi
4	makinoi
5	degronianum var. heptamerum
6	keiskei
7	degronianum var. hondoense
12	degronianum subsp. degronianum
13	brachycarpum subsp. brachycarpum
14	japonicum
15	brachycarpum subsp. brachycapum

KYUSHU (INCLUDING YAKUSHIMA), JAPAN EXP. (1965)

8	kiusianum
9	degronianum var. yakushimanum
10	degronianum var. yakushimanum

HONSHU, JAPAN EXP. (1967)

21	degronianum subsp. heptamerum
22	degronianum subsp. heptamerum
26	japonicum
27	japonicum
28	brachycarpum subsp. brachycarpum

KYUSHU, JAPAN EXP. (1967)

32	weyrichii aff.
35	degronianum var. heptamerum
37	kiusianum
38	degronianum var. heptamerum
39	keiskei
40	degronianum var. heptamerum
41	degronianum var. heptamerum
42	degronianum var. heptamerum
43	kiusianum

SHIKOKU, JAPAN EXP. (1967)

40	pentaphyllum
44	pentaphyllum
45	degronianum var. heptamerum
50	degronianum var. heptamerum
52	tschonoskyi
53	brachycarpum subsp. brachycarpum

HONSHU, JAPAN EXP. (1967)

70	degronianum var. hondoense
81	degronianum var. degronianum
89	brachycarpum subsp. brachycarpum
123	degronianum var. kyomaruense

OKI ISLAND, JAPAN (1967)

75	degronianum var. hondoense

KYUSHU (INCLUDING YAKUSHIMA), JAPAN EXP. (1970)

41	(re-collected) degronianum var. heptamerum
202	keiskei
205	kiusianum var. sataense
212	degronianum var. yakushimanum
219	nudipes aff.
221	nudipes aff.
228	tashiroi

HONSHU, JAPAN EXP. (1971)

503	aureum

509	× nikomontanum (hybrid)
510	tschonoskyi var. trinerve
518	aureum
521	brachycarpum subsp. brachycarpum
523	degronianum var. degronianum
527	brachycarpum subsp. brachycarpum
529	degronianum var. degronianum
531	degronianum subsp. heptamerum
536	kaempferi aff.
537	kaempferi aff.
541	degronianum var. heptamerum
543	keiskei
544	degronianum var. heptamerum

HOKKAIDO & HONSHU EXP., JAPAN (1983)

821	brachycarpum subsp. brachycarpum
823	brachycarpum subsp. brachycarpum
824	brachycarpum subsp. brachycarpum
825	kaempferi
827	brachycarpum subsp. brachycarpum
829	brachycarpum subsp. brachycarpum

Edinburgh Makalu, Nepal Exp. (EMAK - 1991)

234	vaccinioides (Sect. Vireya)
304	pumilum
557	nivale subsp. nivale
569	wightii
641	wightii
685	pumilum
730	camelliiflorum
916	wightii
1055	grande

Edinburgh Sikkim Exp. (ESIK - 1992)

151	leptocarpum
163	pendulum
220	lanatum

Edinburgh Taiwan Exp. (ETE - 1993)

42	morii
67	morii
99	lasiostylum
180	oldhamii aff.
248	nakaharae
250	sp.
264	rubropilosum
395	rubropilosum aff.
412	pseudochrysanthum
439	pseudochrysanthum
442	pseudochrysanthum
443	pseudochrysanthum
444	pseudochrysanthum
452	pseudochrysanthum
475	oldhamii
485	oldhamii
613	kawakamii
623	kanehirae

Erskine, C., Fliegner, H., Howick, C. & McNamara, A.
TIBET & SICHUAN EXP. (1995)

S1610	lutescens
S1630	calophytum
S1643	ambiguum
S1648	oreodoxa
S1656	calophytum
T 001	sp.
T 023	sp.
T 041	sp.
T 044	sp.

Farrer, R.
GANSU (KANSU), CHINA EXP. (1914)

63	oreodoxa var. oreodoxa
79	invictum
88	primuliflorum aff.
104	przewalskii
119	capitatum
510	thymifolium
510c	przewalskii
511	capitatum
512	capitatum

584	anthopogonoides

UPPER BURMA EXP. (1919)

801	moulmainense
811	araiophyllum
812	tanastylum var. tanastylum
813	sulfureum
814	anthosphaerum
815	mallotum
842	edgeworthii
848	pseudociliipes
863	arizelum
872	sidereum
873	basilicum
874	fulvum subsp. fulvum
875	rubiginosum
876	trichocladum var. trichocladum
877	neriiflorum subsp. neriiflorum
878	heliolepis var. heliolepis
887	habrotrichum
887a	glischrum subsp. glischrum
888	sperabile var. sperabile
918	megacalyx
926	stewartianum
937	camplylocarpum subsp. caloxanthum
938	megeratum
959	sinogrande
979	decorum
980	zaleucum
1022	facetum
1024	dichroanthum subsp. scyphocalyx
1044	maddenii subsp. crassum
1045	calostrotum subsp. calostrotum
1046	campylogynum
1047	rupicola var. rupicola
1065	heliolepis var. heliolepis
1196	lepidotum
1196a	campylogynum
1444	kyawii

Forestry Commission & RBG Edinburgh Exp.
YUNNAN, CHINA (1995)

61	racemosum
62	rubiginosum
63	vernicosum
143	vernicosum
146	phaeochrysum
147	oreotrephes
205	yunnanense
206	beesianum
209	phaeochrysum
210	phaeochrysum var. levistratum
227	uvariifolium var. uvariiflorum
253	selense subsp. selense
254	uvariifolium var. uvariiflorum
302	aganniphum aff.
305	wardii aff.
308	beesianum
311	rupicola var. chryseum
328	rex subsp. fictolacteum
365	heliolepis
367	wardii var. wardii
439	decorum subsp. decorum
440	vernicosum

Forrest, G.
BURMA/YUNNAN EXP. (1910)

4152	campylogynum
5843	rex subsp. fictolacteum
5847	fastigiatum
5848	anthosphaerum
5851	irroratum subsp. irroratum
5862	saluenense subsp. chameunum
5863	fastigiatum
5864	lepidotum
5865	rupicola var. rupicola
5866	primuliflorum
5868	adenogynum
5869	decorum subsp. decorum
5870	traillianum var. traillianum
5871	adenogynum
5872	traillianum var. traillianum
5873	oreotrephes
5874	yunnanense
5876	impeditum
5877	rubiginosum
5879	telmateium
5880	vernicosum
5881	vernicosum
5882	racemosum
6755	trichocladum var. trichocladum
6756	cephalanthum subsp. cephalanthum

6757	fastigiatum	10075	vernicosum
6761	dichroanthum subsp.	10086	racemosum
	dichroanthum	10113	adenogynum
6762	heliolepis var. heliolepis	10114a	vernicosum
6767	xanthostephanum	10156	traillianum var. traillianum
6769	arboreum var. delavayi	10195	beesianum
6770	virgatum subsp. oleifolium	10204	traillianum var. traillianum
6771	rigidum	10210	oreotrephes
6772	taliense	10213	oreotrephes
6773	haematodes subsp. haematodes	10278	trichostomum
6774	balfourianum	10284	fastigiatum
6775	cyanocarpum	10285	saluenense subsp. chameunum
6776	decorum subsp. decorum	10292	uvariifolium var. uvariiflorum
6777	sulfureum	10297	oreotrephes
6778	lacteum	10311	complexum & impeditum
6779	cyanocarpum	10312	primuliflorum
6780	neriiflorum subsp. neriiflorum	10314	rupicola var. rupicola
6781	dichroanthum subsp.	10333	hippophaeoides var.
	dichroanthum		hippophaeoides
		10347	mollicomum

BURMA/YUNNAN, SW CHINA EXP. (1912-14)

		10367	rupicola var. rupicola
		10423	cuneatum
		10428	wardii var. wardii
7463	arboreum var. delavayi	10429	adenogynum
7504	microphyton	10434	telmateium
7505	microphyton	10435	cuneatum
7516	pachypodum	10438	heliolepis var. brevistylum
7673	moulmainense	10460	beesianum
7832	simsii var. mesembrinum	10477	beesianum
8172	edgeworthii	10481	orthocladum var. orthocladum
8905	trichocladum var. trichocladum	10540	roxieanum var. roxieanum
8923	zaleucum	10546	beesianum
8938	heliolepis var. heliolepis	10547	phaeochrysum var.
8939	neriiflorum subsp. neriiflorum		phaeochrysum
8987	dichroanthum subsp. apodectum	10616	wardii var. puralbum
8989	fulvum subsp. fulvum	10639	uvariifolium var. uvariiflorum
8990	basilicum × arizelum (hybrid)	10651	anthosphaerum
9021	sinogrande	10680	wardii var. wardii
9048	habrotrichum	10857	clementinae
9054	dichroanthum subsp. apodectum	10974	rex subsp. fictolacteum
9055	aff. callimorphum	10991	roxieanum var. roxieanum
9342	virgatum subsp. oleifolium	11031	scabrifolium var. scabrifolium
9431	maddenii subsp. crassum	11073	arboreum var. delavayi
9919	roseatum	11074	irroratum subsp. irroratum
10014	polycladum	11246	trichostomum
10035	yungningense & impeditum	11299	tatsiense
10056	impeditum	11312	selense subsp. dasycladum
10057	rubiginosum	11313	beesianum
10071	cuneatum	11317	wardii var. wardii
10073	rubiginosum	11321	phaeochrysum var.
10074	rubiginosum		phaeochrysum

11421	uvariifolium var. uvariiflorum
11450	orthocladum var. orthocladum
11466	wardii var. wardii
11486	clementinae
11487	hippophaeoides var. hippophaeoides
11503	anthosphaerum
11547	pachypodum
11575	lacteum
11579	taliense
11583	taliense
11597	dichroanthum subsp. dichroanthum
11601	aff. callimorphum
11626	fastigiatum
11629	cyanocarpum
11630	trichocladum var. trichocladum
11736	cuneatum
11875	sinogrande
11896	dichroanthum subsp. apodectum
11910	sulfureum
11958	decorum subsp. diaprepes
12054	habrotrichum
12078	basilicum
12094	dichroanthum subsp. apodectum
12095	habrotrichum
12096	neriiflorum subsp. neriiflorum
12100	virgatum subsp. oleifolium
12109	basilicum
12113	arboreum var. delavayi
12461	hippophaeoides var. hippophaeoides
12505	trichostomum
12568	telmateium
12607	clementinae
12623	telmateium
12889	anthosphaerum
12893	floccigerum
12899	lukiangense
12901	glischrum subsp. glischrum
12934	saluenense subsp. saluenense
12942	megeratum
12944	crinigerum var. crinigerum
12947	roxieanum var. oreonastes
12948	rex subsp. fictolacteum
12950	selense subsp. dasycladum
12968	saluenense subsp. chameunum
12969	wardii var. wardii
12982	selense subsp. dasycladum
13005	roxieanum var. oreonastes

13023	praestans
13032	beesianum
13143	beesianum
13244	crinigerum var. crinigerum
13258	saluenense subsp. chameunum
13259	forrestii subsp. forrestii
13299	floccigerum
13301	martinianum
13302	brachyanthum var. hypolepidotum
13303	campylogynum
13304	sanguineum var. sanguineum
13315	wardii var. wardii
13348	proteoides
13380	lukiangense
13383	saluenense subsp. chameunum
13387	anthosphaerum
13438	anthosphaerum
13439	martinianum
13440	floccigerum
13508	facetum
13512?	sulfureum
13518	campylogynum
13526	cephalanthum subsp. platyphyllum
13550	brachyanthum subsp. hypolepidotum
13568	beesianum

NE BURMA, YUNNAN, SICHUAN & TIBET FRONTIERS EXP. (1917-19)

13768	telmateium
13789	× detonsum (hybrid)
13791	hippophaeoides var. hippophaeoides
13792	hippophaeoides var. hippophaeoides
13793	hippophaeoides var. hippophaeoides
13794	hippophaeoides var. hippophaeoides
13798	racemosum - pure white
13799	hippophaeoides var. hippophaeoides
13800	hippophaeoides var. hippophaeoides
13803	racemosum
13804	racemosum
13841	primuliflorum

13842	hippophaeoides var. hippophaeoides	14102	aganniphum var. flavorufum
13847	telmateium	14114	phaeochrysum var. levistratum
13852	anthophaerum	14115	phaeochrysum var. levistratum
13853	irroratum subsp. irroratum	14116	beesianum
13864	irroratum subsp. irroratum	14119	aganniphum var. aganniphum
13881	leptothrium	14128	wardii var. wardii
13896	lukiangense	14134	aganniphum var. aganniphum
13897	selense subsp. dasycladum	14135	heliolepis var. brevistylum
13899	polycladum	14138	forrestii var. forrestii
13900	mekongense var. mekongense	14142	roxieanum var. roxieanum
13904	saluenense subsp. chameunum	14145	phaeochrysum var. levistratum
13905	dasypetalum	14160	mekongense var. mekongense
13905a	polycladum	14166	sanguineum var. haemaleum
13915	russatum	14181	lukiangense
13931	oreotrephes	14190	wardii var. wardii
13933	selense subsp. selense	14195	albertsenianum
13935	floccigerum	14208	alutaceum var. russotinctum
13936	× erythrocalyx (hybrid)	14209	praestans
13938	× erythrocalyx (hybrid)	14210	heliolepis var. brevistylum
13947	rupicola var. chryseum	14226	beesianum
13949	martinianum	14231	rex subsp. fictolacteum
13990	uvariifolium var. uvariiflorum	14233	praestans
13996	glischrum subsp. glischrum	14242	microgynum
14000	rupicola var. chryseum	14243	alutaceum var. iodes
14004	campylogynum	14245	eudoxum var. eudoxum
14005	rupicola var. chryseum	14268	sanguineum var. didymoides
14008	crinigerum var. crinigerum	14269	sanguineum var. cloiophorum
14009	selense subsp. selense	14270	sanguineum var. cloiophorum
14011	forrestii subsp. forrestii	14271	citriniflorum var. citriniflorum
14012	sanguineum var. sanguineum	14272	citriniflorum var. citriniflorum
14021	aganniphum var. aganniphum	14274	citriniflorum var. citriniflorum
14024	phaeochrysum var. levistratum	14286	crinigerum var. crinigerum
14038	vernicosum	14291	heliolepis var. brevistylum
14041	phaeochrysum var. levistratum	14331	calvescens var. calvescens
14043	saluenense subsp. chameunum	14334	primuliflorum
14050	aganniphum var. aganniphum	14344	cephalanthum subsp. cephalanthum
14052	brachyanthum subsp. hypolepidotum	14345	aganniphum var. flavorufum
14054	saluenense subsp. saluenense	14352	beesianum
14055	caphalanthum subsp. cephalanthum	14356	citriniflorum var. citriniflorum
14057	selense subsp. selense	14364	temenium var. temenium
14059	megeratum	14365	temenium var. temenium
14060	nakotiltum	14368	aganniphum var. flavorufum
14061	roxieanum var. roxieanum	14372	rubiginosum
14062	crinigerum var. crinigerum	14416	citriniflorum var. citriniflorum
14063	rex subsp. fictolacteum	14421	microgynum
14066	selense subsp. setiferum	14432	roxieanum var. roxieanum
14094	aganniphum var. aganniphum	14450	beesianum
14095	wardii var. wardii	14452	rubiginosum
		14458	selense subsp. selense
		14461	beesianum

14464	calvescens var. duseimatum	15126	primuliflorum
14485	eclecteum var. eclecteum	15127	primuliflorum
14488	beesianum	15128	adenogynum
14492	alutaceum var. russotinctum	15129	sp.
14499	fulvum subsp. fulvoides	15130	vernicosum
14508	comisteum	15132	telmateium
14509	proteoides	15137	trichostomum
14519	phaeochrysum var. levistratum	15154	telmateium
14605	beesianum	15155	primuliflorum
14685	proteoides	15159	complexum
14686	beesianum	15164	adenogynum aff.
14718	× bathyphyllum (hybrid)	15165	vernicosum
14732	aganniphum var. flavorufum	15166	primuliflorum
14774	eudoxum var. eudoxum	15168	rex subsp. fictolacteum
14790	beesianum	15169	primuliflorum
14809	traillianum var. dictyotum	15171	adenogynum
14810	aganniphum var. flavorufum	15203	mollicomum
14811	beesianum	15204	tatsienense
14911	crinigerum var. crinigerum	15210	telmateium
14987	haematodes subsp. chaetomallum	15216	uvariifolium var. uvariiflorum
14988	fulvum subsp. fulvoides	15218	cuneatum
15002	pleistanthum	15219	rubiginosum
15004	augustinii subsp. chasmanthum	15222	oreotrephes
15018	selense	15243	adenogynyum
15023	floccigerum	15245	primuliflorum
15035	mekongense var. mekongense	15249	fastigiatum
15038	aganniphum var. aganniphum	15251	hippophaeoides var.
15039	alutaceum var. iodes		hippophaeoides
15043	alutaceum var. russotinctum	15259	trichostomum
15070	adenogynum	15263	tatsienense
15071	heliolepis var. brevistylum	15264	hippophaeoides var.
15072	adenogynum		hippophaeoides
15076	impeditum	15265	hippophaeoides var.
15077	primuliflorum		hippophaeoides
15079	primuliflorum	15266	racemosum
15080	primuliflorum	15267	complexum
15085	telmateium	15268	telmateium
15086	primuliflorum	15269	complexum
15087	trichostomum	15270	rupicola var. rupicola
15088	primuliflorum	15271	primuliflorum
15091	impeditum & fastigiatum	15278	fulvum subsp. fulvoides
15092	primuliflorum	15293	eclecteum var. eclecteum
15093	primuliflorum	15305	traillianum var. traillianum
15095	anthosphaerum	15354	phaeochrysum var. agglutinatum
15096	trichostomum	15356	tapetiforme
15097	irroratum subsp. irroratum	15367	rupicola var. rupicola
15102	arboreum var. delavayi	15370	telmateium
15103	scabrifolium var. scabrifolium	15391	rupicola var. rupicola
15120	telmateium	15392	complexum
15123	traillianum var. traillianum	15399	primuliflorum
15124	beesianum	15400	complexum

15412	wardii var. wardii	15706	araiophyllum
15414	selense subsp. dasycladum	15719	arboreum var. delavayi
15415	phaeochrysum var. agglutinatum	15734	annae
15417	wardii var. puralbum	15736	leptothrium
15418	oreotrephes	15745	tanastylum var. pennivenium
15427	cuneatum	15756	moulmainense
15444	uvariifolium var. uvariiflorum	15761	rubiginosum
15446	tatsienense	15764	basilicum
15448	cuneatum	15766	tanastylum var. tanastylum
15449	trichostomum	15767	meddianum var. meddianum
15450	hippophaeoides var. hippophaeoides	15770	sulfureum
		15774	megacalyx
15452	trichostomum	15776	trichocladum var. trichocladum
15459	hippophaeoides var. hippophaeoides	15777	fulvum subsp. fulvum
		15778	habrotrichum
15462	racemosum	15779	neriiflorum subsp. neriiflorum
15464	cuneatum	15782	sulfureum
15465	oreotrephes	15791	decorum subsp. diaprepes
15466	primuliflorum	15808	callimorphum var. callimorphum
15467	telmateium	15815	griersonianum
15468	telmateium	15816	decorum subsp. diaprepes
15487	brachyanthum subsp. brachyanthum	15887	maddenii subsp. crassum
		15898	arizelum
15497	balfourianum	15899	valentinianum
15504	scabrifolium var. scabrifolium	15908	campylogynum
15520	cyanocarpum	15917	facetum
15521	haematodes subsp. haematodes	15932	dichroanthum subsp. apodectum
15570	cyanocarpum	15933	heliolepis var. heliolepis
15575	dimitrium	15954	annae
15578	rigidum	15967	praestans
15579	selense subsp. jucundum	15968	aganniphum var. aganniphum
15581	rigidum	15969	balfourianum
15588	cyanocarpum	15976	arboreum var. peramoenum
15589	rigidum & sulfureum	15977	rex subsp. fictolacteum
15594	sulfureum	15998	moulmainense
15606	vernicosum	16000	araiophyllum
15609	bureavii	16002	basilicum
15612	fastigiatum	16006	habrotrichum
15613	fastigiatum	16032	pachypodum
15614	fastigiatum	16084	moulmainense
15615	fastigiatum	16128	hippophaeoides var. hippophaeoides
15645	telmateium		
15651	schistocalyx	16249	tatsienense
15658	trichocladum var. trichocladum	16250	hemitrichotum
15659	sinogrande	16252	rupicola var. muliense
15660	fulvum subsp. fulvum	16257	telmateium
15663	neriiflorum subsp. neriiflorum	16277	impeditum
15665	diphrocalyx	16282	yungningense
15667	roseatum	16284	impeditum
15673	leptothrium	16291	oreotrephes
15688	zaleucum	16292	impeditum

16295	primuliflorum	16477	roxieanum var. cucullatum
16296	telmateium	16488	aganniphum var. aganniphum
16300	telmateium	16489	phaeochrysum var. agglutinatum
16301	eudoxum var. eudoxum	16493	wardii var. wardii
16302	phaeochrysum var. phaeochrysum	16508	roxieanum var. oreonastes
		16509	proteoides
16305	nivale subsp. boreale	16511	wardii var. wardii
16306	primuliflorum	16531	uvariifolium var. uvariiflorum
16307	nivale subsp. boreale	16533	floccigerum
16308	primuliflorum	16543	oreotrephes
16311	trichostomum	16555	glischrum subsp. glischrum
16312	primuliflorum	16576	heliolepis var. brevistylum
16313	telmateium	16577	tapetiforme
16314	roxieanum var. cucullatum	16579	rupicola var. chryseum
16315	adenogynum	16580	rupicola var. chryseum
16316	balfourianum	16581	esetulosum
16318	selense subsp. dasycladum	16584	oreotrephes
16319	phaeochrysum var. agglutinatum	16591	anthosphaerum
16320	mimetes aff.	16595	primuliflorum
16321	wardii var. wardii	16597	rubiginosum
16351	protistum var. protistum	16604	proteoides
16352	leptopeplum	16606	roxieanum var. roxieanum
16353	lukiangense	16609	proteoides
16354	anthosphaerum	16616	roxieanum var. cucullatum
16356	primuliflorum	16631	irroratum subsp. irroratum
16360	augustinii var. chasmanthum	16632	arboreum var. delavayi
16361	coriaceum	16637	roxieanum var. oreonastes
16362	pleistanthum	16643	adenogynum
16363	cephalanthum subsp. cephalanthum	16652	clementinae
		16655	rex subsp. rex
16364	coriaceum	16656	phaeochrysum var. levistratum
16367	lukiangense	16667	alutaceum aff.
16375	beesianum	16668	× bathyphyllum (hybrid)
16377	sphaeroblastum	16673	phaeochrysum var. levistratum
16378	lukiangense	16677	aganniphum var. aganniphum
16379	roxieanum var. cucullatum	16679	selense subsp. selense
16380	phaeochrysum var. levistratum	16680	aganniphum
16428	alutaceum var. alutaceum	16683	beesianum
16436	primuliflorum	16684	selense subsp. selense
16439	phaeochrysum var. agglutinatum	16687	microgynum
16449	saluenense subsp. chameunum	16688	anthosphaerum
16450	tapetiforme	16691	haematodes subsp. chaetomallum
16451	aganniphum var. aganniphum	16692	augustinii var. chasmanthum
16455	adenogynum	16693	beesianum
16459	phaeochrysum var. agglutinatum	16695	erastum
16464	phaeochrysum var. agglutinatum	16699	beesianum
16467	phaeochrysum var. levistratum	16702	temenium var. temenium
16469	roxieanum var. cucullatum	16711	eudoxum var. eudoxum
16472	aganniphum var. aganniphum	16713	anthosphaerum
16473	adeonogynum	16721	fulvum subsp. fulvoides
16474	beesianum	16724	beesianum

16726	aganniphum var. aganniphum	17495	anthosphaerum
16727	sanguineum var. himertum	17501	trichocladum var. trichocladum
16728	sanguineum var. himertum	17539	roseatum
16729	alutaceum var. iodes	17551	decorum subsp. diaprepes
16734	traillianum var. dictyotum	17559	roseatum
16735	beesianum	17560	dichroanthum subsp. apodectum
16736	sanguineum var. haemaleum	17572	maddenii subsp. crassum
16739	saluenense subsp. saluenense	17586	decorum subsp. diaprepes
16742	alutaceum var. iodes	17588	virgatum var. oleifolium
16743	beesianum	17596	valentinianum
16745	alutaceum var. iodes	17610	facetum
16746	beesianum	17616	facetum
16749	wardii var. wardii	17622	heliolepis var. heliolepis
16750	selense subsp. selense	17626	neriiflorum subsp. neriiflorum
16751	eudoxum var. mesopolium	17636	fulvum subsp. fulvum
16752	× bathyphyllum (hybrid)	17637	schistocalyx
16753	aganniphum var. flavorufum	17650	basilicum
16754	phaeochrysum var. agglutinatum	17651	callimorphum var. callimorphum
16755	traillianum var. dictyotum	17665	pseudociliipes
16760	aganniphum var. flavorufum	17678	basilicum
16764	aganniphum var. flavorufum	17681	fulvum subsp. fulvum
16765	proteoides	17696	griersonianum
16771	aganniphum var. flavorufum	17703	meddianum var. meddianum
16778	aganniphum var. flavorufum	17708	arboreum var. peramoenum
16779	alutaceum var. iodes	17735	rubiginosum
16780	phaeochrysum var. levistratum	17750	trichocladum var. trichocladum
16790	yunnanense	17819	moulmainense
16806	balfourianum	17824	genestierianum
16811	balfourianum	17827	anthosphaerum
16816	yunnanense	17829	tanastylum var. tanastylum
16836	phaeochrysum var. levistratum	17832	moulmainense
17100	phaeochrysum	17835	tanastylum var. tanastylum
17110	spaeroblastum	17836	araiophyllum
17165	trichostomum	17851	neriiflorum subsp. agetum
17205	rex subsp. fictolacteum	17852	facetum
17220	sp.	17853	mallotum
17227	dendricola	17854	fulvum subsp. fulvum
17330	haematodes subsp. chaetomallum	17900	pseudociliipes
17333	alutaceum aff.	17918	microphyton
17357	alutaceum var. russotinctum	17920	rubiginosum
17406	sinogrande	17927	basilicum
17407	beesianum	17928	kyawii
17447	alutaceum var. iodes	17930	arboreum var. peramoenum
17456	augustinii var. chasmanthum	17937	zaleucum
17461	lukiangense	17943	anthosphaerum
17463	lukiangense	17950	neriiflorum subsp. neriiflorum
17464	rubiginosum	17963	valentinianum
17466	aganniphum	17996	neriiflorum subsp. neriiflorum
17473	phaeochrysum var. levistratum	18000	yunnanense
17476	augustinii var. chasmanthum	18022	trichocladum var. trichocladum
17483	rubiginosum	18028	arizelum

18030	campylogynum	19007	vernicosum
18036	meddianum var. meddianum	19008	sanguineum
18041	cephalanthum subsp.	19009	sanguineum
	platyphyllum	19010	beesianum
18042	zaleucum	19011	beesianum
18044	callimorphum var. callimorphum	19015	rubiginosum
18045	arizelum	10919	selense subsp. selense
18049	griersonianum	19154	proteoides
18052	basilicum	19165	proteoides
18054	sidereum	19169	sanguineum subsp. cloiophorum
18069	habrotrichum	19193	vernicosum
18108	basilicum		
18153	dichroanthum subsp. apodectum	**CHINA, NW YUNNAN EXP.**	
18167	dichroanthum subsp. apodectum	**(1921-22)**	
18168	anthosphaerum		
18171	facetum	19355	protistum var. giganteum
18173	maddenii subsp. crassum	19404	racemosum
18210	maddenii subsp. crassum	19437	saluenense subsp. chameunum
18273	facetum	19440	russatum
18310	fulvum subsp. fulvum	19450	polycladum
18329	genestierianum	19458	russatum
18349	trichocladum var. trichocladum	19467	wardii var. wardii
18355	pseudociliipes	19468	anthosphaerum
18393	protistum var. protistum	19479	saluenense subsp. saluenense
18394	protistum var. protistum	19492	cephalanthum subsp.
18395	kyawii		cephalanthum
18458	protistum var. giganteum	19512	wardii var. wardii
18475	moulmainense	19515	forrestii subsp. forrestii
18548	protistum var. protistum	19540	martinianum
18686	sanguineum var. cloiophorum aff.	19541	brachyanthum subsp.
18900	virgatum subsp. oleifolium		hypolepidotum
18901	eclecteum var. eclecteum	19544	oreotrephes
18902	decorum subsp. decorum	19552	beesianum
18903	augustinii var. chasmanthum	19554	lukiangense
18904	yunnanense	19555	rex subsp. fictolacteum
18905	saluenense subsp. saluenense	19562	alutaceum var. russotinctum
18906	augustinii var. chasmanthum	19567	alutaceum var. iodes
18907	heliolepis var. brevistylum	19569	sanguineum var. didymoides
18908	moulmainense	19570	megeratum
18909	mekongense var. mekongense	19574	alutaceum var. iodes
18912	alutaceum var. iodes	19597	nivale subsp. boreale
18914	praestans	19607	rupicola var. chryseum
18917	haematodes subsp. chaetomallum	19674	tapetiforme
18918	calostrotum subsp. keleticum	19701	pleistanthum
18920	aganniphum var. flavorufum	19704	alutaceum var. russotinctum
18933	rubiginosum	19713	aganniphum var. aganniphum
18934	sanguineum var. haemaleum	19714	phaeochrysum var. agglutinatum
18937	eudoxum var. mesopolium	19716	aganniphum var. aganniphum
18938	citriniflorum var. citriniflorum	19733	phaeochrysum var. agglutinatum
18943	eclecteum var. eclecteum	19743	wardii var. wardii
19006	proteoides	19744	aganniphum var. aganniphum

19758	aganniphum var. aganniphum
19769	floccigerum
19772	lukiangense
19773	aganniphum var. aganniphum
19781	lukiangense
19783	phaeochrysum
19793	phaeochrysum var. levistratum
19798	phaeochrysum var. levistratum
19814	augustinii subsp. chasmanthum
19819	lukiangense
19822	phaeochrysum var. agglutinatum
19825	augustinii subsp. chasmanthum
19827	alutaceum var. alutaceum
19828	aganniphum var. aganniphum
19844	monanthum
19866	rupicola var. chryseum
19872	brachyanthum subsp. hypolepidotum
19911	haematodes subsp. chaetomallum
19911a	× hemigymnum (hybrid)
19912	mekongense var. mekongense
19913	saluenense subsp. saluenese
19915	calostrotum subsp. keleticum
19917	genestierianum
19919	calostrotum subsp. keleticum
19930	mekongense var. mekongense
19952	eclecteum var. eclecteum
19954	selense subsp. setiferum
19955	haematodes subsp. chaetomallum
19956	monanthum
19958	sanguineum var. haemaleum
19959	haematodes subsp. chaetomallum
19960	temenium var. dealbatum
19977	pocophorum var. pocophorum
19978	haematodes subsp. chaetomallum
19982	sanguineum var. didymoides
19983	pocophorum var. pocophorum
19993	rupicola var. chryseum
19994	saluenense subsp. chameunum
20003	sperabiloides
20005	heliolepis var. heliolepis
20008	lukiangense
20015	haematodes subsp. chaetomallum
20019	pocophorum var. pocophorum
20020	fulvum subsp. fulvoides
20021	xanthostephanum
20023	campylocarpum subsp. caloxanthum
20025	haematodes var. chaetomallum
20026	haematodes var. chaetomallum
20027	forrestii subsp. forrestii
20028	pocophorum var. hemidartum
20062	cephalanthum subsp. cephalanthum
20063	augustinii subsp. chasmanthum
20064	augustinii subsp. chasmanthum
20067	virgatum subsp. oleifolium
20071	temenium var. temenium
20075	fulvum subsp. fulvoides
20078	catacosmum
20085	anthosphaerum
20090	citriniflorum var. citriniflorum
20094	megacalyx
20095	rubiginosum
20106	protistum var. protistum
20118	maddenii subsp. crassum
20120	rex subsp. fictolacteum
20176	pleistanthum
20185	pleistanthum
20196	primuliflorum
20208	tepetiforme
20213	phaeochrysum var. agglutinatum
20215	haematodes subsp. chaetomallum
20218	citriniflorum var. horaeum
20220	sanguineum subsp. didymum
20230	tephropeplum
20235	calostrotum subsp. keleticum
20239	sanguineum subsp. didymum
20246	martinianum
20253	sanguineum var. haemaleum
20255	calostrotum subsp. keleticum
20262	habrotrichum
20286	aganniphum
20291	vernicosum
20297	bainbridgeanum
20299	haematodes subsp. chaetomallum
20302	stewartianum aff.
20305	floccigerum aff.
20306	arizelum
20318	phaeochrysum var. levistratum
20321	floccigerum
20322	coryanum
20323	bainbridgeanum
20330	phaeochrysum var. levistratum
20332	megeratum
20333	haematodes subsp. chaetomallum
20338	selense subsp. setiferum
20347	phaeochrysum var. agglutinatum
20381	rex
20387	sinogrande
20388	nuttallii
20415	adenogynum

20416	sphaeroblastum
20418	phaeochrysum var. levistratum
20419	mimetes
20425	roxieanum
20426	alutaceum var. iodes aff.
20428	mimetes var. simulans
20429	primuliflorum
20430	yunnanense
20432	rupicola subsp. muliense
20434	yunnanense
20440	sphaeroblastum
20442	phaeochrysum var. levistratum
20444	adenogynum
20445	sphaeroblastum
20446	sphaeroblastum
20447	sphaeroblastum
20450	intricatum
20451	beesianum
20452	primuliflorum
20454	impeditum
20455	balfourianum
20456	balfourianum
20457	telmateium
20460	yungningense
20461	telmateium
20462	nivale subsp. boreale
20463	yungingense
20464	rupicola var. rupicola
20465	primuliflorum
20470	wardii var. wardii
20476	trichostomum
20477	telmateium
20480	trichostomum
20481	oreotrephes
20482	tatsienense
20484	racemosum
20485	yunnanense
20486	tatsienense
20488	orthocladum var. orthocladum
20489	oreotrephes
20492	impeditum
20498	rex subsp. rex
20525	mollicomum
20625	rubiginosum
20629	oreotrephes
20648	tatsienense × siderophyllum (hybrid)
20678	irroratum subsp. irroratum
20693	lepidotum
20708	rupicola var. rupicola
20783	oreotrephes
20793	pleistanthum
20795	pleistanthum
20814	anthosphaerum
20816	fulvum
20817	rex subsp. fictolacteum
20819	sinogrande
20821	rex
20824	trichocladum var. longipilosum
20825	sperabiloides
20826	martinianum
20832	coryanum
20834	wardii var. wardii
20835	brachyanthum subsp. hypolepidotum
20840	oreotrephes
20845	genesstierianum
20861	calostrotum subsp. keleticum
20863	protistum var. protistum
20864	calostrotum subsp. keleticum
20865	anthosphaerum
20877	floccigerum aff.
20879	monanthum
20880	xanthostephanum
20881	bainbridgeanum
20884	tephropeplum
20885	floccigerum aff.
20886	stewartianum hybrid
20888	sanguineum subsp. didymum
20889	temenium var. temenium
20891	sanguineum
20893	sanguineum
20895	catacosmum
20896	calostrotum subsp. riparium
20897	megacalyx
20899	nuttallii
20905	sanguineum
20906	megeratum
20910	sanguineum
20911	sanguineum
20912	saluenense subsp. saluenense
20917	maddenii subsp. crassum
20923	pleistanthum
20926	pleistanthum
20934	lukiangense
20950	russatum
20956	rupicola var. chryseum
20961	hylaeum
20973	augustinii subsp. chasmanthum
20978	lukiangense
20987	mekongense var. mekongense
21000	selense subsp. selense

21006	oreotrephes	21405	sphaeroblastum
21009	sphaeroblastum	21408	roxieanum var. cucullatum
21010	sphaeroblastum	21409	adenogynum
21011	phaeochrysum var. levistratum	21410	adenogynum
21012	phaeochrysum var. levistratum	21442	tatsienense
21013	eclecteum var. eclecteum	21462	hippophaeoides var. occidentale
21017	wardii var. wardii	21463	xanthostephanum
21018	phaeochrysum var. levistratum	21470	yunnanense
21019	phaeochrysum var. levistratum	21475	irroratum subsp. irroratum
21020	phaeochrysum var. agglutinatum	21476	hippophaeoides var. occidentale
21021	phaeochrysum	21478	lukiangense
21027	rubiginosum	21487	polycladum
21030	cuneatum	21488	racemosum
21031	intricatum	21490	russatum & rupicola var. rupicola
21039	sphaeroblastum	21492	nivale subsp. australe
21040	sphaeroblastum	21507	fastigiatum
21045	phaeochrysum var. agglutinatum	21528	polycladum
21047	phaeochrysum var. levistratum	21529	russatum & rupicola var. rupicola
21048	phaeochrysum var. levistratum	21531	neriiflorum subsp. phaedropum
21049	roxieanum var. cucullatum	21533	fastigiatum & rigidum
21051	sphaerblastum	21539	rex subsp. fictolacteum
21052	phaeochrysum var. levistratum	21546	roxieanum
21055	balfourianum	21547	nivale subsp. australe
21056	balfourianum	21549	racemosum
21239	telmateium	21551	wardii var. wardii
21241	orthocladum var. orthocladum	21559	polycladum
21248	intricatum	21560	racemosum
21250	telmateium	21563	selense subsp. dasycladum
21252	racemosum & tatsienense	21564	edgeworthii
21253	trichostomum	21577	telmateium
21265	saluenense subsp. chameunum	21582	maddenii subsp. crassum
21270	tatsienense	21586	beesianum
21274	orthocladum var. orthocladum	21680	(= 22751) nuttallii
	× impeditum (hybrid)	21681	(= 22803) floccigerum
21282	yungningense	21682	lukiangense
21287	phaeochrysum var. levistratum	21683	lukiangense
21288	orthocladum var. orthocladum	21685	(= 22733) lukiangense
21292	elegantulum	21686	(= 22884) anthosphasrum
21299	trichostomum	21687	(= 22702) stewartianum aff.
21306	racemosum	21688	(= 22846) bainbridgeanum
21321	racemosum	21689	(= 22899) selense subsp. selense
21323	irroratum subsp. irroratum	21690	sp.
21344	intricatum	21692	genestierianum
21348	heliolepis var. brevistylum	21693	coryanum
21351	racemosum	21694	(= 22938) eurysiphon
21358	yunnanense	21695	(= 22939) megacalyx
21377	telmateium	21697	(= 22901) bainbridgeanum
21390	phaeochrysum var. phaeochrysum	21699	mekongense var. mekongense
		21700	(= 22885) anthosphaerum
21400	phaeochrysum var. phaeochrysum	21701	megeratum
		21702	(= 22804) floccigerum

21703 (= 22806) floccigerum
21704 (= 22805) floccigerum
21705 (= 22761) sinogrande
21706 tephropeplum
21707 (= 22652) xanthostephanum
21708 (= 22610) stewartianum
21709 (= 22886) pocophorum var.
         hemidartum
21710 haematodes subsp.
         chaetomallum
21711 (= 22912) pocophorum var.
         pocophorum
21712 (= 22913) pocophorum var.
         pocophorum
21713 (= 22909) pocophorum var.
         pocophorum
21714 (= 22831) edgeworthii
21716 (= 22833) virgatum subsp.
         oleifolium
21718 chamaethomsonii/forrestii
21720 (= 22916) pocophorum var.
         pocophorum
21721 pocophorum var. pocophorum
21723 (= 22674) chamaethomsonii var.
         chamaethomsonii
21724 (= 22923) forrestii aff.
21725 (= 22863) × xanthanthum (hybrid)
21727 (= 22910 = 22015) catacosmum
21728 × hemigymnum (hybrid)
21729 (= 22847) × xanthanthum (hybrid)
21730 (= 22649) × xanthanthum aff.
         (hybrid)
21731 (= 22656) × xanthanthum (hybrid)
21732 (= 22705) sanguineum var.
         haemaleum
21733 (= 22697) temenium var. gilvum
21734 temenium var. temenium
21735 (= 22677) sanguineum var.
         haemaleum
21736 (= 22633) × hillieri (hybrid)
21737 × hillieri (hybrid)
21738 eudoxum var. eudoxum
21739 (= 22676) sanguineum var.
         cloiophorum
21740 (= 22687) sanguineum var.
         haemaleum
21741 × erythrocalyx (hybrid)
21743 (= 2273) selense subsp. selense
21744 temenium var. dealbatum
21745 (= 22860) haematodes subsp.
         chaetomallum aff.

21746 (= 22667) sanguineum var.
         didymoides
21747 sanguineum var. didymoides
21748 sanguineum var. didymoides
21750 (= 22852) sanguineum subsp.
         didymum
21751 citriniflorum var. citriniflorum
21752 (= 22679) citriniflorum
21753 (= 22670) haematodes subsp.
         haematodes
21754 (= 22694) sanguineum var.
         didymoides
21755 (= 22767) campylocarpum subsp.
         caloxanthum
21756 calostrotum subsp. keleticum
21757 (= 22659) calostrotum subsp.
         keleticum
21758 (= 22688) haematodes subsp.
         chaetomallum
21759 (= 22862) haematodes subsp.
         haematodes
21760 (= 22666) saluenense subsp.
         saluenense
21761 (= 22721) bainbridgeanum
21763 (= 22621) stewartianum
21764 eudoxum var. mesopolium
21765 (= 22685) sanguineum subsp.
         didymoides
21766 (= 22718) bainbridgeanum
21767 eudoxum var. eudoxum
21768 (= 22706) chamaethomsonii var.
         chamaedoron
21769 (= 22710) eclecteum var.
         eclecteum
21770 (= 22850) eclecteum var.
         bellatulum
21771 rex subsp. fictolacteum
21772 saluenense subsp. saluenense
21773 anthosphaerum
21774 (= 22735) lukiangense
21775 (= 22940) martinianum
21776 mekongense var. mekongense
21777 (= 22807) floccigerum
21778 (= 22653) xanthostephanum
21779 (= 22809) floccigerum
21780 (= 22810) floccigerum
21781 (= 22619) stewartianum
21782 sanguineum/temenium
21783 sanguineum var. didymoides
21784 (= 22709) temenium var.
         gilvum aff.

21785 (= 22858) haematodes subsp. chaetomallum aff.

21786 (= 22924) forrestii subsp. forrestii

21787 (= 22611) stewartianum

21809 temenium var. temenium

21810 (= 22918) fulvum subsp. fulvum

21811 (= 22856) leptocarpum

21812 glischrum subsp. glischrum

21813 glischrum subsp. glischrum

21814 (= 22902) fulvum subsp. fulvoides

21815 fulvum

21816 (= 22762) uvariifolium var. uvariiflorum

21817 uvariifolium var. uvariiflorum

21818 coriaceum

21819 (= 22724) sanguineum var. haemaleum

21821 (= 22713) bainbridgeanum

21822 oreotrephes

21823 sanguineum var. haemaleum

21824 (= 22808) sperabiloides

21825 (= 22654) monanthum

21826 (= 22657) haematodes subsp. chaetomallum

21827 eudoxum var. eudoxum

21828 (= 22894) pocophorum var. pocophorum

21829 (= 22720) bainbridgeanum

21830 (= 22911) pocophorum var. pocophorum

21831 (= 22883) haematodes subsp. chaetomallum

21832 (= 22719) bainbridgeanum

21833 (= 22715) bainbridgeanum

21834 (= 22717) bainbridgeanum

21835 (= 22622) oreotrephes

21836 campylocarpum subsp. caloxanthum

21837 × hemigymnum (hybrid)

21828 (= 22893) eclecteum var. bellatulum

21839 (= 22708) eclecteum var. bellatulum

21840 eclecteum var. eclecteum

21841 (= 22618) stewartianum

21842 (= 22892) eclecteum var. eclecteum

21843 coriaceum

21844 (= 22730) temenium var. gilvum

21845 eudoxum var. mesopolium

21846 (= 22707) stewartianum hybrid

21848 (= 22665) haematodes subsp. chaetomallum aff.

21849 (= 22859) haematodes subsp. chaetomallum aff.

21850 (= 22690) temenium hybrid

21851 (= 22668) citriniflorum var. horaeum

21852 (= 22680) citriniflorum var. horaeum

21853 haematodes subsp. haematodes

21854 (= 22675) citriniflorum var. horaeum

21855 citriniflorum var. horaeum

21856 sanguineum var. didymoides

21857 (= 22693) haematodes subsp. chaetomallum

21858 (= 22683) × hillieri (hybrid)

21860 citriniflorum var. horaeum

21861 (= 22770) rex

21862 (= 22784) arizelum

21863 (= 22771) rex subsp. fictolacteum

21864 (= 22703) arizelum

21865 (= 22786) arizelum

21866 (= 22772) rex

21867 (= 22785) rex subsp. fictolacteum

21868 (= 22787) rex subsp. fictolacteum

21869 (= 22788) rex

21870 (= 22738) semnoides

21871 (= 22890) rex subsp. fictolacteum

21872 (= 22658) haematodes subsp. chaetomallum

21873 (= 22857) haematodes subsp. chaetomallum

21874 (= 22898) selense subsp. selense

21875 campylocarpum subsp. caloxanthum

21876 (= 22800) selense subsp. selense

21877 (= 22895) selense subsp. setiferum

21878 (= 22906) selense subsp. selense

21879 (= 22905) selense subsp. selense

21880 crinigerum var. crinigerum

21881 (= 22891) eclecteum var. eclecteum

21882 (= 22647) eclecteum var. eclecteum

21884 (= 22728) × hemigymnum (hybrid)

21885 (= 22612) stewartianum

21886 (= 22648) eclecteum var. bellatulum

21887	(= 22711) eclecteum var. bellatulum
21888	(= 22620) stewartianum
21889	(= 22613) stewartianum
21891	(= 22615) stewartianum
21892	(= 22758) selense subsp. selense
21893	(= 22729) bainbridgeanum
21894	(= 22716) bainbridgeanum
21895	(= 22722) bainbridgeanum
21896	(= 22903) fulvum subsp. fulvoides
21897	(= 22768) fulvum subsp. fulvoides
21898	(= 22917) fulvum subsp. fulvoides
21899	coriaceum
21900	(= 22802) chamaethomsonii var. chamaethomsonii
21901	temenium var. dealbatum
21902	(= 22698) temenium var. dealbatum
21903	(= 22695) temenium var. dealbatum
21904	(= 22699) temenium var. dealbatum
21905	(= 22904) temenium var. gilvum aff.
21906	(= 22900?) × hillieri (hybrid)
21907	(= 22726) sanguineum var. haemaleum
21908	(= 22671) × hillieri (hybrid)
21909	(= 2270) eudoxum
21910	stewartianum hybrid
21911	(= 22731) × hillieri (hybrid)
21912	(= 22692) × hillieri (hybrid)
21914	(= 22701) temenium var. gilvum
21916	chamaethomsonii var. chamaedoron
21917	(= 22897) selense subsp. selense
21918	(= 22617) stewartianum
21919	(= 22614) stewartianum
21923	cephalanthum subsp. cephalanthum
21932	telmateium
21934	traillianum var. traillianum
21936	maddenii subsp. crassum
21944	roxieanum var. cucullatum
21948	cuneatum
21954	wardii var. wardii
21955	racemosum
21965	racemosum
21969	arboreum var. delavayi
21972	nivale subsp. australe
21974	nivale subsp. australe
21975	rupicola var. rupicola
21977	lukiangense
21981	anthosphaerum
21988	orthocladum var. longistylum
22014	roxieanum var. cucullatum
22019	selense subsp. dasycladum
22020	rex subsp. fictolacteum
22187	roxienaum var. cucullatum
22197	cuneatum
22202	clementinae
22295	russatum & rupicola var. rupicola
22299	polycladum
22300	campylogynum
22320	primuliflorum
22610	(= 21708) stewartianum
22611	(= 21787) stewartianum
22612	(= 21885) stewartianum
22613	(= 21889) stewartianum
22614	(= 21919) stewartianum
22615	(= 21891) stewartianum
22617	(= 21918) stewartianum
22618	(= 21841) stewartianum
22619	(= 21781) stewartianum
22620	(= 21888) stewartianum
22621	(= 21763) stewartianum
22647	(= 21882) eclecteum var. eclecteum
22648	(= 21886) eclecteum var. eclecteum
22649	(= 21730) haematodes subsp. chaetomallum aff.
22652	(= 21707) xanthostephanum
22653	(= 21778) xanthostephanum
22654	(= 21825) monanthum
22656	(= 21731) × xanthanthum (hybrid)
22657	(= 21826) haematodes subsp. chaetomallum
22658	(= 21872) haematodes subsp. chaetomallum
22659	(= 21757) calostrotum subsp. keleticum
22665	(= 21848) × xanthanthum (hybrid)
22666	(= 21760) saluenense subsp. saluenense
22667	(= 21746) sanguineum var. didymoides
22668	(= 21851) citriniflorum var. horaeum
22670	(= 21753) haematodes subsp. haematodes

22671 (= 21908) haematodes subsp. haematodes

22674 (= 21723) chamaethomsonii var. chamaethomsonii

22675 (= 21854) citriniflorum var. horaeum

22676 (= 21739) sanguineum var. cloiophorum

22677 (= 21735) sanguineum var. haemaleum

22679 (= 21752) citriniflorum var. citriniflorum

22680 (= 21852) citriniflorum var. citriniflorum aff.

22682 (= 22725 = 21915) sanguineum var. haemaleum

22683? (= 21858) citriniflorum var. citriniflorum

22685 (= 21765) sanguineum var. didymoides

22687 (= 21740) sanguineum var. haemaleum

22688 (= 21758) haematodes subsp. chaetomallum

22690 (= 21850) citriniflorum var. horaeum

22694 (= 21754) citriniflorum var. horaeum

22695 (= 21903) temenium var. dealbatum

22697 (= 21733) temenium var. gilvum

22698 (= 21902) temenium var. dealbatum

22699 (= 21904) temenium var. gilvum

22700 (= 21909) eudoxum

22702 (= 21687) stewartianum

22703 (= 21864) rex subsp. fictolacteum

22705 (= 21732) sanguineum

22706 (= 21768) chamaethomsonii var. chamaedoron

22708 (= 21839) eclecteum var. bellatulum

22709 (= 21781) temenium var. gilvum aff.

22710 (= 21769) eclecteum var. eclecteum

22711 (= 21887) selense subsp. selense

22713 (= 21821) bainbridgeanum

22714 (= 21762) bainbridgeanum

22715 (= 21833) bainbridgeanum

22716 (= 21894) bainbridgeanum

22717 (= 21834) bainbridgeanum

22718 (= 21766) bainbridgeanum

22719 (= 21832) bainbridgeanum

22720 (= 21829) bainbridgeanum

22721 (= 21761) bainbridgeanum

22722 (= 21895) bainbridgeanum

22723 brachyanthum subsp. hypolepidotum

22724 (= 21819) sanguineum var. haemaleum

22725 (= 22682 = 21915) sanguineum

22726 (= 21907) sanguineum var. haemaleum

22728 (= 21884) eclecteum var. eclecteum

22729 (= 21893) bainbridgeanum

22730 (= 21844) temenium var. gilvum

22733 (= 21685) lukiangense

22735 (= 21774) lukiangense

22739 (= 21743) selense subsp. selense

22751 (= 21680) nuttallii

22758 (= 21892) selense subsp. selense

22761 (= 21705) sinogrande

22767 (= 21755) selense subsp. setiferum

22768 (= 21898) fulvum subsp. fulvoides

22770 (= 21861) rex

22771 (= 21863) arizelum

22772 (= 21866) rex

22784 (= 21862) rex

22785 (= 21867) rex subsp. fictolacteum

22786 (= 21865) arizelum

22787 (= 21868) arizelum

22788 (= 21869) rex

22800 (= 21876) selense subsp. selense

22802 (= 21900) chamaethomsonii var. chamaethomsonii

22803 (= 21681) floccigerum

22804 (= 21702) floccigerum

22805 (= 21705) floccigerum

22806 (= 21703) floccigerum

22807 (= 21777) floccigerum

22808 (= 21824) floccigerum aff.

22809 (= 21779) floccigerum

22810 (= 21780) floccigerum

22822 (= 21696) megacalyx

22831 (= 21714) edgeworthii

22833 (= 21716) virgatum subsp. oleifolium

22846 (= 21688) bainbridgeanum

22847 (= 21729) × xanthanthum (hybrid)

22850	(= 21770) eclecteum var. eclecteum
22842	(= 21750) sanguineum subsp. didymum
22853	eclecteum var. eclecteum
22856	(= 21811) leptocarpum
22857	(= 21873) haematodes subsp. chaetomallum
22858	(= 21785) haematodes subsp. chaetomallum aff.
22859	(= 21785) haematodes subsp. chaetomallum aff.
22860	(= 21745) haematodes subsp. chaetomallum aff.
22862	(= 21759) citriniflorum var. horaeum
22863	(= 21725) haematodes subsp. chaetomallum aff.
22883	(= 21831) haematodes subsp. chaetomallum
22884	(= 21686) anthosphaerum
22885	(= 21700) anthosphaerum
22886	(= 21709) pocophorum var. hemidartum
22890	(= 21871) rex subsp. fictolacteum
22891	(= 21881) eclecteum var. eclecteum
22892	(= 21842) eclecteum var. eclecteum
22893	(= 21838) eclecteum var. eclecteum
22894	(= 21828) pocophorum var. pocophorum
22895	(= 21877) selense subsp. setiferum
22897	(= 21917) campylocarpum subsp. caloxanthum
22898	(= 21874) selense subsp. selense
22899	(= 21689) selense subsp. selense
22900?	(= 21906) sperabiloides
22901	(= 21697) bainbridgeanum
22902	(= 21814) fulvum subsp. fulvoides
22903	(= 21896) fulvum subsp. fulvoides
22905	(= 21879) selense subsp. selense
22906	(= 21878) selense subsp. selense
22909	(= 21713) pocophorum var. pocophorum
22910	(= 22915 = 21727) catacosmum
22911	(= 21830) pocophorum var. pocophorum
22912	(= 21711) pocophorum var. pocophorum

22913	(= 21712) pocophorum var. pocophorum
22915	(= 21727 = 22910) catacosmum
22916	(= 21720) pocophorum var. pocophorum
22918	(= 21810) fulvum subsp. fulvoides
22922	forrestii subsp. forrestii
22923	(= 21724) forrestii hybrid
22924	(= 21786) forrestii subsp. forrestii
22938	(= 21694) eurysiphon
22939	(= 21695) martinianum
22940	(= 21775) martinianum
22941	pocophorum var. hemidartum

YUNNAN & SE TIBET, CHINA & NE BURMA EXP. (1924-25)

24009	arboreum var. delavayi
24060	tanastylum var. tanastylum
24070	tanastylum var. tanastylum
24091	neriiflorum subsp. neriiflorum
24101	zaleucum
24104	meddianum var. meddianum
24107	diphrocalyx
24110	fulvum subsp. fulvum
24113	dichroanthum subsp. apodectum
24116	griersonianum
24117	annae
24131	sulfureum
24138	valentinianum
24139	basilicum
24140	sinogrande
24149	tanastylum var. pennivenium
24154	shweliense
24160	trichocladum var. trichocladum
24193	arizelum
24201	facetum
24219	meddianum var. meddianum
24220	neriiflorum subsp. neriiflorum
24225	basilicum
24228	virgatum subsp. oleifolium
24229	sulfureum
24235	sulfureum
24283	pseudociliipes
24305	dichroanthum subsp. apodectum
24308	pseudociliipes
24312	tanastylum var. tanastylum
24314	fulvum subsp. fulvoides
24315	habrotrichum
24331	dichroanthum subsp. apodectum
24350	callimorphum var. callimorphum

24496	maddenii subsp. crassum	25065	dichroanthum subsp. scyphocalyx
24528	stewartianum	25067	mallotum
24530	stewartianum	25076	fulvum subsp. fulvum
24532	dichroanthum subsp. scyphocalyx	25090	sidereum
24535	rubiginosum	25100	(= 26081) basilicum
24542	kyawii	25340	sulfureum
24544	dichroanthum subsp. scyphocalyx	25446	yungchangense
24546	dichroanthum subsp. scyphocalyx	25447	(= 25923) sperabile var. weihsiense
24562	zaleucum	25449	(= 25938) rubiginosum
24563	sidereum	25474	(= 25920) sperabile var. sperabile
24570	campylogynum	25481	(= 25919) sperabile var. weihsiense
24571	cephalanthum subsp. cephalanthum	25494	(= 25978) wardii var. wardii
24572	calosstrotum subsp. calostrotum	25496	(= 25930 ?) fastigiatum
24574	rupicola var. rupicola	25498	(= 25912) polycladum
24575	trichocladum var. trichocladum	25500	(= 25908) russatum
24577	heliolepis var. heliolepis	25503	(= 25921) calostrotum subsp. riparioides
24592	facetum	25505	(= 25891) roxieanum var. cucullatum
24598	stewartianum		
24600	anthosphaerum	25506	calostrotum subsp. riparioides
24603	dichroanthum subsp. scyphocalyx	25507	(= 25957) sanguineum var. didymoides
24616	dichroanthum subsp. scyphocalyx	25508	(= 25895= ?25923) saluenense subsp. chameunum
24618	yunnanense	25509	(= 25988) mekongense var. mekongense
24620	dichroanthum subsp. scyphocalyx		
24633	(= 26115) lepidostylum	25512	(= 25896) rex subsp. fictolacteum
24660	hylaeum	25513	(= 25893) beesianum
24680	kyawii	25514	(= 25883) roxieanum
24683	dichroanthum subsp. scyphocalyx	25515	(= 25926) roxieanum var. oreonastes
24688	megacalyx	25516	(= 25983) beesianum
24712	dichroanthum subsp. apodectum	25518	(= 25906) sanguineum var. sanguineum
24728	dichroanthum subsp. apodectum	25520	(= 25966) aganniphum var. aganniphum
24729	(= 25999) megacalyx		
24730	maddenii subsp. crassum	25521	(= 25943) sanguineum var. sanguineum
24739	facetum		
24740	arizelum	25524	(= 25961) chamaethomsonii/ forrestii
24742	sidereum		
24747	maddenii subsp. crassum	25526	(= 25982) yungningense
24748	facetum	25529	(= 25941) rupicola var. rupicola
24774	dendricola	25532	(= 25931) rupicola var. rupicola
24775	protistum var. protistum	25534	(= 25979) wardii var. wardii
24831	genestierianum	25535	(= 25880) selense subsp. dasycladum
25011	calostrotum		
25020	fulvum	25542	(= 25922) calostrotum subsp. riparioides
25064	preptum		

25543   (= 25913) sanguineum var.
        sanguineum
25553   russatum
25555   polycladum
25560   (= 25835) saluenense subsp.
        chamaeunum
25563   (= 25878) aperantum hybrid
25564   (= 25942) chionanthum
25565   haematodes subsp. chaetomallum
        aff.
25569   (= 25935) sperabile var.
        weihsiense
25570   (= 25808) charitopes subsp.
        charitopes
25572   (= 25775) tephropeplum
25574   (= 25857) maddenii subsp.
        crassum
25575   (= 25843) brachyanthum subsp.
        hypolepidotum
25576   (= 25796) zaleucum
25577   (= 25787) dichroanthum subsp.
        septentrionale
25578   (= 25861) dumicola
25579   (= 25855) dichroanthum subsp.
        scyphocalyx
25580   (= ?25993) dumicola
25581   (= 25789) charitopes subsp.
        charitopes
25584   kyawii
25585   (= 25850) crinigerum var.
        crinigerum
25586   (= 25854) maddenii subsp.
        crassum
25588   (= 25612) leptocarpum
25593   (= 25806) × erythrocalyx (hybrid)
25597   (= 25877) haematodes subsp.
        chaetomallum
25601   (= 25862) haematodes subsp.
        chaetomallum
25602   (= 25856) haematodes subsp.
        chaetomallum
25603   eclecteum
25604   (=? 25873) eclecteum var.
        eclecteum
25605   (= 25845) × hemigymnum
        (hybrid)
25606   (= 25765) zaleucum
25607   (= 25786) haematodes subsp.
        chaetomallum
25608   (= 25782) arizelum
25609   (= 25790) zaleucum

25610   (= 25785) glischrum subsp.
        glischrum
25611   (= 25799) zaleucum
25612   (= 25588) leptocarpum
25614   (= 25811) martinianum
25615   (= 25864) stewartianum
25616   glischrum subsp. glischrum
25617   (= 25858) monanthum
25618   (= 25859) stewartianum
25619   (= 25794) crinigerum var.
        euadenium
25620   (= 25814) stewartianum
25622   (= 25822) coriaceum
25624   (= 25853) nuttallii
25625   (= 25870) coelicum
25627   (= 25841) arizelum
25629   (= 25767) maddenii subsp.
        crassum
25630   (= 25784) coriaceum
25631   (= 25852) sulfureum
25633   crinigerum var. euadenium
25634   crinigerum var. euadenium
25636   (= 25821) calvescens var.
        calvescens
25639   (= 25830) semnoides
25640   (= 25800) floccigerum aff.
25641   (= 25803) crinigerum var.
        crinigerum
25642   (= 25869) stewartianum
25644   (= 25766) tephropeplum
25645   (= 25777) glischrum subsp.
        rude
25646   stewartianum
25647   (= 25834) coelicum
25683   (= 25817) calostrotum subsp.
        riparioides
25684   (= 25825) protistum var.
        giganteum
25697   (= 25902) aganniphum var.
        aganniphum
25701   (= 25940) proteoides
25705   (= 25917) clementinae
25707   nivale subsp. australe
25714   (= 25820) tephropeplum
25716   (= 25992) praestans
25717   (= 25949) rothschildii
25718   (= 25929) roxieanum var.
        oreonastes
25719   rex subsp. fictolacteum
25725   (= 25927) glischrum subsp.
        glischrum

25737	(= 25899) selense subsp. dasycladum
25738	(= 25938) roxieanum var. cucullatum aff.
25740	(= 25918) traillianum var. traillianum
25742	(= 25916) clementinae
25744	fulvum subsp. fulvoides
25765	(= 25606) zaleucum
25766	(= 25644) tephropeplum
25767	(= 25629) maddenii subsp. crassum
25775	(= 25572) tephropeplum
25777	(= 25645) glischrum subsp. rude
25782	(= 25608) arizelum
25784	(= 25630) coriaceum
25785	(= 25610) glischrum subsp. glischrum
25786	(= 25607) pocophorum aff.
25787	(= 25577) dichroanthum subsp. septentrionale
25789	(= 25581) charitopes subsp. charitopes
25794	(= 25619) crinigerum var. euadenium
25796	(= 25576) zaleucum
25799	(= 25611) zaleucum
25800	(= 25640) floccigerum aff.
25803	(= 25641) crinigerum var. crinigerum
25806	(= 25593) calvescens var. calvescens
25808	(= 25570) charitopes subsp. charitopes
25811	(= 25614) martinianum
25814	(= 25620) stewartianum
25817	(= 25683) calostrotum subsp. riparium
25818	crinigerum var. euadenium
25820	(= 25714) tephropeplum
25821	(= 25636) eclecteum hybrid
25822	(= 25622) coriaceum
25825	(= 25684) protistum var. giganteum
25830	(= 25639) semnoides
25831	floccigerum aff.
25834	(= 25647) coelicum
25835	(= 25560) saluenense subsp. chameunum
25841	(= 25627) arizelum

25843	(= 25575) brachyanthum subsp. hypolepidotum
25845	(= 25605) × hemigymnum (hybrid)
25850	(= 25585) crinigerum var. euadenium
25852	(= 25631) sulfureum
25853	(= 25624) nuttallii
25854	(= 25586) maddenii subsp. crassum
25855	(= 25579) dichroanthum subsp. scyphocalyx
25856	(= 25602) coelicum
25857	(= 25574) maddenii subsp. crassum
25858	(= 25617) monanthum
25859	(= 25618) stewartianum
25862	(= 25601) haematodes subsp. chaetomallum
25864	(= 25616) stewartianum
25865	taggianum
25869	(= 25642) stewartianum
25870	(= 25625) coelicum
25872	coriaceum
25873	(= 25604) stewartianum
25875	(= 25679) sinogrande
25877	(= 25597) haematodes
25878	(= 25563) aperantum hybrid
25880	(= 25535) selense subsp. dasycladum
25883	(= 25514) roxieanum var. cucullatum
25891	(= 25505) roxieanum var. cucullatum
25896	(= 22512) rex subsp. fictolacteum
25899	(= 25737) selense subsp. dasycladum
25901	citriniflorum var. horeaum aff.
25902	(= 25697) aganniphum var. flavorufum
25904	(= 25555) polycladum
25906	(= 25518) sanguineum var. sanguineum
25907	rupicola var. rupicola
25913	(= 25543) citriniflorum var. horeaum aff.
25914	augustinii subsp. rubrum
25915	alutaceum var. russotinctum
25916	(= 25742) clementinae
25917	(= 25705) clementinae

25918 (= 25740) traillianum var. traillianum
25919 (= 25481) sperabile var. weihsiense
25920 (= 25474) sperabile var. sperabile
25921 (= 25503) calostrotum subsp. riparioides
25922 (= 25542) calostrotum subsp. riparioides
25923? (= 25985=25508) saluenense subsp. chameunum
25926 (= 25515) roxieanum var. oreonastes
25927 (= 25725) glischrum subsp. glischrum
25928 (= 25738) alutaceum var. russotinctum
25929 (= 25718) roxieanum var. oreonastes
25923 (= 25447) sperabile var. weihsiense
25935 (= 25569) sperabile var. weihsiense
25936 (= 25483) fulvum subsp. fulvoides
25938 (= 25449) rubiginosum
25941 (= 25529) rupicola var. rupicola
25942 (= 25564) sanguineum
25943 (= 25521) sanguineum var. didymoides
25944 fulvum subsp. fulvoides
25945 (= 25739) roxieanum
25947 (= 25717) rothschildii
25957 (= 25507) sanguineum var. didymoides
25958 fulvum subsp. fulvoides
25959 rex
25960 (= 25520) aganniphum var. aganniphum
25961 (= 25524) chamaethomsonii/ forrestii
25978 (= 25494) wardii var. wardii
25979 (= 25534) wardii var. wardii
25981 fastigiatum
25982 (= 25526) fastigiatum
25983 (= 25516) beesianum
25984 irroratum var. irroratum
25984a anthospaerum
25988 (= 25509) mekongense var. mekongense
25992 (= 25716) praestans

25993 (= 25580) selense subsp. dasycladum
25999 (= 24729) megacalyx
26023 tanastylum var. tanastylum
26040 tanastylum var. tanastylum
26043 basilicum
26045 facetum
26046 neriiflorum subsp. neriiflorum
26048 griersonianum
26066 arboreum var. peramoenum
26068 maddenii subsp. crassum
26071 facetum
26078 tanastylum var. pennivenium
26081 (= 25100) basilicum
26091 megacalyx
26092 sinogrande
26093 sp.
26109 maddenii subsp. crassum
26112 (= 24347) valentinianum
26113 sulfureum
26120 maddenii subsp. crassum
26122 sp.
26157 arboreum var. delavayi
26316 protistum var. protistum
26419 (= 27378) genestierianum
26421 (= 27620) araiophyllum
26422 (= 27622) sulfureum
26423 (= 26618) edgeworthii
26424 (= 27627) tanastylum var. tanastylum
26425 (= 27600) glischroides
26426 (= 27470) glischroides
26427 (= 27619) tanastylum var. tanastylum
26428 (= 27609) glischroides
26429 (= 27614) protistum var. protistum
26430 (= 27478) anthosphaerum
26431 (= 27611) tephropeplum
26432 (= 27612) anthosphaerum
26433 (= 27464) anthosphaerum
26434 (= 27581) sperabile var. sperabile
26435 (= 27635) sperabile var. sperabile
26436 (= 27653) anthosphaerum
26347 (= 27457) tanastylum var. tanastylum
26438 (= 27460) araiophyllum
26439 (= 27455) tephropeplum
26440 (= 27638) taggianum
26441 (= 27722) dendricola

26442 (= 27601) sperabile var. sperabile
26443 (= 27607) anthosphaerum
26444 (= 27669) pseudociliipes
26445 (= 27427) araiophyllum
26446 (= 27595) sperabile var. sperabile
26447 (= 27458) sulfureum
26448 (= 27625) glischroides
26449 (= 27466) neriiflorum subsp.
         neriiflorum
26452 (= 27671) anthosphaerum
26453 (= 27639) sperabile var.
         weihsiense
26454 (= 27608) anthosphaerum
26455 (= 27463) glischroides
26456 sinogrande
26457 (= 27670) tephropeplum
26458 (= 26634 etc., see 26633) sidereum
26459 (= 27690) dendricola
26461 (= 27655) pseudociliipes
26462 (= 27689) dendricola
26463 (= 27405) yunnanense
26464 (= 27628) pseudociliipes
26465 (= 27469) sperabile var. sperabile
26466 (= 27498) arboreum var. delavayi
26472 (= 27661) pseudociliipes
26473 brachyanthum subsp.
         hypolepidotum
26474 (= 27598) oreotrephes hybrid
26475 (= 27370) arboreum var. delavayi
26476 (= 27465) meddianum var.
         atrokermesinum
26477 (= 27377) tanastylum var.
         pennivenium
26478 (= 27605) sperabile var.
         weihsiense
26480 (= 27456) anthosphaerum
26481 (= 27376) araiophyllum
26482 (= 27473) rubiginosum
26483 (= 27610) araiophyllum
26484 (= 27632) tanastylum var.
         tanastylum
26486 (= 27402) yunnanense
26487 (= 27637) neriiflorum subsp.
         neriiflorum
26488 (= 27631) rubiginosum
26489 (= 27372) tanastylum var.
         tanastylum
26490 (= 27367) araiophyllum
26491 (= 27368) araiophyllum
26492 (= 27374) araiophyllum
26494 (= 27426) araiophyllum

26495 (= 27606) meddianum var.
         atrokermesinum
26449 (= 27623) meddianum var.
         atrokermesinum
26528 (= 27698) araiophyllum
26615 (= 27688) pseudociliipes
26618 (= 27617 =26423) edgeworthii
26629 (= 27399) habrotrichum
26632 (= 27400) habrotrichum
26633 (= 27677 =26634 =26458 =27679
         =27673) sidereum
26634 (= 26633) sidereum
26636 (= 27687) leptocarpum
26791 (= 27761) sidereum
26792 (= 27702) araiophyllum
26797 (= 27700) araiophyllum
26798 (= 27739) caesium
26921 (= 27484) stewartianum
26922 (= 27459) basilicum
26923 (= 27593) maddenii subsp.
         crassum
26924 (= 27585) dichroanthum subsp.
         scyphocalyx
26925 (= 27597) aperantum
26926 (= 27587) aperantum
26927 (= 27485) dichroanthum subsp.
         scyphocalyx
26928 (= 27489) heliolepis var.
         brevistylum
26929 (= 27492) stewartianum
26930 (= 27651) aperantum
26931 (= 27474) aperantum
26932 (= 27629) stewartianum
26933 (= 27590) aperantum
26934 (= 27584) aperantum
26935 (= 27616) arizelum
26936 (= 27467) aperantum
26937 (= 27480) aperantum
26938 (= 27604) aperantum
26961 (= 27642) heliolepis var.
         heliolepis
26962 (= 27586) stewartianum
26963 (= 27599) dichroanthum subsp.
         scyphocalyx
26964 (= 27636) aperantum
26965 (= 27471) dichroanthum subsp.
         scyphocalyx
26966 (= 27494) dichroanthum subsp.
         scyphocalyx
26974 (= 27641) dichroanthum subsp.
         scyphocalyx

26978 (= 27589) dichroanthum subsp.
         scyphocalyx
26980 (= 27643) stewartianum
26981 (= 27592) stewartianum
26984 (= 27475) stewartianum
26985 (= 27574) campylocarpum subsp.
         caloxanthum
26986 (= 27667) stewartianum
26987 (= 27591) rupicola var.
         rupicola
26988 (= 27503) campylogynum
26991 (= 27656) campylogynum
26992 (= 27659) stewartianum
26993 (= 27482) stewartianum
27002 (= 27491) aperantum
27003 (= 27580) dichroanthum subsp.
         scyphocalyx
27011 (= 27487) dichroanthum subsp.
         scyphocalyx
27012 (= 27481) dichroanthum subsp.
         scyphocalyx
27013 (= 27588) stewartianum
27018 (= 27477) dichroanthum subsp.
         scyphocalyx
27019 (= 27573) dichroanthum subsp.
         scyphocalyx
27020 (= 27645) aperantum
27022 (= 27666) aperantum
27025 (= 27483) aperantum
27050 (= 27626) dichroanthum subsp.
         scyphocalyx
27051 (= 27662) dichroanthum subsp.
         scyphocalyx
27052 (= 27650) dichroanthum subsp.
         scyphocalyx
27054 (= 27583) dichroanthum subsp.
         scyphocalyx
27057 (= 27461) dichroanthum subsp.
         scyphocalyx
27059 (= 27633) dichroanthum subsp.
         scyphocalyx
27061 (= 27644) dichroanthum subsp.
         scyphocalyx
27063 (= 27663) dichroanthum subsp.
         scyphocalyx
27065 (= 27497) calostrotum subsp.
         calostrotum
27067 arizelum
27069 facetum
27071 (= 27568) dichroanthum subsp.
         scyphocalyx

27073 (= 27648) aperantum
27075 (= 27579) aperantum
27077 (= 27640) aperantum
27079 (= 27493) aperantum
27081 (= 27486) aperantum
27083 (= 27576) aperantum
27085 (= 27462) glischrum subsp.
         glischrum
27089 (= 27672) dichroanthum subsp.
         scyphocalyx
27093 (= 27646) dichroanthum subsp.
         scyphocalyx
27095 (= 27654) dichroanthum subsp.
         scyphocalyx
27097 (= 27499) dichroanthum subsp.
         scyphocalyx
27099 (= 27570) dichroanthum subsp.
         scyphocalyx
27101 (= 27621) megacalyx
27103 (= 27603) zaleucum
27105 (= 27468) facetum
27108 (= 27624) arizelum
27109 (= 27476) pseudociliipes
27110 (= 27615) maddenii subsp.
         crassum
27111 (= 27572) aperantum
27113 (= 27496) dichroanthum subsp.
         scyphocalyx
27115 (= 27657) dichroanthum subsp.
         scyphocalyx
27116 (= 27613) dichroanthum subsp.
         scyphocalyx
27117 (= 27660) trichocladum var.
         trichocladum
27118 (= 27569) campylogynum
27119 (= 27571) rupicola var. rupicola
27121 (= 27658) calostrotum subsp.
         calostrotum
27122 (= 27501) cephalanthum subsp.
         cephalanthum
27123 (= 27664) campylocarpum subsp.
         caloxanthum
27125 (= 27495) campylocarpum subsp.
         caloxanthum
27126 kyawii
27128 (= 27578) kyawii
27129 (= 27577) stewartianum
27131 (= 27479) stewartianum
27132 (= 27665) dichroanthum subsp.
         scyphocalyx
27133 (= 27652) stewartianum

27134	(= 27594) dichroanthum subsp. scyphocalyx
27135	(= 27500) stewartianum
27136	(= 27582) stewartianum
27137	(= 27490) dichroanthum subsp. scyphocalyx
27138	(= 27647) stewartianum
27140	(= 27575) dichroanthum subsp. scyphocalyx
27142	(= 27488) callimorphum var. myiagrum
27143	(= 27596) stewartianum
27144	(= 27649) stewartianum
27250	(= 27678) kyawii
27343	habrotrichum
27355	(= 27730) protistum var. giganteum
27357	campylogynum
27358	neriiflorum subsp. agetum
27359	dichroanthum subsp. apodectum
27367	(= 26490) araiophyllum
27368	(= 26491) araiophyllum
27370	(= 26475) arboreum var. delavayi
27372	(= 26489) tanastylum var. tanastylum
27374	(= 26492) araiophyllum
27376	(= 26481) araiophyllum
27377	(= 26477) tanastylum var. pennivenium
27378	(= 26419) genestierianum
27389	callimorphum aff.
27399	(= 26629) habrotrichum
27400	(= 26632) habrotrichum
27404	(= 26596) yunnanense
27405	(= 26463) yunnanense
27413	basilicum
27415	annae
27416	annae
27426	(= 26494) araiophyllum
27427	(= 26445) araiophyllum
27455	(= 26439) tephropeplum
27456	(= 26480) anthosphaerum
27457	(= 26437) tanastylum var. tanastylum
27458	(= 26447) sulfureum
27459	(= 26922) basilicum
27460	(= 26438) araiophyllum
27461	(= 27057) dichroanthum subsp. scyphocalyx
27462	(= 27085) glischrum subsp. glischrum

27463	(= 26455) glischrum subsp. glischrum
27464	(= 26433) anthosphaerum
27465	(= 26476) meddianum var. atrokermesinum
27466	(= 26449) neriiflorum subsp. neriiflorum
27467	(= 26936) aperantum
27468	(= 27105) facetum
27469	(= 26465) sperabile var. sperabile
27470	(= 26426) glischroides
27471	(= 26965) dichroanthum subsp. scyphocalyx
27473	(= 26482) rubiginosum
27474	(= 26931) aperantum
27475	(= 26984) stewartianum
27477	(= 27018) dichroanthum subsp. scyphocalyx
27478	(= 26430) anthosphaerum
27479	(= 27131) stewartianum
27480	(= 26937) dichroanthum subsp. scyphocalyx
27482	(= 26993) stewartianum
27483	(= 27025) aperantum
27484	(= 26921) stewartianum
27485	(= 26927) dichroanthum subsp. scyphocalyx
27486	(= 27081) aperantum
27487	(= 27011) dichroanthum subsp. scyphocalyx
27488	(= 27142) callimorphum var. myiagrum
27489	(= 26928) heliolepis var. brevistylum
27490	(= 27137) dichroanthum subsp. scyphocalyx
27491	(= 27002) aperantum
27492	(= 26929) stewartianum
27493	(= 27079) aperantum
27494	(= 26966) dichroanthum subsp. scyphocalyx
27495	(= 27125) campylocarpum subsp. caloxanthum
27496	(= 27113) dichroanthum subsp. scyphocalyx
27497	(= 27065) calostrotum subsp. calostrotum
27498	(= 26466) arboreum var. delavayi
27499	(= 27097) dichroanthum subsp. scyphocalyx

27500 (= 27135) stewartianum
27501 (= 27122) cephalanthum subsp.
       cephalanthum
27502 (= 26977) dichroanthum subsp.
       scyphocalyx
27503 (= 26988) campylogynum
27568 (= 27071) dichroanthum subsp.
       scyphocalyx
27569 (= 27118) campylogynum
27570 (= 27099) dichroanthum subsp.
       scyphocalyx
27571 (= 27119) rupicola var. rupicola
27572 (= 27111) aperantum
27573 (= 27019) dichroanthum subsp.
       scyphocalyx
27574 (= 26985) campylocarpum subsp.
       caloxanthum
27575 (= 27140) dichroanthum subsp.
       scyphocalyx
27576 (= 27083) aperantum
27577 (= 27129) stewartianum
27578 (= 27128) kyawii
27579 (= 27075) aperantum
27580 (= 27003) dichroanthum subsp.
       scyphocalyx
27581 (= 26434) sperabile var. sperabile
27582 (= 27136) stewartianum
27583 (= 27054) dichroanthum subsp.
       scyphocalyx
27584 (= 26934) aperantum
27585 (= 26924) dichroanthum subsp.
       scyphocalyx
27586 (= 26962) stewartianum
27587 (= 26926) aperantum
27588 (= 27013) stewartianum
27589 (= 26978) dichroanthum subsp.
       scyphocalyx
27590 (= 26933) aperantum
27591 (= 26987) rupicola var. rupicola
27592 (= 26981) stewartianum
27593 (= 26923) maddenii subsp.
       crassum
27594 (= 27134) dichroanthum subsp.
       scyphocalyx
27595 (= 26446) sperabile var. sperabile
27596 (= 27143) stewartianum
27597 (= 26925) aperantum
27598 (= 26474) oreotrephes
27599 (= 26963) dichroanthum subsp.
       scyphocalyx
27600 (= 26425) glischroides

27601 (= 26442) sperabile var. sperabile
27603 (= 27103) zaleucum
27604 (= 26938) aperantum
27605 (= 26478) sperabile var.
       weihsiense
27606 (= 26495) meddianum var.
       atrokermesinum
27607 (= 26443) anthosphaerum
27608 (= 26454) anthosphaerum
27609 (= 26428) glischroides
27610 (= 26483) araiophyllum
27611 (= 26431) tephropeplum
27612 (= 26432) anthosphaerum
27613 (= 27116) dichroanthum subsp.
       scyphocalyx
27614 (= 26429) protistum var.
       protistum
27615 (= 27110) maddenii subsp.
       crassum
27616 (= 26935) rex subsp. arizelum
27617 (= 26618 = 26423) edgeworthii
27620 (= 26421) araiophyllum
28621 (= 27101) megacalyx
27622 (= 26422) sulfureum
27623 (= 26499) meddianum var.
       atrokermesinum
27624 (= 27108) arizelum
27625 (= 26448) glischroides
27626 (= 27050) dichroanthum subsp.
       scyphocalyx
27627 (= 26424) tanastylum var.
       tanastylum
27628 (= 26464) pseudociliipes
27629 (= 26932) stewartianum
27630 (= 26964) aperantum
27631 (= 26488) rubiginosum
27632 (= 26484) tanastylum var.
       tanastylum
27633 (= 27059) dichroanthum subsp.
       scyphocalyx
27635 (= 26435) sperabile var. sperabile
27636 (= 26964) aperantum
27637 (= 26487) neriiflorum subsp.
       neriiflorum
27638 (= 26440) taggianum
27639 (= 26453) sperabile var. sperabile
27640 (= 27077) aperantum
27641 (= 26974) dichroanthum subsp.
       scyphocalyx
27642 (= 26961) heliolepis var.
       brevistylum

27643   (= 26980) stewartianum
27644   (= 27061) dichroanthum subsp.
            scyphocalyx
27645   (= 27020) aperantum
27646   (= 27093) dichroanthum subsp.
            scyphocalyx
27647   (= 27138) stewartianum
27648   (= 27073) aperantum
27649   (= 27144) stewartianum
27650   (= 27052) dichroanthum subsp.
            scyphocalyx
27651   (= 26930) aperantum
27652   (= 27133) stewartianum
27653   (= 26436) anthosphaerum
27654   (= 27095) dichroanthum subsp.
            scyphocalyx
27655   (= 26461) pseudociliipes
27656   (= 26991) campylogynum
27657   (= 27115) dichroanthum subsp.
            scyphocalyx
27658   (= 27121) calostrotum subsp.
            calostrotum
27659   (= 26992) stewartianum
27660   (= 27117) trichocladum var.
            trichocladum
27661   (= 26472) pseudociliipes
27662   (= 27051) dichroanthum subsp.
            scyphocalyx
27663   (= 27063) dichroanthum subsp.
            scyphocalyx
27664   (= 27123) campylocarpum subsp.
            caloxanthum
27665   (= 27132) dichroanthum subsp.
            scyphocalyx
27666   (= 27022) aperantum
27667   (= 26986) stewartianum
27669   (= 26444) pseudociliipes
27670   (= 26457) tephropeplum
27671   (= 26452) anthosphaerum
27672   (= 27089) dichroanthum subsp.
            scyphocalyx
27673   (= 27679 etc., see 26633) sidereum
27677   (= 26633 etc., see 26633) sidereum
27678   (= 27250) kyawii
27679   (= 26634 etc., see 26633) sidereum
27685   sp.
27686   (= 26626) leptocarpum
27687   dendricola
27688   (= 26615) pseudociliipes
27689   (= 26462) dendricola
27690   (= 26459) dendricola

27697   arboreum var. delavayi
27698   (= 26528) araiophyllum
27700   (= 26797) araiophyllum
27701   arboreum var. peramoenum
27702   (= 26792) araiophyllum
27703   annae
27705   annae
27706   annae
27713   annae
27714   tanastylum var. tanastylum
27715   valentinianum
27717   arboreum var. delavayi
27718   arboreum var. delavayi
27722   (= 26441) dendricola
27724   maddenii subsp. crassum
27725   pseudociliipes
27727   decorum subsp. diaprepes
27730   (= 27355) protistum var.
            giganteum
27737   (= 27738) dendricola
27738   (= 27737) dendricola
27739   (= 26798) caesium
27744   araiophyllum
27745   yunnanense
27746   araiophyllum
27757   tanastylum var. tanastylum
27758   genestierianum
27759   pseudociliipes
27761   (= 26791) sidereum
27768   arboreum var. delavayi
27769   edgeworthii
27771   araiophyllum
27775   araiophyllum
27776   maddenii subsp. crassum
27792   arizelum
27794   arizelum

YUNNAN & SICHUAN EXP. (1930-31)

28236   rubiginosum
28237   taliense
28241   cephalanthum subsp.
            platyphyllum
28248   lacteum
28250   trichocladum var. longipilosum
28253   taliense
28254   campylogynum
28254a russatum
28266   brachyanthum subsp.
            brachyanthum

28283	dichroanthum subsp. dichroanthum	29264	balfourianum
28290	dichroanthum subsp. dichroanthum	29266	intricatum
		29267	primuliflorum
28295	racemosum	29268	impeditum
28297	rigidum	29269	telmateium
28301	neriiflorum subsp. neriiflorum	29271	trichostomum
28302	cephalanthum subsp. cephalanthum	29273	hemitrichotum
		29278	balfourianum
28304	irroratum subsp. irroratum	29280	mimetes var. simulans aff.
28305	edgeworthii	29281	mimetes var. simulans
28311	maddenii subsp. crassum	29282	balfourianum
28312	maddenii subsp. crassum	29293	primuliflorum
28315	decorum subsp. decorum	29305	wardii var. wardii
28319	maddenii subsp. crassum	29312	adenogynum
28323	adenogynum	29313	adenogynum
28326	rigidum	29314	adenogynum
28342	lepidotum	29317	roxieanum var. cucullatum
28343	rupicola var. rupicola	29320	sphaeroblastum
28344	telmateium	29321	sphaeroblastum
28347	sp.	29322	wardii var. wardii
28348	dichroanthum subsp. dichroanthum	29323	yunnanense
		29325	phaeochrysum var. levistratum
28351	haematodes subsp. haematodes	29326	taliense aff.
28353	taliense	29327	phaeochrysum var. levistratum
28355	taliense	29328	taliense aff.
28357	taliense	29329	taliense aff.
29130	taliense aff.	29331	tatsienense
29131	phaeochrysum var. levistratum	29333	sphaeroblastum
29132	taliense aff.	29341	× detonsum (hybrid)
29242	wardii var. wardii	29545	neriiflorum subsp. neriiflorum
29243	phaeochrysum var. levistratum	29599	roseatum
29244	balfourianum	29588	habrotrichum
29245	sphaeroblastum	29647	callimorphum var myiagrum
29246	sphaeroblastum	29655	tephropeplum
29247	beesianum	29663	stewartianum
29248	beesianum	29666	calostrotum subsp. calostrotum
29248	hemitrichotum		
29249	rupicola var. muliense	29685	stewartianum
29250	trichostomum	29687	yunnanense
29251	nivale subsp. boreale	29762	griersonianum
29252	taliense aff.	29763	facetum
29253	phaeochrysum var. levistratum	29785	arizelum
29254	phaeochrysum var. levistratum	29809	megacalyx
29256	adenogynum	29894	rupicola var. rupicola
29257	roxieanum var. cucullatum	29926	kyawii
29258	taliense aff.	29929	kyawii
29259	yungningense	29937	campylogynum
29260	yungningense	29938	aperantum
29262	sphaeroblastum	30375	kyawii
29263	balfourianum	30392	griersonianum
		30393	edgewothii

30394	dichroanthum subsp. scyphocalyx
30395	rupicola var. rupicola
30526	beesianum
30527	mekongense var. mekongense
30528	rothschildii
30531	traillianum var. traillianum
30532	beesianum
30533	stewartianum
30534	aperantum
30535	haematodes subsp. haematodes
30536	aperantum
30539	haematodes subsp. chaetomallum
30540	calostrotum subsp. riparioides
30543	saluenense subsp. chameunum
30880	pronum
30883	campylogynum
30887	decorum subsp. decorum
30888	adenogynum
30889	rupicola var. rupicola
30891	saluenense subsp. chameunum
30892	beesianum
30893	rex subsp. fictolacteum
30894	beesianum
30896	Subsect. Heliolepida
30910	oreotrephes
30911	saluenense subsp. ?
30912	sperabile var. weihsiense
30937	Subsect. Scabrifolia
30940	hemitrichotum
30941	impeditum
30942	rupicola var. muliense
30967	campylogynum
30977	heliolepis var. heliolepis

Fox, S.
BHUTAN EXP. (1990)

9	kesangiae var. kesangiae
12	griffithianum
17	hodgsonii
28	triflorum var. trifloum
41	kesangiae var. kesangiae
43	argipeplum
45	camelliiflorum
47	thomsonii subsp. thomsonii
50	cinnabarinum
53	hodgsonii
55	flinckii
60	arboreum var. cinnamomeum

62	keysii
71	pendulum
93	bhutanense
96	thomsonii subsp. thomsonii
98	wightii

GOSAINKUND EXP., NEPAL (1995)

7	anthopogon subsp. anthopogon
30	barbatum
37	anthopogon subsp. anthopogon
70	anthopogon subsp. anthopogon
103	barbatum
125	sp.

Gould, B.J.
SIKKIM EXP. (1937)

2a	campanulatum subsp. aeruginosum
18	lepidotum
22	niveum
31	hodgsonii
37	barbatum

Halliwell, B. (BH)
NEPAL EXP. (1970)

20	sp.
62	sp.
85	campanulatum
102	sp.
124	campanulatum

JAPAN EXP. (1979)

4013	aureum
4236	brachycarpum
4259	sp.
4283	sp.
4348	japonicum
4355	aureum

Heasman, M.
BHUTAN EXP. (1992)

9	virgatum subsp. virgatum

17a	thomsonii subsp. thomsonii
18a	kesangiae var. kesangiae
20	ciliatum
24	hodgsonii aff.
36	hodgsonii
44	campylocarpum subsp. campylocarpum
46	cinnabarinum subsp. xanthocodon
47	lepidotum
48	succothii
50	camelliiflorum
54	argipeplum
56	pendulum
62	kendrickii
65	dalhousiae var. dalhousiae
68	maddenii subsp. maddeniii

Hedegaard, J.
BHUTAN EXP. (1983)

B100	wightii
B102	campanulatum subsp. aeruginosum
B103	campanulatum subsp. aeruginosum
B107	barbatum
B108	ciliatum
B110	fulgens
B112	lanatum
B113	lepidotum
B114	anthgopogon subsp. anthopogon
B116	campylocarpum subsp. campylocarpum
B117	wightii

Hedge, I.C. & Wendelbo, P.
AFGHANISTAN EXP. (1969)

8975	collettianum
9706	afghanicum

Holmberg, M. & Stringberg, U.
S KOREA EXP. - 1992

92/044	mucronulatum var. mucronulatum
92/148	schlippenbachii
92/232	brachycarpum
92/349	mucronulatum var. mucronulatum
92/423	yedoense var. poukhanense
92/449	weyrichii

Howick, Lord C. & McNamara
NE USA EXP. (1990)

1287	viscosum
1318	maximum
1320	viscosum
1339	periclymenoides
1353	sp.
1355	sp.

SICHUAN & YUNNAN, CHINA EXP. (1990)

1381	dichroanthum subsp. dichroanthum
1386	racemosum
1414	sp.
1414a	sp.
1417	sp.
1420	sp.
1423	sp.
1425	sp.
1440	sp.
1448	sp.
1449	sp.
1450	sp.
1452	traillianum var. traillianum
1463	sp.
1466	rex subsp. fictolacteum
1467	sp.
1468	sp.
1469	williamsianum
1490	sp.
1497	sp.
1509	racemosum
1511	sp.
1529	sp.
1539	sp.
1541	racemosum

1544	dicroanthum subsp.
	dichroanthum
1547	sp.
1553	sp.
1564	sp.

HIMACHAL PRADESH, NW INDIA EXP. (1993)

1784	anthopogon
1801	lepidotum
1805	campanulatum subsp.
	campanulatum
1837	campanulatum subsp.
	campanulatum
1844	lepidotum
1850	anthopogon
1854	campanulatum subsp.
	campanulatum
1923	arboreum subsp. arboreum

Hruby, T.
NEPAL EXP. (1975)

3	campanulatum
4	lepidotum
10	setosum
14	campanulatum
16	wallichii

Kew-Edinburgh Kanchenjunga Exp. (KEKE)
NE NEPAL (1989)

440	lepidotum
635	anthopogon subsp. anthopogon
694	anthopogon subsp. anthopogon
698	wightii
806	Subsect. Maddenia
1110	pendulum
1157	Subsect. Maddenia
1223	sp.

Kew-Quarryhill
S JAPAN EXP. (1989)

8	reticulatum

37	degronianum var. hondoense
99	kaempferi
117	weyrichii
148	weyrichii
294	kiusianum
309	tashiroi
310	degronianum var. yakushimanum
356	indicum
384	kaempferi
399	kaempferi
414	keiskei
434	kaempferi

Kingdon-Ward, F.
N YUNNAN-TIBET FRONTIER, CHINA EXP. (1913)

260	davidsonianum
406	mekongense var. mekongense
529	wardii var. wardii
768	aganniphum var. aganniphum
793	campylogynum

NE UPPER BURMA EXP. (1919)

3038	edgeworthii
3039	zaleucum
3040	neriiflorum subsp. neriiflorum
3042	glischrum subsp. glischrum
3042a	habrotrichum?
3061	sidereum
3095	megeratum
3096	stewartianum
3097	trichocladum var.
	trichocladum
3101	arizelum
3155	hylaeum
3172	campylogynum
3248	maddenii subsp. crassum
3267	euchroum
3267a	dichroanthum subsp.
	scyphocalyx
3299	oreotrephes
3300	stewartianum
3301	aperantum
3302	brachyanthum subsp.
	hypolepidotum
3303	campylogynum
3304	rupicola var. rupicola
3305	trichocladum var. trichocladum

3365	cephalanthum subsp. cephalanthum
3390	calostrotum subsp. keleticum
3391	campylogynum
3392	dichroanthum subsp. scyphocalyx
3408	campylocarpum subsp. caloxanthum
3721	campylocarpum subsp. caloxanthum
3721a	campylocarpum subsp. caloxanthum ?

NE YUNNAN-SICHUAN BORDER, SW CHINA EXP. (1921)

3776	pachypodum
3784	arboreum var. delavayi
3805	decorum subsp. decorum
3948	arboreum var. delavayi
3952	racemosum
3952a	pubescens
3952b	pubescens
3953	pubescens
3998	trichostomum
4023	rupicola var. muliense
4050	hemitrichotum
4102	telmateium
4160	primuliflorum
4170	wardii var. wardii
4177	balfourianum
4184	intricatum
4185	sphaeroblastum
4207	roxieanum
4211	beesianum
4268	telmateium
4308	rubiginosum
4309	oreotrephes
4322	yunnanense
4410	wardii var. wardii
4456	lysolepis
4458	wardii aff.
4465	trichostomum
4486	cuneatum
4487	decorum subsp. decorum
4509	rex subsp. rex
4583	lepidotum
4583a	racemosum?
4733	telmateium
4843	phaeochrysum
4860	traillianum var. traillianum

4974	yunnanense
4994	hemitrichotum
4995	uvariifolium var. uvariiflorum
5001	scabrifolium var. scabrifolium
5002	decorum subsp. decorum
5002a	irroratum
5004	scabrifolium var. scabrifolium
5005	irroratum subsp. irroratum

YUNNAN-SICHUAN-TIBET (CHINA), NE BURMA EXP. (1922)

5384	primuliflorum
5385	tapetiforme
5409	phaeochrysum var. phaeochrysum
5405	vernicosum
5414	selense subsp. selense
5415	anthosphaerum
5416	sanguineum var. sanguineum
5417	forrestii subsp. forrestii
5418	sinogrande
5421	virgatum subsp. oleifolium
5425	moulmainense
5427	crinigerum var. crinigerum
5428	rubiginosum
5430	calostrotum subsp. keleticum
5431	haematodes subsp. chaetomallum
5432	sanguineum
5432a	sanguineum subsp. didymum
5433	sanguineum
5434	martinianum
5435	temenium var. temenium
5436	saluenense subsp. saluenense
5437	brachyanthum subsp. hypolepidotum
5438	arizelum
5438a	arizelum
5438b	Subsect. Heliolepida
5439	edgeworthii
5440	seinghkuense
5445	facetum
5446	xanthostephanum
5447	dendricola
5448	maddenii subsp. crassum
5449	dendricola
5457	Subsect. Thomsonia
5458	anthosphaerum
5466	nuttallii
5469	kyawii
5480	neriiflorum subsp. neriiflorum

5481	brachyanthum subsp. hypolepidotum
5482	calostrotum subsp. riparium
5483	neriiflorum subsp. phaedropum
5484	pocophorum var. pocophorum
5485	sidereum
5487	dichroanthum subsp. septentrionale
5489	mekongense var.mekongense
5490	sp.
5505	Sect. Tsutusi
5533	kyawii
5602	oreotrephes
5607	Subsect. Triflora

TIBET & BHUTAN EXP. (1924-25)

5656	principis
5659	hirtipes
5660	uvariifolium var. griseum
5687	triflorum var. triflorum
5687a	triflorum var. triflorum
5700	kongboense
5718	dignabile
5718a	mekongense var. mekongense
5718b	campylocarpum subsp. caloxanthum
5729	nivale subsp. nivale
5732	faucium aff.
5733	laudandum var. laudandum
5734	fragariiflorum
5735	nivale subsp. nivale
5736	wardii var. wardii
5756	wardii hybrid
5756a	wardii
5759	phaeochrysum var. agglutinatum
5777	nivale subsp. nivale
5778	nivale subsp. nivale
5790	oreotrephes
5792	nivale subsp. nivale
5828	calostrotum var. riparium
5829	mekongense var. mekongense
5830	cerasinum
5842	campylogynum
5843	charitopes subsp. tsangpoense
5844	charitopes subsp. tsangpoense
5845	forrestii subsp. papillatum
5846	chamaethomsonii/forrestii
5847	chamaethomsonii var. chamaethauma
5848	laudandum var. temoense

5849	laudandum var. temoense
5850	kongboense
5851	mekongense var. rubrolineatum
5853	campylocarpum subsp. campylocarpum
5856	pumilum
5861	Subsect. Neriiflora
5862	nivale subsp. nivale
5862a	pumilum
5863	aganniphum var. aganniphum
5874	cinnabarinum subsp. xanthocodon 'Concatenans'
5875	parmulatum
5876	uniflorum var. uniflorum
5877	arizelum
5878	temenium var. temenium
5879	chamaethomsonii aff. var. chamaethauma
5880	stewartianum
5911	sp.
5917a	calvescens aff.
5940	lepidotum
5953	sp.
5971	lanatoides
5994	lepidotum
6020	kongboense
6021	kongboense
6026	cinnabarinum subsp. xanthocodon
6069	virgatum
6069a	lepidotum
6079	sp.
6215	griffithianum
6223	hirtipes
6229	campylocarpum subsp. campylocarpum
6250	megeratum
6250a	baileyi
6251	leptocarpum
6256	glischrum subsp. rude
6257	keysii
6257a	Subsect. Trichoclada
6258a	lanigerum
6261	sinogrande
6261a	montroseanum
6263	triflorum var. triflorum
6273	leucaspis
6275	Subsect. Triflora
6276	maddenii
6276a	maddenii subsp. maddenii
6278	auritum

6279	virgatum subsp.oleifolium
6281	glischrum subsp. glischrum
6283	vaccinioides (Sect. Vireya)
6284	ramsdenianum
6285	venator
6286	megacalyx
6291	leucaspis
6301	pemakoense
6303	tephropeplum
6304	Subsect. Edgeworthia
6307	sp.
6310	taggianum
6311	uvariifolium var. uvariiflorum
6325	scopulorum
6330	Sect. Azaleastrum
6333	nuttallii var.
6335	ovatum
6354	scopulorum
6401	faucium
6403	arboreum var. delavayi
6409	triflorum var. triflorum
6411	Subsect. Lepidota
6413	maddenii subsp. maddenii
6414	Sect. Choniastrum
6415	dalhousiae var. rhabdotum
6457a	keysii

BURMA & ASSAM EXP. (1926)

6676	dendricola
6711	dendricola
6716	sinogrande
6735	insculptum (Sect. Vireya)
6736	maddenii subsp. maddenii
6738	neriiflorum subsp. phaedropum
6751	xanthostephanum
6752	vesiculiferum
6753	sidereum
6769	horlickianum
6781	megacalyx
6782	sinogrande
6792	sidereum
6793	seinghkuense
6794	tephropeplum
6795	martinianum
6805	beanianum
6806	trichocladum var. trichocladum
6807	edgeworthii
6809	taggianum
6818	arizelum
6819	megeratum

6829	beanianum
6831	sanguineum var. didymoides
6832	forrestii subsp. forrestii
6833	hylaeum
6834	tephropeplum
6835	beanianum
6848	leptocarpum
6854	neriiflorum subsp. phaeodropum
6855	exasperatum
6856	vesiculiferum
6868	campylocarpum subsp. caloxanthum
6869	eclecteum var. eclecteum
6884	uniflorum var. imperator
6896	eclecteum var. eclecteum
6900	eclecteum hybrid
6903	calostrotum subsp. riparium
6912	forrestii subsp. papillatum
6913	forrestii subsp. forrestii
6914	cephalanthum subsp. cephalanthum
6920	eclecteum var. eclecteum
6921	eclecteum var. eclecteum
6922	eclecteum var. eclecteum
6923	cerasinum
6924	pruniflorum
6930	campylocarpum
6934	saluenense subsp. saluenense
6935	forrestii subsp. forrestii
6936	eclecteum var. eclecteum
6945	sanguineum
6953	beesianum
6954	phaeochrysum var. levistratum
6955	haematodes aff.
6960	tapetiforme
6961	pumilum
6962	callimorphum var. myiagrum
6965	campylocarpum subsp. caloxanthum
6967	cephalanthum subsp. cephalanthum
6984	calostrotum subsp. riparium
6986	callimorphum var. myiagrum
6991	euchroum
7001	nivale subsp. nivale
7012	saluenense subsp. saluenense
7023	anthopogon subsp. anthpogon
7038	brachyanthum subsp. hypolepidotum
7045	pruniflorum

7046	brachyanthum subsp. hypolepidotum
7048	rupicola var. rupicola
7058	nivale subsp. nivale
7061	calostrotum subsp. riparium (dwarf)
7062	calostrotum subsp. riparium
7084	rupicola
7090	Subsect. Neriiflora
7108	heliolepis var. brevistylum
7121	triflorum var. triflorum
7122	uvariifolium var. uvariiflorum
7123	crinigerum var. crinigerum
7124	sperabile var. weihsiense
7125	hylaeum
7136	maddenii subsp. crassum
7137	edgeworthii
7138	virgatum
7139	megacalyx
7140	arboreum
7171	leucaspis
7184	recurvoides
7185	sanguineum
7187	Sect. Pogonanthum
7188	pruniflorum
7189	selense. subsp. dasycladum
7190	selense subsp. setiferum
7196	campylocarpum subsp. campylocarpum
7229	lepidotum
7259	Subsect.Maddenia
7327	facetum
7426	lukiangense
7427	protistum var. protistum
7428	nuttallii
7455	chrysolepis
7484	hylaeum
7500	sanguineum var. didymoides
7523	calostrotum subsp. riparium
7550	pruniflorum
7553	maddenii subsp. crassum
7606	Subsect. Maddenia
7612	martinianum
7625	tanastylum
7630	dendricola
7633	tapetiforme
7642	sinogrande

ASSAM AND MISHMI HILLS EXP. (1927-28)

7701	formosum
7717	formosum var. inaequale
7723	maddenii subsp. maddenii
7724	macabeanum
7725	elliottii
7731	triflorum var. bauhiniflorum
7732	johnstoneanum
7968	arboreum
8016	walongense
8044	tanastylum var. tanastylum
8052	edgeworthii
8069	protistum var. protistum
8112	neriiflorum subsp. phaedropum
8113	boothii
8130	sinogrande
8163	rex
8164	crinigerum var. crinigerum
8165	tephropeplum
8205	megacalyx
8206	edgeworthii
8225	megeratum
8229	calostrotum subsp. riparium
8238	hookeri
8239	cinnabarinum subsp. xanthocodon
8250	exasperatum
8251	lanigerum
8254	piercei
8256	campylocarpum subsp. campylocarpum
8257	pruniflorum
8258	cerasinum
8259	trichocladum
8260	pemakoense
8288	tsariense var. tsariense
8289	pocophorum var. pocophorum
8293	sanguineum var. sanguineum
8294	stewartianum
8300	fulvum subsp. fulvoides
8326	leptanthum
8337	cephalanthum subsp. cephalanthum
8341	chamaethomsonii var. chamaethauma
8400	maddenii subsp. crassum
8415	pruniflorum
8521	neriiflorum subsp. phaedropum
8522	kasoense

8545   maddenii subsp. crassum

UPPER BURMA AND TIBETAN FRONTIER EXP. (1931)

9130   Subsect. Maddenia
9170   horlickianum
9195   Subsect. Irrorata
9200   magnificum
9210   Sect. Vireya
9220   taggianum
9236   tanastylum var. tanastylum
9250   xanthostephanum
9252   Subsect. Maddenia
9254   seinghkuense
9258   vesiculiferum
9260   arizelum
9261   megacalyx
9263   neriiflorum subsp. phaedropum
9273   maddenii subsp. crassum
        'Manipurense'
9274   nuttallii
9293   neriiflorum subsp. phaedropum
9294   calostrotum
9301   magnificum
9321   neriiflorum subsp.
        phaedropum aff.
9322   hylaeum
9361   horlickianum
9371   chrysodoron
9382   neriiflorum
9385   montroseanum
9394   calostrotum subsp. riparium
9397   arizelum
9399   vaccinioides (Sect. Vireya)
9400   xanthostephanum
9402   taggianum
9403   horlickianum
9405   Sect. Vireya
9413   eclecteum var. eclecteum
9414   campylogynum
9415   genestierianum
9416   tephropeplum
9440   vaccinioides (Sect. Vireya)
9446   nuttallii
9478   triflorum var. triflorum
9479   uvariifolium var. uvariiflorum
9483   neriiflorum subsp. phaedropum
9485   vesiculiferum
9490   genestierianum
9500   selense subsp. selense

9503   crinigerum var. crinigerum
9504   edgeworthii
9505   oreotrephes
9506   neriiflorum
9509   oreotrephes
9517   calostrotum subsp. riparium
9519   trichocladum
9529   virgatum subsp. oleifolium
9543   seingkhuense
9544   arizelum
9561   neriiflorum subsp. phaedropum
9565   tephropeplum
9567   xanthostephanum
9569   megeratum
9584   maddenii subsp. crassum
9591   cephalanthum subsp.
        cephalanthum
9601   beesianum
9608   haematodes subsp. chaetomallum
9609   rupicola var. chryseum & nivale
        subsp. nivale
9621   selense subsp. selense
9629   forrestii subsp. forrestii
9633   saluenense subsp. saluenense
9634   eclecteum var. ecleceum
9635   chamaethomsonii var.
        chamaethauma
9636   rupicola var. chryseum
9637   haematodes subsp. chaetomallum
9641   cephalanthum subsp.
        cephalanthum
9665   sp.
9704   brachyanthum subsp.
        hypolepidotum
9710   rupicola var. rupicola
9717   calostrotum subsp. riparium
9726   vesiculiferum
9735   pruniflorum
9790   campylogynum
9795   praestans
9800   lepidotum
9810   campylogynum
9815   campylogynum
9816   forrestii subsp. forrestii aff.
9909   rupicola var. chryseum
10005   tapetiforme × rupicola var.
        rupicola (hybrid)
10012   traillianum var. traillianum
10020   heliolepis var. heliolepis
10121   campylogynum?
10129   leptocarpum

10134	coelicum
10136	Subsect. Maddenia
10139	Subsect. Glauca
10140	campylogynum
10141	vaccinioides (Sect. Vireya)
10142	boothii
10159	eclecteum var. eclecteum
10160	eclecteum var. eclecteum
10161	Subsect. Campylocarpa
10175	dendricola (taronense?)
10180	dendricola
10231	simsii

ASSAM AND UPPER BURMA EXP. (1933)

10351	virgatum
10379	edgeworthii
10401b	tephropeplum?
10490	trichocladum var. trichocladum
10496	haematodes aff.
10497	beesianum
10498	fulvum
10498a	uvariifolium var. uvariifolium
10500	pruniflorum
10521	tapetiforme & nivale subsp. nivale
10530	campylocarpum subsp. campylocarpum
10531	rupicola var. rupicola & nivale subsp. nivale
10532	calostrotum subsp. anthopogon
10533	phaeochrysum var. levistratum
10541	Sect. Pogonanthum
10542	saluenense forma & calostrotum subsp. riparium
10579	phaeochrysum var. levistratum
10582	saluenense subsp. saluenense & calostrotum subsp. riparium
10595	nivale subsp. nivale
10700	principis
10830	Subsect. Thomsonia
10832	traillianum var. dictyotum
10841	lepidotum
10842	kongboense
10870	campylogynum
10928	maddenii subsp. crassum 'Manipurense'
10929	edgeworthii
10950	tanastylum
10951	Subsect. Thomsonia

10952	glischrum subsp. rude
10959	spilotum aff.
10969	Sect. Pogonanthum
10970	Subsect. Selensia
10971	cinnabarinum?
11002	neriiflorum aff.
11004	Subsect. Heliolepida
11011	cerasinum
11012	Sect. Pogonanthum
11016	nivale subsp. nivale
11029	xanthostephanum
11035	sperabile var. weihsiense
11040	piercei
11043	cerasinum
11050	sanguineum
11052	kasoense
11055	Subsect. Maddenia
11057	dendricola
11060	Subsect. Grandia

TIBET, ASSAM-HIMALAYA FRONTIER TRACT EXP. (1935)

11175	macabeanum
11378	kendrickii
11464	megeratum
11532	'Manipurense'
11565	glaucophyllum
11568	cinnabarinum subsp. xanthocodon 'Concatenans'
11569	anthopogon
11586	phaeochrysum var. phaeochrysum
11587	fulgens
11588	wightii
11605	argipeplum
11612	wallichii
11640	hodgsonii
11915	mekongense var. longipilosum
11964	circinnatum
12404	tsariense var. tsariense
12438	erosum?
12585	formosum var. formosum
12588	triflorum var. bauhiniiflorum
12589	maddenii

NE UPPER BURMA AND TIBET EXP. (1937)

13017	martinianum
13020	Subsect. Grandia

13130	Subsect. Maddenia
13150	coelicum × haematodes subsp. chaetomallum (hybrid)
13151	oreotrephes
13165	Subsect. Neriiflora
13180	Subsect. Neriiflora
13190	Subsect. Saluenensia
13194	Subsect. Neriiflora
13195	monanthum
13210	Subsect. Campylogyna
13225	forrestii subsp. forrestii
13230	monanthum
13324	pocophorum aff.
13327	Subsect. Barbata
13355	Subsect. Neriiflora
13361	pruniflorum
13365	rupicola var. rupicola
13367	calostrotum
13369	praestans
13370	tapetiforme
13371	saluenense subsp. saluenense
13399	campylogynum ?
13405	Subsect. Pogonanthum
13416	sanguineum var. sanguineum
13419	martinianum
13420	selense subsp. dasycladum
13424	sp.
13480	sp.
13494	Subsect. Maddenia
13500	sp.
13550	magnificum hybrid
13606	kendrickii
13625	keysii
13632	edgeworthii
13645	leptocarpum
13647	falconeri hybrid
13648	protistum var. protistum
13649	grande aff.
13650	hookeri (crimson form)
13652	falconeri subsp. falconeri
13653	hodgsonii
13654	falconeri subsp.falconeri
13655	wightii
13662	thomsonii. subsp. thomsonii
13663	tsariense var. tsariense
13665	fulgens
13666	succothii
13670	argipeplum
13681	falconeri hybrid
13683	grande
13699	anthopogon subsp. anthopogon

13705	wallichii
13708	phaeochrysum var. levistratum
13712	thomsonii subsp. thomsonii
13750	lanatum
13758	cinnabarinum
13789	× candelabrum (hybrid)
13965	aganniphum
14314	campanulatum
14342	arizelum

N BURMA EXP. - VERNAY AND CUTTING (1938-39)

5	simsii
51	kyawii
52	dendricola
61	oreotrephes
62	microphyton
71	simsii
87	dendricola
100	decorum subsp. decorum
135	moulmainense
152	dendricola
180	dendricola
203	protistum var. protistum
213	magnificum
227	megeratum
228	eclecteum var. eclecteum
233	oreotrephes
234	neriiflorum
236	arizelum
245	campylogynum
250	moulmainense
251	chrysodoron
252	callimorphum?
280	dendricola
281	dendricola
286	neriiflorum
293	edgeworthii
312	neriiflorum subsp. neriiflorum
346	edgeworthii
347	kasoense?
354	chrysodoron
372	edgeworthii aff.
395	chrysodoron
396	arboreum var. delavayi
400	'Manipurense'
404	habrotrichum
409	habrotrichum
412	vaccinioides (Sect. Vireya)
413	leptothrium?

416	tanastylum var. tanastylum
424	genestierianum
433	moulmainense
438	tanastylum var. tanastylum
440	dendricola
445	neriiflorum subsp. neriiflorum
448	neriiflorum subsp. neriiflorum
460	leptothrium
461	microphyton
499	simsii

KHASIA/JAINTIA HILLS EXP. INDIA (1946)

16029	formosum var. inaequale
16060	sp.

E MANIPUR, (NE INDIA) EXP. (1948)

17044	arboreum
17200	sp.
17215	johnstoneanum
17216	arboreum
17217	'Manipurense'
17361	vaccinioides (Sect. Vireya)
17405	triflorum
17407	macabeanum
17436	Subsect. Maddenia
17700	'Manipurense'
17818	'Manipurense'

ASSAM (NE INDIA) EXPS.(1949)

18540	moulmainense
18541	Subsect. Maddenia
18753	formosum
18811	Subsect. Maddenia
18829	vaccinioides (Sect. Vireya)
18985	johnstoneanum
19082	macabeanum
19083	elliottii
19101	triflorum var. bauhiniiflorum

LOHIT VALLEY, ASSAM/TIBET FRONTIER (1950)

19244	virgatum subsp. virgatum
19245	arboreum var. peramoenum aff.
19259	walongense

19325	virgatum subsp. virgatum
19398	vaccinioides (Sect. Vireya)
19404	maddenii subsp. crassum
19405	neriiflorum hybrid
19406	sidereum
19431	hylaeum
19432	megacalyx
19433	edgeworthii
19447	crinigerum var. crinigerum
19448	triflorum var. triflorum
19449	sinogrande
19450	calostrotum subsp. riparium
19451	uvariifolium
19452	hylaeum
19453	neriiflorum hybrid
19573	mekongense var. rubrolineatum
19588	sanguineum var. sanguineum
19589	eudoxum var. eudoxum
19590	anthopogon
19591	pumilum
19606	nivale subsp. nivale
19620	pruniflorum
19657	'Manipurense'
20260	Subsect. Barbata
20280	Subsect. Maddenia
20285	cerasinum aff.
20305a	johnstoneanum

THE TRIANGLE EXP., N BURMA (1953)

20601	dendricola
20629	moulmainense
20651	dendricola
20679	moulmainense
20680	tanastylum var. tanastylum
20681	sp.
20682	genestierianum
20693	vaccinioides (Sect. Vireya)
20696	neriiflorum aff.
20702	maddenii subsp. crassum
20836	megacalyx
20837	zaleucum
20838	sidereum
20839	edgeworthii
20840	edgeworthii
20843	neriiflorum subsp. neriiflorum
20844	tephropeplum
20845	luteiflorum
20876	protistum var. protistum
20877	sinogrande

20878	chrysodoron
20910	vaccinioides (Sect. Vireya)
20919	sp.
20922	arizelum
20923	dichroanthum subsp. apodectum
20924	haematodes subsp. haemotodes
20925	chamaethomsonii var. chamaethauma
20926	cinnabarinum subsp. tamaense
20927	campylocarpum subsp. caloxanthum
20928	campylogynum
20929	cephalanthum subsp. cephalanthum
20934	trichocladum var. trichocladum
20981	ciliicalyx
21000	dichroanthum subsp. apodectum
21001	sulfureum
21003	cinnabarinum subsp. tamaense
21005	maddenii subsp. crassum
21006	eclecteum var. eclecteum
21007	leptocarpum
21021	cinnabarinum subsp. tamaense
21040	luteiflorum
21072	trichocladum var. trichocladum
21073	forrestii × coelicum (hybrid)
21074	Subsect. Neriiflora
21075	coelicum
21077	coelicum
21078	cephalanthum subsp. cephalanthum
21079	mekongense var. mekongense
21086	neriiflorum subsp. neriiflorum
21111	sinogrande
21130	campylogynum
21481	campylogynum
21494	vaccinioides (Sect. Vireya)
21498	protistum var. protistum
21512	dendricola
21525	moulmainense
21547	martinianum
21556	luteiflorum
21557	martinianum aff.
21559	megeratum
21601	Subsect. Grandia
21602	protistum var. giganteum
21679	tephropeplum

WC BURMA EXP. (1956)

21768	arboreum var. delavayi

21796	sp.
21976	arboreum subsp. albomentosum
21909	sp.
21921	burmanicum
22036	simsii
22200	johnstoneanum
22291	Subsect.Arborea

Kinmouth, F.
BHUTAN EXP. (1990)

78	anthopogon subsp. anthopogon
79	anthopogon subsp. anthopogon
80	barbatum
81	bhutanense
82	camelliiflorum
83	campylocarpum subsp. campylocarpum
84	falconeri subsp. falconeri
85	flinckii
86	glaucophyllum var. tubiforme
87	grande aff.
88	hodgsonii
89	hodgsonii
90	kendrickii
91	kendrickii
92	kesangiae
93	maddenii subsp. maddenii
94	neriiflorum subsp. phaedropum
95	arboreum
96	nivale subsp. nivale
97	pendulum
98	thomsonii subsp. thomsonii
99	thomsonii subsp. thomsonii
100	triflorum var. triflorum
101	triflorum var. triflorum
102	flinckii aff.
103	wallichii
104	wightii

VIETNAM EXP. (1991)

(see also Rushforth, 1991)

150	Sect. Vireya
151	Sect. Vireya
152	irroratum subsp. pogonostylum
153	maddenii

154   tsoi
155   maddenii subsp. crassum
156   excellens
157   maddenii
158   maddenii
159   Sect. Tsutsusi
160   tsoi
194   maddenii
195   Subsect. Arborea
196   Subsect. Arborea
197   protistum var. giganteum
198   maddenii
199   Sect. Vireya
201   Subsect. Boothia
202   sp.
203   Subsect. Irrorata
204   irroratum subsp.
          pogonostylum
205   excellens

Kirkham, T.S. & Flanagan, M.
TAIWAN EXP. (1992)

37   formosanum
195   nakaharae

Kirkham, T.S., Flanagan, M. & Boyce
S KOREA EXP. (1989)

54   dauricum
57   brachycarpum subsp.
          brachycarpum
101   schlippenbachii

Kunming Edinburgh Gothenberg Exp. (KEG)
YUNNAN, CHINA (SPRING 1993)

313   nivale subsp. boreale
317   aganniphum var.
          aganniphum
319   primuliflorum
332   primuliflorum
347   rupicola
799   rupicola var. chryseum
1219   complexum

Kunming Gothenberg Exp. (KGB)
YUNNAN, CHINA (AUTUMN 1993)

19   wardii
20   beesianum
21   phaeochrysum var. levistratum
22   aganniphum var. aganniphum
23   aganniphum var. aganniphum
24   phaeochrysum var. agglutinatum
25   phaeochrysum var. agglutinatum
26   rupicola
28   heliolepis var. brevistylum
136   primuliflorum
137   nivale subsp. boreale
142   beesianum
153   trichostomum
154   vernicosum
172   beesianum
173   oreotrephes
174   rubiginosum
203   rupicola var. chryseum
206   saluenense subsp. chameunum
227   aganniphum var. aganniphum
236   nivale subsp. boreale
243   nivale subsp. boreale
245   yunnanense
262   hippophaeoides
265   hippophaeoides
291   rupicola var. chryseum
292   tapetiforme
293   saluenense subsp. chameunum
294   nivale
295   primuliflorum
296   aganniphum var. aganniphum
365   phaeochrysum var.
          phaeochrysum
366   beesianum
375   rupicola
400   uvariifolium var. uvariifolium
440   rupicola var. chryseum
447   primuliflorum
448   saluenense subsp. chameunum
449   nivale subsp. boreale
484   wardii
486   phaeochrysum var. levistratum
495   vernicosum
496   heliolepis var. brevistylum
558   uvariifolium var. uvariifolium

559	yunnanense
564	phaeochrysum var. agglutinatum
565	wardii
566	oreotrephes
574	phaeochrysum var. phaeochrysum
589	rupicola var. chryseum
597	aganniphum var. aganniphum
654	rupicola
680	anthosphaerum
684	roxieanum
688	roxieanum
691	selense subsp. selense
692	wardii
693	saluenense subsp. saluenense
695	proteoides
699	sanguineum var. sanguineum
700	proteoides
742	rupicola × complexum (hybrid)
745	complexum
750	rupicola
778	wardii
802	haematodes subsp. haematodes
804	cyanocarpum
805	fastigiatum
806	lacteum
808	balfourianum
809	campylogynum
827	lacteum

Kunming Yunnan Exp.(A.Clark *et al.*) (1995)

486	excellens
826	spinuliferum
828	spinuliferum
832	siderophyllum
833	siderophyllum
872	lacteum
873	sikangense
874	bureavii
875	pubicostatum
878	sphaeroblastum
879	sikangense
880	bureavii
897	pubicostatum aff.
901	Subsect. Falconera
903	Subsect. Heliolepida
911	arboreum var. delavayi
914	pubicostatum

930	tsaii aff.
942	campylogynum
982	irroratum
1024	atrovirens
1029	denudatum aff.
1031	oreodoxa var. fargesii aff.
1035	racemosum aff.
1040	Subsect. Fortunea
1054	calophytum var. pauciflorum
1056	ochraceum
1058	lutescens
1073	oreodoxa aff.
1087	denudatum
1088	denudatum
1089	yunnanense aff.
1095	Subsect. Fortunea
1098	Subsect. Heliolepida
1100	Subsect. Fortunea
1103	denudatum
1104	oreodoxa var. fargesii aff.
1106	yunnanense aff.
1108	oreodoxa var. fargesii aff.
1109	yunnanense aff.
1128	ochraceum aff.
1131	moupinense aff.
1132	denudatum aff.
1133	ochraceum aff.
1140	arboreum var. delavayi
1142	irroratum 'Ningyuenense'
1143	denudatum
1145	strigillosum
1146	huianum
1148	huianum
1150	strigillosum
1152	Subsect. Irrorata
1153	strigillosum
1156	Subsect. Irrorata
1157	moupinense
1162	irroratum 'Ningyuenense'
1163	strigillosum aff.
1171	Subsect. Irrorata
1172	Subsect. Irrorata
1174	denudatum
1175	Subsect. Irrorata
1177	sp.
1178	sp.
1184	lutescens
1194	Subsect. Heliolepida
1199	irroratum 'Ningyuenense'
1202	coeloneuron
1205	coeloneuron

1206	calophytum var. openshawianum
1207	strigillosum
1213	sinofalconeri
1217	siderophyllum aff.
1219	flumineum
1225	mengtszense
1229	microphyton aff.
1230	valentinianum var. oblongilobatum
1239	hemsleyanum
1243	Subsect. Irrorata
1258	valentinianum var. oblongilobatum
1268	sp.

Kumar, V.
HIMACHAL PRADESH, NW INDIA (1975)

698	arboreum subsp. arboreum
715	arboreum subsp. arboreum
738	campanulatum subsp. campanulatum

Kurashige, Y.
JAPAN (1987)

16	brachycarpum
100	tashiroi
179	amagianum
180	degronianum var. kyomaruense
183	tschonoskyi var. tschonoskyi
241	nipponicum
269	semibarbatum
276	makinoi
385	tosaense
392	dilatatum
427	lapponicum
441	hidakanum
443	kaempferi
458	camtschaticum var. camtschaticum
461	aureum
491	brachycarpum subsp. fauriei
494	degronianum var. degonianum
498	albrechtii
501	tschonoskyi var. tschonoskyi
510	pentaphyllum
518	kiyosumense

544	kaempferi
545	kaempferi
557	reticulatum
573	albrechtii
594	reticulatum
603	kaempferi
604	kaempferi
656	tschonoskyi var. tschonoskyi
672	kaempferi
711	weyrichii
719	weyrichii
730	weyrichii
751	kaempferi
752	kaempferi
756	kaempferi
759	kaempferi
765	kaempferi
768	kaempferi
771	tsusiophyllum
772	kaempferi
802	semibarbatum
829	semibarbatum
830	degronianum subsp. heptamerum
846	degronianum subsp. heptamerum
876	mayebarae
889	keiskei
934	nudipes var. kirishimense
971	kaempferi var. mikawanum
975	stenopetalum
984	indicum

Ludlow, F. & Sherriff, G.
BHUTAN & S TIBET EXP. (1934)

1081	sp.
1082	campanulatum
1083	tsariense var. tsariense
1084	fulgens
1085	campanulatum
1091	anthopogon subsp. hypenanthum

BHUTAN AND SOUTH TIBET EXP. (1936)

1141	maddenii
1142	maddenii
1181	camelliiflorum
1182	arboreum
1183	camelliiflorum
1193	papillatum

1204	dalhousiae var. rhabdotum
1205	dalhousiae var. dalhousiae
1208	grande aff.
1209	camelliiflorum
1306	wallichii
1352	neriiflorum subsp. neriiflorum
1353	triflorum var. triflorum
1354	cinnabarinum subsp. xanthocodon 'Purpurellum'
2505	megeratum
2552	pumilum
2627	principis
2652	pumilum
2653	forrestii subsp. forrestii
2654	campylogynum
2736	thomsonii subsp. lopsangianum
2738	principis
2739	ciliatum
2743	sp.
2744	lindleyi
2745	edgeworthii
2747	kendrickii
2751	sherriffii
2752	pudorosum
2753	arizelum
2754	fulvum
2755	erosum
2757	ciliatum
2758	trichocladum var. trichocladum
2759	megeratum
2760	camelliiflorum
2761	megeratum
2762	pumilum
2764	glaucophyllum var. glaucophyllum (in cult.)
2765	camelliiflorum
2766	tsariense var. tsariense
2767	sp.
2770	virgatum
2797	principis
2816	Subsect. Taliensia
2817	Subsect. Taliensia
2818	lepidotum
2824	anthopogon?
2825	arboreum
2826	thomsonii subsp. thomsonii
2827	sp.
2828	anthopogon subsp. anthopogon
2833	maddenii
2835	griffithianum
2836	edgeworthii

2837	dalhousiae var. rhabdotum
2843	dalhousiae var. rhabdotum
2845	camelliiflorum
2846	fulgens
2847	thomsonii subsp. thomsonii
2848	Subsect. Thomsonia
2849	camelliiflorum
2850	camelliiflorum
2851	sp.
2852	camelliiflorum
2853	camelliiflorum
2855	camelliiflorum
2856	glaucophyllum var. tubiforme
2857	leptocarpum
2858	tsariense var. tsariense
2859	wightii
2860	sp.
2891	dalhousiae var. dalhousiae
2892	maddenii
2893	arboreum var. roseum
2894	tsariense var. tsariense
2895	wallichii
2896	baileyi
2898	pendulum
2903	campanulatum aff.
2906	campanulatum aff.
2907	sp.
2915	fulgens?
2916	wightii
2917	dalhousiae var. rhabdotum

BHUTAN EXP. (1937)

3026	griffithianum
3039	keysii
3048	campylocarpum subsp. campylocarpum
3061	triflorum var. triflorum
3095	glaucophyllum var. glaucophyllum
3132	edgeworthii
3216	pogonophyllum
3324	camelliiflorum
3578	wallichii

Ludlow, Sherriff & Taylor
SE TIBET EXP. (1938)

3587	principis
3589	sp.

3600	principis	6656	baileyi
3601	primuliflorum	6657	tsariense var. tsariense
3613	thomsonii subsp. thomsonii	6659	wallichii
3618	clementinae	6660	pendulum
3619	Subsect. Taliensia	6661	tsariense var. tsariense
3620	lanatum	6676	maddenii subsp. crassum
3624	hirtipes	6694	dalhousiae var. dalhousiae
3778	charitopes subsp. tsangpoense	6754	maddenii subsp. maddenii
3785	calostrotum subsp. riparium	7012	maddenii subsp. crassum
4751b	forrestii subsp. forrestii	7190	principis
5198b	pumilum	7200	clementinae
5582	trilectorum		
5679	wardii var. wardii		
6302	principis		

6349a cinnabarinum subsp.
      xanthocodon 'Purpurellum'

Ludlow and Sherriff & Elliot
SE TIBET EXP. (1946-47)

6411	arboreum var. roseum	12002	principis
6424	wallichi	12014	triflorum var. triflorum
6533	pumilum	12019	faucium
6538	trichocladum var. trichocladum	12024	virgatum
6548	wardii var. wardii	12045	faucium
6549	lanatum	12117	nuttallii
6556	pumilum	12208	faucium
6560	cinnabarinum subsp.	12231	scopulorum
	xanthocodon	12239	sp.
6561	thomsonii subsp. lopsangianum	12248	maddenii subsp. maddenii
6563	neriiflorum subsp. phaedropum	12505	mekongense var. mekongense
6567	viscidifolium	13251	principis
6568	ciliatum	13269	kongboense
6569	glischrum subsp. rude	13276	campylogynum
6573	'Manipurense'	13278a	forrestii subsp. forrestii
6576	brachyanthum subsp.	13278b	chamaethomsonii
	hypolepidotum	13283	sp.
6579	hookeri	13521	uvariifolium var. griseum
6580	sulfureum	15763	phaeochrysum var. agglutinatum
6586	wardii var. wardii	15764	wardii var. wardii
6587	cerasinum	15765	hirtipes
6588	calostrotum subsp. riparium	15774	principis
6591	wardii var. wardii	15817	uvariifolium var. griseum
6598	forrestii subsp. forestii	15819	oreotrephes
6599	wardii var. wardii	15828	fragariiflorum hybrid (in cult.)
6600	ludlowii	15831	principis
6602	campylocarpum subsp.		
	campylocarpum		

Ludlow, Sherriff & Hicks
BHUTAN EXP. (1949)

6608	clementinae		
6612	phaeochrysum var. agglutinatum		
6633	leptocarpum	15841	virgatum subsp. virgtum
6638	miniatum aff.	16007	arboreum subsp. arboreum
6645	principis	16009	ramsdenianum
6648	erosum	16019	ciliatum
6652	lanatum	16026	arboreum var. roseum

16027	cinnabarinum subsp. cinnabarinum
16054	virgatum subsp. virgatum
16062	triflorum var. triflorum
16068	griffithianum
16090	wallichii
16095	arboreum × barbatum (hybrid)
16096	papillatum
16099	anthopogon subsp. hypenanthum
16100	wightii
16101	succothii
16103	papillatum
16116	thomsonii subsp. thomsonii
16117	pendulum
16120	hodgsonii
16121	wallichii
16123	kendrickii
16126	cinnabarinum subsp. xanthocodon
16128	wallichii
16136	wallichii
16137	hodgsonii
16140	wallichii
16155	lanatum
16157	setosum
16160	campylocarpum subsp. campylocarpum
16168	campylocarpum subsp. campylocarpum
16184	lindleyi
16206	virgatum subsp.virgatum
16246	campylocarpum
16248	wallichii
16249	wightii
16294	nivale subsp. nivale
16324	lanatum
16346	hodgsonii
16351	succothii
16366	campylocarpum subsp. campylocarpum
16371	falconeri subsp. falconeri
16392	keysii
16378	edgeworthii
16419	anthopogon subsp. anthopogon
16442	baileyi
16443	campanulatum
16448	thomsonii subsp. thomsonii
16492	cinnabarinum subsp. xanthocodon
16493	cinnabarinum subsp. xanthocodon
16494	hodgsonii
16495	cinnabarinum subsp. xanthocodon
16510	lepidotum & dalhousie var. rhabdotum
17359	baileyi
17447	baileyi
17448	wallichii
17449	campanulatum
17478	wallichii
17498	ciliatum
17501	trichocladum var. trichocladum
17509	lepidotum
17512	wallichii
17521	cinnabarinum subsp. xanthocodon
17525	barbatum
17526	campanulatum subsp. aeruginosum
17527	wallichii
17531	camelliiflorum
17531a	maddenii subsp. maddenii
17543	setosum
17546	hirtipes
17550	anthopogon subsp. anthopogon
17552	lepidotum
18683	ciliatum
19847	tsariense aff.
19848	'Basfordii' (as in cult.)
19849	triflorum var. triflorum
19850	succothii
19869	sp.
21170	anthopogon subsp. hypenanthum
21184	pumilum
21257	dalhousiae var. rhabdotum
21274	sp.
21282	glaucophyllum var. tubiforme
21283	cinnabarinum var. cinnabarinum
21284	keysii
21285	thomsonii subsp. thomsonii
21286	× candelabrum (hybrid)
21287	papillatum
21289	leptocarpum
21290	neriiflorum subsp. phaedropum
21292	lepidotum
21293	cinnabarinum
21294	arboreum subsp. arboreum
21295	succothii
21296	hodgsonii
21297	baileyi
21298	campanulatum

21299	keysii
21475	(or 21457) baileyi
21483	griffithianum

McBeath, R.
NEPAL EXP. (1981)

1083	vaccinioides (Sect. Vireya)
1110	lepidotum
1120	pumilum
1171	nivale subsp. nivale
1173	setosum
1183	anthopogon subsp. hypenanthum
1208	nivale subsp. nivale
1234	wightii
1235	wallichii
1236	campanulatum
1243	hodgsonii
1254	campylocarpum subsp. campylocarpum
1256	cinnabarinum subsp. cinnabarinum
1262	cinnabarinum
1279	thomsonii subsp. thomsonii

NEPAL EXP. (1983)

1506	lowndesii
1507	anthopogon
1518	lepidotum
1548	anthopogon subsp. hypenanthum

NEPAL EXP. (1990)

2247	cowanianum
2489	vaccinioides (Sect. Vireya)
2491	pendulum
2529	camelliiflorum
2638	neoglandulosum

Mclaren, the Hon. J.
YUNNAN & SICHUAN, CHINA EXPS. (1932-39)

A 29	'Dimitrium'
A 29a	Subsect. Fortunea
A183	coriaceum
A183a	Subsect. Fortunea
A226	arboreum subsp. delavayi
C 01	haematodes subsp. haematodes
C 01a	arboreum var. delavayi
C 03	maddenii subsp. crassum aff.
C 29	'Dimitrium'
C 33	edgeworthii
C 44	neriiflorum subsp. neriiflorum
C 47	microphyton
C 78	virgatum subsp. oleifolium
C184	caesium
C226	arboreum var. delavayi
C226a	Subsect. Irrorata
D 07	sperabile var. weihsiense
D 18	uvariifolium var. uvariiflorum
D 19	Subsect. Irrorata
D105	beesianum
D106	Subsect. Falconera
D148	heliolepis var. brevistylum
D268	sinogrande
D271	fulvum subsp. fulvoides
D272	beesianum
D273	lukiangense
D274	coriaceum
D333	maddenii subsp. crassum
K 50	Subsect. Campylocarpa
L112a	trichocladum var. trichocladum
P 69	oreotrephes
P 70	cuneatum
P 71	vernicosum
S 33	spinuliferum
S 38	spinuliferum
S 39	scabrifolium var. scabrifolium
S122	maddenii subsp. crassum
S124	aganniphum var. flavorufum
S124a	haematodes subsp. haematodes
S127	× erythocalyx (hybrid)
S127a	telmateium
S131	haematodes
S146	Subsect. Fortunea
S158	edgeworthii
T 41	aberconwayi
T 71	venicosum
T107	haematodes subsp. haematodes
T126	lacteum
T133	Subsect. Fortunea
U 35a	aberconwayi
V 11	spinuliferum
V 33	Irroratum 'Ningyuenense'
V 69	decorum subsp. decorum
V 71	irroratum subsp. pogonostylum
V139	'Bodinieri'
V169	pachypodium
V172	decorum subsp. decorum

V187	decorum subsp. decorum	59	camelliiflorum

V187   decorum subsp. decorum
Z 05   concinnum
AA 01   spinuliferum
AA 12   scabrifolium var. spiciferum
AA 16   siderophyllum
AA 17   scabrifolium var. pauciflorum
AA 27   spinuliferum
AA 33   scabrifolium var. pauciflorum
AA 52   spinuliferum
AA121   microphyton
AD 75   prattii
AD106   wasonii
AG 45   Subsect. Triflora
AG344   Subsect. Triflora
AG395   davidsonianum
AG396   polylepis
AH217   Subsect. Triflora
AH270   Subsect. Triflora
AH300   Subsect. Triflora
AH307   oreodoxa var. oreodoxa
AH314   Subsect. Triflora
AH407   Subsect. Triflora
AH440   Subsect. Triflora
AH444   Subsect. Triflora
38/010 ambiguum
38/013 trichanthum
38/016 argyrophyllum subsp.
            argyrophyllum
38/020 wasonii
38/023 bureavii
38/025 orbiculare
38/030 oreodoxa var. oreodoxa
39/117 arboreum var. peramoenum
39/120 Subsect. Triflora
39/279 polylepis
39/284 pachytrichum var.
            pachytrichum
39/297 wasonii
39/329 Subsect.Triflora

Millais, E.G.
BHUTAN EXP. (1988)

51   cinnabarinum subsp.
          xanthocodon
52   triflorum
55   falconeri subsp. falconeri
56   barbatum
57   arboreum
58   grande

59   camelliiflorum
61   kesangiae
62   keysii
64   keysii
65   kesangiae
66   argipeplum
68   campanulatum subsp.
          aeruginosum
69   campanulatum subsp.
          aeruginosum
70   wightii
71   tsariense aff.
72   fulgens
75   bhutanense (grey indumentum)
76   bhutanense (orange
          indumentum)
77   flinckii
79   flinckii
80   hodgsonii
81   hodgsonii aff.
82   campylocarpum subsp.
          campylocarpum
83   flinckii aff.
84   thomsonii
85   cinnabarinum subsp.
          xanthocodon
86   succothii
87   anthopogon
88   cinnabarinum subsp.
          xanthocodon
89   pendulum
90   flinckii
91   cinnabarinum subsp.
          cinnabarinum
92   campylocarpum subsp.
          campylocarpum
93   kendrickii
94   succothii
95   campylocarpum subsp.
          campylocarpum
96   cinnabarinum subsp.
          xanthocodon
97   argipeplum
98   arboreum
100   cinnabarinum subsp.
          cinnabarinum
101   griffithianum
102   hodgsonii
103   falconeri subsp. falconeri
104   succothii
105   lindleyi

SICHUAN EXP. (1990)

106	wiltonii
107	concinnum
108	sikangense
109	watsonii
110	orbiculare
111	faberi
114	Subsect. Lapponica
115	pachytrichum var. pachytrichum
116	argyrophyllum subsp. hypoglaucum
117	polylepis
118	floribundum
118a	calophytum var. calophytum
121	prattii
122	wasonii aff.
124	decorum subsp. decorum
125	intricatum
126	Subsect. Lapponica
127	phaeochrysum var. levistratum
129	phaeochrysum
130	intricatum ?
131	intricatum ?
134	phaeochrysum var. agglutinatum
135	phaeochrysum var. phaeochrysum
136	Subsect. Lapponica
137	oreodoxa subsp. fargesii
138	watsonii
139	souliei
142	phaeochrysum var. levistratum
144	phaeochrysum var. levistratum
146	websterianum
147	prattii
148	phaeochrysum 'Cuprescens' ?
149	davidsonianum
150	floribundum aff.
151	concinnum
152	racemosum
153	lutescens
158	galactinum
155	sikangense
156	nitidulum
157	faberi

Millais, E.G. *et al*
SICHUAN & YUNNAN EXP., CHINA (1995)

(See also Cox, P.A. *et al.* - Sichuan & Yunnan Exp.)

288	polylepis
293	augustinii
294	denudatum
295	rex
300	decorum subsp. decorum
302	fastigiatum
303	polylepis
304	pingianum
305	strigillosum
312	ochraceum
314	asterochnoum
315	sp. nov.
316	huianum
318	calophytum var. openshawianum
321	tatsienense
322	argyrophyllum aff.
323	denudatum
328	longipes
330	huianum
333	siderophyllum
334	denudatum
336	longipes
337	longipes
338	strigillosum/pachytrichum
339	irroratum 'Ningyuenense'
340	irroratum 'Ningyuenense'
341	calophytum
346	siderophyllum
347	glanduliferum
348	vernicosum
349	sikangense var. exquisitum
350	sphaeroblastum var. wumengense
354	lacteum
356	lacteum
357	lacteum
358	heliolepis 'Fumidum'
359	sphaeroblastum var. wumengense
360	arboreum subsp. delavayi

Paterson, D.S. & Clarke, S.
W USA EXP. (1991)

12	occidentale

71	occidentale
72	macrophyllum
136	Subsect. Ledum
155	Subsect. Ledum

Paterson, D.S. & Main, J.
YUNNAN EXP. (1994)

26	decorum subsp. decorum
46	racemosum
47	neriiflorum subsp. neriiflorum
62	cyanocarpum
68	racemosum
70	neriiflorum subsp. neriiflorum
71	sp.
78	sulfureum
79	sulfureum
81	rubiginosum
83	cyanocarpum
88	racemosum
172	yunnanense
187	decorum subsp. decorum
192	sp.
195	yunnanense
198	yunnanense

Patrick, J.R.R. & Hsu, C.C. (Rhododendron Venture, Taiwan)
1968 EXP.

681106	pseudochrysanthum
681107	kawakamii 'White'
681108	moulmainense
681109	morii
681110	morii
681111	morii
681112	rubropilosum
681113	rubropilosum
681114	nakaharae
681115	oldhamii

1969 EXP.

| 69/200 | kawakamii, yellow |
| 69/203 | kawakamii, yellow |

69/212	rubropilosum
69/215	formosanum
69/216	pseudochrysanthum
69/217	kanehirae
69/218	hyperythrum
69/219	moulmainense

1970 EXP.

RV8829	moulmainense
RV9803	oldhamii
RV9804	oldhamii
RV9809	morii
RV9811	morii
RV9812	hyperythrum
RV9814	sikayotaisanense
RV9816	pseudochrysanthum
RV9819	oldhamii
RV9821	kawakamii
RV9829	morii
RV9831	rubropilosum
RV9832	morii
RV9834	morii
RV9835	hyperythrum
RV9837	pseudochrysanthum
RV9840	morii
RV9844	pseudochrysanthum
RV9863	morii
RV9866	taiwanalpinum
RV9880	ovatum
RV9881	hyperythrum
RV9882	lasiostylum
RV9889	morii
RV9890	morii
RV9891	pseudochrysanthum
RV9892	formosanum

1972 EXP.

72/001	pachysanthum
72/002	pseudochrysanthum
72/003	pseudochrysanthum

1973 EXP.

73/100	morii
73/101	sikayotaisanense
73/102	formosanum
73/103	kawakamii
73/104	moulmainense
73/105	mariesii

73/106 oldhamii
73/107 ovatum

1974 EXP.

74/001 morii
74/002 noriakianum
74/003 taiwanalpinum
74/004 morii
74/005 rubropilosum
74/006 formosanum
74/007 formosanum

Pes, T.
NEPAL EXP. (1994)

2585   cowanianum
2588   campanulatum
2590   campanulatum

Polunin, Sykes & Williams
W NEPAL EXP. (1952)

3486   lowndesii

Pradhan, U.C. & Lachungpa, S.T.
SIKKIM (1986)

2   niveum
8   sp.
10   × sikkimense (hybrid)
12   wightii
13   ciliatum
17   cinnabarinum subsp.
            cinnabarinum
19   grande
20   setosum
21   niveum
29   griffithianum
31   fulgens
32   sp.
33   sp.
34   grande
35   virgatum subsp.
            virgatum
39   campanulatum

Rock, J.F.
SE TIBET & NW YUNNAN, CHINA EXP. (1923-24)

6002   yunnanense
6031   yunnanense
6073   rubiginosum
6232   sp.
6249   sinogrande
6253   taliense/roxieanum var.
            cucullatum
6254   sp.
6259   irroratum subsp. irroratum
6269   haematodes subsp. haematodes
6270   heliolepis var. heliolepis
6273   cyanocarpum
6274   trichocladum var. trichocladum
6291   scabrifolium subsp. scabrifolium
6294   irroratum subsp. irroratum
6295   rex subsp. fictolacteum
6296   bureavii
6308   irroratum subsp. irroratum
6309   rex. subsp. fictolacteum
6323   cephalanthum subsp.
            cephalanthum
6334   fastigiatum
6335   neriiflorum subsp. neriiflorum
6346   lacteum
6353   calostrotum subsp. riparioides
6354   campylogynum
6357   selense subsp. jucundum
6364   haematodes subsp. haematodes
6365   taliense/roxieanum var.
            cucullatum
6369   edgeworthii
6370   maddenii subsp. crassum
6450   hemitrichotum
6451   hemitrichotum
6460   thymifolium
6524   Subsect.Triflora
6525   rigidum
6656   arboreum var. delavayi
6681   decorum subsp. decorum
6743   (= USDA 56355) - thymifolium &
            arboreum var. delavayi
6744   (= USDA 56360) - neriiflorum
            subsp. neriiflorum
6745   (= USDA 56361) - edgeworthii
6826   (= USDA 56362) - yunnanense
6827   (= USDA 56363) - racemosum
6828   (= USDA 56357) - rubiginosum

6829	(= USDA 56356) - vernicosum
6830	(= USDA 56364) - hippophaeoides var. hippophaeoides
6831	(= USDA 56359?) - rex subsp. fictolacteum
6832	(= USDA 56358) - traillianum var. traillianum
6999	edgeworthii
7075	sp.
7077	sp.
7272	sp.
7376	sidereum
7377	edgeworthii
7381	sinogrande
7577	stamineum aff.
7640	rubiginosum
7646	leptothrium
7648	facetum
7649	zaleucum
7650	neriiflorum subsp. neriiflorum
7651	sulfureum
7658	habrotrichum
7662	fulvum subsp. fulvum
7663	dichroanthum subsp. apodectum
7664	anthosphaerum
7665	fulvum subsp. fulvum
7666	neriiflorum subsp. neriiflorum
7667	sp.
7794	adenogynum
7795	beesianum
7796	traillianum var. traillianum
7865	(= USDA 56827) - edgeworthii
7866	(= USDA 56828) - stamineum
7906	arboreum var. peramoenum
7907	arboreum var. peramoenum
7911	arboreum var. delavayi
7935	(= USDA 56857) - arboreum var. delavayi
7954	pseudociliipes
10276	sanguineum var. haemaleum
10545	cephalanthum subsp. cephalanthum
10550	oreotrephes
10551	vernicosum
10552	cuneatum × hippophaeoides var. hippophaeoides (hybrid)
10553	telmateium
10572	tatsienense
10882	(= USDA 58598) - vernicosum
10883	(= USDA 58599) - phaeochrysum var. levistratum

10884	(= USDA 58633) - heliolepis var. brevistylum
10885	(= USDA 58634) - sp.
10893	sanguineum var. sanguineum
10894	(= USDA 59031) - sanguineum var. sanguineum
10895	(= USDA 59030) - sanguineum subsp. haemaleum
10896	(= USDA 59032) - beesianum
10897	(= USDA 59033) - sanguineum var. sanguineum
10898	(= USDA 59437) - eudoxum var. eudoxum
10899	(= USDA 59034) - sanguineum var. cloiophorum
10900	(= USDA 59035) - sanguineum
10901	(= USDA 59036) - sanguineum
10902	(= USDA 59037) - sanguineum
10903	(= USDA 59038) - sanguineum var. didymoides
10904	(= USDA 59039) - sanguineum var. didymoides
10905	(= USDA 59040) - citriniflorum var. citriniflorum
10906	(= USDA 59041) - sanguineum var. himertum
10907	(= USDA 59042) - eudoxum var. mesopolium
10908	(= USDA 59043) - beesianum
10909	(= USDA 59044) - temenium
10910	(= USDA 59045) - eclecteum var. bellatulum
10911	(= USDA 59046) - sanguineum var. haemaleum
10912	(= USDA 59047) - martinianum
10913	(= USDA 59048) - praestans
10914	(= USDA 59049) - rupicola var. chryseum
10915	(= USDA 59050) - selense subsp. setiferum
10916	(= USDA 59051) - beesianum
10917	(= USDA 59052) - brachyanthum subsp. hypolepidotum
10918	(= USDA 59438) - haematodes subsp. chaetomallum
10919	(= USDA 59053) - brachyanthum subsp. hypolepidotum
10920	(= USDA 59439) - roxieanum var. roxieanum
10921	(= USDA 59440) - rex subsp. fictolacteum

10922 (= USDA 59441) - sanguineum

10923 (= USDA 59442) - alutaceum var.
       russotinctum

10924 (= USDA 59443) - cephalanthum
       subsp. cephalanthum

10925 (= USDA 59054) - wardii var.
       wardii

10926 (= USDA 59055) - sanguineum
       var. sanguineum

10927 (= USDA 59056) - sanguineum

10928 (= USDA 59444) - sanguineum
       var. sanguineum

10929 (= USDA 59445) - selense subsp.
       selense

10930 (= USDA 59446) - selense subsp.
       selense

10931 (= USDA 59447) - fulvum
       subsp. fulvoides

10932 (= USDA 59448) - eudoxum var.
       brunneifolium

10933 (= USDA 59449) - traillianum var
       dictyotum

10934 (= USDA 59450) - sanguineum

10935 (= USDA 59719) - cephalanthum
       subsp. cephalanthum

10936 (= USDA 59451) - phaeochrysum
       var. levistratum

10937 (= USDA 59452) - augustinii
       subsp. chasmanthum

10938 (= USDA 59453) - sanguineum

10939 (= USDA 59454) - eclecteum var.
       eclecteum

10940 (= USDA 59455) - sanguineum
       var. didymoides

10941 (= USDA 59720) - temenium

10942 (= USDA 59721) -
       anthosphaerum

10943 (= USDA 59714) - rubiginosum

10944 (= USDA 59722) - eclecteum var.
       bellatulum

10945 (= USDA 59723) - sanguineum

10946 (= USDA 59724) - citriniflorum
       var citriniflorum

10947 (= USDA 59456) - sanguineum
       var. haemaleum

10948 (= USDA 59457) - haematodes
       subsp. haematodes

10950 (= USDA 59458) - temenium var.
       mesopolium

10951 (= USDA 59459) - sanguineum
       var. himertum/temenium var.

       gilvum

10952 (= USDA 59460) - temenium var.
       temenium

10953 (= USDA 59725) - sanguineum
       var, didymoides

10954 (= USDA 59726) - oreotrephes

10955 (= USDA 59727) - coriaceum

10956 (= USDA 59728) - roxieanum var.
       roxieanum

10957 (= USDA 59729) - praestans

10958 (= USDA 59730) - martinianum

10959 (= USDA 59057) - floccigerum

10960 (= USDA 59058) - crinigerum var.
       crinigerum

10961 (= USDA 59059) - selense subsp.
       selense

10963 (= USDA 59060) - selense subsp.
       selense

10964 (= USDA 59061) - forrestii subsp.
       forrestii

10965 (= USDA 59461) - martinianum

10966 (= USDA 59462) - praestans

10967 (= USDA 59463) - crinigerum

10968 (= USDA 59464) - cringerum var
       crinigerum

10969 (= USDA 59465) - mekongense
       var. mekongense

10970 (= USDA 59466) - crinigerum var
       crinigerum

10971 (= USDA 59467) - crinigerum var
       crinigerum

10972 (= USDA 59468) - crinigerum var
       crinigerum

10973 (= USDA 59469) - crinigerum var
       crinigerum

10974 (= USDA 59470) - crinigerum var
       crinigerum

10975 (= USDA 59471) - crinigerum var
       crinigerum

10976 (= USDA 59472) - crinigerum var
       crinigerum

10977 (= USDA 59062) - crinigerum var
       crinigerum

10978 (= USDA 59063) - crinigerum var
       crinigerum

10979 (= USDA 59064) - roxieanum var
       roxieanum

10980 (= USDA 59065) - crinigerum var
       crinigerum

10981 (= USDA 59066) - crinigerum var
       crinigerum

10982   (= USDA 59067) - crinigerum var
        crinigerum
10983   (= USDA 59068) - crinigerum var
        crinigerum
10984   (= USDA 59069) - haematodes
        subsp. chaetomallum
10985   (= USDA 59070) - haematodes
        subsp. chaetomallum
10986   (= USDA 59071) - oreotrephes
10987   (= USDA 59072) - beesianum
10988   (= USDA 59073) - beesianum
10989   (= USDA 59074) - haematodes
        subsp. chaetomallum
10990   (= USDA 59075) - beesianum
10991   (= USDA 59076) - brachyanthum
        subsp. hypolepidotum
10992   (= USDA 59077) - crinigerum var
        crinigerum
10993   (= USDA 59473) - forrestii subsp.
        forrestii
10994   (= USDA 59078) - forrestii subsp.
        forrestii
10995   (= USDA 59079) - praestans
10996   (= USDA 59474) - floccigerum
10997   (= USDA 59080) - forrestii subsp.
        forrestii
10998   (= USDA 59475) - proteoides
10999   (= USDA 59081) - floccigerum
11000   (= USDA 59476) - oreotrephes
11001   (= USDA 59082) - saluenense
        subsp. saluenense
11002   (= USDA 59083) - sanguineum
        var. sanguineum
11003   (= USDA 59084) -
        chamaethomsonii var.
        chamaedoron
11004   (= USDA 59477) - beesianum
11005   (= USDA 59478) - saluenense
        subsp. saluenense
11006   (= USDA 59479) - megeratum
11007   (= USDA 59480) - praestans
11008   (= USDA 59481) - praestans
11010   (= USDA 59482) - saluenense
        subsp. saluenense
11011   (= USDA 59483) - sanguineum
11012   (= USDA 59484) - saluenense
        subsp. saluenense
11013   (= USDA 59085) - praestans.
11014   (= USDA 59086) - oreotrephes
11015   (= USDA 59087) - lukiangense
11016   (= USDA 59088) - fulvum subsp.

        fulvoides
11017   (= USDA 59089) - beesianum
11018   (= USDA 59090) - sanguineum
        var. sanguineum
11019   (= USDA 59485) - cephalanthum
        subsp. cephalanthum
11020   (= USDA 59486) - roxieanum var.
        roxieanum
11021   (= USDA 59731) - beesianum
11022   (= USDA 59487) - sanguineum
        var. haemaleum
11023   (= USDA 59091) - fulvum
11024   (= USDA 59092) - sanguineum
        var. sanguineum
11025   (= USDA 59488) - eclecteum var.
        bellatulum
11026   (= USDA 59093) - selense subsp.
        selense
11027   (= USDA 59094) - eclecteum var.
        bellatulum
11028   (= USDA 59095) - selense subsp.
        selense
11029   (= USDA 59096) - sanguineum
        var. sanguineum
11030   (= USDA 59097) - eclecteum var.
        bellatulum
11031   (= USDA 59098) - eclecteum var.
        bellatulum
11032   (= USDA 59099) - eclecteum var.
        eclecteum
11033   (= USDA 59489) - forrestii subsp.
        forrestii
11034   (= USDA 59100) - fulvum subsp.
        fulvoides
11035   (= USDA 59490) - eclecteum var.
        eclecteum
11036   (= USDA 59491) -
        chamaethomsonii var.
        chamaethomsonii
11037   (= USDA 59492) - eclecteum var.
        bellatulum
11038   (= USDA 59101) - eclecteum var.
        eclecteum
11039   (= USDA 59493) -
        sanguineum
11040   (= USDA 59494) - eclecteum var.
        bellatulum
11041   (= USDA 59102) - eclecteum var.
        bellatulum
11042   (= USDA 59103) -
        chamaethomsonii var.

chamaethomsonii

11043 (= USDA 59104) - rex subsp.
fictolacteum

11044 (= USDA 59495) - fulvum subsp.
fulvoides

11045 (= USDA 59105) - uvariifolium
var. uvariiflorum

11046 (= USDA 59496) - sanguineum
var. haemaleum

11047 (= USDA 59106) - sanguineum
var. haemaleum

11048 (= USDA 59497) - fulvum subsp.
fulvoides

11049 (= USDA 59498) - sanguineum
var. haemaleum

11050 (= USDA 59107) - eclecteum var.
bellatulum

11051 (= USDA 59499) - eclecteum var.
eclecteum

11052 (= USDA 59500) - sanguineum
var. didymoides

11053 (= USDA 59501) - eclecteum var.
bellatulum

11054 (= USDA 59108) - eclecteum var.
bellatulum

11055 (= USDA 59109) - eclecteum var.
bellatulum

11056 (= USDA 59110) - eclecteum var.
bellatulum

11057 (= USDA 59111) - eclecteum var.
bellatulum

11058 (= USDA 59502) - selense subsp.
selense

11059 (= USDA 59112) - eclecteum var.
eclecteum

11060 (= USDA 59503) - eclecteum var.
bellatulum

11061 (= USDA 59113) - eclecteum var.
eclecteum

11062 (= USDA 59504) - selense subsp.
selense

11063 (= USDA 59114) - selense subsp.
selense

11064 (= USDA 59115) - selense subsp.
selense

11065 (= USDA 59116) - selense subsp.
selense

11066 (= USDA 59117) - selense subsp.
selense

11067 (= USDA 59505) - × erythrocalyx
(hybrid)

11068 (= USDA 59118) - beesianum

11069 (= USDA 59119) - coriaceum

11071 (= USDA 59506) -
rubiginosum

11072 (= USDA 59120) - heliolepis var.
heliolepis

11073 (= USDA 59121) - floccigerum

11074 (= USDA 59122) - forrestii subsp.
forrestii

11075 (= USDA 59507) - uvariifolium
var. uvariiflorum

11076 (= USDA 59123) - proteoides

11077 (= USDA 59124) - selense subsp.
selense

11078 (= USDA 59125) - eudoxum

11079 (= USDA 59508) - mekongense
var. mekongense

11080 (= USDA 59126) - eclecteum var.
eclecteum

11081 (= USDA 59127) - haematodes
var. chaetomallum

11082 (= USDA 59128) - sanguineum
var. haemaleum

11083 (= USDA 59129) - crinigerum var.
crinigerum

11084 (= USDA 59130) - roxieanum var.
roxieanum

11085 (= USDA 59132) - phaeochrysum
var. agglutinatum

11086 (= USDA 59509) - tapetiforme

11087 (= USDA 59510) - phaeochrysum
var. levistratum

11088 (= USDA 59732) - tapetiforme

11089 (= USDA 59133) - cephalanthum
subsp. cephalanthum

11090 (= USDA 59511) - phaeochrysum
var. levistratum

11091 (= USDA 59733) - tapetiforme

11092 (= USDA 59134) - tapetiforme

11093 (= USDA 59734) - tapetiforme

11094 (= USDA 59735) - esetulosum

11095 (= USDA 59512) - selense subsp.
selense

11096 (= USDA 59736) - phaeochrysum
var. levistratum

11097 (= USDA 59737) - aganniphum
var. aganniphum

11098 (= USDA 59513) - tapetiforme

11099 (= USDA 59738) - beesianum

11100 (= USDA 59514) - alutaceum var.
alutaceum

11101 (= USDA 59515) - alutaceum var.
       russotinctum
11102 (= USDA 59516) - phaeochrysum
       var. levistratum
11103 (= USDA 59517) - phaeochrysum
       var. levistratum
11104 (= USDA 59518) - phaeochrysum
       var. levistratum
11105 (= USDA 59519) - phaeochrysum
       var. levistratum
11106 (= USDA 59135) - phaeochrysum
       var. levistratum
11106a (= USDA 59135a) - alutaceum var.
       alutaceum
11107 (= USDA 59520) - phaeochrysum
       var. levistratum
11108 (= USDA 59521) - phaeochrysum
       var. agglutinatum
11109 (= USDA 59136) - tapetiforme
11110 (= USDA 59137) - beesianum
11111 (= USDA 59138) - selense subsp.
       selense
11112 (= USDA 59139) - beesianum
11113 (= USDA 59522) - alutaceum var.
       russotinctum
11114 (= USDA 59523) - wardii var.
       wardii
11115 (= USDA 59524) - roxieanum
       var. roxieanum
11116 (= USDA 59140) - alutaceum var.
       iodes
11117 (= USDA 59739) - alutaceum var.
       russotinctum
11118 (= USDA 59740) - aganniphum
       var, aganniphum
11119 (= USDA 59141) - phaeochrysum
       var. levistratum
11120 (= USDA 59142) - phaeochrysum
       var. levistratum
11121 (= USDA 59143) - phaeochrysum
       var. levistratum
11122 (= USDA 59144) - alutaceum var.
       russotinctum
11123 (= USDA 59145) - alutaceum var.
       russotinctum
11124 (= USDA 59146) - Subsect.
       Taliensia
11125 (= USDA 59147) - aganniphum
       var. aganniphum
11126 (= USDA 59148) - rupicola var.
       chryseum

11127 (= USDA 59149) - selense subsp.
       selense
11128 (= USDA 59150) - oreotrephes
11130 (= USDA 59152) - tapetiforme
11132 (= USDA 59153) - oreotrephes
11133 (= USDA 59154) - aganniphum
       var. aganniphum
11134 (= USDA 59155) - adenogynum
11135 (= USDA 59741) - aganniphum
       var. aganniphum
11137 (= USDA 59156) - wardii var.
       wardii
11138 (= USDA 59525) - lukiangense
11139 (= USDA 59157) - lukiangense
11140 (= USDA 59158) - lukiangense
11141 (= USDA 59159) - oreotrephes
11142 (= USDA 59160) - crinigerum var.
       crinigerum
11143 (= USDA 59161) - aganniphum
       var. aganniphum
11144 (= USDA 59162) - roxieanum
11145 (= USDA 59526) - wardii var.
       wardii
11146 (= USDA 59163) - alutaceum var.
       russotinctum
11147 (= USDA 59164) - wardii var.
       wardii
11148 (= USDA 59165) - rupicola var.
       chryseum
11149 (= USDA 59527) - phaeochrysum
       var. levistratum
11150 (= USDA 59528) - aganniphum
       var. aganniphum
11151 (= USDA 59529) - aganniphum
       var. aganniphum
11152 (= USDA 59530) - wardii var.
       wardii
11153 (= USDA 59531) - aganniphum
       var. aganniphum
11154 (= USDA 59166) -
       citriniflorum
11155 (= USDA 59532) - pocophorum
       var. pocophorum
11156 (= USDA 59533) - haematodes
       subsp. chaetomallum
11157 (= USDA 59167) - citriniflorum
       var. horaeum
11158 (= USDA 59168) - sanguineum
11159 (= USDA 59534) - rex subsp.
       fictolacteum
11160 (= USDA 59535) - campylogynum

11161 (= USDA 59169) - sanguineum
       var. cloiophorum
11162 (= USDA 59536) - pocophorum
       var. hemidartum
11163 (= USDA 59170) - pocophorum
       var. pocophorum
11164 (= USDA 59171) - haematodes
       subsp. chaetomallum hybrid
11165 (= USDA 59172) - arizelum
11166 (= USDA 59537) - maddenii
       subsp. crassum
11167 (= USDA 59173) - leptocarpum
11168 (= USDA 59538) - fulvum
11169 (= USDA 59174) -
       chamaethomsonii var.
       chamaethomsonii
11170 (= USDA 59539) - haematodes
       subsp. chaetomallum hybrid
11172 (= USDA 59540) - brachyanthum
11173 sinogrande
11174 (= USDA 59541) - coryanum
11175 (= USDA 59175) - haematodes
       subsp. chaetomallum
11176 (= USDA 59176) - sanguineum
       var. sanguineum
11177 (= USDA 59177) - sanguineum
       var. haemaleum
11178 (= USDA 59742) - sanguineum
11179 (= USDA 59178) - pocophorum
       var. hemidartum
11180 (= USDA 59179) - eclecteum var.
       eclecteum
11181 (= USDA 59180) - sanguineum
11182 (= USDA 59181) - pocophorum
       var. hemidartum
11183 (= USDA 59743) - sanguineum
11184 (= USDA 59542) - haematodes
       subsp. chaetomallum
11185 (= USDA 59543) - catacosum
11186 (= USDA 59744) - citriniflorum
       var. horaeum
11187 (= USDA 59544) - rex subsp.
       fictolacteum
11188 (= USDA 59182) - calostrotum
       subsp. keleticum
11189 (= USDA 59183) - crinigerum var.
       crinigerum
11190 (= USDA 59184) -
       bainbridgeanum
11191 (= USDA 59745) - haematodes
       subsp. keleticum

11192 (= USDA 59185) - crinigerum var.
       crinigerum
11193 (= USDA 59186) - crinigerum var.
       crinigerum
11194 (= USDA 59545) - selense subsp.
       setiferum
11195 (= USDA 59187) -
       bainbridgeanum
11196 (= USDA 59188) - crinigerum var.
       crinigerum
11198 (= USDA 59189) - rupicola var.
       chryseum
11199 (= USDA 59546) - sanguineum
       var. cloiophorum aff.
11200 (= USDA 59547) - moulmainense
11201 (= USDA 59190) - pocophorum
       var. pocophorum
11202 (= USDA 59191) -
       genestierianum
11203 (= USDA 59746) - citriniflorum
       var. horaeum aff.
11204 (= USDA 59548) - haematodes
       subsp. chaetomallum
11205 (= USDA 59192) - martinianum
11206 (= USDA 59549) - citriniflorum
       var. horaeum aff.
11207 (= USDA 59550) - arizelum
       'Rubicosum'
11208 (= USDA 59747) - sanguineum
       var. haemaleum
11209 (= USDA 59551) - selense subsp.
       selense
11210 (= USDA 59552) - haematodes
       subsp. haematodes
11211 (= USDA 59193) - sp.
11212 (= USDA 59533) - sanguineum
       aff.
11213 (= USDA 59554) - selense subsp.
       setiferum
11214 (= USDA 59748) - temenium var.
       temenium
11216 (= USDA 59555) - sanguineum
       subsp. didymum
11217 (= USDA 59556) - anthosphaerum
11219 (= USDA 59505) - virgatum
       subsp. oleifolium
11222 (= USDA 59557) - megacalyx
11223 (= USDA 59558) - rex. subsp.
       fictolacteum
11225 (= USDA 59559) - fulvum subsp.
       fulvoides

11227 (= USDA 59560) - haematodes subsp. chaetomallum
11228 (= USDA 59506) - tephropeplum
11229 (= USDA 58507) - vaccinioides (Sect. Vireya)
11233 (= USDA 59561) - nuttallii
11238 (= USDA 59194) - saluenense subsp. saluenense
11239 (= USDA 59508) - sinogrande
11240 (= USDA 59562) - beesianum
11241 (= USDA 59509) - selense subsp. selense
11242 (= USDA 59563) - rex subsp. fictolacteum
11243 (= USDA 59564) - rupicola var. rupicola
11244 (= USDA 59565) - rex. subsp. fictolactum
11246 (= USDA 59566) - traillianum var. traillianum
11247 (= USDA 59567) - wardii var. wardii
11248 (= USDA 59568) - Subsect. Triflora
11249 (= USDA 59569) - nivale subsp. australe
11250 (= USDA 59570) - roxieanum var. cucullatum
11251 (= USDA 59571) - roxieanum
11252 (= USDA 59195) - roxieanum var. cucullatum
11253 (= USDA 59572) - roxieanum var. cucullatum
11254 (= USDA 59749) - clementinae
11255 (= USDA 59573) - clementinae
11256 (= USDA 59750) - anthosphaerum
11257 (= USDA 59574) - anthosphaerum
11257a (= USDA 59574a) - × pallescens (hybrid)
11258 oreotrephes
11259 selense subsp. dasycladum
11260 (= USDA 59196) - trichostomum
11261 (= USDA 59575) - roxieanum var. roxieanum
11262 (= USDA 59576) - oreotrephes
11263 (= USDA 59715) - rubiginosum
11264 (= USDA 59577) - racemosum
11265 (= USDA 59578) - racemosum
11266 (= USDA 59579) - irroratum subsp. irroratum
11267 (= USDA 59751) - rigidum
11268 (= USDA 59580) - rigidum

11269 (= USDA 59197) - selense subsp. dasycladum
11270 (= USDA 59198) - selense subsp. dasycladum
11271 (= USDA 59199) - cuneatum
11272 (= USDA 59200) - lukiangense
11273 (= USDA 59581) - irroratum subsp. irroratum
11274 (= USDA 59582) - irroratum subsp. irroratum
11275 (= USDA 59210) - lukiangense
11276 (= USDA 59752) - maddenii subsp. crassum
11277 (= USDA 59583) - edgeworthii
11278 (= USDA 59202) - edgeworthii
11279 (= USDA 59584) - arboreum var. delavayi
11280 (= USDA 59203) - yunnanense
11281 (= USDA 59585) - yunnanense hybrid
11282 (= USDA 59586) - arboreum var. delavayi
11282a (= USDA 59586a) - arboreum var. delavayi
11283a (= USDA 59204a) - heliolepis var. brevistylum
11284 (= USDA 59587) - russatum × rupicola var. rupicola (hybrid)
11285 (= USDA 59205) - roxieanum var. oreonastes
11286 (= USDA 59588) - rex subsp. fictolacteum
11287 (= USDA 59206) - cuneatum
11288 (= USDA 59207) - rigidum
11289 (= USDA 59208) - selense subsp. dasycladum
11290 (= USDA 59753) - rex subsp. fictolacteum
11291 roxieanum var. roxieanum
11292 (= USDA 59589) - roxieanum
11293 (= USDA 59590) - roxieanum
11294 (= USDA 59209) - russatum
11295 (= USDA 59210) - russatum
11296 (= USDA 59211) - russatum
11297 (= USDA 59212) - irroratum subsp. irroratum
11298 (= USDA 59591) - oreotrephes
11299 (= USDA 59592) - xanthostephanum
11300 (= USDA 59593) - oreotrephes
11301 (= USDA 59213) - roxieanum

11302	(= USDA 59594) - roxieanum var. oreonastes
11303	(= USDA 59214) - fastigiatum
11304	(= USDA 59215) - nivale subsp. australe
11305	(= USDA 59216) - campylogynum
11306	(= USDA 59217) - pronum
11307	(= USDA 59218) - roxieanum var. cucullatum
11308	(= USDA 59219) - xanthostephanum
11309	(= USDA 59595) - roxieanum var. cucullatum
11310	(= USDA 59220) - irroratum subsp. irroratum
11311	(= USDA 59221) - roxieanum
11312	(= USDA 59222) - roxieanum
11313	(= USDA 59223) - traillianum var. traillianum
11314	(= USDA 59224) - traillianum var. traillianum
11315	(= USDA 59225) - hippophaeoides var. occidentale
11316	(= USDA 59226) - molle subsp. molle
11317	(= USDA 59596) - leptothrium
11318	(= USDA 59597) - russatum
11319	(= USDA 59598) - polycladum
11321	(= USDA 59227) - wardii var. wardii
11322	(= USDA 59228) - cephalanthum subsp. cephalanthum
11323	(= USDA 59029) - phaeochrysum var. levistratum
11324	(= USDA 59206) - phaeochrysum var. phaeochrysum
11325	(= USDA 59229) - vernicosum
11326	(= USDA 59207) - vernicosum
11328	(= USDA 59599) - phaeochrysum var. levistratum
11329	(= USDA 59600) - vernicosum
11331	(= USDA 59601) - vernicosum
11333	(= USDA 59602) - phaeochrysum var. levistratum
11334	(= USDA 59603) - beesianum
11335	(= USDA 59230) - phaeochrysum var. agglutinatum
11336	(= USDA 59604) - aganniphum var. aganniphum
11337	(= USDA 59605) - beesianum
11338	(= USDA 59606) - phaeochrysum var. levistratum
11339	(= USDA 59607) - aganniphum var. aganniphum
11339a	(= USDA 59607a) - aganniphum var. aganniphum
11340	(= USDA 59608) - phaeochrysum var. agglutinatum
11341	(= USDA 59231) - phaeochrysum var. agglutinatum
11341a	(= USDA 59231a) - aganniphum
11342	(= USDA 59232) - phaeochrysum var. levistratum
11342a	(= USDA 59232a) - aganniphum
11343	(= USDA 59609) - phaeochrysum var. agglutinatum
11343a	(= USDA 59609a) - aganniphum
11344	(= USDA 59233) - phaeochrysum var. levistratum
11345	(= USDA 59610) - phaeochrysum var. agglutinatum
11346	(= USDA 59611) - anthosphaerum
11348	(= USDA 59234) - sinogrande
11349	(= USDA 59612) - beesianum
11351	(= USDA 59235) - fulvum subsp. fulvoides
11352	(= USDA 59613) - sp.
11354	(= USDA 59236) - anthosphaerum
11355	(= USDA 59237) - wardii var. wardii
11357	(= USDA 59614) - lukiangense
11358	(= USDA 59239) - anthosphaerum
11362	(= USDA 59240) - lepidotum
11363	(= USDA 59615) - hippophaeoides var. hippophaeoides
11364	(= USDA 59241) - hippophaeoides var. hippophaeoides
11365	(= USDA 59616) - hippophaeoides var. hippophaeoides
11366	(= USDA 59242) - anthosphaerum
11367	(= USDA 59617) - adenogynum
11368	(= USDA 59243) - cuneatum
11368a	(= USDA 59248a) - heliolepis
11371	(= USDA 59618) - traillianum var. traillianum
11372	(= USDA 59436) - traillianum var. traillianum
11373	(= USDA 59619) - traillianum var. traillianum
11376	(= USDA 59248) - anthosphaerum
11376a	(= USDA 59248a) - bureavii
11377	(= USDA 59249) - anthosphaerum

11377a (= USDA 59249a) - bureavii
11378 (= USDA 59250) - rex subsp.
       fictolacteum
11379 (= USDA 59754) - beesianum aff.
11380 (= USDA 59251) - irroratum
       subsp. irroratum
11381 (= USDA 59620) - irroratum
       subsp. irroratum
11382 (= USDA 59755) - bureavii
11383 (= USDA 59621) - beesianum aff.
11385 (= USDA 59756) - selense subsp.
       dasycladum
11386 (= USDA 59757) - uvariifolium
       var. uvariiflorum
11387 (= USDA 59758) - oreotrephes
11388 (= USDA 59759) - glischrum
       subsp. glischrum
11389 (= USDA 59622) - wardii subsp.
       wardii
11390 (= USDA 59252) - anthosphaerum
11391 (= USDA 59623) - uvariifolium
       var. uvariiflorum
11392 (= USDA 59253) - cuneatum
11393 (= USDA 59254) - cuneatum
11395 (= USDA 59255) - rex subsp.
       fictolacteum
11396 (= USDA 59256) - traillianum var.
       traillianum
11397 (= USDA 59624) - rex subsp.
       fictolacteum
11401 (= USDA 59257) - trichostomum
11403 (= USDA 59717) - racemosum
11404 (= USDA 59435) - decorum
11408 (= USDA 59625) - vernicosum
11415 (= USDA 59258) - racemosum
11418 (= USDA 59626) - pleistanthum
11419 (= USDA 59760) - oreotrephes ×
       zaleucum (hybrid)
11421 (= USDA 59761) - traillianum var.
       traillianum
11422 (= USDA 59713) - yunnanense
11424 (= USDA 59718) - racemosum
11429 (= USDA 59627) - oreotrephes
11430 (= USDA 59716) - lepidotum
11434 (= USDA 59259) - rupicola var.
       rupicola
11452 (= USDA 59628) - rex subsp.
       fictolacteum
11453 (= USDA 59629) - heliolepis var.
       brevistylum
11454 (= USDA 59630) - traillianum var.

traillianum
11455 (= USDA 59631) - cephalanthum
       subsp. cephalanthum
11459 (= USDA 59260) - traillianum var.
       traillianum
11460 (= USDA 59632) - traillianum var.
       traillianum
11461 (= USDA 59633) - traillianum var.
       traillianum
11463 (= USDA 59261) - beesianum
11465 (= USDA 59262) - telmateium
11468 (= USDA 59634) - primuliflorum
11469 (= USDA 59263) - impeditum
11470 (= USDA 59635) - traillianum var.
       traillianum
11471 (= USDA 59636) - adenogynum
11473 (= USDA 59637) - Subsect.
       Taliensia
11476 (= USDA 59638) - racemosum
11500 phaeochrysum var. levistratum
11501 beesianum
11502 praestans
11503 praestans
11504 uvariifolium var. uvariiflorum
11505 lukiangense
11506 saluenense subsp. saluenense
11507 selense subsp. selense
11567 wardii var. wardii
11597 chamaethomsonii var.
       chamaethomsonii
11634 praestans
11635 selense subsp. selense
11636 beesianum
11640 rex
11642 rex
11644 coriaceum
11702 phaeochrysum var.
       levistratum
11703 sp.
11704 heliolepis var. heliolepis
11706 leptothrium

NW GANSU, CHINA EXP. (1925-26)

13278 przewalskii
13279 anthopogonoides
13302 przewalskii
13303 thymifolium
13596 capitatum
13597 anthopogonoides

13598	thymifolium	18125	sp.
13599	rufum	18138	(= USDA 3791) - phaeochrysum var. levistratum
13600	capitatum		
13601	rufum	18139	(= USDA 3788) - vernicosum
13605	capitatum	18140	(= USDA 3738) - oreotrephes
13610	anthopogonoides	18141	(= USDA 3790) - phaeochrysum var. levistratum
13611	capitatum		
13612	przewalskii	18142	(= USDA 3749) - sikangense
13613	rufum	18143	(= USDA 3741) - sp.
13622	capitatum	18144	(= USDA 3757) - intricatum
13628	rufum	18149	(= USDA 3789) - beesianum
13629	przewalskii	18150	(= USDA 3758) - beesianum
13630	rufum	18152	(= USDA 3751) - aganniphum var aganniphum
13634	capitatum		
13635	capitatum	18153	(= USDA 3761) - balfourianum
13636	anthopogonoides	18155	(= USDA 3763) - roxieanum var. cucullatum
13640	rufum		
13643	rufum	18156	(= USDA 3760) - balfourianum
13645	rufum	18157	(= USDA 3792) - roxieanum var. cucullatum
13647	rufum		
13649	rufum	18158	(= USDA 3750) - balfourianum
13650	rufum	18159	(= USDA 3799) - phaeochrysum var. levistratum
13674	capitatum		
13675	rufum	18160	(= USDA 3752) - balfourianum
13676	przewalskii	18161	(= USDA 3764) - roxieanum
13677	przewalskii	18162	(= USDA 3794) - sphaeroblastum
13678	rufum	18163	(= USDA 3762) - sp.
13679	przewalskii	18164	(= USDA 3756) - balfourianum
13680	rufum	18168	(= USDA 3983) - phaeochrysum var. levistratum
13681	przewalskii		
13682	rufum	18169	(= USDA 3832) - sikangense
13683	rufum	18170	(= USDA 3831) - balfourianum
13684	rufum	18171	(= USDA 3990) - phaeochrysum var. levistratum
13685	przewalskii		
13686	przewalskii	18172	(= USDA 3842) - roxieanum var. cucullatum
13688	capitatum		
13691	rufum	18173	(= USDA 3845) - balfourianum
13692	rufum	18174	(= USDA 3834) - alutaceum var. cucullatum
13693	rufum		
13694	przewalskii	18175	(= USDA 3841) - balfourianum
13695	przewalskii	18176	(= USDA 3833) - roxieanum var. cucullatum
13696	rufum		
13697	rufum	18177	(= USDA 3746) - balfourianum
14928	rufum	18178	(= USDA 3985) - sphaeroblastum
15004	micranthum	18179	(= USDA 3830) - phaeochrysum var. levistratum
15014	rufum		
		18180	(= USDA 3991) - sphaeroblastum

NW YUNNAN, CHINA EXP. (1929)

18181	(= USDA 3936) - primuliflorum
18182	(= USDA 3835) - sphaeroblastum
18185	(= USDA 3988) - aff. mimetes var. simulans
18119	(= USDA 3745) - rubiginosum

18186 (= USDA 3828) - roxieanum var. cucullatum
18187 (= USDA 3829) - rupicola var. chryseum aff.
18189 (= USDA 3987) - rubiginosum
18222 (= USDA 3838) - intricatum
18223 (= USDA 3839) - impeditum
18224 (= USDA 3844) - Subsect. Lapponica
18226 (= USDA 3840) - sikangense
18227 (= USDA 3984) - wardii var. wardii
18228 (= USDA 3837) - adenosum
18234 (= USDA 3800) - rex subsp. rex
18275 (= USDA 3989) - racemosum
18277 (= USDA 3843) - sp.
18281 (= USDA 3986) - uvariifolium var. uvariiflorum
18331 (= USDA 3847) - sinogrande
18332 (= USDA 3848) - wardii var. wardii
18333 (= USDA 3849) - wardii var. wardii
18336 (= USDA 3852) - arizelum
18337 (= USDA 3853) - arizelum
18338 (= USDA 3854) - semnoides
18339 (= USDA 3855) - fulvum
18341 (= USDA 3857) - megeratum
18350 (= USDA 3850) - stewartianum
18351 (= USDA 3851) - oreotrephes
18352 (= USDA 3861) - aperantum
18353 (= USDA 3862) - campylocarpum
18354 (= USDA 3863) - aperantum
18355 (= USDA 3864) - haematodes subsp. chaetomallum aff.
18356 (= USDA 3865) - haematodes subsp. chaetomallum aff.
13357 (= USDA 3866) - haematodes subsp. chaetomallum aff.
18359 (= USDA 3868) - haematodes subsp. chaetomallum
18365 (= USDA 3784) - rupicola var. rupicola
18366 (= USDA 3875) - roxieanum var. cucullatum
18367 (= USDA 3976) - rupicola var. rupicola
18369 (= USDA 3878) - mekongense var. mekongense
18373 (= USDA 3881) - campylocarpum

subsp. caloxanthum
18375 (= USDA 3883) - stewartianum
18376 (= USDA 3884) - stewartianum
18377 (= USDA 3885) - stewartianum
18378 (= USDA 3886) - stewartianum
18379 (= USDA 3887) - aperantum aff.
18380 (= USDA 3888) - calostrotum subsp. riparioides
18381 (= USDA 3889) - calostrotum subsp. riparioides
18382 (= USDA 3890) - haematodes
18383 (= USDA 3891) - campylocarpum subsp. caloxanthum
18384 (= USDA 3892) - rubiginosum
18385 (= USDA 3893) - coriaceum
18386 (= USDA 3894) - glischrum subsp. glischrum
18387 (= USDA 3895) - glischrum subsp. glischrum
18388 (= USDA 3896) - mekonongense var. mekongense
18389 (= USDA 3897) - haematodes subsp. chaetomallum
18390 (= USDA 3898) - semnoides
18391 (= USDA 3899) - rothschildii aff.
18395 (= USDA 3902) - sulfureum
18396 (= USDA 3903) - semnoides
18397 (= USDA 3904) - semnoides
18399 (= USDA 3905) - nuttallii
18400 (= USDA 3906) - sp.
18402 (= USDA 3908) - crinigerum var. crinigerum
18403 (= USDA 3909) - sp.
18404 (= USDA 3910) - maddennii subsp. crassum
18405 (= USDA 3911) - campylocarpum subsp. caloxanthum
18406 (= USDA 3912) - haematodes subsp. chaetomallum
18407 (= USDA 3913) - coriaceum
18407a (= USDA 3913a) - lanigerum
18408 (= USDA 3914) - tephropeplum
18409 (= USDA 3915) - xanthospethanum
18410 (= USDA 3916) - zaleucum
18411 (= USDA 3917) - zaleucum
18412 (= USDA 3918) - tephropeplum
18413 (= USDA 3919) - tephropeplum
18415 (= USDA 3920) - eclecteum var. eclecteum
18416 (= USDA 3921) - eclecteum var.

eclecteum

18418	(= USDA 3923) - zaleucum
18420	(= USDA 3925) - glischrum subsp. glischrum
18421	(= USDA 3926) - martinianum
18424	(= USDA 3929) - sp.
18433	(= USDA 3935) - rothschildii
18434	(= USDA 3936) - maddenii subsp crassum
18435	(= USDA 3937) - roxieanum
18436	(= USDA 3938) - roxieanum var. roxieanum
18437	(= USDA 3939) - traillianum var. traillianum
18438	(= USDA 3940) - traillianum var. traillianum
18439	(= USDA 3941) - traillianum var. traillianum
18440	(= USDA 3942) - beesianum
18441	(= USDA 3943) - traillianum var. traillianum
18442	(= USDA 3944) - rupicola var. rupicola
18443	(= USDA 3945) - beesianum
18444	(= USDA 3946) - traillianum var. traillianum
18445	(= USDA 3993) - beesianum
18446	(= USDA 3947) - clementinae
18447	(= USDA 3948) - rex subsp. fictolacteum
18448	(= USDA 3939) - clementinae
18449	(= USDA 3950) - glischrum subsp. glischrum
18450	(= USDA 3951) - saluenense subsp. chameunum
18451	(= USDA 3952) - rex subsp. fictolacteum
18452	(= USDA 3953) - rex subsp. fictolacteum
18453	(= USDA 3954) - saluenense subsp. riparioides
18454	(= USDA 3955) - saluenense subsp. riparioides
18455	(= USDA 3956) - wardii var. wardii
18456	(= USDA 3957) - oreotrephes
18457	(= USDA 3958) - oreotrephes
18458	(= USDA 3959) - hippophaeoides var. occidentale
18459	(= USDA 3960) - rex subsp.

fictolacteum

18460	(= USDA 3961) - orthocladum var. longistylum
18462	(= USDA 3963) - russatum
18463	(= USDA 3964) - citriniflorum var. horaeum
18464	(= USDA 3965) - sanguineum var. didymoides
18465	(= USDA 3966) - floccigerum
18466	(= USDA 3967) - sperabile var. weihsiense
18467	(= USDA 3968) - sperabile var. weihsiense
18468	(= USDA 3969) - sperabile var. weihsiense
18469	(= USDA 3970) - floccigerum/sperabile
18471	(= USDA 3972) - leptothrium
18473	(= USDA 3974) - leptothrium
18474	(= USDA 3975) - sp.
18475	(= USDA 3976) - leptocarpum
18476	(= USDA 3977) - sp.
18477	(= USDA 3978) - crinigerum var. euadenium
USDA	4007 - sp.
USDA	4012 - sp.
USDA	4020 - sp.
USDA	4021 - sp.
USDA	4022 - sp.
USDA	4023 - sp.
USDA	4082 - sp.
USDA	4083 - sp.
USDA	4084 - sp.
USDA	4085 - sp.

NW YUNNAN, CHINA EXP. (1932)

21993	sanguineum var. haemaleum
21994	sperabiloides
21995	bainbridgeanum
21997	saluenense subsp. saluenense
21999	bainbridgeanum
22000	crinigerum var. crinigerum
22001	pocophorum var. pocophorum
22002	pocophorum var. pocophorum
22003	eclecteum var. eclecteum
22004	haematodes subsp. chaetomallum
22005	stewartianum
22006	genestierianum
22007	xanthostephanum

22013	genestierianum	22122	sperabiloides
22014	xanthostephanum	22123	martinianum
22019	edgeworthii	22126	floccigerum
22021	rex subsp. fictolacteum	22183	sanguineum subsp. didymum
22023	rex subsp. fictolacteum	22184	brachyanthum subsp.
22024	arizelum 'Rubicosum'		hypolepidotum
22025	rex subsp. fictolacteum	22187	haematodes subsp. chaetomallum
22028	selense subsp. selense	22188	haematodes subsp. chaetomallum
22029	selense subsp. selense	22189	citriniflorum var. horaeum
22030	selense subsp. selense	22191	citriniflorum var. citriniflorum
22031	bainbridgeanum	22192	citriniflorum var. horaeum
22032	selense subsp. selense	22193	citriniflorum var. horaeum
22033	selense subsp. selense	22194	citriniflorum var. horaeum
22034	sanguineum var. haemaleum	22196	citriniflorum var. horaeum
22037	rex subsp. fictolacteum	22197	haematodes subsp. chaetomallum
22038	rex subsp. fictolacteum	22198	sanguineum var. sanguineum
22039	rex subsp. fictolacteum	22199	haematodes subsp. chaetomallum
22040	beesianum	22201	sanguineum var. sanguineum
22041	beesianum	22202	sanguineum var. cloiophorum
22042	uvariifolium var. uvariiflorum	22203	sanguineum var. sanguineum
22045	virgatum subsp. oleifolium	22204	sanguineum var. sanguineum
22050	chamaethomsonii var.	22205	citriniflorum var. horaeum
	chaethomsonii	22206	citriniflorum var. horaeum
22056	monanthum	22207	citriniflorum var. horaeum
22058	haematodes subsp. chaetomallum	22208	citriniflorum var. horaeum
22059	haematodes subsp. chaetomallum	22210	citriniflorum
22063	rupicola var. rupicola	22211	haematodes subsp. chaetomallum
22064	sanguineum var. cloiophorum	22212	citriniflorum var. horaeum
22065	haematodes subsp. chaetomallum	22213	citriniflorum var. horaeum
22066	haematodes subsp. chaetomallum	22214	leptocarpum
22069	haematodes subsp. chaetomallum	22215	sanguineum var. himertum
22070	temenium var. dealbatum		× temenium (hybrid)
22090	mekongense var. mekongense	22216	nuttallii
22091	rex subsp. fictolacteum	22219	rex subsp. fictolacteum
22092	fulvum subsp. fulvoides	22220	rex subsp. fictolacteum
22094	arizelum	22221	beesianum
22095	anthosphaerum	22222	eclecteum
22096a	uvariifolium var. uvariiflorum	22223	beesianum
22096b	uvariifolium var. uvariiflorum	22224	eclecteum
22097	fulvum subsp. fulvoides	22225	selense subsp. selense
22100	eclecteum var. eclecteum	22226	× erythocalyx (hybrid)
22102	selense subsp. setiferum	22227	rex subsp. fictolacteum
22106	rex subsp. fictolacteum	22228	crinigerum var. crinigerum
22108	arizelum	22229	rex
22110	arizelum 'Rubicosum'	22230	eclecteum
22111	fulvum subsp. fulvoides	22231	rex subsp. fictolacteum
22112	crinigerum var. crinigerum	22232	arizelum
22117	rex subsp. fictolacteum	22233	rex subsp. fictolacteum
22119	martinianum	22234	beesianum
22120	megeratum	22235	temenium var. gilvum hybrid
22121	floccigerum	22236	sanguineum var. haemaleum

22237	selense var. selense		23338	aganniphum var. aganniphum
22238	sanguineum var. haemaleum		23348	sp.
22269	eclecteum var. eclecteum		23350	phaeochrysum var. levistratum
22271	temenium var. gilvum		23360	rupicola var. chryseum
22272	temenium var. gilvum		23369	phaeochrysum var. levistratum
22277	citriniflorum		23371	aganniphum var. aganniphum
22279	rex subsp. fictolacteum		23394	phaeochrysum var. levistratum
22288	tapetiforme		23398	rupicola var. chryseum
22289	campylogynum		23400	primuliflorum
22290	temenium var. gilvum		23401	aganniphum var. aganniphum
22291	selense subsp. selense		23405	aganniphum var. aganniphum
22292	temenium var. gilvum		23406	phaeochrysum var. levistratum
22293	sanguineum		23407	Subsect. Fortunea
22295	eudoxum var. eudoxum		23408	wardii var. wardii
22297	saluenense subsp. saluenense		23410	nivale subsp. boreale
22298	temenium var. gilvum		23414	wardii var. wardii
22301	floccigerum		23452	beesianum
22302	fletcherianum		23453	rex subsp. fictolacteum
22303	floccigerum		23467	rupicola var. rupicola
22304	haematodes subsp. chaetomallum		23477	augustinii subsp. chasmanthum
22305	haematodes subsp. chaetomallum		23480	crinigerum var. crinigerum
22306	haematodes subsp. chaetomallum		23481	eclecteum var. eclecteum
22307	rex subsp. fictolacteum		23482	martinianum
22345	heliolepis var. brevistylum		23483	megeratum
22440	megacalyx		23485	crinigerum var. crinigerum
22465	catacosmum		23487	fulvum subsp. fulvoides
22466	haematodes subsp. chaetomallum		23488	fulvum subsp. fulvoides
22634	virgatum subsp. oleifolium		23489	crinigerum var. crinigerum
22649	anthosphaerum		23490	crinigerum var. crinigerum
22657	habrotrichum aff.		23491	oreotrephes
22659	fletcherianum		23492	selense subsp. selense
23294	haematodes subsp. chaetomallum		23494	Subsect. Thomsonia
23301	heliolepis var. brevistylum		23495	floccigerum/sperabile
23302	heliolepis var. brevistylum		23496	praestans
23304	haematodes subsp. chaetomallum		23497	fulvum subsp. fulvoides
23305	haematodes subsp. chaetomallum		23498	chamaethomsonii var.
23306	haematodes subsp. chaetomallum			chamaethomsonii
23307	aganniphum var. aganniphum		23502	fulvum
23308	beesianum		23506	floccigerum/sperabile
23310	nivale subsp. boreale		23508	fulvum
23314	wardii var. wardii		23509	eclecteum var. eclecteum
23321	phaeochrysum var. agglutinatum		23510	eclecteum var. eclecteum
23322	primuliflorum		23511	eclecteum var. eclecteum
23324	phaeochrysum var. agglutinatum		23512	eclecteum var. eclecteum
23325	phaeochrysum var. agglutinatum		23513	mekongense var. mekongense
23326	oreodoxa var. fargesii		23514	rubiginosum
23328	aganniphum var. aganniphum		23515	sp.
23330	saluenense subsp. chameunum		23516	eclecteum var. eclecteum
23331	aganniphum var. aganniphum		23517	uvariifolium var. uvariiflorum
23332	pleistanthum		23518	beesianum
23333	aganniphum var. aganniphum		23520	praestans

23521	beesianum		23631	sanguineum
23524	sanguineum		23632	eclecteum var. eclecteum
23526	roxieanum var. roxieanum		23633	cephalanthum subsp.
23527	beesianum			cephalanthum
23528	beesianum		23634	saluenense subsp. saluenense
23529	sanguineum		23635	sanguineum var. himertum
23530	beesianum		23636	sanguineum var. didymoides
23540a	rupicola var. chryseum		23637	sanguineum var. haemaleum
23540b	proteoides		23638	citriniflorum var. citriniflorum
23545	saluenense subsp. saluenense		23639	sanguineum var. haemaleum
23546	saluenense subsp. chameunum		23640	temenium var. gilvum
23548	saluenense subsp. saluenense		23641	sanguineum var. sanguineum
23553	brachyanthum subsp.		23642	sanguineum var. haemaleum
	hypolepidotum		23643	sanguineum
23555	rex. subsp. fictolacteum		23645	sanguineum var. himertum
23556	saluenense subsp. saluenense		23646	eudoxum var. mesopolium
23559	cephalanthum subsp.		23647	citriniflorum var. citriniflorum
	cephalanthum		23648	campylogynum
23560	campylogynum		23649	citriniflorum var. horaeum
23561	roxieanum var. roxieanum		23650	sanguineum var. sanguineum
23562	alutaceum var. iodes		23651	aganniphum var. aganniphum
23563	sanguineum var. sanguineum		23652	aganniphum var. aganniphum
23564	citriniflorum var. citriniflorum		23653	aganniphum var. aganniphum
23569	heliolepis var. brevistylum		23660	alutaceum var. iodes
23575	alutaceum var. iodes		23661	adenogynum
23578	sanguineum var.		23662	adenogynum
23579	citriniflorum var. citriniflorum		23663	eudoxum var. mesopolium
23580	sanguineum		23664	sanguineum var. sanguineum
23581	citriniflorum var. citriniflorum		23666	heliolepis var. brevistylum
23586	rex subsp. fictolacteum		23669	citriniflorum
23587	praestans		24278	impeditum
23588	floccigerum		24280	sphaeroblastum
23589	coriaceum		24281	balfourianum
23590	rubiginosum		24282	rufescens
23591	lukiangense		24283	rubiginosum
23592	edgeworthii		24284	phaeochrysum var. agglutinatum
23593	temenium var. temenium		24285	primuliflorum
23615	mekongense var. mekongense		24295	phaeochrysum var. agglutinatum
23616	nivale subsp. boreale		24296	proteoides
23617	temenium var. temenium		24299	roxieanum var. cucullatum
23618	phaeochrysum var. agglutinatum		24302	phaeochrysum var. agglutinatum
23619	beesianum		24304	primuliflorum
23620	saluenense subsp. saluenense		24306	phaeochrysum var. agglutinatum
23621	eclecteum var. eclecteum		24307	beesianum
23622	sanguineum		24309	yunnanense
23625	beesianum		24310	sphaeroblastum
23626	Subsect. Selensia		24311	sphaeroblastum
23627	saluenense subsp. saluenense		24314	phaeochrysum var. levistratum
23628	sanguineum		24317	phaeochrysum var.
23629	temenium var. temenium			phaeochrysum
23630	eclecteum var. eclecteum		24319	telmateium

24320	thymifolium	24524	phaeochrysum var. agglutinatum
24321	trichostomum	24531	hemitrichotum
24322	sikangense	24540	primuliflorum
24325	sphaeroblastum	24541	hemitrichotum
24336	telmateium	24544	trichostomum
24339	wardii var. wardii (in cult.)	24569	impeditum & rex subsp. rex
24343	sphaeroblastum	24573	rex subsp. rex
24350	sphaeroblastum	24582	beesianum
24359	phaeochrysum var. agglutinatum	24583	beesianum
24360	wardii var. wardii	24591	yunnanense
24361	telmateium	24592	yunnanense
24363	phaeochrysum var. agglutinatum	24599	rubiginosum
24365	phaeochrysum var. agglutinatum	24602	yunnanense
24366	phaeochrysum var. agglutinatum	24604	uvariifolium var. uvariiflorum
24368	wardii var. wardii	25233	Sect. Tsutsusi
24369	impeditum	25234	scabrifolium var. scabrifolium
24381	balfourianum	25235	sp.
24382	balfourianum	25236	sp.
24383	balfourianum	25237	spinuliferum
24384	impeditum aff.	25238	sp.
24385	nivale subsp. boreale	25239	microphyton
24395	phaeochrysum var. agglutinatum	25240	sp.
24403	phaeochrysum var. levistratum	25246	adenogynum
24404	oreotrephes	25247	rubiginosum
24406	balfourianum	25251	uvariifolium var. uvariiflorum
24410	phaeochrysum var. agglutinatum	25252	traillianum var. traillianum
24413	sphaeroblastum	25258	rupicola var. rupicola
24414	phaeochrysum var. agglutinatum	25259	traillianum var. traillianum
24418	phaeochrysum var. levistratum	25260	selense subsp. dasycladum
24421	pleistanthum	25272	preptum aff.
24432	yunnanense	25277	rupicola var. rupicola
24433	decorum subsp. decorum	25278	lepidotum
24434	vernicosum	25301	traillianum var. traillianum
24439	trichostomum	25302	rupicola var. rupicola
24440	sikangense	25303	saluenense subsp. chameunum
24445	phaeochrysum var. levistratum	25305	adenogynum
24446	intricatum	25306	rex. subsp. fictolacteum
24457	phaeochrysum var. levistratum	25308	adenogynum
24458	Subsect. Fortunea	25313	sphaeroblastum
24459	phaeochrysum var. levistratum	25314	phaeochrysum var. phaeochrysum
24460	impeditum		
24461	phaeochrysum var. levistratum	25326	rubiginosum
24464	impeditum	25327	yunnanense
24471	sikangense	25328	traillianum var. traillianum
24481	sphaeroblastum	25329	rubiginosum
24487	wardii var. wardii	25331	vernicosum
24489	primuliflorum	25334	lepidotum
24495	wardii var. wardii	25340	anthosphaerum
24501	proteoides	25345	beesianum
24503	roxieanum	25349	adenogynum
24512	phaeochrysum var. agglutinatum	25350	primuliflorum

25352	uvariifolium var. uvariiflorum	25442	bureavii
25368	traillianum var. traillianum	25443	scabrifolium var. scabrifolium
25370	yungningense	25444	rex subsp. fictolacteum
25372	rubiginosum	25445	bureavii
25373	vernicosum	25446	scabrifolium var. scabrifolium
25375	adenogynum	25447	rex subsp. fictolacteum
25376	primuliflorum	25448	rex subsp. fictolacteum
25377	nivale subsp. australe	25451	irroratum subsp. irroratum
25381	yunnanense	25452	roxieanum var. roxieanum
25384	traillianum var. traillianum	25453	edgeworthii
25386	irroratum subsp. irroratum	25454	edgeworthii
25387	adenogynum	25455	roxieanum var. cucullatum
25388	semnoides aff.	25458	pronum
25389	semnoides	25459	campylogynum
25390	alutaceum var. alutaceum	25462	roxieanum var. cucullatum
25391	wardii var. wardii	25463	roxieanum var. cucullatum
25393	semnoides	25464	roxieanum
25394	semnoides	25465	xanthostephanum
25395	irroratum subsp. irroratum	25466	rex subsp. fictolacteum
25396	rex subsp. fictolacteum	25467	wardii var. wardii
25398	selense subsp. dasycladum	25468	fulvum subsp. fulvoides
25400	irroratum subsp. irroratum	25470	phaeochrysum var. agglutinatum
25401	clementinae	25472	sphaeroblastum
25402	hippophaeoides var. hippophaeoides	25474	phaeochrysum var. levistratum
25405	roxieanum var. cucullatum	25476	sikangense
25406	roxieanum var. cucullatum	25478	sphaeroblastum
25407	roxieanum var. cucullatum	25480	sphaeroblastum
25414	rex subsp. fictolacteum	25482	phaeochrysum var. phaeochrysum
25417	fastigiatum		
25418	rex subsp. fictolacteum		
25419	uvariflorium		

TIBET & YUNNAN, CHINA EXP. (1948-49)

25421	uvariflorium		
25422	roxieanum	1	campylocarpum subsp. caloxanthum
25423	roxieanum	2	crinigerum var. crinigerum
25424	rex subsp. fictolacteum	3	crinigerum var. crinigerum
25425	fulvum subsp. fulvoides	4	Subsect. Irrorata
25426	fulvum subsp. fulvoides	5	saluenense subsp. chameunum
25428	selense subsp. dasycladum	6	temenium var. dealbatum aff.
25429	oreotrephes	6a	sanguineum aff.
25430	clementinae	6b	eudoxum var. eudoxum
25431	fulvum subsp. fulvoides	7	Subsect. Lapponica
25432	clementinae	8	beesianum
25435	bureavii	9	fulvum subsp. fulvoides
25436	bureavii	10	floccigerum
25437	balfourianum	11	sanguineum
25438	rubiginosum	12	brachyanthum var. hypolepidotum
25439	bureavii	13	haematodes subsp. chaetomallum
25440	cephalanthum subsp. cephalanthum	14	arizelum
25441	rex subsp. fictolacteum		

15	xanthostephanum	70	genestierianum
16	arizelum	71	rubiginosum
17	virgatum subsp. oleifolium	72	lukiangense
18	sanguineum	73	uvariifolium var. uvariiflorum
19	alutaceum var. iodes	92	forrestii subsp. forrestii
20	crinigerum var. crinigerum	93	brachyanthum subsp.
21	mekongense		hypolepidotum
22	haematodes subsp. chaetomallum	94	proteoides
23	sanguineum	95	megeratum
24	sanguineum	96	oreotrephes
25	arizelum	97	arizelum
26	fulvum subsp. fulvoides	98	crinigerum var. crinigerum
27	sanguineum	100	crinigerum var. crinigerum
28	rubiginosum	101	temenium var. gilvum aff.
29	eclecteum var. eclecteum	101a	sanguineum var. haemaleum aff.
31	sanguineum var. haemaleum	102	arizelum aff.
32	floccigerum	103	praestans
33	eclecteum var. eclecteum	104	martinianum
34	sp.	105	campylogynum
36	beesianum	106	sanguineum var. sanguineum
37	eclecteum var. eclecteum	107	aganniphum var. aganniphum
38	crinigerum var. crinigerum	108	citriniflorum
39	haematodes subsp. chaetomallum	109	beesianum
40	haematodes subsp. chaetomallum	110	saluenense subsp. saluenense
41	haematodes subsp. chaetomallum	111	sanguineum aff.
42	beesianum	112	sanguineum
42a	Subsect. Neriiflora	113	temenium
43	Subsect. Lapponica	114	temenium
44	sanguineum subsp. didymum	115	Subsect. Neriiflora
45	sanguineum subsp. didymum	116	Subsect. Neriiflora
46	sanguineum	117	beesianum
47	martinianum	118	praestans
48	bainbridgeanum	119	citriniflorum aff.
49	floccigerum	120	coriaceum
50	fulvum subsp. fulvoides	121	anthosphaerum
51	Subsect. Falconera	122	mekongense var. mekongense
51a	arizelum	123	eclecteum var. eclecteum
52	haematodes subsp. chaetomallum	124	citriniflorum var. citriniflorum
53	sanguineum subsp. didymum		aff.
54	sanguineum subsp. didymum	125	sperabiloides
56	saluenense subsp. chameunum	125a	temenium
57	martinianum	125b	sanguineum var. sanguineum
58	calostrotum subsp. keleticum	126	sanguineum var. sanguineum
59	sanguineum	128	sanguineum subsp. didymum
60	temenium var. dealbatum	129	heliolepis var. heliolepis
61	sanguineum subsp. didymum	131	eclecteum var. eclecteum
62	sanguineum subsp. didymum	132	campylogynum
63	alutaceum var. iodes	133	maddenii subsp. crassum
64	alutaceum var. iodes	134	fulvum subsp. fulvoides
65	sanguineum subsp. didymum	135	edgeworthii
69	Subsect. Neriiflora	136	sanguineum var. sanguineum

137	rubiginosum	199	augustinii subsp. hardyi
138	roxieanum var. roxieanum		
139	alutaceum var. iodes		
140	coriaceum		**Russell, J.**
141	alutaceum var. iodes		JAPAN EXP. (1987)
142	roxieanum var. roxieanum		
143	fulvum subsp. fulvoides	871	molle subsp. japonicum
144	floccigerum	893	makinoi
145	heliolepis var. brevistylum	941	kaempferi
146	mekongense var. mekongense	943	quinquefolium
147	proteoides	949	sanctum
148	eclecteum var. eclecteum	965	sanctum
149	sanguineum		
150	sanguineum var. sanguineum		
151	proteoides		**Rushforth, K.**
152	saluenense subsp. saluenense		SICHUAN, CHINA EXP. (1980)
153	praestans		
154	selense subsp. selense	139	ambiguum
155	beesianum	141	calophytum var. calophytum
158	uvariifolium var. uvariiflorum	142	calophytum var. calophytum
159	leptothrium	143b	ambiguum
161	fulvum	143c	wiltonii
162	glischrum subsp. glischrum	143d	calophytum
163	anthosphaerum	150	pingianum
164	beesianum	172	oreodoxa × pachytrichum
165	oreotrephes		(hybrid)
166	haematodes subsp. chaetomallum	172a	davidii?
167	rothschildii aff.	173	sp.
169	stewartianum	176	pachytrichum
170	rothschildii aff.	177	faberi
171	temenium	178a	faberi
172	annae	178c	faberi
173	uvariifolium var. uvariiflorum	184	pingianum
174	Subsect. Irrorata	185	nitidulum var. omeiense
175	saluenense subsp. chameunum	187	ambiguum
176	beesianum	195	ambiguum
177	sperabile var. weihsiense	198	pachytrichum × stigillosum
178	calostrotum subsp. riparioides		(hybrid)
179	rigidum	214	pachytrichum
180	fulvum subsp. fulvoides	336	decorum subsp. decorum
182	sinogrande	337	siderophyllum
184	rubiginosum		
185	irroratum subsp. irroratum		BHUTAN EXP. (1985)
186	rubiginosum		
187	rubiginosum	755	arboreum subsp. arboreum
188	fastigiatum	813	succothii
189	rubiginosum	818	lepidotum
190	rubiginosum	839	lepidotum
191	Subsect. Irrorata	850	wallichii
192	irroratum subsp. irroratum	862	campanulatum subsp.
193	rex subsp. fictolacteum		aeruginosum

870	campanulatum subsp. aeruginosum
873	lanatum
882	wallichii
884	cinnabarinum subsp. xanthocodon
885	lanatum
886	wightii
890	baileyi
901	baileyi
903a	lepidotum
904	lepidotum
905	lepidotum
909	lepidotum
911	baileyi
931	barbatum
938	arboreum subsp. arboreum
954	keysii
958	kesangiae var. kesangiae
966	arboreum subsp. arboreum
974	keysii
1014	edgeworthii
1017	dalhousiae var. dalhousiae

BHUTAN EXP. (1987)

1023	arboreum subsp. arboreum
1047	cinnabarinum subsp. cinnabarinum
1050	arboreum var. roseum
1051	wallichii
1053	campylocarpum subsp. campylocarpum
1059	edgeworthii
1078	camelliiflorum
1084	kesangiae var. kesangiae
1087	barbatum
1091	kesangiae var. kesangiae
1091a	falconeri subsp. falconeri
1093	lindleyi
1100	kesangiae var. kesangiae
1121	falconeri subsp. falconeri
1128	falconeri subsp. falconeri
1130	kesangiae var. kesangiae
1131	arboreum var. delavayi
1135	argipeplum
1136	kesangiae var. kesangiae
1175	kesangiae var. kesangiae
1176	argipeplum
1181	hodgsonii
1181a	sp.

1194	thomsonii subsp. thomsonii
1226	kesangiae var. kesangiae
1231	argipeplum
1232	pendulum
1233	camelliiflorum
1234	flinckii
1235	campylocarpum subsp. campylocarpum
1237	campylocarpum subsp. campylocarpum
1242	kesangiae var. kesangiae
1243	argipeplum
1245	campylocarpum subsp. campylocarpum
1253	camelliiflorum
1257	kesangiae aff.
1270	dalhousiae var. rhabdotum
1277	camelliiflorum
1286	dalhousiae var. rhabdotum
1291	camelliiflorum
1292	edgeworthii
1296	camelliiflorum
1298	camelliiflorum
1304	maddenii
1308	kesangiae
1309	cinnabarinum subsp. cinnabarinum
1310	argipeplum
1312a	glaucophyllum var. glaucophyllum
1333	maddenii
1340	grande
1349	succothii
1371	hodgsonii
1401	falconeri subsp. falconeri
1424	succothii
1432	hodgsonii
1442	flinckii
1453	hodgsonii aff.
1455	cinnabarinum subsp. xanthocodon
1459	glaucophyllum var. tubiforme
1465	flinckii
1472a	kendrickii
1481	kesangiae aff.
1483	hodgsonii
1488	kesangiae aff.
1496	flinckii

E BHUTAN EXP. (1990)

1562	arboreum var. delavayi
1583	virgatum subsp. virgatum
1626	arboreum
1629	kesangiae
1640	kesangiae aff.
1655	thomsonii subsp. thomsonii
1666	wightii
1682	kesangiae × falconeri (hybrid)
1685	kesangiae × falconeri (hybrid)
1695	maddenii subsp. maddenii
1710	grande aff.
1712	kendrickii
1720	grande aff.
1726	argipeplum
1727	kesangiae
1737	kesangiae
1738	thomsonii subsp. thomsonii
1739	arboreum
1743	wightii
1745	nivale subsp. nivale
1750	bhutanense
1751	bhutanense
1752	sp.
1753	bhutanense
1754	sp.
1755	flinckii aff.
1756	bhutanense
1763	thomsonii subsp. thomsonii
1767	kesangiae
1768	campylocarpum subsp. campylocarpum
1771	keysii
1778	neriiflorum subsp. phaedropum
1800	falconeri subsp. falconeri
1811	hodgsonii
1814	argipeplum
1820	lindleyi
1821	griffithianum

VIETNAM EXP. (1991)

1876	poilanei (Sect. Vireya)
1877	Subsect. Maddenia
1880	nuttallii
1881	sp.
1885	sp.
1886	poilanei (Sect. Vireya)
1894	maddenii subsp. crassum
1922	lyi
1922a	Subsect. Maddenia
1924	poilanei (Sect. Vireya)
1925	sp.
1929	lyi
1955	Subsect. Maddenia
1981	Subsect. Irrorata
1986	protistum var. giganteum
1990	arboreum aff.
1992	protistum var. giganteum
1995	excellens aff.
1998	protistum var. giganteum
2002	protistum var. giganteum
2005	Subsect. Maddenia

VIETNAM EXP. (1992)

2108	nuttallii
2116	lyi aff.
2165	maddenii subsp. crassum
2178	protistum var. giganteum
2180	lyi aff.
2184a	sp.
2189	sp.
2199	protistum var. giganteum
2202	sp.
2203	maddenii subsp. crassum
2203a	excellens aff.
2204	Subsect. Parishia
2204a	excellens aff.
2205	protistum var. giganteum
2205a	maddenii subsp. crassum
2214	excellens aff.
2215	lyi
2225	lyi
2229	maddenii subsp. crassum
2231	poilanei (Sect. Vireya)
2246	maddenii subsp. crassum
2247	veitchianum aff.
2247a	veitchianum aff.
2248	ovatum
2251	sp.
2260	veitchianum aff.
2261	nutallii
2270	excellens aff.
2279	sulfureum
2279a	excellens aff.
2279b	sp.
2314	sp.
2319	sulfureum
2321	sp.
2330	edgeworthii

2334	lyi
2356	sororium (Sect. Vireya)
2357	rushforthii (Sect. Vireya)
2359	lyi
2385	excellens aff.

YUNNAN EXP. (1993)

2494	dendricola
2499	decorum subsp. decorum
2553	arboreum var. peramoenum
2559	Sect. Choniastrum
2570	arboreum var. delavayi
2571	decorum subsp. diaprepes
2572	sinogrande
2584	neriiflorum aff.
2586	leptothrium
2610	leptothrium
2628	facetum
2637	sp.
2639	Subsect. Boothia
2651	sinogrande
2657	basilicum
2681	sidereum
2682	neriiflorum
2687	zaleucum
2701	edgeworthii
2710	coriaceum
2711	edgeworthii
2719	Subsect. Maddenia
2720	calostrotum aff.
2725	racemosum
2726	decorum subsp. decorum
2731	neriiflorum
2734	rubiginosum var. rubiginosum
2736	trichocladum
2740	stewartianum
2745	rubiginosum var. rubiginosum
2748	cyanocarpum
2750	rex subsp. fictolacteum
2758	virgatum subsp. oleifolium
2760	lacteum
2761	selense subsp. jucundum
2763	rex subsp. fictolacteum
2764	taliense
2765	balfourianum
2780	racemosum
2793	decorum subsp. decorum
2801	rubiginosum subsp. rubiginosum
2805	yunnanense
2833	vernicosum

VIETNAM EXP. (1994)

2919	sp.
2929	sororium (Sect. Vireya)
2932	sp.
2935	moulmainense
2939	sp.
2941	Subsect. Irrorata
2960	saxicolum
2961	lyi
2976	poilanei (Sect. Vireya)
2978	maddenii subsp.crassum
2983a	sororium (Sect. Vireya)
2987	lyi
2989	Subsect. Irrorata
2992	veitchianum aff.
2998	excellens aff.
3002a	Subsect. Maddenia
3011	chunii aff.
3021	tanastylum
3023	huidongense aff.
3025	sulfureum
3026	maddenii subsp. crassum
3028	sp.
3045	chunii aff.
3057	maddenii subsp. crassum
3080	sororium (Sect. Vireya)
3093	nuttallii
3095	xanthostephanum
3096a	facetum aff.
3097	rushforthii
3097a	Sect. Vireya
3099	excellens aff.
3111	tephropeplum
3112	protistum var. giganteum
3114	protistum var. giganteum
3116	maddenii subsp. crassum
3121	irroratum subsp. pogonstylum
3145	sp.
3148	poilanei (Sect. Vireya)
3212	triumphans
3284	irroratum 'Langbianense'
3285	fleuryi
3295	irroratum 'Langbianense'
3297	triumphans (Sect. Vireya)

XIZANG (TIBET)EXP. (1995)

3325	sp.
3336	principis
3388	triflorum

3423	uvariifolium var. griseum
3440	cerasinum
3446	principis
3448	nivale
3453	lepidotum
3458	uvariifolium var. griseum
3460	cerasinum
3465	faucium
3489	Subsect. Fulgensia
3490	hirtipes
3492	sp.
3501	forrestii
3503	mekongense
3506	chamaethomsonii var. chamaethauma
3516	campylocarpum subsp. caloxanthum
3519	forrestii
3520	sp.
3521	charitopes subsp. tsangpoense
3522	chamaethomsonii var. chamaethauma
3523	charitopes subsp. tsangpoense
3528	aganniphum
3532	wardii
3582	virgatum
3604	triflorum
3628	faucium
3654	principis
3684	wardii
3688	dignabile or pomense aff.
3689	phaeochrysum var. agglutinatum
3720	fragariiflorum
3721	Subsect. Lapponica
3722	kongboense aff.
3723	sp.
3724	sp.
3725	kongboense aff.
3726	principis
3732	wardii
3749	campylogynum
3771	faucium aff.
3774	uvariifolium var. griseum
3783	uvariifolium var. griseum
3784	faucium aff.
3804	principis
3844	principis
3845	anthopogon

YUNNAN EXP.(1996)

3902	spinuliferum
3908	microphyton
3909	arboreum subsp. delavayi
3910	arboreum subsp. delavayi
3939	microphyton
3946	decorum subsp. decorum
3969	fulvum subsp. fulvoides
3979	zaleucum
3980	sidereum
3986	facetum
3997	neriiflorum aff.
4006	valentinianum aff.
4013	Subsect. Parishia
4027	sinogrande
4028	leptothrium
4029	araiophyllum
4049	rubiginosum
4049a	trichostomum
4051	selense subsp. jucundum
4051a	cyanocarpum
4051b	selense subsp. jucundum
4054	rex subsp. fictolacteum
4055	lacteum
4056	taliense aff.
4056a	taliense
4057	lacteum
4084	racemosum
4085	cuneatum or hippophaeoides
4086	vernicosum
4089	Subsect. Lapponica
4099	vernicosum
4103	vernicosum
4104	racemosum
4112	wardii
4113	oreotrephes
4114	beesianum
4131	wardii
4150	beesianum
4154	heliolepis aff.
4158	uvariifolium var. uvariiflorum
4164	yunnanense
4208	vernicosum
4217	yunnanense
4229	arboreum subsp. delavayi
4255	nuttallii or excellens
4256	Subsect. Parishia
4270	rufosquamosum aff.
4278	sororium aff. (Sect. Vireya)
4303	rufosquamosum aff.

Sakhalin-Ussuri Exp. (1994)

135   schlippenbachii

Schilling, A.
NEPAL 1966 EXP.

1111   arboreum subsp. arboreum

NEPAL 1975 EXP.

2047   triflorum var. triflorum
2048   setosum
2049   arboreum var. cinnamomeum

NEPAL 1976 EXP.

2169   campylocarpum subsp.
            campylocarpum
2170   setosum
2171   anthopogon subsp. anthopogon
2172   wallichii
2187   arboreum var. cinnamomeum
2188   campylocarpum subsp.
            campylocarpum
2193   sp.

NEPAL 1977 EXP.

2252   campylocarpum subsp.
            campylocarpum
2259   anthopogon subsp.
            anthopogon
2260   setosum
2264   lepidotum
2269   nivale subsp. nivale
2281   lepidotum
2295   triflorum
2299   barbatum

NEPAL 1978 EXP.

2328   barbatum
2330   triflorum var triflorum
2343   hodgsonii

NEPAL 1983 EXP.

2649   arboreum var. roseum

BHUTAN EXP. (1988)

2963   lowndesii
2980   dalhousiae var. dalhousiae

Simmons, Erskine, Howick & McNamara (SICH)
SICHUAN, CHINA EXP. (1988)

40   polylepis
141   przewalskii
142   nivale subsp.boreale
143   primuliflorum
153   sp.
155   rufum
163   sp.
239   lutescens
240   decorum subsp. decorum
244   sp.
246   polylepis
265   lutescens
284   floribundum
300   polylepis
310   floribundum
316   argyrophyllum subsp.
            argyrophyllum
320   argyrophyllum subsp.
            argyrophyllum
342   nivale subsp. boreale
343   decorum subsp. decorum
349   intricatum
357   przewalskii
377   souliei
378   sp.
380   decorum subsp. decorum
385   sp.
390   sp.
401   pachytrichum var. pachytrichum

SICHUAN, CHINA EXP. (1991)

531   davidsonianum
533   sp.
542   sp.
550   sp.
552   thymifolium
584   souliei
585   sp.
586   sp.

587	sp.
588	bureavii aff.
595	bureavii
611	sp.
622	davidsonianum
650	sp.
676	sp.
685	sp.
698	sp.
702	thymifolium?
712	sp.
713	sp.
756	sp.
785	sp.
786	sp.
818	sp.
819	sp.
820	sp.
821	sp.
823	sp.
832	sp.
846	sp.

SICHUAN EXP., CHINA (1992)

921	decorum subsp. decorum
922	yunnanense
928	lutescens
929	floribundum
930	sp.
943	irroratum
944	decorum subsp. decorum
947	yunnanense
949	racemosum
960	rubiginosum
981	decorum subsp. decorum
990	sikangense var. sikangense
1010	phaeochrysum var. agglutinatum
1014	rubiginosum
1026	davidsonianum
1037	rex subsp. rex
1041	racemosum
1045	davidsonianum
1054	pachytrichum var. monosematum
1065	davidsonianum
1070	intricatum
1071	rupicola var. muliense
1074	beesianum
1075	phaeochrysum var. agglutinatum
1085	wardii
1095	sp.

1124	yunnanense
1134	rex subsp. rex
1151	sp.
1153	rex subsp. rex
1171	ambiguum
1177	spinuliferum
1187	racemosum
1188	racemosum
1198	coeloneuron
1207	yunnanense
1230	polylepis
1236	rex

SICHUAN EXP. (1994)

1317	sp.
1318	sp.
1322	sp.
1352	sp.
1409	sp.
1412	sp.
1428	sp.
1436	sp.
1437	sp.
1445	sp.
1473	rex subsp. fictolaceum
1480	sp.

Simmons, J. & Elsley, J.
E USA EXP. (1981)

18	catawbiense
62	calendulaceum

Simmons, Fleigner & Russell (GUIZ)
GUIZHOU, CHINA EXP. (1985)

74	sp.
75	haofui
120	moupinense aff.
121	maculiferum
125	sp. Subsect. Argyrophylla
148	maculiferum
163	liliiflorum
233	simsii var. simsii

Sinclair, I.
BHUTAN EXP. (1993)

1720	virgatum subsp. virgatum
1721	ciliatum
1722	thomsonii subsp. thomsonii
1724	thomsonii subsp. thomsonii
1725	barbatum
1726	maddenii subsp. maddenii
1727	lindleyi
1728	griffithianum
1730	argipeplum
1731	hodgsonii aff.
1732	hodgsonii
1734	cinnabarinum subsp. xanthocodon
1735	flinckii
1736	wightii
1737	succothii
1738	argipeplum
1739	camelliiflorum
1740	pendulum
1741	falconeri subsp. falconeri
1742	kendrickii
1743	keysii
1744	dalhousiae var. dalhousiae
1748	griffithianum

E USA EXP. (1994)

1753	viscosum

Sinclair, I. & Long, D.G.
BHUTAN EXP. (1984)

5220	campanulatum subsp. aeruginosum
5348	setosum
5671	kesangiae var. kesangiae
5695	falconeri subsp. falconeri
5696	camelliiflorum

Sino-American Exp. (SABE)
SICHUAN & W HUBEI ,CHINA (1981)

863	maculiferum
942	oreodoxa var. fargesii
943	maculiferum

1322	argyrophyllum subsp. hypoglaucum

Sino-British Exp. to Cangshan (SBEC)
YUNNAN, CHINA (1981)

K058	spinuliferum
K059	× duclouxii (hybrid)
K063	decorum subsp. decorum
K064	siderophyllum
K068	spinuliferum
K108	decorum subsp. decorum
K112	decorum subsp. decorum
K113	microphyton
K141	pachypodium
K143a	microphyton
K160	scabrifolium var. spiciferum
K161	siderophyllum
15	pachypodum
42	decorum subsp. decorum
47	arboreum var. delavayi
60	yunnanense
64	irroratum
100	irroratum subsp. irroratum
103	sulfureum
104	sinogrande
115	pachypodum
116	decorum subsp. decorum
119	× agastum (hybrid)
120	arboreum var. delavayi
121	rubiginosum
130	rubiginosum
160	rex subsp. fictolacteum
162	cyanocarpum
163	anthosphaerum
172	neriiflorum subsp. neriiflorum
181	decorum subsp. decorum
182	sinogrande
183	facetum
184	neriiflorum subsp. neriiflorum
194	yunnanense
207	edgeworthii
210	sulfureum
218	yunnanense
228	decorum subsp. decorum
235	lacteum
239	irroratum subsp. irroratum
240	heliolepis var. brevistylum

244	cyanocarpum
249	sulfureum
257	facetum
258	heliolepis
260	cyanocarpum
265	virgatum subsp. oleifolium
295	maddenii subsp. crassum
323	× agastum (hybrid)
331	yunnanense
334	sinogrande
343	haematodes subsp. haematodes
345	lacteum
349	cyanocarpum
350	roxieanum var. cucullatum aff.
351	trichocladum var. trichocladum
361	cyanocarpum
363	heliolepis
364	haematodes subsp. haematodes
365	selense subsp. jucundum
439	decorum subsp. decorum
471	trichocladum var. trichocladum
473	neriiflorum subsp. neriiflorum
474	racemosum
504	trichocladum var. trichocladum
507	neriiflorum subsp. neriiflorum
519	campylogynum
532	sulfureum
533	fastigiatum
534	rex subsp. fictolacteum
535	cyanocarpum
543	selense subsp. jucundum
544	selense subsp. jucundum
545	dichroanthum subsp. dichroanthum
546	taliense
554	balfourianum
555	taliense
557	fastigiatum
561	haematodes subsp. haematodes
565	yunnanense
581	taliense
582	lacteum
583	balfourianum
584	balfourianum × taliense ? (hybrid)
585	haematodes subsp. haematodes
586	haematodes subsp. haematodes
587	campylogynum
601	dichroanthum subsp. dichroanthum
607	edgeworthii
621	virgatum subsp. oleifolium

640	maddenii subsp. crassum
641	brachyanthum var. brachyanthum
664	yunnanense
694	maddenii subsp. crassum
720	arboreum var. delavayi
721	irroratum subsp. irroratum
734	decorum subsp. decorum
749	fastigiatum
750	trichocladum var. trichocladum
751	cephalanthum subsp. cephalanthum
753	fastigiatum pink
804	fastigiatum
805	trichocladum var. trichocladum
806	racemosum
840	anthosphaerum
883	irroratum × facetum (hybrid)
890	facetum
897	rex subsp. fictolacteum
898	irroratum subsp. irroratum
949	facetum ?
957	rex subsp. fictolacteum
969	sp.
971	cyanocarpum
1014	facetum
1058	yunnanense
1059	decorum subsp. decorum
1060	decorum subsp. decorum
1072	maddenii subsp. crassum
1225	decorum subsp. decorum
1227	virgatum subsp. oleifolium

Sino-British Lijiang Exp.(SBLE)

YUNNAN, CHINA (1987)

24	telmateium
25	cuneatum
61	primuliflorum
71	racemosum
81	vernicosum
83	rubiginosum
103	uvariifolium var. uvariiflorum
104	cuneatum
111	orthocladum?
141	fastigiatum
142	decorum subsp. decorum

144	vernicosum
199	cuneatum
200	rubiginosum
201	oreotrephes
202	beesianum
203	adenogynum
204	traillianum var. traillianum
205	Subsect. Lapponica
206	primuliflorum
219	heliolepis
235	adenogynum
236	telmateium
237	traillianum var. traillianum
245	primuliflorum aff.
247	cuneatum
299	trichostomum
305	sp.
306	oreotrephes
316	hippophaeoides var. hippophaeoides
317	rubiginosum
333	telmateium
357	vernicosum
364	fastigiatum
403	mekongense
406	selense subsp. dasycladum
423	lukiangense
424	leptothrium
433	racemosum
435	edgeworthii
437	rex subsp. fictolacteum
438	anthosphaerum
449	fulvum subsp. fulvoides
453	saluenense subsp. chameunum
454	phaeochrysum
457	Subsect.Lapponica
458	russatum
459	wardii var. wardii (litiense)
481	polycladum
489	mekongense var. mekongense
494	polycladum
557	rupicola var. rupicola
560	balfourianum
565	traillianum var. traillianum
568	cuneatum

Sino-Scottish Exp. to NW Yunnan, China (SSNY) (1992)

2a	vernicosum
10	racemosum
14	hippophaeoides var. hippophaeoides
24	oreotrephes
35	vernicosum
46	hippophaeoides var. hippophaeoides
47	racemosum
55	selense subsp. selense
56	wardii var. wardii
63	uvariifolium var. uvariiflorum
65	beesianum
66	heliolepis var. heliolepis
83	russatum
90	rex subsp. fictolacteum
94	decorum subsp. decorum
95	decorum subsp. decorum
99	wardii var. wardii
104	vernicosum
108	phaeochrysum
110a	phaeochrysum var. phaeochrysum
129	telmateium
131	saluenense subsp. chameunum
138	aganniphum var. aganniphum
140	phaeochrysum var. levistatum
143	aganniphum var. flavorufum
144	phaeochrysum var. levistratum
148	primuliflorum
149	rupicola var. chryseum
151	selense subsp. selense
160	tapetiforme
161	primuliflorum
162	sp.
163	phaeochrysum
164	primuliflorum
173	tapetiforme
221	oreotrephes
224	balfourianum
229	hippophaeoides white
230	trichostomum
248	primuliflorum
250	beesianum
270	rupicola var. chryseum aff.
285	trichostomum
292	beesianum

296	complexum	6	campylocarpum subsp.
303	beesianum		campylocarpum
304	heliolepis var. heliolepis	7	campanulatum
305	rupicola var. rupicola aff.	8	campanulatum
320a	aganniphum var. aganniphum	9	hodgsonii
322	balfourianum	10	hodgsonii aff.
323	beesianum	11	campanulatum
350	cephalanthum subsp.	12	campylocarpum subsp.
	platyphyllum		campylocarpum
352	taliense	13	campylocarpum subsp.
354	fastigiatum		campylocarpum
358	lacteum	14	campanulatum
363	brachyanthum subsp.	15	barbatum
	brachyanthum	16	arboreum
364	dichroanthum subsp.	17	wallichii
	dichroanthum	18	arboreum
369	campylogynum	19	camelliiflorum
370	cyanocarpum	20	camelliiflorum
371	haematodes subsp.	21	barbatum
	haematodes	22	arboreum
372	trichocladum var. trichocladum	23	arboreum
374	maddenii subsp. crassum	24	dalhousiae var. dalhousiae
375	virgatum subsp. oleifolium	25	arboreum
		26	arboreum
		27	arboreum

Smith, H.
GANSU, CHINA, ETC. *C.*1934

13979	sp.
13982	phaeochrysum var. levistratum
17920	concinnum

Smitinand, T. - Thailand Exps.
(1962)

7819	ludwigianum

(1974)

6	lyi

Spring-Smythe,T. - E Nepal Exps.
(1961-62)

1	grande
2	arboreum
3	arboreum
4	dalhousiae var. dalhousiae
5	arboreum

28	dalhousiae var. dalhousiae
29	arboreum subsp. cinnamomeum
30	barbatum
31	dalhousiae var. dalhousiae
32	dalhousiae var. dalhousiae
33	camelliiflorum
34	lepidotum
35	lepidotum
36	Subsect. Maddenia
37	grande
38	barbatum
39	camelliiflorum
40	barbatum
41	campanulatum
42	hodgsonii
43	campylocarpum subsp.
	campylocarpum
44	campanulatum
45	arboreum
46	lepidotum
47	Subsect. Maddenia
48	Subsect. Maddenia
49	camelliiflorum
50	arboreum
51	lepidotum
52	lepidotum

53	lepidotum
54	Subsect. Maddenia
55	Subsect. Maddenia
56	lindleyi
57	lindleyi aff.
58	arboreum
59	dalhousiae var. dalhousiae
60	arboreum

(1970)

61a	sp.
61b	arboreum
61c	arboreum
61d	grande
61e	arboreum
62	grande
63	grande
64	grande
65	arboreum
67	arboreum
68	arboreum
69	grande
70	arboreum

Stainton, Sykes & Williams (SSW)

C NEPAL EXP. (1954)

8216	sp.
8251	lowndesii
8274	dalhousiae var. dalhousiae
9090	anthopogon subsp. hypenanthum
9097	cowanianum
9106	campanulatum
9107	campanulatum

Tran, O.V.
VIETNAM (1993)

5	moulmainense
27	excellens aff.
28	sp.
31	nuttallii
32	tanastylum
33	Subsect. Irrorata
34	maddenii subsp. crassum

35	sinofalconeri
36	Subsect. Irrorata
64	sp.

Valder, P.G.
CAMERON HIGHLANDS (1972)

F1	wrayi
F2	wrayi
F3	wrayi
F4	wrayi
F6	wrayi
F7	wrayi
F9	wrayi
F10	jasminiflorum (sect. Vireya)
F12	sp. (sect. Vireya)
F13	javanicum (sect. Vireya)
F14	javanicum (sect. Vireya)

SUMATRA (1994-95)

I1	multicolor (sect. Vireya)
I2	aequabile (sect. Vireya)
I2a	sumatranum (sect. Vireya)

KEDAH (1994-95)

I12	moulmainense
I12a	jasminiflorum (sect. Vireya)
I12b	longiflorum (sect. Vireya)

THAILAND (1994-95)

I19	lyi
I20	lyi
I21	simsii
I29	veitchianum
I30	veitchianum
I38	veitchianum
I39	arboreum subsp. delavayi
I42	veitchianum
I42a	moulmainense

HONG KONG (1974-75)

I47	simiarum
I49	hongkongense
I49a	moulmainense
I50	simsii

I51   farrerae
I51a   championiae

Warner & Howick
EASTERN USA EXP. (1985)

96   maximum
141   Sect. Pentanthera
142   Sect. Pentanthera
177   catawbiense

CALIFORNIA, BRITISH COLUMBIA & WASHINGTON, W USA EXP. (1986)

212   occidentale
235   occidentale

JAPAN EXP. (1987)

576   brachycarpum subsp.
         brachycarpum
632   brachycarpum subsp.
         brachycarpum
633   albrechtii
673   japonicum
691   albrechtii
704   albrechtii
708   brachycarpum?
709   tschonoskyi var. tschonoskyi
757   kaempferi
763   kaempferi
790   makinoi
794   dilatatum
796   stenopetalum
797   keiskei
819   sanctum

PYRENEES EXP. (1989)

964   ferrugineum

Wharton, P.
GUIZHOU, CHINA EXP. (OCT. 1994)

009   coeloneuron
020   Sect. Azaleastrum
034   Subsect. Fortunea

041   Subsect. Fortunea
044   Subsect. Fortunea
049   sutchuenense aff.
050   auriculatum
083   Subsect. Fortunea
090   × agastum (hybrid)
095   × agastum (hybrid)
097   Subsect. Triflora
098   × agastum (hybrid)
099   simsii

Wilson, E.H. - Veitch-Sponsored Exps.
W HUBEI, CHINA (1899-1902)

311   argyrophyllum subsp.
         hypoglaucum
317   latoucheae var. latoucheae
505   adenopodum
517   × geraldii (hybrid)
570   fortunei subsp. discolor
598   augustinii subsp. augustinii
648   fortunei subsp. discolor
683   mariesii
752   argyrophyllum subsp.
         hypoglaucum
885   fortunei subsp. discolor
886   latoucheae var. latoucheae
887   stamineum
887b   fortunei subsp. fortunei
920   auriculatum
938   ovatum
944   maculiferum
1077a fortunei subsp. fortunei
1181   fortunei subsp. discolor
1218   micranthum
1232   sutchuenense
1250   oreodoxa var. fargesii

W SICHUAN, CHINA (1903-05)

1433   concinnum
1435   pachytrichum var. pachytrichum
1519   orbiculare subsp. orbiculare
1520   longesquamatum
1521   argyrophyllum subsp.
         argyrophyllum
1522   pachytrichum var. monosematum
1523   calophytum

1524	concinnum		5137	argyrophyllum subsp.
1525	pachytrichum var. pachytrichum			hypoglaucum
1526	argyrophyllum subsp.		5139	ririei
	argyrophyllum			
1527	faberi?			
1531	davidii			
1535	davidsonianum			
1538	bureavioides			
1539	'Magorianum' (hybrid?)			
1540	souliei			

Wilson, E.H. - Arnold Arboretum-Sponsored Exps.
W HUBEI & W SICHUAN, CHINA (1906-09)

1541	oreodoxa var. oreodoxa			
1543	intricatum		509	sutchuenense
1547	prattii		567	stamineum
1764	wasonii		569	simsii
1766	concinnum		586	fortunei subsp. discolor
1769	bureavii?		608	augustinii subsp. augustinii
1773	flavidum var. flavidum		660	micranthum
1777	vernicosum		800	molle subsp. molle
1779	davidsonianum		879	moupinense
1782	decorum subsp. decorum		882	hanceanum
1800	wasonii		1195	lutescens
1804	wiltonii		1196	amesiae
1808	ririei		1196a	concinnum
1809	stamineum		1197a	lutescens
1810	orbiculare subsp.orbiculare		1198	hunnewellianum subsp.
1857	polylepis			hunnewellianum
1862	trichanthum		1199	lutescens
1863	przewalskii		1200	micranthum
1864	praeteritum		1201	concinnum
1865	pachytrichum var.		1202	flavidum var. flavidum
	pachytrichum		1203	pachytrichum var. pachytrichum
1866	wasonii		1204	longistylum
1867	concinnum		1205	polylepis
1867a	faberi		1206	watsonii
1869	concinnum		1207	augustinii subsp. augustinii
1870	strigillosum		1207a	polylepis
1871	wiltonii		1208	sargentianum
1872	watsonii		1209	decorum subsp. decorum
1873	davidii		1209a	calophytum var. openshawianum
1875	lutescens		1210	argyrophyllum subsp.
1876	wasonii 'Rhododactylum'			argyrophyllum
1878	concinnum		1211	oreodoxa var. oreodoxa
1879	ambiguum		1220	trichanthum
1880	ambiguum		1221	polylepis
1881	ambiguum		1222	souliei
1882	'Planetum' (hybrid?)		1224	calophytum var. calophytum
1885	argyrophyllum subsp.		1225	websterianum
	hypoglaucum		1237	augustinii subsp. augustinii
1887	wongii		1256	vernicosum
1888	sargentianum		1274	davidsonianum
3942a	polylepis		1275	davidsonianum

1276	davidsonianum
1278	longesquamatum
1319	× edgarianum (hybrid?)
1320	micranthum
1324	ambiguum
1325	Subsect. Taliensia
1326	pachytrichum var. pachytrichum
1328	trichostomum
1328a	websterianum
1330	ambiguum
1339	insigne
1341	strigillosum
1342	trichanthum
1343	searsiae
1345	lutescens
1349	pachytrichum var. pachytrichum
1350	williamsianum
1352	davidsonianum
1353	wiltonii
1361	longesquamatum
1367	calophytum var. calophytum
1369	calophytum var. calophytum
1391	ovatum
1686	fortunei subsp. fortunei
1690	ovatum
3412	maculiferum
3414	calophytum var. openshawianum
3415	davidii
3416	oreodoxa var. fargesii
3418	orbiculare subsp. orbiculare
3425	ochraceum
3427	auriculatum
3428	racemosum
3440	pachytrichum var. pachytrichum
3443	argyrophyllum subsp. hypoglaucum
3445	trichanthum
3448	concinnum
3454	sargentianum
3465	nivale subsp. boreale
3467	nivale subsp. boreale
3468	nivale subsp. boreale
3469	nivale subsp. boreale
3473	simsii
3474	simsii

N & NW SICHUAN, CHINA EXP. (1910-11)

| 4041 | concinnum |
| 4231 | przewalskii |

4232	przewalskii
4233	amesiae
4233a	concinnum
4234	faberi
4235	rufum
4236	concinnum
4237	sargentianum
4238	augustinii subsp. augustinii
4239	davidsonianum
4240	ambiguum
4241	concinnum
4242	trichanthum
4243	przewalskii
4244	watsonii
4245	oreodoxa var. oreodoxa
4246	pachytrichum var. pachytrichum
4247	oreodoxa var. oreodoxa
4248	hunnewellianum subsp. hunnewellianum
4249	wasonii
4250	rufum
4251	wasonii
4252	ambiguum
4253	bracteatum
4254	galactinum
4254a	'Peregrinum' (hybrid?)
4255	hanceanum
4256	moupinense
4257	decorum subsp. decorum
4258	srigillosum
4259	watsonii
4260	oreodoxa var.oreodoxa
4261	davidii
4262	micranthum
4263	longesqamatum
4264	wiltonii
4265	ambiguum
4266	floribundum
4267	strigillosum
4268	stamineum
4269	nivale subsp. boreale
4270	pachytrichum var. pachytrichum
4271	oreodoxa var. oreodoxa
4272	faberi
4273	thayerianum
4274	souliei
4275	argyrophyllum subsp. argyrophyllum
4276	argyrophyllum subsp. argyrophyllum
4277	lutescens

4278   polylepis
4279   calophytum var. calophytum
4280   davidsonianum
4726   longistylum

JAPAN EXP. (1914-15)

7192   molle subsp. japonicum
7638   albrechtii
7657   tschonoskyi
7670   molle subsp. japonicum
7676   quinquefolium
7683   pentaphyllum
7683a   quinquefolium
7694   reticulatum
7709   indicum
7709a   kaempferi
7733   semibarbatum
7794   stenopetalum 'Linearifolium'
7801   tosaense
7813   weyrichii

KOREA, JAPAN & TAIWAN EXP. (1917-19)
KOREA

9251   dauricum
9411   weyrichii
9592   schlippenbachii
9595   tschonoskyi

LIUKIU & BONIN ISLANDS

10956   'Obtusum'
11248   kiusianum
11250   kiusianum
11255   kiusianum

TAIWAN

10928   pseudochrysanthum

10939   rubropilosum
10955   morii
11175   oldhamii

Yu, T.T.
YUNNAN (1938-39)

7860   saluenense subsp. saluenense
7867   selense subsp. selense
8611   saluenense subsp. chameunum
8645   saluenense subsp. chameunum
10925   racemosum
10958   decorum aff.
10961   rubiginosum
10993   racemosum
13809   vernicosum
13845   hippophaeoides
13886   rubiginosum
13937   hippophaeoides var.
            hippophaeoides
13961   vernicosum
14641   rupicola var. muliense
14694   vernicosum
14703   rubiginosum
14757   wardii var. puralbum
14843   hemitrichotum
14952   uvariifolium var. uvariiflorum
14955   adenogynum
14990   rubiginosum
15011   racemosum
15012   racemosum
15629   primuliflorum
17431   edgeworthii
19642   lukiangense
19757   calostrotum subsp.calostrotum
20750   fulvum
20817   cephalanthum subsp.
            cephalanthum
21005   dendricola
21031   maddenii subsp.crassum

Glossary

....

ACUMINATE: of an apex that is blunt but with a projecting point

ACUTE: of an apex that is tapering to a sharp point

ADPRESSED: lying close and flat against

AGGLUTINATED: of an indumentum of hairs embedded in a surface film

APICULATE: as for acuminate but with a more pronounced point

AURICULATE: with small ear-like projections at the base of a leaf

AXILLARY: growing from the angle formed by the junction of leaf and stem

BLOOM: waxy covering

CAMPANULATE: bell-shaped(see p.348)

CAPITELLATE: of hairs that are compound, with a tuft of long and flexuous simple branches arising from a short stalk

CARTILAGINOUS: like cartilage, translucent and smooth

CILIATE: fringed with hairs

CLONE: vegetatively propagated progeny of a single individual

CORDATE: heart-shaped

CORIACEOUS: leathery

CRENULATE: with small rounded teeth

CUNEATE: of a leaf base, tapering into the petiole

CUPULAR: cup-shaped

CURVED-CYLINDRICAL: (see p.348)

CUSPIDATE: of an apex that has a substantial protruding point

DECLINATE: of a style that is curved downwards

DEFLEXED: of a style that is abruptly bent downwards

DENDROID: of a hair that is branched like a tree

DETERSILE: of an indumentum that is eventually completely shed

DIMORPHIC: of scales or leaves that are of two distinct kinds

DISC: a fleshy outgrowth at the ovary base that secretes nectar

EGLANDULAR: lacking glands

ELLIPTIC: (see p.347)

EPIDERMIS: the surface layer of a leaf

EPIPHYTE: growing on another plant but deriving no nourishment from it

EVANESCENT: of an indumentum that is gradually lost as the plant matures

FASCICULATE (of hairs): like capitellate but with a broad stalk of several layers of thickened cells

FERRUGINEOUS: rusty brown

FILAMENT: the stalk bearing the anther

FILIFORM-ACICULAR: of a hair that is slender but stiff

FIMBRIATE: of a scale or hair that has a fringed margin

FLAGELLATE: of hairs that are compound, with long whip-like arms

FLOCCOSE: possessing dense, woolly hairs that fall away in tufts

FOLIOLIFEROUS: of hairs that are compound, the stalk and arms of which are composed of leaf-shaped cells

FUNNEL-CAMPANULATE: intermediate between funnel-shaped and campanulate

FUNNEL-SHAPED: (see p348)

GLABRESCENT: becoming glabrous

GLABROUS: without hairs or scales

GLANDULAR: bearing glands

GLAUCOUS: bluish green in colour

HYPOCRATERIFORM: salver-shaped

INDUMENTUM: a hair covering

IMPRESSED: of a style that arises from a sunken pit at the apex of the ovary

INFLORESCENCE: a flower cluster (see also truss)

LANATE: of an indumentum that is thick and woolly

LANCEOLATE: (see p.347)

LEPIDOTE: with scales

LINEAR: (see p.347)

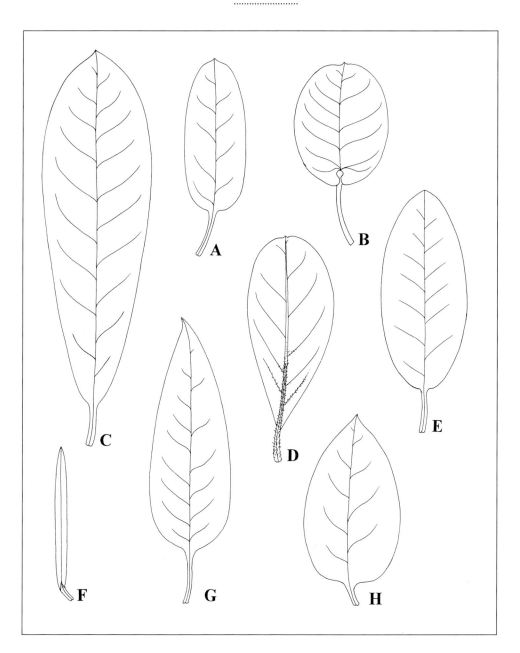

A = oblong,
B = orbicular
C = oblanceolate
D = obovate

E = elliptic
F = linear
G = lanceolate
H = ovate

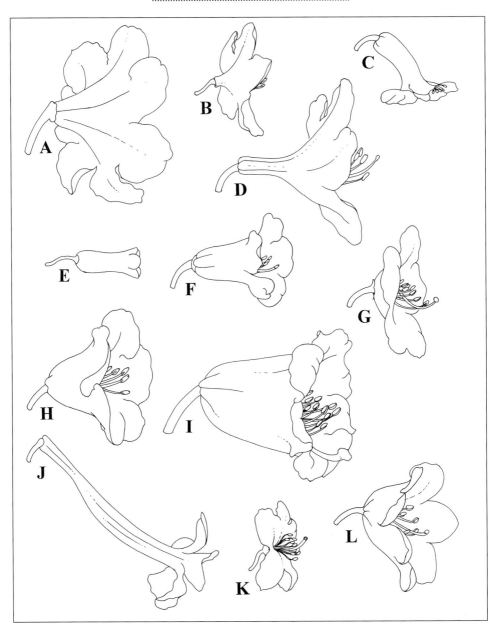

A = funnel-shaped
B = broadly funnel-shaped
C = curved-cylindrical
D = tubular funnel-shaped
E = tubular
F = tubular-campanulate

G = saucer-shaped
H = campanulate
I = ventricose-campanulate
J = trumpet-shaped
K = rotate
L = broadly campanulate

LINGULATE: resembling a tongue

LORIFORM: of a hair that is simple, substantial and wavy

MAMILLATE: of an epidermis that is covered with nipple-like protruberances

MATT: with a dull surface

MUCRONATE: with a short narrow point

NECTAR POUCHES: sac-like protruberances at the base of the corolla, containing nectar

OBLANCEOLATE: (see p. 347)

OBLONG: (see p.347)

OBTUSE: of an apex that is blunt

OBOVATE: (see p.347)

ORBICULAR: (see p.347)

OVARY: the central female part of the flower enclosing the ovules, later becoming the capsule

OVATE: (see p.347)

PAPILLATE: covered by small elongate projections

PEDICEL: the stalk of an individual flower

PERULAE: scales surrounding a bud

PETIOLE: the stalk of a leaf

PILOSE: with long soft hairs

PUBERULOUS: with very short hairs

PUBESCENT: with short hairs

PUNCTATE: dotted or shallowly pitted

PYRIFORM: pear-shaped

RACEME: an inflorescence whose growing point continues to grow, usually lacking a terminal flower and with a lengthened axis

RADIATE: of a compound hair with branches that spread outwards from a common centre

RAMIFORM: of a hair that is branched

RETICULATE: marked with a network of veins

RETRORSE: directed downwards or backwards

RETUSE: of a leaf or bract that has a central depression in a rounded apex

REVOLUTE: rolled downwards

RHACHIS: the axis of the inflorescence

ROSULATE: of compound hairs that resemmbe the radiate type but have longer arms

ROTATE: (see p.348)

RUGOSE: wrinkled

SAUCER-SHAPED: (see p.348)

SCALE: small scale-like multicellular protuberance

SERRULATE: with small sharp teeth

SESSILE: with no stalk

SETULOSE: of an indumentum that is composed of short bristle-like hairs

SINUS: the depression between two lobes or teeth

STAMEN: the male reproductive organ, consisting of the stalk-like filament and the pollen-bearing anther

STELLATE: star-shaped

STIGMA: that part of the style receptive to pollen (usually apical)

STYLE: the usually attenuated beak to the ovary, with the stigma at its apex

STRIGOSE: with stiff adpressed hairs

SUBULATE: awl-shaped, with a long straight sharp point

TOMENTOSE: with a dense covering of short cottony hairs

TRUMPET-SHAPED: (see p.348)

TRUSS: the flower cluster (see inflorescence)

TUBULAR: (see p.348)

TUBULAR-CAMPANULATE: (see p.348)

TUBULAR FUNNEL-SHAPED: (see p.348)

VALVES: the outermost units into which the fruit breaks (excluding the thin skin that often peels away)

VENTRICOSE: swollen or inflated on one side

VENTRICOSE-CAMPANULATE: (see p.348)

VESICLE: a small bladder-like sac containing fluid or air

VESICULAR: like a vesicle

VILLOUS: shaggy

VISCID: sticky

VISCIN: of threads that are sticky, to which the pollen grains are attached

ZYGOMORPHIC: having only one plane of symmetry, hence irregular

New Combinations Published for the First Time in This Handbook

Rhododendron **arboreum** Sm. subsp. **albomentosum** (Davidian) D.F. Chamb., **comb. et stat. nov.** Basionym: *R. delavayi* Franch. var. *albomentosum* Davidian, *The Rhododendron Species Vol. 2* (Series Arboreum - Lacteum) 308 (1989). Type: West Central Burma, Mount Victoria, 10,000ft, 9 April 1956, Kingdon-Ward 21976 (holo. BM).

Rhododendron **fulvum** Balf.f & W.W.Sm. subsp. **fulvoides** (Balf.f. & Forrest) D.F. Chamb., **comb. et stat. nov.** Basionym: *R. fulvoides* Balf.f. & Forrest in *Notes from the Royal Botanic Garden Edinburgh* **12**:112 (1920). Type: China, NW Yunnan, Mekong/Salween divide, 11,000ft, x 1914, Forrest 13400 (holo. E)

Rhododendron **morii** Hayata var. **taitunense** (T.Yamaz.) D.F.Chamb., **comb. nov.** Basionym: *R. pseudochrysanthum* subsp. *morii* (Hayata) T.Yamaz. var. *taitunense* T.Yamaz. in *The Journal of Japanese Botany* **56**:366 (1981); based on *R. rubropunctatum* Hayata in Icones Pl. Formos. 3:141 (1913). Type: Taiwan, Pref. Taipei, Mt Shichisei, March 1991, *S. Sasaki* s.n. (holo. TI).

This new combination is required as *R. morii* is maintained here at specific rank, distinct from *R. pseudochrysanthum*.

Rhododendron **pachytrichum** Franch. var. **monosematum** (Hutch.) D.F.Chamb., **comb. nov.** Basionym: *R. monosematum* Hutch. in *Curtis's Botanical Magazine* **142**: t.8675 (1916). Syn.: *R. strigillosum* Franch. var. *monosematum* (Hutch.) T.L.Ming in *Acta Botanica Yunnanica* **6**:155 (1984). Type: a plant grown at Kew from seed collected by Wilson in 1903 as seed no 1521, from Mt Wu in Sichuan Province (holo. K).

From the plate in *Curtis's Botanical Magazine* it is clear that var. *monosematum* is closer to *R. pachytrichum* than it is to *R. strigillosum*; it may however have originated as a hybrid between these two species.

Selected Bibliography

....

Temperate Rhododendrons

COX, P.A. 1985. *The Smaller Rhododendrons.* B.T. Batsford Ltd, London.

COX, P.A. 1990. *The Larger Rhododendron Species* (ed. 2). B.T. Batsford Ltd, London.

COX, P.A. & COX, K.N.E. (1997). *The Encyclopedia of Rhododendron Species.* Glendoick Publishing, Perth.

CHAMBERLAIN, D.F. 1982. A Revision of *Rhododendron* II Subgenus *Hymenanthes. Notes Roy. Bot. Gard. Edinb.* **Vol. 39**, pp. 209-486.

CHAMBERLAIN, D.F., HYAM, R., ARGENT, G., FAIRWEATHER, G & WALTER, K.S. (1996). *The Genus Rhododendron its classification & synonymy.* The Royal Botanic Garden Edinburgh.

CHAMBERLAIN, D.F. & RAE, S.J. 1990. A Revision of *Rhododendron* IV Subgenus Tsutsusi. *Edinb. J. Bot.* **47**, pp. 89-200.

CULLEN, J. 1980. A Revision of *Rhododendron* I Subgenus Rhododendron. *Notes Roy. Bot. Gard. Edinb.* **Vol. 39**, pp. 1-207.

DAVIDIAN, H.H. 1982 *Rhododendron Species. Vol. 1 - Lepidotes.* Timber Press, Oregon.

DAVIDIAN, H.H. 1989 *Rhododendron Species. 2 - Elepidote Species.* Timber Press, Oregon.

DAVIDIAN, H.H. 1992. *Rhododendron Species 3 - Elepidote Species, Series Neriiflorum - Thomsonii, Azaleastrum and Camtschaticum.* Timber Press, Oregon.

DAVIDIAN, H.H. 1995 *Rhododendron Species. 4 - Azaleas,* pps. 184. Timber Press, Oregon.

FANG, M.Y. (ed.) 1986. *Sichuan Rhododendron of China.* Science Press Beijing.

FENG, G.M. (ed.) 1988. *Rhododendrons of China 1.* Science Press, Beijing.

FENG, G.M. (ed.) 1992. *Rhododendrons of China 2.* Science Press, Beijing.

HU, L.C. & FANG, M.Y. (eds.) 1994. Ericaceae. *Flora Reipublicae Popularis Sinicae* **57**, pt. 2. Science Press, Beijing.

KRON, K.A. 1993. A Revision of *Rhododendron* V Section *Pentanthera. Edinb. J. Bot.* **50**, pp. 249-364.

JUDD,W.S. & KRON, K.A. 1995. A Revision of *Rhododendron* VI Subgenus Pentanthera (Sections Sciadorhodion, Rhodora & Viscidula). *Edinb. J. Bot.* **52**, pp. 1-54.

PHILIPSON W.R. & PHILIPSON, M.N. 1975. Revision of Subsection Lapponica.

PHILIPSON, W.R. & PHILIPSON, M.N. 1986. A Revision of *Rhododendron* III Subgenera *Azaleastrum, Mumeazalea, Candidastrum* and *Therorhodion. Notes Roy. Bot. Gard. Edinb.* **44**, pp 1-29.

SLEUMER, H. 1949. Ein System der Gattung *Rhododendron. Bot. Jahrb.* **74**, pp. 511-53.

SLEUMER, H. 1958. The Genus *Rhododendron* in Indochina and Siam. *Blumea, Suppl. IV.,pp.* 39-59.

SPETHMANN, W. 1987. A new infrageneric classification and phylogenetic trends in the genus *Rhododendron (Ericaceae).* Plant Systematics and Evolution, pp. 9-31.

SPETHMANN, W., OETTING, M. & WALTER, B. 1992. *Rhododendron Bibliography.* Deutsche Rhododendron Gesellschaft, Bremen.

STEVENSON, J.B. 1930, 2nd ed. 1947. *The Species of Rhododendron.* pp. 861. The Rhododendron Society, London.

TAM, P.C. 1983. *A Survey of the Genus Rhododendron in South China* (in Chinese).

YAMAZAKI, T. 1995. *A Revision of the Genus Rhododendron in Japan, Taiwan, Korea and Sakhalin*. Tsumura Laboratory, Tokyo.

Vireya rhododendrons

ARGENT G.C.G. 1988. Vireya Taxonomy in Field and Laboratory. *Proceedings of the Fourth International Rhododendron Conference, Wollongong, New South Wales*. Edited by J. Clyde Smith. The Australian Rhododendron Society Inc. pp.119-33.

ARGENT G., FAIRWEATHER G. & WALTER K. 1996. *Accepted Names in Rhododendron Section Vireya*. Royal Botanic Garden, Edinburgh. pp. 1-39.

ARGENT G., MITCHELL D. & SMITH P. 1993. Introducing the Vireyas, *The Garden* **Vol. 118** pt 11, pp. 492-94.

ARGENT G., LAMB A., PHILLIPPS A. & COLLENTETTE S. 1988. *Rhododendrons of Sabah*, Sabah Parks Publication No. 8 pp.1-145.

CLYDE SMITH J. 1989. *Vireya Rhododendrons*. The Australian Rhododendron Society Inc. p.1-76.

KENYON J. & WALKER J. 1997. *Vireyas for New Zealand Gardens*. Godwit Publishing Ltd., New Zealand pp.1-95. (The same publication as *Vireyas a Practical Gardening Guide* published by Timber Press, Portland, Oregon.)

MURRAY R.A. 1993. *Vireya Names (2nd Ed.)* Clover Springs Computer Services, New Jersey. pp.1-64.

SLEUMER H. 1966. *Rhododendron in Flora Malesiana* **ser. I 6**: Wolters-Noordhoff, Groningen 474-668.